Professional Sports & THE LAW

by Lionel S. Sobel
Instructor in Law, University of Southern California

Foreword by Howard Cosell

Introduction by Dr. Joseph Taubman

LAW—ARTS PUBLISHERS INC.
453 Greenwich St., N.Y.C., N.Y. 10013

Library of Congress Catalogue Card No. 76-51948

ISBN 0-88238-060-5

Printed in the United States of America by

MEILEN PRESS INC., NEW YORK, N. Y.

To the memory of

Steven William Rose

1944-1973

friend, lawyer, and sports fan,
who, like Brian Piccolo and Ernie Davis, was defeated
in life only by an opponent that respected no rules.

TABLE OF CONTENTS

PAGE

Chapter 2

RESERVE AND OPTION CLAUSES

PAGE

Chapter 3

THE PLAYER DRAFT

Chapter 6

LEAGUE MERGERS AND OTHER FORMS OF PEACE

Chapter 7

DISCIPLINE AND ELIGIBILITY

PAGE

Chapter 8

Buying and Moving Team Franchises

Chapter 9

PROFESSIONAL SPORTS AND THE TAX LAWS: TAX ASPECTS OF TEAM AND LEAGUE OPERATIONS

Chapter 10

PROFESSIONAL SPORTS BROADCASTING

PAGE

FOREWORD

By Howard Cosell

On April 28, 1967, at the Federal Customs Building on San Jacinto Street in Houston, Texas, Muhammad Ali, the Heavyweight Champion of the World, refused military induction. Within a relative matter of minutes thereafter, almost as if on signal, the politically appointed Chairman of the New York State Athletic Commission stripped the Champion of his title and also took away his license to fight. The Chairman's action was widely acclaimed. More than 90% of the sportswriters and sports announcers in this country regaled the move. All other boxing jurisdictions subsequently followed suit. Ali would fight no more. America was vindicated. Let the traitor pay the price. That was the general attitude. Everyone was reminded everywhere of the classic Ali utterance, *"I ain't got nothin' against them Viet Cong."*

For one educated at Law and who believes in a government of laws, this whole sequence of events was astonishing and even frightening. The Champion had not been arraigned, there was no Grand Jury presentment, there had been no indictment, no trial, no conviction, no appeal, no appeal to higher court, no appeal to the Court of last resort—the Supreme Court of the United States. In other words, due process of law, as guaranteed by the Fifth Amendment of the Constitution, had not even been initiated and yet Ali had been deprived of his duly achieved property right—the Championship—and his right to earn a living.

At the same time, it was not generally pointed out that the same New York State Boxing official who had struck with such remarkable swiftness against Ali, was routinely issuing boxing licenses to deserters from the military.

That which followed was inevitable in a government of laws. The Supreme Court of the United States by a vote of 8–0 exonerated Ali, and a Federal Court Judge in the Southern District of New York held that the Chairman of the Athletic Commission had denied the Champion equal protection under the laws as prescribed in the Fourteenth Amendment by virtue of his having licensed military deserters to fight.

For three and one-half years, the Champion was idle and there was no one to return those 3½ years to him. It was an incredible time, an incredible experience. What made it so incredible was the fact that during those 3½ years, only a handful of sports communicators kept calling attention to the Law, to the matter of the American legal system and to the terrible injustice that was parceled out to Muhammad Ali. The relevant theme here is that it is no longer possible to communicate accurately in sports without having some knowledge of the law and how sports increasingly relates to it. This is where this book renders a real service. Sportswriters and sports announcers now have a place to turn to so that they can discover in lucid, simple terms what the law is all about and how it relates to sports. They can no longer find a haven in ignorance and bias. This book can bring a highly increased knowledgeability and accuracy to every sports communicator in the nation.

Let's take a look at how the Law relates to other sports. In this country we do not have two standards of Law—one for the rich and one for the poor, one for all businesses and another for just one favored business. Yet, in fact, major league baseball has been set apart from all other businesses in the United States and even further, major league baseball has been placed above the Law. It is the only business in the United States—apart from the public utilities—that is not subject to the Federal anti-trust laws, yet unlike the public utilities it is not subject to government regulation. Professional football, hockey and basketball, for example, are subject to the anti-trust laws. How did this extraordinary situation that sets baseball apart from the real world come about? What has been the foundation at law for a manifest discrimination and apparent anachronism? The explanation is lodged with clarity in this book. How have the major league baseball players forced a change in baseball's onerous but previously legally protected reserve system? The answer is in the recent case of pitchers Andy Messersmith and Dave McNally. The explanation is in this book.

Indeed, professional sports generally are undergoing the greatest upheaval and restructuring in their history and it is happening through the courts of law and through collective bargaining. The professional football reserve system, otherwise known as the *Rozelle Rule,* has been declared invalid in the Mackey case in Minnesota and the Kapp case in California. The NBA owners have collectively bargained out an agreement with the NBA players which ultimately will wipe out any vestige of a reserve system in professional basketball. All of these matters are covered herein meticulously and with clarity. As far as I am concerned, this book should become a must for every library in the country and a desk aid for every sports communicator. Maybe then, and only then can we eradicate such situations as that of a sports writer in the Boston Globe recently characterizing a lockout of the baseball training camps by the owners as a "players strike". I have been waiting for this book for a long time. I'm glad it's here.

INTRODUCTION

"Sports and the Arts"

By Dr. Joseph Taubman

Several years ago, my wife and I went to hear Lionel Hampton and his band play at the Century Plaza Hotel in Century City in Los Angeles. We were introduced by Lionel Hampton to "Mudcat" Grant, a professional baseball pitcher. Before the evening was over, "Mudcat" sang a few numbers with the band. "Mudcat" was looking forward to a career in show business after retirement from baseball.

In November, 1974, the happenstance of athlete-turned-performing-artist took us on a quick trip from Madrid to the Canary Islands. Only this time, it was to see Jim Brown, renowned former back of the Cleveland Browns, turned movie actor, who was one of the stars in a motion picture being produced there. Jim Brown was interested in the lead role in a script written by my client who was then based in Madrid.

More recently, in the early spring of 1976, we met with Dorothy Hamill and her family on the occasion of imminent transition from Olympic champion amateur to professional. As the Variety news item reveals, her manager has in mind another Sonia Heine skating film—and also television —star.

Thus, inspirationally and aspirationally, the world variously known as "show business", "entertainment", and the "performing arts" is a magnet for athletes and has been for a long time, as the career of swimming star, "Tarzan" Johnny Weissmuller can attest.

And yet from the legal end, the marriage has not always been seen as a desirable coming together of heroes of sports and the arts.

In the late 1960's, the Practising Law Institute ("PLI") ran a four-day workshop in New York on athletes and entertainers. The PLI Impresario had some concern as to whether the event might not be a kind of mixing of oil and water. I was to be the first speaker on the third day, i.e., the last to give forth on entertainment before the speakers on sports were to have their innings. The speakers constituted a kind of panel and were requested to be on hand at other times.

In the late afternoon of the second day, Ms. PLI Impresario came up to me with a note of agitation in her voice and wondered if I could go on that afternoon because she felt the athletic part of the audience might be getting restless at the prospect of too much entertainment and too little sports. Not wishing to disappoint our charming program planner, I quickly discarded whatever last minute preparations that might otherwise make my talk seem more prepared and, in the best traditions of the proverbial mouthpiece, I—to borrow a word from television—"winged it" then and there to an entertainment conclusion.

Today, the athletic portion of such a workshop, i.e., lawyers, accountants, players' representatives, business advisors, etc., the infra-structure of the sports world, might be a more understanding lot because they are probably more sophisticated about such matters.

A propos of our entertainment milieu, on one of the network news programs a few weeks ago, there was a five minute sequence in which Edward Villella, the ballet star, commented on the style and grace of "Dr." Julius Erving of the New York Nets, as he leaped through the air making various shots for the basket. The commentary was accompanied by comparison shots of ballet star, Villella, dancing, and basketball star, Erving, soaring to make his shots.

If viewers should fail to make the connection themselves, the media will surely bring it out vis-a-vis the balletic effects of an Olga Korbut and accompanying gymnasts, or the shimmering beauty of our prime figure skaters.

And so the milieu today is one of kinship between sports and the arts. Both are principals in what are commonly called "amusement", "recreation", and, yes, "entertainment" in the definitional sense, although the latter term in the lay sense probably is closer to "show business" than sports.

Sports are the realm of games and contests where the tests are almost entirely physical, and yet the term comprehends the game of chess, the most sedentary of sedentary events. The physicality, however, need not be limited to humans. Cock fights and greyhound racing come to mind.

Athlete and spectator alike are constantly, in theory at least, at nostril sensitivity, perhaps, as it were, by the primal instincts of competition and survival of the fittest, whether the challenge be one of individual or team competitors and/or a race against the clock as in track and speed skating events. Perhaps our interest in sports represents the civilizing impact of organized competition against competitors and/or time or nature, a turning of the savage instincts of violent survival into forms of play.

But organized games and contests, collectively denominated "sports", whose participants are variously called "athletes" and "players" pay a premium in our society to the winner. The prevailing party is endowed with the aura of excellence and crowned with the emoluments of "success". Throughout the world, the winner is a hero. It is as though we have extrapolated the virtues of excellence as the virtues of winning in one of the places where heroes can be created and remain heroes. The Horatio Algers of business may be a vanished breed, but we still extol our Joe Namaths, Hank Aarons, Muhammad Alis, Chris Everts, and many others at the height of their achievements.

Barring corruption, scandal, or reduction by antitrust or even ordinary hard-nosed business factors of sports to a cynical acceptance by a jaded "ripped-off" public, athletics is perhaps our last frontier of heroics, hero-making and hero-worship.

In part, this may be attributable to the fact that sports imply participation under given rules. Indeed, infraction of the rules may, and often does, result in expulsion from the game or event, fine, and even suspension.

The arts, on the other hand, have an entirely different ambit. Yesterday's genre and forms may be today's cliché and a dead art form. The creative urge sets the parameters. Creativity is two-fold: in the fixing of the work by the author thereof, and in its interpretation in performance, with a possible fusion of the two as in improvisation. Creators who are original often strive to break out of old molds so as to create new forms and meanings. Their competition is their own striving to attain their own goals, however much they may be restricted by budgetary considerations and contemporary market place criteria of success—box office, ratings, awards, and so on. But the creative norm and the public welcome, whether in a cash or admission price nexus or by public subsidy or subvention, contributions and/or free admission support, determine the character and characterizations thereof. And so the arts may assume anti-hero, anti-conventional norms. The protagonists may be unheroic. There may be manifestations of violence or, to the contrary, the prototypes may be meek, ineffectual bumblers. Indeed, Aristotle's unities of time and place may be disregarded. The logic of a beginning, a middle and an end may be thrown overboard in the quest for the discrete, the psychological, the bizarre, the dissonant, the abstract, the surreal.

It may be said that excepting where ideology decrees that permissible art be the servant of society, art has no boundaries, no parameters other than the limits of imagination of the creator and performer, even though to the athlete seeking to turn performer in the arts, show business holds out the promise of a kind of continuity of known values, aims, and aspirations.

Like the minimal quantum of creativity required for a copyright under our laws, the term "professional" in both sports and the arts is deceptively simple. Anyone performing or creating for compensation, i.e., gain, *ipso facto,* is a professional. The corollary is a public or audience willing to do homage by payment. In a creative sense, the outstanding amateur is endowed with the broader meaning of excellence inherent in the term "professional", be it an Olympic champion or a Paganini, Heifetz, or Oistrakh who never received a penny for performance.

Recent history of professional sports and the law, as exemplified by Lionel Sobel's perceptive opus, bears out strong similarities between the path trodden by professional sports presently and the antecedent history of entertainment. The hallmarks are litigation, antitrust, business and union parameters. Yet, the past decade, more or less, has also seen the so-called cultural explosion, i.e., the flowering of the non-profit arts, however, weakened in the last few years by cutbacks in public subsidy and recession.

Inevitably, the impact on professional sports must be the freedom of market forces to operate free of unreasonable restraints and the practical aim of maintaining the dignity of the individual athlete in his or her quest for excellence. Perhaps the starting point is the public recognition of the need for maintenance and support of amateur sports including, analogously to the National Endowment for the Arts, federal support for the Olympics, so that our finest amateur performers need not appear to go begging for funding in order to participate in the world Olympic games.

In 1972, I wrote as the concluding paragraph of my section on "Sports" in my introductory chapter of my treatise, "Performing Arts Management and Law":

> "In sports, in most instances, there is no underlying literary or artistic property, be it play, novel, or musical composition, which is the basis of ownership via copyright, proprietorship, and the licensing and transformation of the bundle of rights. In the performing arts, as a result, creativity becomes inextricably entwined with artistry so as to affect the very legal, business, and yes, artistic, matrix of the performing arts thereby making the latter fundamentally different in their parameters from sports."[1]

And yet, for the sports owners, there are broadcasting and cable-casting of events, let alone radio, and for the

[1] Taubman, Joseph, 1 Performing Arts Management and Law 20 (1972), at the end of Sec 1.11, Sports; see, also Sec 1.8, Show Business at p. 12, Sec 1.9, Recreation at p. 15, and Sec 1.10, Leisure, at p. 16.

athletes, there are not only commercials and endorsements, but the end of the player's rainbow may be entré into that other fabulous world of competition, dreams and heroics—show business and the arts.

ACKNOWLEDGMENTS

A great many people took time from their demanding schedules to respond, graciously and gratuitously, to my questions and to my requests for documents, pleadings, reports and transcripts. This book would not have been possible without their cooperation and assistance. In particular, I should like to thank the following individuals (none of whom, of course, should be held accountable for the opinions and conclusions I have expressed): Clarence Campbell, President, National Hockey League; Don Weiss, Director of Public Relations, National Football League; John Thompson, Executive Director, NFL Management Council; Patty Davidson, World Hockey Association; Paula Van Hoose, World Team Tennis; Jack Teele, Los Angeles Rams; Al Campanis, Vice President, Los Angeles Dodgers; Edward R. Garvey, Executive Director, and Richard Berthelsen, Staff Counsel, NFL Players Association; Dr. Roger G. Noll and Dr. Benjamin A. Okner, The Brookings Institution; Francis Breidenbach, Esq., Cummins, White & Breidenbach, Los Angeles; Tim Grandi, Esq., Nagel, Regan & Davidson, Inc., Newport Beach; Philip R. Hochberg, Esq., O'Connor & Hannan, Washington, D.C.; James B. Jalenak, Esq., Hanover, Walsh, Barnes & Jalenak, Memphis; Ronald L. Johnson, Esq., Chief Deputy City Attorney of San Diego; Ellis S. Rubin, Esq., Miami Beach; John E. Thomas, Esq., Cochrane & Bresnahan, P.A., St. Paul; Alan Pearce, Office of the Chairman of the Federal Communications Commission; Congressman Emanuel Celler, Chairman, House Judiciary Committee; Senator Sam J. Ervin, Jr.; Senator Philip A. Hart, Chairman, Senate Subcommittee on Antitrust and Monopoly; Congressman Torbert Macdonald, Chairman, House Subcommittee on Communications; Senator John O. Pastore; Congressman Harley O. Staggers, Chairman,

House Committee on Interstate and Foreign Commerce; Senator John V. Tunney; and Nicholas Zapple, Esq., Communications Counsel, Senate Committee on Commerce.

Special thanks are due to Leslie S. Klinger, Esq., of Manatt, Phelps & Rothenberg, in Los Angeles. Not only was he a very valuable source of knowledge and information, he also tolerated, above and beyond the call of friendship, countless hours of talk about sports and law, all in apparent good cheer.

Special thanks are also due to my students at the University of Southern California Law Center, particularly Dennis Gibala of the Class of 1975 who promoted my Professional Sports Law course with the School's faculty and administration in the first place. The tremendous interest and enthusiasm which my students expressed for this subject sustained my own. And their questions and comments taught me as much as I hope they learned.

Finally, though especially, I should like to thank my wife, Carol. Her encouragement and support were the most essential elements of this book, and they were constant, even though my research and writing made her a "book widow" on far too many weekends and evenings. If she was less interested in this project than I, she masked that feeling well, and she and her help made the writing of this book far less solitary a task than it otherwise would have been. Our 2½ year old daughter, Lindsay, deserves credit as well, for throughout her young life, she has been living under a permanent injunction "not to touch Daddy's papers"—a very difficult order to abide by for as curious and intelligent a person as she is.

Lionel S. Sobel
Beverly Hills, California
July, 1976

Chapter 1

PROFESSIONAL SPORTS AND THE ANTITRUST LAWS: THE ANOMALY THAT IS BASEBALL

§1.1 Origins of the baseball exemption

§1.1(a) The Federal League "war"

Professional sports came into existence in this country shortly after the end of the Civil War. In its earliest years, barnstorming teams of baseball players traveled thousands of miles each season, mounting exhibition games wherever opponents and paying audiences could be found. In 1871, several of these teams organized themselves into the first professional league. And from then until just before the beginning of World War I, teams and entire leagues appeared and vanished, often warring with one another in modern fashion for the services of the best players.[1]

By 1913, however, a certain stability had been achieved. The American League had completed metamorphosis from its minor league beginnings as the Western League into full fledged, if junior major league status. It had entered into an affiliation contract, called the "National Agreement," with the older, more established National League, providing that each would respect the player contracts of the other. Professional baseball was then enjoying a period of prosperity.

That pre-World War I prosperity encouraged new entrants into the professional baseball market place. In March of 1913, several wealthy sportsmen incorporated

[1] Organized Baseball: Report of the Subcommittee on the Study of Monopoly Power of the Committee on the Judiciary, House of Representatives, H.Rep. 2002, 82d Cong., 2d Sess. 16-50 (1952).

the Federal League of Professional Baseball Clubs and issued franchises to Brooklyn, Pittsburgh, Buffalo, Baltimore, St. Louis, Kansas City, Indianapolis, and Chicago. During its first season, the Federal League stocked its teams with players who were not under contract to American or National League teams, and it enjoyed moderate success.

Prior to the start of the 1914 season, the Federal League sought to become a party to the National Agreement between the American and National Leagues. It was rebuffed, however, on the grounds the country was not big enough for three major leagues. In response, the Federal League declared war. It systematically sought to raid American, National, and minor league teams of their best players. Organized Baseball, as these affiliated leagues had come to be known, responded by threatening its players with blacklisting if any jumped to the Federal League—and reinforced those threats with increased salary offers. Nonetheless, of the 264 baseball players who performed in the Federal League during the 1914 and 1915 seasons, 18 had broken American or National League contracts, 25 had broken minor league contracts, 63 had ignored American or National League reserve clauses, and 115 had ignored minor league reesrve clauses. Only 43 had not been under contract to any club in Organized Baseball at the time they signed with the Federal League.[2]

The Federal League set out to become major in another way as well. Between the 1913 and 1914 seasons, each of its teams built a new baseball stadium. Whether by virtue of player allocation methods, luck, or some other design, the Federal League pennant races in 1914 and 1915 were

---

[2] *Id.* at 50-55.

close. All of these things suggested the new league should have been a financial success, but it was not.

Attendance was disappointing. The Chicago Federal League team finished the 1914 season in second place in the standings and in first place in total attendance. By comparison, the Chicago American League team had greater attendance, even though it finished sixth in the standings of its league. Even Organized Baseball's financial picture was no longer as bright as it had been, however. Competition from the Federal League, general economic depression and World War I caused American and National League teams to lose money as well.[3]

On January 5, 1915, the Federal League initiated what was to become a time honored tradition. It filed an antitrust lawsuit against its established competitors. Though Organized Baseball had not sued any players who simply ignored their reserve clauses to play in the Federal League, it had sued those who broke their current season's contracts to do so. In the antitrust suit which the Federal League filed in Chicago, it asked for a judicial declaration that the National Agreement was illegal and that Organized Baseball's player contracts were void. The Federal League also sought an injunction, requiring Organized Baseball to dismiss all lawsuits against players then in the Federal League and prohibiting Organized Baseball from filing any more.

The case was tried before Judge Kenesaw Mountain Landis, who later was to become the first Commissioner of Baseball. Eleven months after the trial was completed, Judge Landis had not rendered his verdict. The Federal League, uncertain whether it could survive the 1916 season,

---

[3] *Id.* at 56.

was unable to wait any longer, and in December of 1915 it made peace with Organized Baseball.

The so-called "Peace Agreement" was in reality a death certificate, for it provided that the American and National Leagues were to pay the owners of Federal League teams $600,000 to dissolve it. In addition, the owners of the Chicago Federals were permitted to buy the American League Chicago Cubs, and the owners of the St. Louis Federals were permitted to buy the National League St. Louis Browns. All blacklisted players were reinstated, and Federal League teams were permitted to sell their player contracts to American and National League teams.

Left unsatisfied, however, were the owners of the Baltimore Federal League team. They wanted to buy the St. Louis Cardinals and move the team to Baltimore. Although the City of St. Louis had not been supporting, and was probably unable to support, both the Browns and the Cardinals, National League owners refused to permit the purchase. The Baltimore Federal owners complained to the Antitrust Division of the Department of Justice, but were told that Assistant Attorney General Todd saw no violations. Thereupon, the American, National and Federal Leagues finalized their agreement, excluding the Baltimore owners entirely.[4]

Section 1 of the Sherman Act declares illegal every contract, combination or conspiracy restraining trade or commerce among the states.[5] Section 2 of the Sherman Act makes it a crime to monopolize, or attempt to monopolize, trade or commerce among the states.[6] And Section 4 of

[4] *Id.* at 56-57.

[5] 15 U.S.C. § 1.

[6] 15 U.S.C. § 2.

the Clayton Act provides that any person who is injured by a violation of the Sherman Act may recover three times the amount of his injury.[7] Relying upon these sections, the Federal Baseball Club of Baltimore, Inc., filed suit on March 29, 1916, against the American and National Leagues, all of their teams, the presidents of the two leagues, and several people who had been active in the Federal League but were instrumental in agreeing to its demise.

The suit contended that American and National League player contracts restrained the trade and commerce of baseball in violation of Section 1 of the Sherman Act, because the reserve clauses they contained, and the blacklisting threats used to enforce them, prevented Federal League teams from being able to hire quality players, all of whom were under contract to teams in Organized Baseball at the time the Federal League came into existence. This inability to hire quality ball players was alleged to be the reason attendance had been low, and low attendance was alleged to be the reason the Federal League had been driven out of business.

Further, the suit contended that by using such player contracts, and by tying up all of the best playing talent, and particularly by paying the Federal League money to go out of business, the American and National Leagues had monopolized all baseball trade and commerce in the United States in violation of Section 2 of the Sherman Act.

The case was tried in Washington, D.C., in April of 1919, and the Baltimore owners were victorious. District Judge Stafford instructed the jury that the American and National Leagues and their teams were engaged in inter-

[7] 15 U.S.C. § 15.

state commerce and that they had monopolized baseball. He asked the jury to determine whether they had also conspired to destroy the Federal League, and if so, the amount of damages the Baltimore owners had suffered as a result.

The jury decided the defendants had conspired to destroy the Federal League, and that as a result the Baltimore owners had been damaged by $80,000. In accordance with the provisions of Section 4 of the Clayton Act, Judge Stafford tripled the $80,000 verdict and entered judgment for $240,000.[8]

By its terms, the Sherman Act applies only to "trade or commerce" "among the states." The defendants had contended that baseball was neither trade or commerce nor conducted among the states, and that therefore the Sherman Act did not apply to them at all. The Court of Appeals agreed, and reversed the $240,000 judgment.[9]

"The players, it is true, travel from place to place . . ." —places which were in different states. But the players "are not the game," the Court of Appeals said. "Not until they come into contact with their opponents on the baseball field and the contest opens does the game come into existence. *It is local in its beginning and in its end.*" Thus, the Court held, baseball was not conducted "among the states." [10]

Nor was it trade or commerce. The Court of Appeals explained that:

---

[8] National League of Professional Baseball Clubs v. Federal Baseball Club of Baltimore, 269 Fed. 681, 682 (D.C. Cir. 1921).

[9] National League v. Federal Baseball, 269 Fed. 681 (D.C. Cir. 1921).

[10] *Id.* at 684-685 (emphasis added).

> ". . . Trade and commerce require the transfer of something, whether it be persons, commodities, or intelligence, from one place or person to another. . . . A game of baseball is not susceptible of being transferred. . . . Nothing is transferred in the process to those who patronize it. The exertions of skill and agility which they witness may excite in them pleasurable emotions, just as might a view of a beautiful picture or a masterly performance of some drama; but the game effects no exchange of things according to the meaning of 'trade and commerce'. . . ." [11]

Baseball, said the Court, "is not trade or commerce; it is sport." [12]

The United States Supreme Court affirmed in a unanimous opinion by Justice Oliver Wendell Holmes—an opinion which established a precedent which has survived to this day.[13] Baseball games, said Justice Holmes, "are purely state affairs." [14] They are not interstate. Furthermore, a baseball game, "although made for money, would not be called trade or commerce in the commonly accepted use of those words." [15] Since baseball was neither interstate nor trade or commerce, the Sherman Act did not apply to it, and has not ever since.

§1.1(b) The Mexican League "war"

From the demise of the Federal League to the end of World War II, Organized Baseball was not challenged in any significant way. Commissioner Kenesaw Mountain

---

[11] *Id.* at 684-685.

[12] *Id.* at 685.

[13] Federal Baseball Club v. National League, 259 U.S. 200 (1922).

[14] *Id.* at 208.

[15] *Id.* at 209.

Landis—formerly Judge Landis—was himself sued in 1930 by the Milwaukee American League team when he declared one of its players a free agent because it assigned him to its farm system in violation of baseball's rules.[1] But baseball's exemption from the antitrust laws was not put in jeopardy nor even questioned during that period.

Then in 1946, postwar prosperity again generated competition. This time the challenger was foreign rather than domestic. Don Jorge Pasquel, president of the Mexican League, came to the United States and began hiring major league baseball players. Don Jorge Pasquel and his brother Bernardo, who was vice president of the League, were brazen in their approach. On May 3, 1946, for example, Bernardo Pasquel held a news conference in New York City at which he announced that Phil Rizzuto "will leave the Yankees and go to Mexico when I give the word. . . . I will not leave New York without taking a Yankee regular of the first rank with me." [2] In response, the Yankees went to court, and only seventeen days after the news conference, were awarded a temporary injunction restraining the Mexican League and those acting on its behalf, including the Pasquel brothers, from making any further attempts to induce Yankee players to repudiate their contracts.[3]

Nonetheless, the Mexican League did succeed in signing 18 major league players.[4] Three of these were Danny Gar-

---

[1] Milwaukee American Assn. v. Landis, 49 F.2d 298 (N.D. Ill. 1931).

[2] American League Baseball Club of New York v. Pasquel, 63 N.Y.S. 2d 537, 538 (1946).

[3] *Id.* See also § 5.2(b)(2)(C), *infra.*

[4] Organized Baseball: Report of the Subcommittee on the Study of Monopoly Power of the Committee on the Judiciary, House of Representatives, H.Rep. 2002, 82d Cong., 2d Sess. 77 (1952).

della of the New York Giants, and Fred Martin and Max Lanier of the St. Louis Cardinals.

Gardella was a Giant outfielder during the 1944 and 1945 seasons. Before signing his 1946 contract, he and the team's management had a dispute, the exact cause of which is not known for certain, though Gardella reportedly claimed it was because he refused to wear a necktie.[5] Whatever the reason, Gardella played in the Mexican League in 1946, and as a result was suspended from Organized Baseball for five years by Commissioner Albert "Happy" Chandler.

Max Lanier and Fred Martin both played for the Cardinals during the 1945 season and had signed 1946 contracts as well. Nevertheless, they, too, played in the Mexican League during the 1946 season, reportedly because they had been offered more money than the Cardinals were going to pay them.[6] They, too, were suspended from Organized Baseball for five years, as were all of the other players who played in Mexico that year.

According to a Congressional Report issued several years later, few of the 18 Americans who played in Mexico enjoyed the experience.[7] Unfortunately, they found, Commissioner Chandler would not reinstate them. Some of the 18, including Martin and Lanier, organized independent barnstorming teams and toured the United States putting on exhibition games. The tour was a financial loss, however, because, Martin and Lanier alleged, Organized Baseball teams refused to allow the barnstormers the use of their parks and threatened the owners of independent parks

---

[5] Topkis, Monopoly in Professional Sports, 58 Yale L.J. 691 (1949).

[6] Martin v. Chandler, 1949 CCH Trade Cases ¶ 62,397 (S.D.N.Y. 1949).

[7] Organized Baseball, *supra* note 4, at 79.

with penalties if they allowed the barnstormers to use theirs. The barnstormers also found that many professional baseball players refused to play against them for fear that they, too, would be blacklisted.[8]

Some of the 18 found employment in semi-professional leagues, and for a short time, in other foreign leagues. The Cuban Professional League, whose season was during the winter rather than the summer, hired Martin and Lanier and several others. Dr. Sanguilly, part owner of the Cuban League, was apparently pleased to have major league players on his teams, because he came to the United States to seek permission from American and National League team owners to hire more. When the owners found out that blacklisted players were in his league, they not only denied Dr. Sanguilly the permission he sought, they also declared the Cuban League an "outlaw" and approved a newly formed competitive league in Cuba.[9]

The competitive league went out of business before its first season ended. The next year, when Dr. Sanguilly's Cuban League again sought permission to hire major league players for the winter, permission was granted on condition that no blacklisted players be permitted to play.[10]

In 1947 and 1948, Organized Baseball entered into similar agreements with the Panama Professional Baseball League, the Venezuela Professional Baseball League, and the Puerto Rico Professional Baseball League. Barred from all of these leagues, some blacklisted players joined professional teams in the Quebec Provincial League in

[8] *Id.*
[9] *Id.* at 80.
[10] *Id.* at 81.

Canada. But in 1949, that League, too, was taken into Organized Baseball's fold as a Class C minor league.[11]

The Mexican League itself was finally neutralized also. Don Jorge Pasquel stopped his raids for financial reasons and retired as league president. His successor, Dr. Eduardo Pitman, discovered that not only had the Mexican League failed to induce many major league players to jump to it, Organized Baseball had, in fact, induced several Mexicans to join American teams. Thus, in March of 1949, Dr. Pitman and Commissioner Chandler reached an "oral understanding" that each would respect the player contracts of the other, including their reserve clause paragraphs.[12]

Barred from what must have been almost every professional baseball league in the Western Hemisphere, if not the world, Danny Gardella went to court. Though *Federal Baseball* v. *National League*[13] seems to have been decided correctly in its time, baseball grew substantially between 1922 and the late 1940s, and relevant principles had changed as well.

One of the precedents relied upon heavily by Justice Oliver Wendell Holmes in 1922 had been *Hooper* v. *California*.[14] In that case, the Supreme Court had ruled that an insurance company was not engaged in interstate commerce, even though it sold insurance policies in several states. By the time Danny Gardella filed his suit, *Hooper* v. *California* had been overruled by the Supreme Court in *United States* v. *South-Eastern Underwriters Association*[15] where the court held that the sale of insurance in more than one state did constitute interstate commerce.

---

[11] *Id.* at 81-82.
[12] *Id.* at 82.
[13] 259 U.S. 200 (1922), discussed in § 1.1(a), *supra*.
[14] 155 U.S. 648 (1895).
[15] 322 U.S. 533 (1944).

Also, Justice Holmes had said that personal services unrelated to the production of some object were not trade or commerce. The Supreme Court later ruled, however, in a case involving doctors, that "trade" and "commerce" do include personal services, whether or not some object is produced.[16]

Furthermore, in 1922 courts could say, as they did in the *Federal Baseball* case, that a baseball game "is local in its beginning and in its end." [17] But by the time Gardella went to court in 1948, radio and television, both nonexistent in 1922, were broadcasting live games across state lines.

For all of these reasons, Gardella had cause to be hopeful when he sued Commissioner Chandler, the presidents of the American, National, and minor leagues, and the New York Giants, alleging that they had a monopoly on professional baseball and that by blacklisting him they were restraining interstate trade and commerce in violation of the Sherman Act. He further claimed that their acts had caused him $100,000 in damages. The defendants, naturally unwilling to concede that anything of significance had occurred since *Federal Baseball* v. *National League,* moved to dismiss the case on the grounds that baseball was exempt from the Sherman Act.

District Judge Goddard acknowledged the changes that had taken place since 1922, but agreed with Organized Baseball that *Federal Baseball* was still controlling. He therefore dismissed the case.[18]

But on February 9, 1949, Danny Gardella won a victory in the Court of Appeals which made and continues to make

---

[16] American Medical Assn. v. United States, 317 U.S. 519 (1943).

[17] 269 Fed. at 685.

[18] Gardella v. Chandler, 79 F.Supp. 260 (S.D.N.Y. 1948).

him unique in baseball's legal history. In a two to one decision, that Court reversed the dismissal of his case and sent it back to Judge Goddard with instructions that a trial should be conducted to determine whether Gardella's allegations were true.[19] If those allegations were in fact true, said Judge Frank,

> ". . . We have here a monopoly which, in its effect on ball-players like the plaintiff, possesses characteristics shockingly repugnant to moral principles that, at least since the War Between the States, have been basic in America, as shown by the Thirteenth Amendment to the Constitution, condemning 'involuntary servitude,' and by subsequent Congressional enactments on that subject. For the 'reserve clause,' as has been observed, results in something resembling peonage of the baseball player. By accepting the 'reserve clause'—and all players in organized baseball must 'accept' it—a player binds himself not to sign a contract with, or play for, any club other than the club which originally employs him or its assignee. Although many courts have refused to enforce the 'reserve' clause, yet severe and practically efficacious extra-legal penalties are imposed for violation. The most extreme of these penalties is the blacklisting of the player so that no club in organized baseball will hire him. In effect, this clause prevents a player from ever playing with any team other than his original employer, unless that employer consents. Since the right to play with organized baseball is indispensable to the career of a professional baseball player, violations of the clause by such players are infrequent. The violator may perhaps become a judge (with a less exciting and

---

[19] Gardella v. Chandler, 172 F.2d 402 (2d Cir. 1949).

> often less remunerative occupation) or a bartender or a street-sweeper, but his chances of ever again playing baseball are exceedingly slim.
>
> "As one court, perhaps a bit exaggeratedly, has put it, 'While the services of these baseball players are ostensibly secured by voluntary contracts a study of the system as . . . practiced under the plan of the National Agreement, reveals the involuntary character of the servitude which is imposed upon players by the strength of the combination controlling the labor of practically all of the players in the country. . . . There is no difference in principle between the system of servitude built up by the operation of this National Agreement, which . . . provides for the purchase, sale, barter, and exchange of the services of baseball players —skilled laborers—without their consent, and the system of peonage brought into the United States from Mexico and thereafter existing for a time within the territory of New Mexico. . . . The system created by "organized baseball" in recent years presents the question of the establishment of a scheme by which the personal freedom, the right to contract for their labor wherever they will, of 10,000 skilled laborers, is placed under the dominion of a benevolent despotism through the operation of the monopoly established by the National Agreement.' "[20]

The precedent established by *Federal Baseball* was not fatal to Gardella's suit, as far as Judge Frank was concerned. Indeed, he felt that subsequent decisions of the Supreme Court may well have "left that case but an im-

[20] *Id.* at 409-410.

potent zombie."[21] Rather than simply treat it as such, however, Judge Frank chose instead to distinguish the case.

> "In that earlier case, the court held that the traveling across state lines was but an incidental means of enabling games to be played locally. . . . Here the games themselves, because of radio and television, are, so to speak, played interstate as well as intrastate."[22]

Judge Learned Hand agreed. ". . . The situation appears," he said, ". . . the same as that which would exist at a 'ball-park' where a state line ran between the diamond and the grandstand."[23]

As might have been expected, the decision touched off a storm of controversy. The day after it was announced, Florida Congressman Syd Herlong, formerly an official of the Class D Florida State League, made a speech on the floor of the House of Representatives lamenting that the Gardella case "could well sound the death knell for the sport that has kindled the fires of ambition in the breasts of so many thousands of young Americans."[24]

But such an argument had already been considered by Judge Frank. "Defendants suggest that 'organized baseball' which supplies millions of Americans with desirable diversion, will be unable to exist without the 'reserve clause' " he had written in his opinion. "Whether that is true, no court can predict. In any event, the answer is that the public's pleasure does not authorize the courts to con-

---

[21] *Id.* at 408-409.

[22] *Id.* at 410-411.

[23] *Id.* at 407.

[24] Quoted in Liebling, The Wayward Press—The Doldrums: George & Danny, The New Yorker Magazine, March 12, 1949, pg. 50.

done illegality, and that no court should strive ingeniously to legalize a private (even if benevolent) dictatorship."[25]

Furthermore, not everyone agreed that without the reserve clause baseball's death knell had been sounded. Red Smith, the sports columnist of the *New York Herald Tribune,* responded to Congressman Herlong's speech by writing,

> "It is no time to keep quiet when a Congressman gets up in the House and implores a citizen to abandon his test of something that may be unfair and illegal. . . . Gardella has planted a tack in teacher's chair, but it is nonsense to suggest that the wound thus inflicted might prove fatal to baseball. If some aspects of the baseball monopoly are illegal, they can be altered and the game can go on in health and rectitude. If some of baseball's business methods are illegal, then they bloody well ought to be changed to conform with the law."[26]

Commissioner Chandler was, of course, not happy with Judge Frank's ruling. Said the Commissioner of the Judge's statement that the reserve clause results in something very like peonage, "No major leaguer makes less than $5,000 a year and some make up to a hundred thousand dollars. If you call that peonage, then a lot of us would like to be in it."[27] Perhaps anticipating such a remark, Judge Frank had already pointed out in his written opinion, ". . . If the players be regarded as quasi-peons, it is of no moment that they are well paid; only the to-

[25] Gardella v. Chandler, *supra* note 19, at 415.
[26] Quoted in Liebling, *supra* note 24.
[27] *Id.*

talitarian-minded will believe that high pay excuses virtual slavery."[28]

In addition to controversy, the *Gardella* decision touched off more litigation. Encouraged by Danny Gardella's success in the Court of Appeals, Fred Martin and Max Lanier filed a lawsuit of their own less than one month later.

Though Gardella, Martin, and Lanier were entitled to their days in court, those days would still have been several months away at least. It was then spring and the 1949 season was about to start. The wait for a trial date would likely have meant another season lost—seasons which none of the three could afford to lose for athletic reasons, if not financial. By 1949, Martin had been playing professional baseball for fourteen years, and Lanier for sixteen, and even younger players need to play every season in order to maintain their high-level skills.

Thus, anxious to be reinstated for the new season and buoyed by Judge Frank's strong words, the three ballplayers applied for preliminary injunctions preventing Organized Baseball, while their trials were being awaited, from continuing to keep their names on the list of suspended or ineligible players, and from refusing to negotiate with them in good faith for their services.

Then the first flush of success was quickly dissipated. Injunctions were denied to all three players, and the denials were upheld on appeal.[29] Preliminary injunctions would have given the players all of the relief they would have been entitled to after trial, without proving their cases, the

---

[28] Gardella v. Chandler, *supra* note 19, at 410.

[29] Martin v. Chandler, 1949 CCH Trade Cases ¶ 62,397 (S.D. N.Y. 1949), *aff'd,* 174 F.2d 917 (2d Cir. 1949); Gardella v. Chandler, 1949 CCH Trade Cases ¶ 62,412 (S.D.N.Y. 1949), *aff'd,* 174 F.2d 919 (2d Cir. 1949).

courts held. Further, injunctions would have disturbed the status quo, because all three had voluntarily resigned from the teams they sought to rejoin. Also, they could have been compensated adequately with money damages for the lost season if they eventually won their suits. Most important, serious questions of fact and law remained to be resolved; though the allegations of their complaints may have been sufficient to distinguish *Federal Baseball,* those allegations had not been proved as yet, nor had it been established yet that Organized Baseball's conduct did constitute illegal restraint of trade.

In fact, the allegations were never proved; they were never even tried. For shortly after their motions for preliminary injunctions were denied, Commissioner Chandler reinstated all of the blacklisted players, including Gardella, Martin, and Lanier. Later, Commissioner Chandler explained his reasons for doing so to a House of Representatives Subcommittee as follows:

> "Gardella sued us and then Martin and Lanier sued us, and I was under some pressure from the club owners and the lawyers to put the fellows back. But I would not do it until the court said I did not have to.
>
> "They had asked for a mandatory injunction which would have required the Commissioner to reinstate them. After they went down there and the thing was not as good as they thought it was, they were sadder and wiser, you understand, and they came back and wanted to play. . . .
>
> "They said they were sorry they went, and I was sorry they went. And it was no fun punishing kids like that, a lot of good kids. It was not all their fault. Some of them wanted more money and they could not

get it. Some of them thought they could get more money down there. . . ."[30]

Congressman Wilson then said, "I take it that after you felt the court had upheld your power of suspension, you could afford to be magnanimous."[31]

Commissioner Chandler answered, "Congressman, I thought that I could not only afford to be, but I thought I was bound to temper justice with mercy."[32]

Chandler tempered justice not only with mercy, but with money as well. Danny Gardella reportedly received $60,000 to drop his case.[33] He probably needed that money, too. While his case was pending, he was called the Dred Scott of baseball and had been compared to Sampson. He had also been working in a Mount Vernon hospital as an orderly at a salary of $36.00 per week.[34]

§1.1(c) Legislative proposals, 1951

Organized Baseball undoubtedly settled with the blacklisted players so as not to jeopardize its antitrust exemption. It soon discovered, however, that many considered the *Gardella*[1] opinion to be controlling. By 1951, only two years after the Gardella settlement, Commissioner Chandler and Organized Baseball found themselves defendants in eight federal antitrust lawsuits seeking treble damages

---

[30] Organized Baseball, *supra* note 4, at 83-84.

[31] *Id.* at 84.

[32] *Id.*

[33] Maher, Danny Gardella Case Didn't Settle Anything, L.A. Times, Sept. 24, 1975, Part III.

[34] Liebling, *supra* note 24.

[1] Gardella v. Chandler, 172 F.2d 402 (2d Cir. 1949), discussed in § 1.1(b), *supra*.

totaling several million dollars.[2] Uncertain what the courts might decide, they went to Congress for relief.

Three bills were introduced in the House of Representatives and one in the Senate, all of which would have granted complete exemption from the antitrust laws to all "organized professional sports enterprises or to acts in the conduct of such enterprises." The House Subcommittee on the Study of Monopoly Power conducted extensive hearings on the bills, and then issued a 232 page Report recommending they *not* be passed.[3] The Subcommittee's reasons have been misrepresented or ignored ever since, and thus warrant careful attention.

First, it must be emphasized that the Subcommittee did *not* believe that Organized Baseball would continue to enjoy the exemption originally granted by the Supreme Court in *Federal Baseball* v. *National League.* The Report was clear about that.

> "The Supreme Court's decision in the Federal League case has not been over-ruled. Nevertheless, as the various opinions in the recent case of *Gardella* v. *Chandler* demonstrate, it may be seriously doubted whether baseball should now be regarded as exempt from the antitrust laws. Since 1922, there have been important changes both in the operations of organized baseball and also in the Supreme Court's interpretation of the scope of the statutes enacted pursuant to Congress' constitutional power to regulate interstate commerce.

[2] Organized Baseball: Report of the Subcommittee on the Study of Monopoly Power of the Committee on the Judiciary, House of Representatives, H.Rep. 2002, 82d Cong., 2d Sess. 1 (1952).

[3] *Id.* at 230.

"Only in recent years has it been possible for millions of baseball fans to watch baseball being played through the medium of television. This fact together with the development of radio broadcasting, which has largely taken place since the decision in the Federal League case, affords the principal ground for contending that baseball now has an interstate character which it did not have in 1922. . . .

"Another important development since 1922 is the extensive growth of farm systems. Now each major league baseball club exercises control by means of either stock ownership or contract, over the activities of several minor league clubs located in various States. There may be no legal difference between the geographic disbursal of farm clubs which exist today and the geographic distribution of the major league clubs at the time of the Federal League decision. If, however, the extensive farm systems do not afford a sufficient ground for distinguishing the Federal League case, they nevertheless serve to point up the question whether the Supreme Court might now be inclined to overrule that case. . .

"There is no need to review here the authorities. . . . It is sufficient to state that their disagreement discloses a substantial possibility that the Federal League case would no longer be regarded by the Supreme Court as controlling."[4]

Nor did the Subcommittee believe that Organized Baseball's activities were legal in any event, and that exemption was therefore unnecessary. The Report pointed out the potential illegalities, and concluded,

[4] *Id.* at 135-136.

"The Subcommittee need not resolve any of these issues of legality. It is important, however, to stress the fact that if the legal issues are determined adversely to baseball the courts must enforce the law even though they may believe that organized baseball cannot exist without the reserve clause, and that millions of Americans would lose a desirable form of diversion if it is held illegal." [5]

The reason the Subcommittee recommended the bills not be passed was that it concluded that professional baseball should not be granted a complete immunity from the antitrust laws. This conclusion has been so completely ignored or overlooked ever since, that the exact language of the Report warrants reproduction here.

"If a blanket immunity were granted, all appeal to the courts from a possibly arbitrary decision by the rulers of professional baseball would be foreclosed. In the past the reserve clause has been employed as a 'war measure' to fight the development of competing leagues, sometimes at the expense of individual players. Although instances of arbitrary exercise of power have been rare, they have occurred in the past. The possibility, however remote, that power will be misused in the future makes it unwise perpetually to preclude resort to the courts in such cases.

"The above considerations are fully recognized by men prominent in baseball. One of the leading major league club owners frankly stated to the Subcommittee that he 'would not be in favor of baseball being exempt from the antitrust laws.' Other representatives of baseball management expressed similar opinions, as

---

[5] *Id.* at 139.

did certain players and sportswriters. Even the sponsors of the carte blanche legislation conceded, under questioning, that it would be unwise for the Congress to enact their bills into law without any amendment. Accordingly, the Subcommittee has decided to report unfavorably H.R. 4229, 4230, and 4231 [the three House bills]." [6]

Although the Subcommittee was opposed to the blanket immunity the bills would have granted, it was not completely opposed to baseball's reserve system. In fact, its Report flatly stated that the reserve system should not be outlawed by legislation, explaining, "The Subcommittee concludes, on the basis of the evidence reviewed in this Report, that professional baseball could not operate successfully and profitably without some form of reserve clause." [7] The Report therefore went on to consider whether some form of limited exemption for the reserve system should be enacted. In view of subsequent courtroom developments, the Subcommittee's conclusion is—in retrospect—quite surprising.

> "A statute granting a reasonably limited exemption for the reserve clause would avoid the principal objections to either a blanket immunity or a flat condemnation of organized baseball's reserve rules. For this reason the Subcommittee has carefully considered the wisdom of recommending the enactment of broadly phrased legislation intended to accomplish this objective. Such a bill would state in general terms that the antitrust laws shall not apply to reasonable rules and regulations which promote competition among baseball clubs, even though they restrain competition for

[6] *Id.* at 230.
[7] *Id.* at 228.

player's services—as does the reserve clause—provided that such rules guarantee players a reasonable opportunity to advance in their profession and to be paid at a rate commensurate with their ability. This type of legislation would lay down a rule of reason for baseball. It would give no protection to activities designed to thwart geographic realignment of major league franchises, or to arbitrary blacklisting of players in the course of a 'war' against an independent league. On the other hand, the reasonable and necessary utilization of the reserve clause would be protected against successful antitrust attack.

"There is however, no need to enact a special rule of reason for baseball unless such a rule is not already applicable to this industry. *Organized baseball, represented by eminent counsel, has assured the Subcommittee that the legality of the reserve clause will be tested by the rule of reason.* Though lawsuits have been filed against organized baseball in recent years, in none of them has the court *yet* passed on the reasonableness of the reserve clause. The Department of Justice has not disputed baseball's position that the reserve clause is legal under the rule of reason.

"It would therefore seem premature to enact general legislation for baseball at this time. *Legislation is not necessary until the reasonableness of the reserve rules has been tested by the courts.* If these rules are unreasonable in some respects, it would be inappropriate to adopt legislation before baseball has had an opportunity to make such modifications as may be necessary. Moreover, the type of general legislation now under consideration would require a series of court actions before the legality of the various reserve rules and regulations could be finally settled. A series of lawsuits under such a new statute might not differ materially from the situation confronting organized baseball today. In either event, the courts may have to differentiate the unreasonable features of baseball's rules and regulations from those which are reasonable and necessary. For these reasons, *together with the Subcommittee's earnest desire to avoid influencing pending litigation,* it is unwise to attempt to anticipate judicial action with legislation.

"Accordingly, the Subcommittee has determined . . . to recommend no legislative action at this time." [8]

The Subcommittee's recommendation was accepted by the full House of Representatives, and no legislation was enacted.

What is remarkable about the last quoted portion of the Report is this. While Organized Baseball was assuring the Subcommittee "that the legality of the reserve clause will be tested by the rule of reason," Organized Baseball was arguing to several judges that the rule of reason was irrelevant to the reserve clause, because baseball was not interstate trade or commerce and was thus entirely exempt from the antitrust laws.[9]

§1.1(d) The baseball exemption reaffirmed

Three of the eight lawsuits which had provoked introduction of the immunity bills the Subcommittee recom-

[8] *Id.* at 231-232 (emphasis added).

[9] Toolson v. New York Yankees, 101 F.Supp. 93 (S.D. Cal. 1951), *aff'd,* 200 F.2d 198 (9th Cir. 1952); Kowalski v. Chandler, 202 F.2d 413 (6th Cir. 1953); Corbett v. Chandler, 202 F.2d 428 (6th Cir. 1953); *all aff'd, sub nom.,* Toolson v. New York Yankees, 346 U.S. 356 (1953), discussed in § 1.1(d), *infra.*

mended against eventually worked their way to the United States Supreme Court where they were decided together under the name *Toolson* v. *New York Yankees.*[1] George Earl Toolson, the plaintiff in one of the cases, was a player in the Yankees' farm system. Unhappy about his assignment from the Newark, New Jersey club to one in Binghamton, New York, Toolson refused to report. He was thereupon placed on Binghamton's "ineligible list," and as a result was barred from playing professional baseball. His case was dismissed without a trial by District Judge Harrison who said as he did so, "If the *Federal Baseball Club* case is, as Judge Frank intimates, an 'impotent zombi,' I feel that it is not my duty to so find but that the Supreme Court should so declare." [2]

Judge Harrison also stated,

> "It is a matter of common knowledge that the status of organized baseball is the subject of a Congressional hearing and it may pass legislation that will be determinative of the issue before this court. I believe it is my clear duty to endeavor to be a judge and should not assume the function of a pseudo legislator." [3]

If George Toolson felt frustrated, he could not have been blamed. Congress, assured by Organized Baseball that the reserve clause would be tested by the rule of reason in the courts, and because of an earnest desire to avoid influencing pending litigation, enacted no legislation. Judge Harrison, not wishing to assume the function of a pseudo legislator, accepted Organized Baseball's argument that the

[1] 346 U.S. 356 (1953).

[2] Toolson v. New York Yankees, 101 F.Supp. 93, 95 (S.D. Cal. 1951).

[3] *Id.*

rule of reason was irrelevant because of the *Federal Baseball* ruling almost thirty years before.

Nor were Toolson's frustrations relieved on appeal. The Court of Appeals affirmed the dismissal "On the grounds and for the reasons stated in [Judge Harrison's] opinion. . . ."[4] And on November 9, 1953, the United States Supreme Court revitalized the "impotent zombi" with this one paragraph opinion:

> "In *Federal Baseball Club of Baltimore* v. *National League of Professional Baseball Clubs* . . . this Court held that the business of providing public baseball games for profit between clubs of professional baseball players was not within the scope of the federal antitrust laws. Congress has had the ruling under consideration but has not seen fit to bring such business under these laws by legislation having prospective effect. The business has thus been left for thirty years to develop, on the understanding that it was not subject to existing antitrust legislation. The present cases ask us to overrule the prior decision and, with retrospective effect, hold the legislation applicable. We think that if there are evils in this field which now warrant application to it of the antitrust laws it should be by legislation. Without re-examination of the underlying issues, the judgments below are affirmed on the authority of *Federal Baseball Club of Baltimore* v. *National League of Professional Baseball Clubs* . . . so far as that decision determines that Congress had no intention of including the business of baseball within the scope of the federal antitrust laws. Affirmed."[5]

[4] Toolson v. New York Yankees, 200 F.2d 198, 199 (9th Cir. 1952).

[5] Toolson v. New York Yankees, 346 U.S 356-7 (1953).

The *Toolson* opinion is vulnerable to criticism on four grounds. First, although Congress had had the *Federal Baseball* ruling under consideration, it was incorrect of the Supreme Court to state that Congress had not seen fit to bring baseball under the antitrust laws by legislation. As is apparent from the Subcommittee Report, Congress thought it unlikely that Organized Baseball continued to enjoy the exemption granted it by *Federal Baseball.*[6] The legislation Congress had considered and rejected shortly before the Court's decision in *Toolson* v. *New York Yankees* was not legislation to overturn *Federal Baseball,* as the Court implies in its short *Toolson* decision; rather it was legislation that would have reactivated the exemption Congress believed no longer existed. Thus, the Supreme Court did in *Toolson* precisely that which Congress had refused to do. Congress' refusal to enact the proposed legislation was therefore no basis for the *Toolson* result; it should have been a ground for the Court to expressly overrule *Federal Baseball.*

Second, the Supreme Court stated in *Toolson* that it was acting on the authority of *Federal Baseball* "so far as that decision determines that Congress had no intention of including the business of baseball within the scope of the Federal antitrust laws." That statement has no factual basis. *Federal Baseball* did not in any way determine that Congress had no intention to include baseball under the antitrust laws. The case simply determined that given the facts and law then existing, Organized Baseball was not engaged in interstate commerce. As Supreme Court Justices Harold H. Burton and Stanley F. Reed put it in their dissent from the *Toolson* decision,

---

[6] See § 1.1(c), *supra.*

> "In the *Federal Baseball Club* case the Court did not state that even if the activities of organized baseball amounted to interstate trade or commerce those activities were exempt from the Sherman Act. The Court acted on its determination that the activities before it did not amount to interstate commerce." [7]

Third, while the Court correctly stated the result it had reached in *Federal Baseball,* it completely ignored subsequent opinions of its own which were the basis for Judge Frank's "impotent zombi" intimation.[8]

Fourth, since George Toolson's complaint had been dismissed by Judge Harrison without a trial, there was nothing in the record to indicate whether Organized Baseball had in fact relied upon its exemption. If it had not in fact relied, that it may have "been left" to do so is irrelevant. Moreover, all of the actions which gave rise to the lawsuits decided by the Court in *Toolson* were taken after the decision of the Court of Appeals in *Gardella* v. *Chandler.*[9] Even if Organized Baseball had in fact relied upon its exemption prior to *Gardella,* reliance thereafter hardly would have been justified.

Whether the *Toolson* decision was correct or not, however, it stood. A petition for rehearing was routinely denied,[10] and thereafter *Toolson* v. *New York Yankees* afforded Organized Baseball many years of peace, as far as lawsuits and courtrooms were concerned.

---

[7] 346 U.S. at 360.

[8] See, Gardella v. Chandler, 172 F.2d 402, 412 fn. 7a, b, & c (2d Cir. 1949).

[9] 172 F.2d 402 (2d Cir. 1949).

[10] 346 U.S. 917 (1953).

§1.2 Other sports: the creation of an anomaly

While baseball was at peace, other segments of the entertainment industry were not. In 1953 the Federal Government filed an antitrust suit against Lee and Jacob Shubert, Marcus Heiman and three corporations they controlled, charging them with restraining trade and monopolizing the business of producing, booking and presenting legitimate theatrical plays, musicals and operettas. Following the Supreme Court's decision in *Toolson* v. *New York Yankees,*[1] the trial judge in the *Shubert* case dismissed the Government's suit, saying, "In principle, I can see no valid distinction between the facts of this case and those which were before the Supreme Court in the cases of *Federal Baseball* . . . and *Toolson*. . . ."[2] Indeed, the business of legitimate theater is not substantially different from that of professional baseball. In both, entertainers perform in enclosed places before assembled crowds of viewers who pay for the privilege of watching the performances in person. If the presentation of professional baseball games was not "interstate trade or commerce," a holding that plays, musicals and operettas were not either seems reasonable.

The Government, however, saw distinctions the trial judge had not, and in an opinion by Chief Justice Earl Warren, the Supreme Court agreed with the Government.[3]

> "In *Toolson,* where the issue was the same as in *Federal Baseball,* the Court was confronted with a unique combination of circumstances. For over 30 years there had stood a decision of this Court specifically fixing the status of the baseball business under the anti-

---

[1] 346 U.S. 356 (1953), discussed in § 1.1 (d), *supra.*

[2] United States v. Shubert, 120 F.Supp. 15, 16 (S.D.N.Y. 1953).

[3] United States v. Shubert, 348 U.S. 222 (1955).

> trust laws and more particularly the validity of the so-called 'reserve clause.' During this period, in reliance on the *Federal Baseball* precedent, the baseball business had grown and developed . . . . And Congress, although it had actively considered the ruling, had not seen fit to reject it by amendatory legislation. Against this background, the Court in *Toolson* was asked to overrule *Federal Baseball* on the ground that it was out of step with subsequent decisions reflecting present day concepts of interstate commerce. The Court, in view of the circumstances of the case, declined to do so. But neither did the Court necessarily reaffirm all that was said in Federal Baseball. Instead, 'without re-examination of the underlying issues,' the Court adhered to *Federal Baseball* 'so far as that decision determines that Congress had no intention of including the business of baseball within the scope of the federal antitrust laws.' . . . In short, *Toolson* was a narrow application of the rule of *stare decisis*."[4]

Legitimate theater, the Court held, fell outside the area protected by the narrow application of *stare decisis*,[5] and thus was subject to the antitrust laws.

§1.2(a) Boxing

In an opinion rendered by the Supreme Court the same day as *Shubert*,[1] the Court even refused to follow the base-

[4] *Id.* at 229-230.

[5] Latin, meaning, that which has been decided should stand. In law, the doctrine requires a case having the same facts as one already decided to be decided in the same manner. See, however, § 1.3(b)(3)(A), *infra*.

[1] United States v. Shubert, 348 U.S. 222 (1955), discussed in § 1.2, *supra*.

ball precedents in a case involving professional boxing. In *United States* v. *International Boxing Club,* the Government charged several defendants with restraining trade and monopolizing the business of promoting professional championship boxing matches. The trial judge dismissed the Government's case, believing that *Federal Baseball* and *Toolson* exempted boxing from the antitrust laws.[2] Again the Supreme Court reversed the dismissal, saying,

> ". . . *stare decisis* cannot help the defendants here; for, contrary to their argument, *Federal Baseball* did not hold that all businesses based on professional sports were outside the scope of the antitrust laws. The issue confronting us is, therefore, not whether a previously granted exemption should continue, but whether an exemption should be granted in the first instance. And that issue is for Congress to resolve, not this Court." [3]

Justice Felix Frankfurter, however, dissented. "It would baffle the subtlest ingenuity," he said, "to find a single differentiating factor between other sporting exhibitions . . . and baseball. . . ." [4] His notion of *stare decisis* was that it applied whenever there were substantially similar facts; identical facts were not necessary. "I cannot translate even the narrowest conception of *stare decisis* into the equivalent of writing into the Sherman Law an exemption of baseball to the exclusion of every other sport different not one legal jot or tittle from it." [5]

Justice Sherman Minton joined Justice Frankfurter in dissent. Said he,

---

[2] 348 U.S. 236 (1955).

[3] *Id.* at 243.

[4] *Id.* at 248.

[5] *Id.* at 250.

"When boxers travel from State to State, carrying their shorts and fancy dressing robes in a ditty bag in order to participate in a boxing bout, which is wholly intrastate, it is now held by this Court that the boxing bout becomes interstate commerce. What this Court held in the *Federal Baseball* case to be incident to the exhibition now becomes more important than the exhibition. This is as fine an example of the tail wagging the dog as can be conjured up." [6]

§ 1.2(b) Football

If after the *International Boxing Club*[1] case there was any doubt that baseball stood alone in the eyes of the law, that doubt was laid to rest in 1957 when the Supreme Court decided *Radovich* v. *National Football League.*[2] William Radovich, a University of Southern California graduate, played with the Detroit Lions from 1938 until 1941, when he joined the Navy because of World War II. In 1945, the All-Pro guard returned to the Lions, but the next year asked to be traded to the Los Angeles Rams so he could be near his ailing father who lived in California.

The Lions refused. Having played the entire 1945 season as required by his 1945 contract, and not having signed a contract for the 1946 season, Radovich moved to Los Angeles and joined the Los Angeles Dons, a member of the then-new All-America Conference, with whom he played for two years. In 1948, the San Francisco Clippers of the Pacific Coast League offered Radovich employment as a player-coach, but withdrew the offer before Radovich could accept. The reasons for its withdrawal led to his lawsuit.

[6] *Id.* at 251.

[1] United States v. International Boxing Club, 348 U.S. 236 (1955), discussed in § 1.2(a), *supra.*

[2] 358 U.S. 445 (1957).

The Detroit Lions were and are members of the National Football League. The NFL, like Organized Baseball, required all of its member teams to use Uniform Player Contracts which in those years contained reserve clauses—clauses which gave NFL teams perpetual rights to the services of every player in the league.

The All-America Conference, however, was not affiliated with the National Football League, and for that reason the Dons ignored the Lions' reserve rights. When Radovich signed with the Dons, the National Football League blacklisted him for five years.

The blacklist did not affect Radovich during the two years he played for the Dons. Since the All-America Conference was not affiliated with the NFL, it did not penalize Radovich for being blacklisted by the NFL, just as it had honored the Dons' 1946 contract with him, even though he was under reserve to the Lions.

However, the effects of the blacklist were felt by Radovich when he wanted to accept the offer of the San Francisco Clippers. The Pacific Coast League, of which the Clippers were a member, was affiliated with the National Football League in a fashion similar to the affiliation of major and minor league baseball teams. After the Clippers had offered Radovich employment as a player-coach, the NFL advised the team that he had been blacklisted, and that if it did sign him, it would suffer severe penalties. The offer was withdrawn immediately, and thereafter the Clippers refused to sign Radovich to any position.

When the All-America Conference went out of business in 1949, Radovich was unable to find employment with any professional football team, for all were then NFL members. His lawsuit followed. In it he charged the NFL, its member clubs and commissioner, the Pacific Coast League and its commissioner, and the San Francisco Clippers with conspiring to monopolize professional football in the United States by destroying the All-America Conference and by blacklisting him.

All of the defendants moved to dismiss the case on the grounds that football, like baseball, was exempt from the antitrust laws. And after the Supreme Court rendered its decision in *Toolson,* the District Court judge dismissed Radovich's complaint. By the time the dismissal was reviewed by the Court of Appeals, however, the Supreme Court had rendered its decision in the *International Boxing Club* case. With the defendants relying on *Toolson* and *Federal Baseball,* and Radovich relying on *International Boxing Club,* the Court of Appeals expressed its dilemma thusly, "Which of the two tides catches professional football? We confess that the strength of the pull of both cases is about equal." [3]

On the one hand, the Court of Appeals considered sound Radovich's argument that baseball's immunity was an historical accident confined strictly to that sport. On the other hand, the professional football business is more similar to the business of baseball than to the business of boxing. "Football is a team sport," said the Court.

> "Its operation has just about the same aspects as baseball. Boxing is an individual sport. In professional football, very good arguments do exist for the indulgence of restraints on individual players. . . . In boxing, arguments for restraints on the individual's right to contract seem rather hollow." [4]

---

[3] Radovich v. National Football League, 231 F.2d 620, 622 (9th Cir. 1956).

[4] *Id.*

The Court of Appeals decided football was caught in the tide of *Toolson* and *Federal Baseball.* "Further," it said in bolstering its affirmance of the dismissal of Radovich's complaint, "It appears reasonable to us to assume that if Congressional indulgence extended to and saved baseball from regulation, then the indulgence extended to other team sports." [5]

While the Court of Appeals' thinking was reasonable, a majority of the Supreme Court disagreed with its conclusion. In an opinion on behalf of six of the nine members of the Court, Justice Tom Clark said, ". . . we now specifically limit the rule . . . established [in *Federal Baseball* and *Toolson*] to the facts involved, i.e., the business of organized professional baseball." [6] Justice Clark explained the Court's reasons for doing so as follows:

> "In *Toolson* we continued to hold the umbrella over baseball that was placed there some 31 years earlier by *Federal Baseball.* The Court did this because it was concluded that more harm would be done in overruling *Federal Baseball* than in upholding a ruling which at best was of dubious validity. Vast efforts had gone into the development and organization of baseball since that decision and enormous capital had been invested in reliance on its permanence. Congress had chosen to make no change. All this, combined with the flood of litigation that would follow its repudiation, the harassment that would ensue, and the retroactive effect of such a decision, led the Court to the practical result that it should sustain the unequivocal line of authority reaching over many years. . . .

---

[5] *Id.*

[6] 352 U.S. at 451.

"If this ruling is unrealistic, inconsistent, or illogical, it is sufficient to answer, aside from the distinctions between the businesses, that were we considering the question of baseball for the first time upon a clean slate we would have no doubts. But *Federal Baseball* held the business of baseball outside the scope of the Act. No other business claiming the coverage of those cases has such an adjudication. We, therefore, conclude that the orderly way to eliminate error or discrimination, if any there be, is by legislation and not by court decision. Congressional processes are more accommodative, affording the whole industry hearings and an opportunity to assist in the formulation of new legislation. The resulting product is therefore more likely to protect the industry and the public alike. The whole scope of congressional action would be known in advance and effective dates for the legislation could be set in the future without the injustices or retroactivity and surprise which might follow court action." [7]

Justice Felix Frankfurter, who dissented in the *International Boxing Club* case because he could see no relevant distinction between baseball and boxing, dissented again. Conscious as he was, said he, of his "limited competence in matters athletic," he had not as yet heard of any consideration which led the Court to rule as it did in *Toolson* "that is not equally applicable to football." [8] Unable to distinguish football from baseball, and finding "no basis for attributing to Congress a purpose to put baseball in a class by itself," [9] Justices John Marshall Harlan and William J. Brennan dissented as well.

---

[7] 352 U.S. at 450-452.
[8] 352 U.S. at 455.
[9] 352 U.S. at 456.

§1.2(c) Legislative proposals, 1957-1965

§1.2(c)(1) 85th Congress: the Celler bill and the per se doctrine

Football executives did find the *Radovich*[1] decision to be unrealistic, inconsistent and illogical, and they immediately did as the Supreme Court suggested. They went to Congress, hoping and probably expecting that its processes would be "more accommodative." Several bills were immediately introduced in the House of Representatives, and in the summer of 1957—only months after the Supreme Court's ruling—approximately 50 witnesses testified during 15 days of hearings before the House Antitrust Subcommittee.[2]

The bills were of three types. Some were similar to those the Subcommittee had recommended against in its 1952 Organized Baseball Report—bills which provided for complete antitrust exemption for professional sports and all of their acts. Others would have subjected all sports to the requirements of the antitrust laws, but also would have permitted courts to determine, based on the facts of each case, whether any particular agreement or practice constituted a reasonable and thus legal restraint of trade. The third group of bills also would have placed all professional sports under the dictates of the antitrust laws; however, rather than allow courts to determine which practices or agreements were reasonable, and legal, this third group expressly exempted certain practices.

---

[1] Radovich v. National Football League, 352 U.S. 445 (1957), discussed in § 1.2(b), *supra*.

[2] Hearings on H.R. 5307, et al., before the Antitrust Subcommittee of the House Committee on the Judiciary, 85th Congress, 1st Sess. (1957).

Despite the extensive hearings, no action was taken by the House of Representatives on any of these bills. Then in January of 1958, Congressman Emanuel Celler, Chairman of the House Judiciary Committee (and also Chairman of the Subcommittee that issued the 1952 Organized Baseball Report), introduced a bill of his own, H.R. 10378. The Celler bill subjected the professional team sports of baseball, football, basketball and hockey to the requirements of the antitrust laws, but expressly exempted activities which were "reasonably necessary" to equalize competitive playing strengths, to grant exclusive franchise territories, and to preserve public confidence in the honesty of professional sports.

Because extensive hearings had been held the previous summer, no further hearings were considered necessary, and on May 13, 1958 the House Judiciary Committee reported favorably on its Chairman's bill, recommending to the full House of Representatives that it be passed.[3] In its Report, a majority of the Committee sought to convey the impression that Celler's bill was favorable to professional sports, or at least as favorable as it could be short of exempting professional sports completely. Thus, the bill's exemption of "reasonably necessary" activities was said to be a favor to the industry; and in a way it was.

Although the language of the Sherman Act prohibits all contracts, combinations and conspiracies that restrain trade, the courts have long held that only "unreasonable" restraints are illegal, not all restraints.[4] However, the Supreme Court has held that certain kinds of restraints

---

[3] H.Rep. 1720, 85th Cong. (1958).

[4] Standard Oil Co. v. United States, 221 U.S. 1 (1911).

have such a "pernicious effect on competition"[5] that they are always illegal, whether or not they may be reasonable under particular circumstances. These kinds of practices are said to be "per se" violations of the Sherman Act. In the Committee's view, "Allocation of territories and group boycotts to enforce the player selection system, the reserve clause recognition system, and the exercise of the Commissioner's powers, particularly, might be subject to the per se doctrine of antitrust law."[6] Hence the favor to professional sports.

> "It is the intent of the committee in this bill to assure, with respect to the classes of activities enumerated therein, that the antitrust per se doctrine shall not apply. On the contrary, whenever an activity in an organized professional team sport is challenged under the antitrust laws, the bill requires that such activity shall not be found to violate the antitrust laws if the activity is reasonably necessary to accomplish the results enumerated in the bill."[7]

Many members of the House Judiciary Committee did not view Congressman Celler's bill as a relief measure at all, however. In fact they viewed it as presenting a serious threat to professional sports.

> "Under the terms of H.R. 10378, unless it can be shown in actual court proceedings that these practices are 'reasonably necessary' for the continuation of the sport involved they will become illegal . . . . Instead of confirming the legality of these practices, the present bill would force organized professional team sports

---

[5] Northern Pacific v. United States, 356 U.S. 1, 5 (1957).

[6] H.Rep. 1720, *supra* note 3, at 7.

[7] *Id.*

> to run a gauntlet of legal proceedings to save themselves from complete ruin."[8]

As they viewed it, "This bill is an open invitation to every disgruntled player to litigate the fine points of the game in courts throughout the land."[9]

The dissenters had a better idea. By simply eliminating the words "reasonably necessary" from Congressman Celler's bill, the player draft, the reserve clause, exclusive territories, and actions taken to preserve confidence in the honesty of sports would be absolutely exempt. Thus when the bill was brought up for a vote on the floor of the House of Representatives on June 24, 1958, the dissenters introduced substitute bills that omitted mention of "reasonably necessary"; and after extensive debate, H.R. 10378 was passed, but without those two words.

Three days later, on June 27th, the House-passed bill was introduced in the Senate; and in July, the Senate Antitrust Subcommittee held 12 days of hearings at which 37 witnesses testified.[10] Then, for reasons now unknown, the Subcommittee tabled the bill; no further action was taken by the time the 85th Congress adjourned, killing the bill entirely. Congress never again came so close to enacting a comprehensive sports antitrust law.

§1.2(c)(2) 86th Congress: the Kefauver bills and the Continental League

By the time the 86th Congress convened in January of 1959 the temptation to tinker had taken hold. Or perhaps

---

[8] *Id.* at 10.

[9] *Id.* at 11.

[10] Hearings on H.R. 10378 and S. 4070 before the Subcommittee on Antitrust and Monopoly of the Senate Committee on the Judiciary, 85th Cong., 2d Sess. (1958).

tinkering was thought necessary to placate those who may have been responsible for the demise of the amended Celler bill. Senator Hennings introduced a bill at the outset of the 86th Congress which was substantially similar to the House-passed bill of the year before.

It was quickly followed in February of 1959 by another which severely limited the scope of exempted activities. Introduced by Senator Estes Kefauver, this bill subjected professional team sports to the antitrust laws, while absolutely exempting practices designed to equalize team playing strengths, exclusive territory arrangements, actions taken to preserve the honesty of sports, and the regulation of radio and television broadcasting of sports contests. However, Senator Kefauver's bill provided that none of the exemptions would apply to any professional baseball team that controlled more than 80 players at one time. Further, Kefauver's bill provided that players had to consent before they could be subjected to a league-wide draft. Exclusive territories, to be exempt, had to be no larger than a circle having a 35 mile radius from the ballpark, and were not exempt in any event in cities that had a population of more than two million. The exemption relating to radio and television broadcasting would apply only if the Federal Communications Commission found agreements relating thereto were reasonably necessary. And finally, Kefauver's bill provided that it was to be effective for only four years, thus enabling Congress to reexamine the situation later.

Hearings were held on both the Hennings and Kefauver bills,[1] and at their conclusion Senator Kefauver introduced yet another. Kefauver's second bill did not apply to base-

---

[1] Hearings on S. 616 and S. 886 before the Subcommittee on Antitrust and Monopoly of the Senate Committee on the Judiciary, 86th Cong., 1st Sess. (1959).

ball, because, he said, the Antitrust Subcommittee had been unable to agree on a bill that would cover all sports equally. He said that baseball was fundamentally different from other team sports because of its extensive minor league system for developing major league playing talent. The Subcommittee wanted more time to study baseball, and Kefauver touted his new bill as one that in the meantime would eliminate the existing discrimination among the team sports.

In September of 1959, Kefauver's second bill was reported favorably by the Antitrust Subcommittee to the full Judiciary Committee, and the following June his first bill and Senator Hennings' bill were reported as well. By that time however, Senator Kefauver had introduced a third bill, S. 3483.

S. 3483 contained two parts. Title I applied to football, basketball and hockey, but not to baseball. It provided that the antitrust laws would not apply to the activities of those three sports to the extent they related to the equalization of competitive playing sports, to the employment, selection, or eligibility of players or to the reservation, selection or assignment of player contracts, to exclusive franchise territories (not to exceed 35 miles in radius and not to exist in cities of over two million), to the preservation of public confidence in the honesty of sports, and to certain agreements or practices relating to radio and television broadcasting.

Title II related to baseball alone, and was for the most part the mirror image of Title I. That is, Title II provided that the antitrust laws would apply to baseball, except those activities exempted by Title I. In addition, however, Title II contained a proviso which Title I did not contain.

With respect to football, basketball and hockey, Title I exempted from the antitrust laws those activities relating to the employment, selection or eligibility of players, or to the reservation, selection or assignment of their contracts. Title II did the same on behalf of baseball, but then provided that notwithstanding such exemption, all baseball players with four or more years of professional experience who were directly or indirectly owned or controlled by a major league team would be subject to an unrestricted draft, every year after the World Series, by any other major league team, except for forty players which each team could reserve for itself. The effect of this proviso was to make it an antitrust violation for major league teams to reserve more than forty veteran players a year. There was no similar limitation on the number of players a football, basketball or hockey team could reserve.

The ostensible difference between baseball and the other three team sports was that baseball had extensive farm systems, thereby enabling major league teams to own or control not only the players on their own rosters, but also hundreds of minor league players as well. While it is true that football and basketball do not have farm systems, hockey does, but no explanation was offered by the advocates of S. 3483 as to why hockey was to be treated more kindly than baseball.

S. 3483 puzzled some Senators in another respect, too. Up until the time that bill was considered by the Senate, baseball had been completely exempt from the antitrust laws by reason of the *Federal Baseball* and *Toolson* decisions. Football on the other hand, and presumably basketball and hockey as well, were completely subject to those laws. Yet, the effect of S. 3483 was not only to equalize the treatment of all four sports; it actually went further and made baseball subject to antitrust restrictions to a greater degree than the other three.

The reason that S. 3483 went so far and reversed the positions of the sports was that the organizers of a proposed new major baseball league, the Continental League, had convinced many Senators that it would not be able to begin operations so long as existing American and National League teams had a virtual lock on all of the available player talent. Especially convinced were Senators representing states that did not have an American or National League franchise, but who hoped to be awarded a Continental League team.

American and National League owners were naturally opposed to Title II, as were many owners of minor league franchises, most of whom received subsidies from the majors in exchange for supplying players. Senators Everett Dirksen and Roman Hruska, for example, received telegrams from the presidents of 75 minor league clubs urging them to oppose Title II on the grounds it would "mean the total emasculation of the minor leagues as presently constituted." [2] Said one telegram to Senator Dirksen from the president of the New York Penn League,

> "It is highly inconceivable that anyone would invest substantial amounts of money in scouting, signing, and assigning players to us and meeting the financial obligations of working agreements which are substantial without the assurance of a return of their investment." [3]

Members of the existing Organized Baseball establishment, as indicated by their use of the word "investment," thought of players as their private "property." As a result,

[2] S.Rep. 1620, 86th Cong., 2d Sess. 22 (1960).

[3] *Id.* at 22-23.

they were highly contemptuous of the promoters of the Continental League, who under Title II would have had the right to draft players from existing teams. It would have had this right because Title II insisted that all "major league" teams be able to draft, but did not define "major league." Organized Baseball's attitude was, "Why should any group . . . naming themselves 'major league' be extended this same privilege without having proved themselves as successful. . . ." [4]

While S. 3483 was still in Committee, this conflict between Organized Baseball and the Continental League was shown to be virtually irreconcilable. Two significant amendments were offered in Committee by Senators who were sympathetic to Organized Baseball's position. One would have added baseball to the sports covered by Title I and would have stricken Title II entirely. The other would have allowed Title II to remain in the bill, but would have added a definition of the term "major league." Essentially, the proposed definition would have left it to the American and National Leagues to determine whether another league was "major" and thus entitled to participate in the draft. (Senators Dirksen and Hruska would have prohibited the existing leagues from unreasonably withholding such recognition and approval, but as originally introduced by Senator Philip Hart, the amendment would not have imposed even that limitation on the power of the American and National Leagues to determine whether a competitor had become "major.")

Both proposed amendments were rejected by a majority of the Committee, but the minority refused to accept defeat. As a result, the Committee could not reach agreement on whether to recommend passage of the bill to the

[4] *Id.* at 23.

full Senate and therefore reported the bill to the Senate without a recommendation. Instead, the Report contained seven separate statements expressing the individual views of nine Senators.[5]

Extensive debate on the bill was conducted on the floor of the Senate on June 28, 1960. Again Organized Baseball's supporters proposed the amendment adding baseball to Title I and dropping Title II. This time the amendment passed, 45 to 41. As soon as it had, Senator John Carroll of Colorado, a state without an American or National League team, and a supporter of Title II, said, ". . . the hour is late. The deed has been done. I move to recommit the bill to the Senate Judiciary Committee without instructions . . . so that the committee may study the bill further."[6]

The motion to recommit then passed 73 to 12, suggesting two things. First, the vote to drop Title II probably resulted from the absence of an understanding of what the bill was intended to accomplish, rather than from a desire to protect Organized Baseball from the competition of the Continental League. The lack of understanding was probably caused by the seven separate statements which accompanied the Committee Report in lieu of the single majority report and individual dissents that are customary. Thus, the 73 Senators who voted to recommit the bill to Committee probably hoped the Committee would make up its own collective mind and then inform the Senate what decision had been reached.

Second, promoters of the Continental League were not helped by the recommission of the bill to Committee, be-

---

[5] S.Rep. 1620, 86th Cong., 2d Sess. 1, 8, 14, 16, 18, 19, 21 and 25 (1960).

[6] 106 Congressional Record, 86th Cong., 2d Sess. (June 28, 1960).

cause in the absence of legislation, baseball would continue to enjoy complete exemption from the antitrust laws and could thus continue to control most, if not all, of the nation's players. However, Senator Carroll may have thought or hoped that representatives of professional football, basketball and hockey would lobby those Committee members who objected to Title II into accepting it in order to get the bill out of Committee again. For in the absence of legislation, those three sports would continue to be subject to the antitrust laws in full.

Whatever the Senators' thoughts may have been, neither S. 3483 nor any other sports bill emerged from the Senate Judiciary Committee again during the 86th Congress.

In the House of Representatives seven sports bills were considered during the 86th Congress. Six were substantially similar to H.R. 10378—the Celler bill as amended —that had passed the House during the 85th Congress.[7] The seventh bill would have completely exempted professional team sports from the antitrust laws. Hearings were held on all seven bills in September of 1959,[8] but no further action was taken. With the close of the 86th Congress at the end of 1960, all sports bills in both houses died. Baseball was still exempt, completely; football, basketball, and hockey were not at all.

§1.2(c)(3) 87th Congress

By the time the 87th Congress convened in January of 1961, the Supreme Court's *Radovich* v. *National Football*

[7] See § 1.2(c)(1), *supra*.

[8] Hearings on H.R. 2370 et al. before the Antitrust Subcommittee of the House Committee on the Judiciary, 86th Cong., 1st Sess. (1959) (not printed).

League[1] decision was almost four years old, and it had caused no damage whatever to professional football. The Continental League had never begun play, possibly because of Congress' failure to pass Title II of S. 3483; and thus its promoters were no longer lobbying members of Congress to break up Organized Baseball's monopoly. With other important matters of state demanding its attention, Congress began to feel less pressured to clarify the status of professional sports under the antitrust laws.

New bills were introduced. Senator Kefauver introduced one similar to S. 3483 providing for the unrestricted draft of unreserved baseball players by all major league teams. And Senator Hart introduced one that treated all team sports absolutely the same. No hearings were held on either of these bills however, and though they were reported to the full Judiciary Committee by its Antitrust Subcommittee, the Judiciary Committee did no more than discuss and forget them.

Three bills similar to Senator Hart's were introduced in the House of Representatives early in the 87th Congress, but they, too, were ignored by the committee to which they had been referred.

During the summer of 1961, Congress did quickly pass a bill permitting sports leagues to enter into package contracts with television networks for the sale of broadcast rights to the league's entire schedule of games.[2] But other than the television law, Congress gave no further consideration to professional sports during the 87th Congress, and the bills that had been introduced at its outset quietly died.

---

[1] 352 U.S. 445 (1957), discussed in § 1.2(b), *supra*.

[2] Discussed in § 10.2(b), *infra*.

§ 1.2(c)(4) 88th Congress

On December 16, 1973, midway through the 88th Congress, Senator Hart introduced a bill similar to those he had introduced in previous years. Hearings were conducted in January and February of 1964,[1] and on July 20, 1964, the Judiciary Committee reported the bill to the full Senate, recommending that it be passed.[2] The Senate, however, took no action.

Fourteen bills identical to Senator Hart's were introduced in the House of Representatives during the 88th Congress, but those, too, were ignored.

For a while it seemed that all of the steam that had once propelled Congress through weeks of hearings consisting of volumes of testimony from scores of witnesses had finally dissipated entirely. Then in August of 1964, the Columbia Broadcasting System announced that it had purchased control of the New York Yankees; and the Organized Baseball monopoly issue once again became one of concern.

§ 1.2(c)(5) 89th Congress: the Hart bill and the CBS-Yankees purchase

Since August 1964 came too close to adjournment for the 88th Congress to consider Senator Hart's pending bill, the Senator waited until the beginning of the 89th, and on February 2, 1965, he introduced a new one substantially similar to those he had introduced before. Hearings were held immediately, limited to the antitrust

---

[1] Hearings on S. 2391 before the Subcommittee on Antitrust and Monopoly of the Senate Judiciary Committee, 88th Cong., 2d Sess. (1964).

[2] S.Rep. 1303, 88th Cong. (1964).

implications of CBS' acquisition of the Yankees,[1] and on July 16, 1965, the Judiciary Committee reported the bill to the full Senate, recommending that it be passed.[2]

The bill was called up on the floor of the Senate on August 31, 1965, and extensive debate was conducted over several proposed amendments. Senator Sam Ervin introduced one which would have removed the antitrust exemption for the draft of college students prior to the conclusion of their senior playing seasons. Several senators, and apparently some schools who supported the amendment, thought it was designed to prohibit professional teams from drafting college students. While basketball and football had their own rules against doing so, the bidding war between the American Football League and the National Football League was then in full force, and several teams had signed promising college seniors before they had played in post-season bowl games.[3]

In fact, however, Senator Ervin's amendment was not intended to prohibit the *signing* of college students. It was simply intended to prohibit professional teams from *drafting* them. The result sought would have enabled college students to bargain with every team that might be interested, rather than only the one team per league that would hold draft rights to him after graduation. If college students were going to drop out of school to become professional athletes, Senator Ervin reasoned, the least Congress could do was assure them the opportunity to make the best deal they could for themselves.

[1] Hearings on S. 950 before the Subcommittee on Antitrust and Monopoly of the Senate Judiciary Committee, 89th Cong., 1st Sess. (1965).

[2] S.Rep. 462, 89th Cong. (1965).

[3] See § 5.2(a), *infra*.

Some senators, however, thought that Ervin's amendment would actually encourage students to drop out of school, because those that continued their educations until graduation would then be subject to the player draft and would then have only one team per league with which to bargain. For that and probably other reasons as well, Senator Ervin's amendment was defeated.

Then Senator William Proxmire of Wisconsin proposed an amendment which would have required teams to divide evenly all of the revenue received by them from the sale of television broadcast rights. The purpose of the amendment, he said, was to assist financially weaker teams, who were often the athletically weaker teams, too. A second purpose, he said, was to discourage teams from moving from one city another.

The Milwaukee Braves had recently announced plans to move to Atlanta, even though, over the years, Milwaukee had had the second highest average attendance in its league.[4] Senator Proxmire understood the Braves were moving because an Atlanta television station was willing to pay more for broadcast rights than Milwaukee stations, because no other major league baseball teams were located in the southeastern part of the country, while Milwaukee was hemmed in by two Chicago teams and the Minnesota Twins. If revenue was divided equally among all teams, the Braves would have no such incentive to move.

However, some senators thought the Proxmire amendment would be unfair to teams that had developed large television audiences in their parts of the country and were therefore paid accordingly. The New York Yankees, for example, had much greater television revenues than other

---

[4] See § 8.3(a), *infra*.

teams—revenue which the Yankees did not think should have to be shared with others. The Proxmire amendment did not pass either.

Senator Allott of Colorado proposed an amendment that would have required that there be only one player draft in each sport, which would be participated in at the same time by all leagues "at the same level." In other words, he would have done away with the separate drafts that were then being conducted by the American and National Football Leagues, and would have required the two leagues to participate in a single draft as they have done ever since their merger in 1966. "What I object to" he said, for reasons he did not explain, "are the exorbitant salaries promised these young men, as a result of team bidding against team, when the young man has never participated in the sport professionally." [5]

His amendment was offered at the behest of the war-weary American Football League. Had it passed, it would have effectively constituted a merger of the then separate leagues. It did not pass however. Neither the amendment, nor anything remotely similar to it, had been considered by the Judiciary Committee, nor had any hearings been conducted on the effects of such a proposal. Recognizing the sweeping effects the amendment would have had, the Senate defeated it on a voice vote.

An amendment proposed by Senator Pearson of Kansas would have stricken from the list of exempted activities the one that authorized exclusive franchise territories. He argued that by eliminating that exemption, teams could, in some way, be prevented from moving from city to city. How this would be accomplished was never made clear

[5] 117 Congressional Record 22327, 89th Cong., 1st Sess. (August 31, 1965).

during the very short debate that followed the amendment's introduction, and it, too, was defeated on a voice vote.

It seems that after years of consideration and volumes of testimony at weeks of hearings, the Senate had finally put its mind to enactment of a comprehensive sports antitrust bill, and no further tinkering was going to be permitted. Finally, the time came for a vote on Senator Hart's bill, and finally, too, it passed. When it did, there was a round of congratulatory speeches concluding with one in which Senator Jacob Javits congratulated Senator Hart, saying he

> "... has done a splendid job in piloting through the Senate intricate and difficult legislation, which will be of great value to millions of Americans, old and young alike, who will thank him for having brought regularity and order to what has often been the subject of uncertainty." [6]

Apparently, the House of Representatives, or at least Judiciary Committee Chairman Emanuel Celler, failed to perceive the bill's great value however. On September 1, 1965, it was referred to the House Committee on the Judiciary and never emerged.

That was the last time either House of Congress made any attempt to enact comprehensive sports antitrust legislation. The following year, Congress did enact legislation authorizing the merger of the American and National Football Leagues,[7] but as matters stood at the close of the 89th Congress, baseball was still entirely exempt from the antitrust laws, and football, basketball and hockey were still subject to them.

---

[6] *Id.* at 22329.

[7] See § 6.1 (b) & (c), *infra.*

§1.3 The baseball anomaly reaffirmed

§1.3(a) Continued attacks on the baseball exemption

While *Radovich* v. *NFL*[1] is principally remembered as the case which held football subject to the antitrust laws, it also reaffirmed the earlier *Federal Baseball*[2] and *Toolson*[3] decisions as well. "As long as the Congress continues to acquiesce we should adhere to—but not extend—the interpretation of the Act made in those cases," the Court said.[4]

Nevertheless, despite three Supreme Court rulings and continued Congressional acquiescence, antitrust suits continued to be filed against Organized Baseball. One was filed in 1960 by the owners of the Portland minor league team against the Baltimore Orioles. In the hope of overcoming *Federal Baseball* and *Toolson,* Portland argued that the conditions of restraint in professional baseball had become even more aggravated that when those cases had been decided, and that *Radovich* had "undercut" their effect. However, both the trial court and the court of appeals were so unpersuaded by those arguments, that they dismissed the case with an opinion so short that the nature of the dispute that gave rise to it in the first place is not even disclosed.[5]

In 1969, a dispute that became significant for other reasons[6] led to the filing of an antitrust suit by American

---

[1] 352 U.S. 445 (1957), discussed in § 1.2(b), *supra.*

[2] Federal Baseball Club v. National League, 259 U.S. 200 (1922), discussed in § 1.1(a), *supra.*

[3] Toolson v. New York Yankees, 346 U.S. 356 (1953), discussed in § 1.1(d), *supra.*

[4] 352 U.S. at 451.

[5] Portland Baseball Club, Inc. v. Baltimore Baseball Club, Inc., 282 F.2d 680 (9th Cir. 1960).

[6] See § 4.1(b), *infra.*

League umpires Alexander Salerno and William Valentine. The two had been fired the previous summer by league president Joe Cronin for supposed "incompetence." Salerno and Valentine denied they were incompetent, and charged that they had really been fired because of their efforts to organize the twenty-five American League umpires into a labor union for the purpose of collective bargaining. Although the two men added a significant chapter to the legal history of professional sports,[7] they lost their antitrust lawsuit.[8] In an opinion by Judge Friendly, the Second Circuit Court of Appeals affirmed the dismissal of their case without a trial, saying,

> "We freely acknowledge our belief that *Federal Baseball* was not one of Mr. Justice Holmes' happiest days, that the rationale of *Toolson* is extremely dubious and that, to use the Supreme Court's own adjectives, the distinction between baseball and other professional sports is 'unrealistic,' 'inconsistent' and 'illogical.' . . . However, . . . we continue to believe that the Supreme Court should retain the exclusive privilege of overruling its own decisions, save perhaps when opinions already delivered have created a near certainty that only the occasion is needed for pronouncement of the doom. While we should not fall out of our chairs with surprise at the news that *Federal Baseball* and *Toolson* had been overruled, we are not at all certain the Court is ready to give them a happy dispatch."[9]

As the *Curt Flood*[10] case was soon to prove, Judge Friendly's uncertainty was prescient.

---

[7] *Id.*

[8] Salerno v. American League of Professional Baseball Clubs, 429 F.2d 1003 (2d Cir. 1970).

[9] *Id.* at 1005.

[10] See § 1.3(b), ***infra.***

§1.3(b) The Curt Flood case

§1.3(b)(1) The facts

Curtis Charles Flood began his professional baseball career in 1956 at the age of 18 and at an annual salary of $4,000. By 1968, the St. Louis Cardinals were paying him $90,000 per year. In his twelve years as a major-leaguer—all of them with the Cardinals—Flood won the Golden Glove Award as the best center fielder in the National League seven seasons in a row. He committed no errors at all during the 1966 season and ranks among the top ten outfielders in lifetime fielding averages. He batted .335 in 1967, .301 or better in six of his twelve years as a Cardinal, and had an overall battling average of .293. The Cardinals played in the World Series in 1964, 1967, and 1968, and Flood was co-captain of the team from 1965 to 1969.[1]

St. Louis—in addition to being the Cardinals' home town—was also Curt Flood's home. He had friends and business interests there. Nonetheless, in October of 1969, the Cardinals traded Flood to the Philadelphia Phillies in a multi-player transaction, without his consent or knowledge. He first learned of the trade on October 8th, when Jim Toomey, an assistant to Cardinal General Manager Bing Devine, phoned Flood at his home and told him, "Curt, you've been traded to Philadelphia. You, McCarver, Hoerner and Byron Browne. For Richie Allen, Cookie Rojas and Jerry Johnson. Good luck, Curt." [2]

Flood later said of the call, "If I had been a foot-shuffling porter, they might have at least given me a pocket watch. But all I got was a call from a middle-echelon cof-

---

[1] Flood v. Kuhn, 407 U.S. 258, 264 (1972).

[2] C. Flood, The Way It Is 185 (New York: Trident Press, 1971).

fee drinker in the front office. Was I not entitled to a gesture from the general manager himself?" [3]

Flood did in fact receive a gesture from the general manager the following day. It was a letter which said,

> "Dear Curt:
>
> Enclosed herewith is Player Report Notice #614 covering the OUTRIGHT assignment of your contract to the Philadelphia Club of the National League, October 8, 1969. Best of luck. Sincerely yours, Bing Devine General Manager." [4]

By virtue of Major League Rule 9, Flood, "upon receipt of written notice of such assignment," was "bound to serve the assignee." In paragraph 6(a) of his Uniform Player Contract, Flood had agreed that it could be assigned.[5]

On their face, Major League Rule 9 and Player Contract paragraph 6(a) made Flood's trade seem entirely proper. It certainly was routine; professional baseball teams engage in countless player-for-player trades every year. Players have been sold for as little as 25¢ and traded for a bulldog, a bird dog, a turkey and an airplane.[6] What was unusual about Flood's trade was that he refused to accept it, even though the Phillies offered him $100,000 for the 1970 season.

"It violated the logic and integrity of my existence," he later explained. "I was not a consignment of goods. I was

---

[3] *Id.* at 187-188.

[4] Note, The Balance of Power in Professional Sports, 22 Maine L.Rev. 459, 468 fn. 47 (1970).

[5] Flood v. Kuhn, *supra* note 1, at 260 fn. 1.

[6] Comment, Monopsony in Manpower: Organized Baseball Meets the Antitrust Laws, 62 Yale L.J. 576, 587 fn. 59 (1953).

a man, the rightful proprietor of my own person and my own talents."[7]

Although the 1969 season was already over when Flood's 1969 contract was assigned, he was not free to seek employment with any team but the Phillies. This was because Flood's contract—like the contract of every other major and minor league baseball player in the United States and several other countries as well—contained a "reserve clause." Paragraph 10(a) of the contract provided that by January 15th of 1970, the Cardinals, or any team to which the 1969 contract had been assigned, could mail Flood a new contract for the 1970 season, and if Flood and the team had not agreed on a salary for 1970 by March 1st, and therefore Flood had not signed the new contract by then, the team itself could renew the old one for an additional year as long as it did not cut his salary more than twenty percent.[8] Thus, even though Flood did not want to play in Philadelphia, the Phillies could simply send him a contract for 1970, and unless Flood agreed on a salary and signed the contract, the Phillies could unilaterally renew his 1969 contract and cut his salary by $18,000 to boot.

Flood explained his problem:

> "A salesman reluctant to transfer from one office to another may choose to seek employment on the sales force of a different firm. A plumber can reject the dictates of his boss without relinquishing his right to plumb elsewhere. At the expiration of one contract, an actor shops among producers for the best arrangement he can find. But the baseball monopoly offers no such option to the athlete. If he elects not to work for

---

[7] C. Flood, *supra* note 2, at 15.

[8] Flood v. Kuhn, *supra* note 1, at fn. 1.

> the corporation that 'owns' his services, baseball forbids him to ply his trade at all. In the hierarchy of living things, he ranks with poultry."[9]

Unwilling to be so treated, Flood decided to file a lawsuit to invalidate the reserve clause that bound him to the Phillies. The Executive Board of the Major League Baseball Players Association unanimously voted to support Flood's case and authorized Marvin Miller, the Association's executive director, to retain a lawyer at Association expense.

Prior to becoming executive director of the Major League Baseball Players Association, Marvin Miller had been chief economic advisor and assistant to the president of the United Steelworkers of America. The Steelworkers' legal counsel at the time had been Arthur J. Goldberg, who later became Secretary of Labor under President Kennedy, then Associate Justice of the United States Supreme Court, and then United States Ambassador to the United Nations. By December of 1969, Mr. Goldberg was practicing law privately with the New York City law firm of Paul, Weiss, Goldberg, Rifkind, Wharton & Garrison, and it was Goldberg whom Miller retained to represent Curt Flood.

To be certain that Organized Baseball had actual knowledge of Flood's feelings about the trade and his desires as a result of it, before suit was filed, Flood sent the following letter to Bowie Kuhn, the Commissioner of Baseball, on December 24, 1969:

> "Dear Mr. Kuhn:
>
> After twelve years in the major leagues, I do not feel that I am a piece of property to be bought and

[9] C. Flood, *supra* note 2, at 15.

> sold irrespective of my wishes. I believe that any system which produces that result violates my basic rights as a citizen and is inconsistent with the laws of the United States and of the several States.
>
> It is my desire to play baseball in 1970, and I am capable of playing. I have received a contract offer from the Philadelphia club, but I believe I have the right to consider offers from other clubs before making any decisions. I, therefore, request that you make known to all Major League clubs my feelings in this matter, and advise them of my availability for the 1970 season." [10]

Commissioner Kuhn replied that he certainly agreed that "as a human being" Flood "was not a piece of property to be bought and sold. That is fundamental to our society," he acknowledged, "and I think obvious. However," he went on,

> "I cannot see its applicability to the situation at hand. You have entered into a current playing contract with the St. Louis club, which has the same assignment provisions as those in your annual Major League contracts since 1956. Your present contract has been assigned in accordance with its provisions by the St. Louis club to the Philadelphia club. . . ." [11]

With that response, issue was joined, and the matter ripe for litigation—litigation which eventually wound up before the United States Supreme Court upon which Flood's lawyer, Arthur Goldberg, had served only three years before.

---

[10] Brief for Petitioner, Flood v. Kuhn, *supra* note 1; C. Flood, *supra* note 2, at 194-195.

[11] *Id.*

§1.3(b)(2) Rulings

Curt Flood's lawsuit was filed in Federal District Court in New York City on January 16, 1970. Named as defendants were Commissioner of Baseball Bowie Kuhn, National League President Charles Feeney, American League President Joseph Cronin, and each of the twenty-four major league teams. The complaint contained four causes of action, each charging that Organized Baseball's reserve system was illegal. The first cause of action asserted that the reserve system violated the Sherman Act. The second cause of action claimed the reserve system violated the antitrust statutes of New York, California and certain other states. The third cause of action alleged the reserve system violated the common law of various states. And the fourth cause of action asserted that the system created a form of peonage and involuntary servitude in violation of federal civil rights and labor statutes and the Thirteenth Amendment to the Federal Constitution. (A fifth cause of action was based upon the alleged beer selling practices of the St. Louis Cardinals and their owner, Anheuser-Busch, Inc., and the alleged broadcasting policies of the New York Yankees' owner, the Columbia Broadcasting System, Inc. That cause of action was dismissed early in the case, apparently without strenuous objection by Flood, because it was not related to the reserve system.[1])

The trial began May 19, 1970 before Judge Irving Ben Cooper, a man who considered baseball to be the national pastime and who believed its "status in the life of the nation is so pervasive" that he could properly say "that baseball is everybody's business." [2] The trial lasted until June 10th, producing some 2,000 pages of testimony tran-

[1] Flood v. Kuhn, 312 F.Supp. 404 (S.D.N.Y. 1970).

[2] Flood v. Kuhn, 309 F.Supp. 793, 797 (S.D.N.Y. 1970).

script and 56 exhibits. Judge Cooper explained that he had resolved to be very liberal in allowing the introduction of evidence so that "each theory or contention advanced by the litigants would be amply covered and dealt with when all the proof was in."[3] Thus, those 2,000 pages of testimony contained, in detail, Flood's reasons for believing that Organized Baseball's reserve system was unnecessarily restrictive and his lawyers' reasons for asserting it was illegal. Judge Cooper heard testimony on alternatives to the reserve system and modifications of it that the Major League Baseball Players Association had suggested to the team owners. And he heard from league officials and owners why they believed the reserve system was reasonable and the alternatives unsuitable.

But after all the evidence was in and all of the briefs had been submitted and studied, Judge Cooper did not decide whether the reserve clause was reasonable or legal. Instead he ruled that Organized Baseball was exempt from the requirements of all federal and state antitrust laws, and that the reserve system did not subject Flood to involuntary servitude. His judgment in favor of Organized Baseball and against Curt Flood was by no means the product of any unwillingness on Judge Cooper's part to reach the underlying issues. Rather he simply found that the precedents mandated Organized Baseball's victory, and he so ruled on August 12, 1970.[4]

By the time the Court of Appeals heard oral argument on January 27, 1971, the entire 1970 season had long since passed, and Flood had not played so much as a single inning of it. Spring training for the 1971 season was fast approaching and Flood's contract had been as-

[3] Flood v. Kuhn, 316 F.Supp. 271, 273 (S.D.N.Y. 1970).

[4] *Id.*

signed again, this time by the Philadelphia Phillies to the Washington Senators.

On April 7, 1971, Judge Waterman announced that the Court of Appeals was "compelled" to affirm Organized Baseball's victory.[5] In a concurring opinion, Judge Moore let it be known that he not only felt compelled to do so, but also felt it the prudent and correct thing to do on the merits of the controversy. "If baseball is to be damaged by statutory regulation," he said, "let the congressman face his constituents the next November and also face the consequences of his baseball voting record." As far as Judge Moore was concerned, he "would limit the conduct of baseball's affairs to the throwing out by the Chief Justice (in the absence of the President) of the first ball of the baseball season."[6]

So Curt Flood's case went to the Supreme Court while Curt Flood himself went to the Washington Senators. An agreement had been reached between Flood and Organized Baseball allowing Flood to sign with the Senators for the 1971 season without prejudicing his lawsuit. He did sign, for $110,000. Unfortunately, the one year lay-off had its feared consequences. Flood played the first two months of the 1971 season without distinction, and then suddenly retired from baseball. His case lingered in the Supreme Court a year after his retirement, but on June 19, 1972, the Court affirmed the decisions below, telling the former Golden Glove Award Winner that his "remedy, if any is indicated, is for congressional, and not judicial, action."[7]

The Supreme Court, too, did not consider the merits of Flood's claim that the reserve system was illegal. Rather,

---

[5] Flood v. Kuhn, 443 F.2d 264, 265 (2d Cir. 1971).

[6] *Id.* at 272, 273.

[7] Flood v. Kuhn, 407 U.S. 258, 285 (1972).

it simply agreed with Judge Cooper and the Court of Appeals that Organized Baseball was exempt from the requirements of all federal and state antitrust laws. In his opinion for the five-man majority, Justice Harry Blackmun acknowledged that Organized Baseball was now engaged in interstate commerce and that unlike baseball, "Other professional sports operating interstate—football, boxing, basketball, and presumably, hockey and golf—are not so exempt."[8] Thus, the Supreme Court was well aware of the unique treatment it was affording baseball. Said Justice Blackmun, ". . . baseball is, in a very distinct sense, an exception and an anomaly. . . . If there is any inconsistency or illogic in all this, it is an inconsistency and illogic of long standing that is to be remedied by the Congress and not by this Court."[9]

§1.3(b)(3) Issues

In order to so decide, the Supreme Court had been required to consider five issues:

1. Whether the principle of *stare decisis* required the Court to follow *Federal Baseball* and *Toolson* and thus hold that baseball continues to be exempt from federal antitrust laws.

2. Whether Congress' failure to enact any of the exemption-related legislation it had considered over the years was evidence that Congress intended baseball to retain its exemption.

3. Whether baseball's supposed reliance on its exemption would make it unfair to overturn it now.

[8] *Id.* at 282-283.

[9] *Id.* at 282, 284.

4. Whether baseball was exempt from state antitrust laws even if it continued to be exempt from federal antitrust law.

5. Whether baseball's reserve clause was exempt from antitrust attack because the clause was contained in a uniform player contract that had been collectively bargained for by the Major League Baseball Players Association.

Each of these issues was difficult.

§1.3(b)(3)(A) Stare decisis

Even *stare decisis* did not permit simple application of the precedents. In the fifty years that had passed since *Federal Baseball,*[1] and even in the nineteen years that had passed since *Toolson,*[2] the legal definition of "interstate commerce" had broadened considerably. Cases relied upon by the Supreme Court in 1922 in holding that baseball was not "interstate commerce" had been squarely overruled even before *Toolson.*[3] And the interstate aspects of Organized Baseball's business operations had dramatically increased between 1922 and 1953 and again between 1953 and 1972.

Furthermore, the doctrine of *stare decisis* was not without its critics. In fact, Justice Oliver Wendell Holmes, the author of the *Federal Baseball* decision, had himself once written in an article in the Harvard Law Review,

> "It is revolting to have no better reason for a rule of law than that it was laid down in the time of Henry

---

[1] Federal Baseball Club v. National League, 259 U.S. 200 (1922), discussed in § 1.1(a), *supra.*

[2] Toolson v. New York Yankees, 346 U.S. 356 (1953), discussed in § 1.1(d), *supra.*

[3] See § 1.1(b), *supra.*

IV. It is still more revolting if the grounds upon which it was laid down have vanished long since, and the rule simply persists from blind imitation of the past."[4]

As recently as in 1970, the Supreme Court said in an antitrust case unrelated to sports, ". . . *stare decisis* is a principle of policy and not a mechanical formula of adherence to the latest decision, however recent and questionable. . . ."[5]

And Justice Marshall, in his own opinion in the *Flood* case itself, said, "We do not lightly overrule our prior constructions of federal statutes, but when our errors deny substantial federal rights, like the right to compete freely and effectively to the best of one's ability as guaranteed by the antitrust laws, we must admit error and correct it."[6]

Nevertheless, Justice Marshall's opinion was a dissent.

A majority of the Court decided to "adhere once again to *Federal Baseball* and *Toolson* and to their application to professional baseball." The Court had already held baseball exempt twice, and "Under these circumstances," Justice Blackmun wrote for the Court, "there is merit in consistency even though some might claim that beneath that consistency is a layer of inconsistency."[7]

§1.3(b)(3)(B) Congressional inaction

Likewise, Congress' failure to enact any of the exemption-related legislation it had considered over the years offered no guides to what Congress' intentions were. Fre-

[4] Holmes, Path of the Law, 10 Harv. L.Rev. 457, 469 (1897).

[5] Boys Market v. Retail Clerks Union, 398 U.S. 235, 240 (1970).

[6] Flood v. Kuhn, 407 U.S. 258, 292-293 (1972).

[7] *Id.* at 284.

quently, Congressional inactivity in the wake of a Supreme Court ruling is considered by the courts to be an acceptance of the ruling. That would be particularly so where, as here, specific legislation had been introduced in response to a decision, hearings had been held, but then no statute enacted. Indeed, Supreme Court Justice Hugo Black was of the opinion that once Congress considers an issue that has been dealt with in a case and then has not acted, Congressional inaction indicates a willingness to let the decision stand, and judicial reconsideration of the case thereafter actually amounts to legislation[1]—something in which courts are not supposed to engage.

On the other hand, not all judges agree with that analysis. Justice Douglas, in his dissent to the decision of the Court in the *Flood* case, quoted a majority opinion of the Court in a 1940 case which said,

> "It would require very persuasive circumstances enveloping Congressional silence to debar this Court from reexamining its own doctrines. To explain the cause of non-action by Congress when Congress itself sheds no light is to venture into speculative unrealities. ... Various considerations of parliamentary tactics and strategy might be suggested as reasons for the inaction . . . of Congress, but they would only be sufficient to indicate that we walk on quicksand when we try to find in the absence of corrective legislation a controlling legal principle." [2]

Justice Marshall, in his dissent in the *Flood* case, suggested some persuasive considerations of his own why he

[1] Boys Market v. Retail Clerks Union, 398 U.S. 235, 257-259 (1970).

[2] Helvering v. Hallock, 309 U.S. 106, 119-121 (1940), quoted in Flood v. Kuhn, 407 U.S. 258, 287 fn. 3 (1972).

did not think Congress had acquiesced in the Court's *Federal Baseball* and *Toolson* decisions.

> "Had the Court been consistent and treated all sports in the same way baseball was treated, Congress might have become concerned enough to take action. But, the Court was inconsistent, and baseball was isolated and distinguished from all other sports. In *Toolson* the Court refused to act because Congress had been silent. But the Court may have read too much into this legislative inaction.
>
> "Americans love baseball as they love all sports. Perhaps we become so enamored of athletics that we assume that they are foremost in the minds of legislators as well as fans. We must not forget, however, that there are only some 600 major league baseball players. Whatever muscle they might have been able to muster by combining forces with other athletes has been greatly impaired by the manner in which this Court has isolated them. It is this Court that has made them impotent, and this Court should correct its error."[3]

A majority of the Court felt otherwise, however. Justice Blackman, in his majority opinion, said, "Remedial legislation has been introduced repeatedly in Congress but none has ever been enacted. The Court, accordingly, has concluded that Congress as yet has had no intention to subject baseball's reserve system to the reach of the antitrust statutes."[4] In that regard, the Court may well have been correct. The two bills which did pass one house of Congress, though not the other, both exempted reserve and

[3] Flood v. Kuhn, *supra* note 2, at 292.
[4] *Id.* at 283.

option systems from the antitrust laws.[5] And the only sports antitrust bills ever to have been actually enacted, the Sports Broadcasting Act of 1961 and the Football Merger Act of 1966, both granted professional sports exemptions not enjoyed by most other businesses.[6]

§ 1.3 (b) (3) (C) Reliance and retroactivity

Baseball's supposed reliance on the exemption granted it in 1922 was another troubling factor to be considered in deciding how to dispose of the *Curt Flood* case properly. On the one hand, at least four baseball executives testified during the trial that they did indeed consider the exemption at the time they invested in baseball, and that they would not have made the investments which they did make, had the exemption not existed.[1]

On the other hand, football is subject to the antitrust laws, and the value of NFL franchises are, on the average, greater than the value of baseball franchises. Furthermore, several entirely new leagues have come into existence since *Radovich* v. *NFL* made clear that all sports but baseball are subject to antitrust requirements.[2] For these reasons, it seems difficult to believe that any investments have been made in baseball that would not otherwise have been made, particularly in light of Congress' ability to enact legislation at any time imposing antitrust requirements on baseball. Baseball's exemption, after all,

[5] See §§ 1.2(c)(1) and 1.2(c)(5), *supra.*

[6] See Chapter 10 and § 6.1(b) & (c), *infra.*

[1] Flood v. Kuhn, 407 U.S. 258 (1972).

[2] 352 U.S. 445 (1957), discussed in § 1.2(b), *supra;* New Leagues: American Football League (merged into National Football League, see § 6.1, *infra*), World Hockey Association, American Basketball Association, World Football League, North American Soccer League, World Team Tennis, International Volleyball Association.

is based on the comparatively weak reed of judicial interpretations. Other exemptions, such as those for farm cooperatives, insurance sales and labor organizations, are based on acts of Congress.[3] Just as Congress has not enacted legislation subjecting baseball *to* the antitrust laws, it has not enacted any exempting baseball *from* the antitrust laws either.

While Organized Baseball recognized that Congress could at any time enact legislation subjecting it to the antitrust laws, it argued that if Congress did so, at least such a law would have effect only from the date it was enacted. On the other hand, Organized Baseball argued, a decision by the Supreme Court overruling *Federal Baseball* and *Toolson* would have retroactive effect as well as prospective effect, and that would subject Organized Baseball to treble damage liability for conduct it engaged in at a time when it thought, in good faith, that it was exempt.

It is true that a ruling by the Supreme Court could have the retroactive effect feared by Organized Baseball. That is because, traditionally, court rulings have been thought of as announcements of the law *as it always has been.* While legislatures make new laws, in theory, courts simply interpret existing law. Thus, even when the Supreme Court reverses an earlier decision of its own, in theory the Court is announcing what the law has always been and is merely correcting a mistake it made in the earlier case; the Court is not said to be making new law.

The potential unfairness of this theory has caused the Supreme Court to begin to announce that certain of its

---

[3] **Farm Cooperatives: Clayton Act, 15 U.S.C. § 17, and Capper-Volstead Act, 7 U.S.C. §§ 291 & 292; Insurance: McCarran Act, 15 U.S.C. §§ 1011-1015; Labor Organizations: Clayton Act, 15 U.S.C. § 17.**

rulings will have prospective effect only. That is, despite the traditional fiction that the Court is merely announcing the law as it always has been, the Court is now beginning to say, in certain cases, that its rulings will be precedents only for actions that are taken after the dates they are announced. Curt Flood sought such a prospective ruling only. Had it been granted, its impact on Organized Baseball would have been no greater than the impact of any legislation that might have come from Congress.

The Supreme Court rejected that possibility, however. Without explaining why it could not issue a prospective ruling itself, it referred to "the confusion and the retroactivity problems that inevitably would result with a judicial overturning of *Federal Baseball*" and said that it preferred legislative action "that, by its nature, is only prospective in operation." [4]

§1.3(b)(3)(D) State antitrust law

If federal antitrust law did not apply to baseball, then, Flood's lawyers argued, state antitrust must. The argument had a great deal of surface appeal, for state governments are permitted to regulate business affairs, so long as that regulation does not conflict with federal policy. In the event there is a conflict, the United States Constitution provides that federal law is supreme and thus preempts state law.[1] If federal law does not apply, however, Flood's lawyers argued there could be no conflict. Baseball cannot have it both ways, they said. One of the two bodies of law—federal or state—must apply.

The courts did not agree. Federal law does not apply only because of old cases so holding—not because Organ-

[4] Flood v. Kuhn, *supra* note 1, at 283.

[1] U.S. Constitution, Article 6, Section 2.

ized Baseball is not engaged in interstate commerce. Baseball is engaged in interstate commerce, and state regulation would interfere with it. Since the federal government has pre-empted the entire field of interstate commerce regulation, state law cannot be applied to baseball, even though federal law does not regulate baseball in particular. Some judges who have considered the question of state regulation of baseball, have said that Congress' refusal to enact legislation applying to baseball shows that Congress intends baseball to be left unregulated. Thus, state regulation would conflict with federal policy they say.[2]

In holding that state antitrust law could not be applied to baseball, the Court of Appeals acknowledged that Flood was "caught in a most frustrating predicament," a predicament which Organized Baseball "zealously seized upon with great perspicacity."

> "On the one hand, the doctrine of *stare decisis* binds the plaintiff because of an initial holding that baseball is not 'interstate commerce' within the Sherman Act, and, on the other hand, after there have been significant changes in the definition of 'interstate commerce,' he is told that baseball is so uniquely interstate commerce that state regulation cannot apply. However, in our own defense, we do not consider our decision to be internally inconsistent. In disposing of the Sherman Act count in plaintiff's complaint, we are bound by Supreme Court decision, while in our disposition of the state and common law counts, we must of necessity decide this question of first impression by present Commerce Clause standards and not the standards applicable in 1922. Any apparent incon-

[2] Wisconsin v. Milwaukee Braves, Inc., 31 Wis.2d 699, 144 N.W.2d 1 (1966), *cert. den.*, 385 U.S. 990 (1966). Accord, Matuszak v. Houston Oilers, Inc., 1974-2 CCH Trade Cases ¶ 75,373 (Tex. Ct. Civ. App. 1974), discussed in § 5.2(b)(2)(A), *infra.*

sistency results not from faulty logic, but from the vagaries of fate and this court's subordinate role to the Supreme Court." [3]

It seems that Organized Baseball has long been the beneficiary of the "vagaries of fate." As Flood's lawyers pointed out in their brief to the Supreme Court, "For half a century, Organized Baseball has succeeded in persuading one forum after another that 'some other forum' is the appropriate one to deal with the abuses of the reserve clause." [4] In Organized Baseball's brief to the Supreme Court in the *Federal Baseball* case, it argued that baseball should be exempt from federal regulation because states were "entirely competent to reach and deal with any evil in the field of sport." [5] In 1951, Organized Baseball told the Celler Subcommittee that the legality of the reserve clause would be tested in federal courts by the Sherman Act's rule of reason.[6] But in 1953, it argued in the *Toolson* case that the Supreme Court should not apply the Sherman Act to the reserve clause, because baseball was only a local affair subject to the regulatory powers of state and local governments.[7] Then in 1966, Organized Baseball argued in a Wisconsin state court case that only federal law could regulate baseball adequately,[8] while in 1969, it told the National Labor Relations Board that any labor dispute

---

[3] Flood v. Kuhn, 443 F.2d 264, 268 (2d Cir. 1971).

[4] Petition for Certiorari 19-20, Flood v. Kuhn, 407 U.S. 258 (1972).

[5] Respondent's Brief 67, Federal Baseball Club v. National League, 259 U.S. 200 (1922), quoted in Petition for Certiorari, *supra* note 4.

[6] H.Rep. 2002, 82d Cong., 2d Sess. 231 (1952), quoted in Petition for Certiorari, *supra* note 4.

[7] Respondent's Brief 30, Toolson v. New York Yankees, 346 U.S. 356 (1953), quoted in Petition for Certiorari, *supra* note 4.

[8] Wisconsin v. Milwaukee Braves, Inc., *supra* note 2.

in professional sports would not affect interstate commerce substantially.[9] Finally, in 1972, Organized Baseball told the Supreme Court that the reserve clause was exempt from antitrust attack because the *Flood* case was only a labor dispute over a mandatory collective bargaining issue.[10]

§1.3(b)(3)(E) Labor exemption

Whether the reserve clause is insulated from antitrust attack because it is contained in a collective bargaining agreement was not decided by any of the three courts which considered Curt Flood's case, because each court held baseball exempt for other reasons. It is however, a serious and complex issue, and one that has received attention in a Yale Law Journal article which begins as follows:

> "For years the impact of antitrust principles on the arrangements allocating players among teams in professional sports has been hotly disputed. Now recent events seem to have brought this issue to a head. A malaise among good athletes like Curt Flood has increased the tempo of litigation, and an important voice in the United States Senate, Senator Sam J. Ervin, Jr., has responded to a petition for an antitrust exemption for the proposed basketball merger by calling for a full scale review of the issue. We enter this crowded arena, not to solve the antitrust dilemma, but to put it to rest. For, in the form in which it is generally debated, it is an issue whose time has come and gone, an issue which has suffered that modern fate worse than death: irrelevancy." [1]

---

[9] American League & Association of Umpires, 180 NLRB No. 30, 72 LRRM 1545 (1969).

[10] Flood v. Kuhn, 407 U.S. 258, 285 (1972).

[1] Jacobs & Winter, Antitrust Principles and Collective Bargaining by Athletes: Of Superstars in Peonage, 81 Yale L.J. 1 (1971).

As discussed in Chapter 4, subsequent cases have failed to confirm its irrelevance, perhaps because irrelevance would have been too provocative an epilogue to more than 50 years of litigation, three Supreme Court rulings, more than 50 Congressional bills, and thousands of pages of Subcommittee hearings.

§1.4 The scope of the baseball exemption

As sweeping a reaffirmation of Organized Baseball's antitrust exemption as *Flood* v. *Kuhn*[1] was, even it has not laid the exemption issue to rest entirely. Since *Flood* was decided, at least two federal antitrust lawsuits have questioned the scope of baseball's exemption by asserting that the particular practices challenged in them were not exempt, even though the reserve clause is.

One of these cases was *Portland Baseball Club, Inc.* v. *Kuhn.*[2] There the Portland franchise of the Pacific Coast League alleged that the awarding of major league franchises to Seattle and San Diego constituted an invasion of Pacific Coast League territory in violation of the Sherman Act (and in breach of Rule 1(a) of the Professional Baseball rules requiring just and reasonable compensation for such invasions). Though the Portland club argued that *Toolson* and *Flood* exempted the reserve rule only, its antitrust claim was summarily dismissed (and ultimately the Rule 1(a) claim was as well).

The second case was *San Diego* v. *National League.*[3] There the City of San Diego alleged a violation of the

[1] 407 U.S. 258 (1972).

[2] 491 F.2d 1101 (9th Cir. 1974), *aff'g,* 368 F.Supp. 1004 (D.Or. 1971).

[3] U.S.D.C. S.D.Cal., Civ. No. 73-529-T (Filed Dec. 12, 1973): related case arising from same facts discussed in §8.3(b), *infra.*

antitrust laws by virtue of an agreement for the sale of the San Diego Padres to buyers whose expressed intentions were to move the team to Washington, D.C., with the approval of the National League, in violation of the Padres' long-term stadium lease. In response to a motion to dismiss based on *Flood* v. *Kurn,* San Diego set forth three reasons why the baseball exemption should not defeat its suit.

First, it contended that the exemption applies "only to the business of baseball, and more specifically the player reserve clause."[4] When professional baseball deals with other businesses—such as the stadium rental business—which are "outside the interworkings of baseball's dynasty,"[5] the city contended that baseball was, indeed, subject to the antitrust laws.

Second, the Supreme Court had held in *Flood* and in *Toolson* that the job of overruling baseball's longstanding exemption belongs to Congress, and not to the courts. San Diego alleged the existence of conspiracy among several Congressmen and baseball executives to prevent the enactment of exemption-repealing legislation in exchange for a Washington franchise; and for that reason, San Diego contended that the "philosophy . . . that the courts are waiting for Congress to act, is no longer a valid or reasonable consideration."[6] "It is submitted", San Diego said, "the courts are now obligated to act in view of the clearly biased and prejudiced position of Congress."[7]

---

[4] Memorandum of Points and Authorities in Support of Motion for Temporary Restraining Order and Preliminary Injunction 5, San Diego v. National League, *supra* note 3.

[5] *Id.*

[6] *Id.* at 6.

[7] *Id.*

Third, San Diego argued that the defendants had monopolized and restrained not only the professional baseball business, where their exemption might protect them, but also the sports stadia business where their exemption did not apply; and thus they were liable for that reason, even if no other.

Because the Padres were ultimately sold to a buyer who kept the team in San Diego, the case was dismissed before the city's contentions were ruled upon by the court. Nevertheless, there is some authority in support of San Diego's position that Organized Baseball's exemption would not have protected it from charges that it had monopolized and restrained the separate business of stadia operation.

In 1953, the federal government filed suit against the National Football League, alleging that certain NFL bylaws requiring radio and television blackouts were in violation of the antitrust laws. The case was decided shortly after the Supreme Court's decision in the *Toolson* case; and the National Football League argued, among other things, that like baseball it too was exempt from the antitrust laws. Since the case was decided some four years prior to ***Radovich*** **v.** ***NFL,***[8] it was a reasonable position for it to take at the time.

District Judge Grim nevertheless rejected the argument, saying,

> "The only restriction alleged in the baseball cases was in the internal operation of professional baseball itself. . . . The present case, on the other hand, primarily concerns the League's restraint of interstate commerce in the radio and television industries. It is

[8] 352 U.S. 445 (1957), discussed in § 1.2(b), *supra.*

> obvious that whether professional football itself is or is not engaged in interstate commerce is immaterial in the present case and that the decisions in the baseball cases referred to do not control the present case."[9]

It seems to follow that even though baseball's "internal operation" is exempt, that exemption would not protect it from allegations that it had restrained trade in some other area or industry. Baseball executives apparently were of the same view on at least two occasions in the past.

At the same time the government challenged the NFL's broadcast policies, and prior to the Supreme Court's decision in *Toolson,* the government also challenged Organized Baseball's policy of blacking out broadcasts of major league games in cities that had minor league franchises. Though Organized Baseball had on its side the benefit of the holding in *Federal Baseball,* it chose not to litigate the dispute. Rather, it capitulated to the government, rescinded the objected to rule, and went to Congress for legislation expressly authorizing its blackout policy. Though the Senate Committee on Interstate and Foreign Commerce reported favorably on the proposed bill,[10] it was never enacted.

Early in 1958, after the decisions of the Supreme Court in *Toolson* and the District Court in *United States* v. *National Football League,* Organized Baseball's lawyer, Paul Porter, wrote a letter to the head of the Antitrust Division, Assistant Attorney General Victor Hansen, submitting for consideration a proposed new broadcasting rule which

---

[9] United States v. National Football League, 116 F.Supp. 319, 328 (E.D. Pa. 1953), discussed in § 10.2(a)(2), *infra.*

[10] S.Rep. 387, 83d Cong., 1st Sess. (1953).

in Mr. Porter's judgment conformed to the holding in *U.S.* v. *N.F.L.*[11] Mr. Hansen refused to approve the proposed rule, however, saying that it was different in important respects from those portions of the NFL rule which had been sanctioned by the District Court. Again, rather than challenge the government, Organized Baseball acquiesced, this time despite the antitrust exemption which had been reaffirmed for it by the Supreme Court in *Toolson* less than five years before. Though Organized Baseball may have acquiesced for a number of reasons, it seems fair to presume that at least one was a concern that its exemption was not broad enough to include radio and television policies.

Organized Baseball also became concerned about its exemption when, in 1964, the Columbia Broadcasting System acquired an 80% interest in the New York Yankees. At the time of the purchase, the Commissioner of Baseball asked Paul Porter for an opinion on certain aspects of the transaction, including an analysis of its antitrust implications. Porter was asked to give particular attention to its possible impact on baseball's exemption under the *Toolson* case. Porter advised the Commissioner that the antitrust aspects were not free from doubt and that no experienced lawyer could predict with assurance what the response of the Justice Department might be.

Porter also advised the Commissioner that if the Justice Department brought suit to set aside CBS' purchase of the Yankees, ". . . it was possible that baseball's judicial immunity under the *Toolson* decision could be placed in

---

[11] Letters published in Hearings on H.R. 10378 and S.4070 before the Subcomm. on Antitrust and Monopoly of the Sen. Comm. on the Judiciary, 85th Cong., 2d Sess. 686-689 (1958), discussed in § 10.2(a)(3), ***infra***.

jeopardy." [12] He said this could happen "if the defendants in such a proceeding sought to invoke *Toolson* as extending general immunity to organized baseball, including broadcast aspects as well as the sale and transfer of league franchises." [13] Porter further informed the Commissioner that baseball could preserve its exemption if "it was recognized that the *Toolson* case limited baseball's immunity to essential sports activities." [14]

As a result, the Commissioner instructed Porter to do whatever was necessary "to obtain the maximum assurance that, in the event of a legal attack upon this acquisition, the parties would not rely upon the *Toolson* case as extending an antitrust exemption to a commercial transaction that might be questioned on other grounds." [15] Porter then telephoned Leon Brooks, general counsel of CBS, and told him of the Commissioner's concerns. Brooks replied that it was his own view, supported by an opinion from outside counsel, that CBS could acquire the Yankees without violating the antitrust laws, but that in the event a proceeding was brought by the Justice Department, CBS would defend it without relying upon baseball's antitrust exemption under the *Toolson* case. Porter reported to the Commissioner that "Mr. Brooks also expressed the opinion that the *Toolson* case probably did not extend any exemption beyond the essential sports practices of organized baseball." [16]

---

[12] Memorandum to the Commissioner of Baseball from Paul A. Porter, published in Hearings on S.950 before the Subcomm. on Antitrust and Monopoly of the Sen. Comm. on the Judiciary, 89th Cong., 1st Sess. 159, 160 (1965).

[13] *Id.*

[14] *Id.*

[15] *Id.*

[16] *Id.* at 161.

CBS' pledge not to invoke *Toolson* proved to be academic, for its purchase of the Yankees was never challenged by the Justice Department. While the thinking of the lawyers for the Commissioner and CBS may have been conservative—because asked for in a pre-litigation, planning context—it does not seem to have been too conservative. For example, in a recently decided antitrust case between the Oakland Athletics and a stadium concessionaire, the exemption issue was never mentioned.[17]

Thus it seems that Organized Baseball's internal operations involving essential sports activities or practices are exempt from the antitrust laws, while all others are not. The only question remaining for future litigation is which of baseball's "internal operations" are "essential sports activities or practices."

[17] Twin City Sportservice v. Charles O. Finley Co., Inc., 512 F.2d 1264 (9th Cir. 1975).

Chapter 2
RESERVE AND OPTION CLAUSES

§2.1 Origins of the reserve clause

At the outset of Senate hearings held in 1971 on a bill to authorize the merger of the National and American Basketball Associations, Senator Sam Ervin of North Carolina said,

> "Many years ago, the term 'chattel' was used to denote the legal status of slaves. That is, they were considered a type of chattel which was owned as a piece of furniture or livestock was owned. This use of the term 'chattel' applied to human beings and the condition it stands for are so abhorrent that we don't even like to acknowledge that they ever existed. Yet, in a real sense that is what these hearings are about today—modern peonage and the giant sports trusts."[1]

More than any other reason, reserve and option systems are why many people compare highly paid professional athletes to slaves or peons. These systems grant each team the exclusive right to negotiate with and employ, year after year, all of the players assigned to it. Players are prohibited by these systems from negotiating with or playing for any team other than the one to which they have been assigned, without regard to any personal, professional or financial reasons they may have for wanting to switch.

Though commonly referred to as reserve or option "clauses," these systems are much more than clauses in player contracts. In fact, the first reserve system was

---

[1] Hearings on S.2373 before the Subcomm. on Antitrust and Monopoly of the Sen. Comm. on the Judiciary, 92d Cong., 1st Sess. 12 (1971).

adopted in 1879 by secret agreement among the owners of National League baseball teams, and no mention of it appeared in the players' contracts or elsewhere. Rather, because eight of the fifteen National League teams had gone bankrupt that year as the result of an intra-league bidding war for talented players, the surviving owners simply agreed that each could reserve for his team a certain number of players which the others would not hire. Because the National League was then the only professional league in existence, each owner could pay his reserved players whatever he pleased without worry that another team would lure them away with higher salaries.[2]

This secret agreement worked well, and the National League prospered. Its prosperity, however, attracted competitors, and in 1881 another professional league was formed called the American Association. Naturally, the owners of the teams in the new league were not parties to the secret agreement permitting reservation of players, and a new bidding war was immediately begun. Several teams in both leagues were threatened with financial ruin, and before long the leagues were willing to make peace with one another.

The peace pact between the National League and the American Association was known as the "National Agreement," and its most important feature was a provision affording each of the teams in both leagues the right to reserve a stated number of players which none of the other teams would hire. At the time the National Agreement was signed, the players' contracts still made no mention of the teams' right to reserve them. However, the contracts did

---

[2] History of reserve clause recited in H.Rep. 2002, 82d Cong., 2d Sess. 34 (1952) and in Metropolitan Exhibition Co. v. Ewing, 42 Fed. 198 (S.D.N.Y. 1890).

contain a clause by which players agreed to be bound by all of the provisions of the National Agreement. Since the teams' right to reserve was spelled out in the National Agreement, the players were said to have assented to their reservation.

Before long, the players realized that many of them were being reserved, and though they did not like it, at least some of them considered it to be a necessary evil. One prominent player of the day wrote, "The reserve rule itself is a usurpation of the player's rights; but it is, perhaps, made necessary by the peculiar nature of the ball business, and the player is indirectly compensated by the improved standing of the game." [3]

The players were not content with the wording of their contracts, however. Changes were made in the National Agreement from time to time, and the players had to keep track of the changes in order to know precisely what their rights and obligations were. As a result, in November of 1887, player representatives met with representatives of the owners, and the two groups agreed on a new contract form. The clause by which players agreed to be bound by the National Agreement was removed, and in its place the first "reserve clause" was inserted. It read,

> "It is further understood and agreed that the party of the first part [the team] shall have the right to 'reserve' the said party of the second part [the player] for the season next ensuing the term mentioned in paragraph 2, herein provided, and that said right and privilege is hereby accorded to said party of the first part upon the following conditions, which are to be taken and construed as conditions precedent to the

[3] Metropolitan Exhibition Co. v. Ewing, *supra* note 2, at 203.

> exercise of such extraordinary rights or privileges, viz.: (1) That the said party of the second part shall not be reserved at a salary less than that mentioned in the 20th paragraph herein, except by the consent of the party of the second part; (2) that the said party of the second part, if he be reserved by the said party of the first part for the next ensuing season, shall not be one of more than 14 players then under contract—that is, that the right of reservation shall be limited to that number of players, and no more."[4]

In plain English, the clause gave teams the right "to reserve" 14 players for the following season, providing their salaries were not cut.

The National Agreement and the "reserve clause" had their intended effect, and the National League and the American Association both prospered. Again that prosperity attracted competition. This time the competition came not from wealthy businessmen, but rather from some players themselves. John Montgomery Ward, a New York player who later became a practicing attorney, organized many of his contemporaries into the first union of professional athletes, the National Brotherhood of Professional Baseball Players. Among the early goals of the Brotherhood was the abandonment of the reserve clause, and when the owners refused to capitulate, the Brotherhood formed its own league in 1890, aptly called the "Players League."[5]

Among the athletes who had agreed to perform in the Players League in 1890 were two men named Ward and Ewing who had played for the National League's New York team during the 1889 season. Of course, the contracts the

[4] *Id.* at 200.

[5] H.Rep. 2002, *supra* note 2, at 32.

two had signed with New York contained clauses which said that they understood and agreed that New York had the right to reserve them for the 1890 season. When New York learned that Ward and Ewing intended to join the Players League in 1890, it went to court to stop them from doing so, claiming that it had exercised its right to reserve both of them. Both players argued that though New York had the right "to reserve" them for the 1890 season, it did not have the right to prevent them from playing baseball for teams in another league. They had not agreed to play for New York in 1890, they said; they had simply agreed that New York could reserve them. That agreement, they argued, was only effective within the National League and American Association, as the history of the reserve clause made clear.

New York's suit against Ewing was filed in federal court, and its suit against Ward was filed in state court. The federal judge agreed with Ewing that the term "right to reserve" was ambiguous by itself, but in light of its history, its meaning was clear. ". . . [T]he right of reservation" said the judge, "is nothing more or less than a prior and exclusive right, as against the other clubs [who were parties to the National Agreement], to enter into a contract securing the player's services for another season." [6] But, the judge added, the reserve clause was not a basis for a suit to enjoin an athlete from playing for a team that was not a party to the National Agreement —as none of the Players League teams were.

This interpretation of the reserve clause was precisely the one given it by the man who created it. A. G. Mills, president of the National League in 1879 when the first

[6] Metropolitan Exhibition Co. v. Ewing, *supra* note 2, at 204.

reserve rule was adopted, is considered to be the "father" of the reserve clause, and in a letter dated May 31, 1888 to *Sporting Life* magazine, Mills wrote,

> "The 'reserve rule,' as I formulated it for the use of the clubs of our alliance, placed its obligation upon *clubs,* and prohibited them from employing or negotiating with players reserved to other clubs; the penalties prescribed for the violation of such reserve rule were placed upon the *clubs* and the Association of which they were members, and not upon the players, who were not parties to the compact." [7]

In state court, Ward did not have success with this argument. There the judge said that whether or not the history of the reserve clause was considered, he agreed with New York's contention that "to reserve" means "to hold" or "to keep for future use," and that with this meaning the reserve clause applies within the National League and American Association, and outside of them as well. However, said the judge, New York was not entitled to an injunction preventing Ward from playing in the Players League for other reasons.

Ward's 1889 contract with New York did not state the terms and conditions of his employment during the 1890 season, and thus was too indefinite and uncertain to warrant a court order that he comply with it. New York, of course, argued that the judge should simply infer that the terms and conditions of Ward's 1890 employment were to be the same as those of his 1889 contract. But the judge doubted that he should draw such an inference, and said that if he did, he would have to infer that all of the pro-

[7] H.Rep. 2002, *supra* note 2, at 34.

visions of the 1889 contract applied during 1890—including the reserve clause. Thus, New York would have the right to reserve Ward again for the 1891 season, and again and again for every season thereafter. Were that the case, said the judge, the contract would lack mutuality and would be so unfair as to be unenforceable, because the contract gave New York the right to terminate on ten days' notice even though Ward would be bound by it perpetually. In short, said the judge, the contract was either too uncertain and indefinite to enforce, or, if it was certain, it was perpetual, and thus too unfair to enforce. Ward, like Ewing, was held free to join the Players League.[8]

As one would expect, the National League and the American Association rewrote the reserve clause after losing the *Ward* and *Ewing* cases and amended it from time to time thereafter.

While all professional team sports leagues have systems similar to baseball's reserve system, there are significant distinctions between them.

§2.2 Current reserve and option systems

§2.2(a) Baseball

Organized Baseball's reserve system consists of several inter-related player contract provisions and major league rules. Prior to October of 1973, the player contract reserve clause itself provided that the team had the right to mail the player a new contract by January 15th following the close of the last season covered by his old contract, and the player then had until March 1st to agree on salary and term. If no agreement was reached by March 1st, the team

[8] Metropolitan Exhibition Co. v. Ward, 9 N.Y.S. 779 (1890).

itself had the right to renew the old contract for a year and to cut the player's salary by 20%.[1]

In other paragraphs of the contract, the player promised not to play baseball for anyone else "while under contract," and agreed that the team was entitled to an injunction preventing him from doing so, should he have breached that covenant.[2] The player also agreed that he could be assigned to any other team—in other words, that he could be sold or traded.[3]

The player contract provisions were, and are, reinforced by a Major League Rule which requires all major league teams to use the uniform contract form prescribed by the Major League Executive Council,[4] and by another rule which prohibits teams from eliminating the reserve clause unless the Commissioner of Baseball approves in writing[5] —something he never does.

To insure that no player would have reason to ignore his reserve clause, the Major League Rules prohibit negotiations between a player and any team other than the one with which he is under contract or by which he is reserved.[6] Thus, players never know whether other teams would be interested in them or what salary other teams might be willing to pay.

Finally, the rules provide that teams may assign player contracts to other teams—that is, teams may trade or sell

---

[1] Uniform Player's Contract ¶ 10(a); Flood v. Kuhn, 407 U.S. 258, 260 fn. 1 (1972).

[2] *Id.* at ¶ 5(a) and ¶ 4(a).

[3] *Id.* at ¶ 6(a).

[4] Rule 3(a) of the Major League Rules; Flood v. Kuhn, *supra* note 1, at 259 fn. 1.

[5] *Id.*

[6] Rule 3(g) of the Major League Rules; Flood v. Kuhn, *supra* note 1, at 259 fn. 1.

players to other teams—and, after the assignment, all rights and obligations of the player's former team become the rights and obligations of his new team.[7]

The total effect of these contract provisions and league rules was this. Once a player signed his first professional baseball employment contract, he became the property of his team. His contract could be renewed by the team, year after year, without his consent and at salaries he never agreed to accept. His only options were to play or to retire from professional baseball, because no other team would even consider hiring him as long as he was under contract. Further, he could be traded from team to team, with or without his consent. If he was traded, he was as bound to the new team as he had been to the former team, because the new team then had the right to reserve him perpetually.

In October of 1973, two important changes to Organized Baseball's reserve system were announced, both of which give players significant new rights. First, teams no longer have the right to unilaterally cut salaries 20%. Beginning with the player-team negotiations which established salaries for the 1974 season, teams make their initial offers by December 20th, and between that date and February 1st, ordinary negotiations with players are conducted. If those negotiations result in agreement on salary, a new contract for the coming season is executed, as before. However, in the event agreement is not reached by February 1st, either the player or the team may refer the matter to one of a panel of fifteen neutral arbitrators selected in advance by the Players Association and the Major Leagues. Between February 10th and February 20th, the arbitrator hears and

---

[7] Rule 9(a) of the Major League Rules; Flood v. Kuhn, *supra* note 1, at 259-260 fn. 1.

considers evidence on such factors as the player's overall performance, the quality of his leadership and public appeal, the length and consistency of his career, comparable salaries, and the player's physical and mental qualities. (The arbitrator is not permitted to consider the financial position of the player or of the ball club, press comments, or testimonials other than "recognized player awards.") The arbitrator is required to announce his decision concerning the player's salary for the coming season within three days after final argument. The unique feature of this arbitration system is that the arbitrator must select the last offer made by either the team or the player. That is, the arbitrator's decision may not be a compromise between the positions taken by the player and the team, nor may it be more than the player's last demand nor less than the team's last offer.[8]

For example, a team may offer a player $30,000 on December 20th for the coming baseball season. The player may respond a few days later with a demand to be paid $80,000. Thereafter, ordinary negotiations may be carried on, during which the team may increase its offer to $45,000 while the player decreases his demand to $65,000. If that is how matters stand on February 1st, either side may ask for arbitration. The arbitrator, after hearing evidence, must then select either $45,000 or $65,000; no other figure is available to him. Thus, as February 1st approaches, both the team and the player are compelled to be serious and realistic about their respective offers and demands. If either side insists on an unreasonable figure, loss is invited,

---

[8] Bernstein, Baseball Adopts Plan to Eliminate Holdouts, L.A. Times, Oct. 11, 1973, Part III, Pg. 1; Newhan, Oakland Club Expected to Get An 'A' in Arbitration, L.A. Times, Feb. 1, 1974, Part III, Pg. 1.

because the arbitrator is likely to select the other side's figure, even if it may be somewhat too high or too low.

During the first year this arbitration procedure was in effect, approximately 45 players asked for arbitration, and approximately 29 were actually heard, 9 of them involving the Oakland Athletics alone. Of the 9 involving the Athletics, team owner Charley Finley won 5 and lost 4.[9] According to newspaper accounts, management won 16 over-all, while the players won 13;[10] and, again according to newspaper reports, the ratio seems to have remained the same during 1975.[11]

This "high-low" or "last offer, last demand" method of arbitration was first proposed in the late 1940's as a method of settling labor disputes, as an alternative to the national emergency dispute procedures contained in the Taft-Hartley Act. It was not adopted, however, probably because most industrial controversies involve several issues in addition to wages. Terms and conditions of employment do not lend themselves as well to this sort of arbitration as do money issues only. Therefore, because terms and conditions other than salary are negotiated by the Major League Baseball Players' Association, professional baseball is thought to be the first business that has used this system.[12]

Peter Seitz, one of the neutral arbitrators, has commented on some of the unique aspects of the hearings. He says, for example, that the arbitrators were "inundated by

---

[9] L.A. Times, Feb. 12, 1974, Feb. 23, 1974.

[10] Maher, Arbitrator: Either Way He Rules, He's Called Arbitrary, L.A. Times, Mar. 16, 1974, Part III, Pg. 1.

[11] L.A. Times, Feb. 14, 16, 21, 22, 1975.

[12] Seitz, Footnotes to Baseball Salary Arbitration, 29 The Arbitration Journal 98 (1974).

a torrent of statistical data."[13] While the accuracy of the statistics was never challenged, their significance almost always was. Seitz cited as illustrative the hypothetical case of the team that sought to justify its refusal to give a pitcher a raise with statistics showing that the pitcher's earned-run average and win-loss record had deteriorated from previous seasons. The pitcher then pointed out that in the games he lost, the margin of defeat was slight, and that in most of those games, the team hit well below its season's batting average. Seitz asks,

> "What weight should be given to the raw yearly statistics presented by the club in the face of this kind of explanation? Are a pitcher's yearly statistics the result of his own efforts or failure exclusively, or are they the product of the mutual efforts and performance of his teammates? Are all accidental and unfortuitous circumstances wiped out by the process of averaging?"[14]

Seitz also cited the example of an outfielder whose generally high batting average and RBI figures fell off in one year, causing his team to offer him a smaller raise than he wanted for the following year. The player explained that his poorer than expected performance was the result of a playing injury and the fact that he returned to the lineup earlier than he should have, under normal medical circumstances, because he was urgently needed. He pointed out that his batting average declined immediately after his return, but, as the season progressed, improved considerably. Therefore he argued that yearly statistics are misleading, and that the arbitrator should give more weight to

---

[13] *Id.* at 100.
[14] *Id.*

his performance at the end of the season. The player also pointed out that his RBI's fell off, because he had been batting second, third or fifth in the lineup before his injury, but that after his return, he was assigned to bat seventh or eighth. As a result, there were fewer runners on base when he came to bat, and therefore fewer to bat in. Seitz remarks,

> "Does this explain his comparatively poor showing last year? What weight should be given to these considerations in ascertaining his value to the club in the *next* year; which, after all, is the question to be answered by the Arbitrator."[15]

It is thus apparent, as Seitz has reported, that "the battle of raw statistics did not furnish easy answers for the arbitrator."[16] Ultimate decisions, he noted, were affected by "imponderables less objective and susceptible to measurement."[17]

The second important change to Organized Baseball's reserve system was one that would have prevented the St. Louis Cardinals from trading Curt Flood against his wishes, had it been in effect at the time. It provides that where a player has had ten years of service, the last five of them with one team, he cannot be traded without his written consent.[18]

With these changes in effect, a player's circumstances are far better. However, he may still be bound to one team perpetually, or traded from team to team against his wishes unless he has 10 years' experience, the last five with one

[15] *Id.* at 101.
[16] *Id.*
[17] *Id.*
[18] Bernstein, *supra* note 8.

club. Because of the requirement that the last five years be with one club, it is possible that a veteran with far more than ten years' service will still be subject to trade against his wishes, if he is traded so often he is not able to accrue five years with one club, or if he consents to a trade after five years with one club and is traded again before he accrues five more with his new team. As a result, Marvin Miller, the executive director of the Major League Baseball Players Association, has said that players will continue and even intensify their efforts to have Congress outlaw the reserve clause altogether.[19]

Moreover, the recent arbitration decision in the Messersmith and McNally case construes the reserve clause as not being perpetual at all. Thus, baseball players may now play-out the renewal year in their contracts and become free agents after all.[20]

§2.2(b) Hockey

§2.2(b)(1) National Hockey League

Prior to 1974, the reserve system used by the National Hockey League was very similar to the one used by major league baseball. Like baseball, the National Hockey League's reserve system was perpetual for the lifetime of the player. As in baseball, the National Hockey League had adopted an arbitration scheme for determining a player's salary in the event he and the team could not agree. The reserve clause contained in the National Hockey League Standard Player's Contract provided that the club would tender to the player, on or before September 1st, a contract containing the same terms, except with respect

[19] *Id.*

[20] See § 2.4(c)(2), ***infra.***

to salary. The contract further provided that the player thereby undertook that at the request of the club he would enter into a contract for the following season upon the same terms and conditions except as to salary. Salary was determined by mutual agreement, failing which, arbitration under an Arbitration Agreement between the League and the NHL Players' Association was conducted.[1]

The Arbitration Agreement referred to in the reserve clause provided that in the event a player and his team were unable to agree on the player's salary for the coming season, the matter was referred to an independent arbitrator selected in advance by the president of the NHL and the executive director of the Players' Association. The arbitrator then fixed the salary to be paid. However, unlike the baseball arbitrator, the NHL arbitrator could fix whatever salary he considered appropriate and was not bound by the last offer and demand of the team and player. The NHL Arbitration Agreement would have expired by its own terms at the end of the 1974-1975 season. Before the Arbitration Agreement had been entered into, salary disputes had been referred to the president of the NHL.[2]

The total effect of the reserve clause and the Arbitration Agreement was this. The team agreed to send the player a contract for the coming season, and the player agreed to sign it. If they could agree on a salary for the coming season, the agreed upon figure was inserted in the contract, and nothing further had to be done until the following year when the team would send the player another contract for the player's signature. Year after year the team had

[1] Standard Player's Contract ¶ 17; Philadelphia World Hockey Club, Inc. v. Philadelphia Hockey Club, Inc., 351 F.Supp. 462, 475 (E.D. Pa. 1972).

[2] *Id.* at 482.

the right to send the player a new contract, and year after year the player agreed that he would sign it. In the event an impasse was reached with respect to the player's salary, the matter was referred to an independent arbitrator who fixed the salary, and the player was then required to sign the contract. The player was thus bound to his team perpetually, unless he was sold or traded, in which case he was bound to his new team.

As in baseball, the reserve clause found in the player contract was reinforced with several league rules. National Hockey League By-Laws, for example, provided that no team could change any of the provisions of the Standard Players' Contract without the authorization of the NHL Board of Governors.[3] Thus every player in the NHL was required to have, and did have, a reserve clause in his contract.

The NHL By-Laws also prohibited "tampering" with players owned by another team. "Tampering" meant discussing, negotiating, or offering employment, and also included the making of any public or private statement indicating a desire, interest or intention of acquiring the services of a player owned by another team.[4]

If a player refused to sign a Standard Player Contract after the arbitrator made his decision as to salary, the player could be expelled or suspended from the League. A player could also be expelled or suspended if he played for any other team or league.[5] In addition, the player

---

[3] By-Laws § 2.2(a); Philadelphia World Hockey Club, Inc. v. Philadelphia Hockey Club, Inc., *supra* note 1, at 476.

[4] By-Laws § 15; Phil. World Hockey etc., *supra* note 1, at 477.

[5] By-Laws § 17.5; Phil. World Hockey etc., *supra* note 1, at 478.

agreed in his contract that his team could enjoin him by court order from playing hockey for any other team.[6]

In November of 1973, the NHL Board of Governors adopted a new player contract clause to replace its old perpetual reserve clause.[7] In essence, this new clause gives the team an option on the player's services for one additional year, at the conclusion of which the player becomes a free agent able to negotiate with any team in either the NHL or World Hockey Association. As is the case in the National Football League,[8] the new NHL option clause and accompanying by-laws require an "equalization payment" to be made by NHL teams that sign NHL players who become free agents, which payment is to be made to the NHL team that formerly employed the player. Unlike the National Football League, however, the NHL President is not the person who determines the amount of the equalization payment in the event the two teams involved cannot agree on a mutually satisfactory payment. Rather, a neutral arbitrator is to be appointed by a majority vote of the NHL Board of Governors, and it is the neutral arbitrator who decides between the proposals made by each team (no compromise between them being possible, as in baseball salary arbitrations). The proposals made by each team may only be assignments of player contracts, and/or draft choices, and/or cash (cash to be used only as a last resort).[9]

The new NHL option clause has additional features as well—in fact it consists of six sub-paragraphs—which make

[6] Standard Player's Contract ¶ 6; Boston Professional Hockey Assn. v. Cheevers, 348 F.Supp. 261 (D.Mass. 1972).

[7] L.A. Times, Dec. 4, 1973.

[8] See § 2.2(c)(1), *infra*.

[9] By-Laws § 9A.

it unique in the professional sports industry, and which make it as complicated to read as many sections of the Internal Revenue Code. Not only is the team given an option on the player's services for one additional year, but the player is also given an option to require the team to employ him for another year at his previous salary. The player's option may be exercised in either of two situations. If the team intends not to exercise its option for another year, it must notify the player of that fact by August 10th, telling him that he is about to become a free agent unless he wants to exercise his option to require the team to employ him for one more year. The player is then free to become a free agent or to exercise his option to require the team to employ him by sending the team a signed "Player's Termination Contract" covering one year.[10]

In other sports, a "player's option" to require a team to employ him for an additional year would be meaningless. This is because in all other sports, unless a player has a "no-cut" contract, the team has the right to terminate the contract (including the obligation to pay salary) if the player's performance, in the opinion of the club's management, is insufficient for him to qualify as a team member.[11] In other words, in all other sports, the team has the right —but not the obligation—to employ the player for the term of the contract. The club's obligations under the contract may be terminated by it at any time, simply by cutting the player from the team. In hockey, on the other hand, players may not be cut from major league teams because of insufficient ability. They may be assigned to minor

[10] Standard Player's Contract (1974 form) ¶ 17.

[11] See, e.g., NFL Standard Player Contract ¶ 6; NBA Uniform Player Contract ¶ 20(b); Major League Baseball Uniform Player's Contract ¶ 7(b).

leagues at a lower salary (the amount of which is specified in advance in the NHL contract), but once signed, an NHL player appears assured of at least the salary payments called for in his contract.[12] In this context, the NHL's Player's Termination Contract appears to be quite significant, especially for players who are approaching the end of their professional careers.

If the team does want to exercise its option on the player's services for an additional year, it simply sends him a new contract for the coming season containing option clause for the season after that. If the player does not wish to sign this new contract—because he wants to "play out" the option and become a free agent—the player refuses to sign it and asks instead for a "Player's Option Contract" which he signs and returns to the team. The "Player's Option Contract"—like the "Player's Termination Contract"—calls for only one year of additional employment.[13]

If the player does not want to play out the option and become a free agent, he simply signs the new standard player's contract tendered to him; his salary in such a case would be arrived at either by mutual agreement, or by arbitration if agreement could not be reached, or (in the absence of a current collective bargaining agreement establishing the mechanism for arbitration) the salary would be the same as in the previous year.[14]

There is an additional feature of the new NHL option clause which applies to rookies only. The first professional contract of every NHL player signed after the new option clause came into effect contains an addendum which has

---

[12] NHL Standard Player's Contract (1974 form) ¶ 1 and ¶ 13.

[13] *Id.* at ¶ 17(c).

[14] *Id.* at ¶ 17(d).

the effect of giving NHL teams an option on the rookie's services for two additional seasons, rather than only one.[15]

These changes substantially liberalized the National Hockey League's player control practices, and the League had hoped to obtain NHL Players Association approval for them. The Players Association, however, did not agree to the changes. In fact, it terminated the negotiations with the League preceding their adoption.[16] However, because the changes conferred benefits on the players without increasing their obligations, the League was able to make the changes unilaterally.

The new NHL option clause appears in player contracts covering the 1974-1975 and subsequent seasons. Though there were many players in the NHL with long term contracts which had been signed before the new clause was adopted, those players were also given the benefit of the new clause and by-laws. The NHL did so by formally waiving, in writing, all of its claims to rights under the old reserve clause to services for any season after 1974-1975.[17]

§2.2(b)(2) World Hockey Association

The World Hockey Association, whose first season was 1972-1973, has an option system which appeared, at the time it was adopted and from the point of view of the players, more liberal than that used by any other profes-

[15] NHL Addendum to Standard Player's Contract for certain amateurs.

[16] Letter dated Nov. 30, 1973 from each NHL team to all NHL players, attached as a portion of Appendix A to Consent Decree signed by District Judge Higginbotham on Feb. 19, 1974 settling virtually all litigation between the NHL and WHA. See § 6.3, *infra*.

[17] *Id.*

sional sport league. The WHA Player's Contract contains no actual reserve or option clause. However, players are not free to move from team to team as they please. Rather, the contract provides that in the event the player and the team fail to sign a new contract by June 1st for the season following expiration of the existing contract, both player and team appoint a mediator of their own choosing to hear and determine the dispute. If the two mediators are able to resolve the dispute by July 15th, a new contract is signed and no further proceedings are necessary.

However, in the event the two mediators are unable to resolve the dispute by that date, they select a third, impartial mediator whose decision is to be reached by July 31st. If the player and the team agree that the impartial mediator's decision is fair, a new contract is signed. However, in the event the player or the team disagrees with his decision, either may refuse to enter into a contract for the coming season, and on August 1st the player automatically enters a special "secondary draft" pool. The secondary draft is held on August 15th, and the player is then selected by another team in the WHA. In the event the player and the team selecting him are unable to agree on a contract by September 1st, the player re-enters the secondary draft pool, and another draft is held on a date designated by the league president.[1]

In addition to this unique provision for mediation, the World Hockey Association Player's Contract also contains provisions by which the player agrees that his team may enjoin him from playing for another team

[1] WHA Player's Contract ¶ 16.

during the contract term,[2] and the player agrees that he may be sold or traded to another team.[3]

The total effect of these provisions is to give the WHA team holding the player's contract something similar to a right of first refusal on the player's services for the following season. If a player wants to insist on a certain salary, he may re-enter the secondary draft pool repeatedly until a team willing to pay him that salary finally has the opportunity to draft him. Thus, this procedure was a creative response to some of the objections professional athletes in all sports have had to reserve and option systems.

On the other hand, the mediation and secondary draft procedure devised by the WHA seems to assume that the only reason a player and a team might not sign a new contract is because of a dispute over the amount of salary the player is to receive. There are, of course, other possible reasons why agreement might not be reached. For example, when the St. Louis Cardinals assigned Curt Flood's contract to the Philadelphia Phillies, Flood refused to sign with the Phillies even though they offered him more money than he had received from the Cardinals. In Flood's case, the amount offered by Philadelphia was not the real issue. Rather, Flood objected to his being traded like a consignment of goods, in complete disregard of his dozen years of service to the Cardinals and his social and business ties to the City of St. Louis.[4]

In such situations, the WHA mediation procedure can be of no help. Moreover, if the dispute between the player

---

[2] *Id.* at ¶ 6.

[3] *Id.* at ¶ 9.

[4] See § 1.3(b)(1), ***supra.***

and the team is based on the player's dislike of the team's hometown, or the player's desire to live and play in a particular town, the mediators cannot resolve that. The only way a player can change cities is to enter the secondary draft pool and hope to be drafted by the team he wants. However, the mediation procedure may not allow the player to insist on entering the secondary draft pool for the purpose of changing cities. Though the Player's Contract is unclear as to this, it permits the player to enter the secondary draft pool only if he disagrees with the decision of the impartial arbitrator, because he believes "in good faith" that the arbitrator's decision is unfair.[5] In the context of professional team sports, where trades are made routinely and in large numbers, and where the player is aware and has agreed in his contract that he may be sold or traded, it may not be "unfair" for the impartial arbitrator to decide that a player cannot refuse to sign a player contract simply because he does not like the team to which he has been traded.

Consider another example. Players often demand to be traded because they feel their coaches are not playing them as often or as much as they would like. If a player refused to sign a new contract with his team for that reason, mediation would be of no help whatever. Team owners cannot agree with a player that he will be played any particular amount; that decision is for the coach alone to make. Again, it may not be "unfair" for the impartial arbitrator to decide that a player cannot refuse to sign a player contract simply because he feels he should be played more often. If it would not be unfair of the arbitrator to so decide, then the WHA Player's Contract does not seem to permit the player (who must mediate "in good faith")

[5] WHA Player's Contract ¶ 16.2.

to disagree with the impartial mediator's decision in order to compel his being included in the secondary draft pool.

§2.2(c) Football

§2.2(c)(1) National Football League

The option clause contained in the National Football League Standard Player Contract provides that the team has the right to renew the contract and retain the player's services for an additional year—but only one year—at 90% of his prior year's salary.[1] The one year limitation on the team's right to renew is a significant departure from the practice in Organized Baseball, where the right to renew was perpetual. Because of the one year limitation, the system in the National Football League is referred to as an "option" rather than a "reserve" system. In effect, the NFL Player Contract gives the team an option on the player's services for the following year.

Other provisions of the NFL Player Contract give the team the right to sell or trade the player and to enjoin him from playing for any other team.[2] It also provides that in the event the player retires from professional football prior to the expiration of the contract or the renewal year, then the contract or the renewal year is extended for so long as the player remains in retirement.[3] With respect to those players who truly retire from professional football, this extension is perpetual but without significance. The law does not permit the team to prevent a player from retiring or even from going into some business or profession other

[1] Standard Player Contract ¶ 10.

[2] *Id.* at ¶ 9 and ¶ 8.

[3] *Id.* at ¶ 13.

than professional football.[4] In other words, NFL teams cannot compel players to play football until the contract and the renewal year expire. However, this contract clause became very significant in at least one case where a player came out of retirement to join a newly-formed league.[5]

The NFL Standard Player Contract option clause is supported by specific provisions of the By-Laws of the National Football League. One provision prohibits tampering or negotiating with, or offering employment to any player belonging to another NFL team.[6] Another authorizes assignment of player contracts to other teams, and provides that upon receiving notice of such assignment, players are to report to their new teams "as promptly as possible." [7]

If there were no other By-Laws relating to the operation of the NFL option system, it is possible players might not object to it as strenuously as they do. Unlike baseball, an NFL player is permitted to obtain his "freedom" and is permitted to negotiate with any and all teams who might be interested in employing him. He may do this simply by allowing his team to exercise its option and by playing during the renewal year without a new contract. When a player does this, he is said to be "playing out his option," though in reality it is the team's option he is playing out, not his own.

Playing out an option is an expensive and risky thing to do, and may not produce the freedom and opportunity

[4] See, e.g., Flood v. Kuhn, 316 F.Supp. 271, 280-282 (S.D.N.Y. 1970).

[5] Dallas Cowboys Football Club, Inc. v. Harris, 348 S.W.2d 37 (Tex. Ct. Civ. App. 1961), discussed in § 2.3(a)(1), *infra.*

[6] NFL Constitution and By-Laws § 9.2.

[7] *Id.* at §§ 16.1 and 16.2.

that theoretically comes from doing so. It is expensive because any football player doing so will be paid only 90% of the salary he received the year before. In all probability, he will actually lose more than 10%. Why this is so was explained by Bernie Parrish, a former member of the Cleveland Browns and author of the book *They Call it a Game,* in testimony before the Senate Subcommittee on Antitrust and Monopoly.[8] Prior to May 1, 1966, the Browns sent Parrish a registered letter, as they had every preceding year since he joined the team, telling him the team had exercised its option on his services for the 1966 season at 90% of his 1965 salary. Since his 1965 salary was $18,500, it at first appears that Parrish could have bought his freedom from the Browns for $1,850 by playing the 1966 season without a new contract ($1,850 being the 10% cut in pay he would have had to accept). Parrish, however, thought he was worth more in 1966 than he had earned in 1965, not less, and the Browns agreed. In fact, the Browns were willing to pay Parrish $23,000 for the 1966 season, but only if he would sign a new Standard Player Contract containing a new option clause for the 1967 season. Because Parrish was under option to the Browns for the 1966 season, no other team in the National Football League would hire him; and, thus, with or without a new contract, he had to play with the Browns in 1966, or else not play professional football at all. Parrish was faced with choosing between signing a new contract with a new option clause for $23,000, or playing without a new contract, to obtain his freedom for the 1967 season, at a salary of $16,650 (90% of $18,500). Parrish signed the new contract.

---

[8] Hearings on S. 2373 before the Subcomm. on Antitrust and Monopoly of the Senate Comm. on the Judiciary, 92d Cong., 2d Sess., Part 2 (1971-1972) at 885-969.

Had he not done so, he would have received $6,450 less in 1966 than he actually was paid.

Playing out an option is a risky thing for a professional athlete to do for several reasons. First, a player might find himself without any employment or income at all during the option year as a result of lingering injuries from the year before, despite the Standard Player Contract provision that players are to be paid for the entire season if they are injured while playing, and even if the player had a "no-cut" clause in his contract.[9] Second, injuries sustained during the option season might make the player less valuable to any future team he wished to join, or even end his career entirely. Third, and perhaps most important, because of the anti-tampering rule, a player has no way of knowing, until the option season is entirely over, whether or not any other team might be interested in hiring him or what his salary might be.

Thus, in order to play out an option, a player must accept at least a 10% cut in pay, which in reality could amount to a much greater cut from what the player could have earned had he been willing to sign a new contract. If the player has any lingering injuries, he must accept the risk that he will have no employment or income during the option year, even though his contract calls for full payment in the event of injury and even though his contract may have a "no-cut" clause. The player must face the risk he might be injured while playing out the option. And he must do all this without knowing in advance what salary any other team might be willing to pay him, or even if there is another team that might want to hire him.

---

[9] See, e.g., Hennigan v. Chargers Football Company, 431 F.2d 308 (5th Cir. 1970), discussed in § 2.5, *infra*.

Despite all these factors, players would probably not object to football's option system as vigorously as they do, if the system did not contain one additional factor which many say effectively prevents players from playing out options in any event. This last critical factor is a provision of the NFL Constitution and By-Laws which has come to be known as the "Rozelle Rule." It provides:

> "Any player, whose contract with a League club has expired, shall thereupon become a free agent and shall no longer be considered a member of the team of that club following the expiration date of such contract. Whenever a player, becoming a free agent in such manner, thereafter signs a contract with a different club in the League, then, unless mutually satisfactory arrangements have been concluded between the two League clubs, the Commissioner may name and then award to the former club one or more players, from the Active, Reserve, or Selection List (including future selection choices) of the acquiring club as the Commissioner in his sole discretion deems fair and equitable; any such decision by the Commissioner shall be final and conclusive." [10]

In other words, whenever a player plays out his option, thus earning his freedom to negotiate with all of the teams in the NFL, and thereafter is hired by another team, the team that hires him must give the player's former team something in return—either cash, another player, or future draft choices. Thus, a player who plays out his option is really doing nothing more than forcing his old team to trade him to another team of his own choice. The requirement that the team hiring the player compensate his former team reduces the amount of salary the new team would

---

[10] NFL Constitution and By-Laws § 12.1(H).

otherwise be willing to pay, because the cost to the new team is not only the player's salary, but also the value of whatever must be given in addition.

Furthermore, in the event the player's new team and former team cannot agree on the compensation to be given, the "Rozelle Rule" empowers the NFL Commissioner, Pete Rozelle, to decide what compensation will be paid. That is, the Commissioner is given the power to award the former team players or future draft choices from the roster of the new team. This power is said to put a damper on the ability of NFL players to find new employment in the league after playing out their options, because teams that might be interested in hiring them do not know in advance whether or not they will be able to reach agreement with the player's former team and who or what Commissioner Rozelle might award the former team in the event agreement is not reached.

The Rozelle Rule has not always been a part of the NFL Constitution and By-Laws. In the League's early years, it had a baseball-type perpetual reserve clause. In 1947, the clause was replaced by the one-year option clause that now appears in the NFL player contract. But the Rozelle Rule was not added until the spring of 1963, as a result of R. C. Owens' playing out his option with the San Francisco 49ers, then signing with the Baltimore Colts, with the 49ers receiving nothing in return. In testimony before a Senate Subcommittee on Antitrust and Monopoly in 1964, Creighton Miller, attorney for the NFL Players Association, interpreted the then-new rule to be for the purpose of discouraging players from playing out their options.[11] Commissioner Rozelle, on the other hand,

[11] Hearings on S. 2391 before the Subcomm. on Antitrust and Monopoly of the Senate Comm. on the Judiciary, 88th Cong., 2d Sess. 99 (1964).

testified that the rule was in response to the concerns of the owners "that if a number of players from a given team played out their option and went elsewhere, it could tend to destroy the balance in the league that has meant so much to the growth of the NFL."[12] Rozelle testified further that since the rule was adopted a player, John Adams, had played out his option with the Chicago Bears and signed with the Los Angeles Rams, as he wanted, because his home was in that area, and the Rams and the Bears had negotiated the Bears' compensation—a high draft choice—without Rozelle's intervention.

Commissioner Rozelle has intervened on several occasions since, however; and at least one "award" made by him was interpreted as a warning to team owners that they would be dealt with harshly in the event they sign players who have played out their options. The player involved was David Parks. He had played out his option with the San Francisco 49ers and had been hired by the New Orleans Saints. When the Saints and 49ers were unable to agree on the compensation the 49ers should receive, Rozelle awarded them Kevin Hardy, whom the Saints had just chosen as their 1968 first round draft choice, plus the Saints' first round draft right for 1969. Thereafter, so few players successfully changed clubs after playing out their options, that in May of 1972 NFL Players Association president, John Mackey, and thirty-three other professional football players filed suit against the National Football League in the Federal District Court in Minnesota. The suit sought a judicial declaration that the Rozelle Rule violated the Sherman Antitrust Act, and included allegations that ten of the player-plaintiffs had

[12] *Id.* at 119.

previously played out their options but, because of the Rozelle Rule, had been unable to sign with other teams.[13]

Naturally, the National Football League denied that the Rozelle Rule violates the Sherman Act, but seems not to deny that it discourages team jumping. In an interview published just a month after the suit was filed, Commissioner Rozelle said that from 1966 (when the National and American Football Leagues merged) through 1970, forty-two players played out their options. Of the forty-two, only thirteen signed with new teams, eleven without invoking the Rozelle Rule. Twenty-four players re-signed with the clubs they had been playing for, two went to Canada, and three retired. Although Rozelle stated that his figures indicated that the twenty-four who re-signed with their original clubs had "healthy" pay increases, he went on to acknowledge that ". . . there would have been more moves if there were no Rozelle Rule." "But" he said, "we think reason substantiates the rule. If you had movement without compensation, you would decimate franchises, hurting owners and fans." [14]

§2.2(c)(2) World Football League[1]

The World Football League Player's Contract provided that the "Club and Player shall each have the option to extend the term of this Contract . . . for an additional one year period . . ." [2] The option was to be exercised by written notice, to be given prior to December 31st of the final year of the contract. When notice was given,

---

[13] Mackey v. National Football League, 407 F.Supp. 1000 (D.Minn. 1975), discussed in § 2.4(b)(1), *infra.*

[14] Maher, Sports' Option Clause: The Issue Is Freedom, L.A. Times, June 29, 1972, Part III, Pg. 1.

[1] The World Football League disbanded on October 22, 1975.

[2] WFL Player's Contract ¶ 15.3.

it automatically bound the other party for an additional year, during which all of the terms and conditions of the original contract remained in effect, except for the option and salary provisions. The contract specified that the option was to be for a single year only, and that neither the club nor the player would have the right to extend it further. It also provided that (unlike the practice in the NFL), "After the termination of this Contract (whether or not the one year option has been exercised by either party) Club shall have no right to compensation, arising from this Contract, from any other Club which subsequently employs Player." [3]

The player's salary during the option year was not automatically reduced, as in the NFL. The WFL contract provided that upon exercise of the option, the player and the club "agree to make a good faith effort to agree on Player's compensation." [4] If, however, they were unable to agree by May 1st, then an arbitration system quite similar to Organized Baseball's new "last offer, last demand" system was to be used. The player and club each were to have submitted a salary amount to the league office "together with any reasons each might have on the fairness of the proposed compensation." [5] The figures and supporting information were then to be submitted by the league president to an independent arbitrator, who had to select one figure or the other. The arbitrator's decision could have been based solely on the information submitted to him, or he could have held a hearing, should he have desired to do so.

The WFL option system seemed to be quite fair to players. It was a true one-year option, without subsequent compensation rights to hinder the player from realizing the

[3] *Id.* at ¶ 15.3.4.

[4] *Id.* at ¶ 15.3.5.

[5] *Id.* at ¶ 15.3.5.1.

benefit of playing out his option. And it incorporated the unique baseball salary arbitration scheme for the option year. On the other hand, WFL players should not have been mislead into thinking they really had the option of requiring their teams to employ them for an additional year, as National Hockey League players apparently do. Even though the WFL contract provided that the player as well as the club had the option to extend the contract for a year, one of the terms and conditions of the contract that remained in effect during the option year was entitled **"Standards of Performance." It read:**

> "Player understands that he is competing with other players for positions on Club's roster and that the number of players on the roster is limited by League rules and practical necessity. If, at any time during the term of this Contract, in the sole opinion of Club, Player's skill, performance, or conduct is not sufficient to enable him to stay on Club's active roster, or within some other League authorized numerical limit, Club shall have the right to terminate this Contract . . ."[6]

Upon termination, the player was to be paid only that portion of his annual salary that was equal to the portion of league games his team had already played that season.[7] Thus, even if a player exercised his option to extend the contract for an additional year, the player might be cut from the team before any league games had been played, and in that event the team would not owe the player any salary at all for the option year.

The WFL contract contained a paragraph in which the player represented and agreed that he had unique skill, ex-

[6] *Id.* at ¶ 12.
[7] *Id.*

perience, knowledge, and ability, and that therefore the Club could enjoin him from playing football for anyone else during the term of the Contract.[8] It also provided that the Club could sell or trade the contract to another WFL team, and in that event, the player agreed to report promptly to the new team and perform faithfully for it.[9]

§2.2(d) Basketball

§2.2(d)(1) National Basketball Association

Through the end of the 1976-1977 season, the National Basketball Association Uniform Player Contract will contain an option clause which provides that by September 1st following the last season covered by the contract, the Club may mail the player a contract for the next season. Thereafter, only one-year rookie contracts will have an option clause. If the player does not sign and return the new contract to the Club by October 1st, then the old contract "shall be deemed renewed and extended for the period of one year, upon the same terms and conditions in all respects as are provided herein."[1] Prior to 1971, the player's salary could be reduced 25%, but in that year the contract was modified so that the salary now remains the same. This clause seems to be a "reserve" clause. That is, it appears to permit NBA teams to renew player contracts perpetually, because in the event a player fails to return an executed copy of a contract for the coming season, the clause provides that the prior season's contract "is deemed renewed and extended . . . upon the same terms and conditions . . ."[2] One of the renewed and extended conditions is the clause

[8] *Id.* at ¶ 6.2.

[9] *Id.* at ¶ 16.1.

[1] NBA Uniform Player Contract ¶ 22.

[2] *Id.*

itself, and thus it would seem to permit further renewals and extensions, year after year, forever. Nevertheless, courts have held that the NBA contract simply grants NBA teams a single one year option on their players' services; the option clause does not renew or extend itself.[3]

In another paragraph of the NBA contract, the player agrees that the team shall have the right to enjoin him from playing for any other team during the term of the contract.[4] Yet another paragraph gives the team the right to sell or trade the player, and the player agrees to accept the trade or sale and to "faithfully perform" for the new team.[5]

As in other sports, the NBA Uniform Player Contract is supported by provisions of the NBA Constitution and By-Laws. All player contracts must be in the form prescribed and adopted by the NBA.[6] Tampering with players under contract to another team in the league is prohibited, and may be punished by suspension or expulsion from the NBA, a $5,000 fine, or both.[7]

Interestingly, however, the NBA Constitution and By-Laws do not contain a compensation rule similar to the NFL's Rozelle Rule. The NBA did not have occasion to consider what the consequence would be in the event an NBA player played out his option and then joined another NBA team until 1974, when Cazzie Russell became the first NBA player to do so. Nevertheless, although the NBA Constitution and By-Laws do not contain a compensation

[3] Central New York Basketball, Inc. v. Barnett, 181 N.E.2d 506 (Ohio Ct. of Com. Pl. 1961); Lemat Corp. v. Barry, 80 Cal. Rptr. 240 (Cal. Ct. App. 1969), discussed in § 2.3, *infra*.

[4] NBA Uniform Player Contract ¶ 9.

[5] *Id.* at ¶ 10.

[6] NBA Constitution and By-Laws § 4.01.

[7] *Id.* at ¶ 35(g).

rule, one does exist, according to an affidavit submitted by former Commissioner Walter Kennedy to a federal judge in the *Oscar Robertson* case.[8]

However, when the *Robertson* case was settled in February of 1976, it was agreed that the compensation rule would be terminated in 1980 and would be replaced with a "right of first refusal" in favor of the player's then-current team. Thus, beginning in 1980, an NBA player whose contract has expired will be free to negotiate with all of the teams in the league. His current team will have the right to retain his services by matching any offer he has received from another team. But if it does not match that offer, the player will be able to join the other team and no compensation whatever will be due his former team.[9]

§2.2(d)(2) American Basketball Association

The American Basketball Association Uniform Player Contract contains a true option clause which provides that on or before the date the contract expires, the Club may renew the contract for one year on the same terms, except that the compensation to be paid during the period of renewal need only be 90% of the amount paid during the preceding season. After such renewal, the Club does not have the option to renew again.[1]

Other paragraphs give the team the right to enjoin the player from playing elsewhere while the contract is in effect,[2] and the right to sell or trade the player to another

[8] Robertson v. National Basketball Association, 389 F.Supp. 867, 891 (S.D.N.Y. 1975), discussed in §§ 2.4(b)(2), 2.4(b)(3), 3.5 and 4.3(b)(4), *infra*.

[9] L.A. Times, Feb. 4, 1976, Part III.

[1] ABA Uniform Player Contract ¶ 15.

[2] *Id.* at ¶ 5.

team.[3] As in NBA contracts, ABA players agree that if traded or sold they will "faithfully perform" for their new teams.[4] In addition, the ABA contract has a paragraph—very similar to the one appearing in National and World Football League player contracts—providing that in the event the player retires from professional basketball, any unexpired portion of the contract or option year is extended for the period of the player's retirement.[5] As with NFL and WFL contracts, the ABA retirement clause has no practical effect if the player truly retires. However, the clause could be very significant if the player's "retirement" is only temporary.

ABA By-Laws require teams to use the League's Standard Player Uniform Player Contract, though the Commissioner is granted authority to approve changes made by a team.[6] And the By-Laws also prohibit tampering with players belonging to another ABA team.[7]

§2.2(e) Team tennis

The Standard Player's Contract used by the World Team Tennis League provides that the team shall have the option to renew the contract for an additional year "on the same terms and conditions" that were in effect during its prior WTT playing season. Notice must be given to the player at least three months prior to the start of the option year season. Once exercised, the team thereafter has no further option on the player.[1]

---

[3] *Id.* at ¶ 6.
[4] *Id.*
[5] *Id.* at ¶ 16.
[6] ABA By-Laws Article XVII.
[7] *Id.* at Article XII.
[1] WTT Standard Player's Contract ¶ 7.2.

Among the terms and conditions which remain the same during the option year is the provision concerning salary. The contract also contains the customary clause providing that the team may sell or trade the player to another team in the league, and that if sold or traded, the player agrees to accept the assignment and to perform faithfully for the new team.[2]

§2.3 Enforcibility in court by teams

Almost since the beginning of professional sports, the meaning and effect of reserve and option systems have been explored in numerous significant lawsuits. While the cases have arisen in at least three different contexts, the most usual by far has involved a player leaving a team in one league—in disregard and alleged violation of a reserve or option clause—and joining a team in a separate competitive league. The practice is often called "league jumping," and in such cases, teams from which players jumped frequently sought injunctions barring them from playing for their new teams.

§2.3(a) Enforcing personal service contracts by injunction

As a general rule, courts will not order the performance of personal services.[1] This is so for several reasons. One is that such orders might compel involuntary servitude in violation of the Thirteenth Amendment to the United States Constitution. Another is that courts would find it difficult, if not impossible, to enforce them. Usually, court orders requiring that some act be done or not be done are enforced

---

[2] *Id.* at ¶ 6.

[1] See, e.g., Metropolitan Exhibition Co. v. Ward, 9 N.Y.S. 779 (1890); Metropolitan Exhibition Co. v. Ewing, 42 Fed. 198 (S.D. N.Y. 1890); and Flood v. Kuhn, 316 F.Supp. 271, 280-282 (S.D. N.Y. 1970).

by holding a violator in contempt. If an order required the performance of personal services, and the employer thereafter contended that the employee was not performing as well as he or she could and should, the court would have to determine whether or not the employee was performing as ordered. In professional sports, as in many other businesses, it would be impossible to make such a determination. Players who are not under court order and who strive for success with all their ability, often have bad days and even bad seasons. There would be no way for a judge to determine whether a player who had been ordered to play for one club, rather than permitted to play for another, and who then played poorly, was simply having a bad day or was actually violating the order.

Although courts usually will not order the performance of personal services, under certain circumstances they may prohibit a person who is under contract to one employer from rendering services to another during the term and in breach of the contract. In legal contemplation, the affirmative covenant to render services is not enforced; rather the negative covenant (not to render services for another during the contract term) is enforced. Involuntary servitude is not compelled and no difficult judgments are required to determine whether or not the order has been complied with.

§2.3(a)(1) Unique services requirement

Personal service contracts may be enforced in this backhand fashion if, but only if, the services called for are unique.[1] If the services are common and available from

[1] See, e.g., Philadelphia Ball Club v. Lajoie, 51 Atl. 973 (Pa. S.Ct. 1902); Dallas Cowboys Football Club, Inc. v. Harris, 348 S.W.2d 37 (Tex. Ct. Civ. App. 1961); Central New York Basketball, Inc. v. Barnett, 181 N.E.2d 506 (Ohio Ct. Com. Pl. 1961).

others, an employer's remedy—if an employee breaks a contract by working for someone else—is to hire another employee, and to sue the first one for any damages suffered. If the services are common and available from someone else, at worst the employer may have to pay more for them. The difference will be his recoverable damages. But no special damage will be suffered if the first employee goes to work elsewhere, not even if he goes to work for a competitor.

Unique services, on the other hand, by definition, are not readily available from someone else. Injunctions prohibiting employees from rendering such services to a second employer in breach of contract with a first employer, have been issued by courts ever since 1852 when an English court did so in *Lumley* v. *Wagner,* a case involving a then-famous opera singer who agreed to perform in two separate opera houses on the same night.[2] Even in the United States, such injunctions date back at least to the mid-1870's, when a New York state court issued one to prevent actress Fanny Morant Smith from breaking a contract she had made for the 1874, 1875 and 1876 theatrical seasons.[3]

Like opera singers and actresses, it was held in an early sports case that professional ball-players "of peculiar fitness and skill to fill a particular position" also render unique services, and thus may be enjoined "in a proper case" from breaching their contracts.[4] Because the Court did not consider that to be a "proper case" for other reasons, no special consideration was given to what constitutes "peculiar fitness."

---

[2] 1 De Gex, M. & G. 604 (1852).

[3] Daly v. Smith, 38 N.Y. Super. Ct. 158.

[4] Metropolitan Exhibition Co. v. Ward, 9 N.Y.S. 779, 781 (1890).

That question was discussed extensively in a case decided shortly thereafter, *Philadelphia Ball Club* v. *Lajoie*.[5] The trial judge in that case refused to issue an injunction, saying that in order to do so the ball-player's "services must be unique, extraordinary, and of such a character as to render it impossible to replace him." The Court found that Lajoie did not meet that standard even though it did find that he was

> ". . . an expert baseball player in any position; that he has a great reputation as a second baseman; that his place would be hard to fill with as good a player; that his withdrawal from the team would weaken it, as would the withdrawal of any good player, and would probably make a difference in the size of the audience attending the game." [6]

The Pennsylvania Supreme Court reversed, saying the trial judge had "taken extreme ground" in holding that an injunction could be issued only where it was impossible to replace a player. A "more just and equitable rule," that Court stated, is that an injunction may be granted,

> "Where one person agrees to render personal services to another, which require and presuppose a special knowledge, skill, and ability in the employee so that in case of a default the same service could not easily be obtained from others. . ." [7]

Lajoie did meet this standard, the Court held, because he had been with the club for several years, his salary constantly increased from year to year, he was thoroughly

---

[5] 51 Atl. 973 (Pa. S.Ct. 1902).

[6] *Id.* at 974.

[7] *Id.* at 973.

familiar with the actions and methods of the other players on the team, his own team work was especially good, he was well known to the public, and he was an attractive drawing card.

> "He may not be the sun in the baseball firmament, but he is certainly a bright particular star. We feel, therefore, that the evidence in this case justifies the conclusion that the services of the defendant [Lajoie] are of such a unique character, and display such a special knowledge, skill, and ability, as renders them of peculiar value to the plaintiff [Philadelphia Ball Club], and so difficult of substitution that their loss will produce 'irreparable injury,' in the legal significance of that term, to the plaintiff." [8]

The *Lajoie* standard of uniqueness has been used almost exclusively ever since. Indeed, the *Lajoie* standard is incorporated, almost word for word, right into the National Football League Standard Player Contract. Paragraph 8 of that document contains a representation by the player that "he has special, exceptional and unique knowledge, skill and ability as a football player" and an agreement by the player that the team may therefore enjoin him from playing for anyone else.

The NFL contract clause and the "unique services" requirement for an injuction were one of the principal issues in a case that arose almost immediately upon the formation of the American Football League in 1960 between the NFL's Dallas Cowboys and Jimmy Harris, a University of Oklahoma star of the mid-1950's. Harris had played for the Los Angeles Rams in 1958 pursuant to an NFL Standard Player Contract which contained the usual

[8] *Id.* at 974.

clause giving the team an option on Harris' services for the 1959 season. The Rams did exercise that option, but, because of a dispute involving the option and other matters, Harris did not play football at all during the 1959 season. Instead, he re-enrolled in the University of Oklahoma as a student and worked for the school as an assistant football coach. Then, in April of 1960, Harris signed a player contract for the 1960 season with the Dallas Texans (now the Kansas City Chiefs) of the new American Football League. Upon learning that Harris had signed with an AFL team, the Rams immediately assigned his contract to the Dallas Cowboys, which was then a new NFL expansion club. On July 22, 1960, the Cowboys filed suit against Harris, seeking to enjoin him from playing professional football for any other team.

The Cowboys alleged that because Harris' NFL player contract had been assigned to them, they had the exclusive right to his services as a player for the 1960 season. In support of their application for an injunction, the Cowboys' representatives testified that Harris had unique ability, while in an attempt to block an injunction, Harris and the Texans testified to the contrary.

The Cowboys also argued that since Harris had represented in his NFL contract with the Rams that he was special, exceptional and unique, he should not have been allowed to testify to the contrary in order to avoid fulfillment of his obligations. That argument was apparently thought to have some merit, for the player contracts used by all professional sport leagues to this very day contain similar clauses in which players represent they are unique. However, neither the trial judge nor the judges of the appellate court accepted the Cowboys' "estoppel" argument. While people are bound by their representations of "fact," the Court indicated, they are not by representations of mere "opinion." The Player Contract clause "is properly to be interpreted as an expression of opinion. . . ." [9] Harris' testimony was therefore proper, and he successfully convinced the jury that he was just an ordinary football player, thereby winning his freedom from the NFL at the trial court level.

The Cowboys appealed, however, and Harris was unable to convince the appellate judges that he was just ordinary. "Unique" does not mean impossible to replace, they held. It simply means not easily replaced. By that standard, Harris was unique, because the testimony indicated that he had above average and even exceptional skill and that other players of Harris' ability were not available to the Cowboys. Though Harris must have been pleased with that appraisal of his abilities, it meant he could be enjoined from playing for the Texans, and he was.[10]

On the very day the Texas Court of Appeals announced its decision in the *Jimmy Harris* case, events were set in motion in New York which eventually resulted in a landmark basketball decision rendered by a state court in Ohio. On May 26, 1961, Central New York Basketball, Inc., a corporation that owned the Syracuse Nationals of the National Basketball Association, mailed Richard "Dick" Barnett an NBA Uniform Player Contract for the upcoming 1961-1962 season. Barnett had been the Nationals' number one draft choice in 1959, and he had played for the team with some distinction during the 1959-1960 and 1960-1961 seasons. Ordinarily, Barnett would have signed the contract which had been mailed him on May 26, 1961—perhaps after some negotiations for a pay raise—and

[9] Dallas Cowboys Football Club v. Harris, *supra* note 1, at 43.
[10] *Id.*

returned it to the team. He had done so the year before, as had all of his teammates.

However, the summer of 1961 was not an ordinary time in the basketball business. Abe Saperstein, owner of the Harlem Globetrotters, had been piqued by the NBA's transfer of the Minneapolis Lakers to Los Angeles, because he believed he had been promised a league franchise in that city in exchange for Globetrotter schedule changes designed to bolster attendance for weak NBA franchises. A double-header featuring a Globetrotter exhibition as the preliminary game often produced a much-needed sell-out. Thus, when the Lakers were moved to Los Angeles, Saperstein decided to organize a league of his own which began play in October of 1961 in eight cities from Washington, D.C. to Honolulu, Hawaii. The Cleveland Pipers of Saperstein's short-lived American Basketball League (not to be confused with the subsequent American Basketball Association), offered Dick Barnett an ABL contract for the 1961-1962 season, and he accepted it. Whereupon, the Nationals filed suit in the state court of Ohio seeking an injunction preventing Barnett from playing basketball for the Pipers, or any team other than the Nationals, until the 1961-1962 season was over.

As in the *Jimmy Harris* case, the *Dick Barnett* case[11] involved the issue of Barnett's basketball ability. Barnett and the Pipers' management testified that Barnett had no exceptional ability, while the Nationals' management—which had offered Barnett a smaller salary than had the Pipers—testified that he was one of the game's "greatest . . . players." When all the evidence was in, the Court found Barnett to be an "outstanding professional basketball player of unusual attainments and exceptional skill and

[11] Central New York Basketball v. Barnett, *supra* note 1.

ability"[12]—a finding that must have gratified Barnett's ego, even though it meant he could be enjoined from playing for the Pipers. In making this finding, the Ohio Court stated,

> ". . . it would seem that mere engagement as a basketball player in the N.B.A., or A.B.L., carries with it recognition of his excellence and extraordinary abilities. . . . Professional players in the major baseball, football, and basketball leagues have unusual talents and skills or they would not be so employed."[13]

The view that all professional athletes have unique skills now seems to be universally accepted. In fact, in a rare lawsuit between a Canadian Football League team and a National Football League team, it was held that two rookies who had not as of then played any professional football at all had unique skills sufficient to justify an injunction in favor of the Canadian team with which they had orginally signed, barring them from playing for the Cleveland Browns.[14] The Court held that the appraisal of the ability of recent college graduates had to depend upon their prospects and potential, for otherwise contracts with players who only had college experience would rarely be enforceable.

Indeed, there has never been a reported case in which a player was permitted to jump leagues on the grounds that he lacked unique skill. Furthermore, following the decision in the *Dick Barnett* case, the testimony which characterized cases until then—by the player that he was average, and by his former team that he was very good—has never been

---

[12] *Id.* at 514.

[13] *Id.* at 514, 517.

[14] Winnipeg Rugby Football Club v. Freeman, 140 F.Supp. 365 (N.D. Ohio 1965).

duplicated. In some subsequent cases, the player conceded his greatness. In others, the issue simply never arose.

It therefore can be said that the "unique talent" requirement for enforcing personal service contracts ". . . is met prima facie in cases involving professional athletes."[15] But for opinions which arose during the recent National Hockey League-World Hockey Association "war,"[16] this entire issue could have been called "well settled." In two of the opinions resulting from that "war," the talent of the players involved was found to be unique, in accordance with the principles applied in preceding sports cases;[17] and none of the cases found the players' talents not to be unique.

However, two other opinions ignored the "unique talent" question altogether, and found, for other reasons, that the NHL teams involved would not be irreparably injured, even if stars jumped to the WHA. In *Boston Professional Hockey Association, Inc.* v. *Cheevers,*[18] a federal District Court held that the Boston Bruins would not suffer irre-

---

[15] Nassau Sports v. Peters, 352 F.Supp. 870, 876 (E.D.N.Y. 1972); see also, Long Island American Assn. Football Club, Inc. v. Manrodt, 23 N.Y.S. 2d 858 (1940). But see Matuszak v. Houston Oilers, Inc., 1974-2 CCH Trade Cases ¶ 75,373 (Tex. Ct. Civ. App. 1974), discussed in § 5.2(b)(2)(A), *infra,* where the Court held that because the Oilers' owner and coach ". . . took occasion to disparage the abilities of Matuszak . . . an ultimate finding of non-uniqueness would be supportable," even though Matuszak had been the NFL's number one draft choice and had made the All-Rookie Team in 1973. The Court also eliminated that portion of an injunction which prevented Matuszak from engaging in "activities related to football," on the ground, in part, that he had not been demonstrated to be unique "with reference to any activity other than as a football player."

[16] See §§ 2.3(b)(2) and 6.3, *infra.*

[17] Nassau Sports v. Peters, *supra* note 15; Nassau Sports v. Hampson, 355 F.Supp. 733 (D. Minn. 1972), both discussed in § 2.3(b)(2), *infra.*

[18] 348 F.Supp. 261 (D. Mass. 1972), *remanded,* 472 F.2d 127 (1st Cir. 1972), discussed in § 2.3(b)(2), *infra.*

parable harm if Gerry Cheevers and Derek Sanderson jumped to the WHA, because the Bruins had enjoyed substantial earnings for years and were a "solidly established commercial operation." [19] Similarly, in *Philadelphia World Hockey Club* v. *Philadelphia Hockey Club,*[20] it was held that "The NHL is no shaky institution which will collapse if it loses a few superstars or even many average players during the pendency of this preliminary injunction," [21] barring it from attempting to enforce its reserve clause in any further legal proceedings.

These two opinions seem at first to be inconsistent with other cases in this area. While it may well have been true, as a matter of fact, that NHL teams could survive the loss of some of their players to the WHA, it has been clear since *Lajoie* that the loss of the unique services of a professional athlete constitutes "irreparable injury" as a matter of law. The *Cheevers* opinion was in fact modified by the Court of Appeals to indicate that the Bruins would suffer irreparable damage from the loss of Cheevers and Sanderson, and thus that case no longer differs from the others.[22] Only the *Philadelphia* case takes a different approach and it can probably be explained in light of the unique way in which it arose. As explained more fully hereafter,[23] the WHA and its teams not only defended suits filed by NHL teams, they also filed antitrust cases against the NHL seeking injunctions which would prevent NHL teams from attempting to enforce the NHL reserve clause. Five such cases were consolidated before federal

---

[19] *Id.* at 268.

[20] 351 F.Supp. 462 (E.D. Pa. 1972), discussed in § 2.3(b)(2), *infra.*

[21] *Id.* at 516-517.

[22] 472 F.2d 127 (1st Cir. 1972).

[23] See § 2.3(b)(2), *infra.*

District Judge A. Leon Higginbotham and thereafter referred to as *Philadelphia World Hockey Club* v. *Philadelphia Hockey Club*. The opinion which accompanied the injunction issued by Judge Higginbotham should be read to mean that *even though* the NHL would suffer irreparable injury from the loss of the unique services of some of its players, that irreparable injury would not be financially fatal to the NHL. Therefore, until the merits of the WHA's claims could be fully litigated, it would be proper to enjoin the NHL from attempting to enforce its reserve clause. If not temporarily enjoined, the WHA might not have survived until trial, because of the total control over almost all players which the NHL reserve system gave it.

§2.3(a)(2) Significance of rivalry between player's former and new teams

In the *Rick Barry* case, the Court held that the Warriors would suffer irreparable injury if Barry jumped to the Oaks, not only because Barry had unique talents as a basketball player, but also because "The Warriors and the Oaks directly compete with each other for attendance within the same market [the San Francisco Bay Area] . . ."[1] As a matter of fact, it may have been true that the Warriors suffered additional injury because Barry jumped to a local rival. Nevertheless, according to previous cases, the loss of his unique services, by itself, would have been sufficient irreparable injury to warrant an injunction.

In a subsequent case between NBA and ABA teams, however, the ABA argued that an injunction should not be granted, because the teams involved were *not* local rivals.[2]

---

[1] Lemat Corp. v. Barry, 80 Cal. Rptr. 240 (Cal. Ct. App. 1969), discussed in § 2.3(b)(1), *infra.*

[2] California Sports Incorporated v. Chamberlain, unpublished ruling, L.A. Times, Oct. 11, 1973, Part III, Pg. 1.

The case was filed in 1973 by the Los Angeles Lakers when Wilt Chamberlain signed with the San Diego Conquistadors as a player-coach for the 1973-1974 and succeeding seasons, in disregard of the option clause in his Lakers contract. In opposition to the Lakers' motion for a preliminary injunction, the Conquistadors contended that irreparable injury is not suffered unless there is direct competition between the two teams for customers, as there had been in the *Rick Barry* case. Judge Campbell Lucas, of the Los Angeles Superior Court, rejected the argument, pointing out that it is the loss of the right to display a player's unique talents that causes the losing team irreparable injury. Further, Judge Lucas held that although the San Diego and Los Angeles teams may not have competed with one another directly for the in-person attendance of any particular basketball fans (because of the distance between the two cities), nevertheless there was general competition between them and their leagues for publicity, television coverage, and fan support in a broader, though still significant, way.[3]

Judge Lucas' decision was correct. The argument of the Conquistadors, while innovative, was simply unsupported by law. For example in the *Dick Barnett* case,[4] Barnett sought to jump from a team in Syracuse, New York, to one in Cleveland, Ohio. The American Basketball League did not have a franchise in Syracuse (or anywhere else in the State of New York); and the National Basketball Association did not have a franchise in Cleveland. Nevertheless, without any mention of this lack of intra-city rivalry, Barnett was enjoined from jumping. Most of the

---

[3] *Id.*

[4] Central New York Basketball, Inc. v. Barnett, 181 N.E.2d 506 (Ohio Ct. Com. Pl. 1961), discussed in § 2.3(a)(1), *supra.*

cases have involved teams in widely separated cities, and though injunctions have been denied in some, neither separation nor absence of a local rivalry between leagues has ever been the basis for the denial of an injunction.

§2.3(a)(3) Character of services to be rendered to new employer

A thus far unresolved issue concerns the significance of any difference in the character of the services to be rendered by a player to a new employer. For example, Jimmy Harris' NFL contract provided that he would play football and "engage in activities related to football" only for the Rams or another NFL team to which he might be traded. It also provided that he could be enjoined from playing football "or engaging in activities related to football" for anyone else, during the contract term.[1] While it is clear that he could not have been prevented from becoming a doctor, lawyer, stockbroker, or anything else unrelated to football, it seems as though the contract might have prohibited him from becoming an assistant football coach at the University of Oklahoma. An assistant football coach engages in activities "related to football," as Harris himself argued in an unsuccessful attempt to defeat the NFL retirement clause. The Court construed the word "football" in the retirement clause to mean "professional football." And it seems likely that a court would have construed the word "football" in the "related activities" clause to mean professional football as well. It is most unlikely that Harris would have been enjoined from college coaching, even had the Rams or Cowboys attempted to do so.

---

[1] Dallas Cowboys Football Club, Inc. v. Harris, 348 S.W.2d 37, 42 (Tex. Ct. Civ. App. 1961), discussed in § 2.3(a)(1), *supra.*

But suppose Harris had signed as a coach with an AFL team. When Wilt Chamberlain signed as a player-coach with the San Diego Conquistadors, in disregard of his Laker option clause, the Lakers sought to enjoin him only from playing. They did not attempt to prevent him from coaching. And in fact, although Chamberlain was enjoined from playing for a year, he did coach the Conquistadors. As coach, Chamberlain brought the San Diego team and the ABA a great deal of publicity—publicity about which, it seems safe to assume, the Lakers and the NBA probably were not happy. The NBA contract grants the team only the right to enjoin the player "from playing basketball" for anyone else; it does not refer to "related activities."[2] This may have been the reason the Lakers did not attempt to prevent Chamberlain from coaching. But whatever the reason, the issue was not posed.

The issue was posed, but not resolved, during the NHL-WHA "war." When the Boston Bruins sued Gerry Cheevers and Derek Sanderson, the Bruins sought to enjoin the two not only from playing for any other team, but also from "aiding, promoting, sponsoring, coaching, managing, or otherwise assisting any other professional hockey club in derogation of their duties of loyalty and promotional assistance to the Bruins."[3] For a few weeks, until the term of their respective NHL contracts expired, Cheevers and Sanderson actually were restrained from making appearances or performing other functions on behalf of the World Hockey Association. But, because injunctions for the renewal years were denied altogether, the Court did not have to decide how broad they could be.

---

[2] NBA Uniform Player Contract ¶ 9.

[3] Boston Professional Hockey Assn. v. Cheevers, 348 F.Supp. 261, 263 (D. Mass. 1972), *remanded,* 472 F.2d 127 (1st Cir. 1972).

The issue was touched upon once again during the brief "war" between the National and World Football Leagues. In *World Football League* v. *Dallas Cowboys Football Club, Inc.*,[4] the Texas Court of Civil Appeals in Dallas held that the signing of a WFL contract for future services (to commence after the expiration of the NFL option year) did not constitute an "activity related to football" prohibited by the NFL Standard Player Contract, even though a great deal of publicity for the WFL resulted from it. The Court did add, however, that "other promotional and publicity activities" for the benefit of the WFL might have been subject to restraint, had equitable relief limited to such activities been sought.

On the other hand, in *Matuszak* v. *Houston Oilers, Inc.*,[5] the Texas Court of Civil Appeals in Houston held that although Matuszak could be enjoined from playing football in the WFL, he could not be enjoined from engaging in "activities related to football" because the term was "too general and non-specific to be a legitimate part of an injunctive order," and because Matuszak was not shown to have had any unique ability other than as a football player.[6]

In support of an injunction prohibiting non-playing services, it could be argued that playing services are not the only ones that are unique. If the team and player have agreed that the player will play and engage in related activities only for the team, a player's rendering related

---

[4] World Football League v. Dallas Cowboys Football Club, Inc.. 513 S.W.2d 102 (Tex. Ct. Civ. App. 1974), discussed in § 5.2(b)(2)(C), *infra.*

[5] Matuszak v. Houston Oilers, Inc., 1974-2 CCH Trade Cases ¶ 75,373 (Tex. Ct. Civ. App. 1974), discussed in § 5.2(b)(2)(A), *infra.*

[6] See §2.3(a)(1), *supra.*

services to someone else in breach of that agreement may also cause the team irreparable injury, from which it should be entitled to injunctive relief.

On the other hand, an agreement which restrains a person from earning a living is illegal, at common law, under the Sherman Act, and, to the extent it requires that services be rendered to someone in particular, under the Thirteenth Amendment.[7] The question then becomes to what extent the athlete is restrained from earning a living. The broader the contract and the more things he is prevented from doing, the greater the possibility, in theory at least, that he will be so restrained.

It is interesting to note that the National Football League, which seems to have the broadest of the player contracts, broadened its contract further after the *Jimmy Harris* case was decided. The NFL contract Harris signed provided that he could be enjoined from playing football or engaging in activities relating to football for anyone else. Today, the NFL contract provides that the player may be enjoined from "playing football *or any other professional sport,* without the consent of the Club, or engaging in activities related to football."[8] Thus, today an NFL player may retire from football to become a doctor, lawyer, stockbroker and other things; but he may not retire to become a coach, official or talent scout for another professional football league, nor may he retire to become a professional baseball player, golfer, tennis player, boxer, wrestler or bowler, without the consent of his old team. It seems the NFL would be hard pressed to justify such sweeping restraints on an athlete's ability to support him-

[7] See, Comment, Monopsony in Manpower: Organized Baseball Meets the Antitrust Laws, 62 Yale L.J. 576, 622-623 (1953); Flood v. Kuhn, 316 F.Supp. 271, 280-282 (S.D.N.Y. 1970).

[8] NFL Standard Player Contract ¶ 8.

self after leaving the League, and therefore it would seem such restraints would be unenforceable.

§2.3(b) Defenses to attempted injunctive enforcement

§2.3(b)(1) Equitable defenses: perpetuality, lack of mutuality and harshness

Injunctions are considered to be "equitable" remedies, available only to those who have acted "equitably." As a result, injunctions may be denied even in cases where all of their prerequisites admittedly exist. Thus, where professional athletes have established that it would be inequitable to enforce reserve and option clauses, injunctions have been denied and they have been permitted to jump to new teams. Typically, courts have refused to issue injunctions, on the grounds that it would be inequitable to do so, in cases where the player's first contract was deemed to be perpetual or harsh or was deemed to lack mutuality—simiiliar concepts which are often interchangeable.

The early case of *Metropolitan Exhibition Co.* v. *Ward*[1] was one in which an injunction was denied. There the Court held that the "renewal paragraph" either was too vague to enforce, or else was renewed along with all of the rest of the contract. If renewed, the contract would thereby be perpetual; it would never expire—unless the team terminated it. The contract gave the team the right to terminate on ten days' notice, which meant that the player was bound forever, while the team was bound for little more than a week. Under those circumstances, the Court held that it would be inequitable to enjoin Ward from playing for his

[1] 9 N.Y.S. 2d 779 (1890).

new team. The same result was reached, for the same reason, in other cases as well.[2]

The contract at issue in *Philadelphia Ball Club* v. *Lajoie*[3] also gave the team the right to cancel on ten days' notice. When Lajoie argued that it therefore lacked mutuality and should not be enforced, the Court did not agree. It stated that he knew from the outset when he first signed the contract that he could be cut from the team, and thereafter not paid. That possibility was part of the bargain he had made, and the Court did not consider that bargain to be unreasonable. According to *Lajoie,* mutuality exists as long as each party has the possibility of compelling the performance of mutually agreed upon promises. Lajoie had that possibility because he could always enforce his right to ten days' pay.

The *Ward* and *Lajoie* cases are not inconsistent as they may appear at first. The distinction between them is that Ward's contract bound him perpetually, while Lajoie's contract was for a definite period, no longer than three years. Thus, while it may have been reasonable for Lajoie to have committed himself for three years, even though he could be cut after ten days, it seems probable that the Court would have held a perpetual commitment unreasonable if the team had the same termination rights.

This distinction between contracts of definite and indefinite duration was a key issue in the *Dick Barnett* case.[4] Barnett had argued that even if he had unique basketball

---

[2] Brooklyn Baseball Club v. McGuire, 116 Fed. 782 (E.D. Pa. 1902); Cincinnati Exhibition Co. v. Johnson, 190 Ill. App. 630 (1914).

[3] 51 Atl. 973 (Pa. S.Ct. 1902), discussed in § 2.3(a)(1), ***supra.***

[4] Central New York Basketball, Inc. v. Barnett, 181 N.E.2d 506 (Ohio Ct. Com. Pl. 1961), discussed also in § 2.3(a)(1), ***supra.***

talent, he should not be enjoined from jumping to the American Basketball League, because his NBA contract with the Nationals was perpetual. The NBA Uniform Player Contract provided (and still provides) that in the event a player fails to sign and return a new contract within a specified period of time, the team has the right to renew the old contract for one year "on the same terms." Since one of the terms that would be renewed would be the term giving the team the right to renew, an NBA team would seem to be able to renew a player contract, year after year, in perpetuity. Unlike the contracts used in some other leagues, the NBA contract does not limit the number of times the team may renew. Because the contract is perpetual, Barnett argued, it lacks mutuality because the player is bound for life while the team is not.

Though the wording of the NBA contract made the argument seem sound, it was not successful. The Nationals contended that the NBA contract was not perpetual; they said the right to renew is for one year only and ". . . at the close of the renewal year, the contract has been completed and is at an end." [5] The Court, quoting from an encyclopedia of Ohio law, said that if a contract has two possible meanings, one of which makes it invalid and the other of which leaves it valid, courts should adopt the meaning which leaves the contract valid. The interpretation urged by the Nationals was "reasonable, rational, practical" and "just," [6] and the Court adopted it. Since under that interpretation the NBA contract was not perpetual, Dick Barnett was enjoined from playing for the Cleveland Pipers or any team other than the Syracuse Nationals during the option year.

---

[5] *Id.* at 509.
[6] *Id.* at 510.

The American Basketball League died December 31, 1962, in the middle of its second season and at a cost to Abe Saperstein of several million dollars.[7] Yet, only four years later, another group of wealthy businessmen sought to succeed where Saperstein had failed so expensively. The American Basketball Association was born, its franchise owners encouraged by the success of the American Football League which had just won Congressional approval for its merger with the NFL.

Naturally, the infant ABA needed players to stock its franchises, and that resulted in highly publicized bidding against the NBA for the services of graduating college basketball stars. An entire new league could not be built with college stars alone, however, and ABA teams looked to their NBA competitors and to professional minor league basketball teams as potential sources of additional playing talent. In several cases, ABA teams found established professional players in both the NBA and the minors who were willing to join their new league. In two cases, the "jump" generated significant legal decisions. One decision involved superstar Rick Barry's move from the NBA to the ABA, and the other, Artie Heyman's move from the Eastern Professional Basketball League to the ABA.

Rick Barry was an All-American in his senior year at the University of Miami and was drafted by the San Francisco Warriors in 1965. His first contract was for 1965-1966, and at its conclusion he signed another for the 1966-1967 season. These contracts were the standard NBA Uniform Player Contract forms, and they contained a paragraph providing that the Warriors could mail Barry a new contract prior to the following season, and if he failed or

[7] D. Wolf, Foul! The Connie Hawkins Story 164-165 (New York: Warner Paperback Library, 1972).

neglected to sign and return it before a certain date, the existing contract would "be deemed renewed and extended for the period of one year, upon the same terms and conditions . . ."[8] Pursuant to that paragraph, the Warriors mailed Barry a contract on June 20, 1967 for the 1967-1968 season. However, Barry did not sign it, because the day before he had granted Pat Boone, one of the owners of the ABA Oakland franchise, an option on his services for 1967-1968, receiving in return an interest in Boone's team. Several weeks later, Barry signed an ABA contract to play for the Oakland Oaks, but by that time the Warriors had already filed suit to enjoin him from playing for the Oaks or any other team.

Less than three weeks after filing their action, the Warriors applied for and received a preliminary injunction barring Barry from playing for any other team until the 1967-1968 season was over, or trial was concluded, whichever came first. Barry immediately appealed, but the appeal process took so long that the season was over before it even was heard. Rather than play for the Warriors however, Barry "sat out" the 1967-1968 season, thus missing an entire year. Once the season was over, the appeal became moot and the Court dismissed it;[9] the Court of Appeals could not bring back the season he had missed, even if it agreed with his position. However, at least one aspect of Barry's argument was so intriguing that it warrants discussion, even though it was never ruled upon. Like Dick Barnett several years before, Rick Barry argued that the NBA Uniform Player Contract was perpetual, because one of the "terms and conditions" which is "deemed

[8] Lemat Corp. v. Barry, 80 Cal. Rptr. 240, 242 fn. 4 (Cal. Ct. App. 1969).

[9] *Id.* at 241 fn 1.

renewed and extended" if a player refuses to sign a new contract is the clause giving the team the right to renew. Thus, an NBA team always has the right to renew, whether or not a player signs any other contract after his first. Since this was so, Barry argued—as had Barnett before him—the NBA Uniform Player Contract lacks mutuality, because the player is bound for life while the team is not. The Syracuse Nationals had responded to that argument by saying that the right to renew could be exercised only once, and that when the option year was over the contract was terminated. The Ohio court had accepted that interpretation, and when Rick Barry made the argument again, the Warriors offered the California court the same interpretation.

This time however, Barry had a rejoinder. The National Basketball Association By-Laws provide that no person is eligible to play in a season game unless and until he signs "a formal contract" with his team.[10] Any time a person who has not signed a formal contract does play in a season game, the By-Laws provide that his team shall be deemed to have lost that game regardless of the final score.[11] Furthermore, Warrior representatives acknowledged that in fact those By-Laws were always complied with and no player anywhere in the National Basketball Association was ever permitted to play in a season game unless and until he signed a contract.[12] Thus, regardless of the interpretation placed on the contract by the NBA, in actual practice "option" years never expired, because players never played without current contracts containing "options" for the following year. (Today, the NBA does permit players

---

[10] NBA Constitution and By-Laws § 2.07.

[11] *Id.* at § 2.08.

[12] Deposition of Franklin Mieuli, President of Lemat Corp., owner of the Warriors.

to play out options. Cazzie Russell was the first to do so, going from the Warriors to the Lakers in 1974.)

Apparently the California court was unconcerned with what the league practice had been, because it did grant a preliminary injunction. Although Barry chose to "sit out" the option year, it was clear that had he chosen to "play it out" with the Warriors, he would not have had to sign a new contract. It is interesting to speculate whether the Warriors would have been deemed the losers of every game in which he played, as provided in the NBA By-Laws.

The question came close to being much more than an academic one, because the Warriors did not drop their suit when the 1967-1968 season was over. The case came to trial in July of 1968, and at that time the Warriors contended that they were entitled to a permanent injunction (for as long as seven years, if need be) preventing Barry from playing elsewhere until he actually "played out" the option. (The Warriors acknowledged that the injunction could not last longer than seven years, even if Barry continued to refuse to play for them, because of a California statute which provides that personal service contracts may not be enforced against employees for a period longer than seven years.[13]) Alternatively, the Warriors contended the injunction should remain in effect until Barry paid them for the monetary damages they suffered as a result of his refusal to play during the year he sat out.

These contentions, coming as they did after the preliminary injunction had already been in effect throughout the 1967-1968 season, were remarkable. It has long been the law—not only in connection with professional sports, but

[13] Calif. Labor Code § 2855, quoted in Lemat Corp. v. Barry, *supra* note 8, at fn. 8.

in all areas—that an injunction may be granted only when the loss complained of cannot be compensated for in money.[14] The loss of the services of a professional athlete had generally been considered to be that kind of loss, and the preliminary injunction preventing Barry from playing for the Oaks for a year had been granted on that premise. Thus, when the year had passed and the Warriors claimed they were entitled to money damages too, the Court refused to award them.

Equally surprising was the Warriors' contention that their injunction should be made permanent (for up to seven years) for so long as Barry refused to play. They had obtained the preliminary injunction in the first place based on their interpretation of the NBA contract, permitting the right to renew to be exercised only once. At trial, however, they contended that they could renew again and again until Barry actually played out the renewal year. The Court refused to accept that argument. Thus, at the conclusion of the trial, the Court entered judgment enjoining Barry from playing for any team other than the Warriors during the 1967-1968 season—which by then was already over.

The Warriors appealed, but the California Court of Appeal affirmed the trial court in all respects.[15] In response to the Warriors' claim that it should have been awarded a permanent injunction preventing Barry from playing elsewhere until he played out the renewal year, the Court of Appeal said,

> ". . . in our view, [such an interpretation of the player contract] would condemn professional ball players to

---

[14] **42 American Jurisprudence 2d, Injunctions §§ 48 and 49.**

[15] Lemat Corp. v. Barry, *supra* note 8.

the involuntary servitude repugnant to the Thirteenth Amendment to the United States Constitution. . ." [16]

In other words, requiring professional athletes to "play out" the options in their contracts, rather than permitting them to "sit them out" would constitute involuntary servitude, in the view of the California Court of Appeal. This raises an interesting question concerning the legality of the "retirement" clause in the National Football League contract. The question is made even more so because the American Basketball Association, which urged the "involuntary servitude" argument on the court in the *Rick Barry* case, also has a retirement clause in its player contract.

The NFL retirement clause gave rise to a key issue in *Dallas Cowboys* v. *Jimmy Harris*.[17] There Harris had argued that even if he had unique talent, he should not be enjoined from playing in the American Football League, because, he said, the NFL contract assigned by the Rams to the Cowboys had already expired by its own terms, option and all. This argument seemed to have merit, because the contract the Cowboys were seeking to enforce was signed by Harris for the 1958 season with an option for the 1959 season. The Cowboys were seeking to prevent him from playing for the Texans during the 1960 season.

However, the NFL contract signed by Harris also contained a paragraph which said that in the event he retired from football before the option expired, then the contract term, including the option term, would be extended for so long as Harris remained in retirement. Since Harris had retired for a year, the Cowboys argued that his contract was extended for a year, and thus covered 1960. The Court

[16] *Id.* at 245 fn. 9.

[17] 348 S.W.2d 37 (Tex. Ct. Civ. App. 1961), discussed also in § 2.3(a)(1), *supra.*

agreed. (The Court rejected Harris' contention that he had not actually "retired," because he had been an assistant football coach at the University of Oklahoma.) If Harris had refused to play for the Cowboys during 1960, it is interesting to wonder whether or not he would have remained in "retirement," so that the NFL option year would have been extended still further. If the NFL were to concede that Harris would have been out of retirement even though not playing football, on the grounds he was not playing only because he had been ordered not to by a court, that would mean that professional players may not voluntarily "sit out" option years, but rather must provoke lawsuits so as to be enjoined. The *Rick Barry* case, however, held that a player cannot be compelled to play out the option year.

The *Jimmy Harris* case and the *Rick Barry* case are therefore at odds with one another. Either the retirement clause is illegal because it compels involuntary servitude, in which case *Harris* was decided incorrectly; or the Warriors were correct in contending that they could continue to renew Barry's contract until he actually played another year, in which case *Barry* was decided incorrectly. It seems that the *Barry* case must have been correct, and *Harris* incorrect. A professional athlete should not be required to play for a team against his wishes—thereby subjecting himself to risk of injury, without even being able to negotiate an acceptable salary—in order to be free to join another team in another league. It is ironic that Barry was finally permitted to join a team in the ABA as the result of a judicial ruling which seems to outlaw a provision of the ABA Uniform Player Contract.

Although the National Basketball Association was the only major basketball league in existence when the ABA was formed, there were a number of minor leagues. Minor league teams were not affiliated with NBA teams the way minor league baseball teams are with the majors, however. Nor were the minor league basketball leagues used very often for grooming major league prospects the way minor league baseball teams are. Instead, the basketball minors were a place players went to if they were not successful in the NBA, rather than a place they came from. Nevertheless, some minor league players, particularly those playing in the Eastern Professional Basketball League, had real talent, and were actively sought out by the infant ABA. Artie Heyman was one of these.

Heyman, nicknamed "Crazy Artie" while in college, had been an All-American at Duke and had been signed by the NBA's New York Knickerbockers as their number one draft choice in 1963. Within a couple of years, Heyman had been traded to the San Francisco Warriors, and from there to the Cincinnati Royals, the Boston Celtics, and then to the Eastern League.

Heyman signed a contract with the Hartford Capitols of the Eastern Professional Basketball League in October of 1966 agreeing to render to it his exclusive services as a basketball player through August 31, 1967. In exchange, he was to be paid $125 in salary plus $50 in expenses for each game he played. The Eastern League contract also gave the Capitols the right to renew for the 1967-1968 season and to terminate at any time, simply by giving Heyman written notice. During the 1966-1967 season, Heyman played in all of the Capitols' games, was the team's most valuable player, and was the Eastern League's highest scorer. Since the team played 28 games that season, he earned a total of $4,900.

Early in 1967, while the ABA was being formed, Heyman signed a contract with the New Jersey Americans pursuant to which he was to receive $15,000 for the 1967-1968 season. The Hartford Capitols then exercised their option on Heyman's services for 1967-1968 and immediately filed suit to enjoin him from playing for any other team. In this case, the ABA was successful from the start. A federal judge refused to issue the preliminary injunction the Capitols had asked for, on the grounds that the Eastern League player contract was "too harsh and one sided to permit equitable enforcement." [18] The judge came to this conclusion because the contract purported to bind Heyman for two years (the original year plus the option year), while permitting the Capitols to terminate at will. In addition, Heyman was to be paid only for those games he actually played, while the Capitols were not required to schedule any particular number of games. Thus, if Heyman were to become ill or injured, or if the Capitols failed to schedule games, Heyman might be paid little or nothing even though he would still be bound by his contract.

Since it had also been argued—unsuccessfully—in the *Jimmy Harris, Dick Barnett* and *Rick Barry* cases that the NFL and NBA contracts were too harsh and one-sided to warrant enforcement, it is interesting to compare those player contracts with the one used in the Eastern League to see how little difference there actually was among them. First, the Eastern League contract purports to bind players for two years while permitting teams to terminate at will. The National Basketball Association contract also purports to bind players for two years at least, and within the league at that time, possibly forever. Similarly, the National Football League contract binds players for two

[18] Connecticut Professional Sports Corp. v. Heyman, 276 F.Supp. 618, 620 (S.D.N.Y. 1967).

years. While the NBA contract does not permit termination "at will," it does permit termination for such subjective reasons as failing, refusing or neglecting to conform personal conduct to standards of good citizenship, good moral character and good sportsmanship; or failing, in the sole opinion of the team's management, to exhibit sufficient skill or competitive ability.[19] The NFL player contract likewise permits termination if in the opinion of the head coach the player does not maintain himself in excellent physical condition, or fails to demonstrate sufficient skill and capacity to play professional football of the caliber required by the NFL or his team, or, if in the opinion of the head coach, the player's work or conduct is unsatisfactory compared with the work and conduct of other team members.[20]

Second, the Eastern League contract provided that players were to be paid only for those games actually played, so that in the event of injury, illness, or lack of scheduled games, players might be paid little or nothing. NBA and NFL contracts appear substantially different in this regard, because they specify salary on an annual basis, not per game. However, closer inspection reveals the distinctions to be more of form than effect. The NBA contract provides that if a player is injured or becomes ill so that he is unable to play, the team has the right to suspend the player without pay, unless the injury or illness resulted directly from playing basketball for the team.[21] The NFL player contract is not as clear on the consequences of non-football related illness or injury, but it too appears to permit the team to suspend salary payments for as long as the athlete is unable to play.[22]

---

[19] NBA Uniform Player Contract ¶ 20.

[20] NFL Standard Player Contract ¶ 6.

[21] NBA Uniform Player Contract ¶ 6.

[22] NFL Standard Player Contract ¶ 14.

Since Artie Heyman was able to avoid the stated obligations of his Eastern League contract in order to perform pursuant to an American Basketball Association contract he had signed, on the grounds the Eastern League contract was "too harsh and one sided," it is also interesting to compare those two agreements. Like the Eastern League player contract, the ABA contract binds the player for two years. Though the ABA contract does not permit termination "at will," it does—like the NBA contract—permit termination for such subjective causes as failing, in the opinion of the team's management, to exhibit sufficient skill or competitive ability.[23] The ABA contract does specify salary on a yearly basis, rather than on a per game basis. But it also provides—again like that NBA contract—that if a player is injured or becomes ill so that he is unable to play, the team has the right to suspend the player without pay, unless the injury or illness resulted directly from playing basketball for the team.[24]

§2.3(b)(2) Legal defenses: restraint of trade and monopolization

Because injunctions are deemed to be an equitable remedy, courts do not issue them when it would be inequitable to do so.[1] Courts will also decline to issue injunctions when doing so would result in the violation of law. In the sports business, as in many others, it has frequently been argued that the antitrust laws would be violated if an injunction were granted prohibiting an athlete from playing for a new team. Apparently the first time such an argument was made was during the Federal Baseball League war in 1914 in the case of *American League Base-*

[23] ABA Uniform Player Contract ¶ 12.

[24] *Id.* at ¶ 4.

[1] See § 2.3(b)(1), *supra.*

ball Club of Chicago v. *Chase.*[2] While the Court held that baseball was not trade or commerce, and thus not subject to the Sherman Act,[3] it did refuse to enjoin Chase from jumping to the Federal League on the grounds that Organized Baseball's monopolistic practices constituted "unclean hands" and "a court of equity . . . will not lend its aid to promote an unconscionable transaction . . ."[4]

In more recent years, it was argued in the *Jimmy Harris,*[5] *Dick Barnett,*[6] and *Rick Barry*[7] cases that injunctions would restrain trade in violation of the Sherman Act, because if granted, those athletes would have been prevented from engaging in their occupations. In *Harris,* the Court found no such violation on the grounds that the Cowboys were "eager to employ his services."[8] In *Barnett* and *Barry,* the Courts determined that the NBA player contract was not perpetual, and therefore held it was not in restraint of trade. Had the NBA contract been perpetual, it might well have been held to violate the antitrust laws, for that is in fact what happened when the formerly perpetual National Hockey League reserve clause was challenged in the NHL-WHA hockey "war."

The National Hockey League was formed in 1917 with only two teams, Montreal and Toronto. It took seven years, until 1924, before a third team was added in Boston, and

---

[2] 149 N.Y.S. 6 (1914).

[3] *Id.* at 16.

[4] *Id.* at 20.

[5] Dallas Cowboys Football Club v. Harris, 348 S.W.2d 37 (Tex. Ct. Civ. App. 1961), discussed in § 2.3(a)(1), *supra.*

[6] Central New York Basketball, Inc. v. Barnett, 181 N.E.2d 506 (Ohio Ct. Com. Pl. 1961), discussed in §§ 2.3(a)(1) and 2.3(b)(1), *supra.*

[7] Lemat Corp. v. Barry, 80 Cal. Rptr. 240 (Cal. Ct. App. 1969), discussed in § 2.3(b)(1), *supra.*

[8] Dallas Cowboys Football Club v. Harris, *supra* note 5, at 47.

1926 brought three more in Chicago, Detroit and New York. Those six franchises then constituted the entire NHL for more than forty years.

The mid-sixties were a time of growth in professional sports. The American Football League had established itself sufficiently to force a merger with the NFL. And the American Basketball Association came into existence to challenge the NBA for a share of the professional basketball market. It was in this climate that the National Hockey League literally doubled its size in 1967, adding franchises in six new cities, Los Angeles, Philadelphia, Pittsburgh, California, Minnesota, and St. Louis. And in 1970, Nassau County (New York), and Atlanta joined the league as well.

While it might have seemed to most that this phenomenal growth had depleted the possibilities for a competitive hockey league, it did not appear that way to Gary Davidson, a southern California lawyer who earlier had been instrumental in organizing the American Basketball Association and later participated in the organization of the World Football League.[9]

The World Hockey Association was formed in 1971. It began play the following year with teams in twelve cities—Philadelphia, Edmonton, Winnipeg, Ottawa, Quebec, Boston, New York, Cleveland, Chicago, Minneapolis-St. Paul, Houston and Los Angeles. Players of course were an immediate need, but potential sources were somewhat limited. While hockey is played in eastern colleges in the United States, it is not generally the major sport that intercollegiate football and basketball are, and college hockey stars do not have the national reputations that football and basketball players have. Thus, graduating col-

[9] G. Davidson, Breaking the Game Wide Open (New York: Atheneum, 1974).

legians were not by far a sufficient pool of player talent for the WHA. On the other hand, in professional hockey—as in professional baseball—there are minor and semi-professional leagues, as well as the majors. Thus, NHL, minor league and semi-pro players whose contracts had "expired" were available to the WHA—in theory. Whether any of these players were available in fact—and in law—was, however, another question. And that question was, when, if ever, did the contracts of any of these players expire? Again, as had been the case when the AFL and ABA came into existence, the player contract reserve clause was in issue. (There are also amateur hockey leagues which play organized schedules on a regular basis. However, even these leagues had signed an agreement with the NHL in which they recognized the NHL and its associated minor leagues as the ". . . sole and exclusive governing bodies of professional hockey in Canada and the United States of America . . ." and agreed that ". . . in all matters relating to professional hockey and its relations to amateur hockey. . . " the amateur associations will deal only with the NHL).[10]

Prior to its amendment in 1973, the National Hockey League player contract contained a perpetual reserve clause, and the reserve clauses in minor league player contracts were identical in all material respects. It was thus possible for NHL teams and their minor league associates to prevent the player contracts of every professional hockey player in North America from ever expiring, thereby making it virtually impossible for the World Hockey Association to ever begin operations. In fact, when the World Hockey Association began its first season of play in 1972,

---

[10] Philadelphia World Hockey Club, Inc. v. Philadelphia Hockey Club, Inc., 351 F.Supp. 462, 478 (E.D. Pa. 1972).

over 200 of the 345 players in the new league were subject to reserve clauses in contracts they had signed for the previous season. Approximately 60 of the 200 had played in the NFL during 1971-1972, while 140 had played in the minor leagues. Fewer than 145 players were not subject to a reserve clause.[11]

As had happened earlier in other sports, the signing of NHL players by WHA teams gave rise to lawsuits in which NHL teams sought injunctions preventing such stars as Bobby Hull, Derek Sanderson, Gerry Cheevers, John McKenzie, Edward Hampson, Garry Peters, and Norman Ferguson from playing in the WHA. However, unlike the earlier football and basketball "wars" which seemed to center around a few select test cases, the National Hockey League filed a rash of suits in state and federal courts from coast to coast. Temporary restraining orders were issued in some cases, pending hearings on motions for preliminary injunctions; but they were denied in others. This complicated maze of cases generated immediate procedural issues. largely involving the efforts of the World Hockey Association to get all of the cases into federal courts and then to consolidate as many of them as possible before one judge.

By the time the cases were ready for argument on the motions of NHL teams for preliminary injunctions, the cases had been consolidated into some four groups, two before Judge Caffrey of the District Court for the District of Massachusetts, five before Judge Higginbotham in the District Court for the Eastern District of Pennsylvania, and one each before Judge Neaher of the District Court for the Eastern District of New York and Judge Larson of

[11] Nassau Sports v. Peters, 352 F.Supp. 870, 880 (E.D.N.Y. 1972).

the District Court for the District of Minnesota. Though the facts in all four groups of cases were virtually identical, and though the same issues were argued in each, no two of the four decisions were the same.

Judge Caffrey had before him two cases filed by the NHL Boston Bruins. One was against Gerry Cheevers who had signed a seven-year contract with the WHA Cleveland Crusaders, pursuant to which he was to play goalie in exchange for $1,400,000 ($200,000 per year), plus bonuses contingent on the Crusaders' league standing and his personal performance. The other was against Derek Sanderson who had signed a ten-year contract with the WHA Philadelphia Blazers calling for total compensation of $2,325,000. Pursuant to the reserve clauses contained in their last NHL contracts, the Bruins had tendered the two stars new contracts calling for $70,000 and $80,000 per year respectively.

The primary defense relied upon by Cheevers and Sanderson was that their NHL contracts for the previous season were illegal and unenforceable because the reserve clause violated the federal antitrust laws. The clause, they said, restrains trade because it binds a player to a single team for "so much of his entire hockey-playing life as that team elects to keep him in its service. . ." [12] Though this defense had not been successful in the *Jimmy Harris, Dick Barnett* or *Rick Barry* cases, neither the NFL nor the NBA option system purports to be as binding as the National Hockey League's reserve system was. Only Organized Baseball's reserve system is as binding as was the NHL's, and the legality of Organized Baseball's system has never

[12] Boston Professional Hockey Assn. v. Cheevers, 348 F.Supp. 261, 265 (D. Mass. 1972), *remanded,* 472 F.2d 127 (1st Cir. 1972).

been tested under the antitrust laws, because the courts had always held baseball exempt.[13]

Hockey is not exempt, however. Judge Caffrey reviewed the NHL reserve clause, the agreement between the NHL and the minor leagues, the NHL By-Laws, and then stated,

> ". . . I do find, that the record establishes that this integrated group of contracts, constitutions, by-laws, and agreements, all of which are in evidence, and which in their totality run to hundreds of pages of legal verbiage, effectively and totally control the careers of any hockey player in the United States or Canada from the time he first joins any organized team which plays in a league on up through amateur leagues, semi-pro leagues, and minor professional leagues, to the major professional hockey league. In light of the fact that this complex system dominates and controls a hockey player's career all of his hockey-playing life as a practical matter, . . . there is a probability that this tangled web of legal instruments will . . . be found to restrain trade in professional hockey." [14]

Judge Caffrey also noted that the Bruins had realized substantial profits for at least several years, and that the trend was one of increasing profits. As a result, they were "in a strong, healthy, and steadily improving financial condition," [15] and there had been no showing that loss of Cheevers and Sanderson would cause irreparable harm to the Bruins' financial affairs and fortunes.[16] Furthermore,

---

[13] See Chapter 1, *supra.*

[14] Boston Professional Hockey Assn. v. Cheevers, *supra* note 12, at 267.

[15] *Id.* at 269.

[16] *Id.*

the Court ruled, in the event it was ultimately decided that the two players breached valid employment contracts,

> ". . . there is available to the Bruins a complete and adequate remedy at law, consisting of a suit for money damages for breach of contract against Cheevers and Sanderson, as well as a suit against . . . the World Hockey Association, the Philadelphia Blazers and the Cleveland Crusaders, in the nature of an action in tort for interference with advantageous contractual relations." [17]

On the other hand, preliminary injunctions preventing Cheevers and Sanderson from playing in the WHA until their cases could be tried in full "would signal the death of the World Hockey Association," [18] according to the testimony of the president of the Philadelphia Blazers. As a result, Judge Caffrey denied the Bruins' motions for preliminary injunctions. And the Bruins headed straight for the Court of Appeals.

The Court of Appeals neither affirmed nor reversed, but instead remanded the case to Judge Caffrey with instructions to consider three questions which had not been considered before.[19] The first was whether—apart from antitrust considerations and simply as a matter of contract law—the two players were obligated to arbitrate their 1972-1973 salaries with the Bruins and be bound by the decisions of the arbitrators. The second was whether the NHL reserve clause purported to bind the players perpetually or only for so long as the Players Association Arbitration Agreement was in effect. And the third was whether, if the

---

[17] *Id.*

[18] *Id.*

[19] 472 F.2d 127 (1st Cir. 1972).

reserve clause was not perpetual, the restraint it imposed might not be reasonable and therefore legal. The Court of Appeals said that the answers to these questions might not affect Judge Caffrey's decision to deny preliminary injunctions, and it did not intend to intimate any views as to the likelihood of the Bruins' ultimate success. It did state however, that it disagreed with Judge Caffrey on whether the Bruins had demonstrated that they would probably suffer irreparable damage by the loss of Cheevers and Sanderson; the Court of Appeals thought the Bruins had demonstrated such injury because damages other than monetary were at stake and they would be unable to show the extent of the monetary damages they would suffer.

Apparently, however, the answers to the questions the Court of Appeals instructed Judge Caffrey to consider did not change the Judge's decision to deny a preliminary injunction. Both Cheevers and Sanderson began the 1972-1973 season with their new World Hockey Association teams. (For reasons having nothing to do with the Bruins' lawsuit, however, Sanderson played only the first eight games of the WHA season. Thereafter, he was benched by the Blazers who claimed he was physically unfit to play. Sanderson claimed the Blazers were in financial trouble, could not afford to pay him, and were hoping to get out of his $2,325.000 contract by inducing him to breach it. Breach it he would not, however, and for the next 30 games Sanderson sat in the stands dressed in street clothes. Finally, Sanderson let the Blazers out of his contract in exchange for $1,000,000 and the right to rejoin the Bruins, which he did.)

Several weeks after Judge Caffrey refused to enjoin Cheevers and Sanderson from playing in the WHA, Judge Neaher issued an injunction at the request of the NHL New

York Islanders preventing Garry Peters from playing for the WHA New York Raiders.[20] Peters, like Cheevers and Sanderson, had been under contract to the Boston Bruins during the 1971-1972 season. Prior to the 1972-1973 season, the National Hockey League expanded for the third time in five years, adding franchises in Nassau County, New York, and Atlanta, Georgia. The owners of these two teams paid the National Hockey League $6,000,000 for their franchises and for the right to staff their teams with 21 players to be selected from other NHL teams in an "expansion draft." The New York Islanders, who were to play their home games on Long Island in Nassau County, drafted Garry Peters from the Bruins, and the Bruins duly assigned his NHL player contract—containing a reserve clause—to the Islanders.

At virtually the same time the National Hockey League was conducting its 1972 expansion draft, the fledgling World Hockey Association also was conducting a draft in anticipation of its first season. Garry Peters was drafted by the WHA New York Raiders. Peters, who had had a $20,000-plus-bonuses contract with the Bruins for the 1971-1972 season, was offered $37,500 for 1972-1973 by the NHL Islanders and $55,000 by the WHA Raiders (as part of a three-year contract calling for $60,000 and $65,000 for the next two seasons). Peters signed with the Raiders, and the Islanders went to court.

As had Cheevers and Sanderson before him, Peters argued that the contract which the Islanders were seeking to enforce was illegal, because the reserve clause binds a player to a team perpetually, thus restraining trade in violation of the antitrust laws. The Islanders countered with the argument that the reserve clause was not per-

[20] Nassau Sports v. Peters, 352 F.Supp. 870 (E.D.N.Y. 1972).

petual, but in fact lasted for three years only, until the Players Association Arbitration Agreement expired in 1975. Interestingly, Judge Neaher said that he found it "unnecessary to choose between these conflicting views of the duration of the NHL reserve clause." [21] Actually, what Judge Neaher ultimately did was not fail to choose. Rather, he chose neither, and instead, Solomon-like, he issued an injunction preventing Peters from playing hockey for any team other than the NHL New York Islanders for one year. He further ordered that "Peters, should he elect to perform his option commitment to [the Islanders], shall not be required to sign a contract for the current season which contains a further renewal option." [22]

This he did because, in his view, the fact that every major professional team sport uses some sort of a reserve or option system,

> ". . . reflects the widespread recognition of the unique character of the business of professional sports and the need for some form of protective system to insure the recoupment of investments—often large—made both to develop and to acquire talented players." [23]

Furthermore, he said the facts simply did not support the claim that "the NHL reserve clause bars access to pools of professional player talent and makes it impossible for newcomers to effectively enter or compete in the business of major league professional hockey." [24] Almost 145 of the 345 players signed by the WHA for its first season were not under a reserve clause, he noted. And of the more than 200 that were, ". . . only five or six including Peters have

[21] *Id.* at 879.
[22] *Id.* at 882 fn. 30.
[23] *Id.* at 879.
[24] *Id.* at 880.

been enjoined or restrained as a result of unilateral suits instituted by NHL clubs. . ." [25] Judge Neaher felt that the balance of hardships tipped in favor of the NHL team in this case, because it had paid some $300,000 for the rights to Peters ($6 million divided by 21 players), and by the time the WHA's antitrust contentions could be litigated, ". . . the option season to which [the Islanders are] entitled under its assignment will have long expired and [the Raiders and Peters] will have had the benefit of rights which [the Islanders] made a substantial payment to acquire." [26]

"In short," Judge Neaher stated in granting the one-year injunction,

> ". . . it appears to this court that [the Raiders] and the other WHA clubs made a calculated decision to risk possible enforcement of the NHL reserve clause and have in large measure succeeded. No good reason is shown why the continued success of that raiding tactic is of such paramount public interest as to be preferred to contract rights legitimately acquired by [the Islanders] for substantial consideration. . . . Peters voluntarily accepted employment under the allegedly illegal contract when his playing talents had no other outlet. He raises the antitrust question only when it appears to be no longer in his economic interest to comply with his agreement. That was not heretofore regarded as a sufficient excuse for breach of contract and should not become so when the claimed illegality, if any, is clearly divisible from the personal services commitment made." [27]

[25] *Id.*
[26] *Id.* at 881.
[27] *Id.* at 880-881.

The decision was a victory of sorts for the National Hockey League. But, in winning that particular battle, the NHL may well have lost the war. For Judge Neaher did not support the League's interpretation of its reserve clause, which interpretation would have required Peters to continue to play for the Islanders, or no one at all, until at least the end of the 1974-1975 season. Furthermore, in reaching his decision, the Judge used language that was supportive of the need for and legality of reserve systems. Nevertheless, he excused Peters from having to sign a new contract for the 1972-1973 season, thus implying, it would seem, that the perpetual reserve system devised by the NHL did indeed violate the law. Why else would Judge Neaher have enjoined Peters for one year only, and excused him from signing a new contract, when there was not one single word anywhere in the NHL Standard Player Contract, NHL Constitution and By-Laws, or any other document whatever, allowing athletes to play in the League without written contracts under any circumstances? The player contract which the Judge purported to enforce provided that, "The Player hereby undertakes that he will at the request of the Club enter into a contract for the following playing season. . ."[28] In effect, Judge Neaher made a new contract for Peters and the NHL, and though it meant that Peters would be unavailable to the WHA and the Raiders for a year, he and other players that might be so enjoined would be available the following season.

While the *Peters* decision appears to be a compromise, it should be noted that in reaching it, Judge Neaher relied upon two facts which are subject to some dispute. One supposed fact was that the Islanders had paid the NHL

---

[28] NHL Standard Player's Contract ¶ 17; quoted in Nassau Sports v. Peters, *supra* note 20, at 875.

approximately $300,000 for the rights to Peters' services. That figure was obtained by dividing the $6 million franchise fee by the 21 players the Islanders were permitted to select in the expansion draft. In reality, however, not all of the franchise fee was paid for draft rights. The NHL franchise itself was worth a great deal of money, even had the Islanders' initial source of players been limited strictly to the minor and amateur leagues.[29]

The second assumption was that the NHL reserve clause did not bar access to professional hockey players, as evidenced by the fact that only five or six players were enjoined from playing in the WHA out of the 345 the new league had signed. The reason only five or six players had been enjoined was that most judges had refused to grant the requested injunctions on the ground that the reserve clause probably restrained trade. It was only because most judges refused to grant injunctions, and because the NHL did not file all of the lawsuits it might have, that Judge Neaher was able to find that there had been no showing that trade was being restrained. In fact, as Judge Neaher himself indicated, over 200 of the 345 players in the WHA its first year had reserve clauses in their prior season's contracts identical to the clause which led Judge Neaher to issue the injunction against Peters. Had the NHL been able to file 200 lawsuits in Judge Neaher's court, or had other judges agreed with Judge Neaher's analysis, the WHA would have been left with only 42% of all of its players. Had that happened, the restraint would have been clear.

Though the NHL New York Islanders were able to retain the services of Garry Peters for a year, they were unsuccessful in their attempt to retain another of the players

[29] See §§ 9.4 & 9.5, *infra*.

they had acquired in the NHL expansion draft, Edward Hampson. Hampson had been under contract to the NHL Minnesota North Stars during 1971-1972; but when the World Hockey Association was formed, he signed a four year contract with its Midwest Saints—a contract later found to be "in conflict" with his 1971-1972 NHL agreement because of the reserve clause it contained.

Hampson's response to the Islander's request for an injunction barring him from playing for the Saints was the same one asserted by Cheevers, Sanderson and Peters—that the NHL reserve clause was an unenforceable device to restrain and monopolize trade in violation of the Sherman Act. The Islanders responded by arguing that the NHL reserve clause bound the player for one year only—not the three years they had sought in the *Peters* case. This change in tactics was probably in recognition of the one-year result in the *Peters* case, and was possibly in recognition of the success the National Basketball Association had earlier had with such an argument in the *Dick Barnett*[30] and *Rick Barry*[31] cases.

Judge Larson was not persuaded by the Islander's new position, however. Without referring to *Barnett* or *Barry,* he said that since the NHL reserve clause required the player to sign a new contract for another year on "the same terms," including the reserve clause itself, there was no reason apparent to him why the reserve clause could be considered "anything but a requirement of perpetual contracting for succeeding one year periods." [32] While Judge Larson agreed with the Islanders that Hampson's skills

[30] Central New York Basketball, Inc. v. Barnett, *supra* note 6.

[31] Lemat Corp. v. Barry, *supra* note 7.

[32] Nassau Sports v. Hampson, 355 F.Supp. 733, 735 (D. Minn. 1972).

were unique, and that their loss would cause them to suffer irreparable injury because they could not acquire precisely the same services from anyone else, he denied their request for an injunction, saying that the NHL's perpetual reserve clause ". . . seems, plausibly, one aspect of a contractual scheme constituting a violation of sections 1 and 2 of the Sherman Antitrust Act . . ."[33]

While the results of the *Cheevers, Sanderson, Hampson,* and even *Peters* cases were favorable to the World Hockey Association, the new league's most significant success came in the cases that had been consolidated before Judge Higginbotham in the Eastern District of Pennsylvania. In those cases, the WHA sought not to defend against requests for injunctions; rather the WHA itself sought an injunction prohibiting the National Hockey League from attempting to enforce its reserve clause. After an extensive hearing which generated over 2000 pages of exhibits and more than 500 pages of briefs and proposed findings, Judge Higginbotham enjoined the NHL and its member teams

> ". . . from further prosecuting, commencing, or threatening to commence any legal proceeding pursuant to and/or to enforce the so-called 'reserve clause' . . . of the National Hockey League Standard Player's Contract, against any player, coach or other person whose contract, but for the reserve clause, expired on or before November 8, 1972 [the date the injunction was issued]."[34]

While the granting of this injunction was consistent with the denials of the injunctions the NHL had sought in the

---

[33] *Id.*

[34] Philadelphia World Hockey Club, Inc. v. Philadelphia Hockey Club, Inc., *supra* note 10, at 519.

Hampson, Cheevers and *Sanderson* cases, Judge Higginbotham's reasoning—explained in a comprehensive 57 page opinion—differed somewhat. In *Hampson, Cheevers* and *Sanderson,* the Courts considered section 1 of the Sherman Act, prohibiting restraint of trade, and section 2 of the Act, prohibiting monopolization, together, and found the NHL reserve clause to be a violation of both. Judge Higginbotham, on the other hand, considered the sections separately, and based his injunction solely on section 2.

With respect to section 1, he found that because of the nature of the professional hockey industry, he was uncertain whether the restraints imposed by the reserve clause were illegal.

> "The sports field is in some ways a hybrid, in that it is both similarly and dissimilarly affected by the normal economic variables governing business success. For a corporation producing aluminum, any entrant in the field is a competitor. From a traditional oligopolist's or monopolist's view, one might consider any new entrant as an adversary and thus undesirable. But by the nature of a sports contest, there must always be an adversary. By analogy, who would enjoy Vida Blue blazing strikes across home plate when the batter's box was empty, or Mark Spitz' triumphs, if he were the only one in the pool. Sports teams need competition, and if there are more than two teams, some type of league is probably desirable.
>
> "For maximum customer receptivity and profit it is in the best interest of any club that its opponents not generally be viewed by the public as totally incompetent and utterly unable to compete effectively. For if the latter occurs, thousands of customers will not spend their dollars for tickets to view hundreds of games

when the contest seems to present no more of a challenge than an ant confronting an elephant. Thus, if it is not possible to keep the competitive challenge of all teams within some reasonable parameters, some type of intra-league reserve clause or system may be desirable and in fact necessary."[35]

While Judge Higginbotham had doubts about the existence of a section 1 violation, he said he had "*no* such doubts"[36] about the existence of a section 2 monopolization violation. It was clear, he said, that through the use of the reserve clause and agreements with the minor, semi-professional and amateur leagues, ". . . the NHL overwhelmingly controls the supply of players who are capable and available for play in a new league. . ."[37] It was that total control which he held was "proscribed by section 2 of the Sherman Act."[38]

In support of his holding that the National Hockey League had monopolized the supply of available player talent, Judge Higginbotham contrasted the situation then existing in the hockey industry with the one that had existed when the American Football League was formed some dozen years before. While most of the ablest football players were then under contract to NFL teams, large numbers of talented players graduated from college each year, many good players were released by NFL teams after training camp each year, and even NFL stars could become free agents after a definite period by playing out their options. In hockey on the other hand, NHL, minor-

[35] *Id.* at 503-504.
[36] *Id.* at 504.
[37] *Id.* at 509.
[38] *Id.*

league and semi-professional players were bound by reserve clauses for at least three years, and perhaps perpetually.

The NHL's intent to monopolize the hockey business was shown not only by the contract clauses and agreements it used, but also by League President Clarence Campbell's announcement that the NHL's expansion would make it ". . . the only major professional hockey league operating from coast-to-coast in the United States and Canada." [39]

Though the injunction Judge Higginbotham issued was only preliminary, to last until the cases could be tried, the trial was not to take place for more than a year. Thus, the preliminary injunction gave the WHA protection until its second season had almost been completed.

Perhaps in anticipation of the coming trial, or perhaps under pressure from the NHL Players' Association, the National Hockey League announced in December of 1973 that the perpetual reserve clause would not appear in player contracts for the 1974-1975 season and thereafter. In its place, there is a one-year option clause very similar to the one found in National Football League contracts. Like the NFL, the National Hockey League will require a team signing a player who has played out his option to compensate the player's former team. However, in the event the teams cannot agree on the compensation to be paid, an arbitrator will make the award, not the NHL's president. In that respect, the NHL compensation rule differs slightly from the NFL's where League Commissioner Pete Rozelle makes the award.[40]

---

[39] *Id.* at 512.

[40] NFL Constitution and By-Laws § 12.1(H), quoted and discussed in § 2.2(c)(1), *supra*.

§2.4 Legality of intra-league, non-judicial enforcement

Unlike the many cases involving players who have sought to "jump" leagues, the *Curt Flood* case,[1] and others filed since,[2] have involved challenges to the enforcement of reserve and option systems within a single league. In such cases, the "enforcement" that is objected to is based on an agreement between the teams in a league—in the form of league by-laws—that no team will hire a player who has been reserved by or is under option to another league team. Courts are not involved in enforcing reserve and option clauses intra-league, as they are when a team seeks an injunction preventing a player from joining a team in another league. Courts have been involved, however, in the efforts of some players to prevent intra-league enforcement by agreement.

§2.4(a) Involuntary servitude principles

When Senator Sam Ervin spoke of slavery and peonage at the outset of hearings on the Basketball Merger Bill,[1] he was not without support from the courts. In 1944, the United States Supreme Court stated that the "undoubted aim of the Thirteenth Amendment . . . was not merely to end slavery but to maintain a system of completely free and voluntary labor throughout the United States."[2] And in 1949, Judge Frank of the Court of Appeals said in the *Danny Gardella* case,

> ". . . we have here a monopoly which, in its effect on ball-players . . ., possesses characteristics shockingly

[1] Flood v. Kuhn, 407 U.S. 258 (1972), discussed in § 1.3(b), *supra*.

[2] See §§ 2.4(b)(1) and 2.4(b)(2), *infra*.

[1] See § 2.1, *supra*.

[2] Pollock v. Williams, 322 U.S. 4, 7 (1944).

> repugnant to moral principles that, at least since the War Between the States, have been basic in America, as shown by the Thirteenth Amendment to the Constitution, condemning 'involuntary servitude' . . . For the 'reserve clause' . . . results in something resembling peonage." [3]

As recently as 1972, the Senate Judiciary Committee Report on the Basketball Merger Bill said, "The Committee believes that the present use of option clauses, reserve clauses, and other devices designed to tie a player to a team deny him fundamental rights . . ." [4]

Nevertheless, recent judicial analysis of the reserve clause concluded it was not prohibited by the Thirteenth Amendment, or legislation enacted pursuant to it. In his lawsuit against Bowie Kuhn, Curt Flood contended (among other things) that the reserve system violated the Thirteenth Amendment, and legislation enacted to enforce it, prohibiting "involuntary servitude." Though that issue was not considered by the Supreme Court, it was given careful thought by District Judge Cooper, who, after reviewing the relevant cases decided that

> "A showing of compulsion is . . . prerequisite to proof of involuntary servitude. Concededly, [Flood] is not compelled by law or statute to play baseball for Philadelphia. We recognize that, under the existing rules of baseball, by refusing to report to Philadelphia [Flood] is by his own act foreclosing himself from continuing a professional baseball career, a consequence to be deplored. Nevertheless, he has the right

---

[3] Gardella v. Chandler, 172 F.2d 402 (2d Cir. 1949), discussed in § 1.1(b), *supra.*

[4] S.Rep. 92-1151, 92d Congress, 2d Sess. 8 (1972).

to retire and to embark upon a different enterprise outside organized baseball. The financial loss he might sustain may affect his choice, but does not leave him with 'no way to avoid continued service . . .' "[5]

Therefore, Judge Cooper held that Flood had not satisfied the essential element of his involuntary servitude claim, compulsory service.

The ruling, while correct, is reminiscent of Anatole France's adage that the law, in all of its majesty, prohibits the rich as well as the poor from sleeping under bridges.

§2.4(b) Antitrust principles

The Senate Judiciary Committee Report on the Basketball Merger Bill also stated the Committee's belief that reserve and option systems "constitute a violation of the antitrust laws."[1] On this score, there was substantial support, even when the Report was issued in 1972, and more has been published since. At the Supreme Court level in the sports context, there is Justice William O. Douglas' dissent to the majority opinion in the *Flood* case:

> "The owners, whose records many say reveal a proclivity for predatory practices, do not come to us with the equities. The equities are with the victims of the reserve clause. I use the word 'victims' in the Sherman Act sense, since a contract which forbids anyone to practice his calling is commonly called an unreasonable restraint of trade . . . Had this same group boycott occurred in another industry, or even in another sport,

[5] Flood v. Kuhn, 316 F.Supp. 271, 281 (S.D.N.Y. 1970); to same effect, see also Augusta Baseball Assn. v. Thomasville Baseball Club, 93 S.E. 208 (Ga. S.Ct. 1917).

[1] S.Rep. 92-1151, 92d Cong., 2d Sess. 8 (1972).

we would have no difficulty in sustaining [Flood's] claim." [2]

Indeed, in one case decided in 1957, a federal Court of Appeals did rule illegal an agreement remarkably similar to reserve and option systems. The agreement had been entered into by magazine subscription solicitation agencies —companies that hired men to sell magazine subscriptions door-to-door. These companies had agreed that none of them would hire any person who had been employed by another agency during the preceding year. The Federal Trade Commission ruled that this agreement constituted an unreasonable restraint of trade in violation of the Sherman Act, and the Court of Appeals upheld that determination. The Court reasoned that the agreement reduced competition in the subscription business, because new agencies would find it more difficult to obtain salesmen since potential employees would be afraid of being out of work for a year, in the event the new agency went out of business. The companies that were parties to the agreement argued that they entered into it in order to discourage fraudulent sales practices. Before the agreement, they said, salesmen were not necessarily inhibited by company rules prohibiting fraud, because salesmen were free to change employers whenever they were caught. Both the Commission and the Court of Appeals rejected this motive —admirable and desirable for the industry though it was— as a justification for engaging in a practice which restrained trade.[3]

---

[2] Flood v. Kuhn, 407 U.S. 258, 287 (1972).

[3] Union Circulation Co. v. F.T.C., 241 F.2d 652 (2d Cir. 1957); see also, Nichols v. Spencer International Press, 371 F.2d 332 (7th Cir. 1967), which held an agreement between book publishers not to hire one another's sales employees for at least 6 months after their employment had been terminated impaired competition and thus might violate the Sherman Act.

Furthermore, the United States Supreme Court ruled, as long ago as 1930, that an agreement between several motion picture exhibitors not to license movies to theaters except by use of a standard form contract they had developed—similar to league by-laws requiring the use of uniform or standard player contracts—constituted a restraint of trade in violation of the Sherman Act.[4]

The Supreme Court has also declared illegal agreements to manipulate prices, and over twenty years ago the *Yale Law Journal* published an article which concluded that the reserve system appeared to fall squarely within the rule of that case, because it eliminates competition for players and permits teams to set their own prices for players.[5] The owners of many teams might dispute their ability to set salaries and point to ever rising salary levels despite reserve and option systems. Nevertheless, while salaries in all sports have increased over the years, the most dramatic salary spurts have always come at a time when separate leagues in a single sport have bid against one another for players. The reserve clause was first adopted to hold down salary levels,[6] and there can be little doubt that it has in fact had that effect. For example, Organized Baseball has not faced competition from a competitive league within the United States in over fifty years. And, during the trial of the *Curt Flood* case, Organized Baseball's own expert witness on economics, Mr. John Clark, testified that compensation paid to players has been a declining percentage of the industry's expenses since at least 1929. In that year, player salaries constituted 35.3% of the total

[4] Paramount Famous Lasky Corp. v. United States, 282 U.S. 30 (1930).

[5] Comment, Monopsony in Manpower: Organized Baseball Meets the Antitrust Laws, 62 Yale L.J. 576, 621-624 (1953).

[6] See § 2.1, *supra.*

expenses of major league teams. In 1943, salaries were down to 28.9% of expenses. In 1946, they dropped to 24.8%; in 1950, to 22.1%; and in 1970, to only 19 or 20%.[7]

Finally, reserve and option systems are enforced within a single league by the concerted refusal of all other teams to deal with a player. This sort of concerted refusal is also called a group boycott, and has been held illegal *per se* by the Supreme Court, regardless of its purpose, even if that purpose was entirely reasonable, desirable, and necessary to the industry.[8]

Recently, the antitrust principles articulated in these non-sports cases have been applied in football and basketball cases of utmost significance.

§2.4(b)(1) Applied to NFL rules

The first published ruling on the merits of intra-league enforcement of reserve and option clauses came in *Joe Kapp* v. *National Football League*.[1] Kapp was an All-American quarterback while at the University of California, and was drafted by the Washington Redskins. He signed instead with a team in the Canadian Football League where he played for eight years. Then in 1967, Kapp signed a two year contract with the Minnesota Vikings (after it paid his Canadian team $50,000 to release him from its option for that year, and after it apparently made arrangements with the Redskins). Dissatisfied with the offer the Vikings made him at the expiration of that contract in 1968, Kapp "played out" his option during

[7] Brief for Petitioner, Flood v. Kuhn, *supra* note 2.

[8] Fashion Originators' Guild v. F.T.C., 312 U.S. 457 (1941).

[1] Kapp v. National Football League, 390 F.Supp. 73 (N.D. Cal. 1974).

the 1969 season (leading the team to the Super Bowl while doing so) and became a "free agent" at its conclusion.

Despite the success he had enjoyed during the 1969 season, no team made him an offer prior to the start of the 1970 season. This was because of the "Rozelle Rule," Kapp claimed, and the inability of interested teams to know in advance what compensation they might have been required to give the Vikings if they did hire him. Shortly after the start of the 1970 season, however, the New England Patriots did make a deal with the Vikings, trading a future number one draft choice and a prior number one selection for Kapp.

The three year contract Kapp signed with the Patriots was not an NFL Standard Player Contract, and it contained no option clause. Apparently, the League did not object to the form of the contract during the 1970 season, and Kapp played and was paid ($154,000) for the season, in accordance with the terms of the agreement. Early in 1971, however, Commissioner Rozelle directed the Patriots to have Kapp sign a Standard Player Contract. Though the team sent him one, Kapp refused to sign it. In May of 1971, Rozelle reminded the Patriots that the NFL Constitution and By-Laws provide that no player may play or practice with a team unless a signed Standard Player Contract is on file with the Commissioner. When Kapp continued to refuse to sign one, "he was, in effect, told by the Patriots to leave" training camp.[2]

Kapp's suit followed, and in it he alleged that the National Football League, its Commissioner, and all of its members caused him to be discharged by the Patriots by conspiring to restrain trade and monopolize football in

---

[2] *Id.* at 77.

violation of the federal antitrust laws. In a motion (for partial summary judgment) made shortly before the trial was to begin, Kapp sought a declaration that the defendants had violated sections 1 and 2 of the Sherman Act, as a matter of law. He contended that the Option, Tampering, and Rozelle Rules, and the rules requiring players to sign Standard Player Contracts, constituted a combination among the defendants to refuse to deal with players except under certain conditions, and that the refusal amounted to a boycott which was illegal *per se* under the antitrust laws without regard to whether or not reasonable purposes might exist for them. Kapp further contended that the rules were in fact unreasonable, and that therefore the "rule of reason" would not save them even if it applied.

The question of whether or not the *per se* doctrine applied was a very significant question in the *Kapp* case—as it is in all sports antitrust cases. For if the doctrine did apply, then the trial would be considerably shorter, because the NFL would not be permitted to introduce evidence of the rules' purposes—those purposes being irrelevant in cases involving *per se* violations—and Kapp would not have to counter that evidence with evidence of his own that the rules were unreasonable. Inquiries into the reasonableness of business practices require elaborate economic analyses, which may be complex and therefore expensive; and this is one of the reasons the Supreme Court has ruled that some practices must be deemed to be illegal without the need for such inquiries. Otherwise, it has been reasoned, the victims of anti-competitive practices would find legal redress prohibitive.

In support of his contention that the Option, Tampering, Standard Player Contract, and Rozelle Rules were illegal *per se,* Kapp cited several cases, among them the group boycott and motion picture licensing agreement cases mentioned above,[3] as well as others that had involved professional sports in particular.[4]

The National Football League, on the other hand, denied that its rules constituted a *per se* violation of the antitrust laws or a violation of any sort. In support of its position, the NFL argued that professional sport league activities must be distinguished from other kinds of business activities, because sport league activities are unique. The League argued that although its teams compete with one another on the field, they are not and cannot be competitors in business, because the very purpose of a professional sports league is to provide reasonably matched teams for field competition in order to attract and sustain the interest and patronage of fans. If each member was allowed to engage in free-for-all competition for the best or better players, then the most strongly financed or otherwise better-advantaged clubs would be able to sign up and thereby monopolize the best or better players, leaving only average or mediocre players for the other clubs with the effect of destroying the evenly matched field competition that brings fans to the games. Thus, the NFL said,

> ". . . there must be league agreements and rules which, restricting the freedom of the clubs to compete for

[3] In § 2.4(b); see 390 F.Supp. 87.

[4] Washington State Bowling Prop. Assn. v. Pacific Lanes, Inc., 356 F.2d 371 (9th Cir. 1966), discussed in § 7.3(e)(1), *infra*; Denver Rockets v. All-Pro Management, Inc., 325 F.Supp. 1049 (C.D. Cal. 1971), discussed in § 7.3(e)(2)(A), *infra;* Boston Professional Hockey Assn., Inc. v. Cheevers, 348 F.Supp. 261 (D. Mass. 1972), discussed in § 2.3(b)(2), *supra;* Blalock v. Ladies Professional Golf Assn., 359 F.Supp. 1260 (N.D. Ga. 1973), discussed in § 7.3(e)(2)(B), *infra;* Gardella v. Chandler, 172 F.2d 402 (2d Cir. 1949), discussed in § 1.1(b), *supra.*

players, impinge to some extent upon the freedom of players to choose their own clubs." [5]

In support of its position, the NFL claimed that the uniqueness of sports "has been long and widely recognized" by Congress, the Department of Justice, and even by the players themselves. Congress, it was pointed out, has enacted legislation exempting the National Football League from the antitrust laws to permit its merger with the American Football League,[6] and to permit it to sell television rights in a package.[7] Further, in the specific area of player control mechanisms, the only bills to be passed by either house of Congress would have granted the League exemption with respect to the kinds of rules Kapp's suit attacked.[8]

Federal District Judge William T. Sweigert seems to have seen merit in the positions taken by both sides. On the one hand, he recognized that "There is authority to the effect that combinations of the kind shown by the record here, constitute *per se* antitrust violations," [9] and that "Under the holdings of those cases the combination here shown would be a *per se* violation of the antitrust laws." [10]

On the other hand, District Court opinions in the *Curt Flood* case and in one of the major hockey cases suggested that the "rule of reason," rather than the *per se* rule, should be applied in sports cases.[11] Judge Sweigert found

---

[5] Kapp v. National Football League, *supra,* note 1 at 79.
[6] See § 6.1, *infra.*
[7] See § 10.2(b)(1), *infra.*
[8] See § 1.2(c), *supra.*
[9] Kapp v. National Football League, *supra* note 1, at 80.
[10] *Id.*
[11] *Id.* at 81.

those cases to be significant, and he was also persuaded by the Congressional and Executive actions referred to by the NFL. In addition, the judge pointed out that restrictive provisions—such as no-competition clauses—in employment contracts used in other industries, where there is no agreement among several employers, are judged according to their reasonableness. And while he recognized that it is *combinations* that are prohibited by the antitrust laws, he nevertheless thought it arguable "that in this unique field of sports . . . the test of legality of league rules . . . should be the same . . . as would be applicable to the individual player-club contract," [12] that is, the "reasonableness test."

Finally, Judge Sweigert was also influenced by the fact that player-club relationships lent themselves well to collective bargaining.

> "Application of the absolute *per se* rule to *all* league rules enforcing restrictions upon the players' free choice of employment tends to preclude collective bargaining negotiations for league enforcement of some rules in this category which, considering the unique nature and purpose of league sports, may be regarded by both players and clubs as reasonably necessary in furtherance of their long-range *mutual* interests." [13]

For all of those reasons, Judge Sweigert concluded that,

> ". . . in this particular field of sports league activities the purposes of the antitrust laws can be just as well served (if not better served) by the basic antitrust

---

[12] *Id.*

[13] *Id.* at 81-82.

reasonableness test as by the absolute *per se* test sometimes applied by the courts in other fields." [14]

While this much of the opinion was favorable to the National Football League, it was not to be victorious. For although Judge Sweigert agreed with the NFL that the "rule of reason" should be applied, he agreed with Kapp that it did not save the objected to practices from being illegal. "[L]eague enforcement of most of the challenged rules is so patently unreasonable that there is no genuine issue for trial," [15] he held. Discussing each of the individual rules in turn, Judge Sweigert acknowledged that the option clause—which gives teams an option to players' services for one additional year at 90% of the contract salary—would not *by itself* be patently unreasonable. However, he said, a "conceivable effect" of the Rozelle Rule "would be to *perpetually* restrain a player from pursuing his ocupation . . ." [16] and therefore that rule was illegal. He held,

> "We conclude that such a rule imposing restraint virtually unlimited in time and extent, goes far beyond any possible need for fair protection of the interests of the club-employers or the purposes of the NFL and that it imposes upon the player-employees such undue hardship as to be an unreasonable restraint and such a rule is not susceptible of different inferences concerning its reasonableness; it is unreasonable under any legal test . . ." [17]

The Tampering Rule and the rule requiring use of the Standard Player Contract were also held to be "patently

[14] *Id.* at 82.

[15] *Id.*

[16] *Id.*

[17] *Id.*

unreasonable insofar as they are used to enforce other NFL rules in that area."[18]

Thus victory, at least preliminarily, was Kapp's. Ed Garvey, Executive Director of the NFL Players Association, called Judge Sweigert's opinion "the most significant development in the history of professional sports from the point of view of the athlete."[19] Bill Curry, President of the NFL Players Association, predicted the case was "certainly going to have a profound effect on player-club relationships."[20] And Kapp's attorney said that if the opinion were upheld, "the structure of organized football is going to be changed pretty radically."[21]

Just before the start of the 1975 season, the Rozelle Rule was tested again in court in a case that could have been even more significant than Kapp's. That case was the result of events which began the year before, when wide-receiver Ron Jessie played out his option with the Detroit Lions and became a free agent. After talking with a number of NFL clubs, as he had a right to do, Jessie signed with the Los Angeles Rams in July of 1975. Interestingly, Jessie's agent, Bob Felton, told reporters that "A half-dozen Clubs made strong offers for Ron, and it was obvious the Rozelle Rule was no deterrent."[22]

The Rams and Lions were unable to agree on who or what fair compensation for Jessie would be, and therefore,

---

[18] *Id.*

[19] Hager, Football Player-Reserve Rule Held Illegal, L.A. Times, Dec. 21, 1974, Part I, Pg. 1.

[20] Maher, Rozelle Rule's Extinction: It Got What It Deserved, L.A. Times, Dec. 21, 1974, Part III, Pg. 1.

[21] Hager, *supra* note 19. In April of 1976, a jury decided that Kapp had not suffered any damages as a result of the NFL's illegal rules. L.A. Times, April 3, 1976.

[22] Hall, Around Town, L.A. Times, July 10, 1975, Part III.

Commissioner Rozelle awarded Ram running back Cullen Bryant to the Lions. Bryant was about to begin his third year in the National Football League, and thus his selection by Rozelle as the "compensation" to be awarded the Lions was unusual in one respect. Although Rozelle had been called upon to award compensation four previous times since the rule bearing his name was adopted in 1963,[23] never before had he awarded a veteran player. One prior award had been a rookie, and the other three awards had been draft choices only.[24] The award was also unusual in another respect; Bryant refused to report to the Lions.

On July 30, 1975, U.S. District Judge Warren J. Ferguson issued a temporary restraining order preventing the National Football League from requiring Bryant to report to the Lions. "I think the Rozelle Rule, in conjunction with the Standard Player Contract and the Option Clause, violates §1 of the Sherman Antitrust Act," [25] Judge Ferguson stated from the bench when he issued the order, explaining,

> "With all power goes correlative responsibility of fair dealing and fair play. The economic power of the NFL, as demonstrated by this case, truly is awesome. That may be the way it has to be, if there is going to be an NFL. The awesome control of the Commissioner may be necessary for the effective management of the League. A trial might well show that. But the rule of reason cannot merely be wiped aside by such necessities. Football owes more to Mr. Bryant than

---

[23] See § 2.2(c)(1), *supra*.

[24] *Id.;* L.A. Times, July 26, 1975, Part III; Mackey v. National Football League, 407 F.Supp. 1000 (D. Minn. 1975).

[25] Rawitch, Bryant Is a Ram, At least For Now, L.A. Times, July 31, 1975, Part III.

is seen in this case. Cullen Bryant is entitled to better treatment than fiat." [26]

The temporary restraining order was to have remained in effect until August 12, 1975 only, on which date Judge Ferguson scheduled a hearing on Bryant's motion for a preliminary injunction. On August 1st, however, Rozelle reversed his decision awarding Bryant to the Lions, and instead he gave them a 1976 first round draft choice, that the Rams had previously acquired from the Green Bay Packers in a trade, and "such additional compensation in the form of a draft choice, as this office may determine appropriate after the conclusion of the 1975 season." [27] Rozelle did this, he stated, because the NFL preferred that the legality of the Rozelle Rule be decided in another case brought by former NFL Players Association President, John Mackey, and several player representatives, in the federal District Court in Minneapolis. A fifty-five day trial had just been concluded in the *Mackey* case, resulting in some twelve thousand pages of testimony transcript. Rozelle explained that,

> "That trial, for the first time in NFL history, produced a complete record of all relevant facts and arguments, both in support of and in opposition to the legality of the Rule. We believe a legal decision on an issue of this importance should be made only on the basis of a record of that nature. We are advised by counsel that it would be impossible to develop such a complete record in a preliminary injunction hearing involving Bryant." [28]

---

[26] *Id.*

[27] L.A. Times, Aug. 2, 1975, Part III.

[28] *Id.*

When the decision in the *Mackey* case was finally handed down in December of 1975, it was not the one the National Football League had been hoping to receive. District Judge Earl R. Larson held that "The Rozelle Rule constitutes a *per se* violation of the antitrust laws," because it constitutes "a concerted refusal to deal, and a group boycott," and because it "is so clearly contrary to public policy." [29]

The National Football League had contended that the *per se* standard[30] was not applicable to it, and that the "rule of reason" should have been applied. The NFL further contended that under the rule of reason, the Rozelle Rule would be legal because it is reasonable, because professional football is a form of entertainment which depends upon competitive balance, and because the Rozelle Rule is necessary to maintain that balance. Given these facts, the NFL argued, the Rozelle Rule has served both player and club interests, and is "absolutely necessary to the existence of professional football and the structure of the game." [31]

Judge Larson, however, disagreed. He found that the freedom which a player "theoretically gains" by playing out his option "appears to be illusory." [32] This is so, he stated, because the unknown compensation that may be awarded if agreement cannot be reached with the player's former team, has made clubs extremely reluctant to sign free agents, and has acted as an effective deterrent to their doing so. As a result, the Rozelle Rule was also found to act as a substantial deterrent to athletes playing out their options and becoming free agents, because

[29] Mackey v. National Football League, 407 F.Supp. 1000, 1007 (D.Minn. 1975).

[30] See § 7.3(e)(2)(A)(iii), *infra*.

[31] Mackey v. National Football League, *supra* note 29, at 1003.

[32] *Id.* at 1006.

players are aware of the possibility that they will simply have to return to their present team in any event.

In addition to the fact that "The Rozelle Rule substantially restricts players' freedom of movement," [33] Judge Larson also found that "The existence of the Rozelle Rule substantially decreases players' bargaining power in contract negotiations . . . (and) as a result, the salaries paid by each club are lower than if competitive bidding were allowed to prevail." [34]

Although Judge Larson specifically held that the Rozelle Rule constituted a *per se* violation of the antitrust laws, he also responded to the NFL's contention that the Rozelle Rule would be legal if measured by the rule of reason, and he found the Rozelle Rule to be "invalid under the Rule of Reason standard," [35] as well. Judge Larson found it to be "unreasonably broad in its application." [36] He noted that the testimony indicated that NFL members are concerned with the effects of unrestricted movement by the best players in the League. Little or no concern was expressed, he noted, with respect to average or below average players. "However, the Rozelle Rule is not limited to superstars or even the better players. It covers, includes and affects every player, no matter how marginal his status or ability." [37]

Judge Larson also found the Rozelle Rule to be unreasonable because it provided no procedural safeguards whatsoever.

---

[33] *Id.* at 1007.

[34] *Id.*

[35] *Id.*

[36] *Id.*

[37] *Id.*

> "There is no hearing or opportunity to be heard. The free agent player may not even be aware that other clubs are interested in him and are negotiating with the club to which he was formerly under contract. There is no safeguard against the club to which the player was formerly under contract being unreasonable or refusing to even state any compensation demand. A club can, and often does, effectively discourage interest by other clubs in a free agent player, simply by telling them that they are interested in signing the player, and that they intend to do so." [38]

Judge Larson also found the Rozelle Rule to be unreasonable because it is unlimited in duration. "It is a perpetual restriction on a player, following him throughout his career. He is at no time truly free to negotiate for his services with any NFL club." [39]

The National Football League had presented evidence supporting several justifications it claimed demonstrated the Rule was reasonable. Judge Larson found, however, that these justifications failed to prove the Rule reasonable. One such justification was the need to protect the club's investment in established players, such as scouting expenses and player development costs. Judge Larson found that the expenses incurred in the selection, training, and development of professional football players is not unlike similar hiring and training expenses incurred in other businesses, and he held that "there is no right to compensation for this type of investment." [40]

---

[38] *Id.*
[39] *Id.*
[40] *Id.* at 1008.

Another justification was the need to preserve player continuity because of the length of time that is required for players to be able to work together effectively as a team. Judge Larson rejected this justification on the grounds that the elimination of the Rozelle Rule would affect all teams equally, and thus, "The quality of play in the NFL will not decrease with the elimination of the Rozelle Rule, and consequent freedom of employment."[41] Even assuming that the quality of play would decrease, according to Judge Larson that fact would not justify the anticompetitive nature of the Rozelle Rule in any event.

Another justification was the need to maintain competitive balance between the teams in the League. Judge Larson found, however, that "the existence of the Rozelle Rule and the other restrictive devices on players have not had any material effect on competitive balance in the National Football League."[42]

Finally, the Rozelle Rule was said to be necessary to prevent disruption of and irreparable damage to the NFL. Judge Larson found that eliminating the Rule "would have no significant immediate disruptive effect on professional football . . . [and] will not spell the end of the National Football League, or even cause a decrease in the number of franchises in the National Football League."[43]

As a result of these findings, Judge Larson directed the entry of a judgment declaring the Rozelle Rule to be in violation of the antitrust laws and enjoining the National Football League and all of its members from continuing to enforce it.

---

[41] *Id.*
[42] *Id.*
[43] *Id.*

§2.4(b)(2) Applied to NBA rules

Less than two months after the decision in the *Joe Kapp* case,[1] a pre-trial order was issued in another sports lawsuit involving virtually identical issues. That case, *Oscar Robertson* v. *National Basketball Association,*[2] was filed in 1970 by the player representatives of each NBA team, following reports that the NBA and the American Basketball Association were considering merger.[3] Though the immediate purpose of the suit was to enjoin any such merger, on the grounds that a merger would create a monopoly in violation of the Sherman Act, it also sought to bar the continued use of the player draft and reserve or option system, on the grounds that their use restrained trade in violation of the Sherman Act. A number of pre-trial motions were ruled upon by federal District Judge Robert L. Carter in February of 1975, including a motion for summary judgment by the National Basketball Association seeking, in effect, judicial approval of the draft and reserve or option system.

Not only did Judge Carter deny the NBA's motion for judgment in its favor, but he did so in language strongly suggesting that had the case gone to trial, judgment might well have been entered for the players. While Judge Carter's own views on whether the "rule of reason" or the *per se* doctrine should be used were not made fully clear, he did discuss the possibility that the *per se* doctrine might apply.

> "Among the practices which have been declared *per se* violations of the Sherman Act are horizontal price-

[1] Kapp v. National Football League, 390 F.Supp. 73 (N.D. Cal. 1974), discussed in § 2.4(b)(1), *supra.*

[2] 389 F.Supp. 867 (S.D.N.Y. 1975).

[3] See § 6.2, *infra.*

fixing at the same level of competition . . .; territorial division of markets . . .; and secondary or group boycotts . . . The player draft and perpetual reserve system are readily susceptible to condemnation as group boycotts based on the NBA's concerted refusal to deal with the players save through these uniform restrictive practices . . . The two control mechanisms are also analogous to price-fixing devices condemned as *per se* violative of the Sherman Act, for the draft and a perpetual reserve system allow competing teams to eliminate competition in the hiring of players and invariably lower the cost of doing business . . . In addition the player draft and a perpetual reserve system can be viewed as devices creating illegal horizontal territorial allocations and product market divisions . . ."[4]

On the other hand, he also expressed the view that,

"Some degree of economic cooperation which is inherently anti-competitive may well be essential for the survival of ostensibly competitive professional sports leagues . . . Without these mechanisms unrestrained price wars for the service of the most proficient players will ensue, or so runs the argument, with the wealthiest teams capturing the top talent and the poorer teams facing demise due to the loss of fans and profit . . ."[5]

Though Judge Carter did not decide which of the two approaches, *per se* or "rule of reason," should be taken,[6]

[4] Robertson v. National Basketball Assn., 389 F.Supp. 867, 893 (S.D.N.Y. 1975).

[5] *Id.* at 892.

[6] In a subsequent pre-trial motion, the players contended that Judge Carter had ruled the complained-of practices to be illegal

he—like Judge Sweigert in the *Joe Kapp* case and like Judge Larson in the *John Mackey* case—did suggest the possibility that even the "rule of reason" might not save the draft and reserve rules from illegality. "Because survival necessitates some restraints, however, does not mean that insulation from the reach of the antitrust laws must follow," he said. "Less drastic protective measures may be the solution." [7]

§2.4(b)(3) Issues to be resolved

§2.4(b)(3)(A) Standard to be applied

While it was not necessary in the *Oscar Robertson* case[1] for Judge Carter to decide whether the "rule of reason" or the *per se* doctrine should be used in order for him to deny the NBA's motion for summary judgment, his full discussion of the issue without a resolution of it suggests that he found it to be a difficult question. Similarly, Judge Sweigert's acknowledgement in the *Kapp*[2] case that there

---

per se, and that therefore the reasonableness of those practices could not be considered. Judge Carter stated, "While that earlier opinion made clear the court's belief that the restraints in controversy are illegal under the antitrust laws . . ., no final determination as to the invalidity of the provisions and practices in question was made. . . . Accordingly, defendants are not barred from raising all possible defenses to plaintiffs' action, including one based on the economic necessity of retaining the challenged restraints. Plaintiffs, of course, are free to move to strike the rule of reason defense once all pre-trial discovery has been concluded. . . . A full hearing to determine whether the issue is appropriate for consideration by a jury will then be in order." Robertson v. NBA, 1975-2 CCH Trade Cases ¶ 60,448 (S.D.N.Y. 1975). No such hearing was ever held, because the case was settled in February of 1976. See § 2.2(d)(1), *supra.*

[7] Robertson v. National Basketball Assn., *supra* note 4, at 892.

[1] Robertson v. National Basketball Association, 389 F.Supp. 867 (S.D.N.Y. 1975), discussed in § 2.4(b)(2), *supra.*

[2] Kapp v. National Football League, 390 F.Supp. 73 (N.D. Cal. 1974), discussed in § 2.4(b)(1), *supra.*

is authority showing that the restraints in question were illegal *per se,* followed by his decision to use the "rule of reason," suggests that he too was troubled by the prospect of holding long-standing League rules illegal *per se.*

The issue of the applicability of the *per se* doctrine to professional sports league practices is one which has generated a great deal of disagreement. In some cases there is disagreement—not silent, but express—not only as to the conclusions reached, but even as to reasoning in cases where the conclusions are the same.[3]

The reasons for such sharp disagreements are not difficult to understand. The practices under attack are, for the most part, old and familiar features of professional sports—features which many current day sports fans were aware of even as children. Moreover, the sincerity of the beliefs of sports executives (with respect to the need for draft, option, and related rules) is doubted only by the most cynical of their critics. Even some professional athletes, active as well as retired, have agreed to the need for some player control mechanisms.[4]

There also can be little doubt that many league practices, especially those of the older, established leagues, are virtually indistinguishable from practices which have been declared to be illegal *per se* by the Supreme Court. It is therefore not surprising that some courts have been reluctant to declare these practices illegal *per se,* without even giving the leagues an opportunity to explain their

[3] Compare Blalock v. Ladies Professional Golf Association, 359 F.Supp. 1260 (N.D. Ga. 1973), discussed in § 7.3(e) (2) (B), *infra,* with Denver Rockets v. All-Pro Management, Inc., 325 F.Supp. 1049 (C.D. Cal. 1971), discussed in § 7.3(e) (2) (A), *infra.* See also, § 7.3(e) (2) (C), *infra.*

[4] Flood v. Kuhn, 316 F.Supp. 271, 276 (S.D.N.Y. 1970).

positions, while other courts have felt bound to declare them illegal and have done so.

The reluctance of courts to apply the *per se* doctrine in sports, while understandable, has little if any support in the law. Except under certain unique circumstances,[5] reasonable motives and business justifications are not relevant in deciding whether or not the *per se* doctrine or the rule of reason should be used. Certain categories of practices are deemed to be illegal *per se,* without regard to motive, justification, or effect. While the doctrine is harsh, it is both acknowledged and intended to be so. On balance, the benefits of the doctrine to business as a whole are believed to outweigh its admitted defects.

Inquiry into motives, justifications, and effect is relevant only if and after it has been determined that the practices complained of do not fall into one of the prohibited *per se* categories. Thus, the uniqueness of the professional sports business is relevant, but only if the practice at issue is not a *per se* violation. If the NFL and NBA draft and option/reserve rules are *per se* violations, as the *Kapp* and *Robertson* cases accurately suggest, and as the *Mackey*[6] case holds, they are and should be held illegal, as they were in the *Mackey* case.

When the *Mackey* decision was released, Commissioner Rozelle issued a statement saying, "The National Football League is, of course, disappointed with the decision of the Minneapolis Court. We had hoped that the court would find the antitrust laws to be sufficiently flexible to accommodate the unique and special needs of a professional

[5] See § 7.3(e)(2)(A)(iv), *infra.*

[6] Mackey v. National Football League, 407 F.Supp. 1000 (D. Minn. 1975), discussed in § 2.4(b)(1), *supra.*

football league."[7] The answer is that the antitrust laws are not sufficiently flexible to accommodate the NFL's current rules; but, other "less drastic measures" have been suggested to accomplish professional sports' unique objectives,[8] and, as Judge Carter stated, they "may be the solution."[9]

In addition, as Judge Larson said in his opinion in the *Mackey* case,

> "If the effects of this decision prove to be too damaging to professional football, assuming justification existed, Congress could possibly grant special treatment to the National Football League based upon its claimed unique status."[10]

§2.4(b)(3)(B) Significance of perpetuality

The ultimate impact the *Kapp*[1] and *Mackey*[2] decisions will have on NFL rules is not immediately apparent. First, Rozelle told reporters almost immediately after the *Kapp* decision was handed down that the NFL would appeal, and that in the interim nothing would be done by the League as a consequence of the ruling. "It is just one District Judge's opinion," Rozelle said.[3] Shortly after the *Mackey* case was decided, Rozelle announced that that decision would be appealed as well.[4]

---

[7] L.A. Times, Dec. 31, 1975, Part III, Pg. 4.

[8] See § 2.7, *infra.*

[9] Robertson v. National Basketball Association, *supra* note 1, at 892.

[10] Mackey v. National Football League, *supra* note 6, at 1008.

[1] Kapp v. National Football League, 390 F.Supp. 73 (N.D. Cal. 1974), discussed in § 2.4(b)(1), *supra.*

[2] Mackey v. National Football League, 407 F.Supp. 1000 (D. Minn. 1975), discussed in § 2.4(b)(1), *supra.*

[3] L.A. Times, Dec. 22, 1974, Part III.

[4] L.A. Times, Jan. 17, 1976, Part III.

Moreover, the extent to which the *Kapp* opinion itself requires fundamental changes in NFL practices is open to question. It appears that in Judge Sweigert's opinion, the principal defect in the present system of rules is that they can "*perpetually* restrain a player."[5] It is therefore possible that even he would approve rules which were limited in duration.

While Judge Larson held the Rozelle Rule to be illegal *per se* in the *Mackey* case, he too added that the Rule was unreasonable, in part, because it was unlimited in duration, and therefore was a perpetual restriction.[6]

§2.4(b)(3)(C) Standing to object

Because the National Football League capitulated to Cullen Bryant just two days after he obtained a temporary restraining order barring the NFL from requiring him to report to the Detroit Lions,[1] his case never resulted in a published opinion. In a way, that is unfortunate, because Bryant's case was more than a simple extension of the principle announced in the *Kapp*[2] and *Mackey*[3] decisions. In those cases, the Rozelle Rule was held to be an unlawful restraint of trade because of its impact on the athlete who has played out his option. In those cases, the issue was presented precisely by those who were injured by the restraint which the Rule was held to impose.

Cullen Bryant, on the other hand, was not the victim of that particular restraint. His case was the first to charge

---

[5] Kapp v. National Football League, *supra* note 1, at 82.

[6] Mackey v. National Football League, *supra* note 2.

[1] See § 2.4(b)(1), *supra*.

[2] Kapp v. National Football League, 390 F.Supp. 73 (N.D. Cal. 1974), discussed in § 2.4(b)(1), *supra*.

[3] Mackey v. National Football League, 407 F.Supp. 1000 (D. Minn. 1975), discussed in § 2.4(b)(1), *supra*.

that the Rozelle Rule might also be illegal because of its effect on the player who is awarded to the free agent's former team.

This is not to say that Bryant did not feel the impact of the Rule as severely as any free agent. The Rozelle Rule does not prevent free agents from signing anywhere. It simply restrains a free agent's ability to play with the team of his choice. Even under the Rozelle Rule, free agents are permitted to re-sign with their old teams. And, as a matter of fact, from 1966 through 1970, of the 42 athletes who played out their options, 24 did re-sign with their original clubs.[4]

The Los Angeles Rams was the team of Bryant's choice. And, for a time, the Rozelle Rule threatened to prevent him from playing with it. While Bryant thus felt its effects in the same way a free agent would, Bryant did not feel them because of the Rule's restraint on trade. Bryant was not a free agent. He was under contract and could be traded at any time. He was, in effect, simply assigned to the Detroit Lions in a trade induced by the Commissioner.

Although there seems to be no difference between the effect of the Rozelle Rule on Bryant and on a free agent, there is a distinction which made the Bryant case so significant. In order to prevail in an antitrust case, not only must the plaintiff have been injured in his business or property "by reason of" an antitrust violation, he also must have been within the "target area" of the economy which was endangered by the violation in the first place.[5]

---

[4] Maher, Sports' Option Clause: The Issue Is Freedom, L.A. Times, June 29, 1972, Part III, Pg. 1.

[5] San Francisco Seals, Ltd. v. National Hockey League, 379 F. Supp. 966, 971 (C.D. Cal. 1974).

People who are injured "by reason of" antitrust violations, but who are not within this "target area," are said to lack "standing" to sue. A recent case involving the San Francisco Seals of the National Hockey League illustrates that a person may be injured by an antitrust violation, even though not in the target area.[6] The Seals wanted to move to Vancouver, but were denied permission by the NHL, allegedly so that the NHL could preserve its control over professional hockey in the Bay Area, and thereby monopolize the industry. A federal District Court held that even if the NHL had conspired to monopolize hockey by preventing a competing league from placing a team in the Bay Area, the victims of that conspiracy were other leagues, not the Seals. Therefore, the court held, although the Seals were injured because they were prevented from moving, they were not in the target area and did not have standing to sue.

Similarly, Bryant was not within the target area of the restraint imposed by the Rozelle Rule on *free agents.* Therefore, had Bryant's case been fully litigated and won by him, his victory would have necessarily established one of the following propositions, both of which define the restraint broadly enough to include him within its target:

1. Either that the illegal restraint which affected Bryant was the one which threatened to prevent him from being able to play with the team of his choice; or

2. That it was illegal for the Los Angeles Rams to delegate to the Commissioner of the NFL their right to trade Bryant.

---

[6] *Id.,* discussed in § 8.2(b), *infra.*

If the first proposition were established, it would seem to outlaw fully all of professional sports' player control mechanisms, including the draft and the right of teams to trade players against their wishes. If the second proposition were established, it would seem substantially, if not completely, to wipe away the authority of the Commissioner in all matters relating to player-team relationships.

§2.4(c) Contract principles

Ironically, after a quarter century of antitrust litigation in which players sought to overturn Organized Baseball's reserve system, largely on the grounds that the system was perpetual and bound players to their teams for their entire careers,[1] the first successful blows to that system were made in recent cases where arbitrators ruled that the system was not in fact perpetual after all.

§2.4(c)(1) The Catfish Hunter case

Organized Baseball's long-standing reserve system first began to break down in an arbitration proceeding initiated by Jim "Catfish" Hunter, then of the Oakland Athletics. Hunter was originally signed by the Athletics in 1964, when the team was still in Kansas City and when Hunter was but a nineteen year old high school graduate. He reportedly received a $75,000 bonus and never played in the minor leagues. In his first year as a professional, he had an 8-8 record in the majors. Although his records during the next four years were only fair, he won 106 games during the five seasons from 1970 through 1974—more than any other major league pitcher. In 1974 in particular, he won twenty-five games and was given the Cy Young Award as the American League's best pitcher.

---

[1] See Chapter 1 and § 2.2(a), *supra.*

Through the conclusion of that season, he had been selected to the All-Star team six times and had a 7-1 record in play-off and World Series games.[1]

Hunter was to have been paid $100,000 in 1974, pursuant to a contract which specified that one-half was to be paid to him as salary, and the other half to be applied in any manner he designated. Intending to minimize the amount of income taxes he would have to pay, Hunter instructed the Athletics' owner, Charles O. Finley, to apply half to the purchase of a non-taxable annuity from a North Carolina insurance company. Finley balked at this instruction, however, stating that while he would pay Hunter all of the money in cash, he would not purchase the annuity because it would not be a deductible expense on the team's own tax returns.

In response to Finley's refusal, Hunter terminated his contract with the Athletics pursuant to the provisions of paragraph 7(a) of the American League Uniform Player's Contract which provides:

> "The Player may terminate this contract, upon written notice to the Club, if the Club shall default in the payments to the Player provided for in paragraph 2 hereof or shall fail to perform any other obligation agreed to be performed by the Club hereunder and if the Club shall fail to remedy such default within ten (10) days after the receipt by the Club of written notice of such default."

The collective bargaining agreement that had previously been entered into between the Major League Baseball Players Association and the National and American

[1] L.A. Times, Dec. 17, 1974, Part III.

Leagues established a grievance procedure for the resolution of disputes concerning the interpretation of, or compliance with, the provisions of any agreement between the Players Association and the Leagues, or any agreement between a player and a club. In accordance with this procedure, Hunter initiated a grievance seeking an award of the amounts still due him and, more importantly, seeking to be declared a free agent and eligible to negotiate with all of the teams in both major leagues.

Hunter's grievance was heard by an arbitration panel consisting of Marvin Miller, Executive Director of the Players Association, John J. Gaherin, counsel to the major leagues, and Peter Seitz, a neutral arbitrator who was designated Chairman. On December 16, 1974, the panel ruled, 2-1 with Gaherin dissenting, that Hunter was a free agent, and ordered the Athletics to pay him the $50,000 still due, with interest.

The decision caused baseball officials to express "dismay" and "shock." An aide to American League President Lee MacPhail explained to reporters, "We expected that the arbitrator might say he had to pay it, even perhaps pay interest, but we never expected Hunter to be declared a free agent." [2] Actually, they should not have been so surprised. Although Hunter was the first baseball player to be declared a free agent by the arbitration panel, as long ago as 1930 Organized Baseball's first Commissioner, Kenesaw Mountain Landis, declared one of the Milwaukee American League team's players to be a free agent when it assigned him to its farm system in violation of baseball's rules—a ruling which was upheld by the courts.[3]

---

[2] *Id.*

[3] Milwaukee American Assn. v. Landis, 49 F.2d 298 (N.D. Ill. 1931).

Finley sought to overturn the ruling with a lawsuit filed in the California Superior Court, in which his attorney argued that declaring Hunter a free agent was "akin to giving the death penalty for a parking violation." [4] The Court, however, refused to either vacate the arbitrators' ruling or to issue a temporary injunction preventing Hunter from signing elsewhere.[5]

Sign elsewhere is precisely what Hunter did. On New Year's Eve, 1974, the New York Yankees announced that they had signed the pitcher to a five year playing contract reportedly worth $3.75 million, thus making Hunter the highest paid player in the history of professional baseball.[6]

The sheer size of the compensation the Yankees agreed to pay Hunter can be interpreted in at least two ways. One baseball executive said, "This shows the necessity of the reserve clause. We have to have some semblance of order and this is an example of what would happen if we didn't." [7] On the other hand, it could be said that Hunter's situation demonstrates the unconscionable manner in which the reserve system artificially depresses the amount of pay baseball players would otherwise be able to earn. In reality, it has been suggested with seeming accuracy that the truth is probably somewhere in between.[8] If many baseball superstars became free agents each year, it is unlikely they would all be offered multi-million dollar contracts. Hunter was, it would seem, only because all of the teams in both major leagues were focusing on him alone. If several superstars were available, the bidding would be

[4] L.A. Times, Jan. 4, 1975, Part III.

[5] *Id.*

[6] L.A. Times, Jan. 1, 1975, Part III.

[7] Maher, Hunter Case Only Remotely Tied to Reserve Clause, L.A. Times, Jan. 4, 1975, Part III.

[8] *Id.*

defused and not likely to go as high. Elementary principles of economics indicate that prices decline as supplies increase.

As a legal matter, the Hunter case did not appear at first to present a threat to the continuing vitality of the reserve system, because it was based upon unique facts. The decision was predicated upon a finding that the Athletics had breached Hunter's contract by refusing to pay him all of the compensation agreed upon. So long as other teams in Organized Baseball satisfied their contract obligations, other players would not have the grounds he had for becoming free agents. Subsequently, however, the *Hunter* case became a precedent for one aspect of the most significant ruling to be issued in connection with professional baseball since the Supreme Court declared baseball to be exempt from the antitrust laws back in 1922.[9]

§2.4(c)(2) The Messersmith and McNally case

Pitcher Andy Messersmith signed a one year, $90,000 contract with the Los Angeles Dodgers in 1974. The Dodgers renewed that contract for 1975 in accordance with paragraph 10(a) which reads:

> "On or before December 20 . . . in the year of the last playing season covered by this contract, the Club may tender to the Player a contract for the term of that year. . . . If prior to the March 1 next succeeding said December 20, the Player and the Club have not agreed upon the terms of such contract, then on or before ten days after said March 1, the Club shall have the right by written notice to the Player . . . to renew this contract for the period of one year on the same terms,

[9] Federal Baseball Club v. National League, 259 U.S. 200 (1922), discussed in § 1.1(a), *supra*.

> except that the amount payable to the Player shall be such amount as the Club shall fix in said notice; provided, however, that said amount . . . shall be an amount not less than 80% of the rate stipulated for the next preceding year and at a rate not less than 70% of the rate stipulated for the year immediately prior to the next preceding year."

Although the Dodgers fixed Messersmith's 1975 salary at a reported $115,000, he played the entire 1975 season without signing a new contract, because the Dodgers refused his request to include either a no-trade clause or a clause giving him the right to approve any trade involving him.[1] At the conclusion of the 1975 season, Messersmith and the Players Association took the position that he was a free agent—a position with which the Major Leagues did not agree.

So, on October 7, 1975, the Players Association filed a grievance on Messersmith's behalf, alleging that he had played for the Dodgers in 1975 under a renewed contract; that he had completed the "renewal year" on September 28, 1975; that because his contract with the Dodgers expired on September 29, 1975, as of that date "there was no longer any relation" between the Dodgers and Messersmith and he "became free to negotiate with any of the twenty-four clubs with respect to his services for 1976"; but that the clubs "have conspired to deny Mr. Messersmith that right and have maintained the position that the Los Angeles Club is still exclusively entitled to his services."[2]

[1] Newhan, Messersmith Still Stalled, L.A. Times, Oct. 30, 1975, Part III.

[2] In the Matter of the Arbitration Between the Twelve Clubs Comprising the National League of Professional Baseball Clubs and the Twelve Clubs Comprising the American League of Pro-

On October 9, 1975, the Players Association filed a companion grievance on behalf of Dave McNally, who had played a portion of the 1975 season under a renewed contract for the Montreal Expos before retiring from baseball in mid-season. In answer to both grievances, the Major Leagues alleged that the claims were not within the scope of the grievance procedure established by the collective bargaining agreement and that, therefore, the arbitration panel had no authority to consider them. The Major Leagues also contended that the claims were totally without merit and that both players remained properly reserved by their respective teams.

Hearings were scheduled for late November of 1975, but on October 28th the Kansas City Royals filed a suit in the United States District Court in the Western District of Missouri, seeking to enjoin the Players Association from submitting the cases to arbitration and seeking a judicial declaration that the grievances were not in fact arbitrable. The other twenty-three major league teams immediately intervened in the case in support of the Royals and a hearing was scheduled on their application for a preliminary injunction. After the hearing, however, at the suggestion of Judge John W. Oliver, the Players Association and the Major Leagues entered into a stipulation in which they agreed that the scheduled arbitration proceeding would be held, that the arbitration panel would hear and decide whether it had jurisdiction to consider the grievances, and that the jurisdictional question could later be presented to Judge Oliver for his own determination.

Filing this lawsuit before the arbitration hearing was held was a wise tactical decision, because a party may

---

fessional Baseball Clubs and Major League Baseball Players Association, Decision No. 29, Grievance Nos. 75-27 & 75-28 (Dec. 23, 1975) at 2, referred to below as the Arbitration Decision.

waive his objections to arbitration by voluntarily participating in arbitration proceedings. By filing the lawsuit in advance of the hearing, the Major Leagues preserved their objections to the jurisdiction of the arbitration panel and the stipulation gave them, in effect, the opportunity to present their objections to two separate hearing officers, the arbitration panel and Judge Oliver. Had the Major Leagues been able to convince the arbitration panel that it had no jurisdiction, the matter would have gone no further. However, even if the arbitration panel decided it did have jurisdiction, the Major Leagues were still free to renew their objections to the Court. Similarly, the stipulation was a wise tactic for the Players Association as well, because it enabled the Players Association to get a ruling from the arbitration panel without first incurring the expense of litigation and appeal. Had the arbitration panel decided that it lacked jurisdiction, that would have been the end of the grievances entirely. While the Players Association was thereafter put to the expense of litigation, it then knew it was spending money to preserve a victory.

The Players Association contended that the arbitration panel had jurisdiction to hear the grievances, because the collective bargaining agreement between it and the Major Leagues provided, " 'Grievance' shall mean a complaint which involves the interpretation of or compliance with the provisions of any agreement between the Association and the Clubs . . . or any agreement between a Player and a Club. . . ."[3] The baseball reserve system is comprised of paragraph 10(a) of the Uniform Player's Contract—clearly an "agreement between a Player and a Club"—which gives clubs the right to renew for a successive year,

[3] Article X, quoted in the Arbitration Decision at 27, fn. 2.

and of Major League Rules 4-A and 3(g), which authorize clubs to reserve 40 players and which prohibit tampering with other clubs' players, respectively. The Major League Rules are incorporated into the Uniform Player's Contract in paragraph 9(a) which provides that the Club and the Player agree to accept, abide by and comply with all of their provisions. In sum, the Players Association took the position that the Messersmith and McNally grievances involved disputes over the proper interpretation of and compliance with provisions of agreements between a player and a club, and, because the Uniform Player's Contract was incorporated by reference into the collective bargaining agreement, between the Players Association and the Major Leagues.

The Major Leagues, on the other hand, took the position that the grievance procedure established by the collective bargaining agreement did not authorize grievances concerning the reserve system, because Article XV of that collective bargaining agreement expressly provided that "this Agreement does not deal with the reserve system." [4] Apparently, it was contended that the phrase "this Agreement does not deal with the reserve system," had two-fold significance. First, it meant that the grievance procedure established by the collective bargaining agreement could not be used to arbitrate disputes over the reserve system, because the grievance procedure "does not deal with the reserve system." Second, it was contended that inasmuch as the collective bargaining agreement "does not deal with the reserve system" there had not in fact been any agreement between the Major Leagues and the Players Association with respect to the reserve system; and because there had been no agreement about the reserve system, disputes

[4] Arbitration Decision, *supra* note 2, at 9.

concerning it were not disputes involving "the interpretation of or compliance with the provisions of any agreement between the Association and the Clubs" and were not, therefore, the kind of disputes over which the arbitration panel had jurisdiction.

Peter Seitz, Chairman of the Arbitration Panel, noted that the Leagues' position presented a paradox. On the one hand, he stated, Article XV declared that the collective bargaining agreement "does not deal with the reserve system," while on the other hand, the collective bargaining agreement incorporated the Uniform Player's Contract which both contains the renewal clause and itself incorporates the Major League rules concerning player reservation and tampering. "It is not easy to understand" he said, "how the [collective bargaining] agreement could state that it does *not* 'deal' with the Reserve System, when, at the same time, its own provisions and the provisions of the Players Contract and the Major League Rules which are absorbed into the [collective bargaining] agreement *patently do* 'deal' with such rule." [5]

According to Seitz, the paradox was resolved by the Players Association's explanation of the manner in which Article XV came to be incorporated into the collective bargaining agreement in the first place. The phrase first appeared in the 1970 collective bargaining agreement, which was signed while the *Curt Flood* case[6] was pending. It "provided a kind of 'cease fire" interlude, pending the conclusion of the *Flood Case* litigation—and during that period the reserve system . . . *was acquiesced in, by the Players Association,* however reluctantly. . . ." [7]

---

[5] *Id.* at 20.

[6] **Flood v. Kuhn, 407 U.S. 258 (1972), discussed in § 1.3(b),** *supra.*

[7] **Arbitration Decision, *supra* note 2, at 24.**

Having acquiesced in the reserve system, the Players Association was then concerned "that it had opened itself to litigation by any player who claimed to be adversely affected by that system."[8] It was this apprehension of litigation directed against it, as a participant in a system which the Players Association itself believed to be illegal, that prompted it to initiate its request for a provision declaring that the collective bargaining agreement "does not deal with the reserve system." The Players Association hoped that such a provision would be an effective defense, in the event a player initiated legal action against it as a co-conspirator in agreements claimed to be in violation of the antitrust laws.[9]

Seitz found this to be "an understandable and reasonable explanation of the genesis and rationale of the provision in light of the apparent paradox and contradiction mentioned above."[10] So understood, the provision clearly did not prohibit the filing of grievances for the arbitration of disputes concerning whether or not the various elements of the reserve system were properly interpreted and applied. In fact, Seitz pointed out, the Players Association and the Major Leagues had previously arbitrated a number of disputes involving several aspects of the reserve system without any question having been raised as to the jurisdiction of the Arbitration Panel to act on those grievances. The Major Leagues contended that those disputes dealt only with peripheral aspects of the reserve system and did not affect its "core." Seitz, however, was unconvinced. Jurisdiction, he said, does not depend upon the importance of the issues involved in the case, nor upon its

[8] *Id.* at 25.

[9] See § 4.3, *infra.*

[10] Arbitration Decision, *supra* note 2, at 25.

impact. Rather, jurisdiction depends upon the essence or nature of the case. Moreover, Seitz pointed out that no jurisdictional objection was voiced before the arbitration panel in the "Catfish" Hunter case[11] (though the alleged lack of jurisdiction was raised in the California Superior Court), even though Hunter had been declared to be a free agent because of the breach of his contract—a dispute which seems to go to the "core" of the reserve system as much as any. As a result, Seitz held that the Messersmith and McNally grievances were within the scope of the grievance provision of the collective bargaining agreement and that, accordingly, the arbitration panel had the duty and the power to arbitrate them.

On the merits, the Major Leagues contended that when a club renews a player's contract for the renewal year, the contract in force during that renewal year contains the "right of renewal" clause as one of its terms, thus entitling the club to renew the contract for successive years, in perpetuity, for so long as the player is alive and the club has duly satisfied all conditions required of it. Furthermore, the Major Leagues contended that even if the Uniform Player's Contract was not perpetually renewable, nevertheless clubs could reserve players who had been under contract to them by filing with the Commissioner the reserve list called for in Major League Rule 4-A, and that players so reserved could not then be negotiated or dealt with by other teams because of Major League Rule 3(g) prohibiting tampering.

The Players Association took the position that all contractual relationships between clubs and players terminate at the end of the first renewal year and that thereafter there is no longer any contractual bond whatsoever between

[11] See § 2.4(c)(1), *supra*.

them. Further, the Players Association contended that the only players who could be reserved under Major League Rule 4-A are players who are under contract, and that, therefore, no player who has played out the renewal year may be reserved thereafter. Since the tampering rule, Rule 3(g), prohibits negotiations or dealings only with players who are under contract to or reserved by other teams, the Players Association asserted that players who had played out their renewal years were free to negotiate with all of the teams in the Major Leagues.

Seitz agreed with the Players Association. While acknowledging that the law does not prevent parties from agreeing to successive renewals of the terms of their bargain, even into perpetuity, the contract must express that intention explicitly. The right of subsequent renewals, he said, cannot be determined by implication only. Nothing in paragraph 10(a) of the Uniform Player's Contract expressly provides that it may be renewed for any period beyond the first renewal year. Although the Uniform Player's Contract does provide that it may be renewed "on the same terms," Seitz found great difficulty in implying or assuming a right to renew the renewal clause itself. Because the contract is one which provides for the rendition of personal services, he said that a more explicit expression of such an intention would be expected.

In support of his finding that the Uniform Player's Contract could be renewed only once, Seitz cited and discussed the *Rick Barry* case[12] and the *Dick Barnett* case,[13] both of which construed National Basketball Association renewal

---

[12] Lemat Corp. v. Barry, 80 Cal. Rptr. 240 (Cal. Ct. App. 1969), discussed in § 2.3(b)(1), *supra.*

[13] Central New York Basketball, Inc. v. Barnett, 181 N.E.2d 506 (Ohio Ct. Com. Pl. 1961), discussed in § 2.3(a)(1), *supra.*

clauses virtually identical to that found in baseball contracts to be renewable for one year only.

Seitz also found that in the absence of an existing contractual relationship, players cannot be reserved. This he said was apparent from various Major League Rules which indicated that a contract must be in existence to permit reservation under Rule 4-A. For example, Rule 2(a) provides that a club may not have "title" to more than "forty players' *contracts*"—the same number of players which a club is permitted to place on its reserve list "for an ensuing season" pursuant to Rule 4-A. Rule 4-A provides that no player on the reserve list shall be eligible to play for or negotiate with any other club "until his *contract* has been assigned or he has been released." Rule 8, dealing with the unconditional release of a player, requires that the player's *contract* be tendered to all Major League clubs in accordance with the waiver rules. Rule 9 provides that "A club may assign to another club an existing *contract* with a player." And Rule 7 provides for the termination of a "relation between the club and the player created by *contract*. . . ."

In the face of all of these rules which assume the existence of a contractual relationship, Seitz found the Major Leagues' claim that teams may reserve players by placing their names on a list even in the absence of an existing contract to be unpersuasive.

> "It is like the claims of some nations that persons once its citizens, wherever they live and regardless of the passage of time, the swearing of other allegiances and other circumstances, are still its own nationals and subject to the obligations that citizenship in the nation imposes. This 'status' theory is incompatible with the doctrine or policy of freedom of contract in the eco-

nomic and political society in which we live and of which the professional sport of baseball ('the national game') is a part." [14]

Seitz took pains to emphasize that his opinion should not be read as a statement of his views either for or against a reserve system or, for that matter, the reserve system then in use. It was not his function to do so, he said. Further, he emphasized that his decision

> ". . . strikes no blow emancipating players from claimed serfdom or involuntary servitude such as was alleged in the *Flood Case*. It does not condemn the Reserve System presently in force on constitutional or moral grounds. It does not counsel or require that the System be changed to suit the predilections or preferences of an arbitrator acting as a Philosopher-King intent upon imposing his own personal brand of industrial justice on the parties. It does no more than seek to interpret and apply provisions that are in the agreements of the parties." [15]

Seitz also noted that he was not unmindful of the testimony of the Commissioner of Baseball and the presidents of the National and American Leagues on the importance of maintaining the integrity of the reserve system. He said that it had been represented to him that a decision of the arbitration panel sustaining the Messersmith and McNally grievances would have "dire results, wreak great harm to the Reserve System and do serious damage to the sport of baseball." [16] He was told that a decision favoring

[14] Arbitration Decision, *supra* note 2, at 52.

[15] *Id.* at 37.

[16] *Id.* at 57.

Messersmith and McNally would encourage many other players to become free agents and that this would encourage clubs with the greatest financial resources to hire free agents, thus unsettling the competitive balance between clubs which is so essential to the sport. He stated that he was told that driven by the compulsion to win, team owners would over-extend themselves financially in improvident bidding for players in an economic climate in which some clubs were already straining financially; and that investors would be discouraged from putting money into franchises where several star players could become free agents and no continuing control over their services could be exercised. Seitz reported that he was told that even the integrity of the sport itself may be placed in hazard under certain circumstances.

"I do not purport to appraise these apprehensions,"[17] Seitz responded.

> "They are all based on speculations as to what may ensue. Some of the fears may be imaginary or exaggerated; but some may be reasonable, realistic and sound. After all, they were voiced by distinguished baseball officials with long experience in the sport and a background for judgment in such matters superior to my own. However, . . . it is not for the Panel (and especially the writer) to determine what, if anything, is good or bad about the reserve system. The Panel's sole duty is to interpret and apply the agreements and understandings of the parties. If any of the expressed apprehensions and fears are soundly based, I am confident that the dislocations and damage to the reserve system can be avoided or minimized through good faith collective bargaining between the parties. There are

[17] *Id.* at 58.

numerous expedients available and arrangements can be made that will soften the blow—if this decision, indeed, should be regarded as a blow. This decision is not the end of the line by any means. The parties, jointly, are free to agree to disregard it and compose their differences as to the reserve system in any way they see fit." [18]

Accordingly, the opinion ordered the Major Leagues to inform and instruct their members without delay that the provisions of Major League Rules 4-A and 3(g) did not inhibit, prohibit or prevent them from negotiating or dealing with Messersmith and McNally for employment purposes.

In an affidavit submitted to Judge Oliver at the time the Kansas City Royals filed their suit to enjoin the arbitration, the Royals' owner, Ewing Kauffman, stated that he would not have invested millions of dollars in baseball but for the presence of the reserve system, and he "would not have approved any collective bargaining agreement between the clubs and the Association which placed the power to destroy the reserve system in the hands of the Arbitration Panel." [19] No doubt it is true that he would not have agreed to permit the Arbitration Panel to rule on the enforceability of the reserve system. In retrospect, it is now clear that the collective bargaining agreement should have been more specific than to say, "this Agreement does not deal with the reserve system." Rather, its provision authorizing grievance arbitrations should have defined "grievance" to mean complaints involving the interpretation of or compliance with provisions of "any agreement between the Association and the Clubs . . . or

[18] *Id.* at 58-59.
[19] Newhan, *supra* note 1.

any agreement between a Player and a Club . . . , *except* complaints concerning the interpretation of or compliance with any provision comprising an element of the reserve system." (Indeed, the collective bargaining agreement did provide that "grievance" was *not* to include disputes concerning the clubs' use of players' pictures for publicity purposes.)

Of course, in law as in sports, hindsight is superior to foresight. In support of those who participated in the drafting of the collective bargaining agreement, it seems only fair to point out that throughout the long history of baseball's renewal clause, it has always been understood by players and owners alike to be perpetual in nature. Indeed, as long ago as 1890, the perpetual nature of baseball's renewal clause was given as the reason for refusing to enforce it against a player who had jumped from one league to another.[20] Moreover, as recently as the *Curt Flood* case, the perpetual nature of the reserve system was cited as one of the principal reasons the system was alleged to violate the antitrust laws.

In construing contracts, the aim is to determine the understanding of the parties. Thus, while it might have been difficult to imply or assume that baseball's renewal clause renews even itself in the absence of its long history, that history might well have made implication and assumption altogether unnecessary.

Moreover, the *Rick Barry* and *Dick Barnett* cases discussed by Seitz and cited in support of his interpretation that the renewal clause does not renew itself were not fully

[20] Metropolitan Exhibition Co. v. Ward, 9 N.Y.S.2d 779 (1890), discussed in § 2.3(b)(1) *supra*; accord, Brooklyn Baseball Club v. McGuire, 116 Fed. 782 (E.D. Pa. 1902), Cincinnati Exhibition Co. v. Johnson, 190 Ill. App. 630 (1914).

relevant to the Messersmith and McNally grievances. In both *Barry* and *Barnett,* the players themselves—not the NBA—alleged that the NBA renewal clause was perpetual, in the hope of convincing the courts that it was too unconscionable to enforce. When confronted with this argument, the NBA itself suggested the "once only" interpretation—a suggestion accepted by the courts. Naturally, the National Basketball Association is free to construe its own contract in any way it sees fit. But, that construction—particularly when offered for tactical reasons in litigation—is not transferable to the language of baseball's Uniform Player's Contract under the different circumstances presented by the Messersmith and McNally grievances. Even the National Basketball Association has itself, on occasion, argued that under certain circumstances its renewal clause confers rights whose duration exceeds one additional year.[21]

Nevertheless, the only issue Judge Oliver reconsidered was whether the Arbitration Panel had jurisdiction to hear and consider the grievances. He refused to reconsider the merits of the decision, despite the Major Leagues' charge that Seitz had adopted a "baseless," "disingenuous," "spurious and arrogant theory of contract 'interpretation' . . . fundamentally upsetting baseball's status quo and putting at risk millions of dollars," that he had stated "his own personal prejudice without authority or precedent to support his extra-legal views," and that he had "misstated indisputable facts, ignored massive and conclusive evidence contrary to his desired conclusion and indicated nothing less than an obsessive desire to change (rather than interpret) the rules of the game." [22] Judge Oliver

[21] See § 2.3(b)(1), *supra.*

[22] Kansas City Royals Baseball Corporation v. Major League Baseball Players Association, 409 F.Supp. 233, 251, fn. 12 (W.D. Mo. 1976).

responded to these charges by stating that he found nothing in any statements by Seitz during the hearing, in the manner in which the arbitration proceedings were conducted, or in the opinion or award "which can fairly be said to support the charge that Mr. Seitz did anything other than discharge the duties imposed upon him . . . with the highest sense of fidelity, responsibility and intelligence." [23] Moreover, in his opinion dated February 3, 1976, Judge Oliver held that,

> "The question of interpretation of the collective bargaining agreement is a question for the arbitrator. It is the arbitrator's construction which was bargained for; and so far as the arbitrator's decision concerns construction of the contract, the courts have no business overruling him because their interpretation of the contract is different from his." [24]

Judge Oliver was careful to explain that his holding was not meant to say that if he had reconsidered the merits of the grievances he would have come to a different conclusion. His holding simply provided, he explained, that under applicable federal labor law, when parties to a collective bargaining agreement agree, as did the Major Leagues and Players Association, that grievances involving the interpretation of agreements shall be submitted to arbitration, the parties have agreed to abide by the arbitrator's decision, and it would not have been proper for him to state how he would have decided the merits, had he been the arbitrator.

On the question of whether or not the Arbitration Panel had jurisdiction to consider the grievances in the first place,

---

[23] *Id.*

[24] *Id.* at 253, quoting United Steelworkers of America v. Enterprise Wheel & Car Co., 363 U.S. 593, 599 (1960).

Judge Oliver found "that the parties were under obligation to submit the Messersmith and McNally grievances to arbitration, and that the Arbitration Panel established under Article X of the 1973 Basic Agreement [the collective bargaining agreement] had jurisdiction to hear and decide the grievances." [25] This decision was based on the authority of three cases decided by the United States Supreme Court in 1960 known as the "Steelworkers Trilogy," [26] and a 1974 decision in *Gateway Coal Co.* v. *United Mine Workers.*[27]

In the *Steelworkers* Trilogy, the Supreme Court enunciated a presumption in favor of the arbitrability of labor disputes. In the *Gateway Coal Co.* case, the Supreme Court explained that this federal policy favoring arbitration of labor disputes is grounded upon a congressional command contained in §203(d) of the Labor Management Relations Act, which reads, "Final adjustment by a method agreed upon by the parties is declared to be the desirable method for settlement of grievance disputes arising over the application or interpretation of an existing collective bargaining agreement." [28]

In the *Gateway Coal Co.* case, this presumption in favor of arbitration was held to be so strong that arbitration was required, even though the party resisting arbitration had argued that a provision, other than the arbitration clause, showed that the particular dispute involved in the case was to be excluded from arbitration. The dispute was whether or not mine safety issues were to be arbitrated.

[25] *Id.* at 249.

[26] United Steelworkers of America v. American Mfg. Co., 363 U.S. 564 (1960); United Steelworkers of America v. Warrior & Gulf Navigation Co., 363 U.S. 574 (1960); and United Steelworkers of America v. Enterprise Wheel & Car Corp., 363 U.S. 593 (1960).

[27] 414 U.S. 368 (1974).

[28] 29 U.S.C. § 173(d).

One clause of the collective bargaining agreement specifically provided for an employee mine safety committee which had the authority to make binding recommendations to remove all workers from areas found to be unsafe by reason of immediate danger. Despite the existence of this committee, and despite a holding of the Circuit Court of Appeals that the presumption in favor of arbitration was overcome in this case by a public policy against forcing miners to stake their lives on the judgment of an arbitrator, the Supreme Court held that mine safety issues were arbitrable. The Supreme Court held that inasmuch as the clause providing for a mine safety committee did not constitute a clear, express exception to the arbitration clause, the presumption in favor of arbitration enunciated in the *Steelworkers* Trilogy was controlling.

Judge Oliver found the Messersmith and McNally case to be quite analogous to the *Gateway Coal Co.* case. The Major Leagues had acknowledged to him that if Article XV, which provided "this Agreement does not deal with the reserve system," had not been in the collective bargaining agreement, then even they would agree that the Messersmith and McNally grievances would have been within the terms of the arbitration clause. At most, Judge Oliver thought, Article XV created the same sort of ambiguity that the mine safety committee clause had created in *Gateway Coal Co.* Since the Major Leagues acknowledged that arbitration would be proper in the absence of Article XV, and that Article created only an ambiguity at most, and ambiguities are required to be resolved in favor of arbitration, Judge Oliver entered an order directing the Major League club owners "to specifically comply with the Award of the Arbitration Panel in all particulars and respects." [29]

---

[29] Kansas City Royals Baseball Corporation v. Major League Baseball Players Association, *supra* note 22, at 260.

§2.5 Team obligations upon exercise of option

Almost always, disputes over the meaning and effect of reserve and option systems have centered on the rights of the teams and the obligations of the players. But contracts—including player contracts—create rights and obligations that flow in both directions. Players are given certain rights by contract, and teams incur certain obligations. The question thus arises, what obligations to the player does a team incur when it exercises its right to his services for the reserve or option year; and what rights does the player have when he honors his obligation to play for the team during that year? This precise question was litigated several years ago in a lawsuit involving football player Charles Hennigan, the Houston Oilers, and the San Diego Chargers.[1]

In March of 1964, Hennigan signed a three-year player contract with the Houston Oilers for the 1964, 1965 and 1966 seasons. The contract contained a standard clause which provided that in the event Hennigan was injured while performing services under his contract, he would be paid for the entire season even if he was unable to play. The contract also contained a "no-cut" clause, which while not standard, was often offered to outstanding players in those heady days of the AFL-NFL "war" as an extra inducement to sign. The "no-cut" clause provided, in effect, that even if the team determined Hennigan was not sufficiently talented to play football for it, nevertheless, he would not be cut from the team, his contract would not be terminated, and he would continue to be paid.

Hennigan played for the Oilers for the three years of his contract, but injured his knee while playing during the

[1] **Hennigan v. Chargers Football Company, 431 F.2d 308 (5th Cir. 1970).**

1965 season and again during the 1966 season. Prior to the start of the 1967 season, Hennigan underwent surgery on the injured knee, and a month after the surgery the Oilers assigned Hennigan's contract to the San Diego Chargers. The Chargers immediately exercised the option on Hennigan's services for the 1967 season, and Hennigan duly reported to training camp that summer. Unfortunately, because of his knee surgery, Hennigan did not pass the pre-season physical examination and was sent home. He did not play and was not paid for the 1967 season.

As a result, Hennigan filed suit against the San Diego Chargers to recover his 1967 salary; and the Chargers cross-sued the Houston Oilers. Hennigan claimed that he was entitled to his 1967 salary by virtue of the "injury" and "no-cut" clauses in his contract. The federal District Court in Texas which heard the case agreed, and entered judgment in Hennigan's favor. The Chargers, however, appealed, and the Court of Appeals, in a 2 to 1 decision, reversed and entered judgment for the team.

The majority of the Court of Appeals reached its conclusion by noting that Hennigan's contract referred to both "extensions" and "renewals." The contract was "extended" if a player retired or joined the Armed Forces. It was "renewed" when the option was exercised. The majority therefore concluded that there must be a distinction between "extensions" and "renewals," and the distinction settled upon was this: an extension lengthens the term of the *original* contract, while a renewal creates a *new* contract on the same terms. Since the injury clause required the Chargers to pay Hennigan for a full season only if he was injured while performing services pursuant to the contract *then in effect,* the distinction drawn by the Court of Appeals between his "original" Oiler contract and the "new" Chargers contract was crucial. Hennigan had been injured while playing pursuant to his original Oiler contract, not while playing under his "new" Charger contract. Thus, the majority said, the Chargers had no obligation to pay him for 1967 under the injury clause.

Similarly, the majority of the Court of Appeals felt that the no-cut clause takes effect only after a player passes his pre-season physical; until then, the team has no obligations at all under the contract. Though Hennigan had passed his pre-season physical in 1964, when the Chargers exercised the option for 1967 a "new" contract was created, requiring Hennigan to again pass a pre-season physical before the Chargers had any obligations under that "new" contract. Since Hennigan did not pass the physical in 1967, the Chargers were held to have no obligation to pay him pursuant to the no-cut clause.

The majority's interpretation of the effect of the option clause gave the Chargers all of its benefits and none of its obligations, and they unabashedly said so.

> "[The option clause] is not included in the AFL Contract for the player's benefit. An interpretation of [the option clause] that obligates the Club, upon its exercise of the option, to compensate the player for the option year notwithstanding that the player is physically incapable of passing the physical examination required of him before the option-year season begins —and thus is unable to perform any services as a player for the Club, is an unreasonable interpretation of a provision plainly meant to be for the sole benefit of the Club. Hennigan's interpretation would have this effect, and we reject it." [2]

[2] *Id.* at 317.

Whether Hennigan's interpretation was correct or not was, of course, more difficult than the majority of the Court of Appeals let on. Its difficulty was evidenced by—if nothing else—the fact that the District Court and the dissenting member of the Court of Appeals agreed with Hennigan. The dissenting judge of the Court of Appeals expressed the opinion that "extend" means continuation of the player contract by operation of its own terms, as when the contract is automatically extended by the retirement clause when a player joins the armed forces or retires. "Renew" means continuation of the contract as a result of action taken by the team, as when the team exercises the option. In fact, said the dissenting judge, Webster's Third New International Dictionary defines "renew" as meaning "extend." By this analysis, Hennigan's injury did take place during the term of the continued contract, and thus the Chargers should have paid him for the 1967 season as provided by the injury clause. Furthermore,

> ". . . the Club blindly exercised the option because they wanted Hennigan to play football for them if he could play football for any team. To receive this benefit they exercised an option. . . . As I read the words of the document, the continuation of the contract by the exercise of this option continued the injury clause in the same manner that it continued the restrictions on Hennigan's activities . . . . The Club had the option but the Club also had to take the risk." [3]

Though the four judges who considered Hennigan's case divided 2 to 2 on the proper result, the ultimate decision may not have been as harsh on Hennigan as it seems at first. It is probable that at least one reason Hennigan re-

[3] *Id.* at 318.

ported to the Charger training camp in 1967 without having signed a 1967 contract was that he suspected he might not pass the physical or make the team, and he was hoping to preserve the benefits of his old "no-cut" contract.

Also, the pre-season physical is one of the first things that takes place at training camp. Thus, had Hennigan felt that he was in condition to pass a physical, he still had time to contact all of the other teams in the League for an invitation to their training camps. When the Chargers terminated his contract, Hennigan became a free agent with the right to negotiate with any team.

Furthermore, the doctrine of the *Hennigan* case would only apply in a relatively unique set of circumstances. A player would have to be attempting to play out his option, and the injury which disqualifies him for professional football would have to be one he suffered in a previous season. If a team exercises an option on a healthy player who passes the pre-season physical, and the player thereafter injures himself while playing during the option season, the injury clause in the player's contract would require the team to pay him for the entire season, as though he had signed a new contract covering that season in particular.

Nevertheless, when in other contexts courts consider the extent to which player contracts—and reserve and option clauses in particular—are "mutual," the *Hennigan* case is a good example of one way in which they are not.

(As an aside, it is interesting to note that if an NFL player is injured during the first year of a multi-year contract, his salary will be continued throughout the term of that contract.[4] However, if a multi-year agreement is docu-

[4] NFL Standard Player Contract ¶ 14.

mented with a series of one-year contracts all executed at the same time, the player may not be so protected. This may be why many, if not most, NFL teams ask players to sign a separate contract for each separate season.[5] On the other hand, such a series of one-year contracts could be construed as constituting but a single, integrated contract, thereby entitling an injured player to salary throughout the contract term. All other major sport leagues have avoided this ambiguity by providing expressly in their player contracts that in the event a player is injured performing thereunder, his salary shall be continued, but not beyond the end of the season in which the injury occurred.[6])

§2.6 Rationale for reserve and option systems

In light of players' objections to reserve and option systems, their industry-wide use despite possible illegality, and the tremendous expense involved in their repeated courtroom defenses, it is apparent that team owners and league officials sincerely and absolutely believe that these systems are fundamentally necessary for the continued health and success of professional sports. The reasons for their believing the systems necessary are several and are supported, at least in part, by some documented facts.

§2.6(a) Crushing Dynasty prevention

The principal reason asserted in support of reserve and option systems is that without them the wealthiest franchises would hire all of the best players. This reason has

[5] Matuszak v. Houston Oilers, Inc., 1974-2 CCH Trade Cases ¶ 75,373 (Tex. Ct. Civ. App. 1974), discussed in § 5.2(b)(2)(A), *infra.*

[6] See, e.g., Major League Baseball Uniform Player's Contract ¶ 7(c); WFL Player's Contract ¶ 7.3; NBA Uniform Player's Contract ¶ 6.

been christened the "Crushing Dynasty Theory" by *Sports Illustrated,*[1] which was once told by Washington Redskin president Edward Bennett Williams, "If you didn't have the option clause you wouldn't have a league." [2] This dire prediction is predicated on two assumptions, at least one of which may well be true. The assumptions are that (1) the wealthy teams would in fact "buy up the . . . best players," [3] to use Pete Rozelle's words, and (2) the resulting imbalance in the strengths of the teams would lead to drastically diminished attendance.

It is the second of these assumptions that seems to have been documented. The House of Representatives Report on Organized Baseball published in 1952,[4] stated that a a club that wins 63% of its games will draw twice as many fans as it would draw if it won 42% of its games, and three times as many fans as it would draw if it won only 25%.[5]

On the other hand, what is good for a single team is not necessarily good for the entire league. The league as a whole will derive 50% more revenue from gate receipts if its pennant winner wins 57½% of its games rather than 75% of them.[6] This principle was apparently at work in 1968 when that year's runaway National League pennant race cost the League an estimated $50,000 a day in lost gate receipts.[7]

---

1 Brown, Because of a Clause, A Cause, Sports Illustrated, May 1, 1972, Pg. 62.

2 *Id.*

3 Playboy Interview: Pete Rozelle, Playboy Magazine, Oct. 1973 at 78.

4 H.Rep. 2002, 82d Con., 2d Sess. (1952).

5 *Id.* at 103.

6 *Id.* at 104.

7 Sports Illustrated, Aug. 19, 1968, Pg. 19.

National Football League executives are fond of pointing to the old and defunct All-America Conference which is now but a footnote in sports history at least in part because the Cleveland Browns beat all of the other teams in that league so easily that fans stopped coming to any of their games.[8]

It is also believed that team balance is necessary to maintain the high value of television broadcast rights, particularly in football where all of the games are sold to the networks in a package years in advance. Though the networks do not know what games in particular they will be showing, they are nevertheless willing to buy broadcast rights "because of the old cliché that any team can win on any given day."[9]

Another reason cited in support of the need for reserve and option systems is that, "Certain cities like New York, Los Angeles and Chicago, in that order, would always be favored because they can offer tremendous fringe benefits to a player. Weather and glamour would be important factors in attracting top players to Miami, New Orleans and San Francisco."[10]

Despite these often repeated arguments, the Crushing Dynasty Theory is not subscribed to by many who view reserve and option systems through the eyes of players. Ed Garvey, Executive Director of the National Football League Players' Association, called it "crazy" to say that the wealthy owners would hire all the best players. "We assume the owners are reasonable businessmen, in football to make a profit. They're not going to throw in a lot of their money—money not generated by the game—to buy

[8] Playboy Interview, *supra* note 3, at 78.

[9] Brown, *supra* note 1.

[10] ***Id.***

a super team. It wouldn't make sense from a business point of view," he has said.[11] George Burman, then a Washington Redskin center and a Ph.D. candidate in Labor Economics, expressed the view that no owner "would be willing to build a dynasty, and keep it, in a dying industry. An NFL franchise now goes for $20 million. What owner would want to see the value of his franchise drop to $3 million or to zero?" [12]

Furthermore, the assumption that the wealthiest and best teams would always be willing to offer the most pay is not supported by example. In football, players may switch teams under current contract provisions and league rules, after playing out their options. Not many years ago, quarterback Joe Kapp left the Minnesota Vikings for what was then one of the worst teams in the NFL, the New England Patriots. Apparently, because of the Patriots' special need for him, they were prepared to make him the best offer.[13]

Roger Noll and Benjamin Okner, both economists with The Brookings Institution at the time, testified before the Senate Subcommittee on Antitrust and Monopoly while it was considering the Basketball Merger Bill, and they explained why they believed wealthy teams would not hire all of the best players.

> "[A] good player is worth more to a poor team, all other things being equal. While New York will have more good players, on average, than Memphis, they will not have them all, for the first good player in Memphis will have a greater impact on team revenues

[11] Maher, Sports' Option Clause: The Issue Is Freedom, L.A. Times, June 29, 1972, Part III, Pg. 1, at 13.

[12] Brown, *supra* note 1.

[13] See § 2.4(b)(1).

than adding another star to a star-studded New York team. What the final balance of talent will be is difficult to understand, but it will never be a situation in which most teams are completely uncompetitive, for that costs both the bad and the good teams fan interest and revenues." [14]

Furthermore, it seems baseless to presume that all players will invariably go to the team offering top dollar, if it means being second or third string as well. Professional athletes have a great deal of personal pride, and it seems very likely that many if not most of them would prefer to be a starter at less salary rather than a bench-warmer at more. Indeed, in the judgment of John Mackey, former president of the NFL Players' Association, "The biggest movement you'd see [if the option clause was done away with] would be by players who are now sitting on the bench. A lot of them haven't been treated too well by management. A conservative guess is that there are 25 or 30 backup guys [in the NFL] who could be starters on other clubs." [15]

While it is true that some cities are more desirable to live in than others, even cities will have only a limited influence on players' team choices. In the words of Ed Garvey, ". . . how many superstars can L.A. absorb? Alan Page is a big name in Minneapolis. If he moved to L.A., with all the superstars on the Lakers, Rams and Dodgers, he'd be another ballplayer." [16] Moreover, as George Burman has pointed out, professional athletes,

---

[14] Hearings on S.2373 before the Subcomm. on Antitrust and Monopoly of the Sen. Comm. on the Judiciary, 92d Cong., 1st Sess. 388 (1971).

[15] Brown, *supra* note 1, at 67.

[16] Maher, *supra* note 11, at 13.

like most other people, do not want to continuously move their homes from city to city.[17] In fact, that was one of the reasons Curt Flood did not want to be traded to Philadelphia, even though the Phillies offered him more money than he had been paid in St. Louis.

According to Burman, humane treatment by coaches and management is also an important factor in determining where athletes like to play. "Right now," he said in 1972, "coaches like George Allen, Don Shula, Tommy Prothro, Dick Nolan, and a few others, would have a tremendous advantage in a competitive market. They treat their players like grown men." [18]

§2.6(b) Anti-cheating protection

A second reason sometimes given in support of the need for option and reserve systems relates to the anathema of all sports, cheating. The contention has been made that reserve and option systems protect the integrity of professional sports by preventing suspicions and accusations that might otherwise occur should a player have a bad day against a team which thereafter hired him. Apparently such accusations were in fact made in the nineteenth century, before baseball adopted the first reserve clause.[1]

Modern proponents of this theory have carefully phrased it in terms of preventing suspicion and accusation, rather than preventing cheating itself; because to suggest that reserve and options systems prevent cheating would be to suggest that some professional athletes have a propensity for felonious conduct. Rather, the argument is that all

[17] Brown, *supra* note 1, at 67.

[18] *Id.*

[1] H.Rep. 2002, 82d Cong., 2d Sess. 213-214 (1952).

athletes, even superstars, have occasional bad days on which they do not perform as well as expected. Should a player be hired the next season by a team which did better than expected because the player had a bad day against it the season before, some people might suspect that the player's poor performance was arranged in advance between the player and his future team.

Using reserve and option systems to prevent such suspicions from arising is overcaution in the extreme. Gambling scandals involving athletes have been rare. This is undoubtedly due in major part to the personal integrity of all of the people involved in professional sports and in part to their recognition that gambling by participants can virtually destroy the sport involved by loss of its audience. (If the result is to be preordained, the Harlem Globetrotters provide far better entertainment than teams using conventional play techniques.) All leagues in all sports have rules and contract provisions prohibiting gambling, and the authority of league executives to bar gamblers from further participation has been upheld in the face of court attacks.[2] Furthermore, at least some professional leagues have personal security personnel whose jobs include policing the sport and investigating rumors. The National Football League, for example, spends $200,000 per year on its security department.[3]

Nevertheless, suspicions do arise on occasion, sometimes from the most unlikely sources. Pete Rozelle was once asked by an interviewer why—in view of the NFL's oppo-

---

[2] Molinas v. Podoloff, 133 N.Y.S.2d 743 (1954), discussed in § 7.3(b)(1), *infra*; Molinas v. National Basketball Assn., 190 F.Supp. 241 (S.D.N.Y. 1961), discussed in §§ 7.3(e)(1) and 7.3(e)(2)(C), *infra*.

[3] Playboy Interview: Pete Rozelle, Playboy Magazine, Oct. 1973 at 80.

sition to legalized gambling on football games—the League supplies newspapers with weekly injury lists "which are invaluable aids to bettors."[4] The reason it is done is to avoid suspicion that people involved in the NFL are gambling, not to aid gamblers, Rozelle explained.

> "If we didn't force the clubs to disclose injuries, inside information about disabled players would almost certainly seep to gambling interests, and then heavy money would be placed the other way on a given game. The game might then be taken off the boards, meaning that bookmakers wouldn't accept bets on it. Whenever that happens, it creates suspicion about the honesty of our games; we make spot checks with bookmakers about three times a week to see what the point spreads are, and if we learn that bookies aren't accepting bets on a specific game, we immediately investigate. Normally, these things have to do with an injury situation, and that's why we force disclosure: so there can't be inside information for gamblers to act upon."[5]

Another example of unfounded suspicion came at the end of the 1958 NFL championship game between the New York Giants and the Baltimore Colts. The game's regular period of play had run out with the score tied, thus pushing it into a sudden-death overtime to be won by the team that first broke the tie with any number of points. The Colts drove into field goal range, but instead of attempting that three-point play they went instead for a six-point touchdown, which they scored. Because they had won by scoring a touchdown, the suspicion arose that Colt owner Carroll Rosenbloom had ordered his team to go for the six points,

[4] *Id.*

[5] *Id.*

rather than the easier three, in order to win a big bet he had allegedly made on his team that required a greater than three-point victory.[6] What many of the suspicious apparently had forgotten was that the Colts scored their game winning touchdown on third down, so that even had they not scored on that touchdown attempt play, they still would have had one more down in which to attempt a field goal. Had they attempted a field goal on third down and missed, they would not have had another chance to score on that sequence of downs.

In sum, gambling is prohibited and is policed, and suspicions can and have arisen from irrational sources and even from league efforts to dispel it. Thus, using reserve and option systems to dispel suspicion, particularly on the theory that players will be suspected of cheating for future employers, is an unnecessary, ineffectual and overly burdensome thing to do.

§2.6(c) Uproar and chaos prevention

A third reason occasionally offered in support of reserve and option systems is that they have a stabilizing effect on sports. According to this theory, they prevent players from putting themselves on the auction block each year, thereby preventing the "chaos" that would ensue from open bidding for players at the end of every season. Proponents of this theory also contend that reserve and option systems are necessary to develop team continuity and fan identification. One "informed" but otherwise unidentified "baseball man" once told a reporter that baseball could not survive even using the sort of option clause and compensation rule used by the National Football League. He said,

---

[6] *Id.*

"... suppose I'm Cincinnati and the player is Johnny Bench. Suppose he goes to San Diego. What's San Diego going to give me for Bench? I wouldn't take their whole team for Bench! You know the uproar that would take place in Cincinnati if I lost a player like that?"[1]

The Chaos and Uproar Theory might have been persuasive had the leagues also prohibited teams from trading players amongst themselves. Since teams do trade and sell players, however, there is in fact an "auction block" each year, and it does in fact cause chaos—for the players. The only reason owners do not perceive the auction as creating chaos is because they—and not the players—are the auctioneers. Furthermore, teams have traded players despite community "uproar" when they deemed it in their own best interests to do so. Thus, the Chaos and Uproar Theory does not seem particularly persuasive either.

§2.6(d) Salary restraint

A fourth reason for reserve and option clauses—holding down player salaries—is rarely mentioned today, though it was the reason that led to the creation of the first reserve system. Following a meeting of National League owners on September 29, 1879, the League announced,

"The financial results of the past season prove that salaries must come down. We believe that players in insisting on exorbitant prices are injuring their own interests by forcing out of existence clubs which cannot be run and pay large salaries except at a

[1] Maher, Sports' Option Clause: The Issue Is Freedom, L.A. Times, June 29, 1972, Part III, p. 1, at 14.

> large personal loss. The season financially has been a little better than 1878; but the expenses of many clubs have far exceeded their receipts, attributable wholly to large salaries. In view of these facts, measures have been taken by this league to remedy the evil to some extent in 1880."[1]

The reserve rule adopted by the National League had the effect of actually cutting salaries in 1880 and again in 1881, at which time the rival American Association was formed and salaries again rose.[2]

It has been reported that NFL players and owners believe that if the Rozelle Rule were done away with, player salaries in the NFL would increase 15 or 20%.[3] From the players' point of view, that is one good reason for doing away with it.

Some people think that doing away with reserve and option systems would actually tend to equalize team playing strengths, because second or third-string players who could start on other teams would make the move, thereby strengthening those teams, while weakening teams which have two or more first-string caliber players at a single position.[4]

Finally, Senator Ervin sees another reason to do away with such systems.

> "The reserve clause denies players their freedom of contract, a liberty guaranteed through both the Fifth and Fourteenth Amendments to the U.S. Constitution.

---

[1] H.Rep. 2002, 82d Cong., 2d Sess. 22 (1952).

[2] *Id.* at 22-26.

[3] Brown, Because of a Clause, a Cause, Sports Illustrated, May 1, 1972, Pg. 62, at 67.

[4] *Id.*

The reserve clause reduces a human being to a chattel, a possession like a piece of furniture. Management may sell a man, trade him for another piece of property, or dump him on the open market when it considers him of no more value. The player isn't a human being any more, just a depreciating asset like a machine. I am shocked by anyone who would want to put another human being under such legal obligation in order to maximize his dollar return. It's downright inconsistent with the principles of free enterprise competition, and with the basic virtues that sports are supposed to exemplify."[5]

§2.7 Alternatives to present systems

Though all of the arguments in favor of reserve and option systems can be answered, and though there are reasons for doing away with them, there does not exist a consensus—even among professional athletes—for scrapping the systems entirely. The 1952 House of Representatives Report on Organized Baseball concluded that on the basis of the evidence reviewed in it, professional baseball could not operate successfully and profitably without some form of reserve clause.[1] Similarly, Judge Cooper, before whom Curt Flood's suit was tried, stated,

> "Prior to trial we gained the impression that there was a view, held by many, that baseball's reserve system had occasioned rampant abuse and that it should be abolished."[2]

---

[5] Ervin, What Congress Must Do About Professional Sports, Sport Magazine, March 1972, reprinted in Hearings on S. 2373 before the Subcomm. on Antitrust and Monopoly of the Sen. Comm. on the Judiciary, 92d Cong., 2d Sess. (1971-1972), at 1270, 1271.

[1] H.Rep. 2002, 82d Cong., 2d Sess. 208 (1952).

[2] Flood v. Kuhn, 316 F.Supp. 271, 276 (S.D.N.Y. 1970).

Indeed, in his earlier opinion denying Flood's request for a preliminary injunction, Judge Cooper had said, ". . . the baseball reserve rule appears excessively restrictive. . . ."[3] But, after trial, Judge Cooper stated,

> "We were struck by the fact, however, that the testimony at trial failed to support that criticism; we find no general or widespread disregard of the extremely important position the player occupies.
>
> "Clearly the preponderance of credible proof does not favor elimination of the reserve clause. With the sole exception of [Flood] himself [who testified that he wanted the whole system struck down and declared illegal because he believed no provision in it to be beneficial to the players or to Organized Baseball], it shows that even [Flood's] witnesses do not contend that it is wholly undesirable; in fact they regard substantial portions meritorious."[4]

Jackie Robinson, a witness on Flood's behalf, testified that he favored modification, but not destruction, of the reserve system. And Hank Greenberg, another of Flood's witnesses, testified that he thought that the players recognized that clubs have some equity in their services.[5]

Similarly, a poll of the 1200 members of the NFL Players' Association, taken in 1971, found that 7% wanted no change in football's option system, 62% wanted it modified, while only 31% wanted it eliminated altogether.[6]

---

[3] Flood v. Kuhn, 309 F.Supp. 793, 801 fn. 26 (S.D.N.Y. 1970).

[4] Flood v. Kuhn, *supra* note 2, at 276.

[5] *Id.*

[6] Brown, Because of a Clause, a Cause, Sports Illustrated, May 1, 1972, Pg. 62, at 67.

There are in fact several possible modifications, the exact number depending upon which of the several leagues' systems one is considering.

§2.7(a) Independent competitive leagues

Independent leagues now exist in basketball and hockey and existed recently in football, and the resulting competition for players substantially improved not only player salaries, but also fringe benefits such as pension and insurance plans, and even the quality of travel accommodations. Of course, within each of the competing leagues, players are restricted to dealing with a single team, so that the total number of potential employers is still only two. But the threat of signing with the other league has often prompted teams to make a trade desired by the player, as a condition to joining or staying in a particular league. National championship games between the top-ranked team in each of the competing leagues would be perfectly legal, even though they may be independent of one another in every respect.

§2.7(b) Limitation of control to a fixed term

Limiting a club's control over a player to a fixed term could be accomplished by the adoption of a multi-year contract without any reserve or option clause. Because the average professional athletic career is short—4½ years in professional football, 7 years in basketball, 5 years in baseball—teams could, in most cases, realize all of the benefits of even a perpetual reserve system simply by signing players to four or five year contracts. Multi-year contracts are common in other industries, and though many players would retire before the expiration of the term of their contracts, and thus not attain free agent status, the feeling of being a chattel might disappear.

§2.7(c) Free agent status following option years

As owners and league executives so often point out, option clauses are very common in contracts of all types. It is the compensation rule, called the "Rozelle Rule" in football, which distinguishes the sports option from others and which prevents players from being true free agents at the conclusion of the option year.[1] Thus, it has been suggested that player contracts continue to have one-year option clauses in them, so that each contract executed by an athlete would extend his team's option on his services for another season. Because teams could and would make salary increases dependent upon the player's signing a new contract, teams would retain their player options, except in those cases where players were so dissatisfied that they were prepared to go without a raise, or even take a cut in pay as some player contracts are written now, in order to become a free agent at the conclusion of the option year. Having once played out the option, however, the absence of a compensation rule would make the player's free agent status meaningful, because he could freely seek employment with other teams, without those other teams being concerned that they might have to give up stars from their own rosters or first round draft rights. A possible refinement to this suggestion might be to grant a player's former team a right of first refusal by permitting it to match any offer made to the player by another team.

§2.7(d) Trade veto for veteran players

The act which sparked Curt Flood's attack on the reserve system was his being traded by the Cardinals to the Phillies without his consent or knowledge, after he had

[1] See, e.g., §§ 2.2(c)(1) and 2.2(d)(1), *supra*.

spent twelve years of his life living in St. Louis. A trade veto for veterans would simply have given Flood the right to know of the proposed trade in advance and to say no to it. Of course, if a player is no longer of great use to his former team, there would be no requirement that the team pay him as much money as it paid the year before or even that it keep him on the team at all. But, the theory behind the veteran trade veto suggestion is that once a player has devoted a certain number of years to a sport, he should have some control over his destiny; and if his former team does not want him any longer, he should be made a free agent unless he is traded someplace acceptable to him.

Interestingly, though Flood lost his lawsuit, in 1973 Organized Baseball adopted a trade veto for veterans. Now, a player with 10 years in professional baseball, the last 5 with one club, cannot be traded without his consent. Less than two months after the trade veto was adopted, Ron Santo of the Chicago Cubs vetoed a proposed trade that would have sent him to the California Angels after 14 years with the Cubs. He did not want to leave Chicago because he had business interests there. "This is a difficult situation," he acknowledged. "Now I know they want to get rid of me." [1] Nevertheless, he told the Cub management that he preferred to remain with the organization in any capacity that would be in the best interests of the team. He did say, however, that he would be willing to go to the Chicago White Sox, because that would permit him to stay in the city. Shortly thereafter, he was in fact traded to the White Sox. Similarly, when Willy McCovey of the San Francisco Giants was told the team wanted to trade him, McCovey told the Giants which teams he would not go to.

[1] L.A. Times, Dec. 5, 1973, Part III, at Pg. 6.

The San Diego Padres was one of the acceptable ones, and that is where he was in fact traded in a deal that was satisfactory to him and both teams.[2]

§2.7(e) Minimum salary progression

In 1969, 109 of the 600 major league baseball players earned only the minimum salary specified in their collective bargaining agreement,[1] and thus the primary concern of many players with the reserve system is its effect on their pay. The reserve and option systems used in all sports not only do not provide for salary increases, some permit teams to exercise their reserve or option rights while simultaneously reducing an athlete's salary. It has been suggested that reserve and option rights ought to be granted teams only if they are willing to increase the player's salary from the year before; and if the teams are not willing to do so, the player should become a free agent able to negotiate with all other teams. This proposal too could be coupled with a right of first refusal for the original team.

§2.7(f) Reduction in number of reserved players

As reserve and option systems now work, each team has future rights to at least all of the players on its current playing roster, and usually many other players as well (some minor leaguers, retired players, injured players, and drafted but unsigned athletes, for example). There is no immutable logic which requires reserve and option systems to operate on an all-or-nothing basis however. League by-laws could be amended to provide that each team may enter into player contracts containing option

---

[2] *Id.*

[1] Brief for Petitioner, Flood v. Kuhn, 407 U.S. 258 (1972), discussed in § 1.3(b), *supra.*

clauses with only a specified number of athletes, and all other players must be offered contracts without such clauses in them. This might result in some unfairness to the superstars who are most likely to be reserved. But the indications are that the superstars are less affected than their teammates—at least in terms of salary—by reserve and option systems. Even with a reserve system and no competitive league to turn to, Curt Flood earned $90,000 for the 1969 season and was offered $100,000 by Philadelphia for 1970.

§2.7(g) Salary arbitration

Again despite Flood's loss in the courts, salary arbitration is a proposal that was adopted by Organized Baseball in 1973. It was also adopted by the National Hockey League in 1972, by the World Hockey Association when it was formed in 1972, and by the World Football League when it was formed in 1974. In the National Football League and in basketball, players and owners simply negotiate salary prior to the execution of each new contract. In basketball, players can—after playing or sitting out their options—join teams in the opposite league, and that has provided them with a good measure of bargaining power. In baseball and hockey, however, a third person can be called into the push-and-pull of salary negotiations, the neutral arbitrator. Particularly in baseball, where no rival leagues exist, the arbitrator should be of real assistance to players in the salary determining process, even though the reserve system remains.[1]

§2.7(h) Revenue division between clubs

More equalized division of revenues between clubs is the most radical of the proposed alternatives, because it

[1] See § 2.2(a), *supra,* for description of the baseball arbitration system.

contemplates doing away with reserve and option systems altogether and replacing them with a method designed to provide all teams in a league with the means to compete financially for players on a more equal basis. The primary justification for reserve and option systems is equalization of team playing strengths. Without these systems, it is said, the wealthiest franchises would buy up all the best players. Of course, a franchise can be "wealthy" because its owner has personal wealth derived from other sources. Equalizing the wealth of team owners is obviously not possible through changes in league rules or practices. But teams can be wealthy or poor as well, because of the amount of income generated by club operations themselves.

In all sports, the primary source of income is gate receipts. (Television and radio broadcast rights also bring in substantial sums, particularly in football. The amount of parking and concession income varies from sport to sport, and even within a single sport depending upon the particular contractual arrangements made by the teams with stadia or arena owners.) In the National Football League, the gate proceeds are divided 60% to the home team and 40% to the visiting team.[1] In baseball, the gate proceeds are divided 80%—20%.[2] And in basketball, the live gate is divided 94% to the home team, 6% to the league Commissioner's office, and nothing to the visiting team.[3] Since some teams enjoy larger stadia or arenas than others, and since some teams enjoy a greater following than others, the more equally the gate proceeds are divided, the more equal the teams' financial strengths are

[1] NFL Constitution and By-Laws, Article XIX.

[2] S.Rep. 92-1151, 92d Cong., 2d Sess. 5 (1972).

[3] *Id.*

going to be. Many believe that the NFL's 60-40 split is the league practice most responsible for football's financial health, and that basketball's 94-6-0 split is most responsible for basketball's financial spotiness.[4]

The theory behind the proposal to do away with reserve and option systems and replace them with fairly equal divisions of revenues is that by doing so all teams will have a more equal financial opportunity to bid for the services of the players they need. Radical though this proposal is, it was in fact the one insisted upon by the Senate Judiciary Committee as a condition to its approval of the proposed Basketball Merger Bill. The minimum division called for by amendments made in Committee to the Basketball Merger Bill was 70-30, with reserve or option clauses prohibited under penalty of fine and imprisonment.[5]

§2.7(i) Comments by owners and league officials

Could professional sports live with any of these proposed modifications? Judging only from the public statements of league officials, the answer would appear to be "no." For example, Clarence Campbell, president of the National Hockey League, was once asked whether the NHL was in a position to make concessions on player control. His answer was, "I don't see how."[1] (He also added, incredibly it seems, "I don't see any reason we'd need to, or why the players would want us to. Outside of

[4] See, e.g., Testimony of Roger Noll and Benjamin Okner in Hearings on S. 2373 before the Subcomm. on Antitrust and Monopoly of the Sen. Comm. on the Judiciary, 92d Cong., 1st and 2d Sess. (1971-1972) at 340-419, 1125-1128.

[5] S.Rep. 92-1151, *supra* note 2, at 4.

[1] Maher, Sports' Option Clause: The Issue Is Freedom, L.A. Times, June 29, 1972, Part III, Pg. 1, at 14.

the clash of personalities, I know of no reason a hockey player would want to be free."[2]) Yet, less than a year and a half after making that statement, the National Hockey League did in fact do away with its reserve system, and it adopted in its place a football-type option system not nearly as restrictive as the one Campbell said was needed. Similarly, baseball adopted two of the changes that had been asked for by the players in Curt Flood's case, without apparent damage to that sport.

It seems that what is possible in professional sports is determined more accurately by what leagues have in fact done than by what their executives have said. Or perhaps sports' mavericks should be consulted for insight, rather than its brahmins. Sam Schulman, part owner of the Seattle Supersonics of the NBA and the San Diego Chargers of the NFL, and a premier maverick,[3] once told a reporter,

> "It is my feeling that sports would be better off with no reserve clauses. There is no reason why athletes should be chattels of the owners. Every performer should be free to negotiate for himself as people do in other businesses. If a guy in any sport doesn't want to play for Seattle or Los Angeles or Buffalo, or any other team, why should he be made to do so because the owners have decided that reserve clauses are good for the game? If all reserve clauses were thrown out, you would find after a while that everything would level off and no significant changes would be made." [4]

---

[2] *Id.*

[3] See § 8.2(a), *infra.*

[4] Quoted in Brief for Petitioner, Flood v. Kuhn, 407 U.S. 258 (1972), discussed in § 1.3(b), *supra.*

When asked what would happen to an owner if richer ones decided to gather up all the talent, Schulman replied,

> "He would be left with a choice. He would compete the best way he could or get out of sports. In other businesses of mine, I sign people to contracts of maybe one to five years. At the end of that time, they are free to stay or move elsewhere. And life goes on. It would no different in sports." [5]

---

[5] *Id.*

Chapter 3
THE PLAYER DRAFT

§3.1 Current draft rules

Whenever there exists a pool of players to be divided into teams of equal size, some form of choosing up sides must take place. At the professional level, a pool is created every year when high school and college athletes graduate, and the player draft is the means by which sides are chosen.

Generally speaking, each professional league holds an annual player selection meeting at which teams select—in rounds, and in inverse order to the previous season's league standings—those amateurs who appear from scouting reports or national reputation to have professional potential. Then, by league rule, each team has the exclusive right to negotiate with and hire those players selected by it. Unless there is a competing league, if a player is unable to reach agreement on the terms of his employment with the team that drafted him, or if he simply does not want to live in the home city of that team, he is usually in the same general position as the dissatisfied reserved veteran. He can go into another profession.

The precise details of the ways in which the various professional leagues conduct their drafts vary somewhat. And as is so often the case in the law, the distinctions between the various plans are as helpful as their similarities in gaining an understanding of the nature and significance of the drafting process.

§3.1(a) National Basketball Association

The National Basketball Association holds its annual draft in the spring, at the end of each season. The team with the poorest won-lost record during the season just concluded selects first, with the other teams selecting thereafter in inverse order of their won-lost percentages. After each team has selected one player, successive rounds are conducted the same way until a majority of the teams vote to end the meeting.[1] Prior to the *Spencer Haywood* case,[2] the only players who were eligible to be drafted were those college students whose classes were to be graduated during the June immediately following the draft; college students whose classes had already graduated; and non-college students who had graduated from high school four years before.

In response to the *Haywood* decision, the NBA adopted a "hardship exemption" to its usual eligibility requirements.[3] In May of 1976, it relaxed its eligibility standards still further. Now, any player whose high school class has graduated, may become eligible for selection in the NBA draft simply by giving the League written notice at least 45 days in advance renouncing his collegiate eligibility.[4]

As a result of the settlement of the *Oscar Robertson* case,[5] the duration of a team's draft rights were changed in May of 1976 as well. Now, draft rights last one year only. If the player is not signed during that year, he may be redrafted the following spring by another team. And if he does not sign with that team for a year, he becomes a free agent the next.[6]

---

[1] NBA Constitution and By-Laws, Article VI.

[2] Denver Rockets v. All-Pro Management, Inc., 325 F.Supp. 1049 (C.D.Cal. 1971), discussed in § 7.3(e)(2)(A), *infra.*

[3] See § 7.3(e)(2)(A)(v), *infra.*

[4] L.A. Times, May 4, 1976, Part III.

[5] Robertson v. National Basketball Association, 389 F.Supp. 867 (S.D.N.Y. 1975), discussed in § 2.4(b)(2), *supra.*

[6] L.A. Times, Feb. 4, 1976, Part III.

§3.1(b) American Basketball Association

The wording of the American Basketball Association by-laws concerning the draft and eligibility is quite different from that of the NBA by-laws, but the effect is virtually identical. One significant difference that existed prior to the *Haywood* case,[1] was that the ABA by-laws provide that "in special circumstances" the ABA may waive eligibility requirements, thereby qualifying players for employment in that league who would not otherwise be eligible.[2] Prior to the *Haywood* case, the NBA by-laws had no such waiver provision.

§3.1(c) National Football League

The National Football League holds its annual draft meeting in January, shortly after the Super Bowl. The team with the poorest won-lost record selects first in each round, the others selecting thereafter in inverse order to their standings according to their regular season won-lost records, with the Super Bowl victor selecting last, and the Super Bowl loser selecting next-to-last. The NFL conducts 17 rounds, and any player not drafted during those rounds is considered a free agent and may be negotiated with by all teams and hired by any.[1] Players eligible to be drafted are those who will have graduated by the following September 1st, those whose college football eligibility has expired, and those who first entered college at least five years before.[2]

---

[1] Denver Rockets v. All-Pro Management, Inc., 325 F.Supp. 1049 (C.D.Cal. 1971).

[2] ABA By-Laws, Article XV, § 5.

[1] NFL Constitution and By-Laws, Article XIV.

[2] NFL Constitution and By-Laws, Article XII.

§3.1(d) Organized Baseball

Organized Baseball holds two drafts each year, one in January and the other in June. There are two significant differences between the baseball draft and the football and basketball drafts. First, any player who is still unsigned by the team that drafted him automatically returns to the draft pool and may be redrafted by another team[1] when the next draft meeting takes place approximately six months later. This, of course, is of tremendous theoretical benefit to the players, because they are not compelled to reach agreement with just any team or on any terms offered. On the other hand, unsigned players drafted at the June selection meeting who wait out the months until the following January do so at the cost of missing an entire season, which, it seems safe to say, would be a prohibitively expensive price to pay for most baseball draftees. This is particularly so because, unlike the practice in basketball and football, baseball players become eligible for the professional draft upon their graduation from high school. However, if a high school graduate enrolls in college without signing a baseball contract, he becomes ineligible again until his 21st birthday, after which he may be redrafted.[2] (Major league teams also draft players from the minors. However, inasmuch as minor leaguers are already signed to professional contracts containing reserve clauses, the draft of minor leaguers is the equivalent of a player trade or sale, and thus gives rise to the same issues discussed in the previous chapter.)

---

[1] Hearings on H.R. 1206 et al., before Antitrust Subcommittee of House Comm. on the Judiciary, 92d Cong., 2d Sess. 195 (1972).

[2] *Id.* at 177.

§3.1(e) National Hockey League

The National Hockey League conducts an annual draft of amateur players who reach 20 years of age by January 1st of the following season. Unlike football, basketball and baseball, hockey eligibility requirements make no mention of college or high school graduation, because most amateur hockey is played in leagues, usually supported financially by the NHL, that are not affiliated with schools. Once drafted, an amateur is the exclusive property of the team that selects him for so long as that team offers him employment, either in the NHL or as a member of one of its affiliated minor league teams.[1] (NHL teams also draft players from the minor leagues, from other NHL teams, and may have their players drafted from them by minor league teams under certain circumstances. Again, because all professional hockey players in the NHL and its affiliated minor leagues are signed to contracts containing option clauses, these drafts are equivalent to trades or sales, and the issues that arise from them are the same as those discussed in the previous chapter.)

§3.2 Purposes of draft

§3.2(a) Equalization of team playing strengths

The player draft serves essentially two purposes. The principal purpose asserted in support of the draft by team owners and league officials is that the draft is designed to equalize the playing strengths of the teams within a league. As is said with respect to the need for

---

[1] **Philadelphia World Hockey Club, Inc. v. Philadelphia Hockey Club, Inc., 351 F.Supp. 462, 477-479 (E.D.Pa. 1972); NHL By-Laws § 16B5(b).**

reserve and option systems,[1] owners and league officials contend that in the absence of a player draft, the wealthiest teams would hire the most promising amateur talent, thereby perpetuating their playing-field success and with that, their wealth. Indeed, prior to 1965, Organized Baseball had no amateur draft. All of the teams in both the National and American Leagues bid against one another for the services of the most outstanding high school graduates each year. And when critics of baseball's reserve clause argued that the phenomenal success of the New York Yankees was evidence that the reserve system did not equalize playing strengths, baseball executives responded by blaming the Yankees' success on the absence of a draft and the Yankees' hiring of all the best high school players.[2]

§3.2(b) Salary restraint

A second but less frequently cited reason for the player draft is that it serves to hold down player salaries. Simple principles of elementary economics suggest that a seller will receive a higher price for his product if he has two or more potential buyers bidding for it than if he has only one. In those sports where only one league exists, a player who has been drafted can be hired only by one team. If the player believes the salary offered by that one team is too low, but the team refuses to increase its offer, the player has no choice but to accept the team's offer or enter some other profession. In 1969, more than one-sixth of all major league baseball players,

---

[1] See § 2.6(a), *supra.*

[2] See, e.g., Letter, dated Sept. 18, 1972, from Baseball Commissioner Bowie Kuhn to Congressman Emanuel Celler, published in Hearings on H.R. 1206, et al., before the Antitrust Subcomm. of the House Comm. on the Judiciary, 92d Cong., 2d Sess. 194 (1972).

including veterans, were paid only the minimum salary called for by the collective bargaining agreement that had been negotiated by their Players' Association.[1]

§3.3 Extent to which purposes are realized

§3.3(a) Equalization of team playing strengths

The extent to which these various purposes are—or should be—actually fulfilled has been the subject of vigorous debate. There is little agreement even on the extent to which the draft serves to equalize the playing strengths of teams within a single league. For example, football player John Mackey, in testimony before the Senate Subcommittee on Antitrust and Monopoly, expressed the opinion that the draft was unimportant in equalizing team playing strengths.[1]

Mackey's analysis was that the team that finishes last in the NFL picks first in the first round of the NFL draft, while the Super Bowl winner picks last. That means that the last place team makes the first selection, while the Super Bowl winner makes the 26th selection. The last place team then begins round two by making the 27th selection, and in due course the Super Bowl winner picks 52nd. While the last place team has an advantage over the Super Bowl winner in each round, the draft lasts 17 rounds, and on 16 occasions the last place team actually makes its selection immediately after the Super Bowl winner. By finishing last, a team gets to make selections 1, 27, 53, 79, 105, 131, and so forth, while the Super Bowl winner gets to make selections

[1] Brief for Petitioner, Flood v. Kuhn, 407 U.S. 258 (1972).

[1] Hearings on S.2373 before the Subcomm. on Antitrust and Monopoly of the Sen. Comm. on the Judiciary, 92d Cong., 2d Sess. 1296 (1971-1972).

26, 52, 78, 104, 130, and so forth. In other words, as a group, the last place team's 17 selections are little higher, numerically, than the Super Bowl winner's selections. And, as a matter of fact, aside from the first and last selections, the Super Bowl winner actually drafts before the last place team. The only handicap imposed upon the Super Bowl winner is that it must select the final 442nd draft choice, while the last place team does get to pick the first choice in the first round. Presumably the first draft choice will be a better football player than the 442nd, while all of the two teams' other 16 draft choices will be approximately evenly matched players. Thus, the last place team will get only one player better than those received by the Super Bowl winner, and as *New York Times* sportswriter Leonard Koppett remarked in commenting on Mackey's analysis, ". . . that one player . . . isn't closing the gap very much."[2] Koppett believes that it would take at least eight new outstanding players to transform a last place team into a champion, and in order to get eight first draft picks it would have to finish last eight years in a row. Moreover, since the average professional football career lasts only 4½ years, by the time the eighth player joined the team, the first ones would be on their way to retirement. "It is fair to say, then," Koppett concluded,

> "that the draft procedure has no significant effect at all on whether teams are 'evenly matched.' It is purely and simply an economic device to prevent clubs from bidding against one another for talent. As an economic device, it may or may not be justified—but it should be judged entirely in those terms."[3]

---

[2] *Id.*
[3] *Id.* at 1297.

Former football player Bernie Parrish also testified before the Senate Subcommittee on Antitrust and Monopoly, saying of the draft, "The equalization it allegedly produces is incidental and inconsequential."[4] In support of his opinion, he pointed out that of the eight NFL teams to reach the 1971 playoffs, three had quarterbacks who had been signed as free agents, two had tenth round draft choices at quarterback, one had a quarterback who had once been claimed as an expendable player in a new franchise expansion draft, and only two had quarterbacks who had been their number one draft choices. "The much-heralded player draft had little if anything to do with six of the eight best NFL teams acquiring their key player," he concluded.[5]

On the other hand, Baseball Commissioner Bowie Kuhn is of the opinion that "No one can doubt that the free agent draft has in fact accomplished its objective: to improve competition."[6] In a letter to Congressman Emanuel Celler written in the fall of 1972, Kuhn cited these examples of the ways in which he believed the draft had tended to equalize competition in his sport.

> "The Athletics, a hopeless second division team for decades, has become a contender largely because of Reggie Jackson, Rick Monday and Sal Bando, all of whom Oakland was able to select first or second in the draft because of earlier low finishes in the pennant race. The A's became a division winner in 1971 because of the meteoric rise to stardom of another draft pick, by the name of Vida Blue.

[4] *Id.* at 902.

[5] *Id.* at 903.

[6] Hearings on H.R. 1206, et al., before the Antitrust Subcomm. of the House Comm. on the Judiciary, 92d Cong., 2d Sess. 194 (1972).

"Cincinnati, a team that had won only one pennant since 1940, captured the National League flag in 1970, largely because of its selection of Johnny Bench, Gary Nolan, Don Gullett, Wayne Simpson and Bernie Carbo in the draft. Pittsburgh, en route to its second straight championship, has six draftees on its team—Dave Cash, Richie Hebner, Bob Moose, Bruce Kison, Gene Clines and Milt May. The Pirates were also-rans from 1961 until their championship season of 1971.

"Tom Seaver, a draftee, was the biggest single reason for the miracle performed by the New York Mets in capturing the National League pennant and World Series in 1969, after finishing last the year before. Nolan Ryan, Gary Gentry and Jim McAndrew, other starting pitchers on the 1969 Mets, were also draftees.

"On the other hand, the draft was a primary factor in breaking the New York Yankees' dominance of the American League. Until the institution of the draft the Yankees had won 11 of the 13 previous American League pennants. They were able to sign most of the more promising youngsters because of their reputation, tradition and location. They cannot do so under the present system, however, a fact that undoubtedly has contributed to their failure to win a pennant since 1964, the year before the draft was instituted. The fact that the Yankees are contending for the pennant this year results from their finishing at or near the bottom in recent years, thus being able to acquire, via the draft, key players in their current pennant drive like Thurman Munson, Ron Blomberg and Steve Kline." [7]

---

[7] *Id.* at 194-195.

In basketball, the Milwaukee Bucks finished the 1968-1969 season in last place in their division in the NBA and were thus able to draft Kareem Abdul-Jabbar. With and largely because of Jabbar, the Bucks won the NBA title in 1970-1971.

§3.3(b) Salary restraint

The extent to which the player draft has served to hold down player salaries is also disputed. In his 1972 letter to Congressman Celler, Baseball Commissioner Kuhn asserted that ". . . an analysis of player compensation since the institution of the draft in 1965 shows that it has not in fact resulted in smaller bonuses and salaries being paid to new players."[1] The analysis was made in connection with the trial in Curt Flood's lawsuit, and it showed, Kuhn claimed,

> ". . . that while the draft may have resulted in fewer of the enormous bonuses that were paid in the past to a maximum of one or two outstanding new players every year in order to induce them to sign, the initial inducements paid to all new players were, on the average, higher in the years immediately following the institution of the draft than they were in the years immediately before."[2]

The statistical tables submitted to Congressman Celler with Commissioner Kuhn's letter did in fact show that from 1965 through 1968, the average first year salary of all professional baseball players increased each season (from $6333 in 1965 to $7132 in 1968), though it fell in 1969 (to

[1] Hearings on H.R. 1206, et al., before the Antitrust Subcomm. of the House Comm. on the Judiciary, 92d Cong., 2d Sess. 194 (1972).

[2] *Id.*

$6425), the last year for which statistics were submitted. Interestingly, however, this average increase included the salaries of those first year players who had *not* been drafted, as well as those who had. A separate table, not discussed by Kuhn in his letter to Congressman Celler though submitted with it, showed that both the average first year salary and the average bonus paid to drafted players decreased each year (from $10,517 in salary and $9350 in bonuses in 1965 to $9390 in salary and $8142 in bonuses in 1969) with the exception of 1968.[3] Thus it would appear that drafted players did in fact feel the depressing financial effect of the draft, and the only reason the average salaries of all players appeared to increase was because the average salary and bonuses of the non-drafted players increased (as Kuhn's own tables showed they did each season from 1966 through 1968).

The impact of the draft on salaries can also be seen, in part, from a comparison of the average salaries of players in the different sports. According to a survey conducted by the Associated Press in the fall of 1972, the existence of two separate leagues, and thus two separate drafts, in basketball made that sport's athletes by far the highest paid. Separate leagues in professional hockey, which had only existed for a matter of weeks when the survey was made, had already resulted in hockey players being the second most highly paid athletes. Football, whose own inter-league war was halted with a merger in 1966, paid its players the third highest average salaries in that pre-WFL year. And baseball, which had not suffered any competition within the United States in decades, was a distant fourth.[4]

---

[3] *Id.* at 197-198.

[4] L.A. Times, Oct. 18, 1972, Part III, Pg. 1.

Of course, the high salaries in basketball and hockey cannot be attributed solely to the existence of two separate drafts. The ability of veterans to change leagues also drove up their salaries, thus illustrating the financial impact that reserve and option systems have on veterans. And if the draft were the sole cause of the pay differentials between sports, it would be expected that baseball's average salary would be at least equal to football's, because baseball had no draft at all until 1965.

§3.4 Objections to the draft

Objections to the draft are at least twofold. Naturally, players are upset with salary levels that would be higher, but for the draft. In this regard, team owners and league officials have sought to pit the rookies against the veterans by arguing that money spent on "exorbitant" bonuses and salaries for "untried and unproven" rookies leaves just that much less for payment of the salaries of veterans. As Commissioner Kuhn put it in his letter to Congressman Celler, ". . . to the extent the draft reduced amounts spent —frequently unproductively—on large bonuses to untried rookies, dollars were freed up to be paid to experienced players who had proven their abilities in the major leagues."[1] Undoubtedly, many veterans were envious of the large bonuses and salaries some rookies were receiving, but there is no evidence that any substantial number of veterans accepted the owners' contentions that the draft operates to "free up" money for payment of veterans' salaries. Judging from the public statements of the heads of the various players' associations, the feeling among veterans seems to be that any dollars "freed up" by the

[1] Hearings on H.R. 1206, et al., before the Antitrust Subcomm. of the House Comm. on the Judiciary, 92d Cong., 2d Sess. 194 (1972).

draft—and by reserve and option systems, too, for that matter—are finding their way into the paychecks of front office personnel (who are often the owners or their relatives) and into profits as dividends. Indeed, during the trial of Curt Flood's lawsuit, Organized Baseball's own economic expert witness, John Clark, testified that between 1965, when the baseball player draft was first adopted, and 1969, the median player salary increased 17.7%, while front office expenses increased three times as much.[2]

In addition to the economic objection, however, many people object on principle to the entire concept of a player draft. Senator Sam Ervin is one of these. The draft, he said, is ". . . comparable to the newspaper profession deciding that a college journalism graduate could either work for the newspaper in Anchorage, Alaska, at the salary offered or not work at all."[3] Graduating collegians, no less than veterans, often have ties to particular communities they do not want to leave. The draft, like the reserve and option system and the right to trade players, disregards these ties entirely. Because the draft is an amateur's first formal contact with professional athletics, he may begin his career with the feeling—felt by Curt Flood only after he had become a superstar—that in the scheme of professional sports, athletes are simply materials and not human beings.

§3.5 Legality of the player draft

The legality of the player draft has been challenged in actual litigation far less often than reserve and option systems. This is probably because the draft's impact is

[2] Brief for Petitioner, Flood v. Kuhn, 407 U.S. 258 (1972).

[3] Hearings on S.2373 before the Subcomm. on Antitrust and Monopoly of the Senate Comm. on the Judiciary, 92d Cong., 1st Sess. 15 (1971).

felt only once in an athlete's professional career, at the moment of transition from amateur to professional, and then never again. Once an athlete signs a professional contract, the mechanism which controls his employment opportunities thereafter is the reserve or option system.

Furthermore, the point in an athlete's career where the draft has impact is precisely the point where an athlete is least able to object. It is a point of anxious anticipation and eagerness to begin; and thus far, few if any athletes have been prepared to defer their professional careers in order to litigate the legality of the procedure limiting their choice of teams to one per league. Indeed, given the many years such a lawsuit could take, an athlete would actually have to choose litigation rather than sports as a career in order to challenge the draft.

In May of 1975, a classic test case against the draft was filed, but lasted just one week. The case was brought by a veteran superstar, George McGinnis of the American Basketball Association, against the National Basketball Association and all of its members.[1] McGinnis had joined the ABA's Indiana Pacers following his sophomore year; and after four years with that team, he wanted to join the New York Knicks of the NBA. The NBA's Philadelphia 76ers had drafted McGinnis however, when his college class graduated, in accordance with NBA by-laws. Because NBA draft rights are perpetual, the 76ers claimed he was theirs, and that led to McGinnis' lawsuit seeking to invalidate the draft entirely.

The case was dismissed only one week after it had been filed, because despite the 76ers' claims, the Knicks signed McGinnis anyway, giving him a half million dollar bonus

[1] L.A. Times, May 24, 1975, Part III, Pg. 2.

when they did so.[2] A week after that, NBA Commissioner Larry O'Brien declared the Knicks-McGinnis contract invalid,[3] thereby re-establishing test conditions for a new suit. But in July of 1975, McGinnis signed a six year contract with the 76ers after all, wisely choosing to continue his basketball career in lieu of one as a plaintiff. Various newspaper accounts placed the value of his six-year contract at between $2.5 and $3.25 million.[4]

Those who object to the player draft claim that like reserve and option rules, the draft violates the antitrust laws. In 1926, the United States Supreme Court decided a case involving a hiring system substantially similar to the player draft, *Anderson* v. *Shipowners Association of the Pacific Coast*,[5] in a manner which lends support to that claim. Members of the Shipowners Association owned, operated or controlled substantially all merchant vessels registered in the United States engaged in interstate and foreign commerce from Pacific coast ports. The Association had established offices in San Francisco and San Pedro where every seaman seeking employment on ships belonging to members was required to register. Upon registering, seamen were given numbers establishing the order in which they were offered employment. Association regulations required each seaman to accept the employment he was offered, or none at all, without regard to whether or not the particular assignment was suited to his qualifications and without regard to whether the seaman desired to work on the particular ship he had been offered. In a suit brought by a seaman to enjoin continued use of this hiring system and for damages, the Supreme Court ruled

[2] L.A. Times, May 31, 1975, Part III, Pg. 1.

[3] L.A. Times, June 6, 1975, Part III, Pg. 1.

[4] L.A. Times, July 11, 1975, Part III.

[5] 272 U.S. 359 (1926).

that the effect of the system "is precisely what [the Sherman Act] condemns." [6]

The first judicial discussion of the player draft in particular came as recently as 1971, in a preliminary phase of the *Spencer Haywood* case.[7] Haywood had signed with the Seattle Supersonics of the National Basketball Association before he had been drafted by any team in that league. NBA Commissioner Walter Kennedy disapproved the contract (on the grounds that Haywood was ineligible under the league's four-year rule) and threatened the Supersonics with sanctions if they played him. In the course of granting a motion by Haywood for a preliminary injunction barring the NBA from interfering with his employment by the Supersonics, federal District Judge Warren J. Ferguson found that there was a "substantial probability . . . that the so-called 'college draft' system . . . constitutes a violation of the antitrust laws," because it eliminates all competition among teams for players and thereby "constitutes an arbitrary and unreasonable restraint upon the rights of . . . potential NBA players to negotiate freely for the rendition of their services to NBA teams." [8]

Because the *Spencer Haywood* case was settled, it produced no final decision on the draft's legality. Since the settlement, however, both the National Football League and the National Basketball Association drafts have been held illegal in cases of utmost significance. In *Kapp* v. *National Football League,* the NFL draft was held to be

---

[6] *Id.* at 363.

[7] Denver Rockets v. All-Pro Management, Inc., 325 F.Supp. 1049 (C.D.Cal. 1971).

[8] *Id.* at 1056.

> ". . . patently unreasonable insofar as it permits virtually *perpetual* boycott of a draft prospect even when the drafting club refuses or fails within a reasonable time to reach a contract with the player." [9]

And in *Robertson* v. *National Basketball Association,* the NBA draft was similarly held illegal.

> "Among the practices which have been declared *per se* violations of the Sherman Act are horizontal price-fixing at the same level of competition . . . ; territorial division of markets . . . ; and secondary or group boycotts . . . The player draft and perpetual reserve system are readily susceptible to condemnation as group boycotts based on the NBA's concerted refusal to deal with the players save through these uniform restrictive practices. . . The two control mechanisms are also analogous to price-fixing devices condemned as *per se* violative of the Sherman Act, for the draft and a perpetual reserve system allow competing teams to eliminate competition in the hiring of players and invariably lower the cost of doing business. . . In addition the player draft and a perpetual reserve system can be viewed as devices creating illegal horizontal territorial allocations and product market divisions." [10]

While these two opinions held the NFL and NBA drafts —in their present form—to be illegal, they do not necessarily rule out the legality of player drafts in all forms. Of immediate note is Judge Sweigert's own emphasis on the "perpetual" nature of the National Football League

[9] 390 F.Supp. 73, 82 (N.D.Cal. 1974).

[10] 389 F.Supp. 867, 893 (S.D.N.Y. 1975).

draft. Thus, it is possible that even under the *Joe Kapp* case, Organized Baseball's draft may be legal. Its rules permit a drafted but unsigned player to re-enter the draft pool each six months to be re-selected by another team.[11] On the other hand, while a player who wants to join a particular baseball team may re-enter the draft pool as many times as is necessary to permit that team to draft him, this can be done only at the expense of deferring the start of the player's professional career for at least six months, and perhaps a year or more. At the outset of a professional career, a wait of even six months to a year may be a long time. Furthermore, so long as a player may be traded, at least some of the benefits players would derive from eliminating or shortening draft rights could be eliminated at will by the teams.

It is also worth noting that although the *Oscar Robertson* case suggests that player drafts are illegal *per se,* there is a certain narrow exception to the *per se* doctrine which has been discussed in professional sports cases. That exception exists under certain unique circumstances—circumstances which sports leagues may be able to fulfill. When applied, the exception provides that practices which would otherwise be illegal *per se* are instead to be tested by the "rule of reason"; and if found reasonable, they are legal.[12] One of the necessary circumstances is the existence of procedural safeguards for the benefit of the person who would otherwise be the victim of the objected-to practices.[13] Arguably, the National Football League has a by-law which may satisfy this procedural safeguard re-

---

[11] See § 3.1(d), *supra.*

[12] Denver Rockets v. All-Pro Management, Inc., *supra* note 7, at 1064-1065.

[13] *Id.* at 1065.

quirement. Article XIV, Section 14.7 of the NFL Constitution and By-Laws provides,

> "If for any valid reason it would be impossible for a player to play in the city by which he has been selected, or the player can show reasonable cause why he should be permitted to play in a city other than that designated for him, then through such arrangements as can be made by sale or trade with another club, he shall be permitted to play in the city he prefers if the Commissioner of the League approves his reasons as valid."

Thus, NFL by-laws appear to afford newly-drafted players an opportunity to "show cause" why the draft should not apply to them. On the other hand, although the by-law appears to permit a graduating collegian to designate the team with which he wishes to play, if he has a "valid" reason, there is nothing in the NFL by-laws to prevent him from being traded to another team after he has once signed a Standard Player Contract. Since the laudable result of this NFL by-law may be set aside immediately and at will, it hardly seems to satisfy the "procedural safeguard" requirement which must exist before courts may consider the League's arguments as to why its draft is "reasonable" and therefore legal, rather than a *per se* violation of the law.

Chapter 4

PROFESSIONAL SPORTS AND THE LABOR LAWS

§4.1 The metamorphosis of players associations into labor unions

§4.1 (a) Metamorphosis in fact

Today, unions of professional athletes are as familiar a feature in sports as unions of actors in motion pictures, musicians in music, and auto workers in the automobile industry. Football, baseball and basketball have all experienced player strikes. And the names Marvin Miller, Ed Garvey and Larry Fleisher (heads of baseball, football and basketball unions, respectively) are familiar to most readers of the nation's sports pages. Unlike unions in many other fields, however, those in professional sports do not have the words "union" or "united" in their names, nor did they begin their lives as full-fledged or traditional labor organizations. Sports' unions are actually the various Players Associations, and only in recent years have they engaged in the principal function of a union, collective bargaining.

§4.1 (a) (1) Major League Baseball Players Association

Players' unions are not an entirely new phenomenon. As long ago as 1889, the National Brotherhood of Professional Players was organized under the leadership of John Montgomery Ward, a New York ballplayer and later a practicing attorney. A principal goal of the Brotherhood, even then, was the elimination of the reserve rule, and when team owners refused to acquiesce, the Brotherhood formed its own league, aptly called the "Players League." [1]

The Brotherhood, and other baseball-player unions that followed it in the early decades of the twentieth century, "thrived for a fleeting moment, made their impact . . . and then faded into history." [2]

The modern era of sports' labor history begins in 1946, when a former examiner for the National Labor Relations Board named Robert Murphy formed the American Baseball Guild. Among the Guild's stated objectives were a minimum wage of $7500 per year, security, insurance, bonus and other welfare payments, and the submission of disputes between players and management over salaries and other conditions of employment to collective bargaining. Murphy reportedly enrolled members in the Guild during spring training in 1946; and by May of that year, he claimed membership comprising a majority of six major league teams and over 90% of the Pittsburgh Pirates. Collective bargaining was demanded of the Pirate management; and when it refused to bargain or to recognize the Guild as its players' representative, Murphy threatened a strike unless the Pirates would conduct a representation election to determine whether team members in fact wished to be represented by the Guild.[3]

In response to the strike threat, Pirate President William Benswanger told his players that the 1946 season was then upon them, and asked them to please postpone their union activity until it was over. The players responded by voting to strike immediately, unless an election was agreed

---

[1] H.Rep. 2002, 82d Cong., 2d Sess. 32 (1952).

[2] *Id.*

[3] Krasnow & Levy, Unionization and Professional Sports, 51 Georgetown L.J. 749, 762-763 (1963).

to. It was not; but when the players met again two days later, a second vote to begin the strike fell short of the two-thirds majority they had agreed would be necessary.[4] The American Baseball Guild was then at a critical point in its infancy. It existed and had members; but management would neither bargain with it nor recognize it; and not enough of its members were willing to strike to enable it to employ that tactic.

The Guild was not the only union, before or since, to find itself in such a frustrating position. In 1935, Congress determined that,

> "The denial by some employers of the right of employees to organize and the refusal by some employers to accept the procedure of collective bargaining lead to strikes and other forms of industrial strife or unrest, which have the intent or the necessary effect of burdening or obstructing commerce . . . ."[5]

Congress also determined,

> "The inequality of bargaining power between employees who do not possess full freedom of association or actual liberty of contract, and employers who are organized in the corporate or other forms of ownership association substantially burdens and affects the flow of commerce, and tends to aggravate recurrent business depressions. . . ."[6]

As a result, Congress passed the National Labor Relations Act,[7] popularly known as the Wagner Act, in which

---

[4] *Id.* at 763; Maher, Players' Association: A United Front . . . To Face Owners, L.A. Times, Feb. 12, 1973, Part III, Pg. 1.

[5] 29 U.S.C. § 151.

[6] *Id.*

[7] 29 U.S.C. § 151 *et seq.*

it granted employees the right to organize or join labor organizations for the purpose of bargaining collectively through representatives of their own choosing. Section 9 of the National Labor Relations Act provides that employees, or a labor organization acting on their behalf, may file a petition with the National Labor Relations Board alleging that a substantial number wish to be represented for collective bargaining, and that their employer "declines" to recognize their representative. When that happens, the Board investigates, and if it has "reasonable cause to believe that a question of representation affecting commerce exists,"[8] it holds a hearing. If the Board determines from the hearing that a question of representation does exist, it directs that an election be held by secret ballot, and it certifies the results.

If, during such an election, the employees vote to be represented in collective bargaining by a particular labor union, their employer must then bargain in good faith with that union.[9] An employer's refusal to bargain collectively at that point would constitute an unfair labor practice,[10] which the Board is empowered to prevent by petitioning a federal Court of Appeals for an enforcement order, if necessary.[11]

When, in 1946, the Pirates' management refused to bargain with or recognize the American Baseball Guild, and when the Guild's members nevertheless failed to authorize a strike, Robert Murphy petitioned the National Labor Relations Board seeking such an election. The Board, however, refused to hold hearings or direct an election.

---

[8] 29 U.S.C. § 159.
[9] 29 U.S.C. § 158.
[10] *Id.*
[11] 29 U.S.C. §160.

Though it never officially explained the reason for its refusal, a *New York Times* report stated that the Board's decision was based on the ground that professional baseball was not "commerce."[12] Since it was not, any question concerning the representation of members of the Pirates was not "a question of representation affecting commerce,"[13] and therefore the National Labor Relations Act did not require or even authorize it to direct the petitioned-for election.

Why was professional baseball not "commerce"? The word "commerce," as used in the National Labor Relations Act, is defined by the Act to mean trade between states, or between the states and foreign countries.[14] In other words, "commerce" means interstate and foreign commerce—precisely that variety of commerce restraint of which is outlawed by the Sherman Antitrust Act.[15] The Board's decision in response to the American Baseball Guild petition was made in August of 1946, six months after the decision of the United States Court of Appeals in *Gardella* v. *Chandler*[16] and twenty-four years after the decision of the United States Supreme Court in *Federal Baseball* v. *National League*.[17] Presumably, the Board decided that those decisions, on whether or not Organized Baseball was engaged in interstate commerce for antitrust purposes, were relevant for determining whether or not it was engaged in interstate commerce for labor law purposes. Presumably, also, the Board decided to follow the older Supreme

[12] Hoffman, Is the NLRB Going to Play the Ball Game?, 20 Labor Law Journal 239, 244 (1969).

[13] 29 U.S.C. § 159.

[14] 29 U.S.C. § 152(b).

[15] 15 U.S.C. § 1.

[16] 172 F.2d 402 (2d Cir. 1949), discussed in §1.1(b), *supra*.

[17] 259 U.S. 200 (1922), discussed in § 1.1(a), *supra*.

Court decision holding that Organized Baseball was not in interstate commerce, rather than the then more current decision of the Court of Appeals that it might well be.

Whatever the Board's motive, Murphy was undaunted by its refusal to act. Instead, he turned to the Pennsylvania Labor Relations Board—whose powers within the state were similar to those of the federal Labor Board—and it did hold an election. The outcome, however, must have been a surprising disappointment to Murphy. Of the 31 Pirates eligible to vote, only 19 did. Fifteen voted not to be represented by the American Baseball Guild, one vote was contested, and only three players voted for the Guild.[18]

The Guild's defeat was no accident. It had been actively sought, not only by the management of the Pittsburgh Pirates, but by all of Organized Baseball. A committee of owners produced the "MacPhail Report" recommending certain changes in league practices. Not surprisingly, the recommended changes were quite similar to those the Guild had demanded. And, as soon as the Guild was defeated—perhaps in exchange for the Guild's defeat—Organized Baseball instituted a pension plan, a minimum salary, a player-representative system and a spring training allowance that to this day is called "Murphy Money." [19]

The player-representative system established by Organized Baseball in 1946 was the forerunner of all present-day players' associations. It was, however, a far cry from a labor union. Baseball owners did not "bargain" with player representatives in any sense of that word. Rather, representatives gathered periodically to compile the players' suggestions or requests which were then communicated to the owners who took whatever action they thought

[18] Krasnow & Levy, *supra* note 3, at 763.

[19] *Id.*; Maher, *supra* note 4, at 6.

prudent at the time. Even after the players formed the Major League Baseball Players' Association in 1954, it operated for more than a decade without a full-time executive officer.

Marvin Miller, the Association's first and present Executive Director, was hired in 1966. Before joining the Association, he had been Chief Economic Advisor and Assistant to the president of the United Steelworkers of America. Since becoming Executive Director, Major League Baseball's minimum salary has more than doubled, pension benefits have more than doubled, widow's benefits have doubled to quadrupled, and permanent total disability payments have tripled. Major League Baseball also struggled with its first season-delaying strike in 1972.[20]

§4.1(a)(2) National Basketball Players Association

The National Basketball Players Association was organized by Bob Cousy in the early 1950's. It, too, operated informally for a decade or so, until it retained New York City attorney Larry Fleisher as General Counsel in 1962. Before it was officially recognized by the league, it threatened coercive action and circulated strike rumors.[1] Since 1965, minimum salaries and pension benefits in the NBA have more than tripled.[2] The Association was also instrumental in preventing the merger of the American and National Basketball Associations,[3] which in turn is the

---

[20] Maher, *supra* note 4.

[1] Krasnow & Levy, Unionization and Professional Sports, 51 Georgetown L.J. 749, 764 (1963).

[2] Maher, NBA Players Militant . . . Still Get Along With Owners, L.A. Times, Feb. 14, 1973, Part III, Pg. 1, at 7.

[3] The Association financed litigation resulting in an injunction preventing a merger, Robertson v. National Basketball Assn., 389 F.Supp. 867, 879-880 (S.D.N.Y. 1975). It also testified against

key reason NBA salaries and benefits have increased as dramatically as they have.

§4.1(a)(3) NHL Players Association

A formal "Recognition Agreement" was executed between the owners of National Hockey League teams and the NHL Players Association in June of 1967, pursuant to which the Association is regarded as the official collective bargaining representative of the players.[1] It took the Players Association some ten years to become recognized in this formal fashion.

When originally formed, the Association's primary goal was to obtain for its pension plan some of the network television revenue the League had begun to receive in 1956. The NHL Board of Governors first tabled a request from the Players Association for a meeting to discuss the pension money issue; and then, when the Montreal and Toronto clubs contended they could not authorize the League to act on their behalf because they operated under Canadian law, the Board of Governors declared that negotiations with the Players Association would not be possible.[2]

Anticipating such a tactic, the Players Association retained attorney J. Norman Lewis, who had earlier repre-

---

merger-authorizing legislation; see, Hearings on S.2373 before the Subcomm. on Antitrust and Monopoly of the Senate Comm. on the Judiciary, 92d Cong., 1st & 2d Sess. 226, 302, 866, 877 (1971, 1972). The NBA Players Association was described as "a far more potent force against merger than the NFL Players Association was in the mid-1960s" when Congress authorized the merger of the AFL and NFL; see, Noll, Alternatives in Sports Policy, in Government and the Sports Business (Washington, D.C.: The Brookings Institution, 1974) at 426.

[1] Philadelphia World Hockey Club, Inc. v. Philadelphia Hockey Club, Inc., 351 F.Supp. 462, 497 (E.D.Pa. 1972).

[2] Parker, The Hockey Rebellion, Sports Illustrated, Oct. 28, 1957, at 19.

sented the major league baseball players in their successful effort to have World Series and All-Star game revenues contributed to their pension plan. In October of 1957, Lewis filed a $3 million antitrust suit against the NHL in order to induce it to meet with the Association as requested.[3]

§4.1(a)(4) NFL Players Association

The National Football League Players Association was organized in 1956 under the guidance of Cleveland attorney Creighton Miller who had himself been an All-American football player at Notre Dame. The Association was not recognized until the following year, and even then recognition came only in fits and starts. Coincidently, the decision of the United States Supreme Court in *Radovich* v. *National Football League*,[1] holding the League subject to the antitrust laws, came within a few months of the Association's formation. Bills were immediately introduced in Congress to extend baseball's antitrust exemption to football and other team sports, and hearings were held by the House Antitrust Subcommittee in the summer of 1957.[2] Bert Bell, then NFL Commissioner, testified that the players did not need antitrust protection, because they were covered by the National Labor Relations Act. That prompted the subcommittee's chairman, Congressman Emanuel Celler, to ask Bell whether he in fact recognized the NFL Players Association. Though Bell had not done so before, he had to answer yes, and he did. Thus it was that the NFL Players Association was first recognized.[3]

[3] *Id.*

[1] 352 U.S. 445 (1957), discussed in § 1.2(b), *supra.*

[2] Hearings on H.R. 5307, et al., before the Antitrust Subcomm. of the House Comm. on the Judiciary, 85th Cong., 1st Sess. (1957).

[3] *Id.*

Negotiations were carried on in the weeks that followed which resulted neither in formal written recognition nor in agreement on any of the players' demands. When negotiations finally broke off, Creighton Miller announced that the Association would file a $4.2 million antitrust lawsuit against Bell and the team owners, unless written recognition was granted and negotiations were resumed within two weeks. On December 2, 1957, precisely two weeks later, the League announced its acceptance of several of the players' demands, including a minimum salary, payment for pre-season games and of medical expenses, and salary in the event of injury. Pointedly missing from the League's announcement, however, was any mention of formal written recognition of the Association.[4]

For the next decade, the NFL Players Association was a "loose knit social organization,"[5] according to an attorney later retained to represent it. Indeed, Creighton Miller did tell a Senate Subcommittee in 1964 that members of the Association never considered it to be a union.[6] Although the "Bert Bell NFL Player Benefit Plan" was instituted in 1959, that was only under the pressure of another $4 million antitrust suit threat.[7]

By 1968, however, players' attitudes had changed. Bernie Parrish had done a great deal of work in an effort to organize a new football players' union to be called "The American Federation of Professional Athletes." If and

---

[4] B. Parrish, They Call It a Game (New York: Signet, 1971) at 230-231.

[5] Shulman & Baum, Collective Bargaining in Professional Athletics—The NFL Money Bowl, 50 Chicago Bar Record 173, 174 (1969).

[6] Parrish, *supra* note 4, at 250.

[7] *Id.* at 113.

when it was actually formed, Parrish favored its affiliation with the International Brotherhood of Teamsters.[8]

During the latter part of the 1967 season, Parrish had traveled around the country meeting with teams and collecting authorization cards from players. The player representatives were scheduled to hold their annual convention in Hollywood Beach, Florida, in January of 1968, and Parrish intended to meet with them in a final effort to sell his Federation. He never addressed the meeting however. About two and a half hours before he was scheduled to do so, Parrish reports that he received a telephone call from Chicago attorney Daniel Shulman who said that he had replaced Creighton Miller as counsel to the Association, and that his first official act was to cancel the meeting.[9]

According to Shulman, the player representatives had voted to maintain the Association's independence from the Teamsters,[10] though whether they did so before or after Parrish's address was cancelled is unclear. Shulman and Parrish both agree that Parrish notified the League that his union had an interest in representing a large portion of the players and would therefore be filing a petition for a National Labor Relations Board election. What happened thereafter is also unclear. Parrish reports that "Immediately, that same day, the owners officially recognized the Players Association in writing for the first time since it was formed in 1956." [11] Shulman reports that after notifying the League of its interest, the Teamsters withdrew, thereby removing one of the two conflicting claims, and doing away with the necessity for a Board directed

---

[8] *Id.* at 257.

[9] *Id.* at 262.

[10] Shulman & Baum, *supra* note 5, at 175.

[11] Parrish, *supra* note 4, at 262.

election. According to Shulman, the owners then agreed to an authorization card check by the American Arbitration Association, which was held at the end of February, 1968, with the owners signing a formal recognition agreement on March 5, 1968.[12]

Regardless of its precise timing, the NFL's formal recognition of the Players Association was a significant event—in 1968—because it did away with the possibility that the National Labor Relations Board might have rejected an Association petition for a certification election, as it previously had in 1946 when the American Baseball Guild filed its petition.[13] It is of course possible that the League cooperated with the Players Association in order to enable the Association to establish itself as the players' union as quickly as possible, before it or the Teamsters reconsidered the desirability of Teamster affiliation.

Negotiations between the newly recognized Association and the owners on increased pay for pre-season games, higher minimum salaries, and increases in the pension and insurance plan were carried on throughout the spring of 1968 without success. On June 25, 1968, the players voted by phone to strike if necessary, and thereafter the owners announced that the training camps would be shut down until matters were resolved. The strike/lock-out lasted ten days, and was finally settled by agreement on a two-year collective bargaining contract.[14]

When that contract expired on January 31, 1970, owner-player relations again turned bitter. More than a year was required for the negotiation of a successor agreement—a period marked by unfair labor practice charges, a lock-

---

[12] Shulman & Baum, *supra* note 5, at 175.

[13] See § 4.1(a)(1), *supra*.

[14] Shulman & Baum, *supra* note 5.

out by the owners and a strike by the players. Finally, on June 17, 1971, a four year collective bargaining agreement was executed and made retroactively effective as of February 1, 1970.

During the course of those 1970 and 1971 negotiations, the Players Association was represented by the Minneapolis law firm of Lindquist & Vennum. A young lawyer in the firm's labor department was Ed Garvey, a recent graduate of the University of Wisconsin Law School, who had been president of the University of Wisconsin student body and the liberal National Student Association. When negotiations were concluded, the Players Association asked Garvey to become its full-time executive director.[15]

Garvey was an active director from the start. Even before the expiration of the four year collective bargaining agreement, his name began to appear in news articles discussing the Association's stand on such issues as artificial turf, the bench-fine rule, and the authority of NFL Commissioner Pete Rozelle.[16] The artificial turf and bench-fine rule issues were taken to the National Labor Relations Board,[17] and aspects of Rozelle's authority were taken to various courts.[18] However, these and other issues became major points during negotiations which followed the expiration of that collective bargaining agreement on January 31, 1974—negotiations which broke down and resulted in the longest strike in the history of professional sports.

The first meeting between the Players Association and the NFL Management Council, the owners' bargaining

---

[15] Maher, A Challenge to Rozelle, L.A. Times, Feb. 13, 1973, Part III, Pg. 1.

[16] See, e.g., Maher, *supra* note 15; and Gildea, Ed Garvey: A Man Rozelle Likes to Avoid, L.A. Times, Dec. 10, 1972, § C, Pg. 3.

[17] See §§ 4.2 and 7.3(f)(2), *infra.*

[18] See §§ 2.2(c)(1) and 2.4(b)(1), *supra.*

agent, took place in March 1974; and at that meeting the players presented a list of some 57 demands. These included the elimination of the "Rozelle Rule," the option clause, the waiver system, and reserve lists; elimination of all fines and of the commissioner's authority to discipline players; granting veterans the right to veto trades in which they are involved; prohibiting clubs from impairing the rights of players to free expression; increasing salaries; and replacing artificial turf with natural grass as synthetic fields wore out.[19]

Those demands which related to the Rozelle Rule, waivers, options, fines, discipline, and the like, quickly became known as "the freedom issues." And they were among the first to be rejected by the Management Council. "These are anarchy issues, not freedom issues," labor lawyer Theodore Kheel said on behalf of the Council.[20] And though players such as the Los Angeles Rams' Tom Mack met with reporters to explain the reasons and justifications for the Players Association's demands, most sports writers apparently agreed more with the Council than with the Association.[21] A strike was predicted by at least one observer as early as April.[22]

Despite the involvement of the director of the Federal Mediation and Conciliation Service, W. J. Usery, strike predictions proved accurate. The players officially went on strike July 1, 1974, two days before the first training camp of the season was scheduled to begin. The strike was accompanied by Garvey's announcement that he was filing

---

[19] L.A. Times, Mar. 17, 1974, Part III.

[20] Hall, The Anarchy Game, L.A. Times, Apr. 30, 1974, Part III.

[21] Oates, Rams' Tom Mack Presents Players' Side of Squabble, L.A. Times, Apr. 1, 1974; Hall, War and Pieces, L.A. Times, Apr. 29, 1974; Hall, The Anarchy Game, L.A. Times, Apr. 30, 1974.

[22] Hall, *supra* note 21.

an unfair labor practice charge against the owners on the grounds they had failed to bargain in good faith and were attempting to undermine the union. It was also accompanied by a request from Association President Bill Curry of the Houston Oilers for the support of the public.[23] In response, an NFL spokesman called the unfair labor practice charge "nonsense." [24] And public support, if it existed, was neither overwhelming nor immediately apparent. Even unionized auto workers, interviewed by an Associated Press reporter outside a Cadillac plant in Detroit, were divided on the propriety of the players' demands.[25]

In the National Football League, rookies—who are not members of the Players Association—come to training camp a week or two before the veterans. One of the Association's early strike tactics was to post pickets at the training sites, in the hope that even the rookies would refuse to report. However, the San Diego Chargers and the Dallas Cowboys, the first two teams to open their camps, brought their rookies in a day ahead of schedule, thereby beating the picket lines. While Player Association representatives were permitted to address the rookies, few if any left camp. One Charger rookie who did leave camp was later reported to have returned in order to avoid losing his bonus.[26]

Though virtually all of the rookies selected to play in the 1974 All-Star game reported to their training camp, the Players Association won its first battle of the strike with them. The Association asked the All-Stars not to play the game, and on July 8th they voted not to, unless the

---

[23] L.A. Times, July 2, 1974, Part III, Pg. 1.
[24] *Id.*
[25] L.A. Times, July 14, 1974, Part III.
[26] L.A. Times, July 3, 4, 5, 7, 1974, Part III.

strike was settled before the July 26th game date.[27] Two days later, the sponsor of the game, Chicago Tribune Charities Inc., cancelled it entirely, saying that plans could not be continued because of the game's uncertain status.[28] The Players Association immediately pledged to donate half the money the game would have raised for charity, while the Miami Dolphins, who by virtue of their Super Bowl victory the previous January would have been the All-Stars' opponents, each lost 1/14 of a year's salary because of the cancellation.[29]

Cancellation of the game was apparently a tremendous victory for the Association, judging from the vitriolic responses of the owners. Wellington Mara, president of the New York Giants and chairman of the Management Council Executive Committee, issued a statement in which he charged that the game had been cancelled "solely because it happened to stand in the way of the union leadership's drive for power," [30] and in which he expressed indignation at the "audacity" [31] of the union. He was appalled, he said, that the Association was "so willing to strike out at anyone or anything in its path." [32] Miami Dolphin owner Joe Robbie said, "This is no longer a strike in the ordinary sense. It is now a mission by the Players Association to search and destroy." [33] Robbie also raised the possibility that the entire season might be cancelled, saying, "If the players wipe out the pre-season, then we can't afford to pay each player for the regular season." [34]

---

[27] L.A. Times, July 8, 9, 1974, Part III.

[28] L.A. Times, July 11, 1974, Part III.

[29] *Id.;* L.A. Times, July 9, 1974, Part III.

[30] *Id.*

[31] *Id.*

[32] *Id.*

[33] L.A. Times, July 12, 1974, Part III.

[34] *Id.*

The tide began to turn once again in favor of the owners when the Cincinnati Bengals opened training camp for their veterans on July 13th, and twelve reported.[35] The next day another Bengal veteran reported, as did one of the Cleveland Browns' veterans and one of the New York Giants' veterans.[36] By July 20th, the National Football League announced that 102 veterans had reported to training camps, out of some 1300 in the league, and not all clubs had opened veteran camps as of that date.[37]

With the exhibition season set to begin the first weekend in August, and with the players and the owners at an impasse as of the last week in July, the Management Council announced it would implement a league-wide policy of issuing ticket refunds to fans who requested them.[38] In the meantime, however, both sides escalated their efforts another notch. The Green Bay Packers had scheduled a scrimmage with the Chicago Bears for July 25th and had obtained an injunction barring picketing veterans from the field grounds. Twenty-one veterans were arrested for allegedly violating the court order.[39]

On its part, members of the Players Association joined United Auto Workers strikers who were picketing a General Motors plant in Ohio, and they in turn promised to join the players in a picket of the annual Hall of Fame Game scheduled for July 27th in Canton, Ohio, between the St. Louis Cardinals and the Buffalo Bills.[40] NFL officials, concerned that either team might refuse or be prevented

---

[35] L.A. Times, July 14, 1974, Part III.
[36] L.A. Times, July 15, 1974, Part III.
[37] L.A. Times, July 20, 1974, Part III.
[38] L.A. Times, July 23, 1974, Part III.
[39] L.A. Times, July 26, 1974, Part III.
[40] *Id.*

from playing, "devised one of the most elaborate logistical plans since the evacuation of Dunkirk."[41] False rumors were spread about the teams' travel plans; empty hotel rooms were reserved and paid for to mislead the striking veterans; an empty equipment truck was dispatched as a decoy to see whether or not it would be hijacked (it was not); and the Cleveland Browns were kept on standby, in the event either team failed to appear. The game was played as scheduled, before about 2400 fewer fans than the year before.[42]

Negotiations resumed July 31st in Washington, after federal mediator W. J. Usery expressed optimism that settlement could soon be reached. A 14 hour session followed by a 3½ hour session the next day were recessed without progress however.[43] On August 4th, the player representatives voted to continue the strike, saying that they estimated that reduced attendance at the season's first exhibition games had cost the owners approximately $3.4 million. Nevertheless, more than 300 veterans, including almost 100 starters, had reported to camps by then.[44]

Negotiations resumed August 6th, continued on the 7th and ran over until the early morning of the 8th. Following a 13 hour session, Usery again expressed optimism, saying that the meeting was the best held, and that he was hopeful for a resolution that week.[45] On the 8th, 9th, and 10th, marathon sessions were again conducted. The week ended without any agreement, however, and it was then reported that some club owners were at odds with others. Teams

[41] Kennedy, Star-Struck Canton, Sports Illustrated, Aug. 5, 1974, Pg. 10.

[42] *Id.;* L.A. Times, July 28, 1974, Part III.

[43] L.A. Times, Aug. 2, 1974, Part III.

[44] L.A. Times, Aug. 5, 1974, Part III.

[45] L.A. Times, Aug. 8, 1974, Part III.

with substantial numbers of veterans in camp were said to be less anxious to reach agreement than those with only a few veterans. The major issue was still considered to be the authority of the Commissioner.[46]

On Sunday, August 11th, the 42 day strike came to an abrupt end. The Players Association agreed with Usery to suspend the strike for two weeks, while reserving the right to resume it if the cooling-off period was unsuccessful.[47]

Congressman John Moss, Congresswoman Bella Abzug, and ten other members of the House of Representatives immediately called upon "both the owners and the players—but . . . particularly the owners, to sit down again . . . and this time reach a fair compromise agreement."[48] In a letter to the Management Council, the Congressmen stated that "if the union is significantly injured, we want it known we will undertake a complete review of the National Football League's antitrust status, and if the facts warrant, introduce appropriate legislation."[49]

Seven of the Houston Oilers' veterans who reported to camp after the start of the cooling-off period were cut from the team within an hour of their arrival. Not long thereafter, Kermit Alexander, Vice-President of the Players Association and a member of its negotiating committee, was cut when he reported to the Philadelphia Eagles' training camp. Bill Curry, President of the Players Association, was also cut by the Houston Oilers. Player representative Ken Reaves was traded by the Atlanta Falcons to the New Orleans Saints. And player representatives

---

[46] L.A. Times, Aug. 9, 1974, Part III.
[47] L.A. Times, Aug. 13, 1974, Part III.
[48] L.A. Times, Aug. 14, 1974, Part III.
[49] *Id.*

Tom Keating, Charlie Evans and Del Williams were cut by the Pittsburgh Steelers, New York Giants, and New Orleans Saints respectively.[50]

Negotiations continued during the two week period. The players withdrew their demand that the Rozelle Rule be eliminated, stating that they were willing to leave that issue for the courts to decide. In other areas, such as trades, waivers, and the option clause, they suggested compromises. But they remained firm on the need for an impartial arbitrator in place of the Commissioner. The owners rejected those proposals.[51]

On their part, the owners offered a grievance procedure which they said "affirms the authority of the commissioner ... to govern the game, yet sets up a system of outside arbitration for specified matters." [52] With respect to the Rozelle Rule, they continued to insist on compensation for the team losing a free agent, but proposed that the Commissioner be required to select the offer made by one of the two teams involved, which could consist of players, draft choices or cash. The owners also offered to modify option and waiver rules, and to increase minimum salaries and pension and insurance payments. The players rejected that offer.[53]

Though negotiations were thereafter recessed for an indefinite period, the Association also voted to continue the cooling-off period indefinitely.[54] And the balance of the 1974 season was played without interruption.

---

[50] L.A. Times, July 20, 1974; Aug. 15, 1974; Aug. 21, 1974; Sept. 4, 1974; Sept. 12, 1974.

[51] L.A. Times, Aug. 19, 1974, Part III.

[52] L.A. Times, Aug. 28, 1974, Part III.

[53] *Id.*

[54] *Id.*

In April of 1975, the Players Association submitted a new list of demands. It did not make mention of the Rozelle Rule, because by then a decision was being awaited from a federal court in Minneapolis on that issue.[55] It did however contain demands with respect to option clauses, waivers, trades, minimum salaries, and pensions—demands which the owners rejected.[56] The 1975 season was nevertheless begun without a renewal of the strike, while the Association and the Management Council continued to negotiate, and the Association pursued unfair labor practice charges it had previously filed with the National Labor Relations Board.

On the 32 charges filed by the Association during the strike, 15 were found to be of sufficient merit to warrant a hearing, and in June of 1975, the Board issued a complaint. Among the charges alleged in the complaint were those that Association officials Bill Curry, Kermit Alexander, Tom Keating and Ken Reaves had been cut or traded by their teams because of their union activities, and that the League had increased pre-season pay for veterans as a means of breaking the strike.[57]

The inability of the Players Association to achieve a collective bargaining agreement, despite the lengthy strike, must be deemed a failure of potential significance to all professional sports. Years ago, legal commentators expressed the near-unanimous view that "unionization in professional sports is neither feasible nor practical." [58] While

---

[55] L.A. Times, Apr. 6, 1975; Mackey v. National Football League, 407 F.Supp. 1000 (D.Minn. 1975), discussed in § 2.4(b)(1), *supra.*

[56] L.A. Times, June 11, 1975, Part III.

[57] L.A. Times, June 10, 1975, Part III.

[58] Krasnow & Levy, Unionization and Professional Sports, 51 Georgetown L.J. 749, 759 (1963).

the subsequent metamorphosis of players associations into true labor unions at first made it seem that those commentators were wrong, or that times had changed, the failure of the NFL player strike in 1974 now suggests that the unionization issue may have to be reconsidered.

Those who believed unionization was neither feasible nor practical, did so for essentially five reasons:[59]

1. Professional sports is a field where jobs depend entirely on individual ability, where emphasis is placed on star performers, and where athletes have varied educational and economic backgrounds.

2. Many if not most athletes are motivated by many factors other than or in addition to financial gain.

3. Employment as a professional athlete is brief, migratory and seasonal.

4. Public opinion is apt to oppose unionization by professional athletes.

5. A strike could result in financial disaster for the league involved.

Early proponents of unionization by athletes responded to these concerns by noting that:[60]

1. A union could bargain for minimum wages and employment conditions only, leaving individual athletes the right to negotiate for more, as do other unionized entertainers.

2. Even those athletes who are motivated by factors other than financial gain are concerned with practices and conditions which may shorten their playing careers.

---

[59] *Id.* at 759-761.
[60] *Id.*

3. The briefness of careers emphasizes the need for optimum conditions and for pension and retirement plans.

4. Public opinion could be made favorable if fans were informed of the less glamorous aspects of a professional athletic career and if stars appealed for public support.

5. Strikes would be no more devastating in sports than in any other seasonal business.

While these responses seem to have been borne out by the experiences of players associations until the 1974 NFL strike, they may no longer be entirely valid. Public opinion during the NFL strike seemed to favor neither side entirely. Attendance at the exhibition games played before the cooling-off period began was off from prior years.[61] But that may have been because of fans' unwillingness to pay as much as $10 per ticket to see unknown rookies and free agents.

Certainly some of the public perceived the players as being pampered performers whose salaries of $30,000 or more for six months' work was more than adequate compensation for whatever rules accompanied such a lush job. Moreover, many fans apparently felt that the financial consequences of the strike would be passed along to them, in the form of higher ticket prices,[62] even though the financial impact of the freedom issues, if any, has never been fully assessed.[63]

While the Players Association attempted throughout the strike to explain the significance of the freedom issues to the public, sympathy seems never to have been aroused.

---

[61] L.A. Times, Aug. 5, 1975, Part III.

[62] Letters to Editor, L.A. Times, July 13, 1974, Part III; and L.A. Times, July 14, 1974, Part III.

[63] See, however, § 2.6(d), *supra*.

In this regard, the players may have been the victims of their own success. For it is possible that the public considers it to be so glamorous to be an NFL player anywhere in the League that to strike over the fine points of employment is to make a mountain out of a molehill.

While players associations successfully overcame some of the inherent individualism of professional athletes by bargaining only for minimum salaries and conditions, other related aspects may have been a factor in the failure of the NFL strike. Just as the owners were reportedly in conflict with one another according to the number of veterans each had in camp, so too the players' interests were not entirely uniform. Almost from the outset of the strike, the Miami Dolphins felt more burdened by it than others, because when the All-Star game was cancelled, they lost the opportunity to earn an additional 1/14 of their annual salaries. The Dolphins asked the Players Association to assess each member $100 to compensate them for this loss. The request was apparently declined, however, because as the exhibition season approached, a member of the Dolphins predicted that the strike would be called off because the players would be unwilling to lose the 10% of their salary that was to be paid during the pre-season.[64]

In addition, while all Association members have a common interest in playing conditions, they do not have a common interest in all terms of employment, nor even in the freedom issues. The average NFL career lasts between four and five years. If a player signs a three year contract out of college, he is committed for those three years and an option year—altogether a period of four years. Thus, many players retire from professional football at or before the time they would have earned their freedom,

[64] L.A. Times, July 26, 1974, Part III.

even under the rule changes demanded by the Players Association.

Another conflict among members of the Players Association—which does not exist between members of unions in other industries—was that not all of them were certain to regain their jobs when the strike was over. Every year, a certain number of Players Association members lose their jobs to rookies, free agents, and even other Association members. Being able to demonstrate one's ability to the coaching staff is the most important thing for a player at the beginning of every year. With 90 or more athletes competing for some 43 jobs,[65] every opportunity is important. Thus, those free agents and veterans who went to camp received attention from the coaches not given to the strikers—attention that could not be ignored even by those strikers who anticipated a settlement would be reached in only a matter of weeks. As many of the veterans who reported to camp explained, even the freedom issues were relevant only to active members of NFL clubs.

One of the issues raised by the failure of the strike was whether or not an independent players association can be strong enough to do economic battle with National Football League club owners. With the exception of an informal exchange of support with an Ohio local of the United Auto Workers, the Players Association was on its own. Its picket lines were respected only by those who were truly sympathetic, and its finances, organization and communications were entirely self-generated.

During the course of the strike, the Rams' Tom Mack predicted that unless a "decent settlement" were reached, two things would happen: the Association would ask its

[65] **NFL Constitution and By-Laws, Article XVII.**

members to report to camp, even without a new collective bargaining agreement; and, at some point in the future, the Association's members would "vote to affiliate with a strong labor organization." [66] Though he did not identify any particular strong union, it was speculated that he was referring to the Teamsters.[67]

There is a difference of opinion on whether or not a players association could become part of a large national union successfully. George Meany, President of the AFL-CIO, does not think so. He has said that he does not believe a players association would "fit into the movement," in part because he could not visualize a highly paid athlete "respecting a picket line to protect a $4-an-hour ticket seller." [68] On the other hand, at least two legal commentators have recommended player association affiliation with a large labor union.[69] And Marvin Miller, Executive Director of the Major League Baseball Players Association, has stated that although his Association is not contemplating such affiliation, he did think it was possible, and that, "if a particular organization is overmatched, perhaps the membership would have to give serious consideration to the question." [70]

§4.1 (b) Metamorphosis in law

In order to appreciate the development of the various players associations into the labor unions they are today, the legal climate of the 1960's must be understood. While

---

[66] L.A. Times, Aug. 7, 1974, Part III.

[67] *Id.*

[68] Maher, The NFL and Unions: Are They Compatible?, L.A. Times, Sept. 27, 1974, Part III, Pg. 1.

[69] Krasnow & Levy, *supra* note 58; Note, The Balance of Power in Professional Sports, 22 Maine L.Rev. 459 (1970).

[70] Maher, *supra* note 68.

economic strength alone may enable employees to unionize successfully, a strike is the only and ultimate weapon they have to encourage employer recognition and cooperation—unless the National Labor Relations Board (or some state counterpart) involves itself. Only the judicially enforceable requirements of labor law—concerning such matters as union recognition, collective bargaining and unfair labor practices[1]—afford employees and employers the means with which to engage in more limited forms of "warfare." As Robert Murphy discovered in 1946, however, professional athletes may be less willing and less able to strike than other kinds of workers, because of the seasonal nature of their employment, the intricate schedule of their games, the extent to which they rely on public support and goodwill in the building of their careers, and their belief that team owners have far greater economic strength, and therefore capacity, to withstand the effects of a strike. Thus, the National Labor Relations Board's rejection in 1946 of the petition of the American Baseball Guild for a representation election[2] had a continuing and dampening impact on the future development of players associations into labor unions.

Furthermore, the Board's 1946 action was repeated in 1959, when it dismissed a Teamsters Union petition for an election among the Pirates' ground crew and maintenance employees, because such an election "would not effectuate the purposes of the National Labor Relations Act," according to a letter from the Board's Regional Director.[3] In the

[1] 29 U.S.C. §§ 158 and 159.

[2] See § 4.1(a)(1), *supra*.

[3] Hoffman, Is the NLRB Going to Play the Ball Game?, 20 Labor Law.J. 239, 244 (1969); Pittsburgh Athletic Co., 44 L.R.R.M. 1274, 1275 (1959).

decade that followed dismissal of the Teamsters Union petition, the jurisdiction of the National Labor Relations Board over professional sports was considered three times, once by the Supreme Court of Alabama, once by the Supreme Court of California, and then again by the National Labor Relations Board.

The Alabama case was decided in 1964 and involved the Birmingham Barons, a Southern League professional baseball team.[4] The Barons played their home games in Rickwood Field which they leased from its owners. Prior to the start of the 1964 season, the field's owners hired non-union workmen to repair, renovate and maintain it. As a result, when the season began, the carpenters' union picketed the field with signs saying, "This park remodeled by non-union labor." The pickets discouraged attendance, and that provoked the Barons into seeking an injunction against further picketing. One of the grounds asserted by the carpenters' union in support of its motion to vacate the temporary injunction the Barons had obtained was that the dispute was within the exclusive jurisdiction of the National Labor Relations Board, and therefore it was improper for Alabama courts to become involved in the matter by granting an injunction. The Alabama Supreme Court upheld the injunction, however, stating that the Board had jurisdiction only over labor practices affecting interstate commerce. Citing *Federal Baseball* v. *National League*[5] and *Toolson* v. *New York Yankees*,[6] it held that professional baseball was not in interstate commerce. Thus, the Court ruled, the Union's picketing did not affect interstate com-

[4] Pennington v. Birmingham Baseball Club, Inc., 170 So.2d 410 (Ala. S.Ct. 1964).

[5] 259 U.S. 200 (1922), discussed in § 1.1(a), *supra*.

[6] 346 U.S. 356 (1953), discussed in § 1.1(d), *supra*.

merce, and the Board did not have jurisdiction over it. While the Alabama Court realized that *Federal Baseball* and *Toolson* both involved the Sherman Antitrust Act, and not the National Labor Relations Act, it also said that if a distinction was to be drawn between antitrust and labor laws, federal courts would have to be the ones to draw it.

In 1968, the California Supreme Court was presented with a similar situation. Charles Finley, owner of the American League Oakland Athletics, tried to hire a union band to play at the opening baseball game of the 1968 season. The Musicians Union was so enthusiastic about the plan that it demanded that Finley hire a union band not only for the opening game of the season, but for all weekend home games. Finley refused to do that, however; so when the season began, the Union stationed pickets at all of the entrances to the Oakland Coliseum carrying signs saying, "This Employer is Unfair to Musicians Union Local No. 6." Finley obtained an injunction against further picketing; and the Union applied to the California Supreme Court for a writ prohibiting its enforcement, on the grounds that the National Labor Relations Board had exclusive jurisdiction over the dispute. Finley, of course, argued that the Board did not have jurisdiction, because baseball was not engaged in interstate commerce, citing in support the *Federal Baseball, Toolson,* and *Birmingham Barons* cases.

The California Supreme Court disagreed both with Finley and its Alabama counterpart. Regardless of the holding in the *Federal Baseball* case, it said, professional baseball has since become an interstate business operation, as a matter of fact. Therefore, Finley's dispute with the Musicians Union did affect interstate commerce and was under the Board's exclusive jurisdiction, baseball's antitrust exemption being no evidence that Congress intended baseball to be exempt from labor laws too.[7]

Finley then argued that even if Organized Baseball were engaged in interstate commerce, the National Labor Relations Board would decline to exercise jurisdiction over it. The Board is given authority to do so by section 14 of the National Labor Relations Act, which provides,

> "The Board, in its discretion, may, by rule of decision or by published rules . . ., decline to assert jurisdiction over any labor dispute involving any class or category of employers, where, in the opinion of the Board, the effect of such labor dispute on commerce is not sufficiently substantial to warrant the exercise of its jurisdiction . . . ."[8]

The Board had refused twice to assert jurisdiction over professional baseball, in 1946 and 1959. But neither refusal constituted a "rule of decision" or a "published rule." Thus, it could still change its mind without changing any rules. It had also once declined to assert its jurisdiction over horse racing; but that was on the ground that horse racing was already subject to extensive and detailed regulation by state agencies.[9] Moreover, in more recent years, the Board had exercised jurisdiction over sports centers, skiing facilities, gambling casinos and theaters.[10] Therefore, the California Supreme Court held that Finley had

[7] Musicians Union, Local No. 6 v. Superior Court, 73 Cal.Rptr. 201 (Cal. S.Ct. 1968).

[8] 29 U.S.C. § 164.

[9] Walter A. Kelley, 139 N.L.R.B. 744, 747 (1962).

[10] Celebrity Sports Center, 169 N.L.R.B. No. 29 (1968); Aspen Skiing Corp., 143 N.L.R.B. 707 (1963); Harrah's Club, 150 N.L.R.B. 1702 (1965), enforced, 362 F.2d 425 (9th Cir. 1966), *cert. den.*, 386 U.S. 915; The League of New York Theatres, Inc., 129 N.L.R.B. 1429 (1961).

failed to show that the Board would have refused to assert jurisdiction over professional baseball.

In 1969, the National Labor Relations Board was given another opportunity to determine whether or not it would assert jurisdiction over baseball. American League umpires Alexander Salerno and William Valentine had organized the twenty-five American League umpires into a union. The League refused to recognize the Umpires Union, and so the Union petitioned the Board for a representation election. Interestingly, the League conceded that the Board had the constitutional and statutory authority to exercise jurisdiction over it, apparently abandoning the argument that *Federal Baseball* and *Toolson* exempted it from labor law as well. It was a concession with which the Board agreed. "[W]e find," the Board said, "that professional baseball is an industry in or affecting commerce, and as such is subject to Board jurisdiction under the Act." [11]

Instead, the League urged the Board, as a matter of policy, not to assert jurisdiction over it, as permitted by section 14 of the Act. It contended that,

> "Because of baseball's internal self-regulation, a labor dispute involving The American League of Professional Baseball Clubs is not likely to have any substantial effect on interstate commerce; and that application of the National Labor Relations Act to this Employer is contrary to national labor policy because Congress has sanctioned baseball's internal self-regulation." [12]

---

[11] The American League of Professional Baseball Clubs and Association of National Baseball League Umpires, 180 N.L.R.B. No. 30, 72 L.R.R.M. 1545, 1546 (1969).

[12] *Id.* at 1547.

The Board, however, decided at long last to assert jurisdiction. In language that evidenced an attitude far different from the one it had in 1946 and 1959, the Board said,

> "Baseball's system for internal self-regulation of disputes involving umpires is made up of the Uniform Umpires Contract, the Major League Agreement, and the Major League Rules, which provide, among other things, for final resolution of disputes through arbitration by the Commissioner. The system appears to have been designed almost entirely by employers and owners, and the final arbiter of internal disputes does not appear to be a neutral third party freely chosen by both sides, but rather an individual appointed solely by the member club owners themselves. We do not believe that such a system is likely either to prevent labor disputes from arising in the future, or, having once arisen, to resolve them in a manner susceptible or conducive to voluntary compliance by all parties involved. Moreover, it is patently contrary to the letter and spirit of the Act for the Board to defer its undoubted jurisdiction to decide unfair labor practices to a disputes settlement system established unilaterally by an employer or group of employers." [13]

In response to the League's contention that Congress had sanctioned baseball's internal self-regulation, the Board said,

> "We do not agree that Congress, by refusing to pass legislation subjecting the sport to the antitrust laws when it considered the regulation of baseball and other sports under the antitrust statutes, sanctioned a government-wide policy of 'non-involvement' in all mat-

[13] *Id.*

ters pertaining to baseball. Indeed, to the extent that Congressional deliberation on the antitrust question has reference to the issue before us, it indicates agreement that players' rights to bargain collectively and engage in concerted activities are to be protected rather than limited."[14]

Thus, the Board ordered an election among the American League umpires. And in so doing, it markedly altered the future course of player-league relationships. For express Board jurisdiction over professional team sports, plus formal league recognition of players associations, meant that henceforth collective bargaining would be the principal feature of those relationships.

§4.2 Mandatory subjects for collective bargaining

According to the National Labor Relations Act, those employers and employees who are subject to it—as is now clearly the case with respect to team owners and professional athletes—have an obligation to meet with one another to bargain collectively over "wages, hours and other terms and conditions of employment."[1] The phrase "wages, hours, and other terms and conditions of employment" covers so wide a range of items, it is possible and even likely that in the long run virtually all aspects of professional sports, from contract provisions to pay, scheduling, equipment design, and game rules, will be the subject of collective bargaining proposals at one time or another.

It has been suggested, for example, that Organized Baseball's rule against bonuses is a rule referring to "wages" and would thus be a subject for collective bar-

[14] *Id.* at 1548.

[1] 29 U.S.C. § 158(d).

gaining.[2] It has also been suggested that "hours" covers the length of games, and "conditions of employment," the amount of travel that is necessary.[3] If so, game rules concerning the number of innings in a baseball game and the number of minutes in a quarter or period of a football, basketball or hockey game would be a subject for collective bargaining, as would the length of a season and the particular scheduling of games. While neither side is compelled by law to agree to any proposal or to make any concessions, both are required to meet at reasonable times and confer "in good faith." [4] The extent to which labor law has changed the face of professional sports will be graphically demonstrated the first time Organized Baseball is asked to meet at a reasonable time to bargain in good faith over a player demand that games be shortened to seven innings, or the first time the NFL is asked to bargain over a player demand that quarters be shortened to twelve minutes. Indeed, the impact of collective bargaining has been felt by Organized Baseball in an historic fashion. After fifty years of rigid adherence to its cherished reserve system, in 1973 it adopted salary arbitration by independent arbitrators and a trade veto power for veteran players.[5]

The National Football League, too, has been apprised of the ways in which collective bargaining requirements have altered the manner in which team owners were accustomed to operating. In 1971, the NFL Players Association became concerned that artificial turf might be responsible for an increasing number of player injuries. It

---

[2] Miller, Some Modest Proposals for Collective Bargaining in Professional Sports, 48 Los Angeles Bar Bulletin 155, 157 (1973).

[3] *Id.* at 157-158.

[4] 29 U.S.C. § 158.

[5] See § 2.2(a), *supra*.

therefore sought the cooperation of individual teams for study of the problem, and was referred to the NFL Management Council, the owners' representative for collective bargaining. Ed Garvey, Executive Director of the Players Association, exchanged correspondence with John Thompson, Executive Secretary of the Management Council, but the two were unable to agree on a study proposal.

Shortly thereafter, the Players Association demanded that the Management Council bargain about future installation of artificial turf and agree, in the meantime, to a moratorium on further installations. The Council replied to the Association's demand by denying that it had any legal obligation to bargain so long as the then-current collective bargaining agreement was in effect, but said that it would have Thompson meet and discuss the matter with the Association in the interest of maintaining a good relationship.

The Association rejected the Council's position and demanded good-faith negotiations, not general discussions. Thompson said he would not discuss legal issues but would listen to what the Association had to say about artificial turf. A meeting was finally held at which Thompson suggested the matter be referred to a joint committee of owners and players for study. The Association rejected the proposal, and on December 10, 1971 it filed a charge with the National Labor Relations Board accusing the NFL of committing an unfair labor practice by refusing to bargain about future installations of artificial turf. The Players Association contended that the use of artificial turf in the place of natural grass was a "condition of employment." [6]

---

[6] **National Football League Management Council and National Football League Players Association, 203 N.L.R.B. No. 165, 83 L.R.R.M. 1203 (1973).**

Had the Board agreed with the Players Association's contention, it would *not* have ordered the League to cease further installation of artificial turf. Use of such turf, even if a condition of employment, is not made legal or illegal by labor law. Rather, the Board would have simply ordered the NFL to bargain about its future installation; and even then the League would not have been required by law to agree to discontinue its use or to make any concessions to the Players Association.[7] On the other hand, if the use of artificial turf is a condition of employment, the law requires the owners to confer about its use with the Association, rather than make decisions concerning its use unilaterally.[8]

After the Players Association filed its charge with the Board, the matter was assigned to an Administrative Law Judge, and a hearing held. The Administrative Law Judge agreed with the Association that the use of artificial turf was a "condition of employment" and that the Management Council had a legal obligation to bargain about its future use. However, the Judge also found that the Council had not refused to do so. When the Board reviewed the Judge's findings, it agreed, saying,

> "While admittedly declining to take a definitive position until after it had studied the material presented by the Union, [the Council] did not take unilateral action which might have prejudiced the matter. Up to this point, [the Council's] conduct was clearly justified and in comport with its obligations under the Act." [9]

---

[7] 29 U.S.C. § 158(d).
[8] *Id.*
[9] NFL Management Council, *supra* note 6, at 1205.

Although the Board dismissed the Association's charge, the Board's decision stated that artificial turf was a condition of employment, about which the NFL had an immediate obligation to bargain in good faith.[10] Prior to the injection of labor law into professional sports, it seems safe to presume that owners and league officials never dreamed that players had to be consulted on the kind of field to be used.

Collective bargaining is not, of course, a one-way street. It is also possible that its impact may be demonstrated by proposals owners might make. For example, team owners have expressed concern over the necessity to bargain twice, once with the players association over such things as pension and insurance plans, and then again with each individual player over his actual salary. Ed Silver, labor counsel for the National Basketball Association, has reported that he receives constant complaints from the owners,

> "that they never know what all the negotiations are going to cost them. When a typical employer finishes negotiations, he can take pencil to paper and tell you what his costs are going to be over the term of the contract. Basketball owners say they get it from both ends. Costs are imposed on them in collective bargaining, but that's only part of the ultimate cost. They still have to deal with the individual players on salaries. So they don't really know what their costs are going to be over the term of the collective-bargaining agreement."[11]

---

[10] *Id.*

[11] Maher, NBA Players Militant . . . Still Get Along With Owners, L.A. Times, Feb. 14, 1973, Part III, Pg. 1.

John Thompson, former executive secretary of the NFL Management Council, has expressed the opinion that because players associations negotiate only fringe benefits and side issues, fringe benefits assume far greater significance than they would in more conventional collective bargaining situations. This is so, he has said, because a union measures its success by the benefits it obtains for its members. In most industries, the principal benefit is pay. In professional sports, however, pay is negotiated individually, and not by the union. Therefore, players associations must focus all of their energies on side issues and fringe benefits, thus making such questions more important than they otherwise would be.[12]

Actually, professional sports' dual level bargaining is not unique. In the entertainment industry in particular, it is not uncommon to find that the collective bargaining agreement negotiated by the union sets a minimum—but not a maximum—salary. Nevertheless, it is true that team owners cannot know what their total player-compensation costs will be over the length of a proposed collective bargaining agreement. However, because bargaining is a two-way street, owners could propose that the players associations negotiate not only minimum salaries, but maximum salaries as well, perhaps on the basis of step increases for additional years of service. Indeed, baseball did use such a maximum salary schedule once, and even in recent years, National Football League collective bargaining agreements have specified the salary to be received by all players for pre-season games. Furthermore, it has even been suggested that players associations might someday propose a salary schedule program applicable to all players, thereby doing away with individual salary bar-

[12] Maher, Owners Fight to Retain Rozelle's Power, L.A. Times, Feb. 13, 1974, Part III, Pg. 1.

gaining, because journeymen athletes could expect to benefit by having the superstars included in their number for salary setting purposes.[13] While such action would seem to discriminate against the best players, it has been said that such discrimination would not be illegal.[14]

§4.3 The impact of collective bargaining on players' recourse to judicial relief

§4.3(a) The theory

The advent of collective bargaining in professional sports is particularly significant for additional reasons. League practices such as reserve and option systems, the player draft, and player discipline are usually discussed and their legality analyzed under principles of federal antitrust law. However, practices which are the product of collective bargaining are sometimes exempt from the requirements of the antitrust laws. And thus attorney Michael Jacobs and Yale law professor Ralph Winter have stated that the "antitrust dilemma" of sports league practices "is an issue whose time has come and gone, an issue which has suffered that modern fate worse than death: irrelevancy."[1]

The Sherman Act, passed in 1890, declares illegal every contract, combination or conspiracy restraining trade or commerce, and prohibits monopolization, or attempts to monopolize, trade or commerce, or to combine or conspire with others to do so.[2] Such language is majestically

---

[13] Lowell, Collective Bargaining and the Professional Team Sport Industry, 38 Law and Contemporary Problems 3, 30 (1973).

[14] *Id.*

[1] Jacobs & Winter, Antitrust Principles and Collective Bargaining by Athletes: Of Superstars in Peonage, 81 Yale L.J. 1 (1971).

[2] 15 U.S.C. §§ 1 and 2.

sweeping in its scope, and appears on its face to outlaw labor unions along with industrial trusts. For labor unions are organizations of workers who combine and agree with one another in an effort to restrain whatever freedom their employers might otherwise have had to conduct commerce without regard to their employees' conditions of employment. In so doing, unions seek to monopolize the labor segment of commerce so that improved working conditions can be exacted in exchange for the supply of labor.

Whether Congress ever intended the Sherman Act to be applied to labor is an issue that has long been debated. Regardless of Congress' intent, however, the United States Supreme Court did apply it to labor in 1908 in the *Danbury Hatters' Case,*[3] where it held that a union's effort to organize a hat factory by means of strikes and boycotts violated the antitrust law. Damages of $80,000 were trebled to $240,000, and the judgment was collected without mercy from poor hatmakers who had been members of the union.[4]

Public protest resulted in certain sections of the Clayton Act, enacted in 1914, which provided that human labor was not commerce; that nothing in the antitrust laws should be construed to forbid the existence or operation of unions; and that unions should not be construed to be illegal combinations or conspiracies.[5] Nevertheless, the words "lawfully" and "legitimate" and others of similar import appeared in the Act in various places and virtually destroyed the intended labor exemption. Decisions of the

---

[3] Loewe v. Lawlor, 208 U.S. 274 (1908).

[4] J. Williams, Labor Relations and the Law (Boston: Little Brown & Co., 1965) at 36.

[5] Clayton Act §§ 6 and 20; 15 U.S.C. § 17; 29 U.S.C. § 52.

courts, including the Supreme Court, during the decade of the twenties repeatedly held labor unions liable for antitrust violations.[6]

Congress again attempted to exempt unions in 1932 by passing the Norris-LaGuardia Act[7] which deprived federal courts of the power to issue injunctions in matters involving most labor disputes. And in 1935, it enacted the National Labor Relations Act,[8] popularly known as the Wagner Act, which expressly provided that employees have the right to engage in concerted activities for the purpose of collective bargaining or other mutual aid or protection. These statutes finally had their intended effect, for in 1941 the Supreme Court dismissed a criminal indictment against union officials, holding that the Norris-Laguardia and Clayton Acts made it apparent that union activities were generally immune to Sherman Act attack.[9]

The scope of this "labor exemption" is not entirely clear even today, decades after the enactment of the statutes from which it is derived. However, certain decisions of the Supreme Court have led some to believe that professional athletes in sports that have been unionized may no longer challenge league practices as being in violation of the antitrust laws.

The most relevant Supreme Court decision on this issue seems to be *Amalgamated Meat Cutters* v. *Jewel Tea Company*,[10] decided in 1965. The Meat Cutters Union represented virtually all butchers working in the Chicago area, and it bargained simultaneously with all of its mem-

---

[6] Duplex Printing Co. v. Deering, 254 U.S. 443 (1921).

[7] 29 U.S.C. §§ 101-115.

[8] 29 U.S.C. § 151, *et seq.*

[9] United States v. Hutcheson, 312 U.S. 219 (1941).

[10] 381 U.S. 676 (1965).

bers' employers. One of the items negotiated in 1957 was a union proposal that meat markets be operated between 9 a.m. and 6 p.m. only, Monday through Saturday only. Jewel Tea Company operated a chain of food stores, most of which were equipped with self-service counters where pre-packaged meats were displayed for sale. Jewel Tea objected to the restriction on marketing-hours, because it felt it should be able to sell pre-packaged meats in the evenings, after its butchers had finished work for the day. Thus, during negotiations, Jewel Tea made a counter-proposal to the union, asking that the operating hours of self-service markets not be limited. Jewel Tea expressed the opinion that a limitation on marketing hours would violate the antitrust laws.

Jewel Tea's counter-proposal was rejected by the Meat Cutters Union, and its members authorized a strike to compel acceptance of its limited-hours proposal, if necessary. Under duress of the strike vote, Jewel Tea signed a collective bargaining agreement containing the marketing-hours restriction. It then sued the Meat Cutters, seeking invalidation of the restrictive provision. After seven years of litigation, the Supreme Court ultimately ruled that even if the restriction violated the Sherman Act, it was exempt, because obtained by the union through bona fide collective bargaining. The Court expressed two separate and inconsistent reasons for its decision. (Indeed, three of the Court's nine justices dissented altogether and voted in favor of Jewel Tea.) Three of the justices who voted for the Meat Cutters Union did so because they believed that all provisions of collective bargaining agreements dealing with "wages, hours, and other terms and conditions of employment" should be exempt. Justice Goldberg, who in future years would represent Curt Flood in his suit against Organized Baseball,[11] explained the reasoning of those three justices in this manner:

> "The National Labor Relations Act . . . declares it to be the policy of the United States to promote the establishment of wages, hours, and other terms and conditions of employment by free collective bargaining between employers and unions. The Act further provides that both employers and unions must bargain about such mandatory subjects of bargaining. This national scheme would be virtually destroyed by the imposition of Sherman Act criminal and civil penalties upon employers and unions engaged in such collective bargaining. To tell the parties that they must bargain about a point but may be subject to antitrust penalties if they reach an agreement is to stultify the congressional scheme.
>
> "Moreover, mandatory subjects of bargaining are issues as to which union strikes may not be enjoined by either federal or state courts. To say that the union can strike over such issues but that both it and the employer are subject to possible antitrust penalties for making collective bargaining agreements concerning them is to assert that Congress intended to permit the parties to collective bargaining to wage industrial warfare but to prohibit them from peacefully settling their disputes. This would not only be irrational but would fly in the face of the clear congressional intent of promoting 'the peaceful settlement of industrial disputes by subjecting labor-management controversies to the mediatory influence of negotiation.' "[12]

[11] See § 1.3(b), *supra*.
[12] 381 U.S. at 711-712.

The other three justices who voted for the Meat Cutters Union did so for more limited reasons. As far as they were concerned, the marketing-hours restriction was exempt from the antitrust laws only because the union had acted on its own in requiring Jewel Tea to agree to it. If the Union had conspired with other employers (who may not have had self-service counters in their stores) to impose the restriction on Jewel Tea, then they would have held that the Union had lost its exemption.

A relevant example of a case in which a union lost its antitrust exemption because it conspired with employers to restrain trade is *Allen Bradley Co.* v. *International Brotherhood of Electrical Workers,*[13] decided by the Supreme Court in 1945. Members of the New York City local of the I.B.E.W. were employed by electrical equipment manufacturers and by electrical contractors who bought and installed the equipment. Collective bargaining agreements between the Union and the manufacturers prohibited the manufacturers from selling equipment to any contractor who failed to employ Union members. And collective bargaining agreements with the contractors prohibited them from buying equipment from any manufacturer who failed to employ Union members. This was done in order to increase employment opportunities for the Union's members and to improve their salaries and working conditions. It also had the effect of giving the Union-manufacturer-contractor "partnership" a monopoly on New York City's electrical equipment business.

Allen Bradley Co. and its co-plaintiffs manufactured electrical equipment outside of New York City. They did

---

[13] 325 U.S. 797 (1945).

not, therefore, employ the Union's members, though some of them did have collective bargaining agreements with other unions and in some cases with other locals of the I.B.E.W. By virtue of the collective bargaining agreements entered into by the New York City manufacturers and contractors, Allen Bradley and its co-plaintiffs were unable to make any sales in New York. They filed suit and were successful. The Supreme Court held that the Union's antitrust exemption had been lost, because it had conspired with non-labor elements of industry—manufacturers and contractors—to monopolize a segment of trade and commerce.

These two cases are relevant to professional sports in the following way. In *Amalgamated Meat Cutters* v. *Jewel Tea,* it was held that Jewel Tea could not attack a provision in a collective bargaining agreement it had entered into, even though it appeared that the provision restrained trade and commerce and thus violated the antitrust laws. Similarly, in the *Curt Flood* case,[14] Organized Baseball argued that Flood should not be permitted to attack a provision in a collective bargaining agreement entered into on his behalf by the Major League Baseball Players Association, even if it did violate the antitrust laws. While the labor exemption generally applies to the union rather than to the employer, the Supreme Court has held that the National Labor Relations Act permits separate employers in the same industry to bargain together as a unit and to present common proposals, just as individual employees are permitted to bargain together in a union.[15] Furthermore, it would seem unfair to permit

---

[14] Flood v. Kuhn, 407 U.S. 258 (1972), discussed in § 1.3(b), *supra.*

[15] NLRB v. Truck Drivers' Union, 353 U.S. 87 (1957).

unions to pretend to accept certain proposals made by employers in exchange for concessions by employers on other issues, only to allow unions to challenge later the legality of the proposals employers thought had been accepted. Thus, it has been suggested that the *agreement* which is the product of collective bargaining is exempt from antitrust challenge, regardless of which side initiates the challenge.[16]

§4.3(b) Its application

§4.3(b)(1) In baseball

The courts never ruled on the issue in the *Flood* case. In his opinion denying Flood's motion for a preliminary injunction, District Judge Cooper held that the questions raised by the conflicting views of the parties as to the labor agreement exemption were substantial and complex and afforded another reason to conclude that Flood had not made a clear showing that he would probably succeed on the merits.[1] Following the actual trial, Judge Cooper held that because he was dismissing the case on the grounds that only the Supreme Court could overrule *Federal Baseball* and *Toolson,* it was not necessary for him to reach "this difficult question."[2]

When the case reached the Supreme Court, it too ruled that its adherence to *Federal Baseball* and *Toolson* made it unnecessary to consider the labor exemption argument.[3] Justice Marshall, who dissented from the majority opinion in the *Flood* case, had a good deal more to say about the

[16] Jacobs & Winter, *supra* note 1, at 27.

[1] Flood v. Kuhn, 309 F.Supp. 793, 806 (S.D.N.Y. 1970).

[2] Flood v. Kuhn, 316 F.Supp. 271, 278 (S.D.N.Y. 1970).

[3] Flood v. Kuhn, 407 U.S. 258, 285 (1972).

labor exemption, though he, too, did not purport to resolve the issue, stating that though he would overrule *Federal Baseball* and *Toolson,*

> "This does not mean that [Flood] necessarily would prevail, however. Lurking in the background is a hurdle of recent vintage that [Flood] still must overcome. In 1966, the Major League Players Association was formed. [Actually, that was the year it hired its first full time executive director. It had been formed twelve years earlier.] It is the collective bargaining representative for all major league baseball players. [Bowie Kuhn and Organized Baseball] argue that the reserve system is now part and parcel of the collective-bargaining agreement and that because it is a mandatory subject of bargaining, the federal labor statutes are applicable, not the federal antitrust laws. The lower courts did not rule on this argument, having decided the case solely on the basis of the antitrust exemption.
>
> "This Court has faced the interrelationship between the antitrust laws and the labor laws before. The decisions make several things clear. First, '[b]enefits to organized labor cannot be utilized as a cat's paw to pull employer's chestnuts out of the antitrust fires.' . . . Second, the very nature of a collective-bargaining agreement mandates that the parties be able to 'restrain' trade to a greater degree than management could do unilaterally. . . . Finally, it is clear that some cases can only be resolved by examining the purposes and the competing interests of the labor and antitrust statutes and by striking a balance.
>
> "It is apparent that none of the prior cases is precisely on point. They involve union-management agreements that work to the detriment of manage-

ment's competitors. In this case, [Flood] urges that the reserve systems works to the detriment of labor.

"While there was evidence at trial concerning the collective-bargaining relationships of the parties, the issues surrounding that relationship have not been fully explored. As one commentator has suggested, this case 'has been litigated with the implications for the institution of collective bargaining only dimly perceived. The labor law issues have been in the corners of the case—the courts below, for example, did not reach them—moving in and out of the shadows like an uninvited guest at a party whom one can't decide either to embrace or expel.' . . .

"There is surface appeal to [Organized Baseball's] argument that [Flood's] sole remedy lies in filing a claim with the National Labor Relations Board, but this argument is premised on the notion that management and labor have agreed to accept the reserve clause. This notion is contradicted, in part, by the record in this case. [Flood] suggests that the reserve system was thrust upon the players by the owners and that the recently formed player's union has not had time to modify or eradicate it. If this is true, the question arises as to whether there would then be any exemption from the antitrust laws in this case. [Flood] also suggests that there are limits to the antitrust violations to which labor and management can agree. These limits should also be explored." [4]

For these reasons, Justice Marshall would have remanded the case to the District Court for consideration of whether or not Flood stated a claim under the antitrust laws despite the collective bargaining agreement, and, if so, whether or not there was an antitrust violation.

---

[4] *Id.* at 293-296.

§4.3(b)(2) In hockey

Players are not the only ones who have been unhappy with reserve and option systems and their restraint on athletes' mobility. Newly-formed competitive leagues, whose efforts to sign up players have been stymied by such systems, have also attacked their legality. In the "war" between the National Hockey League and the World Hockey Association, for example, the WHA filed an antitrust suit against the NHL seeking an injunction against further enforcement of the NHL reserve system. WHA teams also defended NHL suits designed to enforce its reserve system with arguments that the system violated the antitrust laws and thus should not be enforced.[1]

Several of the hockey cases were consolidated before federal District Judge Leon Higginbotham, and one of the issues he considered in his lengthy opinion granting the WHA a preliminary injunction against enforcement of the NHL reserve system[2] was whether the NHL was entitled to invoke the labor exemption. The National Hockey League Players Association had been recognized by the League in 1967, and the NHL argued that its reserve clause was the product of collective bargaining and thus insulated from antitrust attack. After thorough analysis of the issue, Judge Higginbotham concluded that the National Hockey League was not entitled to the labor exemption, particularly in a suit brought by a competing league and not by players.

Judge Higginbotham stated there was little or no evidence that the reserve system was the product of collective bargaining. It "was more than a sturdy teenager

---

[1] See § 2.3(b)(2), *supra.*

[2] Philadelphia World Hockey Club, Inc. v. Philadelphia Hockey Club, Inc., 351 F.Supp. 462 (E.D.Pa. 1972).

when the Players' Association was born," he said, and "Subsequent efforts by the Association to revamp the reserve system have been continually rebuffed by the NHL."[3] Nevertheless, he added,

> "Even if, arguendo, there had been substantial arm's-length collective bargaining by the National Hockey League and the Players' Association to revise the perpetual option provision of the reserve clause. . . , those negotiations would not shield the National Hockey League from liability in a suit by outside competitors who sought access to players under the control of the National Hockey League."[4]

In short, the hockey cases were similar to *Allen Bradley* v. *I.B.E.W.*[5] where manufacturers were permitted to level an antitrust attack on provisions of collective bargaining agreements between competing manufacturers and their employees' union. It was not similar—as the *Flood*[6] case may have been—to the *Jewel Tea*[7] case, where a party to the collective bargaining agreement was barred from attacking it.

§4.3(b)(3) In football

On its face, the *Joe Kapp*[1] case seemed quite analogous to *Jewel Tea*,[2] and the National Football League relied on

[3] *Id.* at 498, 499.

[4] *Id.* at 499.

[5] 325 U.S. 797 (1945), discussed in § 4.3(a), *supra.*

[6] Flood v. Kuhn, 407 U.S. 258 (1972).

[7] Amalgamated Meat Cutters v. Jewel Tea Company, 381 U.S. 676 (1965), discussed in § 4.3(a), *supra.*

[1] Kapp v. National Football League, 390 F.Supp. 73 (N.D.Cal. 1974), discussed in §§ 2.4(b)(1), 2.4(b)(3) and 3.5, *supra.*

[2] Amalgamated Meat Cutters v. Jewel Tea Company, 381 U.S. 676 (1965), discussed in § 4.3(a), *supra.*

it in support of its argument that Kapp could not assert antitrust claims against the League. The NFL pointed out that it had entered into a collective bargaining agreement with the Players Association which provided that "All players in the NFL shall sign the Standard Player Contract. . ." and that, "The Standard Player Contract shall govern the relationship between the clubs and the players. . . ."[3] The Standard Player Contract contains or incorporates all of the rules challenged by Kapp in his case, including the option clause, the Rozelle Rule and the player draft. Thus, the NFL contended that the challenged rules were the result of collective bargaining between the League and the exclusive bargaining agent for all NFL players, including Kapp. Since a labor union, duly certified by the NLRB as the exclusive bargaining agent for employees (as the NFL Players Association had been), has the legal authority to bind all of the employees it represents,[4] the NFL argued that Kapp could not challenge the collective bargaining agreement, because he was one of the employees bound by it.

The issue (raised in the *Curt Flood*[5] case but not decided because of baseball's antitrust exemption) was thus squarely posed. Again, however, the issue was not squarely decided. The principal defect in the NFL's position, Judge Sweigert found, was the timing of the Collective Bargaining Agreement. It covered a four year period from February 1, 1970 through January 31, 1974; and Kapp's contract with the New England Patriots was dated October 6, 1970. While it therefore appeared that Kapp's own contract with the Patriots was entered into while the Collective

[3] 390 F.Supp. at 83.

[4] NLRB v. Allis-Chalmers Mfg. Co., 388 U.S. 175 (1967).

[5] Flood v. Kuhn, 407 U.S. 258 (1972).

Bargaining Agreement was in effect, the Collective Bargaining Agreement had not actually been entered into until June 17, 1971 when it was made "effective as of February 1, 1970."[6] Thus, Judge Sweigert found that the Collective Bargaining Agreement relied upon by the League had not existed when Kapp signed his own contract with the Patriots or during the period when the Commissioner was insisting that the Patriots have Kapp sign a Standard Player Contract. "Defendants may not now assert that the Collective Bargaining Contract of June 17, 1971, retroactively justifies their earlier ouster [Kapp]," he ruled.[7]

Because of the unique timing of the contracts involved in the *Kapp* case, it is unlikely that future cases will arise with parallel facts. On the other hand, because no new collective bargaining agreement was entered into when the 1970-1974 agreement expired, it seems that no "labor exemption" defense may be successfully asserted by the NFL to antitrust claims that may be made against it arising out of actions taken after January 31, 1974.

In addition to the timing question, Judge Sweigert added one paragraph of general applicability, relevant to the NFL during all time periods and to other sports as well. He stated,

> ". . . even if the NFL Standard Player Contract requirement had been accepted through collective bargaining, there would still remain the question, well put by Marshall, J. in *Flood* . . . , as to what are 'the limits to the antitrust violations to which labor and management can agree.' We are of the opinion that, however

[6] Collective Bargaining Agreement, Article XVI, § 1 (1970).
[7] 390 F.Supp. at 86.

> broad may be the exemption from antitrust laws of collective bargaining agreements dealing with wages, hours and other conditions of employment, that exemption does not and should not go so far as to permit immunized combinations to enforce employer-employee agreements which, being unreasonable restrictions on an employee's right to freely seek and choose his employment, have been held illegal on grounds of *public policy* long before and entirely apart from the antitrust laws." [8]

The labor exemption defense was raised again by the National Football League in the *Mackey* case.[9] Again, the court found the defense to be without merit. "There is no labor exemption from the antitrust laws available to defendants," [10] Judge Larson held. "The exemption extends only to labor or union activities, and not to the activities of employers." [11]

Judge Larson went on to say that even assuming the labor exemption can extend to management, derivatively or otherwise, it could not be extended to the National Football League under the facts established during trial. The negotiations which preceded the 1968 and 1970 collective bargaining agreements between the NFL and the Players Association included "nothing which could be legitimately characterized as 'bargaining' between the parties with respect to the Rozelle Rule," [12] he found. The issue was effectively ignored in 1968 by relegating it to a committee

---

[8] *Id.*

[9] Mackey v. National Football League, 407 F.Supp. 1000 (D. Minn. 1975), discussed in § 2.4(b)(1), *supra.*

[10] *Id.*

[11] *Id.*

[12] *Id.*

for study. And in 1970, the clubs took the position that the Commissioner's powers, including the Rozelle Rule, were non-negotiable. "The Rozelle Rule has never been the subject of serious, intensive, arms-length collective bargaining,"[13] he stated. Judge Larson then concluded with the observation that,

> "Defendants are not insulated from antitrust liability simply because of the emergence of collective bargaining with the union in 1968, and the union's inability to date to achieve the elimination of the Rozelle Rule through the collective bargaining process."[14]

§4.3(b)(4) In basketball

The "labor exemption" issue was raised once again in *Oscar Robertson* v. *National Basketball Association.*[1] In that case, the issue was finally met squarely and a decision rendered which, without qualification, favors the players. "There is no operative labor exemption barring or protecting the [National and American Basketball Associations] from being sued for antitrust violations," Judge Robert Carter ruled.[2] "A simple and concise answer to [their] contention is that the exemption extends only to labor or union activities, and not to the activities of employers."[3] Judge Carter acknowledged that employers might also benefit from the exemption, but only "derivatively," in cases where they are sued by third parties on account of the activities of unions. Thus, for example, had Jewel Tea Company sued its competitors along with the

[13] *Id.*

[14] *Id.*

[1] 389 F.Supp. 867 (S.D.N.Y. 1975), discussed in §§ 2.4(b)(2), 2.4(b)(3) and 3.5, *supra.*

[2] *Id.* at 884.

[3] *Id.* at 884-885.

Meat Cutters Union,[4] those competing food markets would have been exempt from antitrust liability along with the Union.

The National Basketball Association had argued that practices are immune from the antitrust laws whenever (1) they are directed only at parties to the collective bargaining relationship, and (2) they are mandatory subjects of collective bargaining (that is, wages, hours, and other terms and conditions of employment). This test, if applied in the hockey cases,[5] would have yielded the same result reached there, because in those cases the challenged reserve clause was directed at someone who was not a party to the collective bargaining relationship between the National Hockey League and the Players Association, namely, the World Hockey Association. In the *Oscar Robertson* case, the NBA contended that its draft and option were (1) aimed only at NBA players, and (2) were mandatory subjects of collective bargaining; therefore, the NBA said, it should be immune.

The NBA's proposed test was based, in part, on Justice Goldberg's concurring opinion in the *Jewel Tea* case, which said that collective agreements on mandatory subjects of bargaining must be immune from antitrust attack, for if not, the labor laws would require employers and employees to bargain over subjects about which the antitrust laws prohibited them from agreeing.[6] While Judge Carter acknowledged that some support could be found for the proposed test in Justice Goldberg's concurring opinion, that support was "completely undermined," Judge Carter

---

[4] See, Amalgamated Meat Cutters v. Jewel Tea Company, 381 U.S. 676 (1965), discussed in § 4.3(a), *supra.*

[5] See § 4.3(b)(2), *supra.*

[6] Quoted in § 4.3(a), *supra.*

held, by a statement made by the Supreme Court in *United Mine Workers* v. *Pennington,*[7] a case decided the same day as *Jewel Tea.*

In *Pennington,* a small coal mining company alleged that the collective bargaining agreement negotiated by the United Mine Workers with all coal companies—large and small—was the product of an antitrust conspiracy between the Union and large companies designed to force small companies out of business. This was so because the wages required by the agreement could only be afforded by large companies. The Supreme Court was satisfied that the facts showed that the Union had agreed with the large companies to impose the same wage demands on small companies, and it held,

> "[W]e think a union forfeits its exemption from the antitrust laws when it is clearly shown that it has agreed with one set of employers to impose a certain wage scale on other bargaining units. One group of employers may not conspire to eliminate competition from the industry and the union is liable with the employers if it becomes a party to the conspiracy. This is true even though the union's part in the scheme is an undertaking to secure the same wages, hours or other conditions of employment from the remaining employers. . ."[8]

In the course of so holding, the Supreme Court explained that an agreement resulting from union-employer negotiations

> ". . . is not . . . automatically exempt from Sherman Act scrutiny simply because the negotiations involve a

[7] 381 U.S. 657 (1965).

[8] *Id.* at 665-666.

> compulsory subject of bargaining, regardless of the subject or the form and content of the agreement . . . [T]here are limits to what a union or an employer may offer or extract in the name of wages, and because they must bargain does not mean that the agreement may disregard other laws." [9]

It was this statement which Judge Carter interpreted as undermining the NBA's proposed test. Thus, according to Judge Carter, even if the NBA draft and option were aimed only at NBA players, and not at any third parties, and even if the draft and option were mandatory subjects of collective bargaining, and even if the draft and option had been agreed to during bargaining with the Players Association, nevertheless that does not mean that the draft and option "may disregard other laws." [10]

§4.3(c) Critique of the theory

The two foremost exponents of the theory that professional sport leagues are exempt from antitrust attack by members of players associations are Yale law professor Ralph K. Winter, Jr., and attorney Michael S. Jacobs. In an article published in the *Yale Law Journal* in 1971,[1] they expressed the view that as between employers and employees engaged in collective bargaining, the antitrust laws neither have nor ought to have any application whatsoever to the determination of terms and conditions of employment. The article was written with grace and style, and it expressed the authors' views in a confident though nonpartisan tone. For these reasons, as well as Professor

---

[9] *Id.* at 664-665.

[10] *Id.*

[1] Jacobs & Winter, Antitrust Principles and Collective Bargaining by Athletes: Of Superstars in Peonage, 81 Yale L.J. 1 (1971).

Winter's national reputation, the article was widely circulated and cited.[2] Yet, as the cases discussed above indicate,[3] their conclusions have not been followed to date.

Careful study of the article suggests reasons why, despite the persuasive impression it leaves on first reading, it has not persuaded judges who have actually decided the issues it discusses. Jacobs and Winter first explained that under the National Labor Relations Act, employees' elected representatives become their exclusive representatives for collective bargaining purposes. As a result, once union representation is decided upon by the majority of workers in a unit, all workers in the unit are represented by the union with respect to mandatory subjects of collective bargaining, namely, wages, hours and other terms and conditions of employment. Under the Act, individual members of the union may not bargain for themselves on those subjects (unless the collective bargaining agreement reserves for them the right to do so, as have player association agreements with respect to maximum wages). And this is true even if particular members of the union possess such superior skills that they could have achieved better employment terms on their own than as union members.[4]

The article next pointed out that although the National Labor Relations Act requires employers and unions to bargain in good faith concerning wages, hours and other

---

[2] The article was reprinted, for example, in Hearings on S.2373 before the Subcomm. on Antitrust and Monopoly of the Senate Comm. on the Judiciary, 92d Cong., 2d Sess., Part 2 at 1189 *et seq.* (1971-1972); and in Hearings on H.R. 1206, *et al.*, before the Antitrust Subcomm. of the House Comm. on the Judiciary, 92d Cong., 2d Sess. at 199 *et seq.* (1972). It was also cited in Flood v. Kuhn, 407 U.S. 258 (1972), in both the majority opinion (fn. 22) and the dissent of Justice Marshall (fn. 8).

[3] See §§ 4.3(b)(1), 4.3(b)(3) and 4.3(b)(4), *supra.*

[4] 81 Yale at 7-10.

terms and conditions of employment, it does not compel either side to make concessions or reach an agreement. All that is required is some reasonable effort towards reconciling differences.[5]

Non-intervention by the government with respect to the substantive terms of collective bargaining agreements was considered by Jacobs and Winter to be sound public policy for two reasons. One was their belief that the parties know what is best for them, and that if the government intervenes, it "increases the danger of imposing terms which are in the long run ill-suited to the peculiar circumstances of the bargaining relationship." [6]

A second reason was that even if the government outlaws a particular demand, bargaining power can be shifted to other issues. "Denying a demand to a party may thus increase the chances of a strike because it lessens the area of possible compromise without affecting the underlying strength of the parties." [7] For example, if reserve and option systems were outlawed, owners might seek maximum salaries or other alternatives which many players could find "less palatable in the long run than the reserve clause." [8]

Jacobs and Winter thought it "obvious" that reserve and option systems are mandatory subjects for collective bargaining, stating that they found it "difficult to construct even a hypothetical argument that a contractual provision so intimately connected with determining the team for which an athlete will play and what salary and other benefits he may extract through individual bargaining is not a term and

[5] *Id.* at 11.
[6] *Id.* at 12.
[7] *Id.* at 13.
[8] *Id.*

condition of employment."[9] Thus, they concluded that leagues and players associations must bargain about reserve and option systems if either side raises the issue, but that agreement is not compelled by law. The stronger side is permitted to use its strength to prevail.

If the owners are stronger, and by virtue of that strength compel the players associations to acquiesce in a reserve or option system, then, according to the article, all of the players must accept such systems, just as they must accept the minimum wage, pension and other provisions that are negotiated on their behalf. Individual players may not challenge reserve and option systems arrived at after collective bargaining any more than other union members may challenge comparable provisions of collective bargaining agreements negotiated for them.

Jacobs and Winter acknowledged that there are certain limits on the kinds of collective bargaining agreements unions may negotiate. But in their opinion, those limits are not exceeded by reserve and option systems. They did not consider reserve and option systems to be unreasonable, for they compared such systems to the union hiring hall so common in other industries. Furthermore, because such systems may be renegotiated each time a collective bargaining agreement expires, they did not consider them to be long term restrictions. Nor would they consider a player association's acquiescence in a reserve or option system to be a violation of the association's duty to represent all of its members fairly.[10]

---

[9] *Id.* at 10-11. See, however, Robertson v. National Basketball Association, 389 F.Supp. 867, 889 (S.D.N.Y. 1975), and Mackey v. National Football League, 407 F.Supp. 1000, 1009 (D.Minn. 1975), for a contrary opinion.

[10] *Id.* at 17-21.

With respect to the antitrust issue in particular, Jacobs and Winter emphasized that just as employees may join together in a union for collective bargaining, so may employers bargain as a group rather than individually. Citing *Allen-Bradley, Jewel Tea* and *Pennington,* they contended that a majority of the Supreme Court "has insisted that one factor be present before the Sherman Act applies to arrangements arrived at through collective bargaining: one group of employers must conspire to use the union to hurt their competitors." [11] From this they concluded, "That the reserve clause, as raised in *Flood,* is strictly a labor market issue seems plain, and, as a result, cannot give rise to antitrust liability." [12]

The article seems to have gone astray in two regards. First, although the reasons cited for non-intervention by government seem sound in theory, they have long since been rejected by Congress in fact. As a result, the article overstates the extent to which unions and employers are free to make demands subject only to their strength to enforce them. In the area of wages and hours, for example, the federal Fair Labor Standards Act establishes a minimum wage below which no collective bargaining agreement may go.[13] The Fair Labor Standards Act also establishes a maximum length work week which no collective bargaining agreement may exceed, unless time and a half is to be paid.[14] Similarly, in the area of working conditions, the federal Occupational Safety and Health Act specifies detailed working conditions which cannot be avoided by any collective bargaining agreement.[15] A col-

---

[11] *Id.* at 26.

[12] *Id.* at 27.

[13] 29 U.S.C. § 206.

[14] 29 U.S.C. § 207.

[15] 29 U.S.C. §§ 651-678.

lective bargaining agreement which violated either of these laws could be attacked by union members, even though the union is its members' exclusive representative.

Second, the article treats the labor exemption cases too narrowly. *Allen-Bradley, Jewel Tea,* and *Pennington* all happened to involve accusations that unions and employers had conspired together to injure the employers' competitors.[16] But they did not hold, as Jacobs and Winter suggest, that employers may bargain collectively with impunity if the target of their conspiracy is their employees, rather than their competitors. As the Supreme Court observed in *Pennington,* and as Judge Carter noted in the *Oscar Robertson* case, "There are limits to what a union or an employer may offer or extract in the name of wages, and because they must bargain does not mean that the agreement reached may disregard other laws." [17]

The substance of agreements between employers and unions may not disregard the Fair Labor Standards Act or the Occupational Safety and Health Act; nor may the substance of those agreements disregard the Sherman Act. While Jacobs and Winter were correct when they asserted, "Surely a union butcher who desired to work at night could not challenge the contractual provision agreed upon in *Jewel Tea,"* [18] the reason they were correct is that the provision violated no law that protected the *butchers.* While it was alleged to have violated antitrust laws protecting the Jewel Tea Company, the butchers would not

---

[16] See §§ 4.3(a) and 4.3(b)(4), *supra.*

[17] United Mine Workers v. Pennington, 381 U.S. 657, 665 (1965), quoted in Robertson v. National Basketball Association, 389 F.Supp. 867, 888 (S.D.N.Y. 1975).

[18] 81 Yale L.J. at 27.

have had standing to assert that violation.[19] On the other hand, reserve and option systems may well violate antitrust laws protecting professional athletes, as well as competing leagues. And thus players, unlike butchers, may challenge such systems on antitrust grounds.

[19] See, San Francisco Seals, Ltd. v. National Hockey League, 379 F.Supp. 966 (C.D.Cal. 1974), discussed in § 8.2(b), *infra*.

Chapter 5

INTER-LEAGUE "WARS"

§5.1 History of inter-league competition

"Wars" between sports leagues have been a familiar and virtually constant feature of the professional sports scene for more than a decade. Even before the modern era, sporadic conflicts took place, beginning in baseball as long ago as the nineteenth century.[1] Though Organized Baseball has suffered no competition for almost three decades, the National League, since its formation in 1871, has battled with the American Association, the Union Association, the Players League, the American League (which survived), the Federal League, and the Mexican League.

The National Basketball Association traces its origins to 1937 when the National Basketball League was formed. An American Basketball League followed, as did the Basketball Association of America. By 1948, five of six American League teams and four of eleven Basketball Association of America teams had gone out of business. The survivors joined forces and competed with the National League, causing financial disaster for all. In 1949, the National League and the BAA merged, forming today's National Basketball Association. The NBA faced competition briefly—for a season and a half—from the American Basketball League in 1960 and 1961. And in 1966, it entered into a new and still lingering "war" with the American Basketball Association.[2]

---

[1] See §§ 1.1(a) and 1.1(b), *supra,* and H.Rep. 2002, 82d Cong., 2d Sess. (1952).

[2] Hearings on S.2373 before the Subcomm. on Antitrust and Monopoly of the Senate Comm. on the Judiciary, 92d Cong., 1st Sess. 187-190 (1971).

The National Football League competed with the All-America Football Conference between 1946 and 1949. In 1950, the NFL absorbed three of its opponents' teams,[3] thereby renewing its monopoly on professional football until 1960, when the American Football League began operations. The NFL-AFL "war" lasted until 1966 when the two leagues received Congressional authorization to merge.[4] And, more recently, the World Football League began yet another, though short-lived war.[5]

What is ultimately at stake in these sports "wars" is the patronage of ticket-buying, television-watching fans. The battles are fought with two weapons—financial and legal—and on three fronts—for players, for stadia, and for cities.

§5.2 Competition for players

The most visible of the battles are those for players—battles which have made some athletes multi-millionaires, and which many say have driven some franchises to the brink of bankruptcy. The battle for players has also generated more litigation than any other single issue in all of professional sports.

§5.2(a) Graduating collegians

Football and basketball are, of course, major sports at the college level, and the better collegians often have nationwide reputations and followings long before gradua-

---

[3] Hearings on S.2373 before the Subcomm. on Antitrust and Monopoly of the Senate Comm. on the Judiciary, 92d Cong., 2d Sess., Part 2 at 767 (1971-1972); American Football League v. National Football League, 205 F.Supp. 60, 65 (D.Md. 1962), *aff'd,* 323 F.2d 124 (4th Cir. 1963).

[4] See § 6.1, *infra.*

[5] See, generally, G. Davidson, Breaking the Game Wide Open (New York: Atheneum, 1974).

tion. Thus, they are actively sought by professional teams even in times of "peace." In times of "war," however, the demand for their services increases virtually without measure. The ability to sign big-name collegians is one early measure of the viability of a new league. And, because most veterans already playing in established leagues are saddled with option clauses, college graduates are the only significant pool of playing talent available to a new league for its first season of play. In theory, a new league may hire all of the college graduates it can get without fear of expensive and time consuming lawsuits. In the AFL-NFL "war" of the early sixties, however, the two leagues managed to wind up in court even over collegians.

§5.2(a)(1) Contracts: offer and acceptance

In the fall of 1959, Billy Cannon was a star on the Louisiana State University football team; the American Football League was organizing for its first season of play the following year; and Pete Rozelle was general manager of the Los Angeles Rams, a team that finished the season in a tie for last place with a record of two wins and ten losses. A coin flip was to decide whether it got the very first draft pick that year, or the second. And the Rams wanted Cannon.

On Saturday, November 28, 1959, Billy Cannon was in New York to accept one of the many honors that were being bestowed upon him for his football prowess. The NFL draft was to take place in Philadelphia the following Monday, and Rozelle spoke to Cannon by phone about the Rams' interest in him. This was done, the Rams later testified, because the right to the first draft pick is so valuable that care is taken to be sure it is not wasted on an athlete who is not interested. On Sunday, November

29th, Rozelle again spoke to Cannon, and told him to come to Philadelphia so that a joint press conference could be held if the Rams were able to draft him. Cannon did, registering in the hotel under the name "Billy Gunn" at Rozelle's suggestion. The Rams did win the flip of the coin on Monday and immediately selected Cannon. Thereafter, Rozelle and Cannon met with the press and reported that the Rams had drafted Cannon and that he intended to play for them. Rozelle and Cannon then went to Rozelle's hotel room where Cannon signed three NFL Standard Player Contracts for the 1960, 1961 and 1962 seasons, and Rozelle gave him a $10,000 bonus check.

The National Football League had thus beaten its rival, the American Football League, to the top draft prospect of the season, only minutes after the battle had begun. This early success was not announced to the press, however, because Louisiana State had been invited to the Sugar Bowl the following January 1st, and Cannon's signing a professional contract made him ineligible to play in it.

Rozelle later testified that he "told Billy Cannon this would be kept in confidence, the signing would not be announced until after the Sugar Bowl and told him to take good care of the money." [1] Testimony also established that Rozelle had earlier told Cannon's college coach that "the Rams will do nothing to impair Cannon's eligibility for the Sugar Bowl." [2] Indeed, Cannon himself had told the press that he would sign with the Rams following the Sugar Bowl on New Year's Day.

---

[1] Los Angeles Rams Football Club v. Cannon, 185 F.Supp. 717, 725 (S.D.Cal. 1960).

[2] *Id.*

Cannon did not endorse his bonus check, but instead simply gave it to his banker for safekeeping. Approximately two weeks after he signed with the Rams, Cannon was contacted by the Houston Oilers of the American Football League, and on December 22, 1959, he signed a contract with that team. On December 30th, Cannon sent the Rams a letter telling them he no longer wanted to play for them, revoking any offer to play for them he may have previously made, and returning the $10,000 bonus check.

Almost immediately, the Rams filed suit against Cannon in the federal District Court in Los Angeles, seeking an injunction preventing him from playing for the Oilers or any other team during the term of their contract and an order declaring those contracts valid. When they filed suit, the Rams probably anticipated a quick and easy judicial victory; only five years before, an NFL team, the Cleveland Browns, had lost such a case when they signed two college stars who had signed the month before with the Winnipeg team of the Canadian Football League. A federal District Judge in Ohio enjoined Robert Freeman and Jack Locklear from playing with the Browns during the 1955 season, holding that their 1955 Canadian Football League contracts were for services of special merit which were of peculiar and particular value to Winnipeg, and that damages, in the event of breach, would be incapable of measurement.[3]

The Rams' case against Cannon was tried before District Judge Lindberg in the spring of 1960; and if the Rams thought that Winnipeg's earlier victory would be the controlling precedent, they were sorely disappointed. Cannon won in time to go to the Oilers' training camp that summer.

---

[3] **Winnipeg Rugby Football Club v. Freeman, 140 F.Supp. 365 (N.D.Ohio 1955).**

After a careful and thorough analysis of the facts and applicable law, Judge Lindberg found that no contract had ever existed between Cannon and the Rams, for a very simple reason. In those days, the NFL Standard Players Contract provided:

> "This agreement shall become valid and binding upon each party hereto only when, as and if it shall be approved by the Commissioner." [4]

Austin Gunsel, Acting Commissioner during the brief period between Bert Bell's death in October of 1959 and Rozelle's appointment in January of 1960, had approved Cannon's contract for 1960, but not the 1961 and 1962 agreements. The 1961 and 1962 documents had not been submitted to the Acting Commissioner, and the evidence showed that he was not even aware of their existence until late in December.

The Rams argued that the Commissioner's approval of contracts was "an unimportant ministerial act concerning the League and the Club." [5] Billy Cannon, of course, took the position that it was "an act absolutely essential to the formation of the contract." [6] Judge Lindberg agreed with Cannon. "The words 'shall become valid' clearly compels the conclusion that—in the absence of approval—it is not yet a valid agreement," Judge Lindberg explained.[7] "The use of the word 'if' clearly suggests that approval might not happen at all. This clause is too definite to be ignored. It jumps out at you." [8]

---

[4] 185 F.Supp. at 721.

[5] *Id.*

[6] *Id.*

[7] *Id.*

[8] *Id.* at 722.

Therefore, the Judge held that the 1961 and 1962 documents were at most offers by Cannon to play for the Rams during those years—offers which he had unquestionably revoked. The Judge also found that the 1960 document was not a binding contract because the testimony showed that all of the negotiations between Cannon and Rozelle had been for a three-year contract, not a one-year contract. Thus, Cannon's offer had been to play for the Rams for three years, and that offer was never accepted by the Rams because they had requested and received approval from the Commissioner for one year only.

The Rams also argued that Cannon's taking of the $10,000 bonus check should have been construed as an acceptance by him of a Ram counter-offer for one year of employment, or as consideration for an option on his services which the Rams could exercise for a reasonable period of time. While both of these arguments were based on sound legal theory, Judge Lindberg did not accept them. He did not because he found that Cannon had not accepted the bonus check in payment, but rather took it sincerely believing it was not his until after the Sugar Bowl game. The Judge was able to make this finding because he noted that Cannon was

> ". . . anything but an astute businessman. His whole life and interest has been directed toward athletics and particularly football; and while he impressed me as being somewhat naive for a college senior I feel certain that he knew he couldn't accept as payment the $10,000 check that was tendered to him and remain eligible to play for his school in the Sugar Bowl, nor do I believe he would intentionally disqualify himself. He didn't need to. With respect to Cannon

> this wasn't a chance in a lifetime to turn professional which he might lose forever if he didn't grab it immediately."[9]

Why Rozelle chose to have Cannon sign three separate one-year contracts, rather than a single three-year document, was never explained in Judge Lindberg's opinion; it may never have been explained to him. But whatever the reason,[10] it was fortuitous; for Cannon's other defenses included allegations that he had been induced to sign the contract documents only as a result of fraud and deceit on Rozelle's part. Allegations of that kind are not uncommon in litigation, and they are far more often made than proved. In this case, Judge Lindberg did not rule on them at all, because he found that no contract ever actually existed. The Judge did say however:

> "Just what language Rozelle used in persuading Cannon to sign the documents I do not know and I doubt if either Cannon or Rozelle have a completely accurate recollection of what was said. I am persuaded, however, that during the 30 to 45 minutes spent in the room Rozelle conveyed the impression to Cannon that the documents would not become effective or binding upon him until after the Sugar Bowl game on New Year's Day."[11]

One of Billy Cannon's LSU teammates was Johnny Robinson, also considered a top professional prospect. Robinson was drafted by the Detroit Lions of the National Football League on November 30, 1959. And on December

---

[9] *Id.* at 725-726.

[10] For a possible reason, see § 2.5, *supra,* and Matuszak v. Houston Oilers, Inc., 1974-2 CCH Trade Cases ¶ 75,373 (Tex.Ct. Civ. App. 1974), discussed in § 5.2(b)(2)(A), *infra.*

[11] 185 F.Supp. at 726.

2nd, the Lions signed him to a one-year $14,500 contract, paying him $2,500 in advance immediately. "It was understood" a judge later found, "that in view of the forthcoming Sugar Bowl game, no public mention of the arrangement would be made until after New Year's."[12]

Later that December, Robinson was contacted by the Dallas Texans of the American Football League. Like Cannon, Robinson too was persuaded to sign with the new league, and on December 29th, he notified the Lions he would not be playing for them. The Lions presented Robinson's contract to the NFL Commissioner for approval on January 6, 1960, and it was approved on January 12th. When Robinson returned his advance the next day, the Lions refused to accept it and filed suit in federal court in Baton Rouge to enjoin Robinson from playing for the Texans or any other team.

The case was heard by District Judge Skelly Wright (now a judge of the Court of Appeals in Washington, D.C.). Judge Wright began his opinion as follows:

> "This case is but another round in the sordid fight for football players, a fight which begins before these athletes enter college and follows them through their professional careers. It is a fight characterized by deception, double dealing, campus jumping, secret alumni subsidization, semi-professionalism and professionalism. It is a fight which has produced as part of its harvest this current rash of contract jumping suits. It is a fight which so conditions the minds and hearts of these athletes that one day they can agree to play football for a stipulated amount for one group, only to repudiate that agreement the fol-

[12] Detroit Football Company v. Robinson, 186 F.Supp. 933, 934 (E.D.La. 1960).

lowing day or whenever a better offer comes along. So it was with Johnny Robinson."[13]

Like Judge Lindberg (nine days before him), Judge Wright concluded that no valid or binding contract existed between a player and an NFL team until the league Commissioner approved the contract. In Johnny Robinson's case, the Commissioner did not approve the contract until two weeks after Robinson withdrew his offer to play for the Lions. The Judge stated:

> ". . . despite its efforts to 'sign up' this player, and 'bait' him with twenty-five one-hundred dollars bills, Detroit failed to land their fish. His struggle to wriggle off the hook has proved successful. But it might not be amiss to remind Robinson of what Judge Rogers said to Sam Etcheverry in a similar case [filed by the Chicago Cardinals in 1956]:
>
> > '. . . in four or five, six or eight years, some day your passes are going to wobble in the air, you are not going to find that receiver. If you keep playing around here, with these professionals, and others, and jumping your contracts—you are all right this time, . . . but . . . some day your abilities will be such that your club won't even send a twice disbarred attorney from Dogpatch to help you. They sent some dandy ones this time . . .'"[14]

LSU's opponent in that New Year's Day 1960 Sugar Bowl game was the University of Mississippi. Ole Miss had a player named Charlie Flowers who had been drafted by the New York Giants of the National Football League

---

[13] *Id.*
[14] *Id.* at 935-936.

and the Los Angeles Chargers of the American Football League. Like Billy Cannon, Charlie Flowers was also in New York City the weekend of the NFL draft. While in New York, he was invited to the office of Giant owner Wellington Mara, and there was urged to sign a two-year contract. Flowers, however, wanted to play in the Sugar Bowl and knew that if he signed he would be ineligible. Mara knew it too of course, and so he proposed that the signing of the contract be kept confidential until after the game. Flowers signed and was given checks for $3,500 as a bonus. "Part of the deceit agreed to . . ." a court later found, "was an agreement that Mara would not submit the contract to the Commissioner until after January 1st." [15]

Flowers returned to Mississippi and had second thoughts about his Giants contract almost immediately. On December 5th, he phoned the Giants to withdraw. In response, the Giants promptly filed his contract with the Commissioner who approved it on December 15th. At Mara's request, however, the Commissioner withheld announcement of his approval until after New Year's Day.

On December 29th, Flowers was offered a better contract by the Los Angeles Chargers, and though he did not formally execute it until after the Sugar Bowl game, he immediately wrote to the Giants withdrawing from his agreement with them and returning the bonus checks. Thereafter, the Giants filed suit in federal court in Mississippi, seeking to enjoin Flowers from playing for the Chargers or any other team.

This case was somewhat different from those involving Billy Cannon and Johnny Robinson, because Flowers'

---

[15] New York Football Giants, Inc. v. Los Angeles Chargers Football Club, Inc., 291 F.2d 471, 473 (5th Cir. 1961).

contract had been approved by the Commissioner before Flowers formally withdrew in writing. Though it seems the Court could have held that Flowers revoked his offer to play for the Giants during his December 5th telephone call—a call which preceded the Commissioner's approval —it found in Flowers' favor for another though related reason. The Court held that because Mara had agreed not to submit the contract for approval until after January 1st, Flowers had the right to cancel until that date, and the Commissioner's prior approval on December 15th was simply not effective.[16]

The Giants, however, were unwilling to accept the loss of Flowers, and though it took an entire year, they pursued their claim to his services to the United States Court of Appeals. There, Flowers' victory was affirmed, but on substantially different grounds.[17]

§5.2(a)(2) Unclean hands and fraudulent inducement

An injunction is considered an "equitable" remedy, said to be available only to those who have "clean hands." The Supreme Court has explained that the "clean hands doctrine" does not require parties to "have led blameless lives . . . as to other matters . . ."[1] It does, however, require "that they shall have acted fairly and without fraud or deceit as to the controversy in issue."[2] Referring to Judge Wright's earlier opinion in the *Johnny Rob-*

---

[16] *Id.*

[17] See § 5.2(a)(2), *infra.*

[1] Precision Instrument Mfg. Co. v. Automotive Maintenance Machinery Co., 324 U.S. 806, 814 (1945).

[2] *Id.*

inson[3] case, the judges of the Court of Appeals who heard the *Flowers*[4] case said:

> ". . . we share his disgust at the sordid picture too often presented in this kind of litigation. So much so, in fact, that we conclude that in an appropriate case the federal . . . court . . . must decline to lend its aid to either party to a transaction that in its inception offends concepts of decency and honest dealing, such as the case before us.
>
> . . .
>
> "When it became apparent from uncontradicted testimony of Mara that this deceit was practiced in order to bring into being the 'contract' sued upon, the trial court should have dismissed the suit without more on the basis of the 'clean hands' doctrine." [5]

Thus, in its first months of operation and almost a year before it played its first game, the American Football League spirited away three top draft choices from the NFL and successfully withstood the NFL's courtroom attacks. The National Football League took stock of its legal position and realizing that it had been skewered by a clause in its own contract providing that an agreement was to become valid and binding only if and when approved by the commissioner, it amended the clause. The National Football League Standard Players Contract now provides:

> "This contract shall be valid and binding upon the parties hereto immediately upon its execution. A copy

[3] Detroit Football Company v. Robinson, 186 F.Supp 933 (E.D. La. 1960), discussed in § 5.2(a)(1), *supra.*

[4] New York Football Giants, Inc. v. Los Angeles Chargers Football Club, Inc., 291 F.2d 471 (5th Cir. 1961).

[5] *Id.* at 472, 474-475.

of such contract shall be filed by the Club with the Commissioner within ten (10) days after execution. The Commissioner shall have the right to terminate this contract by his disapproval thereof within ten (10) days after the filing thereof in his office; . . . in such event, the Commissioner shall give both parties written notice of such termination, and thereupon, both parties shall be relieved of their respective rights and liabilities hereunder." [6]

Since contracts were made immediately valid, players would be limited to arguing that they had been fraudulently induced to sign them or that the doctrine of unclean hands prevented enforcement. Whether for that reason or others, after that first round of lawsuits in early 1960, the National and American Football Leagues managed to stay out of court for five years. Then in the fall of 1964, the University of Oklahoma team was so good that four of its members were drafted by the pros, including Ralph Neely and Lance Rentzel. Oklahoma also received an invitation to play Florida State on New Year's Day in the Gator Bowl. Neely signed with the Houston Oilers of the AFL, and Rentzel signed with the Minnesota Vikings of the NFL, both during the month of December. In his autobiography, Rentzel explained:

"We were all advised by the club representatives that we could save a lot of money by signing in December, before the New Year, splitting the bonus and the salary over two years instead of paying taxes all in one. It made sense enough, and we did it. And it was a widespread practice among all college players who were about to turn professional.

[6] NFL Standard Player Contract ¶ 17.

"But, as it turned out, I couldn't have made a bigger mistake."[7]

After Neely had signed with the Oilers and had accepted a $25,000 bonus check made payable to his father-in-law "as Trustee," he received a better offer from the Dallas Cowboys of the NFL and decided to accept it. On December 29, 1964, Neely sent letters to the Oilers and their owner—letters that had been prepared for his signature by lawyers for the Cowboys—stating that he did not consider himself bound by his Oiler contracts and was withdrawing from them. The Oilers received Neely's letters (and the $25,000 bonus check they had given him) on December 31st, and on that day the Cowboys deposited $25,000 of their own into Neely's account in a Dallas bank.

(Neely told his coach what he had done, and the evening before the Gator Bowl, the story broke publicly. Only hours before the game, Neely, Rentzel, and two teammates who had also signed professional contracts were all declared ineligible; and Florida State beat Oklahoma. After the game, Lance Rentzel met an NFL scout who told him that "five of Florida State's best players, all of whom had done very well that afternoon, had signed professional contracts before the game."[8])

On the evening of January 1, 1965, Neely signed a contract with the Cowboys, and the two leagues went back to court. At trial, Neely argued that the Oilers contracts he had signed were unenforceable because he had been told they would not become effective, and thus he would not lose his college eligibility, until the day after the

[7] L. Rentzel, When All the Laughter Died in Sorrow (New York: Bantam, 1972) at 85-86.

[8] *Id.* at 87.

Gator Bowl. The trial judge agreed, and ruled in Neely's favor on the grounds that the Oilers had fraudulently induced him to sign.[9] So Neely was free to and did play for the Cowboys during the 1965 professional season. The Court of Appeals reversed Neely's victory, however, and enjoined him from playing for the Cowboys until his Oilers contracts expired at the end of the 1968 season.[10] It held that the evidence showed that Neely knew all along that he would lose his college eligibility the moment he signed a professional contract and received bonus money, and that the clear purpose of keeping the signing secret was not to preserve his eligibility, but rather to prevent his ineligibility from becoming known. The Oilers had done nothing amounting to fraud, the Court of Appeals said, and, therefore, the validity of its contracts with Neely were not affected on that ground.

Neely had also relied on the *Charlie Flowers* case, where it was held that the Giants were not entitled to an injunction against Flowers, because they had been guilty of "unclean hands" in inducing him to sign before his own New Year's Day bowl game. The Court of Appeals in Neely's case was not impressed with the *Flowers* decision. Although it acknowledged that the *Flowers* case involved "a somewhat similar situation," [11] it noted:

> "It is quite apparent that the player contract in that case was acquired under circumstances much different from those in this case, but if the rule announced in that case was intended to apply to every instance in which a contract is entered into with a college football player before a post-season game with an under-

[9] Houston Oilers, Inc. v. Neely, 361 F.2d 36, 38 (10th Cir. 1966).

[10] *Id.*

[11] *Id.* at 42.

standing that it be kept secret to permit that player to compete in the game, then we must respectfully disagree with the conclusion." [12]

Why the Court of Appeals felt that Flowers' contract was acquired under circumstances different from those in the *Neely* case is not at all clear; from the opinions written by the courts in the two lawsuits, the circumstances seem identical. It therefore seems that the *Neely* court's respectful disagreement with the conclusion in the *Flowers* case is the significant aspect of the opinion. Some judges are persuaded by the "clean hands doctrine"; others are not. The *Neely* court explained its views as follows:

> "While we do not for a moment condone the ruthless methods employed by professional football teams in their contest for the services of college football players, including the lavish expenditure of money, it must be conceded that there is no legal impediment to contracting for the services of athletes at any time, and the above-mentioned conduct, while regrettable, does not furnish athletes with a legal excuse to avoid their contracts for reasons other than the temptations of a more attractive offer. Although there are many dismal indications to the contrary, athletes, amateur or professional, and those connected with athletics, are bound by their contracts to the same extent as anyone else, and should not be allowed to repudiate them at their pleasure." [13]

Less than six months after the *Neely* decision, Congress enacted legislation authorizing the merger of the National

[12] *Id.*
[13] *Id.* at 41.

and American Football Leagues,[14] thus bringing their "war" for graduating collegians to an end, and leaving unresolved the apparent conflict between the decisions of the two courts in the *Flowers* and *Neely* cases. However, if lessons can be learned from events that did not take place, it may be that sports league promoters accepted the *Neely* decision as the law. For although the AFL actually wound up winning all four of its lawsuits over graduating collegians, when the American Basketball Association came into existence in 1966 there were no dual signings of college basketball stars—or at least none that reached the courts.

§5.2(b) Veterans stars

When the NBA-ABA "war" began, the legal battle for players shifted to litigation over the services of veteran stars. Actually, it might be more accurate to say that the battle returned to litigation over veteran players, because the early baseball "wars" were primarily fights over veterans.[1] Veteran players, by definition, are those who have signed professional contracts previously. Such contracts cover a term of one or more years plus an additional option or reserve year.

§5.2(b)(1) Under reserve or option only

In years past, new leagues typically have signed veterans at the conclusion of the term of their old league contracts, without respecting the reserve or option year that was yet to come. As discussed in Chapter 2, some courts gave effect to the reserve or option year by enjoining the athlete from playing in the new league until that

[14] See § 6.1, *infra*.

[1] See §§ 1.1(b), 2.3(a)(1) and 2.3(b)(1), *supra*.

year expired, while other courts held the reserve or option clause to be unenforceable for one reason or another.

The World Football League signed its first National Football League veteran in February of 1974, before its first season of play. Interestingly, however, the WFL and the man it signed, Richmond Flowers, a defensive back for the New York Giants, decided to avoid costly litigation by simply agreeing that Flowers would play out his NFL option during the 1974 season and begin WFL play in 1975.[1]

§5.2(b)(2) Under current contract

While competing leagues have disregarded reserve and option clauses most often, they have on several occasions ignored current contracts too. That is, competing leagues have signed players whose contracts still had one or more years remaining to the primary term, in addition to the reserve or option year. The earliest reported incidents of this sort took place during the Federal League baseball "war" in 1914, and the consequences were not always uniform.

§5.2(b)(2)(A) Mutuality doctrine

Harold Chase and George Johnson were two of the first to defect from Organized Baseball to the new Federal League. Chase had executed an American League player contract with Chicago in March of 1914, covering the 1914 season. Then, in June of 1914, he notified his team that he intended to cancel, and he signed a Federal League con-

[1] L.A. Times, Feb. 20, 1974, Part III; but see, World Football League v. Dallas Cowboys Football Club, 513 S.W.2d 102 (Tex. Ct. Civ. App. 1974), discussed in § 5.2(b)(2)(C), *infra,* and Matuszak v. Houston Oilers, Inc., 1974-2 CCH Trade Cases ¶ 75,373 (Tex. Ct. Civ. App. 1974), discussed in § 5.2(b)(2)(A), *infra.*

tract, also covering the 1914 season. Johnson had signed a National League player contract with Cincinnati for the 1914 and 1915 seasons, but after playing the first week of the 1914 season, he left and signed to play in the Federal League.

Chicago and Cincinnati filed separate suits against the two players, seeking injunctions preventing them from playing for Federal League teams during the terms of their National and American League contracts. Injunctions were denied in both cases, however, on the grounds that the National and American League contracts lacked mutuality.[1] They lacked mutuality, the courts held, because they gave the teams the right to cancel simply on ten days' notice. In other words, the teams were seeking to hold Chase and Johnson to their contracts for an entire season or more, while the two players could hold the teams to their contracts only for ten days. That was so unfair, the Courts held, that such contracts were unenforceable. (In the *Chase* case, the Court also decided that Chicago was not entitled to an injunction because of its own "unclean hands." The basis for the Court's "unclean hands" finding was Organized Baseball's reserve rule—even though this was not a reserve clause case—which in the Court's judgment amounted to "quasi peonage of baseball players . . . contrary to the spirit of American institutions, and . . . to the spirit of the Constitution of the United States." [2] In fact, it was the *Chase* case which years later Judge Frank quoted in his opinion in *Gardella* v. *Chandler*[3] to the effect that involuntary servitude was imposed upon players by Organized Baseball.)

---

[1] Cincinnati Exhibition Co. v. Johnson, 190 Ill. App. 630 (1914); American League v. Chase, 149 N.Y.S. 6 (1914).

[2] 149 N.Y.S. at 19.

[3] 172 F.2d 402 (2d Cir. 1949), discussed in § 1.1(b), *supra.*

On the other hand, the Cincinnati National League team was successful in preventing Armando Marsans from jumping to a Federal League team. In a very brief opinion that said nothing about the team's right of cancellation on ten days' notice, a federal court in Missouri granted Cincinnati an injunction preventing Marsans from playing elsewhere.[4]

More recently, a Texas Court of Civil Appeals affirmed the issuance of a temporary injunction preventing John Matuszak from playing for any team other than the Houston Oilers, despite the court's express opinion that Matuszak's Oiler "contracts are incredibly one-sided."[5] Matuszak had been an All-American defensive tackle at the University of Tampa and was the National Football League's number one draft choice in 1973. He signed four separate one year contracts with the Houston Oilers for the 1973 through 1976 seasons, received a $55,000 bonus, and was selected to the 1973 All-Rookie Team.

Matuszak supported the NFL Players Association strike in 1974, and reported to the Oilers' training camp only after the strike had come to an abrupt end.[6] According to Matuszak, he began talking to the World Football League when seven of his veteran teammates were cut the day they reported to camp.[7] Matuszak, who is 6′8″ tall and weighs 280 pounds, and who reportedly likes to be called "the Polish god" and has been described by one sports

---

[4] Cincinnati Exhibition Co. v. Marsans, 216 Fed. 269 (E.D. Mo. 1914).

[5] Matuszak v. Houston Oilers, Inc., 1974-2 CCH Trade Cases ¶ 75,373 (Tex.Ct.Civ.App. 1974).

[6] See § 4.1(a)(4), *supra*.

[7] Klemesrud, Me and The Biggest, Esquire Magazine, Oct. 1975, at 208.

editor as "the biggest white man in America,"[8] told the WFL he wanted to stay in Houston. A contract with the WFL Houston Texans was quickly negotiated and signed, and Matuszak played his first game for the Texans immediately thereafter on Wednesday night, August 28, 1974.

Actually, Matuszak only participated in seven plays. While seated on the bench, Matuszak was served with a temporary restraining order obtained by the Oilers in a lawsuit filed that day. "We wanted to serve it before Matuszak got on the field," Oiler owner Bud Adams told reporters, "but they left the sheriff's office too late to issue it before the game started."[9] Although Matuszak's Oilers contracts had four years to run, including the option year, the Texans' owner, Steve Arnold, told reporters that they contained a flaw which permitted Matuszak to jump leagues immediately.[10]

As the case developed, it became apparent that the flaw was not a technical defect. Rather, Matuszak and the Texans claimed that the Oilers contracts were unenforceable because they violated Texas antitrust laws and because they were "unconscionable." The trial court, however, rejected both contentions and issued a temporary injunction enjoining Matuszak from playing football for any team other than the Oilers and enjoining the Texans from inducing, persuading, or encouraging him to repudiate or breach his Oilers contracts.

An immediate appeal was taken to the Texas Court of Civil Appeals, and while the case was pending there, Matuszak was traded by the Oilers to the Kansas City Chiefs.[11]

---

[8] *Id.* at 130, 210.

[9] L.A. Times, Aug. 29, 1974, Part III.

[10] *Id.*

[11] Klemesrud, *supra* note 7, at 208.

Shortly thereafter, the Court of Appeals affirmed the issuance of the temporary injunction. It held that professional football was not subject to state antitrust law, because federal antitrust law had preempted the area,[12] and that "the question of whether Matuszak's contract violates federal law is a question for the Federal Courts." [13]

The Court of Appeals also held that whether the Oilers' contracts were unconscionable was an issue that should be determined during trial. In so deciding, however, the Court added,

> "In making this holding we should not wish to be understood as intimating any view as to the ultimate outcome of this case. . . . The contracts are incredibly one sided. The options rest with the Club [i.e., the Houston Oilers] (except for payment upon performance) and any disputes are ultimately to be decided by the Commissioner and his findings are conclusive and unappealable. The Club signed Matuszak to four separate one-year contracts rather than one contract for four years in order to reduce the Club's financial exposure in the event of an injury to him. Sport contracts arranged so that the team can easily dispose of an injured player have been found unconscionable and unenforceable." [14]

Interestingly, the decision to affirm the temporary injunction against Matuszak and the Texans was not unan-

---

[12] See § 1.3(b)(3)(D), *supra.*

[13] Matuszak v. Houston Oilers, Inc., *supra* note 5; see also, Sobel, Antitrust Defenses to Contract Actions: A Question of Policy Priorities, 16 The Antitrust Bulletin 455, 468-475 (1971).

[14] Matuszak v. Houston Oilers, Inc., *supra* note 5, citing Connecticut Professional Sports Corporation v. Heyman, 276 F.Supp. 618 (S.D.N.Y. 1967), discussed in § 2.3(b)(1), *supra.*

imous. Chief Justice Tunks dissented, stating that although the federal government has preempted the antitrust regulation of interstate commerce, Texas courts are not obliged to enforce contracts which violate Texas public policy as expressed in that state's own antitrust laws. Furthermore, Chief Justice Tunks noted that,

> ". . . the contract which the Houston Oilers seek to have enforced by the court's use of its equitable powers was procured under circumstances where Matuszak had no freedom of choice. As a result of the combination and agreement between the twenty-six teams in the National Football League, Matuszak could deal with and play for only the Houston Oilers. The evidence shows that many of the terms of the standard contract tendered him were not negotiable. He was given only the option of accepting them or not playing professional football in the United States. Standing in such a position of overwhelmingly superior bargaining power, the Oilers compelled Matuszak to sign a contract which is grossly unfair to him. A court should not lend its equitable powers to the enforcement of a contract so termed and so procured." [15]

Because the case never went to trial (it became moot with the demise of the World Football League, if for no other reason), the interesting issues raised by it concerning the conscionability of the National Football League's contracts were never resolved.[16]

---

[15] *Id.*

[16] See, however, Dallas Cowboys Football Club, Inc. v. Harris, 348 S.W.2d 37 (Tex.Ct.Civ.App. 1961), discussed in § 2.3(b)(1), *supra,* holding that NFL contracts are not so unreasonable and harsh as to be unenforceable.

§5.2(b)(2)(B) Unclean hands doctrine

During the Federal League "war," Organized Baseball was not above pirating some of its players back from the Federal League, and in at least one case the new circuit itself fell victim to the "unclean hands" doctrine. Bill Killefer was the player at issue, an excellent catcher for the Philadelphia National League team during the 1913 season. Killefer's 1913 contract, like those of all other players in Organized Baseball, contained a reserve clause. In disregard of his reserve clause, Killefer signed a contract with the Chicago Federal League team in January of 1914 for the 1914, 1915 and 1916 seasons. Less than two weeks after signing the Federal League contract, Killefer signed a new three-year contract with Philadelphia, causing the Federal League to seek an injunction.

The Court held that the reserve clause in Killefer's 1913 contract with Philadelphia would have been unenforceable because it was indefinite and lacked mutuality. However, it said, that did not justify Chicago's enticing him away. Killefer had a moral if not a legal obligation to play for Philadelphia in 1914, and thus Chicago committed a "willful wrong"[1] in hiring him. For that reason, the Court held, Chicago was not entitled to an injunction,

> "not because there are any equities in Killefer's favor which excuse or exempt him from the performance of his engagements, and not because the merits of the controversy are with the Philadelpia Club, but solely because the actions and conduct of the plaintiffs in procuring the contract, upon which their right to relief is and must be founded, do not square with one of the vital and fundamental principles of equity which

[1] Weegham v. Killefer, 215 Fed. 168, 173 (W.D.Mich. 1914), *aff'd,* 215 Fed. 289 (6th Cir. 1914).

> touches to the quick the dignity of a court of conscience and controls its decision regardless of all other considerations."[2]

Fifty-five years after the decision in the *Killefer* case, another lawsuit arose involving substantially similar facts. This time the player involved was Lou Hudson, a star basketball player for the University of Minnesota until his graduation in the spring of 1966, and NBA Rookie of the Year with the St. Louis Hawks in 1967. Hudson's 1966-1967 contract with the Hawks contained the standard NBA renewal clause[3] covering the 1967-1968 season. Nevertheless, on May 3, 1967, Hudson signed a three-year contract with the Minnesota Muskies of the newly-formed American Basketball Association—a contract which included the 1967-1968 season. Although the Muskies and Hudson claimed to be uncertain about the legal effect of the NBA renewal clause (the *Rick Barry*[4] case had not yet been decided, though the *Richard Barnett*[5] case had been), they were clearly aware of the possibility that the Hawks might successfully enjoin Hudson from playing for the Muskies immediately. As a result, Hudson had the Muskies add a paragraph to his contract which provided that in the event he was enjoined from playing during the 1967-1968 season, the Muskies would pay him $25,000 nevertheless, and he would thereafter play the next three seasons for his agreed-upon salary.

The Hawks did file suit to enjoin Hudson (and to recover $3 million in alleged actual and punitive damages from the

[2] *Id.*

[3] See § 2.2(d)(1), *supra.*

[4] Lemat Corp. v. Barry, 80 Cal. Rptr. 240 (Cal.Ct.App. 1969), discussed in § 2.3(b)(1), *supra.*

[5] Central New York Basketball, Inc. v. Barnett, 181 N.E.2d 506 (Ohio Ct.Com.Pl. 1961).

ABA). Whether for that reason or others, Hudson became dissatisfied with his Muskies contract shortly thereafter. Hudson then signed a new five-year NBA Uniform Player Contract with the Hawks, and the Hawks dismissed their lawsuit. When the 1967-1968 season began, the Muskies' general manager wrote to Hudson telling him that the Muskies were agreeable to his "playing out" his one-year option with the Hawks, but that the Muskies expected him to play for them when the 1968-1969 season began. Hudson never answered the letter, so in May of 1968, the Muskies filed suit against him seeking to enjoin him from playing for any other team for the next three years. They lost.

> "Even if the 'reserve clause' in the St. Louis contract is of doubtful validity [the court explained], the fact remains that the Muskies, knowing that Hudson was under a moral, if not a legal, obligation to furnish his services to St. Louis for the 1967-1968 and subsequent seasons, if St. Louis chose to exercise its option, sent for Hudson and induced him to repudiate his obligation to St. Louis. Such conduct, even if strictly within the law because of the St. Louis contract being unenforceable, was so tainted with unfairness and injustice as to justify a court of equity in withholding relief." [6]

Nor was the Court impressed with the Muskies' argument that they were entitled to an injunction even if they had acted improperly, because the St. Louis Hawks were guilty of inequitable and unlawful conduct themselves when they signed Hudson to a second contract, knowing that he had already signed a valid Muskie contract. "The doors of a court of equity are closed to one tainted with unfairness and injustice relative to the matter in which he seeks

---

[6] Minnesota Muskies, Inc. v. Hudson, 294 F.Supp. 979, 990 (M.D.N.C. 1969).

relief 'however improper may have been the behavior of the defendant,'" the Court stated. "It is irrelevant that the conduct of St. Louis may have been more reprehensible than that of the Muskies, since it is the devious conduct of the Muskies that created the problems in this litigation."[7]

Subsequent developments showed, however, that "deviousness"—like beauty—is in the eyes of the beholder. Billy Cunningham, an ABA All Star, had been playing with the Philadelphia 76ers for four years when the Carolina Cougars of the American Basketball Association first put out feelers in 1969 to determine whether he might be willing to jump leagues. Negotiations between the Cougars and Cunningham began in May or June of 1969, at which time Cunningham already had a contract with the 76ers covering the 1969-1970 season. Furthermore, that contract contained the standard NBA renewal clause giving the 76ers an option on his services for the 1970-1971 season.

The Cougars were planning for the long run, however, and they had no desire to challenge Cunningham's NBA contract or its renewal clause. Rather, on August 5, 1969, the Cougars signed Cunningham to a three-year agreement beginning with the 1971-1972 season. Thus he would join the Cougars only after he had fulfilled all conceivable NBA obligations. The deal Cunningham and the Cougars made permitted him to either "play out" or "sit out" his NBA option year, at his choice; but as part of the bonus he received for signing with the Cougars, he was to be paid $80,000 if he sat the season out or up to $20,000 if he played it out. (If he decided to play the option year and was paid less than $100,000 by the 76ers, the Cougars promised to pay him as much as $20,000 to make up any difference between his 76er salary and $100,000.)

[7] *Id.*

By May of 1970, ten months after Cunningham had signed with the Cougars and a year and a half before he was to begin play with them, a dispute arose. In form, the dispute was over the timing and amount of the bonus the Cougars had agreed to pay. In fact, however, it may have been that the 76ers simply decided to fight back by making Cunningham an even better offer than the one the Cougars had made to get him to agree to jump. (Cunningham's 1969-1970 contract with the 76ers called for $40,000. The Cougars contracts provided for salaries of $100,000, $110,000 and $120,000 beginning in 1971. In May of 1970, the 76ers offered Cunningham $225,000 a year for five years.) Whatever the reason, Cunningham notified the Cougars that they had breached the terms of his agreement with them, and that he therefore no longer considered himself bound by it. And on July 15, 1970, he signed new contracts with the 76ers covering the next five seasons.

The Cougars sued, seeking to enjoin Cunningham from playing basketball for any other team during the terms of their three contracts with him. The trial judge denied the injunction and dismissed the Cougars' complaint for two reasons. He found that the team had breached its agreement with respect to the payment of bonus monies, and held that Cunningham was therefore freed of his obligations to it.[8] That however was a make-weight reason, for what really disturbed the judge was the "devious"[9] conduct of the Cougars in negotiating with and signing a player who was still under contract to another team. He expressed no kind words about the Cougars' willingness to wait more than two years for Cunningham to join them, and, if anything, was particularly incensed that they had

[8] Munchak Corporation v. Cunningham, 331 F.Supp. 872 (M.D. N.C. 1971).

[9] *Id.* at 876.

offered to pay him $80,000 if he chose to sit out the option year, even though he had every legal right to do so. As a result, the judge held that "the Cougars, in its dealings with Cunningham, soiled its hands to such an extent that the injunctive relief should be denied." [10]

The Cougars felt they had been treated with undue harshness by the trial judge and pursued the matter to the Court of Appeals. There they received gentler treatment, for the Court of Appeals found no deviousness in their actions. "We think," it held,

> ". . . that there was neither illegality nor unclean hands in the Cougars' contracting for Cunningham's services to be rendered *after* the term of his contract with the 76ers had expired, notwithstanding that the negotiations . . . took place while Cunningham's contract with the 76ers was still in full force and effect. As the *Washington Capitols* case [involving Rick Barry's unsuccessful attempt to jump back to the NBA from the ABA[11]] stated . . ., 'no actionable wrong is committed by a competitor who solicits his competitor's employees or who hires away one or more of his competitor's employees who are not under contract, so long as the inducement to leave is not accompanied by unlawful actions.' Cunningham was under no obligation, option or restraint with respect to the 76ers after October 1, 1971, and the Cougars had a lawful right to bid and contract for his services to be rendered after that date." [12]

---

[10] *Id.* at 875.

[11] Washington Capitols Basketball Club, Inc. v. Barry, 419 F.2d 472 (9th Cir. 1969).

[12] Munchak Corporation v. Cunningham, 457 F.2d 721, 724 (4th Cir. 1972).

Nor did the Court of Appeals think that there was illegal inducement or unclean hands in the Cougars' agreement to pay Cunningham $80,000 if he sat out his NBA option year. He already had the right to do so, and they also agreed to pay him as much as $20,000 on top of his 76er salary if he did play. Finally, the Court of Appeals did not feel that the Cougars' failure to abide by its agreement with respect to payment of Cunningham's bonus was sufficiently material to warrant his voiding the Cougar contract. At most, it was a question of the timing of the payment, and, as events turned out, Cunningham would have had to repay the bonus money to the Cougars if they had paid it on the date he claimed it was due. Therefore, the Court reversed the trial judge's decision, and sent the case back with instructions to enter an appropriate injunction.

Thus, although the Muskies' contract with Hudson was not enforced because it began during a season when Hudson was under option to the Hawks, the Cougars' contract with Cunningham was enforced because it began after the 76ers' option expired, even though it had been signed beforehand.

§5.2(b)(2)(C) Interference with contractual relations

Each of the cases discussed in the preceding section[1] involved similar factual situations. The athlete in question was first under contract to a team in an established league and then "jumped" to a team in a new rival league. In each case, the player in question thereafter "jumped" back to his original team in the old league, thereby causing the team in the new league to seek an injunction preventing him from playing for his original team. In two cases, in-

[1] § 5.2(b)(2)(B), *supra*.

junctions were denied, on grounds of "unclean hands," because the players had been induced to jump to the new league prior to the expiration of their contracts with their original teams.[2] In two other cases, however, injunctions were granted to teams in new leagues, because in both cases the player's contracts with their new league teams —although signed while the players were still under contract to their original teams—did not begin until the option years in their former contracts expired.[3] Under these circumstances, the courts held that the teams in the new league did not have "unclean hands," and therefore could be awarded equitable relief.

The precise question at issue in all four cases was whether the new league team could prevent the player from jumping back to his original team. A somewhat different question has been presented in cases where players have jumped (or have been encouraged to jump) to a new league, and have not thereafter sought to return to their former teams. In those cases, the former teams contended that their contractual relations with their players were interfered with by teams in new leagues. When players have jumped, their former teams have filed lawsuits against the players themselves, seeking to prevent them from playing for any other team.[4] Interference with contractual relations, however, is a separate cause of action which has been asserted, not against the players them-

[2] Weegham v. Killefer, 215 Fed. 168 (W.D.Mich. 1914), *affd.*, 215 Feb. 289 (6th Cir. 1914); and Minnesota Muskies, Inc. v. Hudson, 294 F.Supp. 979 (M.D.N.C. 1969); both discussed in § 5.2(b)(2)(B), *supra.*

[3] Washington Capitols Basketball Club, Inc. v. Barry, 419 F.2d 472 (9th Cir. 1969); and Munchak Corporation v. Cunningham, 457 F.2d 721 (4th Cir. 1972); both discussed in § 5.2(b)(2)(B), *supra.*

[4] See §§ 2.3 and 5.2(b)(2)(A), *supra.*

selves, but instead against the teams to which they jumped (or were encouraged to jump).

The first case to address this issue directly arose during the Mexican League "war." [5] In a press conference held in May of 1946, Mexican League Vice President Bernardo Pasquel told reporters that Phil Rizzuto "will leave the Yankees and go to Mexico when I give the word" and that he would "not leave New York without taking a Yankee regular of the first rank" with him.[6] The Yankees immediately sought, and were granted, a temporary injunction restraining the Mexican League and those acting on its behalf "from inducing or attempting to induce [Yankee] baseball players to repudiate their contracts of employment with [the Yankees]." [7]

The Mexican League had claimed that its actions were legal because "the contracts between [the Yankees] and its players are so inequitable and monopolistic in character as not to warrant the intervention of a Court of Equity for their enforcement." [8] The Court, however, was not persuaded. It said,

> "Attempts of the defendants to induce Plaintiff's players to leave their employment with Plaintiff are wrongful and illegal under well-settled principles of law, and this is so regardess of whether the contracts between Plaintiff and its players would be enforceable in actions between the parties to the contracts . . . . It is not 'essential that the contract should be of such a nature

[5] See § 1.1(b), *supra.*

[6] American League Baseball Club of New York v. Pasquel, 63 N.Y.S.2d 537, 538 (1946).

[7] *Id.*

[8] *Id.*

> that specific performance could be decreed' . . . . Malicious attempts to induce employees to leave their employer are illegal even if there is no contract for a definite term between them and their employer and their employment is terminable at will."[9]

Apparently Rizzuto and another player who Pasquel had contacted both had contracts with the Yankees at that time. Assuming they did, the injunction was proper, although the Court's rationale is excessively sweeping. While it is true that an unenforceable contract may be interfered with, where the contract is terminable at will business competitors are privileged to induce its termination.[10] Naturally, a player contract which has not yet expired is not "terminable at will." On the other hand, when a player contract has expired, the player/team relationship is terminable at any time thereafter. Therefore, it would seem that not only does a team in one league not act inequitably when it induces a player to jump from another league at the complete conclusion of his original contract, but also such an inducement would be privileged and would not be an interference with contractual relations.[11] Such was, in fact, the holding of a recent case that arose during the brief "war" between the National and World Football Leagues.

In December of 1973, or shortly thereafter, a form letter on World Football League stationery was sent to a substantial number of National Football League players. It read:

---

[9] *Id.* at 538-539.

[10] Prosser, Law of Torts § 129, Pg. 932 (St. Paul: West Publ. Co., 4th Ed., 1971).

[11] *Id.* at p. 946.

"Dear Player:

"The World Football League will begin play in 1974 with franchises in twelve areas, including New York, Chicago, Detroit, Toronto, New England, Southern California, Hawaii, and Florida. The remaining franchises will be awarded from some twenty applications for membership under consideration.

"It is the intention of the World Football League to be 'Major League' in every way, particularly in signing the top professional players available. We feel strongly that every player should honor his present contractual obligation. However, we would very much like to talk with you about the possibility of joining our League at the expiration of your present contract.

"In order for us to know your status and to contact you, please fill out and return the enclosed postcard as soon as possible.

"Wishing you a Merry Christmas and a Happy and Prosperous New Year!

R. Steven Arnold
W. F. L. Organizer" [12]

This letter was received by many if not most of the members of the NFL's Dallas Cowboys; and in April of 1974, three Cowboys, Calvin Hill, Craig Morton, and Mike Montgomery, signed contracts to play for WFL teams, beginning in 1975 after the expiration of the option years in their NFL contracts. As a result, the Cowboys immediately filed suit against the World Football League and related parties, alleging that they had engaged "in a concerted program and course of conduct to obtain players

[12] World Football League v. Dallas Cowboys Football Club, Inc., 513 S.W.2d 102, 104 (Tex.Ct.Civ.App. 1974).

for WFL by directly, intentionally, and tortiously interfering with the contractual relationships existing between the [Cowboys] and its players . . . ."[13]

The trial court issued a temporary injunction enjoining the World Football League

> "from directly or indirectly entering into any oral or written contracts with any football players now under contract with the Dallas Cowboys Football Club, Inc. to perform services as football players in the World Football League, or from inducing or attempting to induce any such football players under contract with the Dallas Cowboys Football Club, Inc. to engage in promotional, commercial or advertising activities for the World Football League or anyone acting in its behalf."[14]

This injunction was dissolved, however, within a matter of weeks by the Texas Court of Civil Appeals. Despite the Dallas Cowboys' bitter complaints that the World Football League was "raiding" and "pirating" its players, the Court of Appeals found that the only evidence of any contact between the World Football League and members of the Cowboys' team was the form letter (and the return postcard enclosed with it), and the Court held that the letter did not "suggest an unlawful 'raiding scheme.'"[15] The letter plainly stated that NFL players should honor their existing contract obligations and it merely inquired about the players' interest in joining WFL teams after the expiration of their present contracts.

---

[13] *Id.* at 103.
[14] *Id.*
[15] *Id.* at 104.

The Cowboys contended that the signing of their players by WFL teams, even for services to be rendered after the expiration of their present contracts, was an unlawful interference with the Cowboys' contractual relations with its players. This was so, the Cowboys asserted, because players who signed with the WFL would not use their best efforts for the Cowboys under their current contracts, the morale of the entire team would suffer, enthusiasm of the fans would wane, and WFL teams would reap the benefits of favorable publicity for outstanding performances by the players who signed with them. The Cowboys also argued that the publicity resulting from the signing of WFL contracts for future services was a breach of the NFL Standard Player Contract in which every player agrees "that during the term of this contract he will play football and engage in activities related to football only for the Club. . . ."[16]

The Court of Appeals held, however, that even if these contentions were factually accurate they would not constitute grounds for injunctive relief.

> "We must consider the freedom of contract of the individual players as well as the rights of the Club [i.e., the Dallas Cowboys] under its present contracts. Bargaining for future services is a matter of economics. The Club can assure itself of the continued services and loyalty of its players by offering them long-term contracts and other financial inducements. If it chooses not to do so for economic reasons, it has no legal ground to complain if the players look elsewhere for their future careers and enter into contracts for services to be performed when their present contracts with the Club expire. Signing such contracts is neither

[16] *Id.* at 105.

a breach of the contract by the players nor a tortious interference by the future employers, and the threat to enter into such contracts affords no ground for equitable relief. Neither does the publicity necessarily attendant upon the signing of contracts with well-known players constitute a tort. An injunction restraining the signing of such contracts because of the attendant publicity would be an unreasonable restraint on the freedom of contract of the players and their prospective employers." [17]

Although the Cowboys did not deny that the WFL and its teams had a legal right to contract with any players they chose, the Cowboys did claim for themselves a right not to have any player presently under contract with it enter into a contract with a WFL team to be performed in the future. However, the Court of Appeals held that it had been "clearly enunciated" that the Cowboys had "no such 'right.' " [18]

§5.3 Competition for stadia

Although a team does not exist without players, neither can it operate professionally without a place to play. While the availability of a suitable location is often critical to the successful operation of many kinds of businesses, few businesses have requirements as specialized as professional sports teams. Many kinds of businesses, for example, may be run from high rise office buildings. Even manufacturing businesses can be operated in industrial buildings that would be satisfactory for a num-

[17] *Id.*

[18] *Id.*, citing Washington Capitols Basketball Club, Inc. v. Barry, *supra* note 3, and Munchak Corporation v. Cunningham, *supra* note 3.

ber of industries. Basketball and hockey, on the other hand, require arenas that seat thousands in comfort and that have sufficient parking and public transportation for that many people. Football and baseball require stadia seating many more thousands, and parking, public transportation, and sufficient road access to accommodate such large crowds. Furthermore, sports stadia and arenas are not usually suitable for other uses. Well managed and comfortable arenas may be rented for occasional concerts or conventions, but such uses would only supplement a full schedule of sporting events. They could not support the operation of an arena by themselves. And football and baseball stadia are suitable for virtually nothing else, usually not even for one another, unless specially designed.

For this reason, most cities that have them only have one stadium or arena. Even the greater New York area presently has only two arenas suitable for major league professional hockey, Madison Square Garden and Nassau Coliseum. While city and county governments and even private investors have shown a willingness to build arenas and stadia in places where they do not already exist, the costs of doing so are enormous. San Diego's basketball and hockey arena was built by private investors in 1966 for $6.4 million on land leased from the City for $1. Its football and baseball stadium was built by the City in 1969 at a cost of $28 million. Houston's Astrodome required more than $45 million in 1965.[1] And the New Orleans Superdome cost more than a mind-boggling $163 million.[2]

---

[1] Burck, It's Promoters vs. Taxpayers in the Superstadium Game, Fortune Magazine, March 1973, at 105.

[2] Maher, Domedest Thing You Ever Saw, L.A. Times, Feb. 19, 1974, Part III, Pg. 1.

Builders have therefore gone ahead only when they have known or have reasonably believed they could obtain a major league tenant, preferably in one of the established leagues. Newly-formed leagues have not regularly drawn enough fans to warrant construction of such expensive arenas and stadia to house only their teams. Thus team owners in newly-formed leagues have not only had to scramble for athletes, they have had to search for a place to play as well.

New leagues are attracted to the biggest cities where established leagues already have franchises, despite resulting head-to-head competition, for two reasons. First, economic studies have shown that a certain size population base is necessary for the support of a major league franchise, and that the largest cities can reasonably be expected to be able to support two or even more franchises in a single sport more easily than smaller cities can support one.[3]

Second, where there already is an established franchise, there is an existing facility suitable for major league play. Because every professional team plays as many games away from home as it does at home, arenas and stadia can be used by two teams, each using it while the other is on the road. Of course, such an arrangement would make scheduling quite complicated for the league whose franchise was the second one to enter into an arena or stadium lease. But, when teams share a facility, schedules can be and have been arranged around available dates. For example, before the Chargers football team moved to San Diego, they and the Los Angeles Rams both played their home games in the Los Angeles Memorial Coliseum.

[3] Hearings on S.2373 before the Subcomm. on Antitrust and Monopoly of the Senate Comm. on the Judiciary, 92d Cong., 1st Sess. 401 (1971).

Naturally, established leagues are never happy about the prospect of competition. Few if any businesses are. While reserve and option clauses have been used to hinder the formation of new leagues by making it difficult for them to obtain quality players,[4] another less-publicized clause has also been used on occasion to make it difficult for new teams to obtain a place to play. Such a clause has appeared in stadia leases and has prohibited stadia operators from leasing them to any other professional team playing the same sport.

A lease provision of this sort was brought to judicial attention when prospective owners of an American Football League franchise attempted to lease Robert F. Kennedy Stadium in Washington, D.C. for the team's home games. Though they had offered to lease the stadium on Friday nights, Saturdays and those Sundays when it was not being used by the NFL's Washington Redskins, they were unable to obtain use of the stadium at any time, because the Redskins' lease prohibited its use by any other professional football team. As a result, the prospective owners claimed they were unable to obtain an AFL franchise. When the NFL and AFL merged, the same group continued its unsuccessful attempts to lease the stadium, hoping to obtain a Continental Football League franchise. They even went so far as to incorporate their own league, the United States Football League, Inc., and issue the Washington franchise to themselves.

Ultimately the group went to federal court, alleging that the lease provision in question restrained trade in violation of the Sherman Act and charging the Redskins and the NFL with attempted monopolization of profes-

[4] See § 2.3, *supra*.

sional football in the District of Columbia. The District Judge dismissed the case, on grounds having little to do with the validity of the restrictive clause in the lease (taking care to note in the process that the plaintiffs were the manager and assistant cashier of a branch bank, a part owner and operator of a retail liquor store, and the operator of a restaurant, none of whom had ever owned, operated or been associated with a professional football team).[5]

Robert F. Kennedy Stadium was constructed pursuant to an act of Congress which authorized the Secretary of the Interior to acquire land for the stadium and to enter into a contract with the District of Columbia Armory Board for its construction and operation. The Armory Board, an unincorporated instrumentality of the District, financed the construction of the stadium by issuing and selling municipal bonds. It was based on these facts that the trial court dismissed the complaint of the unsuccessful lease applicants, holding that the actions of the Armory Board were governmental actions and, as such, not subject to the antitrust laws.

The Court of Appeals however reversed.[6] It explained that not all governmental activity was immune from the requirements of the antitrust laws. After reviewing the legislative history of the act which authorized the construction and operation of the stadium, the Court found no intention on the part of Congress to exempt the activities of the Armory Board. So it sent the case back to the trial court with instructions that the lease between the Board and the Redskins "must be tested in accordance

[5] Hecht v. Pro-Football, Inc., 312 F.Supp. 472 (D.D.C. 1970).
[6] Hecht v. Pro-Football, Inc., 444 F.2d 931 (D.C. Cir. 1971).

with the United States antitrust laws as usually applied to contracts between private parties." [7]

Does such a provision violate the antitrust laws? Before the lawsuit was ever filed, a Special Assistant to the Solicitor of the Department of the Interior advised the Armory Board that in the Solicitor's opinion it does.[8] The Board obtained a contrary opinion from a law firm, and on that basis, it adhered to its view that the provision had to be honored.

Another opportunity to obtain a judicial determination was lost when the National Hockey League and the World Hockey Association settled all litigation between them early in 1974.[9] One of the many cases settled was an antitrust action filed by the WHA in which the WHA charged the NHL with attempted monopolization, as evidenced by —among other things—the inability of the WHA New York Raiders to obtain a lease for the Nassau Coliseum. No lease provision was at issue there. The Raiders' application for a lease was simply rejected by the Coliseum's sports consultant, who, coincidently, happened to be a member of the Board of Directors of the Los Angeles Kings, a National Hockey League team. A lease was thereafter entered into by the Coliseum with the New York Islanders, an NHL expansion team.[10]

So the issue remains. On its face and as used, a provision in a lease prohibiting the use of a stadium or arena by another professional sports team certainly appears illegal, both as a restraint on trade and as a device for

---

[7] *Id.* at 947.

[8] *Id.* at 934, fn. 5.

[9] See § 6.3, *infra.*

[10] Philadelphia World Hockey Club, Inc. v. Philadelphia Hockey Club, Inc., 351 F.Supp. 462, 488 (E.D. Pa. 1972).

monopolization. On the other hand, provisions in leases prohibiting lessors from renting to competing businesses have been upheld as legal.[11] Thus, a definite answer will have to await judicial determination.

In the meantime, it would seem that National Football League teams are confident that the clause is valid. The New York Giants will play their home games in a stadium to be located in New Jersey's Hackensack Meadowlands. The stadium and a neighboring racetrack were constructed with funds raised through the sale of tax-exempt government bonds issued by the New Jersey Sports and Exposition Authority. According to the Official Statement by which the underwriters (Merrill, Lynch, Pierce, Fenner & Smith, Inc. and others) offered the bonds for sale to the public, the Giants' 30-year lease with the Sports Authority provides that no professional or semi-professional football games except Giants' home games and the National Football League all-star games may be played in the stadium.[12] (On its face, this restriction would even appear to prohibit the use of the stadium for the Super Bowl, unless the Giants are a participant!)

While this restriction might have been of concern to the World Football League before its demise, because it prevented its use of the Hackensack facility, the restriction should also be of interest to purchasers of the bonds. Unlike many governmental bonds, those issued by the New Jersey Sports and Exposition Authority for construction of the football stadium and racetrack are *not* backed by the taxing power of the state of New Jersey or any

[11] See, e.g., Murdock v. City of Jacksonville, 361 F.Supp. 1083 (M.D. Fla. 1973), upholding exclusive lease of City Coliseum for presentation of wrestling matches.

[12] Preliminary Official Statement, New Jersey Sports and Exposition Authority (Sept. 26, 1973) at 18-19.

other governmental authority. As the Official Statement makes clear, the sole source of funds for the payment of interest and repayment of principal will be profits from operations.[13] In the event profits from operations are insufficient, the bondholders' only security is a mortgage on the property and structures. Thus, if profits from operations are insufficient, the bondholders as a group may foreclose upon the complex, sell it to private investors, divide the purchase price pro rata, and hope to recover as much of their investment as possible. Should there be no purchasers the bondholders may obtain ownership and operate it themselves in an effort to recover the money owed on the bonds.

However, as the Official Statement also makes clear, the bondholders' mortgage is subject and subordinate to the rights and privileges of the Giants under its lease.[14] Thus, it is possible that profits from operations will be insufficient to make the required payments on the bonds, in part because of the Authority's inability to lease the football stadium to other professional football teams on days when the Giants are out of town. Should this occur, the bondholders may foreclose the mortgage. But even after foreclosure, its new operator will also be prohibited from leasing the stadium to other professional football teams, and thus will be in no better position than the Authority to operate the complex in a manner calculated to produce sufficient profits for repayment of the bond obligations.

This is a remarkable but apparently not unique situation. What the Giants—and other teams before them, no doubt—have managed to do is build a private stadium for

[13] *Id.* at 9.
[14] *Id.* at 19.

their exclusive use. Furthermore, they have done so at a cost lower than would otherwise have been possible by using the state of New Jersey's legal authority to issue tax-exempt, and thus lower interest rate, bonds in order to borrow the necessary money.

§5.4 Competition for cities

Although a professional sports league may be "in business" so long as its teams are stocked with athletes and have some place to play, success by any definition depends upon the support of fans. Without fans, a professional league is one in name only. And because of current costs of operation—including player and other personnel salaries and frequent transcontinental transportation—substantial fan support is necessary for a team to break even financially. Experience has shown that the larger the population base upon which a team may draw, the greater the likelihood that it will enjoy sufficient attendance.[1]

In the early 1960's, Lamar Hunt, an organizer of the American Football League, expressed the view that it would take a metropolitan area with a population of 500,000 or more to support a professional football team, providing it had proper management. In those days, there were 52 such metropolitan areas in the United States, 31 of which had populations of more than 700,000, and 24 of which had more than 1 million. Hunt expressed this opinion while testifying in an antitrust action in which the American Football League had charged the National Football League with attempting and conspiring to monopolize,

---

[1] Noll, Attendance and Price Setting, in Government and the Sports Business (Washington, D.C.: The Brookings Institution, 1974), at 115.

and in fact monopolizing—among other things—those cities which could support professional football.[2]

At the time of the trial, the NFL had franchises located in 14 cities. There were therefore 10 cities with more than a million residents, 17 cities with more than 700,000 residents and 38 cities with more than 500,000 residents, completely open to the AFL. The American Football League's monopolization charge was therefore based upon its claim that the NFL had the power to exclude it from any of those cities and that the NFL had exercised that power in 1960, when its announcement of a forthcoming expansion into Minneapolis had the effect of terminating AFL plans for a team in that city.

Although a monopolization charge is proved by evidence that a defendant has monopoly power and exercised it by taking action to exclude or prevent competition, neither the trial court nor the Court of Appeals agreed with the AFL's contention that the NFL had monopolized professional football.[3] First, though the NFL may have excluded the AFL from Minneapolis,

> "It is not sufficient that they might have had the power to exclude a new league from a particular city or group of cities unless the power to exclude from that city or group of cities would have effectively prevented the formation or operation of a new league." [4]

The expansion into Minneapolis obviously had not had the effect of preventing the formation or operation of the AFL, for, as it had announced at the conclusion of its first

[2] American Football League v. National Football League, 205 F.Supp. 60, 76 (D.Md. 1962), *affd.*, 323 F.2d 124 (4th Cir. 1963).

[3] *Id.*

[4] 205 F.Supp. at 64.

season, "Never before in the history of sports has a sports organization gone so far so fast."[5] Nor did the NFL have the power to exclude the AFL from enough cities to prevent its operation. The NFL could expand at most by a couple of teams each year, and therefore could not possibly expand into all cities large enough to support pro football.

Second, the AFL's emphasis on its loss of Minneapolis ignored the fact that it had successfully placed a franchise in Houston in 1960, while the NFL had failed to do so despite NFL plans to do so. It also ignored the fact that the AFL had placed teams in New York, Dallas, Los Angeles and San Francisco in direct head-to-head competition with NFL teams, and also had received applications for franchises from several cities with populations in excess of 700,000, in addition to those that were actually selected for charter franchises. (The AFL Dallas franchise was subsequently moved to Kansas City; the Los Angeles team to San Diego; and the San Francisco club to Oakland.)

Neither were the courts impressed with the AFL's claims that the NFL had conspired or attempted to monopolize potential football cities. This charge was based upon the NFL's expansion into Minneapolis and Dallas in 1960, its attempt to expand into Houston, and attempts during the formative stages of the AFL to lure away potential AFL owners with suggestions that NFL franchises might be made available to them. The expansion was found to be the result of plans which had existed prior to the formation of the AFL, and the attempts to lure away potential AFL owners were found to be nothing more than "informal talks among friends and business associates about their mutual problems."[6]

[5] *Id.* at 75.

[6] 323 F.2d at 133.

In short, the American Football League had accused the NFL of monopolization because it had failed to leave available for the AFL all cities that were without a team on the date the AFL came into existence. That theory was not so far-fetched as to be unreasonable. In fact, in an analysis of the case later published in the *Harvard Law Review,* it was suggested that it might have been "particularly appropriate" for the courts to have interpreted the antitrust laws so as to require the NFL "to refrain from expansion into new cities or from increasing TV coverage when such actions would preempt part of the market which the new league sought to enter." [7]

Appropriate or not, however, the law as it now stands permits an existing league to battle with a new one on a city-for-city basis, so long as the existing league does not expand into so many cities at once that its competitor will be unable to operate, and so long as its expansion is for reasons other than the destruction of the new league.

---

[7] Comment, The Super Bowl and the Sherman Act: Professional Team Sports and the Antitrust Laws, 81 Harvard L.Rev. 418, 431 (1967).

Chapter 6

LEAGUE MERGERS AND OTHER FORMS OF PEACE

§6.1 The NFL-AFL merger

The National Football League was formed in 1920 under the name "American Professional Football Association." It began with eleven teams, five located in Ohio, each of which paid $100 for its franchise. The next year, a twelfth team was added and the name "National Football League" was adopted. In addition, the franchise fee was reduced to $50.[1]

From its birth until 1946, the NFL had the major league professional football business to itself. In 1946, a competing league known as the All-America Football Conference began operations, but it lasted only four seasons. After the 1948 season, two of its franchises merged, and at the end of the 1949 season the Conference disbanded altogether. Three of its teams, Baltimore, Cleveland and San Francisco, were admitted to the NFL; and the National Football League once again became the only organization in the business, until 1960.[2]

§6.1(a) NFL-AFL war and peace agreement

In 1960, the American Football League was formed, and the modern era of inter-league "wars" began. Actually, when the AFL's promoting founders first contemplated the creation of a new league, "war" was not what they intended. Lamar Hunt and K.S. "Bud" Adams, Jr. were two of the

[1] Durso, The All-American Dollar (Boston: Houghton Mifflin, 1971), at 29-30.

[2] American Football League v. National Football League, 205 F.Supp. 60, 65, 66 (D.Md. 1962), *affd.*, 323 F.2d 124 (4th Cir. 1963).

founders, and in 1957 and 1958, both of them had attempted without success to buy the Cardinals (then based in Chicago) and to obtain—also without success—an NFL expansion franchise. In 1958, NFL Commissioner Bert Bell told both men he did not think the league would expand until at least 1961.[1]

Thus, in early 1959, Hunt—then 27 years of age and without any experience in professional sports—began to plan and organize a new league. During the summer of that year, Hunt revealed his intentions to Commissioner Bell, and told him that the new league desired to maintain a friendly relationship with the NFL. In fact, Hunt proposed that Bell serve as the common commissioner of both the AFL and the NFL, suggested that the two leagues hold a common draft, and recommended that arrangements be made to black out television during home games in both leagues.[2] In effect, Hunt proposed that his new league be merged immediately with the NFL; the only aspects of their operations that would have remained separate at first would have been their playing schedules and their profits or losses.

Bell rejected the proposal, however, and Hunt and Adams proceeded to organize the AFL as a completely separate and competing entity.[3] For the first several years of its existence, competition between the leagues for players was limited to competition for graduating collegians. While that aspect of their competition was vigorous indeed—leading in some instances to signings before post-season bowl games[4]—the American and National Football Leagues

---

[1] American Football League v. National Football League, 205 F.Supp. 60, 67 (D.Md. 1962), *aff'd,* 323 F.2d 124 (4th Cir. 1963).

[2] *Id.* at 69.

[3] *Id.*

[4] See § 5.2(a), *supra.*

did not recruit each other's veteran players, until the spring of 1966.[5]

Both leagues were concerned that their competition for graduating collegians had driven rookie salaries so high that the continued financial solvency of many franchises was threatened. Nevertheless, as late as the early months of 1965, the National Football League continued to refuse to agree to a merger or common draft—at least publicly. The American Football League owners of course wanted a merger or at least a common draft, and at their request, Senator Allott of Colorado proposed an amendment to Senator Hart's pending Sports Bill which would have required that there be only one player draft in each sport, to be participated in at the same time by all leagues "at the same level."[6] The Allott amendment was defeated; but when Senator Hart's bill was passed and sent to the House, the AFL arranged for an amendment to be introduced there, requiring a single common football draft for both the AFL and the NFL. NFL Commissioner Pete Rozelle, however, stated publicly that his league did not endorse the proposal and had not—as late as its annual meeting in February, 1966—discussed the possibility of a common draft with the AFL.[7]

The amendment was never debated in the House. The Senate-passed bill was referred to the House Committee on the Judiciary, chaired by Congressman Emanuel Celler, and Congressman Celler refused to schedule hearings on it.[8]

---

5 Parrish, They Call It A Game (New York: Signet, 1971) at 210.

6 See § 1.2(c)(5), *supra.*

7 112 Congressional Record A919 (Feb. 23, 1966).

8 See § 1.2(c)(5), *supra.*

In the spring of 1966, the understanding (if there was one) between the AFL and NFL that neither would recruit the other's veteran players collapsed. Pete Gogolak of the AFL's Buffalo Bills was signed by the NFL's New York Giants. Roman Gabriel of the NFL's Los Angeles Rams indicated he intended to play out his option and then join the AFL's Oakland Raiders. John Brodie of the NFL's San Francisco 49'ers also announced he was going to play out his option and join an AFL team. And the AFL entered into negotiations with Jim Ninowski of the NFL's Cleveland Browns which were intended to induce him to play out his option and make the jump as well.[9]

Then suddenly in early June of 1966 a "truce" between the two leagues was established. It is thought that so long as the AFL limited its quest for players to the ranks of graduating collegians, NFL owners believed they would be able to outlast their upstart rivals. The NFL rejected a common draft, it has been speculated, because agreement on that score would have amounted to public acknowledgment that the AFL was indeed of major league status,[10] and such an acknowledgment would have strengthened and thus lengthened its life expectancy. However, when the AFL also began signing NFL veterans, NFL owners realized that the AFL meant to compete to both leagues' bankruptcies, if necessary, and NFL owners were then unwilling to shoulder the added expense of bidding for veteran players as well as rookies.

Whether or not this speculation is correct, the American and National Football Leagues announced their intention to merge in June of 1966. After that, only the Sherman Act

[9] Parrish, *supra* note 5, at 216, 218; Sports Illustrated, Aug. 29, 1966, at 20.

[10] 112 Congressional Record A919 (Feb. 23, 1966).

stood between Lamar Hunt and Bud Adams and the National Football League franchises they had always wanted. The Sherman Act was an impediment to the agreed-upon merger, because the merger would and was in fact designed to eliminate all business competition in professional football and to create a monopoly. Realizing that they were vulnerable to antitrust lawsuits by players, prospective franchise owners, television networks, concessionaires, stadia operators and possibly others, the two leagues approached Congress for an amendment to the Sherman Act specifically exempting their merger.

§6.1(b) The merger bills

On September 9, 1966, Senators Russell Long and Everett Dirksen introduced a football merger bill which provided that:

> "The antitrust laws . . . shall not apply . . . to any joint agreement by which the member clubs of two or more professional football leagues combine their operations in an expanded single league, if such agreement increases rather than decreases the number of professional football clubs so operating and the provisions of which are directly relevant thereto."[1]

The bill, S. 3817, was referred to the Senate Judiciary Committee which, without holding hearings of any kind, reported it out to the full Senate two weeks later, recommending that it be passed. The Committee report said, in part:

> "The committee is advised that the plan for an expanded league assures that all 24 of the existing professional football teams will continue to operate in

[1] S.3817, 89th Cong., 2d Sess. (1966).

their present locations. The committee was further advised absent the merger, there was danger that some of the less favorably situated franchises in both existing leagues faced dissolution or transfers to other cities.

. . .

"The merger will improve player strength and financial resources of weaker teams in both leagues.

"The committee discussed the effect of the proposed merger on the football players and agreed that the proposed legislation did not in any way diminish their existing rights.

"The committee was advised that while bonuses to college players will be reduced, such action will make possible relatively higher salaries for players generally, based on proven ability in professional football, will eliminate the inequities which were said to be demoralizing established players, and will substantially increase player salary minimums. The retention of all existing teams and the addition of new franchises will increase the overall employment opportunities for professional football players and coaches.

. . .

"The proposed bill would not extend to the combined league any greater antitrust immunity than that now existing for the existing professional football leagues. The proposed legislation does not seek to resolve any of the antitrust problems of professional football or the other professional team sports.

"It is the intent of the committee that the new league will commence operations with no greater antitrust immunity than the existing leagues now enjoy. The sole effect of this legislation is to permit the combination of the two leagues to go forward without fear of antitrust challenge based upon a joint agreement between the member clubs of two leagues to combine in a single league and to conduct their affairs as members of a single league." [2]

On September 26, 1966, the Senate passed the bill on a voice vote, without debate.

In the meantime, however, things were not going smoothly for the merger in the House of Representatives. On September 8, 1966, Congressman Emanuel Celler, chairman of the House Judiciary Committee which would have jurisdiction over a merger bill, told NFL Commissioner Pete Rozelle that he did not favor enactment of such legislation. Curiously, however, Congressman Celler also told Rozelle that he, Celler, saw no reason the two leagues should not go through with their merger, even without approving legislation. Celler said that his committee was not opposed to the merger, nor did he think that the Justice Department would oppose it.[3]

Rozelle, understandably, was not put entirely at ease by Celler's advice. In a statement issued to the press, Rozelle said:

"Chairman Celler is a recognized expert on antitrust legislation. We are pleased to have his assurances concerning the legality of our plan for an expanded league and his advice to go forward. On the other hand, we have responsibilities to 24 franchises in 23 cities as well as to possible expansion cities currently

[2] S.Rep. 1654, 89th Cong., 2d Sess. (1966), 1966 U.S. Code & Admin. News 4378.

[3] Congressional Quarterly, Sept. 16, 1966, Pg. 2178.

> being studied under the total plan. We feel hesitant because of the numerous complex commitments that must be made on a long-range basis. For this reason, we will continue to urge legislation in Congress." [4]

On September 12, 1966, Congressman William Cramer did in fact introduce a football merger bill in the House, and it was duly referred to Congressman Celler's committee, where no action was taken at first.

On September 26, 1966, when the Senate passed its football merger bill, Congressman Celler again stated that he thought the bill was unnecessary and added that he had no intentions of scheduling hearings on it. While Celler's earlier statement on September 8th that merger legislation was unnecessary was curious enough, his reiteration of it on September 26th was even more curious, because on September 9th, in direct response to his advice to Rozelle to proceed with the merger without authorization, a group called the Chicago Football Associates filed a $12 million antitrust lawsuit against the American and National Football Leagues designed to block their merger. Chicago stockbroker Robert Nussbaum, head of the group and the former operator of the semi-professional Chicago Panthers football team, explained that "A week before the merger I thought I had an American League franchise for Chicago. But it came as a bolt out of the blue when I talked to Lamar Hunt of the AFL expansion committee and was told that the merger precluded Chicago getting a franchise from his league." [5] The Chicago Bears had had the National Football League franchise for that city since the League was formed.

---

[4] 112 Congressional Record 22252, 89th Cong., 2d Sess. (Sept. 12, 1966).

[5] *Id.*

Under pressure from his fellow members of the House, Congressman Celler relented and finally scheduled hearings on the bill for October 6, 1966. The pace of those hearings was very leisurely, however, and the 89th Congress was to adjourn within a couple of weeks. Finally, on October 13th, it became very clear to the bill's proponents that Celler intended to block the bill altogether. Pete Rozelle was in the witness chair when the hearing was called off abruptly by a point of order that the House was in session. Celler gave no certain date for the continuation of the hearing, even though one member of the committee indicated he wanted to question Rozelle further, and even though Federal Trade Commission Chairman Paul Rand Dixon was in the audience waiting to testify. Celler had indicated that before the hearings were through he also wanted to hear from Donald Turner, head of the Justice Department Antitrust Division, from the CBS and NBC television networks, and from representatives from high schools, colleges, and the football players' associations. It was obvious that there was not nearly enough time remaining in the 89th Congress to hear from that number of witnesses.

§6.1(c) Parliamentary tactics

A tactic was therefore devised to by-pass Celler and his committee altogether. During those final weeks of the 89th Congress, both the Senate and House were also considering an important bill relating to the investment tax credit provisions of the Internal Revenue Code. Those provisions had granted business a 7% credit against their federal income taxes for monies invested in the purchase of machinery and equipment. They also permitted accelerated depreciation of industrial and commercial buildings. By late 1966, it was thought that these tax provisions were inflationary, and President Johnson recommended that they be suspended temporarily.

On October 14, 1966, while the Senate was debating the bill to suspend the investment tax credit, Senator Dirksen proposed an amendment adding a provision to the bill which would exempt the merger of the American and National Football Leagues from the antitrust laws. After only minutes of discussion, and no disagreement, the Senate approved the amendment, and later passed the entire tax bill. The House of Representatives also passed the investment tax credit bill, but its version said nothing about the proposed football merger. The two versions of the tax bill were referred to a Conference Committee of House and Senate members for reconciliation of the differences between them. In some cases, the Senate conferees acquiesced and accepted the House version; in other cases, the House conferees acquiesced and accepted the Senate version. With respect to the football merger amendment, the House conferees acquiesced, and the football merger amendment stayed in the bill recommended for enactment by the Conference Committee Report.

Naturally, when the Senate took up the Conference Committee Report on October 21, 1966, its members had no objections to the merger provision, and the Report was agreed to. In the House of Representatives, however, the merger provision generated extensive debate. Several Representatives who favored the merger, contended that the bill would not grant any greater antitrust immunity to professional football than it already had, except that the simple act of merger by itself would be made legal. Congressman Celler was not entirely satisfied that would be the case. Although the Conference Report and those Congressmen who supported it, and even Commissioner Rozelle himself, all insisted that only merger would be legalized, the proposed statute itself would be "paramount," Celler said, "and the statute immunizes the contents of a joint agreement."

> "What is this joint agreement? We do not know . . . But we did at the hearings before the Judiciary Committee try to plumb the depths of this so-called joint agreement, and we are in possession of part of that joint agreement. It contains all manner and kinds of operations under the league that would be formed, including the common draft, the division of territory, an arbitrary method of doling out franchises, and all manner and kinds of additional operations which presently come within the four squares of the antitrust laws.
>
> "That is what we will be immunizing by this action today if we pass and approve this rider. That is why I wanted to have some hearings. I did not want to buy a pig in a poke. I did not want to be like a blind man looking for a black cat in a dark room . . . I desire to explore this enigma, inside a riddle, wrapped in a mystery." [1]

Other Congressmen pointed out to Celler that the reason his hearings had not covered all of the topics he wanted to explore was because he himself had refused to schedule hearings until it was so close to the end of the 89th Congress that inadequate time remained to do so. And ultimately, when the vote was taken, the pro-merger forces won. The Conference Committee Report was agreed to 161 to 76, and the football merger authorization bill became law on November 8, 1966.

---

[1] 112 Congressional Record 28231, 89th Cong., 2d Sess. (Oct. 20, 1966).

There is an interesting and amusing sidelight to the parliamentary tactic that was devised to obtain enactment of the merger bill. On the final day of the 89th Congress, October 22, 1966, Senator Long rose on the floor of the Senate to offer a tribute to Senator Dirksen, who was then in the hospital:

> "Some time ago I urged the minority leader to join with me in trying to pass a measure to protect the football teams . . .
>
> "When it was suggested that the football amendment be attached to the tax bill, someone said, 'Oh, my goodness, don't tell me you are going to attach this bill to a tax measure.'
>
> "Well, it was. When that happened, every professional football team, I think, sent flowers. The Baltimore Colts sent a huge wreath shaped like a horseshoe. The Cleveland Browns sent a wreath shaped like a football. There were so many flowers there that it was almost impossible to get inside the room.
>
> "When the Senator from Illinois woke up and looked at the flowers, he said, 'Apparently the bill must have passed.'" [2]

Shortly thereafter, *Congressional Quarterly* magazine reported that the tactic of adding the merger bill to the investment tax credit bill was actually devised by Senator Long along with Congressman Hale Boggs.[3] Long and Boggs were both members of the critical Conference Committee that accepted the amendment. And both men were from Louisiana. New Orleans did not have a professional football team at the time the merger was being considered,

---

[2] 112 Congressional Record 28797, 89th Cong., 2d Sess. (Oct. 22, 1966).

[3] Congressional Quarterly, Oct. 28, 1966, Pg. 2640.

but was thought to be high on the list of likely cities for future expansion. The bill, as proposed and enacted, conditioned antitrust immunity for the merger on there being *more* teams in the combined league than had participated in the two separate leagues.[4] Not long after the merger bill was enacted, the NFL announced that New Orleans was in fact to receive the next expansion franchise, and it did.

§6.2 The NBA-ABA attempt to merge

§6.2(a) NBA-ABA war and peace agreement

Despite the very expensive failure of Abe Saperstein's American Basketball League in 1961, after only a season and a half of operations,[1] the success of the American Football League and Congressional approval for its merger with the NFL[2] encouraged another group of wealthy businessmen to form a new basketball league in 1966 which they named the American Basketball Association. Their competition, the National Basketball Association, had itself had a rocky and unstable history stretching back to 1937 when the National Basketball League was formed. By 1945 the NBL consisted of twelve teams, many of which played in cities so small they do not have professional basketball franchises today. There was also an American Basketball League in 1945, with teams in six cities.

In 1946, a third league was organized called the Basketball Association of America. Four of the BAA's eleven franchises did not survive to its second season, and in

[4] See § 6.1(b), *supra.*

[1] D. Wolf, Foul! The Connie Hawkins Story (New York: Warner Paperback Library, 1972), at 164-165.

[2] See § 6.1, *supra.*

1947, the remaining seven were joined by a team from the American League which by then had ceased to operate. By 1948, the National Basketball League and the Basketball Association of America were competing with one another for the services of college graduates and established veterans. They were also competing with one another—as current day leagues have not—for the allegiance of entire franchises. Thus, in 1948 four entire NBL teams joined the BAA. Then, in 1949, the two leagues merged and renamed themselves the National Basketball Association. The NBA had 17 teams divided into three divisions during that first season. Six teams went out of business before the 1950 season began, however, and three more ceased play by 1954.[3]

The NBA began to expand in 1960, when the price of a franchise was pegged at $200,000. By 1966, when the ABA was being organized, an NBA franchise cost $1,750,000; and at least some ABA organizers were hoping for a quick merger and comparable increases in the values of their own clubs which a merger could be expected to produce.[4]

For the ABA, credibility was the first order of business. Fans had to be convinced that this new league was truly a major professional circuit. And to establish such needed credibility, ABA owners began hiring the best collegiate and NBA veteran players they could sign. Naturally, doing so was expensive, and in the first four seasons of operation not a single ABA team enjoyed even one profitable year.[5]

---

[3] Hearings on S.2373 before the Subcomm. on Antitrust and Monopoly of the Senate Comm. on the Judiciary, 92d Cong., 1st Sess. 187-190 (1971).

[4] D. Wolf, *supra* note 1, at 202, 205.

[5] Hearings, *supra* note 3, at 191, 209.

The ABA's striving for legitimacy was no less expensive for the NBA. In its attempt to retain its senior position in professional basketball, NBA teams responded to ABA salary offers with higher offers of their own. As a result, during the ABA's first four years of existence, the median salary of NBA players almost doubled from $23,000 to $43,000. Moreover, during this period, NBA teams lost money on more than 60% of their seasons. (Indeed, 20% of the seasons were profitable only because of league entry fees received from new expansion franchises.)[6]

By 1970, both leagues had had enough of their "war," and conversations were begun about the possibility of merger. Merger was to be accompanied by a single common draft of college players, and thus the cessation of competitive bidding for their services, and the cessation of veteran player "raids" by teams in one league against the other would also result. In short, merger would put an end to escalating salary expenses, thus increasing the probability of profitable operation in the future.

§6.2(b) NBA players' suit

One man's expenses are another's income. And when the NBA players heard of the proposed merger, they were none too happy. The existence of an alternate place to sell their services had resulted in dramatic increases in their salaries and fringe benefits, and they were anxious to maintain the option of switching employers, even if they had never engaged in actual negotiations to do so. So on April 16, 1970, Oscar Robertson, who was then president of the NBA Players Association, and the player representatives of each NBA team, commenced a class action

[6] S.Rep. 92-1151, 92d Cong., 2d Sess. 8 (1972); Hearings, *supra* note 3, at 192, 210.

on behalf of themselves and all present and future NBA players seeking to enjoin the proposed merger. The suit, filed in the federal District Court in New York City, was based on the obvious contention that a merger of the only two leagues offering professional basketball employment would constitute a violation of the Sherman Act, because it would restrain trade and create a monopoly in that industry. (The suit also sought to invalidate the player draft and the option clause as well.)[1]

On April 17th, District Judge Lloyd MacMahon granted a temporary restraining order blocking the merger, noting that there was "no longer any question that the Sherman antitrust law applies to sports other than baseball in the same way it applies to other commercial enterprises engaged in interstate commerce."[2] Two weeks later, after more extensive briefing and oral argument, District Judge Charles Tenney granted the players a preliminary injunction enjoining both the merger and any "express or implied" agreement between the leagues not to employ or negotiate with one another's players. However, recognizing the leagues' First Amendment right "to petition the Government for a redress of grievances," Judge Tenney's order specifically provided that nothing contained in it was to be construed to prevent the two leagues from meeting with each other for the purpose of soliciting Congress for legislation which would permit their merger.[3]

---

[1] Complaint published in Hearings on S.2373 before the Subcomm. on Antitrust and Monopoly of the Senate Comm. on the Judiciary, 92d Cong., 2d Sess., Part 2 (1971) at 1220-1227.

[2] Robertson v. National Basketball Association, Temporary Restraining Order, published in Hearings on S.2373 before the Subcomm. on Antitrust and Monopoly of the Senate Comm. on the Judiciary, 92d Cong., 1st Sess. (1971) at 25.

[3] *Id.* at 26.

§6.2(c) Merger bills

Over the course of the next year, negotiations were held between the leagues on the terms and conditions of a merger, should Congress approve. Finally, on May 7, 1971, an agreement to seek Congressional approval for a merger was reached, and the two leagues jointly retained former California Senator Thomas Kuchel—who was then practicing law privately in Washington, D.C.—to make the necessary presentation. On July 29, 1971, identical bills were introduced in the Senate and House of Representatives which were virtually the same as the football merger bill passed by Congress in 1966. The bills were short and to the point. They would have simply inserted into the antitrust acts a phrase providing that:

> "The antitrust laws do not apply to any joint agreement by which the member clubs of two or more professional basketball leagues combine their operations in an expanded single league, if such agreement does not decrease the number of professional basketball clubs so operating and the provisions of which are directly relevant thereto."[1]

The teams in the two leagues certainly hoped for and probably expected quick action on their bills, just as the National and American Football Leagues had received quick action on theirs. This time, however, Congress was more time-consuming. As a result the bills were never passed.

The basketball legislation got off to a rough start in Congress for three reasons. First, Senator Philip Hart, who reportedly favored the merger and who was Chair-

[1] S.2373, 92d Cong., 1st Sess. (1971); H.R. 10185, 92d Cong., 1st Sess. (1971).

man of the Antitrust and Monopoly Subcommittee which had jurisdiction over the legislation, permitted Senator Sam Ervin to chair the subcommittee's hearings on it. Senator Ervin was vociferously opposed to the bill.[2] Second, Bob Short, owner of the Washington Senators baseball team, announced his intention to move the club to Texas just before the basketball hearings were scheduled to begin, thereby upsetting most of Congress.[3] Third, though negotiations with the NBA players had been conducted, no agreement had been reached with them concerning what terms, if any, would be acceptable in exchange for their support of a merger. Thus the NBA players actively opposed the merger bill before Congress, as the football players had not because they had been insufficiently organized.

The hearings themselves were thorough. Senator Ervin, with the style that later made him a folk hero during the Watergate Hearings, began by declaring in his opening statement that the football merger bill had been "railroaded through the Congress." He stated:

> "I deeply hope that Congress will not follow the precedent it set in handling the pro football merger question. This committee plans to conduct an extensive and comprehensive inquiry before final action is taken one way or the other on the proposed basketball merger bill. The common draft and the option clause which will result from the merger are issues concerning the economic enslavement of professional basket-

[2] See, e.g., Senator Ervin's opening remarks in Hearings on S.2373 before the Subcomm. on Antitrust and Monopoly of the Senate Comm. on the Judiciary, 92d Cong., 1st Sess. 12-22 (1971).

[3] *Id.* at 18; Hearings on H.R. 1206, et al., before the Antitrust Subcomm. of the House Comm. on the Judiciary, 92d Cong., 2d Sess. 186-187. See also, § 8.3(b), *infra.*

ball players, and are too important for such ephemeral treatment as was accorded the football merger." [4]

The subcommittee's first witness was former California Senator Thomas Kuchel, counsel for the two leagues. Senator Kuchel, as the subcommittee members respectfully called the attorney, spoke of the need for proposed legislation. "The business of professional basketball is in deep economic trouble," he said.

> "Unless merger is promptly consummated, it is my belief that a substantial number of franchises may fail. After the inevitable shaking out and shrinking down, professional league basketball would be confined to a relative handful of the largest cities in the land. That state of affairs would be to the detriment of the basketball fans of America, and of the players, many of whom would no longer have any opportunity to be a part of this great sport, and of the clubs, both those which would remain and those which would disappear.
>
> . . .
>
> "The conditions presently confronting professional basketball result from the annual rites of self-destruction between the two leagues. Teams are quite literally forced, by the need to maintain major league status, to bid against each other annually for those college players entering professional ranks with reputations as potential superstars. The yearly bidding war with its fantastic contracts for a limited number of untested rookies—contracts which bear no relationship whatever to basketball economics—will inexorably end in ruin. Yet neither league can unilaterally

[4] Hearings on S.2373, *supra* note 2, at 18.

retreat from that war, for to do so would be equally ruinous to it.

"In these circumstances, balanced competition, the very essence of professional league sports, becomes impossible. The rich teams become richer in talent and revenue while the poor teams get poorer and face collapse.

"An end to the bidding war will do away with the astronomical contracts entered into each year with new and untested players. It will bring economic stability to the sport. Merger will enhance professional basketball job opportunities. It will promote the development of strong local ties with consequent enlarging fan loyalty. It offers the best prospect of substantial improvement in the pension and other fringe benefits for the ABA players. Player benefits generally will be allocated, it seems to us, far more equitably." [5]

§6.2(d) Economic studies

Though the ex-senator's presentation was good rhetoric, and while the facts stated and opinions expressed may have been accurate, the simple statement of them was not likely to convince doubtful Congressmen. The National and American Basketball Associations were aware that they would have to do more to get approval for their merger than simply ask for it. So, in addition to retaining Senator Kuchel, the leagues retained Robert R. Nathan, a consulting economist of considerable experience and renown, to study the economics of professional basketball, the financial condition of individual teams, and the anticipated economic effects of the hoped-for merger. Nathan

[5] *Id.* at 91, 93.

was an excellent choice for such a study, for not only had he and his firm conducted studies for corporations, unions, and governmental agencies, he had also been an expert witness on behalf of the state of Wisconsin in its lawsuit against the Milwaukee Braves (which sought to keep the Braves from moving to Atlanta) and on behalf of Curt Flood in his lawsuit against Organized Baseball (seeking to invalidate the reserve clause). Thus, Nathan had impressive credentials and had previously done work for interests that were opposed to professional sports leagues, all of which suggested the absence of built-in bias.

In his testimony before the Senate Subcommittee, Nathan described the bleak financial condition of professional basketball, the industry's historic instability, and the consistent and occasionally enormous losses suffered by most teams. Then he said:

> "One factor stands out among all others when we consider the fundamental reasons for the current financial losses and the continuing instability of professional basketball teams. This is the sharp increase in the salaries of a relatively few players, especially rookies and especially over the past four seasons, when both the National Basketball Association and the American Basketball Association were in operation."[1]

It was his conclusion that merger was necessary and would "provide the possibility of financial opportunity and stability . . ."[2]

---

[1] Hearings on S.2373 before the Subcomm. on Antitrust and Monopoly of the Senate Comm. on the Judiciary, 92d Cong., 1st Sess. 194-195 (1971).

[2] *Id.* at 203.

Nathan's testimony confirmed what most non-economists, including team owners, thought was the case—namely, that high salaries were the cause of the owners' financial problems—and had it not been for the concern of some Congressmen, such as Senator Ervin, for the financial welfare of the players, the basketball merger bill probably would have been enacted without controversy. The NBA owners had in fact attempted to enlist the support of their players by making them a generous offer on new player-contract and league by-law provisions. The NBA had offered to do away with option clauses in the contracts of veteran players; and to limit rookie contracts to a period of one year with a one-year option. Upon becoming a free agent, a player would have had the right to negotiate with any team, but his old team would have a "right of first refusal," that is a right to meet the highest offer the player had received, and thereby retain his services. If a player did sign with another team, because his former team had not met its offer, the latter would have had a right to be compensated by the new team with money, draft choices, players, or any combination of the three. The amount of compensation would have been determined by an arbitration panel consisting of three members, one of whom would have been named by the Players Association, the second by the NBA Commissioner, and the third by the other two. The panel members would have been guided by several factors in making their decisions: (1) the impact of the transfer on the revenues and competitive ability of the team losing the player, and (2) any special costs incurred by the team losing out in connection with unusual or exceptional promotional activities relating to the player. However, they were not to consider the difference between the salaries paid by the former and new teams. Nor were they to award compensation so substantial as to materially discourage movement of players from one team to another.[3]

As progressive a proposal as this was, by comparison with existing NBA practices and those of other leagues, the players did not accept it. While they were willing to accept a player draft and an option clause in rookie contracts, they insisted that a player's former team not have a "right of first refusal" or a "compensation" right. Their proposal was not acceptable to the owners.

In the meantime, it developed that The Brookings Institution in Washington, D.C. was conducting an investigation of its own into public policy towards professional team sports as part of its series of Studies in the Regulation of Economic Activity. When the Senate Subcommittee learned of the Brookings study, it invited Roger G. Noll and Benjamin A. Okner, the two Brookings Senior Fellows who were principally in charge of the project, to testify on the proposed basketball merger. Their testimony was truly remarkable in that it introduced several new and previously unconsidered ideas, and was eventually instrumental in changing the thinking of several Senators who had originally favored the merger bill without qualification. For it was the conclusion of Noll and Okner that the merger of the NBA and ABA, by itself, would not in fact improve the financial condition of the basketball industry.

The reasons for their conclusion were even more remarkable than the conclusion itself. The only impact merger would have had on the financial position of the various teams would have been a decrease in the size of player-salaries. Yet, Noll and Okner found from their study of financial information supplied by the two leagues

---

[3] ***Id.* at 95-97.**

that if player salaries were reduced to absolutely zero, five of the eleven teams in the ABA would have continued to operate at a loss![4] In fact, Noll and Okner estimated that player salaries would have to be halved before all but the strongest ABA teams could break even. And even some teams in the NBA would have to reduce their player-salary expenses by half before they could break even. Though player-salaries in professional football did decrease somewhat following the merger of the NFL and AFL, the decrease came nowhere near half. Figures obtained by Noll and Okner with respect to the Philadelphia Eagles indicated that the decrease was closer to 3%. Furthermore, most basketball teams would have reached the minimum salary permitted by the NBA Players Association collective bargaining agreement long before halving their salary costs, even if merger might have given them the bargaining leverage they otherwise needed to do so.[5]

One of the reasons so many professional basketball teams were having such financial trouble—a reason the leagues had not volunteered to Congress—was that costs of operations other than player-salaries, including such things as "front office" salaries and expenses, were larger than player-salaries and had increased more than player-salaries during the years of inter-league competition.[6]

According to Noll and Okner, the principal cause of most teams' financial difficulties was insufficient revenues. Several teams, including one in the NBA, were playing in home arenas whose total seating capacity was so small that even if every home game of the season were sold out they

[4] Hearings on S.2373 before the Subcomm. on Antitrust and Monopoly of the Senate Comm. on the Judiciary, 92d Cong., 2d Sess., Part 2, at 1018 (1971).

[5] *Id.*

[6] *Id.* at 1018-1019.

still could not break even.[7] Therein lay basketball's key problem and the way to its solution. Unlike the practice in football and baseball, home teams in both the NBA and ABA retain all of the proceeds of ticket sales; visiting teams receive nothing. In the National Football League, the visiting team gets 40% of the gate, and in baseball, 20%.[8] While the proceeds of network television contracts are divided equally between all basketball teams in each league, income from that source is comparatively small for NBA teams and virtually negligible for ABA teams. Thus, while professional basketball as a whole operates only slightly in the red, all of the profits go to a few very successful teams, while all of the others are either marginal or money-losing enterprises.

The best way to improve the financial condition of most basketball teams, Noll and Okner stated, was to require the leagues to adopt a gate-sharing system similar to that used in the NFL. They explained that:

> "A typical game in Madison Square Garden yields about $100,000 in gate receipts. This is as much as one ABA team collects all season, and more than half the season revenue of two other ABA teams. If these teams could play the Knicks in New York just twice a year and take home half the gate, they could increase their total revenues by sixty to one hundred percent. To achieve the same effect on profits through the merger route [alone] would require teams to cut their player salaries in half. Quite obviously, ending the competition for players would not benefit the weaker teams nearly as much as would an inter-league playing schedule

[7] Hearings, *supra* note 1, at 409.

[8] NFL Constitution & By-Laws, Article XIX; S.Rep. 92-1151, 92d Cong., 2d Sess. 5 (1972).

that was coupled with a relatively even gate-sharing arrangement. In fact, it is difficult to imagine any other action materially improving the lot of the weak ABA teams."[9]

§6.2(e) Judiciary Committee amendments

The recommendation of Noll and Okner on mandatory gate-sharing was accepted by the members of the Senate Antitrust and Monopoly Subcommittee; and when they reported the bill to the full Judiciary Committee, they amended it to require the visiting team to be given at least 30% of the gate. Likewise, when the Judiciary Committee reported the bill to the full Senate, with the recommendation that it be passed, the bill included an amendment requiring at least a 70-30 split. The Judiciary Committee report stated, "The Committee decided to require the splitting of gate receipts not just to prevent team failures but, equally important, to allow all the teams to compete on a relatively equal financial footing in their bidding for player services."[1]

The Judiciary Committee also added several other significant amendments to the merger bill before sending it to the full Senate. The agreement between the NBA and ABA had required each ABA team (except the Virginia Squires) to pay the NBA $1,250,000 as an entrance or franchise fee. Though this fee was payable over a ten-year period, even that lengthy payout required annual installments of $125,000. "The Committee felt," it said in its report to the Senate, "that this provision of the merger agreement, standing alone, is inconsistent with the purpose for which the exemption from the antitrust laws is re-

---

[9] Hearings, *supra* note 4, at 1040.

[1] S.Rep. 92-1151, 92d Cong., 2d Sess. 6 (1972).

quested; namely, to ensure the survival of the financially weaker teams in the American Basketball Association." [2] As a result, the Committee added an amendment to the merger bill which provided that all entry or franchise fee payments to be made by ABA teams were to be made solely from television revenues received by them as a result of the merger.

The Judiciary Committee also sided with the players on the issue of option rights. Thus, it amended the merger bill to prohibit compulsory option clauses (other than a one-year option clause in one-year rookie contracts), including a prohibition on the NBA's desired plan for a "right of first refusal" and for "compensation" fixed by arbitrators.

Finally, the Judiciary Committee also amended the merger bill to prohibit television blackouts of championship and playoff games in all sports, if those games were sold out five days in advance.[3]

Former Senator Thomas Kuchel told reporters that he was "obviously . . . delighted" that the merger bill had started moving in Congress.[4] More than a year had passed between the date it was introduced and the date the Judiciary Committee reported it to the full Senate. However, at least one of his clients was considerably less than delighted. NBA Commissioner Walter Kennedy stated that the proposed merger could be "wrecked" because of the amendments the Committee had added.[5] And as matters turned out, Kennedy's assessment seems to have been accurate.

---

[2] *Id.*

[3] *Id.* at 6-7.

[4] Wall Street Journal, Sept. 8, 1972.

[5] L.A. Times, Sept. 23, 1972, Part III.

The 92nd Congress was only weeks from adjournment by the time the bill was reported out, and those weeks passed without any further action. By the time the 93rd Congress convened in January of 1973, Watergate was beginning to occupy the attention of Congress, and no serious efforts were made to renew legislative action on the basketball merger. The merger agreement between the two leagues expired by its own terms on January 4, 1974, and on January 30, 1974, the American Basketball Association filed a $600 million suit against the NBA and its 17 teams in federal court in San Francisco alleging antitrust violations, breach of contract and fraud.[6]

§6.3 The NHL-WHA litigation settlement

When in November of 1972, federal District Court Judge Leon Higginbotham ruled that there was "a clear and substantial likelihood" that the National Hockey League's reserve clause and other related agreements would be found to violate the Sherman Act,[1] the NHL must have known that changes would have to be made. Although the ruling came in response to the World Hockey Association's motion for a preliminary injunction against further NHL attempts to enforce its reserve clause pending a full scale trial, and though judges frequently see things differently after a trial has brought out all of the facts, the WHA motion had generated over 2000 pages of exhibits and more than 500 pages of legal briefs. There were, in other words, few facts if any that Judge Higginbotham was likely to learn at a trial that he did not already know at the conclusion of the preliminary injunction hearing.

[6] L.A. Times, Jan. 31, 1974.

[1] Philadelphia World Hockey Club, Inc. v. Philadelphia Hockey Club, Inc., 351 F.Supp. 462, 518 (E.D.Pa. 1972), discussed in § 2.3(b)(2), *supra.*

Thus, it must have seemed to the National Hockey League that it was almost certain that Judge Higginbotham would find in the WHA's favor after trial and therefore award a permanent injunction and possibly a large money judgment as well. Since the NHL Players Association had been bargaining for years for an end to the reserve clause, and since it looked as though the Court might order it ended, it must have become apparent to the NHL that the most prudent course was to amend the reserve clause itself before trial, while it still had some control over its own policies and was not acting pursuant to court order, and before its collective bargaining agreement expired and it had to bargain with the NHL Players Association over the wording of a substitute for the reserve clause.

The replacement clause adopted in November of 1973 was not perpetual,[2] thereby making it possible for the World Hockey Association to gain access to free agent professionals. The new clause thus became the basis for the settlement of all WHA/NHL litigation. The trial of thirteen separately filed lawsuits which had all been consolidated before Judge Higginbotham was scheduled to begin March 18, 1974. The cases were settled February 19, 1974.

The settlement agreement required the World Hockey Association to respect and not contest the legality and enforceability of the NHL's new option system. The NHL agreed to pay the WHA $1,750,000; not to interfere with WHA access to playing arenas owned or controlled by NHL teams; and to play 15 exhibition games with WHA teams during the training period preceding the 1974-1975 season. (For every one of the 15 exhibition games not played during that year, because of the NHL team's failure

[2] See § 2.2(b)(1), *supra.*

to appear, the NHL agreed to pay the WHA $10,000 and to play the game the following year, when in the event of another NHL default, the game would be rescheduled for the following year and another $10,000 would be due, and so on until all 15 games were actually played.) The agreement required both leagues to dismiss all of the lawsuits they or their members had pending against one another, thus bringing to end the WHL/NHL hockey war.[3]

[3] Consent Decree signed by District Judge Higginbotham on Feb. 19, 1974, settling virtually all litigation between the NHL and WHA.

Chapter 7
DISCIPLINE AND ELIGIBILITY

§7.1 Nature and purpose of disciplinary measures

In June of 1973, Baseball Commissioner Bowie Kuhn fined Yankee outfielder Bobby Murcer $500, because Murcer publicly stated that neither Kuhn nor American League President Joe Cronin "had the guts to stop pitchers from throwing spit-balls."[1] If that seems a stiff penalty for a mild and harmless bit of criticism, it was nevertheless not without a good deal of precedent in the world of professional sports. Indeed, Murcer's fine was but a small tile in the mosaic that is the power of professional sport leagues to impose discipline for all manner of conduct deemed "detrimental" or "prejudicial" to their "best interests."

Penalized conduct ranges from activities that most would concede may call into question the integrity and honesty of the sport itself, to simple oral statements concerning matters that have nothing whatever to do with athletics. And the discipline that has been imposed ranges from painless reprimands to career-ending blacklisting.

On one end of the conduct spectrum is game-fixing and gambling. Professional games are exciting, and therefore entertaining, only if spectators believe that the participants are exerting their best efforts and that the score is the product of those efforts. While it is true that the Harlem Globetrotters always win their games, and that their spectators know this in advance, the Globetrotters play basketball far differently from teams in the NBA and ABA. The Globetrotters are comedians as well as athletes, and it is their comedy that makes them entertaining despite the

[1] L.A. Times, June 30, 1973, Part III.

pre-ordained result. If players bet against their own teams, a logical inference would be that the result had been fixed. And without the Globetrotters' comedy, there would be little reason for people to watch fixed games.

Equally important, the financial success of a professional sports league depends upon fan interest in all games played during the season, not merely games played between division contenders. The notion that any team in the league can beat any other team on any given day is the cornerstone upon which season tickets and broadcasting rights are sold. The outcome of every game must be in some doubt prior to its start. Thus, even players who bet only on their own teams to win destroy the cornerstone of professional sports. In such cases, it is not the bet that destroys interest in the game bet on. Rather, it is the failure of the player to bet on other games that destroys interest in those; because the failure of the player to bet some games suggests that in the opinion of someone with intimate inside information concerning the team, the team is not likely to do as well as is generally expected.

Though there have been scandals involving college basketball, most notably in 1951 and 1961,[2] professional sports have remained unscathed since the Chicago Black Sox scandal in 1919. This is not to say, however, that professional athletes have never been caught betting on games. In January of 1954, Jack Molinas, an All-American from Columbia University and then in his rookie year with the Fort Wayne Zollner Pistons of the NBA (now the Detroit Pistons), admitted placing several bets on the Pistons to win. He acknowledged, in writing, that he had telephoned an acquaintance at a candy store in New York

[2] See, D. Wolf, Foul! The Connie Hawkins Story (New York: Warner Paperback Library, 1972).

City who gave him the bookies' point spread on coming games. When Molinas thought the Pistons could beat the point spread, he asked his New York contact to place a bet for him. When he did not think the team would better the spread, he told his contact he did not want to bet those games. An investigation by the Fort Wayne, Indiana, police led to Molinas' arrest; and when he confessed, Maurice Podoloff, President of the NBA, was called to the police station in the middle of the night and was shown his statement. Though Molinas had been caught after placing fewer than a dozen bets, which netted him only $400, and though Molinas insisted that at no time had he ever received or been offered a payoff to throw any games, Podoloff immediately told Molinas that he was "through" as a player and suspended him indefinitely. Molinas made several applications for reinstatement in the following years, and even filed two lawsuits to compel the NBA to reinstate him, but his suspension was never lifted.[3]

Football players Paul Hornung of the Green Bay Packers and Alex Karras of the Detroit Lions fared somewhat better than Molinas, under similar circumstances. In the fall of 1962, NFL security personnel picked up rumors that the two stars were gambling on football games, and a five month investigation confirmed that they were betting "relatively nominal amounts" on their own teams.[4] According to Commissioner Rozelle, no evidence was ever uncovered suggesting Hornung or Karras ever gave less than their best on the field or that they ever bet against their own teams.[5] Nevertheless, they—like Molinas—were also suspended, but only for one year.

---

[3] See §§ 7.3(b)(1) and 7.3(e)(1), *infra.*

[4] Playboy Interview: Pete Rozelle, Playboy Magazine, Oct. 1973, at 82.

[5] *Id.*

Professional sports' aversion to gambling is so intense that leagues not only prohibit their players from betting, but also from associating with gamblers or even appearing or allowing it to appear that they do so. Joe Namath, quarterback of the New York Jets, once owned an interest in a New York City bar and restaurant known as "Bachelors III." In some fashion, the NFL determined that the telephones in Bachelors III were being used to place bets—not that Namath or his partners were placing bets themselves, simply that the phones in their public restaurant were being used by someone to do so—and as a result, Namath was told that he would have to sell his interest or be suspended from football. Ultimately, Namath sold his interest. Thereafter, Commissioner Rozelle forbade him ever from going there and "suggested" that all other NFL players avoid it and similar places as well, so that their reputations would not be "tarnished." [6]

Cheating is to individual sports, such as golf and bowling, what gambling is to team sports. In May of 1972, for example, the Ladies Professional Golf Association suspended Jane Blalock for one year on charges that she illegally moved her ball during the second round of a tournament that month in Louisville, Kentucky.[7] Similarly, professional bowler Ralph Manok was suspended by the American Bowling Congress and the Southeast District Bowling Association, not for cheating himself, but for bowling with another professional who had used someone else's name in order to have a higher handicap.[8]

---

[6] Comment, Discipline in Professional Sports: The Need for Player Protection, 60 Georgetown L.J. 771, 776 fn. 21 (1972).

[7] Blalock v. Ladies Professional Golf Assn., 359 F.Supp. 1260 (N.D.Ga. 1973), discussed in § 7.3(e)(2)(B), *infra.*

[8] Manok v. Southeast District Bowling Assn., 306 F.Supp. 1215 (C.D.Cal. 1969), discussed in § 7.3(e)(1), *infra.*

While gambling and cheating are activities that are directly related to sports, leagues also control conduct that is not directly related. Thus, in April of 1967, the New York State Athletic Commission suspended the boxing license of Muhammad Ali, who was then the World Heavyweight Champion, because he had refused to submit to induction into the Armed Forces of the United States. While Ali's subsequent conviction was being appealed, he applied to the Commission for a renewal of his license, which by then had expired by its own terms. In October of 1969, the Commission unanimously denied his renewal application on the grounds that his "refusal to enter the services and [his] felony conviction in violation of Federal law is regarded by this Commission to be detrimental to the best interests of boxing. . . ."[9]

In the summer of 1973, football player Lance Rentzel was suspended from the NFL after he plead guilty to charges of possession of marijuana. The suspension was based on Commissioner Rozelle's determination that Rentzel's problems with the law, including two prior scrapes he had had with state authorities in Minnesota and Texas, constituted conduct "detrimental to the welfare of the League."[10]

In cases of this nature, leagues (and their counterparts in individual sports, commissions and associations) are concerned not with the integrity of the athletic events themselves, but rather with their saleability to the public. The notion here is that professional sports are not a necessity; people do not have to attend or watch. It is simply entertainment—entertainment which is in vigorous

[9] Ali v. State Athletic Commission of New York, 316 F.Supp. 1246, 1247 (S.D.N.Y. 1970).

[10] See § 7.3(b)(2), *infra.*

competition with other leagues playing the same sport, with other sports, and with other forms of entertainment. Professional athletes are idolized by the young. And the fear is that should athletes develop reputations unworthy of idolatry, viewers and ticket-buyers can and will change their allegiance to other forms of entertainment.

The precise extent to which the financial health of professional sport leagues is jeopardized by the less than pristine conduct of athletes or owners is simply conjecture. Nevertheless, the potential for lost revenue is apparently a fact accepted by all entertainment producers, not only sport leagues; motion picture producers, for example, often include "good morals" clauses in their contracts with actors and actresses.[11] In addition, the fact that high standards are required of athletes by at least some fans has been documented. In his frank and revealing autobiography, *When All the Laughter Died in Sorrow,* Lance Rentzel wrote of the vicious and angry letters that poured into the Cowboys' office following his arrest in Dallas in November of 1971 on charges of indecent exposure.[12]

If gambling is at one end of the conduct spectrum, then conduct unrelated to sports is somewhere in the middle. Though Rentzel, for example, was suspended following his guilty plea to possession of marijuana, he was not suspended following his earlier guilty plea to indecent exposure charges. In the fall of 1973, when Congress was conducting hearings on drug use by athletes, Commissioner Rozelle told interviewers that the NFL did not automatically suspend any player arrested on drug charges; the

---

[11] J. Taubman, Performing Arts Management and Law, Vol. I of Forms, Pg. 195 ¶ 13 (New York: Law-Arts Publishers, Inc., 1973).

[12] L. Rentzel, When All the Laughter Died in Sorrow (New York: Bantam, 1972) at 201-202.

League's reaction, he said, depends on all of the facts of each incident.[13]

Further along on the spectrum would be statements and writings by players concerning professional sports. Bobby Murcer's $500 fine for his statement on spitballs is a good example of punishment meted out in response to a simple, oral statement of opinion. Another example is Jim Bouton's reprimand for publishing his controversial book, *Ball Four*—a reprimand which is thought by some to have helped the book reach the best seller list.[14] The reason for penalties of this kind was explained by NFL Commissioner Rozelle in a published interview. The first question put to Rozelle was whether the accusation that he tries to suppress public awareness of disagreements between players and team owners was true. "Yes, it is," he answered, "because I think squabbling in public will eventually ruin football, and there's no doubt that it's hurting us already. Polls taken for the league by Louis Harris—polls as valid as any political polls—indicate that very clearly."[15] He went on to explain that he believed sports were an emotional outlet, a place to find peace from domestic and international problems of the day. If sports take on "the same problematical coloration as the rest of the news," he said, "it would cease to be the popular escape valve" it now is.[16]

The Harris Poll notwithstanding, the relationship between public statements concerning the business aspects of professional sports and their popularity seems conjectural at best. Furthermore, penalizing and suppressing discussion gives rise to serious—if thus far unlitigated—First

---

[13] Playboy Interview, *supra* note 4, at 76-78.

[14] Padwe, Right of Dissent Doesn't Apply to Athletes, L.A. Times, Aug. 31, 1973, Part III.

[15] Playboy Interview, *supra* note 4, at 66.

[16] ***Id.***

Amendment free speech questions and has disquieting overtones in any event.

At the opposite end of the conduct spectrum from gambling would be statements and writings by players having nothing whatever to do with athletics. Although there apparently has never been a case involving disciplinary action as a result of such a statement or writing, a standard provision of the player contracts used by most leagues prohibits players from writing magazine or newspaper articles or appearing on radio or television programs without the consent of the club.[17] Though it would seem unlikely, such a contract provision could conceivably be used to prevent players from voicing their opinions even on political matters should team owners ever decide that the political philosophies of their players, if known, might discourage attendance of fans whose philosophies differ.

§7.2 Nature and purpose of eligibility requirements

Every league and association has eligibility requirements of one sort or another. Their purposes are essentially three-fold. First, as was true of some disciplinary measures, some eligibility rules are designed to prevent cheating. For example, the Washington State Bowling Proprietors Association once had a rule which limited eligibility for participation in tournaments sponsored by its members to those bowlers who restricted their bowling tc member establishments. The stated purpose of the rule was to insure that claimed handicaps were accurate—something which could be done, the Association claimed, only if all bowling was done at member establishments

[17] See, e.g., Major League Baseball Uniform Player's Contract ¶ 3(c); NBC Uniform Player Contract ¶ 17; NHL Standard Player's Contract ¶ 8(b).

where scores could be verified and recorded continuously. This rule came under attack in a case discussed below,[1] because an incidental though obvious effect was also the reduction of competition between member and non-member bowling establishments.

A second purpose of eligibility rules is to reduce to a manageable size the number of athletes who may participate in individual sport tournaments, such as golf tournaments. A golf course, for example, can physically accommodate only a certain number of players per day; and if the number of golfers who would like to participate exceeds the number that can be accommodated, some must be selected and others eliminated. While this could be done by random lot, eligibility standards are usually used instead, in order to obtain the highest level of play possible.[2]

The third purpose of eligibility requirements is to protect the integrity and health of high school and college athletic programs. This is done by prohibiting the employment of certain amateurs until they have exhausted their high school and college eligibility.[3] College coaches and athletic directors, and the programs they run, often rely heavily on one or two athletes for their success—athletes who may be good enough to play professionally, even before their graduation. Therefore, college officials welcome the restrictions imposed by professional teams with respect to the drafting of student players.

---

[1] Washington State Bowling Proprietors Assn. v. Pacific Lanes, Inc., 356 F.2d 371 (9th Cir. 1966), discussed in § 7.3(e)(1), *infra.*

[2] See, Deesen v. Professional Golfers' Assn. of America, 358 F.2d 165 (9th Cir. 1966), *cert. den.,* 385 U.S. 846 (1966), discussed in § 7.3(e)(1), *infra.*

[3] See, Denver Rockets v. All-Pro Management, Inc., 325 F.Supp. 1049 (C.D.Cal. 1971), discussed in § 7.3(e)(2)(A), *infra.*

The benefits flow in both directions, however. While baseball and hockey have extensive minor league systems that are used for the development of player talent, basketball and football do not. Generally speaking, minor league teams do not break even financially, and therefore must be subsidized by the majors. According to Baseball Commissioner Bowie Kuhn, the cost of supporting minor league teams for player development is substantial;[4] and naturally, the National Football League and the National and American Basketball Associations have no desire to incur similar costs. The NFL, NBA and ABA do not have similar player development costs, only because collegiate football and basketball programs do the developing for them.

If, however, the most talented college stars were to turn professional before their four years of college eligibility were up, collegiate programs would be weakened athletically and financially, and thus would be less able to continue to perform their player development function. In addition, the longer a college star plays as an amateur—and thus at no cost to the pros—the greater his skills and national reputation will become, thereby making him more valuable to the professional team and league he eventually joins.

§7.3 Legality of disciplinary measures and eligibility requirements

§7.3(a) Source of authority

Though league and team executives feel that any disciplinary actions they may take are taken only with the best interests of the league and team in mind, they nevertheless

---

[4] Hearings on H.R. 1206, et al., before the Antitrust Subcomm. of the House Comm. on the Judiciary, 92d Cong., 2d Sess. 184 (1972).

do not purport to have *inherent* disciplinary authority. Rather, any such actions taken by them are said to be authorized in advance by the players in their written player contracts and in league by-laws.

Thus, for example, the National Football League Standard Player Contract provides that the

> "Player acknowledges the right and power of the Commissioner (a) to fine and suspend, (b) to fine and suspend for life or indefinitely, and/or (c) to cancel the contract of, any player who accepts a bribe or who agrees to throw or fix a game or who, having knowledge of the same, fails to report an offered bribe or an attempt to throw or fix a game, or who bets on a game, or who is guilty of any conduct detrimental to the welfare of the League or of professional football." [1]

It also provides that,

> "The Player agrees at all times to comply with and be bound by: the Constitution and By-Laws, Rules and Regulations of the League, of the Club, and the decisions of the Commissioner of the League . . . which shall be final, conclusive and unappealable . . . . If the Player fails to comply with said Constitution, By-Laws, Rules and Regulations, the Club shall have the right to terminate this contract . . . to take such other action as may be specified in said Constitution, By-Laws, Rules and Regulations, subject, however, to the right to a hearing by the Commissioner." [2]

The Constitution and By-Laws provide that whenever the Commissioner, after notice and a hearing, decides that a

---

[1] NFL Standard Player Contract ¶ 11.

[2] *Id.* at ¶ 4.

player has violated any of its terms or "has been or is guilty of conduct detrimental to the welfare of the League or professional football" he has authority to suspend and/or fine the player as much as $5,000.[3]

NFL owners also agree in the Constitution and By-Laws to "be bound by" and to "observe all decisions of the Commissioner. . . ." [4]

The player contracts and by-laws of the other leagues contain similar provisions, and their significance is this. Player contracts impose rights and obligations on both players and teams. Among the obligations assumed by teams is to provide employment to the player for the term of the contract and to pay him a specified salary in exchange for those services. Thus, if player contracts did *not* contain provisions by which players agreed to be subject to the disciplinary authority of the team and the league, a fine or suspension could be construed as a breach of contract by the team, because a fine would reduce the agreed upon salary, and a suspension would be a withdrawal of employment.

On the other hand, the inclusion of contract provisions stating the player agrees he may be fined or suspended for certain conduct is designed to make discipline not only legal, but in fact a recognized part of the player's bargain with his team. Thus, a player with a one-year, $50,000 contract, really has a contract which says, in effect, that the team agrees to employ the player for one year, or such lesser time as may result from any disciplinary suspensions imposed by the team or league, at a salary of $50,000, less any disciplinary fines that may be imposed by the team or league. Read in this light, the one-year term

[3] NFL Constitution & By-Laws, Article 8.13(A).

[4] *Id.* at Article 3.11(a).

and $50,000 salary are both maximums, payable to the player only if his conduct is considered satisfactory by team and league officials. If it is not, the player has actually agreed to play for less, and should discipline be imposed, it is done pursuant to that agreement.

Disciplinary action taken against team owners is similarly taken pursuant to the agreement set forth in the league's by-laws.

In individual sports, such as boxing, golf and bowling, the theory is somewhat different, though the result is the same. Boxing is a sport licensed and controlled by the various states rather than by privately organized and administered associations. The authority of state appointed boxing commissioners to impose discipline is recognized by boxers as a condition of obtaining a license. A boxing license is thus comparable to a city business license, with boxers agreeing to pay fines the same way businesses agree to pay city business taxes. Boxing commissioners also reserve the right to suspend and to refuse to renew licenses, just as state motor vehicle departments reserve the right to suspend and to refuse to renew drivers licenses, under specified circumstances.

Golf and bowling associations are privately organized and administered organizations which sponsor tournaments for the benefit of their members. Each such association might be compared to a single team. While association members compete among themselves, rather than against members of other associations, association membership is comparable to a player contract. It is also comparable to a state license. By the terms of association membership, golfers and bowlers recognize and agree to their associations' authority to impose fines and to suspend eligibility for tournament play, under specified circumstances.

The existence of authority and the propriety of its use are often two separate questions. Thus, it is possible for disciplinary rules or eligibility requirements, which concededly confer authority, to be applied in ways that may be illegal.

§7.3(b) Due process principles

§7.3(b)(1) Procedural

Due process of law requires, at a minimum, that fair procedures be used in imposing discipline or making eligibility determinations. Usually, this means that action may be taken only after the person affected has been given notice of the charges and an opportunity to be heard. Ironically, the earliest reported sport discipline case affirmed a player's indefinite suspension, though he claimed he had not been given either notice or a hearing.[1] But the case did so in a manner that supported the validity of the principle that notice and a hearing are usually required.

The case was the one that Jack Molinas of the Fort Wayne Pistons filed against the National Basketball Association shortly after he was suspended indefinitely for betting on Pistons' games. A New York state court judge displayed little sympathy for Molinas, even though it was alleged that the NBA failed to follow its own by-laws in the process of suspending him. Molinas "wagered, and admitted it," the judge said. "To adjudge the suspension null and void, to bring about a hearing for this plaintiff, that must unquestionably and inevitably result in his expulsion or suspension, would be a mere futile gesture." [2]

[1] Molinas v. Podoloff, 133 N.Y.S.2d 743 (1954).

[2] *Id.* at 747.

Significantly, however, the judge stated,

> "If there was the slightest suggestion that the statement [Molinas' confession] was involuntary or untrue, or a single suggestion offered to question it, if there was a triable issue, this court would have . . . ordered a hearing." [3]

In fact, in a subsequent case involving the National Basketball Association, the court did refuse to enforce discipline that had been imposed on an owner. The case arose out of a dispute between the Philadelphia 76ers and the Seattle Supersonics, both of whom claimed NBA draft rights to John Brisker, formerly a member of the ABA's Pittsburgh Condors. When the Supersonics signed Brisker, the 76ers instituted proceedings before the NBA Board of Governors to revoke the Supersonics' NBA franchise. The Board of Governors voted to table the matter, however, and referred the dispute to then Commissioner Walter Kennedy. Without taking any evidence from the Supersonics on their claim that they had signed Brisker properly, Kennedy ruled that the Supersonics had violated "principles of fair play." Therefore, he awarded their first round draft right for the following year to the 76ers and fined the Supersonics $10,000.

When the Supersonics refused to pay the fine, the 76ers filed a petition in federal District Court in New York City, seeking a judgment confirming Kennedy's arbitration award. The Court, however, refused to confirm the award; instead it dismissed the petition for two reasons. First, under the NBA Constitution, only the Board of Governors could consider the 76ers' original complaint, and thus, the Court said, the Board should not have referred the matter

[3] *Id.*

to the Commissioner. Second, because Kennedy heard no evidence from the Supersonics in support of its position that it had acted properly, the Court held that the "proceeding" before Kennedy was so lacking in fairness that courts should not enforce its result.[4]

§7.3(b)(2) Substantive

Due process requires more than noticed hearings, opportunities to present evidence, and related procedural safeguards. It also requires that actions taken be based on actual evidence.[1] An interesting aspect of the requirement that there be a factual basis for disciplinary actions is this. When the conduct to be punished is gambling or game-fixing, the detriment to the league is not only apparent, but also specifically and explicitly prohibited in player contracts and league by-laws. Beyond those offenses, however, prohibited conduct is identified merely as that which is "detrimental" or "prejudicial" to the "best interests" of the league and sport. That identification is obviously imprecise, and the question has arisen, what kinds of conduct are detrimental or prejudicial, and who makes that determination?

The question was raised by Lance Rentzel of the Los Angeles Rams and the NFL Players Association in a suit filed by them, following Rentzel's suspension from the National Football League in July of 1973. The suspension was provoked by Rentzel's guilty plea to charges of possession of marijuana—a plea which he was then appealing on the grounds that the evidence against him was obtained through an illegal search and seizure. According to Com-

---

[4] Riko Enterprises, Inc. dba Philadelphia 76ers v. Seattle Supersonics Corp., 357 F.Supp. 521 (S.D.N.Y. 1973).

[1] Thompson v. Louisville, 362 U.S. 199 (1960).

missioner Rozelle, the suspension was not based on the marijuana charges alone, however. It was based as well, he said, on Rentzel's earlier guilty pleas to charges of indecent exposure and disorderly conduct.

Rentzel's suit was based on several grounds, including breach of contract, interference with contractual relations, restraint of trade, and failure to provide adequate notice of the hearing that preceded his suspension. In retrospect, however, the most significant allegation of the complaint seems to be that the suspension was "arbitrary, capricious and discriminatory," because his was the first suspension ever imposed by Commissioner Rozelle for something other than gambling, and because there is nothing in the NFL By-Laws or elsewhere indicating that Rentzel's conduct would be considered detrimental to the league.

In fact, an entire Article of the NFL Constitution and By-Laws is entitled "Prohibited Conduct" and states that "The violation of any of the provisions of this Article IX shall constitute conduct detrimental to the League and professional football." [2] But none of the listed prohibitions, which cover six pages of fine print, refers in any way to any criminal conduct other than game-fixing or gambling. The itemized prohibitions deal with conflicts of interest, public criticism, tampering, ownership of minor league teams, and the like. Another Article of the NFL Constitution and By-Laws gives Commissioner Rozelle the authority to impose discipline for conduct detrimental to the League.[3] But in Rentzel's case, Rozelle also assumed the authority, not expressly conferred on him by the Constitution and By-Laws, not only to impose discipline, but also

[2] NFL Constitution & By-Laws, Article 9.1(A).

[3] *Id.* at Article 8.13(A).

to determine what conduct—in addition to the listed prohibitions—was "detrimental."

Furthermore, during Rentzel's hearing at NFL offices in New York, Rozelle took no evidence that Rentzel's conduct had in fact been detrimental to the league. He did not, for example, have NFL counsel, or anyone else, introduce evidence that fans were threatening to boycott games, or that television sponsors were threatening to withdraw advertising support if Rentzel continued to play, or that the popularity of NFL football was in any way jeopardized by Rentzel's continued participation. Rather, Rozelle assumed that he could make such a determination entirely on his own. And Judge David A. Thomas of the California Superior Court in Los Angeles upheld Rozelle in what could be a very significant decision.

In an Informal Opinion explaining his reasons for denying the preliminary injunction requested by Rentzel and the NFL Players Association, Judge Thomas said,

> "It is clear that the constitution and bylaws intend that conduct other than those activities specifically described . . . may be considered 'detrimental' and made the subject of a hearing and discipline . . ., and the NFL long has so construed its constitution. The court adopts the construction of the constitution argued by defendants [Commissioner Rozelle, the NFL and the Rams] . . . .
>
> "[Rentzel] essentially asserts that Rozelle arbitrarily determined that [Rentzel's] conduct was detrimental without said conduct '. . . previously (having been) regarded by the league or the commissioner as . . . detrimental . . . and that, therefore, [Rentzel] was denied due process.' The court concludes otherwise.

"It is clear that the defendants have sought for years to establish a standard of public conduct for professional football participants, including players. This standard (which might be better termed 'image') includes the portrayal of players as hightype, admirable young men who are worthy of the respect and emulation of the young' . . . (Or, to borrow from another segment of the entertainment industry, football seeks to present itself under a 'G' rating.)

"This is understandable, for professional football is a privately owned and operated entertainment enterprise pursued by those in it for their own gain, and they have determined that it is to their best interest to promote an image . . . of the kind described above. . . . It is not up to the court to criticize this standard or attempt to change it unless it impinges on the rights of [Rentzel].

"Rozelle had discussed with him in 1971 [Rentzel's] misconduct, the difficulties his action had created for the league, his obligation to adhere to the highest standard . . . . [Rentzel] acknowledged his awareness of the necessity to adhere to the standard . . . .

"It was not necessary in the hearing of June 20, 1973, to take evidence on the issue of whether a marijuana conviction, coupled with [Rentzel's] previous legal problems, constituted a failure to meet the requisite standard of conduct.

"Rozelle had the jurisdiction to determine whether [Rentzel's] conduct . . . constituted detrimental conduct without having to take evidence thereon, so long as a proper hearing had been conducted to determine the facts of [Rentzel's] conduct.

"Further, the penalty (suspension) is not so harsh that no reasonable man would impose it and, therefore,

> the court cannot say that it is so arbitrary that it constitutes a denial of due process." [4]

In a footnote, Judge Thomas qualified slightly his acknowledgement of this sweeping power of the Commissioner, by adding,

> "Arguably, Rozelle or a successor might apply the standard of conduct to a factual situation in such an unreasonable manner that due process would be denied and the court assumes that in such situation it has the jurisdiction to intervene. Such unreasonable application is not present here, however." [5]

Because Judge Thomas was a trial court judge, rather than an appellate judge, and because his decision was an Informal Opinion on a preliminary aspect of the case, the opinion is not binding as a precedent on other judges, either in California or elsewhere. However, should similar lawsuits against the NFL or other leagues be filed in the future, it is virtually certain that Judge Thomas' opinion will be cited in support of a commissioner's authority to determine what "detrimental conduct" is, and the opinion may well have persuasive impact on other judges even though it is not binding. Conceivably, the focal point of future cases could become Judge Thomas' footnote saying that application of the "detrimental" standard in an "unreasonable manner" would be a denial of due process. However, in view of the general reluctance of courts to second-guess the asserted expertise of league officials, it seems

---

[4] Rentzel v. Rozelle, Cal.Super.Ct., Los Angeles Cty. No. C63828, unpublished "Informal Memorandum" Opinion dated August 23, 1973.

[5] *Id.* at fn. 4.

likely that courts will intervene only when those officials have been so "unreasonable" as to have been "outrageous."

§7.3(c) Equal protection principles

Following the refusal of the New York State Athletic Commission to renew Muhammad Ali's boxing license, on the grounds that Ali's refusal to enter military service and his subsequent conviction were detrimental to the best interests of boxing,[1] Ali filed suit against the Commission and each of its three members. His complaint alleged that the Commission's refusal to renew his license was arbitrary and capricious in that a conviction for draft evasion bore no rational relationship to boxing and was therefore irrelevant to the proper exercise of the Commission's functions. In addition, because Ali's refusal to enter the service had been religiously motivated, he charged that the Commission's action impeded his freedom of religion in violation of the First and Fourteenth Amendments and constituted cruel and unusual punishment in violation of the Eighth Amendment. Ali sought a declaratory judgment that the Commission's actions were indeed unlawful and an injunction compelling it to renew his license.

In response to a motion by the Commission that the case be dismissed, Judge Frankel of the federal District Court in New York City ruled that the Commission's right to deny a boxing license because of an applicant's prior felony conviction had been established beyond doubt, and further stated that Ali's freedom of religion and cruel and unusual punishment claims were without merit. However, Ali had also alleged that the Commission had arbitrarily discriminated against him in violation of the equal pro-

[1] Ali v. State Athletic Commission of New York, 316 F.Supp. 1246, 1247 (S.D.N.Y. 1970).

tection clause of the Fourteenth Amendment. Judge Frankel believed that this broadly alleged claim might have legal merit were it supported by specific, concrete allegations. Thus, although he granted the Commission's motion to dismiss Ali's complaint, Judge Frankel allowed Ali additional time within which to amend his complaint in order to allege, if he could, specific facts of discrimination.[2]

Ali's amended complaint set forth a number of remarkable instances of discrimination. It alleged that although the Commission had refused to renew Ali's license, it had previously licensed Jeff Merritt, who had been convicted of robbery; Joey Giardello, who had been convicted of assault; Rocky Graziano, who had twice been convicted of petty larceny and had been court-martialed and convicted by the Army for being absent without leave and disobeying orders; and Sonny Liston, who had been convicted of armed robbery and assault with intent to kill. The Commission's motion to dismiss Ali's amended complaint was denied by Judge Frankel.

Ali's lawyer then investigated the Commission's files to determine whether it had licensed other convicted boxers as well. The fruits of his investigation were described as "rather astounding" by a federal judge to whom they were submitted.[3] The Commission's records revealed at least 244 instances in recent years in which it had granted, renewed or reinstated boxing licenses to applicants who had been convicted of one or more felonies, misdemeanors or military offenses involving moral turpitude. Some 94 felons thus licensed included men convicted for such crimes as second degree murder, burglary, armed rob-

[2] Ali v. State Athletic Commission of New York, 308 F.Supp. 11 (S.D.N.Y. 1969).

[3] Ali v. State Athletic Commission of New York, *supra* note 1, at 1249.

bery, extortion, grand larceny, rape, sodomy, aggravated assault and battery, embezzlement, arson and receiving stolen property. The misdemeanor convictions, 135 in number, were for such offenses as petty larceny, possession of narcotics, attempted rape, assault and battery, fraud, impairing the morals of a minor, possession of burglar's tools, possession of dangerous weapons, carrying concealed weapons, automobile theft and promotion of gambling. There were 15 military offenses, including convictions or dishonorable discharges for desertion, assault upon an officer, burglary and larceny.

With this evidence in hand, Ali moved for a preliminary injunction preventing the Commission from denying him a license at least until the case came to trial. His motion was granted.[4]

Federal District Court Judge Mansfield, to whom the preliminary injunction motion had been assigned, explained that the question before him, unlike the one which had been before Judge Frankel earlier in the proceedings, was "not whether the Commission may in its discretion deny a boxing license to an applicant because of his conviction of a felony or military offense." Judge Mansfield said he concurred "in Judge Frankel's recognition of such power in the Commission."[5] However, Judge Mansfield continued,

> "Although the state possesses broad powers to regulate boxing . . . it may not exercise those powers in such a way as to deny to an applicant the equal protection of the state's laws, which is guaranteed to him by the Fourteenth Amendment. A deliberate and arbitrary discrimination or inequality in the exercise of

[4] *Id.*
[5] *Id.*

> regulatory power, not based upon differences that are reasonably related to the lawful purposes of such regulation, violates the Fourteenth Amendment. . . . In short, the exercise of state power by a state agency in the issuance of or refusal of licenses to engage in a regulated activity should not represent the exercise of mere personal whim, caprice or prejudice on the part of such agency. . . . It should, and constitutionally must, have some rational basis.
>
> "If the Commission in the present case had denied licenses to all applicants convicted of crimes or military offenses, [Ali] would have no valid basis for demanding that a license be issued to him. But the action of the Commission in denying him a license because of his refusal to serve in the Armed Forces while granting licenses to hundreds of other applicants convicted of other crimes and military offenses involving moral turpitude appears on its face to be an intentional, arbitrary and unreasonable discrimination against [Ali], not the even-handed administration of the law which the Fourteenth Amendment requires." [6]

§7.3(d) The source of due process and equal protection requirements

While the principles of law articulated by Judge Mansfield in the *Muhammad Ali* case[1] probably apply to other sports in addition to boxing, boxing is unique in one respect. The Fourteenth Amendment provides that "No *State* shall . . . deprive any person of life, liberty, or property, without due process of law; nor deny any person . . .

---

[6] *Id.* at 1250.

[1] Ali v. State Athletic Commission of New York, 316 F.Supp. 1246 (S.D.N.Y. 1970), discussed in § 7.3(c), *supra*.

the equal protection of the laws." Because the New York State Athletic Commission is an agency of the state, Judge Mansfield had no problem in ruling that "the acts of the state's duly constituted Athletic Commission or similar agency are deemed to be those of the state itself." [2] Thus the Fourteenth Amendment unquestionably applied to the Commission in the *Ali* case.

However, the Fourteenth Amendment does not apply to purely private organizations and, thus, it is not obvious that it applies to the National Football League, the National Basketball Association, and the other team sport leagues, because they are private. Nevertheless, during the last few decades, the United States Supreme Court has ruled in several cases that private organizations which undertake public functions or which utilize public resources or facilities are subject to the Fourteenth Amendment as well as states, despite their private character. At least one study of discipline in professional sports has concluded that team sports leagues should be considered subject to the Fourteenth Amendment, because most sport stadia are publicly owned and operated, the states have aided in the construction of special transportation facilities encouraging attendance at sporting events, additional law enforcement personnel compensated by government are necessary for crowd control, and other special inducements may be provided by many governmental entities to obtain or retain professional sports franchises in particular localities.[3] Imposing Fourteenth Amendment requirements on private sports leagues for these reasons would, it seems, be stretching the principle of "state action" beyond its

[2] *Id.* at 1250.

[3] Comment, Discipline in Professional Sports: The Need for Player Protection, 60 Georgetown L.J. 771, 790-792 (1972).

outer limits.[4] Nevertheless, Fourteenth Amendment requirements, and particularly "due process" requirements, are binding even on purely private sports leagues for other reasons, if not Constitutional ones.

First, due process standards are written into the constitutions and by-laws of many of the leagues. For example, Jack Molinas was not required to establish that the NBA was subject to Constitutional standards because his right to notice of the charges against him and a hearing was set forth in the NBA By-Laws which were incorporated into his contract with the Fort Wayne Pistons.[5]

Second, in recent years, courts have begun to impose upon certain kinds of private associations the same due process standards which the Fourteenth Amendment imposes upon the states, in cases where associations seek to expel a member. Generally, courts have been protecting members from unreasonable expulsion from private associations where membership is essential to the individual's livelihood, the association performs quasi-public functions, and judicial interference will not impair the association's goals (as it will not when a rule is unfairly enforced or when a rule is not reasonably related to the goals of the association). An "unreasonable expulsion" seems to be one that is not the product of a fair proceeding or one in which rules are applied in an unreasonable or discriminatory manner.[6]

While no case squarely holds that professional sports leagues are the kinds of private associations from which

---

[4] See, e.g., Moose Lodge v. Irris, 407 U.S. 163 (1972), and Jackson v. Metropolitan Edison Co., 419 U.S. 345 (1974); but cf., Gilmore v. Montgomery, 417 U.S. 556 (1974).

[5] Molinas v. Podoloff, 133 N.Y.S.2d 743 (1954), discussed in § 7.3(b)(1), *supra*.

[6] Comment, *supra* note 3, at 782-786.

expulsion must be effected in a reasonable fashion, it has been argued that they are or should be.[7] Furthermore, in the *Lance Rentzel* case,[8] Judge Thomas of the California Superior Court assumed that courts would have jurisdiction to intervene in the event an NFL Commissioner applied the league's "detrimental conduct" standard in such an unreasonable manner that due process was denied.[9]

§7.3(e) Antitrust principles

A professional athlete who is declared ineligible or who is suspended for disciplinary reasons is effectively prevented from plying his or her trade. Since "one of the oldest and best established" restraints of trade is one "which unreasonably forbids any one to practice his calling," [1] it is not surprising that some of the most significant discipline and eligibility cases have involved alleged violations of the antitrust laws. Initially, courts focused on the reasons for the league rules at issue, and upheld them if the rules seemed "reasonable" and did not diminish competition.[2] Recently, however, courts have begun to recognize that in sports, as in other businesses, some restraints are illegal *per se,* without regard for the reasonableness of their purposes or their actual effects on competition. Thus, attention is now being focused on the manner in which league rules are being applied,[3] for only if the rules are applied in certain ways can they survive *per se* illegality.

---

[7] *Id.* Also, the National Collegiate Athletic Assn. has been held to be such an association. California State University, Hayward v. National Collegiate Athletic Assn., 121 Cal. Rptr. 85 (Cal. Ct. App. 1975).

[8] Rentzel v. Rozelle, quoted in § 7.3(b)(2), *supra.*

[9] *Id.* at fn. 4.

[1] Gardella v. Chandler, 172 F.2d 402, 408 (2d Cir. 1949), opinion of Learned Hand, J.

[2] See § 7.3(e)(1), *infra.*

[3] See § 7.3(e)(2), *infra.*

§7.3(e)(1) Rule purpose

When Jack Molinas was suspended from the National Basketball Association in 1954 for betting on his team, the Fort Wayne Pistons,[1] he immediately filed an action in a New York state court seeking reinstatement, on the grounds that he had not had a hearing or notice of the charges against him as required by his contract and the NBA Constitution. After losing,[2] Molinas enrolled in Brooklyn Law School, and eventually became a successful attorney. He also became a player-coach in the Eastern Basketball League.[3]

In 1960, after several requests for reinstatement had been denied, Molinas filed a second lawsuit against the NBA. This case was filed in federal court and alleged that the NBA, its president Maurice Podoloff, and all of its teams had violated the antitrust laws by conspiring to restrain trade in three ways: (1) by allocating players by means of the reserve clause; (2) by suspending and refusing to reinstate him; and (3) by affecting his opportunities to play in exhibition games against NBA players. Molinas sought treble damages of three million dollars, an injunction against the alleged conspiracies, and reinstatement in the league. Judge Irving R. Kaufman dismissed the case in January of 1961 with a four page opinion that has been cited many times since.[4]

In response to the reserve clause charge, Judge Kaufman simply held that after his suspension, the refusal of

---

[1] See §§ 7.1 and 7.3(b)(1), *supra.*

[2] Molinas v. Podoloff, 133 N.Y.S.2d 743 (1954).

[3] Molinas v. National Basketball Association, 190 F.Supp. 241, 242 (S.D.N.Y. 1961).

[4] *Id.*

NBA teams other than the Pistons to deal with Molinas was due to the suspension and not the reserve system. "These other teams would obviously have refused to deal with [Molinas] even if the reserve clause had never existed," he stated.[5]

In response to the charge that NBA teams had conspired to prohibit their players from playing against Molinas even in exhibition games, Judge Kaufman found that Molinas had failed to prove that the players' refusal was the result of a conspiracy. "The proof established at most that several league owners, coaches or players may have felt that it was unwise, possibly because of the likelihood of adverse publicity, to participate in a game in which [Molinas], an admitted gambler, was also involved." [6]

Finally, on the key issues of the legality of Molinas' original suspension and the league's subsequent refusal to reinstate him, Judge Kaufman stated that Molinas had "patently failed to establish an unreasonable restraint of trade within the meaning of the anti-trust laws."

> "A rule, and a corresponding contract clause, providing for the suspension of those who place wagers on games in which they are participating seems not only reasonable, but necessary for the survival of the league. Every league or association must have some reasonable governing rules, and these rules must necessarily include disciplinary provisions. Surely, every disciplinary rule which a league may invoke, although by its nature it may involve some sort of a restraint, does not run afoul of the anti-trust laws. And, a disciplinary rule invoked against gambling

---

[5] *Id.* at 243.

[6] *Id.* at 244-245.

seems about as reasonable a rule as could be imagined."[7]

Several years after Molinas' antitrust suit was dismissed, professional bowler Ralph Manok was suspended from the Southeast District Bowling Association and the American Bowling Congress, for bowling in a tournament with another bowler who was using someone else's name, in violation of the rules, in order to have a higher handicap. Because the Southeast District Bowling Association and the American Bowling Congress were the principal sponsors of professional bowling tournaments, Manok's suspension meant that his ability to earn a living as a professional bowler was severely hampered, if not entirely destroyed. As a result, Manok—like Molinas before him—filed an antitrust suit in federal District Court in Los Angeles. And like Molinas, Manok got short shrift. In an opinion rendered in November of 1969, Judge Williams ruled that Manok had failed to make any showing of the existence of a combination between the defendant associations, the intent and purpose of which was to restrain trade through unreasonable restrictions on membership and re-admittance, or that his suspension was in furtherance of any conspiracy to restrain trade.[8]

A third case in which action taken against an athlete was upheld is *Deesen* v. *Professional Golfers' Association of America.*[9] The PGA sponsors or co-sponsors substantially all professional golf tournaments for men in the United States. To participate in a PGA tournament, a golfer must be either a "member" of the PGA or an

---

[7] *Id.*

[8] Manok v. Southeast District Bowling Assn., 306 F.Supp. 1215 (C.D. Cal. 1969).

[9] 358 F.2d 165 (9th Cir. 1966), *cert. den.,* 385 U.S. 846 (1966).

"approved tournament player." To be a member, a person must have at least five years' experience as a golf pro employed by a club, as an approved tournament player playing at least 25 tournaments a year, or any combination of the two. To become an "approved tournament player," a person must be approved by the PGA, and that requires the ability to finish in the money, the financial responsibility to undertake the tour, and moral character and integrity.

Herbert Deesen was an approved tournament player from 1952 to 1958, and during those years he won a total of $240.35. In 1958, his approval was terminated, not for disciplinary reasons, but on the grounds that he did not have sufficient playing ability and had not participated in the minimum number of tournaments required of approved tournament players. When Deesen's request for reinstatement was denied, he filed a suit in federal court seeking treble damages of $210,000, alleging that the PGA and its members had combined and conspired to monopolize and restrain the business of tournament golf and to boycott him in violation of the Sherman Act, by means of PGA rules and regulations governing eligibility for entering tournaments.

Deesen lost in the trial court and appealed to the Court of Appeals where he made several contentions, none of which was accepted. Deesen first argued to the Court of Appeals that PGA rules governing eligibility were unreasonable restraints on trade because they were indefinite and therefore incapable of non-discriminatory enforcement. The Court agreed that theoretically a PGA committeeman's personal dislike of an applicant could result in the denial of his application, but it said there was no evidence showing that had ever happened. Furthermore, the Court said,

> "The basic purpose of the PGA in requiring persons who seek approved tournament standing to meet certain standards and obtain committee approval appears to be a reasonable one, insofar as the evidence before us indicates. That purpose is to insure that professional golf tournaments are not bogged down with great numbers of players of inferior ability. The purpose is thus not to destroy competition but to foster it by maintaining a high quality of competition." [10]

Deesen next argued that the rules were not applied uniformly to PGA members and non-members, because members do not have to show they have the ability to win or finance themselves, nor are they required to enter any minimum number of tournaments. In response, the Court simply answered that the PGA was formed to give tournament outlets to its members. Since every golfer could become a member of the PGA, its rule permitting non-members to play under certain circumstances was therefore not promulgated to suppress competition, and it did not have that effect.

In response to Deesen's contention that the PGA had monopolized professional golf, the Court stated that although the PGA sponsored or co-sponsored most tournaments, and could exclude applicants from participation, there was no evidence that it used its power to exclude golfers from access to PGA tournaments or to suppress or eliminate competition. The category of "approved players" tends to promote competition, the Court indicated, by facilitating participation by proficient younger players.

Finally, Deesen argued that the PGA had combined and conspired to boycott him. The Court ruled otherwise.

---

[10] *Id.* at 170.

Deesen's record over several years provided an adequate basis for striking his name, and his showing during specially scheduled test rounds justified the PGA's refusal to reinstate him. "PGA is entitled to adopt reasonable measures for holding the tournaments to a manageable number," the Court noted, because ". . . only a limited number of golfers can play an eighteen-hole course under tournament conditions during the daylight hours of a single day."[11]

The "reasonable purpose" test that was used in *Molinas, Manok* and *Deesen* has not always validated eligibility and disciplinary rules. Rules and suspensions which stifle competition have been held to be illegal, even if adopted for legitimate disciplinary purposes. An example of such a disciplinary rule was one adopted by the Washington State Bowling Proprietors Association. As its name implies, the organization is a trade association of bowling establishment owners whose businesses are located in the State of Washington. The Association was alleged to be affiliated with a national trade association known as the Bowling Proprietors Association of America and with local associations whose members did business in particular communities within the state. These associations and their members conducted and sanctioned bowling tournaments participated in by individual bowlers and bowling leagues. They also adopted certain "eligibility rules" which established the qualifications of the bowlers who were permitted to participate in the tournaments they conducted or sanctioned. One such rule made the tournaments open only to persons who restricted their league and tournament bowling entirely to establishments which were members of the affiliated national, state and local associations, and rejected

[11] *Id.* at 172.

and declared ineligible for the associations' tournaments any bowler who did any organized bowling at establishments that were not members of the associations. The stated purpose of this rule was to prevent cheating. The associations contended that if a person did all of his "organized" bowling at a limited number of establishments, he would become known to the operators of those establishments; and this familiarity would prevent such practices as bowling under an assumed name and "sandbagging"—inclusion of substandard scores in computing a bowler's average—in order to have a larger handicap.

Though the prevention of cheating is a reasonable purpose for a rule, this particular eligibility rule had another effect as well. It deprived non-member bowling establishments of the patronage of people who wanted to engage in organized bowling. In other words, it required people who wanted to engage in tournaments sponsored by the associations to do all of their organized bowling at member-establishments and to boycott non-members. This tended to suppress competition and create a monopoly in the bowling industry in Washington State.

Pacific Lanes, Inc., the owner of a non-member bowling establishment in Tacoma, lost the patronage of five bowling leagues as a result of the associations' eligibility rules. This cost Pacific Lanes an estimated $67,000 in profits it would have otherwise realized, and so in December of 1961 it filed a federal antitrust action against the associations and their members, seeking treble damages. At the trial's conclusion in early 1965, the jury found that Pacific Lanes had suffered $35,000 in damages because of a conspiracy among the defendants to restrain trade and monopolize bowling in violation of the Sherman Act. In accordance with the law, the District Court judge trebled the damages and entered judgment for Pacific Lanes in the sum of $105,000, plus $22,500 in attorneys' fees.

The defendants appealed on a number of grounds. One was that the judge had incorrectly refused to instruct the jury that the associations' members had the right to put restrictions on their tournament business designed to prevent cheating. Such an instruction would have presumably indicated to the jury that the eligibility restrictions were designed to promote the sport of bowling rather than to constitute a boycott of non-member establishments. The trial judge had refused to give the jury such an instruction, finding that the evidence introduced during the trial did not justify or support it, apparently because there had been no evidence supporting the defendants' contention that their purpose had been to prevent cheating. The Court of Appeals reviewed the transcript of the trial and agreed with the District Court that the instruction was unwarranted in this case. However, the Court of Appeals went on to hold that

> "Even assuming that abuses in the sport existed, it has been established since the case of *Fashion Originators' Guild of America* v. *Federal Trade Commission* . . . that such circumstances do not justify a private association passing regulations to deal with the problem when their effect is to restrain or regulate interstate commerce." [12]

Although this suit was filed by the owner of a non-member bowling establishment, another class or category of people could have objected to the associations' eligibility rule as well—namely, bowlers declared ineligible for the

[12] Washington State Bowling Proprietors Assn. v. Pacific Lanes, Inc., 356 F.2d 371, 376 (9th Cir. 1966).

associations' tournaments because they had participated in organized bowling at non-member establishments. Had suit been filed by an ineligible bowler, the damage suffered would have been different from that suffered by Pacific Lanes, but there is little reason to believe that the outcome would have differed. *Radovich* v. *National Football League*[13] is analogous, and held that a player blacklisted from the NFL, because he joined an All-America Football Conference team in disregard of his NFL option clause, had an antitrust cause of action against the National Football League.

§7.3(e)(2) Rule application

The *Washington State Bowling Proprietors Association* case[1] constituted the beginning of a departure from the "reasonable purpose" test used by the courts in *Molinas* v. *NBA*,[2] *Manok* v. *Southeast District Bowling Association*[3] and *Deesen* v. *PGA*.[4] The defendants in *Washington State Bowling* had asked for a jury instruction indicating that if the purpose of their eligibility rule was reasonable, then it did not violate the Sherman Act, even though it constituted a group boycott. The instruction was denied on the grounds that there had been no evidence that the defendant had a reasonable purpose. The Court of Appeals noted, however, that even reasonable purposes do not justify rules and regulations which restrain trade.

---

[13] 352 U.S. 445 (1957), discussed in § 1.2(b), *supra*.

[1] Washington State Bowling Proprietors Assn. v. Pacific Lanes, Inc., 356 F.2d 371 (9th Cir. 1966), discussed in § 7.3(e)(1), *supra*.

[2] 190 F.Supp. 241 (S.D.N.Y. 1961), discussed in § 7.3(e)(1), *supra*.

[3] 306 F.Supp. 1215 (C.D.Cal. 1969), discussed in § 7.3(e)(1), *supra*.

[4] 358 F.2d 165 (9th Cir. 1966), *cert. den.*, 385 U.S. 846 (1966), discussed in § 7.3(e)(1), *supra*.

Since *Washington State Bowling,* other courts have been confronted with rules which constituted group boycotts but which were adopted for arguably reasonable purposes. And in those cases, the courts have had to reconcile the conflict between the *per se* illegality of group boycotts and the natural tendency to give effect to reasonable and necessary rules. The most satisfactory reconciliation to date is one that was articulated in what has become known as "the Spencer Haywood case."

§7.3(e)(2)(A) The Spencer Haywood case

§7.3(e)(2)(A)(i) Facts

To say that Spencer Haywood has unique talent as a basketball player is to use the word "unique" in its most literal sense. Professional scouts began to show interest in him while he was only a sophomore in college; but even such early (by standards of the 1960's) interest was not the result of any special insight on their part. By the time Haywood finished his sophomore year, he had already been the star of the United States' gold-medal winning basketball team at the 1968 Olympics, and had been selected All-American, Junior College All-American, and High School All-American.

According to Haywood, a representative of the Cincinnati Royals was among those who showed interest in him during his sophomore year; but because of the NBA's four-year rule, the Royals could not sign him to a player contract for another two years.[1] The Denver Rockets of the ABA were interested, too; and although that league also had a four-year rule, the Rockets' representative told

[1] B. Libby & S. Haywood, Stand Up For Something: The Spencer Haywood Story (New York: Grosset & Dunlap, 1972) at 45.

Haywood that there was a way he could play professionally immediately. "That sounded good," Haywood later said. "I mean I was making $15 a month in school, and when suddenly someone says you can make $100,000 a year, you start listening." [2]

According to Rocket co-owner Don Ringsby, the ABA decided in the summer of 1969 to have a secret draft of undergraduate players, thinking that if ABA owners knew a year or two in advance which collegians were going to be theirs, they would have a better chance of outbidding NBA teams whose own draft would only be a few months before the athletes' graduation. The Rockets drafted Haywood during that secret ABA session, and even before it made "preliminary contact" with him, Steve Arnold, a player agent who was procuring athletes for the ABA, notified them that Haywood was unhappy at Detroit and might be willing to turn professional immediately.[3]

Today, the ABA By-Laws concerning eligibility of players provide, "In special circumstances, the Commissioner with the consent of all of the member clubs, may waive any disability that does not contravene any relevant statutory provision or public policy." [4] But in 1969 there was no such provision. Ringsby explained that Arnold

> ". . . came up with the 'hardship' gimmick whereby we could plead for a waiver of the [four-year] rule on the basis of financial hardship. He knew Spencer came from a poor family in the deep south. Arnold just invented it. It was a gimmick. And Jim Gardner, president of the ABA, OK'd it. . . . To be honest about it, the ABA was just looking for ways to land top

[2] *Id.*

[3] *Id.* at 177-179.

[4] ABA By-Laws, Article XV § 5.

> talent even if it meant bending the rules here and there, but in this case this probably was an unfair rule which deserved to be bent. Ball players like Haywood should have a right to earn a living at what they do best whenever and wherever they can." [5]

Thus, in August of 1969, at the age of 19, Spencer Haywood signed a $450,000 three-year contract with the Denver Rockets. A month or two later, the Rockets' owners arranged for Haywood to meet an investment advisor named Ralph Dolgoff who had developed a plan designed to increase the amount of money eventually realized by a professional athlete, at no greater cost to his employer-team and with greater tax benefits to both. The "Dolgoff Plan," as it came to be known, was being used by several ABA teams as part of the compensation offered outstanding players. It seemed beneficial to Haywood, and therefore, in October of 1969, he and the Rockets entered into a new $450,000, three-year contract incorporating Dolgoff's recommendations.

At the end of his first year as a professional, Haywood was the leading scorer and rebounder in the ABA and was voted that league's Rookie of the Year and Most Valuable Player. He led his team to a divisional title; and—with the NBA-ABA "war" then at its height—National Basketball Association scouts began to entice him. Though Haywood still had another two years to go on his contract, "war" was "war" and the Rockets were concerned some NBA team might lure Haywood away, leaving them only with the right to file an expensive and time-consuming lawsuit to enforce Haywood's agreement. Thus in April, 1970, the Rockets, wanting to be sure Haywood would stay with

[5] B. Libby & S. Haywood, *supra* note 1, at 179.

them, and Haywood, wanting an increase in salary he felt warranted by his Rookie of the Year and MVP awards, entered into yet another contract, this one for six years and said to be worth $1.9 million.

This sum was not all in "hard dollars" however. Rather, the new contract provided that Haywood was to receive $50,000 per season for the first two years and $75,000 per season for the following four years. Thus, in straight salary, Haywood was to receive only $400,000. In addition, the Rockets were to invest $10,000 per year for the next ten years into the "Dolgoff Plan" for Haywood's benefit where the Rockets and Dolgoff estimated it would generate $1.5 million which would be paid to Haywood over a twenty year period beginning at age 40.

With the season over and his new contract signed, Haywood spent the summer traveling, touring with an all-star team, and comparing notes with other players. His new contract, he began to feel, was not as good as it had seemed at first, but when he asked the Rockets' owners to explain it to him, they refused. He had signed it, they said, and there were not going to be any more changes. As a result, Haywood asked a lawyer to look at it for him.

The lawyer Haywood turned to for advice was Al Ross of Los Angeles. Ross had gone to Michigan State on a basketball scholarship and had tried out, unsuccessfully, with a professional basketball team before enrolling in law school. After graduation, Ross organized a management company called All-Pro Management, Inc., which specialized in handling the business affairs of athletes and others who were highly paid. Ross said that his review of the agreement confirmed "every bad suspicion Spencer had about his contract."[6] The only monies Haywood was cer-

[6] *Id.* at 152.

tain to receive were those payable as salary—$400,000 over six years. In order to receive any portion of the remaining $1.5 million, he would have to continue working for the Rockets' owners for four years after his six-year playing contract expired, performing undescribed services at an unspecified salary. Even then, in order to realize the full $1.5 million, the Dolgoff Plan investments would have had to have done better than most optimistic stockbrokers would have predicted was possible.[7]

At Haywood's request, Ross phoned the Rockets' owners, told them he represented Haywood, and said he wanted to get Haywood's contract "clarified and guaranteed."[8] All Haywood and he wanted at that time was to have the contract rewritten so that the $1.9 million dollars that had been promised to Haywood would in fact be paid—without regard to non-basketball services or the strength of the stock market.

A series of meetings followed, but were not fruitful. Eventually, they became so bitter that the Rockets filed a lawsuit in federal court against All-Pro Management and Al Ross—but not Haywood—accusing Ross of inducing Haywood to breach his contract with the team. Though negotiations with the Rockets continued after the suit was filed, the case quickly mushroomed.

Haywood had sent the Rockets a notice rescinding his player contract on the ground that it did not contain the promises that had been made to him and announced to the press. Though he refused to play any further for the Rockets after the notice was sent, Haywood had not jumped to any other team at the time the Rockets filed

---

[7] Simon, The First Great Leap: Some Reflections on the Spencer Haywood Case, 48 Los Angeles Bar Bulletin 149, 150 (1973).

[8] B. Libby & S. Haywood, *supra* note 1, at 154.

their suit, and so Haywood was not named as a defendant in the case. However, when Ross answered the Rockets' complaint, Haywood intervened in the case and cross-complained against the team, seeking judicial confirmation that his Rockets contract was of no further force or effect.

Other teams in both leagues quickly expressed interest in Haywood. Naturally, the ABA was anxious to keep Haywood in the league. Individual teams made him offers that were so good, that Ross later characterized them as "hard to believe." [9] The ABA even went so far as to encourage the Rockets' owners to sell out to new owners in the hopes that fresh faces and an unmarred relationship could save Haywood for the league; but Rocket owner Don Ringsby later said "this didn't come to pass, because we were never made a legitimate offer." [10]

Approximately half of the teams in the NBA contacted Ross about Haywood, either directly or through third parties. Some NBA teams were unwilling to make firm offers until the Rockets' lawsuit was concluded. Others wanted to wait until Haywood's college class graduated. But the Seattle Supersonics were willing to sign and play him immediately, to pay Haywood's and Ross' court costs and attorneys' fees, and to indemnify them against any judgments rendered against them. So, on December 28, 1970, Spencer Haywood signed a six-year, no-cut contract with the Seattle Supersonics calling for payment to him of $1.5 million in cash at the rate of $100,000 per year for 15 years.

Upon learning that Haywood had signed with the Supersonics, the Rockets immediately amended their complaint

---

[9] *Id.* at 156.
[10] *Id.* at 188.

and made a motion to enjoin him from playing for any other team, until the conclusion of the 1975-1976 season when their $1.9 million contract with him would expire. A hearing was held before Judge Warren J. Ferguson in the federal District Court in Los Angeles on January 8, 1971, only eleven days after Haywood had signed his Supersonics contract. Though injunctions had been previously granted in other cases where professional athletes had jumped from one league to another,[11] Judge Ferguson denied the Rockets' request for such an injunction and refused to bar Haywood from playing for the Supersonics, because he found that there was a substantial probability that the Rockets' contract with him would be found to be void.[12]

Because of the "war" then existing between the NBA and ABA, sports fans might have expected the National Basketball Association to have been elated with Judge Ferguson's ruling. However, almost all NBA owners and its Commissioner, Walter Kennedy, were *not* elated. In fact, they were infuriated with the Supersonics for signing Haywood, because of their league's four-year rule and the fact that Haywood had not been subject to an NBA draft.

Several of the NBA clubs who were interested in signing Haywood when his dispute with the Rockets became known had called NBA Commissioner Walter Kennedy to ask if Haywood were eligible. Although he had been a professional athlete for over a year, his class still had not graduated from college and would not graduate until June, 1971. Since NBA By-Laws prohibited the drafting or signing of any player until four years after his high school class graduated, and since the By-Laws made no exceptions for

---

[11] See §§ 2.3 and 5.2, *supra*.

[12] Simon, *supra* note 7, at 151.

athletes who were already professionals or who would suffer hardships if required to wait four years before turning professional, Kennedy advised all of the teams inquiring that Haywood was not yet eligible to be signed. The Los Angeles Lakers even went so far as to prepare a statement in writing as to why they thought Haywood should be an exception to the general rule and should be eligible; but Kennedy ruled otherwise, saying merely that the Haywood matter could be put on the agenda of the NBA's forthcoming all-star meeting in January, 1971.

Thus, when the Supersonics signed Haywood in December of 1970 despite Kennedy's ruling that no team in the league could do so, the stage was set for a legal battle that put in issue the legality of the entire draft system.

The NBA all-star meeting took place in San Diego on January 12, 1971. Though Haywood had already been signed—or perhaps *because* he had been signed—the "Haywood matter" was indeed on the agenda. Commissioner Kennedy had already "disapproved" the contract, and every team which played the Supersonics since Haywood joined the team had protested every game for which Haywood was in uniform, whether or not he actually played and regardless of who won. The Supersonics' owner, Sam Schulman, asked that a vote be taken on his right to play Haywood. The result was 15 to 2 against the Supersonics. Furthermore, at the conclusion of the meeting, Commissioner Kennedy released a statement to the press which said,

> "The Board of Governors, by a 15-2 vote, have passed a resolution directing the Commissioner with the aid of counsel to consider bringing charges against Seattle before the Board of Governors in connection with the Spencer Haywood matter and to advise the Board of

the most drastic penalties lawfully at its command if such charges should be sustained."[13]

Potential "drastic penalties" specifically referred to by Kennedy were fines, suspension of future draft choices and even revocation of Schulman's franchise.

§7.3(e)(2)(A)(ii) Preliminary injunction

Two days after the NBA meeting, Haywood amended his cross-complaint, named the National Basketball Association as an additional cross-defendant, and alleged that the league and its member teams were engaged in an unlawful conspiracy to monopolize and restrain trade in violation of the Sherman Act. The amendment sought an injunction barring the NBA from applying its draft and four-year-rule By-Laws in a manner that would prevent him from playing for the Supersonics immediately. A hearing before Judge Ferguson was held on January 18, 1971, on Haywood's motion for a preliminary injunction, and Judge Ferguson granted it.[1] In so doing, Judge Ferguson noted that with respect to Haywood, the NBA four-year rule had the effect of excluding him from the league until the beginning of the 1971-72 season, some nine months away, by preventing him from contracting with any NBA team, even though he did not desire to attend college and even though he was no longer eligible to participate in collegiate athletics. In light of the evidence presented to him, Judge Ferguson found that there was a substantial probability that the four-year rule constituted a group boycott violating the antitrust laws of the United States.

[13] Denver Rockets v. All-Pro Management, Inc., 325 F.Supp. 1049, 1057 (C.D.Cal. 1971).

[1] Denver Rockets v. All-Pro Management, Inc., 325 F.Supp. 1049 (C.D.Cal. 1971).

Furthermore, with respect to the injury suffered by Haywood if a preliminary injunction were not granted, Judge Ferguson stated:

> "Participating in professional basketball as a player against the best competition which the sport has to offer is as necessary to the mental and physical well being of Haywood as is breathing, eating and sleeping.
>
> . . .
>
> "If Haywood is unable to continue to play professional basketball for Seattle, he will suffer irreparable injury in that a substantial part of his playing career will have been dissipated, his physical condition, skills and coordination will deteriorate from lack of high-level competition, his public acceptance as a super star will diminish to the detriment of his career, his self-esteem and his pride will have been injured and a great injustice will be perpetrated on him." [2]

On the other hand, the only injury to the NBA as a result of a preliminary injunction would have been the uncertainty of the league standings until the case was decided. Judge Ferguson deemed any inconvenience to the league resulting from such uncertainty to be "self-imposed by reason of the substantial probability that any such injury would be caused by nonadherence to the antitrust laws of the United States." [3]

In order to expedite final decision, Judge Ferguson adjusted his court calendar to permit a trial of the entire lawsuit to begin March 2, 1971—only six weeks thereafter. The NBA was unwilling to tolerate even a six weeks de-

---

[2] *Id.* at 1057.
[3] *Id.* at 1058.

lay, however, and immediately appealed the preliminary injunction. On February 16, 1971, the Court of Appeals stayed Judge Ferguson's injunction, pending a hearing and decision by it on the NBA's appeal. The stay had the effect of once again permitting the league to bar Haywood from playing for the Supersonics; and because of the time required to brief, argue and decide cases on appeal, the Court of Appeals' stay was the equivalent of its enforcing the four-year rule. By the time the appellate court would have decided the case, Haywood would have long been eligible for the NBA draft, despite the four-year rule.

Haywood's lawyers then applied to U.S. Supreme Court Justice William O. Douglas for a stay of the Court of Appeals' stay. A stay by Justice Douglas would have had the effect of reinstating Judge Ferguson's preliminary injunction. Because preliminary injunctions are designed to preserve the status quo until a full trial on the merits can be concluded, the issue before Justice Douglas was, what was the status quo. Haywood argued that the last uncontested state of affairs had existed on December 28, 1970 and shortly thereafter, while he was under contract to the Supersonics and before the NBA had threatened the team with drastic penalties if it continued to play him. The NBA, on the other hand, argued that the last uncontested state of affairs existed prior to December 28, 1970, that is, before Haywood signed with Seattle. By the time the case reached Justice Douglas, it was late February of 1971, and the NBA playoffs were scheduled to begin March 23rd. Unless Haywood were permitted to play immediately, the playoffs would have been held without him, because of the time necessary to try the case and decide the appeal. Justice Douglas, recognizing this, ruled:

"Should he be allowed to play and his team not make the playoffs then no one, of course, will have been injured. Should he be allowed to play and his team does make the playoffs but the District Court decision goes in favor of the NBA, then it would be for the District Court to determine whether the NBA could disregard the Seattle victories in all games in which he participated and recompute who should be in the playoffs.

"To dissolve the stay would preserve the interest and integrity of the playoff system, as I have indicated. Should there not be a decision prior to beginning of the playoffs and should Seattle make the playoffs then the District Court could fashion whatever relief it deems equitable.

"In view of the equities between the parties . . ., I have decided to allow the preliminary injunction of the District Court to be reinstated." [4]

The NBA then made a motion to all nine justices of the Supreme Court to vacate Justice Douglas' order, but the motion was denied without opinion. As it happened, the Supersonics failed to make the playoffs that year, even with Haywood.

§7.3(e)(2)(A)(iii) Antitrust "per se" doctrine

While Haywood's right to play pending the conclusion of the lawsuit was being appealed all the way to the Supreme Court, his lawyers were preparing for the soon-to-be-held trial. There were several issues to be resolved during the trial: the validity of the Haywood-Rockets contract; if it were valid, the propriety of an injunction pre-

---

[4] **Haywood v. National Basketball Association, 401 U.S. 1204, 1206-1207 (1971).**

venting Haywood from playing for any other team until it expired; if it were not valid, the validity of the Haywood-Supersonics contract and the legality of the NBA draft and four-year-rule By-Laws. Because each of these issues constituted a full-scale dispute, the trial threatened to become a multi-week marathon, and thus very expensive for all concerned.

In the hopes of simplifying the trial by reducing the number of issues in advance, Haywood asked Judge Ferguson to rule on the legality of the NBA four-year rule before the start of the trial. Haywood's request, made in a motion for partial summary judgment, was based on his contention that there were no *facts* in dispute with respect to the legality of the four-year rule, and therefore no oral testimony was necessary. Haywood contended that all of the facts on that issue were set forth right in the NBA By-Laws and could be read by Judge Ferguson.

The NBA vigorously opposed Haywood's motion on several grounds. Not the least of them was that in the event the jury ruled that the Denver Rockets contract was valid, the question of the legality of the NBA By-Laws would not even be reached, because Haywood would then still be in the ABA. As the NBA argued, it did not want to have twenty-five years of its history and practice obliterated—and certainly not by a player who was going to remain in the competitive league in any event.

The ruling Haywood sought was controversial to say the least, and many—perhaps most—judges would have welcomed any reason or excuse not to decide the issue. Judge Warren Ferguson, however, did not avoid Haywood's motion; and because careful study of the precedents convinced him Haywood was right, he decided in Haywood's favor. Those sections of the NBA By-Laws containing the four-year rule, Judge Ferguson ruled, "are declared to be illegal under Section 1 of the Sherman Act." [1]

According to Judge Ferguson, the four-year rule prevented professional quality basketball players from entering into contracts with NBA teams until four years after their graduation from high school, even though they may not have wanted to attend college, may not have been eligible to attend college, may not have wanted to participate in intercollegiate athletics and may not have been eligible to participate in them. The rule thus constituted a concerted refusal by all NBA teams to deal with a certain group of basketball players. Concerted refusals to deal are also referred to as group boycotts and are prohibited by the Sherman Act.

The National Basketball Association argued that though its four-year rule might have been a concerted refusal to deal, it served very reasonable purposes and was therefore not prohibited by the antitrust laws. Those purposes were to provide a more efficient and less expensive way of training professional basketball players than the "farm team" system used by baseball and hockey, and to guarantee that each prospective player had an opportunity to complete four years of college before beginning his professional career. Judge Ferguson refused to accept these purposes as justifications making the rule legal, however.

"The Sherman Act declares 'every' combination in restraint of trade to be illegal," he explained.[2] It was true that the Supreme Court had ruled that the Sherman Act should be construed "in the light of reason," [3] and that

---

[1] Denver Rockets v. All-Pro Management, Inc., 325 F.Supp. 1049, 1067 (C.D. Cal. 1971).

[2] *Id.* at 1062.

[3] *Id.* at 1063, citing Standard Oil Co. v. United States, 221 U.S. 1 (1911).

so construed, the Act prohibits only unreasonable contracts and combinations in restraint of trade. Nevertheless, the Supreme Court has also ruled that certain agreements and practices have so "pernicious" an effect on competition and so lack any redeeming virtue that they are conclusively presumed to be unreasonable and therefore illegal "without elaborate inquiry as to the precise harm they have caused or the business excuse for their use" in the particular case.[4] Two decisions of the United States Supreme Court demonstrate that group boycotts are an example of practices which are conclusively presumed unreasonable and thus illegal, regardless of the reason for their use.

The first of these cases is *Fashion Originators' Guild* v. *Federal Trade Commission,*[5] decided in 1941. There, an organization of garment and textile manufacturers sought to prevent unscrupulous competitors from copying their designs; and they did this by refusing to sell their products to manufacturers and retail stores that handled the pirated copies. In this fashion it was hoped that those manufacturers and retail stores, when confronted with a cut-off of their supplies of the original textiles and dresses, would refuse to buy from the "style pirates," thus leaving the pirates without markets for their pirated wares. The Federal Trade Commission determined that this practice was illegal and issued a cease and desist order against the Guild and its members. This order was affirmed by the Supreme Court, which held that the FTC's refusal to hear evidence on the reasonableness of the practice was entirely proper, and said further that the boycott would not be legal even if dress and textile copying were against the law in every state in the nation.

---

[4] *Id.*, quoting Northern Pacific v. United States, 356 U.S. 1, 5 (1957).

[5] 312 U.S. 457 (1941).

The second Supreme Court case is *Klor's* v. *Broadway-Hale Stores,*[6] decided in 1959. There, Broadway-Hale Stores, a chain of retail appliance stores, had used its influence to induce several appliance manufacturers not to sell appliances to Klor's, a small appliance store that competed with Broadway-Hale in one location. Klor's sued Broadway-Hale and the appliance manufacturers. The manufacturers' defense was that the entire matter was a "private quarrel" between the two stores. The manufacturers also submitted evidence to show that although they had stopped selling to Klor's, competition in its neighborhood had not been affected. The Supreme Court held that even if there had been no discernible effect on competition, the concerted refusal of the appliance manufacturers to sell to Klor's constituted a violation of the Sherman Act.

§7.3(e)(2)(A)(iv) Silver exception to per se doctrine

The National Basketball Association sought to distinguish these two cases[1] with another Supreme Court case, *Silver* v. *New York Stock Exchange,*[2] decided in 1963. Silver was a securities dealer. Although Silver was not a member of the New York Stock Exchange, he maintained private telephone and ticker tape connections with other securities dealers who were members, with the temporary approval of the Exchange. The Exchange thereafter disapproved, and its member dealers were required to disconnect Silver. As a result, Silver filed an antitrust action, alleging that the cut-off was an illegal concerted

[6] 359 U.S. 207 (1959).

[1] Fashion Originators' Guild v. Federal Trade Commission, 312 U.S. 457 (1941); Klor's v. Broadway-Hale Stores, 359 U.S. 207 (1959), both discussed in § 7.3(e)(2)(A)(iii), *supra.*

[2] 373 U.S. 341 (1963).

refusal to deal. The Supreme Court held that "absent any justification derived from the policy of another statute or otherwise,"[3] the cut-off would have constituted a group boycott illegal *per se* under the Sherman Act. However, the Securities Exchange Act gave the New York Stock Exchange its self-regulation authority; and therefore, although the cut-off was a group boycott, the rule of reason would apply nevertheless. The Supreme Court then ruled that the cut-off was not justified even under the rule of reason. But the case stands for the proposition that the rule of reason may apply in group boycott cases if there is a "justification derived from the policy of another statute or otherwise."

There is no statute which authorizes self-regulation by the National Basketball Association or professional sports in general. However, the NBA argued to Judge Ferguson that there was a policy derived "otherwise" than from a statute which justified self-regulation by the NBA. The justification was derived from the need for separate teams to cooperate with one another in order to create the product they were selling, namely, league championship play.

Judge Ferguson analyzed the Supreme Court's decision in *Silver* to mean that group boycotts are illegal *per se,* with one narrow exception, in which event the rule of reason would apply and, if the boycott were reasonable, it would be legal. Judge Ferguson said that three circumstances must exist in order to qualify for the exception:[4]

1) Self-regulation must be justified by statute "or otherwise."

---

[3] *Id.* at 348-349.

[4] Denver Rockets v. All-Pro Management, Inc., 325 F.Supp. 1049, 1064-1065 (C.D. Cal. 1971).

2) The action taken must be intended to accomplish an end consistent with the justification for self-regulation, be reasonably related to the justification, and be no more extensive than necessary.

3) There must be procedural safeguards assuring that the restraint is not arbitrary and providing a basis for judicial review.

Judge Ferguson ruled that the NBA failed to qualify for the exception from *per se* illegality because it provided no procedural safeguards. He stated,

> "It is clear from the constitution and by-laws of the NBA that there is no provision for even the most rudimentary hearing before the four-year college rule is applied to exclude an individual player. Nor is there any provision whereby an individual player might petition for consideration of his specific case."[5]

From this statement, it appears that Judge Ferguson might have approved a four-year rule if league By-Laws also had provided for a hardship exemption. On the other hand, it may be that exemption only for "hardship" is too strict, and that other grounds would have to be sufficient as well in order to make a four-year rule legal. This is because Judge Ferguson stated,

> "In addition, it is uncontested that the rules in question are absolute and prohibit the signing of not only college basketball players but also those who do not desire to attend college and even those who lack the mental and financial ability to do so. As such they are overly broad and thus improper . . ."[6]

---

[5] *Id.* at 1066.
[6] ***Id.***

Here Judge Ferguson seems to suggest a possible distinction between college players and those who lack the desire or financial ability to attend college. Perhaps the implication is that a four-year rule may be applied to those who enroll in college—so long as they may turn professional at any time if hardship requires it—but may not be applied to those who elect not to enroll in college at all. This is substantially similar to the system now used in professional baseball.[7] Such a rule might provide an acceptable balance between the interests of the colleges and professionals on the one hand, and individual college players on the other. It can be argued, however, that such a rule would make an unfair distinction between those high school graduates who decide immediately they do not want to attend college and those who do not come to that realization until they have actually spent time in college.

§7.3(e)(2)(A)(v) Reaction of sports community to Haywood decision

Judge Ferguson's decision holding the NBA's four-year rule illegal brought forth wails of despair from the sports establishment, both professional and collegiate. NBA Commissioner Walter Kennedy lamented, "This could kill college athletics and seriously injure professional athletics." [1] NFL Commissioner Pete Rozelle agreed. "It could destroy college football and basketball," [2] he contended, though the basis for his concern over football is unclear. Rozelle also announced that despite Judge Ferguson's ruling, the National Football League was going to continue to enforce

[7] See § 3.1(d), *supra*.

[1] Sports Illustrated, April 12, 1971, at 34; B. Libby & S. Haywood, Stand Up For Something: The Spencer Haywood Story (New York: Grosset & Dunlap, 1972) at 105-106.

[2] *Id.*

its eligibility requirements, and it has in fact retained and enforced them to this very day.[3] Northwestern football coach Alex Agase and Furman basketball coach Joe Williams speculated on the dire consequences. "This could eliminate all super-stars from college competition," said the former.[4] "This will take a great deal of incentive out of recruiting good players," the latter asserted.[5] On the other hand, the quality of the consequences was—like beauty—in the eye of the beholder. One college administrator said, "We could always go back to using student athletes." [6] And that is something many colleges have in fact done since, but for financial reasons of their own, and not because of a mass exodus of teenagers into the ranks of professional athletics.

The case which began so tempestuously ended rather suddenly and quietly, leaving at least one significant issue unresolved. After approximately two weeks of testimony, most of which dealt with whether the terms of Haywood's Rockets contract had been misrepresented to him, the case was settled. The Supersonics paid the Rockets a sum of money variously reported as $250,000 or $300,000, in ex-

---

[3] In 1975, Commissioner Rozelle disapproved the contract between Clarence Reece and the Houston Oilers, on the grounds that Reece had not yet satisfied NFL eligibility requirements. Reece had withdrawn from the University of Southern California in 1974, following his sophomore year, and had signed with the Canadian Football League for the 1974 season. In 1975, he signed with the Oilers. When the Commissioner disapproved his Oilers' contract, Reece filed suit in federal District Court in Los Angeles, alleging that the NFL eligibility rules constituted an illegal group boycott. When assured that neither the Oilers nor any other NFL team had encouraged Reece to withdraw from college, the Commissioner rescinded his disapproval of Reece's contract; and Reece was thereafter permitted to report to the Oilers' training camp.

[4] Sports Illustrated and B. Libby & S. Haywood, *supra* note 1.

[5] *Id.*

[6] *Id.*

change for dismissal of their suit.[7] In addition, the NBA dismissed its pending appeals from the preliminary injunction and partial summary judgment granted Haywood by Judge Ferguson. In return, Haywood dismissed his suit against the NBA.

The settlement was a victory for Haywood personally. Though Judge Ferguson never ruled on Haywood's contention that the draft itself was illegal, the settlement permitted the Supersonics to keep him, though they had not drafted him and the NBA's Buffalo Braves had, at the end of the 1970-71 season. The Denver Rockets "lost" the case, in the sense that they gave up Haywood, but they had good reasons of their own for doing so. Rocket co-owner Don Ringsby later stated that the factor that influenced the Rockets the greatest was the feeling of the other ABA team owners that the case was endangering their chance for a merger with the NBA. Ringsby also said that in addition to the money the Rockets received from the Supersonics, the Rockets were also to receive $500,000 from their own league, if and when there was a merger, plus the first ABA draft pick in the first common draft to accompany the merger.[8]

The NBA accepted Judge Ferguson's ruling that its four-year rule was illegal in its then existing form and had to permit Haywood to stay in Seattle, but received, in return, a dismissal of Haywood's claim that the entire draft was illegal. The effect of the decision on the four-year rule apparently was slight on the league. After the settlement, it simply amended its By-Laws to provide that any person ineligible under the four-year rule could petition the NBA Commissioner for classification as a "hardship case,"

[7] B. Libby & S. Haywood, *supra* note 1, at 130 and 189.

[8] *Id.* at 188-189.

and anyone so classified was then immediately eligible for the draft and NBA play. The Commissioner could grant the hardship classification on the basis of the player's written petition alone. But he could not deny the petition without first holding a hearing, at which the player could present oral and written evidence and be represented by counsel. No criteria for "hardship" were specified in the By-Laws, so theoretically all petitions could have been granted consistent with league policy.[9] Indeed, at least one sportswriter has reported that none of the players or coaches he interviewed on the subject had ever heard of an athlete whose petition had been denied. According to NBA Vice President Simon Gourdine, the league's hardship investigation was very thorough and did result in some rejections, though even he conceded that the number of rejections was "relatively small."[10] In the four drafts held between 1971 and 1974, twenty-four basketball players were drafted by NBA teams after obtaining hardship exemptions.[11]

(In May of 1976, the NBA relaxed its eligibility rule still further by doing away with the requirement that a player demonstrate "hardship."[12])

Interestingly, the American Basketball Association, which devised the "hardship exemption" concept in order to beat the NBA to Spencer Haywood, no longer has a four-year rule and thus no need for an exemption of any kind. Its own four-year rule was eliminated, according to the ABA, because requiring a college athlete to petition

---

[9] Distel, Those Hardship Cases: Some Strike It Rich, L.A. Times, July 7, 1974, Part III.

[10] *Id.*

[11] *Id.*

[12] See § 3.1(a), *supra*.

for a hardship exemption causes him to forfeit his college eligibility even if he is not drafted thereafter. The ABA simply drafts undergraduates as well as graduating seniors.[13]

§7.3(e)(2)(B) The Jane Blalock case

A true test of a disciplined athlete's rights under the antitrust laws came in 1972, when professional golfer Barbara Jane Blalock was suspended for one year by the Ladies Professional Golf Association for alleged cheating. According to affidavits filed with the federal District Court in Atlanta, Georgia, the LPGA tournament director appointed four people to observe Blalock during the second round of a tournament in Louisville, Kentucky, in May of 1972. This was done because the director had received complaints that Blalock had previously violated rules of play. The appointed observers reported that Blalock had indeed violated the rules while they had watched, by illegally moving her ball. As a result, the LPGA Executive Board voted on May 20, 1972 to disqualify Blalock from the Louisville tournament, to place her on probation for the rest of the 1972 season, and to fine her $500 for cheating. On May 26, 1972, Blalock was called before the Executive Board and advised of the decision it had reached earlier that week. When asked if she had anything to say, Blalock replied, according to the LPGA minutes, "No, I am guilty of moving my ball from spike marks, out of heel prints and ball marks on several occasions. I've dug my own grave and I guess I'll have to live with it."[1] Later, she vigorously disputed the accuracy of the quote attributed to her in the minutes and contended that she had simply said that if

---

[13] Distel, *supra* note 9.

[1] **Blalock v. Ladies Professional Golf Association, 1972 CCH Trade Cases ¶ 74,111 (N.D. Ga. 1972) at 92,633.**

she had committed any infraction of the rules it was purely unintentional on her part.

Regardless of what Blalock had actually said to the Executive Board, it was the version set forth in the LPGA minutes that apparently became known; because within the next two days a petition signed by 29 player-members of the LPGA was presented to the Board, stating,

> "In view of Jane Blalock's admission to the Executive Board that she had moved the ball not only forward but in addition, out of heel prints, spike marks, and divots on other occasions than previously fined for, we, the undersigned members of the LPGA, demand that the Board take further action by reason of admission of such additional violations of tournament regulations and that she be suspended for the balance of 1972." [2]

On May 28, 1972, the Board convened again to discuss the Blalock matter and voted to suspend Blalock not only for the balance of 1972, as demanded by the player petition, but from June 1, 1972 until May 31, 1973, an entire year. Blalock was informed of the Board decision on May 30, 1972, and she immediately filed suit against the LPGA, its Executive Board members, and its tournament director seeking damages and an injunction against her continued suspension. A temporary injunction against the suspension was granted June 28, 1972, permitting Blalock to play in all LPGA tournaments, so long as she deposited any money she might win with the clerk of the court, or posted a bond to secure repayment in the event she ultimately lost her case.

Approximately a year later, Blalock made a motion for partial summary judgment in which she asked the court

[2] *Id.*

to rule in advance of trial that her suspension constituted an illegal group boycott. And, in what may become a most significant case, Judge Charles A. Moye, Jr., of the federal District Court in Atlanta, ruled that Blalock's suspension was a violation of the Sherman Act, regardless of any justification for it that the LPGA and its Executive Board believed they may have had.[3]

Judge Moye's analysis was similar in many ways to that of Judge Ferguson in the *Spencer Haywood* case.[4] Judge Moye began by noting that golf—unlike baseball—was subject to the antitrust laws, quoting the U.S. Supreme Court decision in the *Curt Flood* case where golf's non-exemption had been presumed.[5] Next Judge Moye noted that the LPGA conducts its business in interstate commerce, and that its Executive Board had agreed to suspend Blalock pursuant to procedures set forth in the LPGA Constitution and By-Laws. Although the Sherman Act prohibits every contract, combination or conspiracy restraining interstate trade, it was noted that the Supreme Court had long ago ruled that only unreasonable contracts, combinations and conspiracies are usually held to be illegal. There are exceptions from the "rule of reason," however, in that certain arrangements are conclusively presumed to be unreasonable. "Once the existence of such an arrangement has been established, no evidence of actual public injury is required . . ., and no evidence of the reasonableness of defendant's conduct will be considered in justification."[6] Collective re-

[3] Blalock v. Ladies Professional Golf Association, 359 F.Supp. 1260 (N.D. Ga. 1973).

[4] Denver Rockets v. All-Pro Management, Inc., 325 F.Supp. 1049 (C.D. Cal. 1971), discussed in § 7.3(e)(2)(A), *supra*.

[5] Flood v. Kuhn, 407 U.S. 258, 282-283 (1972).

[6] Blalock v. Ladies Professional Golf Association, *supra* note 3, quoting E. A. McQuade Tours, Inc. v. Consolidated Air Tour, 467 F.2d 178, 186 (5th Cir. 1972).

fusals to deal, or group boycotts, are one example of arrangements considered to be illegal *per se,* regardless of justification; and, citing *Klor's* v. *Broadway-Hale* and *Fashion Originators' Guild* v. *Federal Trade Commission*[7] (also relied upon by Judge Ferguson in the *Spencer Haywood* case), Judge Moye ruled that Blalock's suspension amounted to a group boycott which was illegal *per se.* "Consequently, it is not necessary that [I] inquire as to the reasonableness of the suspension," [8] he concluded.

Naturally, the LPGA thought its suspension of Blalock for cheating to be entirely reasonable, and argued that the "rule of reason" must apply even if the Court considered the suspension to be a group boycott. In support of its contention that the suspension was reasonable and thus legal, the LPGA cited *Molinas* v. *National Basketball Association*[9] in which the federal District Court in New York City had stated,

> "Every league or association must have some reasonable governing rules, and these rules must necessarily include disciplinary provisions. Surely, every disciplinary rule which a league may invoke, although by its nature it may involve some sort of restraint, does not run afoul of the anti-trust laws." [10]

Judge Moye distinguished *Molinas* by noting that Molinas had been suspended by the president of the NBA and not by Molinas' competitors. On the other hand, the Executive Board of the LPGA was comprised of player-members who competed for prize money with Blalock and other mem-

[7] Discussed in § 7.3(e)(2)(A)(iii), *supra.*

[8] Blalock v. L.P.G.A., *supra* note 3, at 1266.

[9] 190 F.Supp. 241 (S.D.N.Y. 1961), discussed in § 7.3(e)(1), *supra.*

[10] *Id.* at 243-244.

bers in LPGA tournaments, and who therefore were in a position "to gain financially from [Blalock's] exclusion from the market." [11]

§7.3(e)(2)(C) Critique of the Blalock, Molinas and Manok cases

Judge Moye's attempt to distinguish Jane Blalock's case from *Molinas,*[1] on the grounds that Molinas was suspended by the league president,[2] is not entirely satisfying. A group boycott is no less one because imposed by customers or suppliers, rather than by competitors. Though the boycotts in *Klor's* v. *Broadway-Hale*[3] and *Fashion Originators' Guild* v. *FTC*[4] had been instigated by competitors, in both cases the boycotts were participated in by suppliers or customers as well.[5] Furthermore, the illegal boycotts imposed in *Haywood*[6] and in *Radovich*[7] were imposed by the leagues involved and not by Haywood's or Radovich's competitors.

The reason that *Molinas* and *Manok*[8] are weak precedents is that in their brevity they make deceptive and incorrect assumptions about the propriety of disciplinary and eligibility rules. For example, in the *Molinas* case, the Court stated, "Surely, every disciplinary rule which a league may invoke, although by its nature it may involve some sort of

---

[11] Blalock v. L.P.G.A., *supra* note 3, at 1265.

[1] 190 F.Supp. 241 (S.D.N.Y. 1961).

[2] Blalock v. L.P.G.A., 359 F.Supp. 1260, 1267 (N.D. Ga. 1973).

[3] 359 U.S. 207 (1959).

[4] 312 U.S. 457 (1941).

[5] See § 7.3(e)(2)(A)(iii), ***supra.***

[6] Denver Rockets v. All-Pro Management, Inc., 325 F.Supp. 1049 (C.D. Cal. 1971), discussed in § 7.3(e)(2)(A), ***supra.***

[7] 352 U.S. 445 (1957), discussed in § 1.2(b), ***supra.***

[8] 306 F.Supp. 1215 (C.D. Cal. 1969), discussed in § 7.3(e)(1), ***supra.***

restraint, does not run afoul of the antitrust laws." [9] While that may be true, the question is how to distinguish between those that do and those that do not. The Court's further statement that "a disciplinary rule invoked against gambling seems about as reasonable a rule as could be imagined" [10] suggests that the distinction is between reasonable and unreasonable rules, reasonable ones being legal and unreasonable ones, illegal. When the discipline imposed is suspension, simply looking at reasonableness omits several crucial steps, because suspensions may be illegal *per se* boycotts—something which *Molinas* and *Manok* ignored.

Suspensions are legal if, but only if, self-regulation by the league or association is justified by statute or otherwise; the suspension is intended to accomplish an end consistent with the justification for self-regulation, is reasonably related to the justification, and is no more extensive than necessary; and there are procedural safeguards assuring that the suspension is not arbitrary and provide a basis for judicial review.[11] If *Molinas* and *Manok* are considered with these criteria in mind, then the same results are obtained; and the analysis is then more accurate. In *Haywood,* Judge Ferguson never expressly ruled on whether self-regulation by the NBA was justified "otherwise" than by statute (there being no statute conferring such justification), because he found that the NBA lacked necessary procedural safeguards (in connection with its four-year rule). However, the NBA argued there was such a justification in the structure of the industry itself, and Judge Ferguson seems to have accepted that argument.

---

[9] 190 F.Supp. at 244.

[10] *Id.*

[11] Denver Rockets v. All-Pro Management, Inc., *supra* note 6, at 1064-1065.

Thus in *Molinas* and *Manok* it may be said that self-regulation is justified "otherwise" than by statute.

In basketball, the justification is the need for teams to cooperate with each other in order to create the product they are selling, league championship play. In bowling, the justification is the need for individual bowlers to cooperate in order to create their product, championship tournament play. Prohibiting gambling and cheating is consistent with the production of championship play in both sports, and suspensions are intended to enforce those prohibitions. Whether a suspension is more extensive than necessary would depend, it seems, on the particular infraction committed. In *Molinas* and *Manok,* the opinions made it clear that the judges who heard the facts felt that the suspensions were not more extensive than necessary.

Finally, procedural safeguards were in fact provided in *Molinas,* in that his suspension came only after he had admitted in writing that he had violated NBA rules. The procedural safeguards, if any, made available to Manok were not described in the Court's opinion dismissing his suit, though had he alleged the absence of an adequate hearing, it seems likely some mention of the procedure would have been made by the judge.

Thus, though Judge Moye chose to distinguish Blalock's suspension from the LPGA from that of Molinas from the NBA, he could have instead said that Molinas' suspension satisfied all of the strict requirements of the exception to the rule that group boycotts are illegal *per se,* and thus was not necessarily a precedent for Blalock's suspension, unless hers also met the same strict requirements. Interestingly, one reason Judge Moye did not measure Blalock's suspension against those requirements was because he did not agree with Judge Ferguson's decision in *Haywood* that group boycotts could be justified "otherwise" than by statute. "Whatever the 'or otherwise' . . . refers to, it is clear that it necessarily must be of sufficient force and effect impliedly to repeal a federal statute. This Court cannot ascribe that weight to the Constitution and By-Laws of the LPGA," he said.[12]

There are several problems with Judge Moye's rejection of the possibility that self-regulation might be justified "otherwise" than by statute. First is his failure to offer any suggestion as to what the Supreme Court might have meant when it said in *Silver* that "absent any justification derived from the policy of another statute *or otherwise,* the Exchange acted in violation of the Sherman Act." [13] In addition, Judge Moye's sweeping rejection of the LPGA's authority to suspend Blalock for cheating suggests that no league or sports association may ever suspend an athlete for any kind of conduct. Yet, Judge Moye seemed not to disagree with the propriety of the suspension of Molinas from the NBA, saying only that it was imposed by the league president rather than Molinas' competitors—hardly an adequate justification, because Molinas' suspension was no less a group boycott than Blalock's.

Furthermore, Judge Moye seemed not to disagree with the result in another case relied on heavily by the LPGA, *Deesen* v. *Professional Golfers' Association of America.*[14] Judge Moye's decision in *Blalock* distinguished Deesen's loss of approved-player status from Blalock's suspension by noting that the PGA tournament committee was com-

---

[12] Blalock v. L.P.G.A., *supra* note 2, at 1267.

[13] 373 U.S. at 348-349 (emphasis added).

[14] 358 F.2d 165 (9th Cir. 1966), *cert. den.,* 385 U.S. 846 (1966), discussed in § 7.3(e)(1), *supra.*

posed "largely of non-competitors"[15] unlike the LPGA's Executive Board which was composed largely of competitors. However, this distinction seems to be irrelevant in group boycott cases. Judge Moye was also impressed that Deesen's termination "was based upon virtually a mathematical application of predetermined standards. It did not involve a completely unfettered, subjective and discretionary determination."[16] Of course, if the LPGA Executive Board had been asked, it would undoubtedly have said that it too applied pre-determined standards: whenever a player is caught cheating, she is disciplined, the extent of the discipline varying in direct proportion to the extent of the cheating. So this distinction is less than completely satisfying too.

A third distinction between *Blalock* and *Deesen* relied upon by Judge Moye is hardly more significant. Though Herbert Deesen had lost his "approved tournament player" status, and thus was temporarily ineligible for PGA tournaments, he had it within his power to become a full-fledged PGA tournament member by becoming a golf club pro.[17] Thus Deesen was not completely excluded from further participation in PGA tournaments. However, to become a member, Deesen would have to be a golf club pro for five years and was thus effectively barred for that period. Jane Blalock, on the other hand, had been suspended for only one year, and was thus excluded from tournament participation for a much shorter period of time than Deesen and thus affected much less.

In short, Judge Moye's opinion disapproving of Jane Blalock's suspension proves too much, is too broad in

---

[15] Blalock v. L.P.G.A., *supra* note 2, at 1267.

[16] *Id.* at 1268.

[17] See § 7.3(e)(1), *supra.*

its sweep, and his efforts to avoid disagreement with the *Molinas* suspension and the *Deesen* termination are unconvincing. This is not to say, however, that Judge Moye's decision in the *Blalock* case was wrong. It is simply to say that another explanation for it would have been better. The correct analysis, it seems, would be this.

Blalock's suspension was a group boycott, and thus illegal *per se,* unless the structure of the industry justifies self-regulation. It appears from the *Deesen* case that the structure of the tournament golf industry justifies self-regulation. Therefore, if certain conditions exist, the LPGA would be entitled to show that the suspension was reasonable and thus legal. Those conditions, outlined in *Haywood,* are these: the suspension must have been intended to accomplish an end consistent with the justification for self-regulation, must have been reasonably related to that justification, and must have been no more extensive than necessary. Also there must have been procedural safeguards assuring the suspension was not arbitrary and providing a basis for judicial review. The justification for LPGA self-regulation is that tournaments cannot be conducted, especially for prize money, unless all participants play by the same rules. Blalock's suspension was intended to accomplish uniform play in the future and seems reasonably related to that end. Whether the one year period was more or less extensive than necessary is a question of judgment; but assume that it was.

Were there then procedural safeguards? In Blalock's case there were not. The only hearing at which she was present was concluded with a modest fine and six-months probation. Thereafter, she was suspended for a year, based upon facts contained in a statement she denied having made. She was not present or invited to be present at the Board meeting which resulted in her suspension. Furthermore, as Judge Moye emphasized, the Board members who suspended her were her own competitors and thus had a financial interest in whether or not she played. While that fact did not make her suspension any more a group boycott than it would have been even if she had been suspended by a non-competitor Board, the make-up of the Board does heighten the lack of procedural fairness. Finally, Judge Moye felt that the Board's action in increasing the penalty from six-months probation to a one-year suspension was arbitrary. Therefore, by this analysis, the same as in *Haywood* and in *Deesen,* the LPGA was not entitled to argue that Blalock's suspension was reasonable. The result was thus correct.

§7.3(e)(2)(D) NFL rule regarding WFL players

The World Football League went out of business entirely on October 22, 1975, in the midst of its second season, and with debts and losses said to exceed $30 million.[1] Approximately 300 professional football players lost their jobs with WFL teams, and many if not most of them hoped to find employment in the National Football League. The only WFL player who was immediately successful in doing so, however, was Dave Roller, a defensive tackle who had played for the Southern California Sun.[2] He was signed by the Green Bay Packers. Before any other WFL players could do likewise, NFL Commissioner Rozelle amended a recently adopted NFL eligibility rule, and thus barred all NFL teams from signing any other former WFL players for the balance of the 1975 season.

[1] L.A. Times, Oct. 23, 1975, Part III.

[2] L.A. Times, Nov. 6, 1975, Part III.

The eligibility rule in question was adopted by the NFL on September 16, 1975, in apparent anticipation of the folding of the World Football League, or at least some of its teams. The rule read:

> "Resolved, for 1975 only, that any player who has been under a 1975 contract as a player or coach in another major professional football league may not sign with an NFL club for 1975. The foregoing provision shall not apply to players who are without any further contractual obligation within such league, and whose club or league ceases to operate. In no event may any such player be signed for 1975 play after the cessation of intra-conference trading at 4 p.m. Eastern Time Tuesday October 28." [3]

The purpose of this eligibility rule was explained in a statement later issued by Commissioner Rozelle:

> "The trading deadline traditionally has been the deadline for major player movement among NFL teams. We intend to adhere to that resolution in the interest of preserving the competitive integrity of our divisional races, now 5/14ths complete and in deference to those hundreds of players who have worked since July to win places on NFL rosters." [4]

Because the WFL folded a full six days before the deadline for signing, there was sufficient time for those WFL players who could sign with NFL teams to do so. However, John Bassett, the owner of the WFL Memphis Southmen, hoping to obtain an NFL franchise for his team, threatened to file an antitrust lawsuit against the NFL if

[3] Bowman v. National Football League, 402 F.Supp. 754, 755 (D. Minn. 1975).

[4] L.A. Times, Oct. 23, 1975, Part III.

its teams signed former WFL players. Confronted with this threat, Rozelle issued an "edict" moving up the signing deadline from October 28th to October 24th.[5]

Several players who had been unable to sign with NFL teams during the brief two day period between the WFL's collapse on October 22nd, and the new deadline for signing on October 24th, filed an antitrust class action lawsuit of their own on October 29, 1975, alleging that the NFL rule constituted a concerted boycott of former WFL players. On November 5, 1975, District Judge Edward J. Devitt issued an order enjoining the National Football League from taking any action until November 26, 1975 which would prohibit, discourage or prevent any former WFL player (not then under contract to a WFL team or owner) from entering into an employment contract with an NFL team.[6]

Although the opinion does not expressly discuss whether the *per se* doctrine or the "rule of reason" was applied, it is nevertheless apparent that Judge Devitt applied the *per se* doctrine. First, it was reasonable for Commissioner Rozelle to move up the deadline for signing to October 24th in response to the threat of an antitrust suit in the event NFL teams signed former WFL players. Second, in finding it likely that the National Football League and its members were "combining and conspiring to restrain competition for the services of" former WFL players, and in finding it likely that the National Football League and its members were "conducting a concerted boycott against former WFL players,"[7] Judge Devitt cited only cases decided under the *per se* doctrine: *Klor's*

---

[5] L.A. Times, Nov. 6, 1975, Part III.

[6] Bowman v. National Football League, *supra* note 3, at 756-757.

[7] *Id.* at 756.

v. *Broadway-Hale Stores,*[8] *Fashions Originators' Guild* v. *Federal Trade Commission,*[9] *Blalock* v. *Ladies Professional Golf Association,*[10] *Denver Rockets* v. *All-Pro Management,*[11] and *Haywood* v. *National Basketball Association.*[12]

"Plaintiffs are unemployed, but qualified professional football players," he stated, "who are prevented from seeking and obtaining employment in their chosen field by the concerted action of the defendants, to their financial, physical and professional detriment." [13] Under the circumstances, Judge Devitt held that it "would appear to justify the legal conclusion that the antitrust laws are being violated." [14] "Professional sports and the public are better served by open unfettered competition for playing positions," [15] he concluded.

§7.3(f) Labor law principles

§7.3(f)(1) Substantive

On several occasions, it has been suggested that professional sports leagues have taken punitive actions against players and game officials who were active in the organization or administration of their labor unions. In the summer of 1968, for example, American League baseball umpires Alexander Salerno and William Valentine were fired by

[8] 359 U.S. 207 (1959), discussed in § 7.3(e)(2)(A)(iii), *supra.*

[9] 312 U.S. 457 (1941), discussed in §7.3(e)(2)(A)(iii), *supra.*

[10] 359 F.Supp. 1260 (N.D. Ga. 1973), discussed in §7.3(e)(2)(B), *supra.*

[11] 325 F.Supp. 1049 (C.D. Cal. 1971), discussed in § 7.3(e)(2)(A), *supra.*

[12] 401 U.S. 1204 (1971), discussed in § 7.3(e)(2)(A)(ii), *supra.*

[13] Bowman v. National Football League, *supra* note 3, at 756.

[14] *Id.*

[15] *Id.*

League President Joe Cronin for supposed "incompetence." Salerno and Valentine claimed they had not been incompetent, and that they had really been fired because of their efforts to organize the twenty-five American League umpires into a labor union for the purpose of collective bargaining.[1]

Former NFL Players Association President John Mackey testified in 1972 before subcommittees of both the Senate and House of Representatives, telling them that "since 1968 nearly every player representative who participated in collective bargaining for the NFL Players Association was traded or waived out of the League prior to the commencement of the 1970 negotiations."[2] Furthermore, he said, "From 1970 through this season [1971], 10 players representatives have been traded or released."[3]

During the 1974 NFL strike, the Atlanta Falcons' player representative, Ken Reaves, was traded to the New Orleans Saints—a trade which Reaves believed was the result of his involvement in Player Association business.[4]

The baseball umpires' right to organize a union, and the football player representatives' right to bargain collectively with NFL management, are rights expressly conferred and protected by the National Labor Relations Act.[5] Interfer-

---

[1] See, Salerno v. American League of Professional Baseball Clubs, 429 F.2d 1003 (2d Cir. 1970); and, American League of Professional Baseball Clubs & The Major League Umpires Assn., 189 N.L.R.B. No. 85, 76 L.R.R.M. 1645 (1971).

[2] Hearings on S.2373 before the Subcomm. on Antitrust and Monopoly of the Senate Comm. on the Judiciary, 92d Cong., 2d Sess., Part 2, at 843 (1971-1972); Hearings before the Special Subcomm. on Labor of the House Comm. on Education and Labor, 92d Cong., 2d Sess. (1972).

[3] *Id.*

[4] See § 4.1(a)(4), *supra.*

[5] 29 U.S.C. § 157.

ence with them by the employer—be it the league or individual team owner—constitutes an unfair labor practice which the National Labor Relations Board is empowered to prevent.[6]

On the other hand, allegations that unfair labor practices have occurred must be proved; and that is as difficult to do before the National Labor Relations Board as it is in a court of law. Umpires Salerno and Valentine did file unfair labor practice charges with the Board. However, the complaint issued in response was dismissed by the Board, on the grounds that the evidence failed to establish that at the time they were discharged the League had knowledge of the umpires' union activities "beyond mere suspicion or surmise."[7] (Knowledge by the employer of the employee's union activities is a prerequisite to a finding of discharge because of those activities.[8])

§7.3(f)(2) Procedural

The National Labor Relations Act affects the manner in which admittedly proper disciplinary rules may be adopted, as well as the substantive propriety of disciplinary action taken. That this is so was made clear in a case which arose in 1971, when the National Football League adopted a new rule providing that "Any player leaving the bench area while a fight is in progress on the field will be fined $200." The rule had been proposed by Commissioner Rozelle when he became concerned about player injuries resulting from fights on the field, and it was designed to discourage players

[6] 29 U.S.C. §§ 158 and 160.

[7] American League of Professional Baseball Clubs & The Major League Umpires Assn., *supra* note 1, at 76 L.R.R.M. 1651.

[8] *Id.* at 76 L.R.R.M. 1646.

from leaving the bench area and becoming involved in the first place.

The rule became known as the "automatic bench fine rule" and was first used after an exhibition game between the Minnesota Vikings and the San Diego Chargers in August of 1971, when 34 players from both teams were each fined $200 for going onto the field while a fight was in progress. Before the 1971 exhibition season was over, Rozelle had fined 106 players more than $20,000 pursuant to the bench-fine rule, and the Players Association filed an unfair labor practice charge with the National Labor Relations Board.

The theory behind the charge was that the fines constituted a reduction in wages, and as such were a subject for collective bargaining. The League had not bargained about the adoption of the rule, but instead had adopted it unilaterally. In so doing, the Association contended, the League committed an unfair labor practice. In its charge, the Players Association asked that the Board not only order the League to bargain about the bench-fine rule, but also asked for an order requiring the League to rescind the rule and repay the players already fined, on the grounds the rule was adopted without the required bargaining.

The NFL argued that the fines were imposed by Commissioner Rozelle pursuant to authority granted him by the NFL Constitution and By-Laws to discipline players guilty of conduct detrimental to the League.[1]

The Administrative Law Judge ruled in favor of the Players Association, finding that the fines were imposed pursuant to the bench-fine rule unilaterally adopted by the League, and not pursuant to the Commissioner's authority

[1] NFL Constitution & By-Laws, Article 8.13(A).

to penalize conduct detrimental to the League.[2] The Board, however, disagreed with the Judge. The Board stated that since the Commissioner had the authority to impose the fines without regard to the rule, nothing was changed by the League's adoption of the rule, and thus no unfair labor practice had been committed. The Board said that it "would exalt form over substance" to hold that the adoption of the rule constituted a change in the terms of the players' employment, because the Commissioner could have imposed fines without it.[3]

The Players Association then appealed the Board's decision to the United States Court of Appeals, arguing that the Commissioner could have imposed fines without the rule only *after* giving each of the 106 players notice and a hearing.[4] He gave no notices and held no hearings, and thus either exceeded his authority under the NFL Constitution and By-Laws or acted pursuant to a rule adopted without regard for the required collective bargaining.

Ultimately, the Court of Appeals agreed with the Players Association. It held that by unilaterally promulgating and implementing the automatic bench-fine rule, without prior negotiations with the Players Association, the NFL had engaged in an unfair labor practice.[5] The Court therefore ordered the National Labor Relations Board to adopt an appropriate remedy. The Board thereupon ordered the

---

[2] National Football League Management Council & National Football League Players Association, 203 N.L.R.B. No. 165, 83 L.R.R.M. 1203, 1204 (1973).

[3] *Id.* at 1205.

[4] Article 8.13(A) of the NFL Constitution and By-Laws provides that the Commissioner may impose discipline "after notice and hearing."

[5] National Football League Players Association v. National Labor Relations Board, 1974 CCH Labor Cases ¶ 10,284 (8th Cir. 1974).

NFL to rescind the rule and to refund all of the fines that had been collected, with interest at six percent.[6]

§7.4 The Federal Sports Agency proposal

Some measure of disciplinary authority is necessary to maintain the integrity of sports—in fact and in appearance—and its overall image and popularity. However, as many of the cases discussed in this chapter indicate, authority is subject to abuse. To date, players have sought to remedy that abuse in courts of law far more frequently than elsewhere. Often they have been successful, but not always. Courts are still struggling to adapt traditional concepts of commercial and constitutional law to the sometimes unique requirements of professional sports. Both players and team and league officials have been heard to complain that courts are ill-equipped to resolve their special problems. As a result, many have searched for alternative remedies.

In an article published in the *Georgetown Law Journal* in 1972, entitled "Discipline in Professional Sports: The Need for Player Protection,"[1] an editor sympathetic with professional athletes recommended a legislative approach to their problems. However, as the editor himself pointed out, the only bills Congress has been inclined to approve would actually strengthen the authority of teams and leagues to discipline players, rather than counterbalance their existing authority, already judged excessive by the editor.[2] Furthermore, even legislation confining disciplinary authority more tightly than existing laws could be enforced only in court, with all of the delays and expenses that already make litigation a course of very last resort.

[6] L.A. Times, Feb. 6, 1975, Part III.

[1] 60 Georgetown L.J. 771 (1972).

[2] See §§ 1.2(c)(1) and 1.2(c)(5), *supra*.

Several people have considered establishing a Federal Sports Agency similar to such presently existing administrative agencies as the Federal Communications Commission and the Interstate Commerce Commission. In fact, a bill was introduced in the Senate during the 92nd Congress which would have created a sports agency within the Department of Commerce. Reactions to sports agency proposals have been mixed. Senator Sam Ervin, perhaps the foremost legislator-champion of the journeyman athlete, was opposed to it.[3] The *Georgetown Law Journal* favored it.[4]

While the pros and cons of such an agency could be discussed over several pages, in the last analysis, it would certainly be no panacea for the athlete. Experience is evidence enough of that, for in the State of New York, boxing is already administered by a government commission. And Muhammad Ali had to go to court to get protection from it.[5] Even after the New York State Athletic Commission was enjoined from violating Ali's constitutional right to equal protection of the law, the Commission, in disregard of Ali's constitutional right to due process of law, fined Ali and Joe Frazier $5000 each for shoving one another during the taping of a television show preceding their January 1974 match. None of the Commissioners were present at the taping; none of them viewed the tape before assessing the fine; and no hearing was held. They based their action on hearsay and newspaper stories only.[6]

[3] Statement of Senator Sam J. Ervin, Jr., before the Senate Commerce Committee, on S.3445, A Bill to Create A Federal Sports Commission, reprinted in Hearings on H.R. 1206 before the Antitrust Subcomm. of the House Comm. on the Judiciary, 92d Cong., 2d Sess. 239-243 (1972).

[4] Comment, *supra* note 1, at 796-798.

[5] See § 7.3(c), *supra*.

[6] L.A. Times, Jan. 26, 1974, Part III.

Thus, it is clear that the quality of justice depends more on the quality of judges than on any other single factor.

Recently, the development of players associations into full-fledged labor unions has opened new avenues for remedying abuse of disciplinary powers. The players associations' principal power is to seek to limit the authority of teams and leagues through collective bargaining.

Finally, a counter-weight in basketball and hockey is the existence of independent competing leagues. If a player has someplace else to go, there is a limit to the discipline that can—as a practical matter—be imposed upon him.

Chapter 8

BUYING AND MOVING TEAM FRANCHISES

§8.1 League rules: their purpose and potential for abuse

In each of the professional team sports leagues, the creation of a new franchise, the sale of an existing one, and its transfer from one city to another, require approval of the owners of the other teams in the league.[1] Generally speaking, the affirmative vote of three-quarters of the team owners is necessary for any of these things (though ABA and WHA teams may be sold with the approval of only a majority of the other owners). Rules requiring approval for the creation, sale or transfer of franchises are designed to protect the financial stability and integrity of the leagues. However, because the rules do not contain any criteria for approval or disapproval, they may be subject to abuse.

For example, in 1953, the American League voted twice—in votes that were six months apart—not to permit maverick owner Bill Veeck to move his St. Louis team to Baltimore. After the second negative vote, Veeck immediately sold the team, and two days later the League unanimously voted to permit the new owner to make the shift.[2] In 1964, the American League also voted not to permit Charles Finley to move his Kansas City franchise to Louisville, though four years later—after a reported threat by

[1] See, e.g., NFL Constitution and By-Laws, Articles 3.3(C) and 3.5(b); NHL Constitution, Articles 3.3 and 3.5; WHA By-Laws, §§ 4.2 and 4.6; NBA Constitution, Articles 6 and 7; ABA By-Laws, Article VII §§ 1 and 6.

[2] Comment, The Super Bowl and the Sherman Act: Professional Team Sports and the Antitrust Laws, 81 Harvard L.Rev. 418, 429 fn. 59 (1967).

Finley that he would file an antitrust suit—the other owners did permit him to move to Oakland.[3]

Other sports have taken similarly questionable actions. In connection with the 1967 expansion of the National Hockey League, a franchise was awarded to St. Louis even though there had been no applicants from that city, and applicants from other cities had been rejected. This was done, it has been said, as a favor to the man who owned the St. Louis hockey arena, James Norris, who also happened to be an owner of the National Hockey League's Chicago Black Hawks.[4]

The sale of the Chicago Bulls of the National Basketball Association in 1972 was accompanied by an interesting set of approval votes. The team was originally sold to Marvin Fishman for some $5 million. The sale, however, was not approved by the NBA Board of Governors. The reported reason for the disapproval was that Arthur Wirtz, the owner of Chicago Stadium and an owner of the NHL Chicago Black Hawks, had urged his National Hockey League friends, who also owned NBA franchises, to vote against Fishman because Wirtz himself wanted to buy the Bulls. After the sale to Fishman had been disapproved, the Bulls were sold to Wirtz—for $3.3 million—and the sale was approved.[5]

The state of the law on the creation, sale and transfer of sports franchises is not as settled as that in other areas. Purchasers who have been "disapproved" have filed law-

[3] *Id.*

[4] *Id.* at 427 fn. 47.

[5] Logan, Bulls in N.B.A. China Shop Today, Chicago Tribune, Aug. 10, 1972; Logan, NBA Finally Approves Sale of Bulls, Chicago Tribune, Aug. 11, 1972, both reprinted in Hearings on H.R. 1206, et al., before the Antitrust Subcomm. of the House Comm. on the Judiciary, 92d Cong., 2d Sess. 312-314 (1972).

suits in the past, and in at least one case a preliminary ruling was issued suggesting that such purchasers do have some rights.

§8.2 Owner vs. league issues

§8.2(a) Buyer approval requirement

In the mid-1950's, the Washington Professional Basketball Corporation, Inc., was organized for the purpose of owning and operating a major league basketball team in the District of Columbia. In late 1954 or early 1955, the company entered into negotiations with the Receiver for the Baltimore Bullets, Inc.—which had suspended operations in November, 1954—to purchase its NBA franchise, player contracts and other assets. Sufficient agreement was reached that the proposed purchase was submitted to the NBA for approval. Approval was denied, and Washington Professional Basketball Corporation filed an antitrust suit against the league, alleging a conspiracy to exclude it from the NBA and to obtain the services of the Bullets' players for other NBA members.

The NBA claimed that it had disapproved the proposed purchase because the Washington Professional Basketball Corporation indicated it intended to raise needed money by selling bonds which would thereafter require the team to spend $12,000 per year for payment of interest and repayment of principal. The NBA claimed that the $12,000 per annum bond obligation was too likely to undermine the team's financial stability to warrant approval of the purchase.

In an opinion denying an NBA motion to dismiss, the court stated that one of the issues to be determined at trial was whether the NBA's disapproval because of the bond financing was reasonable and made in good faith, or really designed to monopolize professional basketball.[1] The implication of the short and somewhat cryptic decision was that in the event the evidence showed that the purchase had been disapproved because the defendants intended to monopolize basketball, then the Washington Professional Basketball Corporation would be entitled to an injunction requiring the NBA to approve its purchase of the Bullets' franchise, player contracts and other assets. (The lawsuit was apparently lost or settled, however, because the District of Columbia did not thereafter acquire an NBA team. The present Baltimore Bullets team began life as the Chicago Packers in a 1962 expansion, and was transferred to Baltimore in 1964).[2]

Recently, a league's rejection of franchise purchasers was considered more fully in another case involving the National Basketball Association, *Levin* v. *NBA*.[3] Irving Levin and Harold Lipton agreed to buy the Boston Celtics in 1972. Their application for the league's approval of the purchase was denied, however, by a vote of 13 to 2. In the antitrust suit they filed thereafter, Levin and Lipton asserted that they had been rejected because of their friendship and business associations with Sam Schulman, owner of the Seattle Supersonics. Levin testified that NBA Commissioner Walter Kennedy told him that Schulman was "a pain in the neck to the league" and that the owners who had voted against the purchase were "obviously worried" that if Levin and Lipton were "also owners" they

---

[1] Washington Professional Basketball Corp. v. National Basketball Association, 147 F.Supp. 154 (S.D.N.Y. 1956).

[2] Hearings on S.2373 before the Subcomm. on Antitrust and Monopoly of the Senate Comm. on the Judiciary, 92d Cong., 1st Sess. 206 (1971).

[3] 385 F.Supp. 149 (S.D.N.Y. 1974).

would "side with Sam Schulman in all matters in the future and cause the league more trouble than they now have with Sam as it is."[4]

Levin also testified that the president of the Phoenix Suns told him that Schulman was a "renegade," a "rebel," a "troublemaker," and a "craw in the throat" of other NBA owners. "He just doesn't play their game," the Suns' president allegedly said, "and they were obviously worried" that Levin and Lipton would "be siding with him on any matters that come up before the NBA."[5]

The NBA, on the other hand, claimed that Levin and Lipton had been rejected because their business associations with Schulman violated the conflict-of-interest provision of the NBA Constitution, which prohibits members from exercising control, directly or indirectly, over any other member. The facts in support of this contention were that Levin and Lipton were shareholders and officers of the corporation which owned and operated the Supersonics; Levin, Lipton and Schulman were at one time shareholders, officers and directors of National General Corporation; the three had made many investments together; Levin and Schulman were among the principal owners of the San Diego Chargers of the National Football League; and Lipton had been Schulman's personal attorney for a number of years and on occasion had acted as counsel to Levin as well.[6]

In granting the NBA's motion for summary judgment dismissing the case, Judge Owens of the Southern District of New York found that "no matter which reason one credits for the rejection, it was not an anti-competitive

[4] *Id.* at 150-151.
[5] *Id.* at 151.
[6] *Id.* at 151 fn. 1.

reason" nor did it have "an anti-competitive effect." [7] Where the action under attack "has neither anti-competitive intent nor effect, that conduct is not violative of the antitrust laws," he held.[8]

The opinion makes no reference to the *Baltimore Bullets* case.[9] However, the analogy between the NBA's rejection of Levin and Lipton as members and its rejection of Spencer Haywood as a player is so strong that the *Haywood* case[10] had to be dealt with in some fashion. It was covered in a footnote.

> "In reaching this conclusion I have considered and reject the applicability to this case of the holding of Denver Rockets v. All-Pro Management, Inc. . . . There, a by-law of the National Basketball Association which prohibited a qualified player from negotiating with any team until four years after his high school class graduation was declared a 'per se' violation as a 'group boycott'. The distinguishing difference, in my opinion, is that the limiting by-law attacked in *Denver Rockets* prevented a player from entering and *competing* with other players in the *players'* market, whereas in this case the plaintiffs wanted to become partners with, *not competitors of* those who excluded them . . ." [11]

With all due respect, the distinction thus drawn between "the players' market" and the market of NBA "partners" is not a relevant distinction. It compares apples to

[7] *Id.* at 152.

[8] *Id.*

[9] Washington Professional Basketball Corp. v. National Basketball Association, *supra* note 1.

[10] Denver Rockets v. All-Pro Management, Inc., 325 F.Supp. 1049 (C.D. Cal. 1971), discussed in § 7.3(e)(2)(A), *supra.*

[11] 385 F.Supp. at 152, fn. 6.

oranges. The "players' market" does not consist of players who already are members of NBA teams; the players' market consists of non-NBA players who compete with one another for employment by NBA teams. It was that market from which Haywood had been arbitrarily excluded. By analogy, the "owners' market" does not consist of those who already are members of the NBA. Rather, it consists of those who are competing with one another to become NBA members. Levin and Lipton had engaged in that competition with other non-members, and had made the most attractive offer to the owners of the Celtics. By eliminating one of the competitors, Levin and Lipton, the NBA damaged competition in the "owners' market"—just as it had previously damaged competition in the players' market by eliminating one of the competitors, Spencer Haywood.

Moreover, as Judge Ferguson explained in *Haywood,* damage to competition in the relevant market is only one of three separate injuries resulting from group boycotts. The other two are that "the victim of the boycott is injured by being excluded from the market he seeks to enter,"[12] and "by pooling their economic power, the individual members of the NBA have, in effect, established their own private government."[13] Judge Owens, in *Levin,* apparently rejected these injuries as the basis for antitrust liability, stating that "The law is well established that it is competition, and not individual competitors, that is protected by the anti-trust laws."[14] How "well settled" that principle may be is debatable; for it *is* well settled that

[12] Denver Rockets v. All-Pro Management, Inc., *supra* note 10, at 1061.

[13] *Id.*

[14] 385 F.Supp. at 152.

in group boycott cases the actual effect of the boycott, or its lack of actual effect, on competition is irrelevant.[15]

The footnote in *Levin,* quoted above, continues,

> "Further, to the extent *Denver Rockets* may be viewed as applying the *per se* rule in the absence of anti-competitive purpose, the decision, which was not appealed, is not in accord with the law in its own Circuit." [16]

Again with all due respect, the applicability of the *per se* rule depends upon the *practice* involved, and not the defendant's purpose. It is the law in the Circuit where *Denver Rockets* was decided, and throughout the country because the Supreme Court has so held, that group boycotts are illegal *per se,* without regard to their purpose and even in the absence of anti-competitive purpose.[17]

All of this is not to say that the result in *Levin* was *necessarily* incorrect. Though the NBA's disapproval of the Celtics' purchase by Levin and Lipton constituted a boycott, and though such a boycott is usually illegal *per se,* there is an exception to the *per se* doctrine known as the "*Silver* exception." [18] As noted in an earlier chapter, it appears that the NBA may qualify for the *Silver* exception.[19] The *Levin* decision indicates that Levin and Lipton demanded and were granted a personal hearing before the Board of Governors of the NBA before the final vote against them was taken. It therefore appears that the

[15] Klor's, Inc. v. Broadway-Hale Stores, Inc., 359 U.S. 207 (1959), discussed in § 7.3(e)(2)(A)(iii), *supra.*

[16] 385 F.Supp. at 152, fn. 6.

[17] Fashion Originators' Guild v. F.T.C., 312 U.S. 457 (1941), discussed in § 7.3(e)(2)(A)(iii), *supra.*

[18] See § 7.3(e)(2)(A)(iv), *supra.*

[19] *Id.*

procedural safeguard requirement, missing in *Haywood,* may have been satisfied in the *Levin* case.

If the *Silver* exception does apply, then Levin's and Lipton's exclusion from the NBA would be evaluated under the "rule of reason." The conflict-of-interest provision in the NBA Constitution seems reasonable. Its purpose is to preserve the public's confidence that there is intense competition in the league among the teams operated by its members. However, in order to determine whether or not the NBA applied this reasonable rule in order to achieve its acceptable goals, one would have to know why, in reality, Levin and Lipton were rejected. If, as Levin and Lipton contended, they had been rejected in order to prevent them from voting with Schulman on matters of league policy, their rejection would not have been pursuant to the conflict-of-interest provision, and therefore it would have been in violation of the antitrust laws.

(After losing the case, Levin and Lipton sold the Celtics to Robert Schmertz. A few months later, Levin also sold business interests he owned in common with Schulman, and therefore felt the NBA conflict-of-interest rule would no longer bar him. So in January of 1975, Levin repurchased a half interest in the Celtics from Schmertz; and this time he was approved. When Schmertz died the following July, his estate sold Levin the other half as well.)

Interestingly, the editors of the *Harvard Law Review* have taken an extreme stance against league rules requiring approval of proposed franchise sales. In a widely cited article entitled "The Super Bowl and the Sherman Act: Professional Team Sports and the Antitrust Laws," they acknowledged that the requirement for league approval

> ". . . could be defended as protecting the integrity of the sport by preventing gambling interests from ac-

quiring teams, and by guarding against other forms of conflict of interest. In addition, supervision of sales by the other teams might insure that the new owner had finances strong enough to support a competitive team and to enable him to look to the long run interest of the sport." [20]

However, they added,

"Many of the legitimate controls over transfer of ownership—no gamblers, no owners of other teams, or underfinanced buyers—could be secured by league rule, enforceable by injunction, without subjecting every sale to general review by the other owners. Restraints on leaving any business tend to discourage entry, and experience in sports suggests that the sale restrictions are easily subject to abuse, for the power has been used to punish mavericks in a league and to interfere with the business decisions of potential buyers. The tenuousness of the alleged legitimate purposes, the availability of alternatives, the serious restrictive effects on entry, and the possibility of abuse all suggest that these restraints on sale are not sufficiently justified by the peculiarities of the industry to survive antitrust challenge." [21]

§8.2(b) Move approval requirement

In the article cited above,[1] the editors of the *Harvard Law Review* also concluded that rules "which restrict an owner's ability to shift his franchise—at least to a new

[20] 81 Harvard L.Rev. 418, 428 (1967).

[21] *Id.* at 428-429.

[1] Comment, The Super Bowl and the Sherman Act: Professional Team Sports and the Antitrust Laws, 81 Harvard L.Rev. 418 (1967).

territory—should be held illegal."[2] This was so, in the editors' view, because,

> "Territorial restraints are traditionally considered per se illegal, for the division of markets necessarily has the effect of eliminating competition. There seems to be no reason why these restraints are particularly justified in the sports context, at least when a team is moving into virgin territory."[3]

This issue was first considered judicially in 1974, after the National Hockey League Board of Governors voted not to permit the owner of the San Francisco Seals to move the team to Vancouver, British Columbia. In response to that denial, the Seals' owner filed an antitrust action against the League, alleging that the denial constituted both a restraint of trade in violation of section 1 of the Sherman Act[4] and an attempted monopolization in violation of section 2 of the Act.[5]

In support of its section 1 restraint of trade argument, the Seals relied upon the principle that the allocation of exclusive territories generally constitutes a *per se* violation of the Sherman Act.[6] The court, however, found that the cases so holding were

> ". . . not applicable here for they all deal with combinations of independent business enterprises competing economically with each other and with other businesses not included in the combination . . . In the case before us the parties are not economic com-

---

[2] *Id.* at 430.
[3] *Id.* at 429.
[4] 15 U.S.C. § 1.
[5] 15 U.S.C. § 2.
[6] See § 7.3(e)(A)(iii), *supra.*

> petitors, and the territorial restraints of which the plaintiff [the Seals' owner] complains have no effect upon trade or commerce in this relevant market."[7]

While it is true that the Seals and the NHL were not economic competitors—nor were the Seals and other NHL teams—the court's analysis of this issue makes it appear simpler than it really is. NHL teams do not compete with one another economically only because each is situated far enough from the others so that as a practical matter hockey fans can patronize only one. If, however, another NHL team had existed in Vancouver, or in Seattle, then the potential for economic competition between teams would have existed, and the court would not have been able to cast aside so easily the cases which it found "not applicable."

The irony of the *Seals* case is that precisely because there was no NHL team in or near Vancouver, the NHL's refusal to permit the Seals to move there seems more unreasonable than had another team been there. Even the editors of the *Harvard Law Review* noted that "Control of movement is somewhat more justified in the case of a team wishing to move into a city already occupied by another team, since the incumbent team might be sufficiently weakened by the competition to weaken the entire league."[8] Since the cases found "not applicable" would have been applicable had there been a team in or near Vancouver, and since it would have been more reasonable for the NHL to have prohibited the move in that case, it seems incongruous that a League decision which might well have been illegal under reasonable circumstances (because territorial restrictions are

[7] San Francisco Seals, Ltd. v. National Hockey League, 379 F.Supp. 966, 970 (C.D. Cal. 1974).

[8] Comment, *supra* note 1, at 429.

usually illegal *per se*) was found to be legal under unreasonable ones.

The apparent reason for the NHL's obstinate refusal to permit the move was the basis for the Seals' section 2 monopolization claim. The Seals alleged that they had been denied permission to move, because the NHL and its members were engaged in a conspiracy to monopolize the professional hockey industry; and that in furtherance of that conspiracy they wanted to prevent any rival league from placing a franchise in the San Francisco Bay Area—a prestigious and traditionally big league territory. The court did not consider whether this allegation might have been true as a matter of fact, because it held that even were it true, the Seals did not have standing to assert such a claim.

"Standing" is a legal concept that serves to reduce the number and kinds of people who are permitted to bring lawsuits of all kinds, including antitrust lawsuits. In the antitrust field, section 4 of the Clayton Act provides that,

> "Any person who shall be injured in his business or property by reason of anything forbidden in the antitrust laws may sue therefor in any district court of the United States . . ." [9]

The Seals' owner was a person whose business was injured by reason of the NHL's attempt to monopolize hockey, because, assuming the allegations were true, the Seals had been selected by the league and its members to be the sacrificial guardian against rivals establishing a foothold in the San Francisco Bay Area.

Nevertheless, although the Seals' owner satisfied the requirements of section 4 of the Clayton Act, "standing"

---

[9] 15 U.S.C. § 15.

requires more. Courts have interpreted section 4 to mean that a person is injured "by reason of" an antitrust violation only if that person is within the "target area" of the economy which is endangered by the violation.[10] In the *Seals* case, the "target" of the NHL's alleged conspiracy to monopolize was a rival league. Since the Seals were "not a rival hockey league," the NHL's "alleged actions to prevent the formation of rival leagues were not aimed at it." [11]

If the *Seals* case is good law, then a team owner who is denied permission to move can do one of two things: he can stay put, or he can withdraw from the league by selling his team or surrendering his franchise. In either event, the league's denial of move approval will have diminished or obliterated the value of the franchise. If the antitrust laws do not afford a remedy for the damage suffered as a result —because team owners within a league are "partners" rather than "competitors"—some other law should. There is no reason why the owner of one team should be forced to bear special burdens for the benefit of other team owners, particularly if those burdens are the result of illegal action in which the burdened owner is unwilling to participate. Of course in the *Seals* case, the Seals' willingness to participate was apparently disputed. The court found that,

> "Actually, plaintiff does not claim to have been injured by the monopolistic practices of the National Hockey League as such, but that the monopolistic protection which affiliation with the National Hockey League can afford is being denied it at Vancouver." [12]

---

[10] In re Multidistrict Vehicle Air Pollution, 481 F.2d 122, 126, 129-130 (9th Cir. 1973).

[11] 379 F.Supp. at 972.

[12] *Id.*

Nevertheless, assuming a team owner has been required to assume special burdens by his "partners" in the league, and assuming the antitrust laws afford him no remedy, then it may well be that a remedy can be found in the law concerning the fiduciary duties owed by partners to one another. For partners are required by law to act fairly and in good faith with one another in connection with the business of the partnership.[13]

§8.3 Home city vs. team issues

§8.3(a) Antitrust principles: the Milwaukee Braves case

Although the *Harvard Law Review* article discussed above[1] concluded that rules restricting an owner's ability to move his team to a new territory should be held illegal, it considered such rules to violate the antitrust laws only when used to prevent an owner from moving his team. Thus, the article's conclusion would benefit only owners whose desires to move were thwarted and "perhaps the city to which the aborted move would have been made." [2] Where a league approves a team's decision to move, the article had little solace for the abandoned city.

> "In that case it is hard to see how any restraint of trade is involved. Arguments that professional sports teams are somehow municipal enterprises or public utilities which must continue to provide service as long as 'adequately supported' . . . advance a claim to

[13] 60 American Jurisprudence 2d, Partnership § 123.

[1] Comment, The Super Bowl and the Sherman Act: Professional Team Sports and the Antitrust Laws, 81 Harvard L.Rev. 418 (1967).

[2] *Id.* at 430 fn. 61.

interests beyond the scope of the antitrust laws' protection." [3]

Not all of those who have considered the question agree with this conclusion. In a case involving the transfer of the Milwaukee Braves to Atlanta in 1966, a Wisconsin trial court held that the move did violate the antitrust laws.[4] His order requiring the Braves to return to Milwaukee, unless the National League issued the city an expansion franchise to replace them, was reversed by the Wisconsin Supreme Court (with three justices dissenting) only because it held the baseball exemption applied.[5] Therefore, the case remains significant with respect to football, hockey and basketball, which are not exempt; and it stands for the proposition that a team move may indeed violate the antitrust laws under certain circumstances.

The Braves had moved to Milwaukee from Boston (which had been a two-team town) in 1953, and for the next twelve seasons they enjoyed an annual average attendance of over one and a half million—31% higher than the average National League attendance, 52% higher than the average American League attendance, and second only to the Los Angeles Dodgers in major league baseball. Nevertheless, in the fall of 1964, the Braves sought and received National League approval to move to Atlanta, Georgia. Originally, the Braves had intended to begin play in Atlanta at the outset of the 1965 season. However, their lease on Milwaukee County Stadium did not expire until December 31, 1965, and when the County of Milwaukee filed suit to

---

[3] *Id.*

[4] Wisconsin v. Milwaukee Braves, Inc., 1966 CCH Trade Cases ¶ 71,738 (Wisc. Cir. Ct. 1966).

[5] Wisconsin v. Milwaukee Braves, Inc., 144 N.W.2d 1 (Wisc. S.Ct. 1966).

require the Braves to play there for the balance of their lease, the National League authorized the transfer to Atlanta effective with the 1966 season.

Milwaukee was not satisfied that its lease was to be honored, however, for it felt it should not be abandoned at all. And so in August of 1965 the State of Wisconsin filed an antitrust action against the Braves, the National League, and each of its teams, alleging that the plan to move the team away from Milwaukee, without making provision for a replacement franchise for the city, constituted a combination, conspiracy and agreement to illegally restrain trade and monopolize baseball. The particular antitrust statute allegedly violated was not the Sherman Act, but rather was Wisconsin's own state antitrust act. This was done in an effort to get around the decisions of the United States Supreme Court in *Federal Baseball* v. *National League* and *Toolson* v. *New York Yankees*,[6] the theory being that those cases held baseball exempt only from federal—but not necessarily state—law. Wisconsin's state antitrust statute is virtually identical to the Sherman Act, except that it applies only to restraints of trade and monopolies within Wisconsin.

Shortly after suit was filed, the defendants moved for a dismissal, arguing that baseball was exempt from state antitrust statutes as well as the Sherman Act. Though they were eventually successful on this ground in the Wisconsin Supreme Court, the trial judge who heard their motion originally, Judge Elmer W. Roller, denied it, holding that baseball was subject to state antitrust statutes notwithstanding its exemption from federal control.[7] There-

[6] See §§ 1.1(a) and 1.1(d), *supra*.

[7] Wisconsin v. Milwaukee Braves, Inc., 1966 CCH Trade Cases ¶71,666 (Wisc. Cir. Ct. 1966).

after, a lengthy trial was conducted, during which the economic aspects of franchise moves and league expansions were explored in detail.

In a "white paper" presented to the National League by the Braves' themselves, in support of their request for permission to move to Atlanta, it was estimated that during the eleven seasons between 1953 and 1963, over $50 million in out-of-town revenues were brought into Milwaukee by major league baseball. In addition, the Braves paid the county $2.8 million in stadium rent over those years and the county collected another $1.6 million in parking charges. The Braves' payroll over the period exceeded $17.6 million and the team purchased more than $5.5 million worth of food for resale in the stadium during games. On the basis of these figures, the Braves' own "white paper" stated that during the eleven years between 1953 and 1963, the Braves brought to Milwaukee over $77.5 million in income which the city would not otherwise have realized. Robert R. Nathan, an economist retained by the city as an expert witness on its behalf, concluded that the Braves' estimate of their value to the city was too modest. He testified that the team was worth some $18 million annually to Milwaukee.

A book authored by former Baseball Commissioner Ford Frick, entitled "Baseball—An Institution," lent support to Nathan's figures. In a chapter entitled "Baseball As A Factor In The Economy," Commissioner Frick wrote that professional baseball is an important factor in the economy of major league cities "to an extent not usually realized," and that "although the immediate effect of a baseball club's location in a community can pretty well be measured in dollars, the intangible benefits may be of even greater importance through the years." [8] The book also asserted that the presence of a major league baseball team adds to a city's qualifications as a convention site and as an attraction to new industry and investment. In a chapter entitled "Major League Baseball as a Member of the Community," Frick wrote, "No business compares with baseball as a generator of other business in the community in which a major league club is located, according to surveys made by the Chambers of Commerce of many cities." [9]

Given this evidence, Judge Roller had no trouble in concluding that if the Braves did leave Milwaukee, without an expansion franchise being awarded to replace it, Milwaukee would indeed suffer substantial economic injury.

Regardless of the reasons the Braves had for wanting to move to Atlanta, both the County of Milwaukee and a group of private Milwaukee residents felt that the city could and in fact was supporting major league baseball at a profit. Thus, when word of the proposed move became more than rumor, both the County and the group applied to the National League for an expansion franchise. The private group in particular did a great deal of preparatory work in support of its application. First it formed a corporation to own and operate a team, the Milwaukee Brewers Baseball Club, Inc. Then it prepared a prospectus projecting the financial operation of an expansion team based on the actual experiences of the 1960 and 1961 expansion teams and on information concerning the Braves' own operations in Milwaukee over several years. With this prospectus, the corporation was able to obtain the agreement of ten men to invest $150,000 each, and loan com-

[8] 1966 CCH Trade Cases ¶ 71,738 at 82,375-82,376.

[9] *Id.* at 82,376.

mitments from the First Wisconsin National Bank of Milwaukee and from two concession companies. In all, the corporation expected to begin operations—if a franchise were awarded—with capital of $3 million, the same amount with which the California Angels had begun six years earlier.

Despite the careful planning that went into them, however, the applications of the County and the Milwaukee Brewers were both rejected by the National League. "It is the considered judgment of the League" it said in a brief announcement, "that none of the applicants would be able to operate a franchise in 1966 and that League expansion in 1966 is not feasible." [10] The principal reason asserted by several baseball owners whose testimony was heard at the subsequent trial was a shortage of major league quality players.

On the other hand, the testimony of former Commissioner Frick, Bill Veeck (past owner of a number of major league teams), Mr. Bragan (the Braves' field manager), Warren Giles (then President of the National League), and Walter O'Malley (owner of the Los Angeles Dodgers), satisfied Judge Roller that there were sufficient baseball players to stock a team in Milwaukee. Bragan, for example, conceded in his testimony that he had been accurately quoted in two separate newspaper articles, one published in the Milwaukee Journal and the other in the Milwaukee Sentinel, in which he outlined plans for expansion, admitted there were an adequate number of quality players, and named particular players who had made the major leagues precisely because of the 1960 and 1961 expansions. "There's more than enough talent for

[10] *Id.* at 82,398.

expansion," he told the reporter for the Journal. "There are major league players playing minor league ball today. Where would Ron Hunt be if it wasn't for expansion? Or Jim Fregosi or Dean Chance and a lot of others? In the minors, that's where." [11]

Judge Roller also found that Organized Baseball had achieved a monopoly in the professional baseball business, by means of agreements among the teams in each league and between the leagues, and by means of the rules and regulations imposed upon each team and its players.

Having determined that Milwaukee would be injured if the Braves left and no team replaced them, that the National League could expand and provide Milwaukee with a new franchise if it desired to do so, and that Organized Baseball enjoyed a monopoly over professional baseball, it remained only to set forth the legal theories upon which a violation of the antitrust laws could be established. The theories offered by the State of Wisconsin, and accepted by Judge Roller, were these.

First, by refusing to issue Milwaukee a franchise to replace the departing Braves, the National League had engaged in a concerted refusal to deal with and group boycott of those Milwaukee interests who sought to enter the business of professional baseball.

Second, by refusing to issue Milwaukee a replacement franchise, the National League had intentionally protected and extended the professional baseball monopoly, and was thus committing an illegal act of monopolization.

Since the National League had not exercised reasonable controls over the movement of its teams and had not

---

[11] *Id.* at 82,400.

followed reasonable procedures in the issuance of new franchises, Judge Roller enjoined the Braves from playing their home games in any city or place other than Milwaukee County Stadium, Milwaukee, Wisconsin. He stayed his injunction, however, for several weeks so that the National League would have an opportunity to adopt an expansion plan and award Milwaukee an expansion franchise. Were that to be done, the Judge stated, he would not enjoin the Braves from leaving.

The ruling touched off a fury of legal activity. A federal District Court in Houston, Texas enjoined enforcement of Judge Roller's order; and a Georgia state court ordered the Braves to remain in Atlanta.[12] Finally, the Wisconsin Supreme Court resolved these conflicting rulings by overturning Judge Roller's injunction and ordering Wisconsin's case dismissed, on the grounds that Organized Baseball was exempt from state as well as federal antitrust statutes.[13]

Even if Judge Roller's decision states the law that would be applicable to football, basketball and hockey leagues, it does not mean that every franchise move must be accompanied by league expansion in order to be legal. As Howard Cosell has said, "There is no municipal obligation to support a bad product, but neither is there a law that says a businessman must go broke." [14] Judge Roller's decision was based, in large measure, on his finding that the Braves were not becoming insolvent in Milwaukee and that in fact the city was supporting the team quite handsomely.

---

[12] Brief for respondents in opposition to Petition for Certiorari, Flood v. Kuhn, 407 U.S. 258 (1972).

[13] Wisconsin v. Milwaukee Braves, Inc., *supra* note 5.

[14] H. Cosell, Cosell (Chicago: Playboy Press, 1973) at 93.

§8.3(b) Contract principles: the San Diego Padres case

The San Diego Padres began the 1974 baseball season under the new ownership of millionaire Ray Kroc, chairman of the board of McDonald's Corp., the hamburger franchise company noted for its "golden arches." The "hamburger king," as Kroc is occasionally referred to with affection, bought the National League team in January of 1974 from San Diego financier C. Arnholt Smith whose own financial empire was then in the process of crumbling. The sale was not unique. Professional sports teams of all kinds are routinely bought and sold like all other businesses. In fact, Smith himself had sold the Padres twice in the months preceding his deal with Kroc, once to grocery chain owner Joseph Danzansky of Washington, D.C., who intended to transfer the team to the nation's capital, and once to Marjorie Everett, board member and largest stockholder of Los Angeles' Hollywood Park racetrack.

What was unique about Kroc's purchase of the Padres is that it was made possible by lawsuits filed by the City of San Diego designed to prevent Smith, Danzansky or the National League from moving the franchise elsewhere. And it was the first time in sports history that a proposed and league-approved franchise shift had ever been blocked by legal action. Had it not been for the suits filed by San Diego, the Padres would have been the eleventh baseball club to move from one city to another since 1953, when the Braves began this modern "hopscotch" era by moving from Boston to Milwaukee.[1] What is even more remarkable about the success of the San Diego litigation is that it came on

[1] See, Quirk, An Economic Analysis of Team Movements in Professional Sports, 38 Law and Contemporary Problems 42, 48 (1973).

the heels of the similar but unsuccessful litigation filed by the State of Wisconsin when the Braves decided to move from Milwaukee to Atlanta.[2]

The story behind the events which preceded Kroc's purchase of the Padres begins in 1972. It was in that year that the second team to bear the name "Washington Senators" moved from the District of Columbia to a much smaller city in Texas, and called itself the "Texas Rangers." (The first "Washington Senators" left the capital in 1961 to become the "Minnesota Twins," and was replaced immediately with the expansion team that later became the Rangers.) For reasons both sound and curious, Washington's loss of the Senators threw a number of Congressmen into a dither matched only by the closing of a military base whose payroll is the life-blood of a multi-county area. A "D.C. Baseball Steering Committee" was formed immediately, chaired by Congressman B. F. Sisk and subscribed to by more than half the members of the House of Representatives.

Representatives of this Steering Committee met and corresponded with Commissioner Bowie Kuhn and members of Organized Baseball's "Washington Committee" throughout the latter part of 1971 and 1972 in an effort to obtain a new franchise for the capital. Among those participating in the meetings were Joseph Danzansky, a Washington area businessman who was interested in acquiring the District of Columbia franchise. As far as the Washington interests were concerned, either an existing or expansion team seemed to be acceptable. Expansion, however, was not part of Organized Baseball's plans in those years, nor

---

[2] Wisconsin v. Milwaukee Braves, Inc., 144 N.W.2d 1 (Wisc. S.Ct. 1966), discussed in § 8.3(a), *supra*.

were any teams then for sale. So the capital went without major league baseball in 1972 and 1973.

Then, as luck would have it, C. Arnholt Smith began having financial and legal problems and decided to sell the Padres. In May of 1973, he agreed to sell the team to Danzansky for $12 million in a transaction which was the product of "unrelenting pressure upon the baseball fathers," according to the Washington Post in an article that quoted Congressman Sisk as saying that Smith could have received even more money for the Padres from Toronto interests, but he and other members of the Steering Committee "had a hard commitment that Washington would get the first team available." [3]

Though the sale to Danzansky made people in Washington happy, it did little for the disposition of the city fathers in San Diego. Among other things, San Diego had built a $27 million stadium for the Padres when the team came into existence in a National League expansion in 1969. Though the stadium is also "home" to the NFL's San Diego Chargers and a local college football team, those two tenants alone would not have generated sufficient income to justify the stadium's expense. Therefore, San Diego took steps to assure itself a major league baseball tenant by entering into a twenty-year lease with the Padres which was not to end until the conclusion of the 1988 baseball season. When Smith sold the team to Danzansky, only five of the twenty years had passed. In short, it looked to San Diego as though the team was simply going to walk out on a fifteen year obligation; and if it did, the city would lose not only the rent the Padres would have paid for the next fifteen years, but also revenue from parking, concessions and field advertising. In addition, San Diego area

[3] Quoted in L.A. Times, June 30, 1973, Part III.

restaurants, hotels, taxicabs and other tourist oriented businesses would lose customers, and as a result the city would lose tax revenues. These were things San Diego was not going to tolerate if it didn't have to and so the city sued.

On June 15, 1973, the city filed an action in the California Superior Court against the National League, the Padres, Buzzy Bavasi (the Padres' president), C. Arnholt Smith, Joseph Danzansky, and Marvin Willig and Robert Schattner (Danzansky's two partners).[4] The complaint alleged that Smith's announced plans to sell the team to Danzansky and his partners constituted a breach of the twenty-year stadium lease; and that the National League and all of the individual defendants had induced the Padres to commit this breach. The complaint further alleged that San Diego would suffer substantial and irreparable harm if the Padres left the city. Therefore, it asked that an injunction be issued restraining all of the defendants from doing anything to transfer the team elsewhere.

On its face, the city's complaint seemed to have a great deal of merit. Its principal strength lay in the fact that the stadium lease not only gave the Padres the right and obligation to play in San Diego Stadium for twenty years, it also contained a provision by which the Padres expressly agreed to maintain their membership in the National League in good standing, to maintain and hold any and all rights and franchises to play baseball in the City and County of San Diego in accordance with National League rules, and not to do or suffer anything to be done which would cause such right and franchise to be lost or impaired or diminished in any respect or to be transferred to any other city

---

[4] San Diego v. National League of Professional Baseball Clubs, et al., Calif. Super. Ct., San Diego Cty. No. 343508.

or location.[5] In other words, when San Diego decided to build a $27 million stadium for the use of a major league baseball team, it was not ignorant of some seven or eight instances since 1953 in which teams had moved from one city to another; and San Diego required the Padres to promise expressly not to move for at least twenty years.

The transfer of the Padres to Washington, D.C. was not to take place until after the close of the 1973 season. Nevertheless, it was to take place as soon thereafter as possible and no later than January 1, 1974 in any event. Because the '73 season had already begun by the time San Diego learned of the proposed sale and filed its suit, it had to obtain an injunction virtually immediately, if it was to do so at all. Lawsuits usually require several months and often years to come to trial, and once the Padres were out of the city the damage would have been done. The law recognizes this possibility, and, in appropriate cases, provides for temporary relief while the parties are awaiting trial. Thus, the day San Diego filed its suit, it also obtained a temporary restraining order preventing the Padres' sale until such time as a hearing could be held on whether a preliminary injunction should be issued pending trial.

On July 10, 1973, Superior Court Judge Eli H. Levenson denied the city's request for a preliminary injunction. In doing so he said,

> "I am indeed mindful of the possible repercussions that might result from the decision of this Court either way.
>
> "I am particularly mindful of the attitudes and opinions of the people of San Diego who have expressed

---

[5] First Amended Complaint ¶ 11, San Diego v. National League, *supra* note 4.

themselves to me by way of correspondence. Some of that correspondence is rather difficult to answer. I might read one letter that came to me that is of interest. It is dated July 8th. It is written in pencil, and it came to me sealed with a covering letter by the father of this young man who promised his son that he would not look at the letter, so the father was unaware of what it contained. The letter reads:

'Dear Judge Levenson: I am eight years old, and I do not understand why Mr. Smith and other men do not keep their word and keep our San Diego Padres home. My dad has always told me a man's word is his bond, but today many people do not keep their word. Why?

'Please try to help keep our baseball team in town.

'Thank you.'

"And it's signed 'Mike.'

"The other correspondence is not quite as eloquent. It comes from older persons but it is of the same tenor." [6]

There were essentially two reasons Judge Levenson denied the city a preliminary injunction. California law, like that of many if not most jurisdictions, provides that the breach of a contract may not be enjoined unless a court could "specifically enforce" it, in other words, unless a court could order a defendant to comply with it.[7] A sizeable body of law categorizes those contracts performance of which courts can require, and others, performance of which courts cannot. Among those which courts cannot

[6] Transcript of Proceedings at 3-4, San Diego v. National League, *supra* note 4.

[7] California Code of Civil Procedure § 526.

specifically enforce are contracts which call for a succession of acts whose performance cannot be consummated in one transaction.[8] The reason usually given for this limitation is that courts do not like to become involved in continuous and protracted personal supervision of activities of a person or company.

Since the Padres' lease still had fifteen years to run, the team could not fulfill all of its obligations to the city in one transaction. Rather, Judge Levenson felt that he or some other judge would have to supervise the Padres' activities for the entire fifteen years; and this he did not think the law would permit him to do.

The city had analogized the stadium lease to player contracts used by professional sports leagues which courts have enforced on several occasions by enjoining players for a year from performing for any other team.[9] The analogy, however, is not entirely helpful, because contracts for personal services are unique. They are not "specifically enforceable," and yet the law does authorize enjoining their breach under certain circumstances. Nor did Judge Levenson consider the analogy to be authority for his issuing an injunction against moving the Padres. Here the second reason came into play. An injunction is considered an extraordinary remedy, available in breach of contract cases only when the amount of monetary damages suffered because of breach cannot be ascertained, or when money damages, no matter what the amount, could not adequately compensate the injured party.[10] In this case, Judge Levenson considered the stadium lease to be a con-

[8] Thayer Plymouth Center, Inc. v. Chrysler Motors Corp., 255 Cal. App. 2d 300, 303-304 (1967); Long Beach Drug Co. v. United Drug Co., 13 Cal.2d 158, 171 (1939).

[9] See § 2.3, *supra.*

[10] 42 American Jurisprudence 2d, Injunctions §§ 48 and 49.

tract calling for the payment of money. Further, he felt that the amount of the city's damages was ascertainable and that a judgment for that amount would be adequate relief.

However, Judge Levenson continued the temporary restraining order in effect for an additional ten days in order to give San Diego an opportunity to appeal. The city did in fact appeal. However, on July 19, 1973, the California Court of Appeal refused to overturn the denial, principally on the ground that courts may not enjoin the breach of a contract which requires a succession of acts.[11] Although the California Supreme Court agreed to extend the temporary restraining order still further to give it time to consider San Diego's petition for a hearing, on August 16, 1973 that Court ultimately refused to consider the case, and the restraint on the Padres expired of its own accord.

Thus, in mid-August of 1973, San Diego was confronted with what momentarily appeared to be a hopeless dilemma. Nothing prevented Smith from selling the Padres to Danzansky, and Danzansky from moving the team to Washington. The city had been told that it could sue the team for such rent as might be due over the fifteen year balance of the lease, plus other consequential damages, but that was of small comfort for a number of reasons. The lease provided that the Padres were to pay the city 8% of the gross revenue from ticket sales as rent, and there were figures for five years available to enable San Diego to calculate what might have been due in the future. Unfortunately, the Padres had finished last or next to last in the National League every one of those five years, and

[11] San Diego v. National League, Cal.Ct.App., 4th Dist., Div. 1, No. 12741 (1973), unpublished opinion.

therefore it had drawn small crowds. At some time during the course of the coming fifteen years, it could be expected that the team would do much better and thus draw more fans at the gate. But San Diego would have had a hard time proving the extent of future attendance increases, and therefore, how much rental income was really due it. Moreover, the city's loss of tax revenue because of the fall-off in tourism and related business would be even more difficult to compute and prove. Most important of all, San Diego was faced with the prospect of suing a possibly insolvent company for damages which would certainly run into the millions of dollars by anybody's calculations.

The insolvent-defendant problem arose because the Padres' player contracts, National League franchise and equipment, such as uniforms, bats, balls and gloves, were all owned by a corporation known as San Diego Padres, Inc. The stock in San Diego Padres, Inc. was owned by Smith, his daughter and Bavasi. Danzansky was not going to buy the stock, however; he was going to buy the corporation's assets, namely, the player contracts, franchise and equipment. Once Danzansky had done that, the San Diego Padres, Inc. would be out of business altogether, though it would have the purchase price in its bank account. So long as the money stayed in the bank account, the City of San Diego could levy upon it to satisfy any money judgment it might obtain. But the city had little reason to believe the money would stay in the bank long enough for it to do that. (In fact, when Smith finally sold the team to Ray Kroc, an Internal Revenue Service lien for back taxes allegedly owed by Smith almost had the effect of causing the proposed purchase to fall through;[12] and Bankers Life Insur-

[12] L.A. Times, Feb. 1, 1974, Part III.

ance Co. of Nebraska, which had a $1 million judgment against Smith arising out of non-baseball matters, actually obtained a temporary restraining order preventing his distribution of the proceeds of the Padres' sale to any of his creditors.[13])

Naturally, San Diego was not the first creditor to fear that the corporation which owed it money would not have sufficient assets available to satisfy a judgment by the time the trial was concluded. And the law does provide procedures by which such creditors may take immediate steps to assure the preservation of assets. One such procedure is attachment; in appropriate cases, a court order may be issued instructing a marshal or sheriff to take possession of a debtor's assets for safekeeping, pending conclusion of the lawsuit. Attachment is available only in those cases where the amount of damages sustained by the plaintiff is capable of exact determination based upon the terms of the contract itself.[14] Thus, although San Diego had earlier argued that its damages were so difficult to ascertain that only an injunction could protect it, it now had to argue that the damages it was about to sustain were sufficiently certain to warrant the issuance of a writ of attachment.

On August 30, 1974, San Diego filed an amended complaint in the California Superior Court alleging that by reason of the Padres' forthcoming move to Washington, the city would suffer $12 million in damages as a result of lost revenues over the fifteen year balance of the lease. Coincidently, $12 million was also the amount of money Danzansky had agreed to pay for the team. On August 31st, San Diego filed an application for a writ authorizing

[13] Wall Street Journal, March 22, 1974.

[14] California Code of Civil Procedure § 537.1.

the attachment of all of the Padres' player contracts, its National League franchise, all money then in the bank or due to it from others, office equipment and supplies, uniforms, bats, balls and gloves.

Had the attachment been issued, it would have been more valuable tactically than as an ultimate remedy. It would have frozen the team in place in San Diego until the conclusion of the trial a year or two thereafter, and that undoubtedly would have had the effect of cancelling the proposed purchase by Danzansky. Had the city obtained a $12 million judgment, it could then have had the sheriff or marshal auction off the attached assets to satisfy the judgment. Interestingly, however, if the assets were then purchased at auction by someone who wanted to keep the Padres in San Diego, the city would not have suffered any damages at all. Furthermore, according to its Constitution and By-Laws, the National League would still be entitled to approve or disapprove of the purchaser.

As it happened, the application for attachment was denied on December 19, 1973, on the grounds that the amount of damages suffered by the city was not known with sufficient precision. In so ruling, Judge Levenson stated that in denying the city's application,

> "I certainly do not place upon any conduct the stamp of approval because I, like other San Diegans, feel keenly the loss of this franchise, if it is in fact lost. I find it difficult to have to turn down a remedy which might have the effect of keeping that baseball club here, but under the law and under my duty I feel that I have no other recourse than to refuse the writ." [15]

[15] Reporter's Partial Transcript of Proceedings at 6-7, San Diego v. National League, *supra* note 4.

Between the time San Diego had applied for the writ of attachment in August, and the day it was denied in December, a number of significant events had occurred. Another potential buyer had entered the picture, namely Marjorie Everett, the largest shareholder and a member of the board of directors of the corporation that owns Hollywood Park racetrack in Los Angeles. Her interest was greeted with enthusiasm by San Diego, because she promised to keep the Padres there if the team were sold to her.

The National League was far less enthusiastic, however. Though the League's reservations were never publicly stated, it was widely speculated that she was considered unacceptable because of her involvement in a Chicago racetrack scandal that eventually led to the bribery conviction of former Illinois Governor Otto Kerner.[16] The prosecution had contended that Kerner had obtained stock in a track then owned by Mrs. Everett at reduced prices in exchange for a promise of more favorable racing dates. Mrs. Everett was never indicted and she had in fact testified for the prosecution. Furthermore, the California Horse Racing Board conducted a long investigation before issuing the license necessary for her to become a director of Hollywood Park.

Whatever its reasons, when the National League met in Houston on December 6, 1973 to consider the Padres matter, it did not choose to avoid its legal problems with San Diego by approving transfer of the franchise to Everett. Rather, it unanimously approved the team's sale to Danzansky and his partners—subject to certain conditions which were to have been met by December 21st. The most important condition was Danzansky's coming up with a satisfactory indemnity to protect the National

---

[16] L.A. Times, Dec. 7, 1973, Part III.

League and its teams from any liability that might arise out of lawsuits filed by the city.

The exact form and source of this indemnity quickly became a matter of public controversy itself. Danzansky had indicated that the indemnity would be provided, at least in part, by the District of Columbia, Congress, and the District of Columbia Armory Board, operator of Robert F. Kennedy Stadium where the team would have played. This indication was reportedly backed by communications to National League owners from Congressman Sisk's committee to the effect that the District of Columbia would indeed indemnify the League. It was also reported that a number of Congressmen, including Gerald Ford, had wired National League owners that they could expect their help with San Diego's lawsuits.[17] What that meant exactly was never made clear, though it appeared to some sportswriters that federal tax moneys might be made available to satisfy a judgment, should one be awarded San Diego against the National League.[18]

Although in retrospect it seems unlikely that such a proposal would have ever been approved by Congress, there would have been other ways to accomplish the same result by indirect and thus less obvious means. Two years before the Padres situation arose, when Congressman Sisk and members of his Steering Committee had had their first meeting with Bowie Kuhn and members of baseball's Washington Committee, Sisk had stated that he was considering legislation requiring the United States to take over Kennedy Stadium from the District of Columbia and requiring the United States to pay off the stadium bonds

---

[17] Markus, Congress' Role in Padres' Move an Outrage, L.A. Times, Dec. 11, 1973, Part III.

[18] *Id.*

which had been sold to finance its construction.[19] Since funds for the payment of bond interest and repayment of principal come from stadium rental and other operating revenues, such as parking, any leases entered into by the D.C. Armory Board must in fact generate income. On the other hand, if the bonds were paid off, the stadium could be given virtually rent-free to a baseball team. And if that team were the Padres, the money not used to pay rent would then be available to pay any judgment San Diego might obtain.

While some people accused members of Congress of offering federal funds to encourage the Padres' move to Washington, it seemed to others that some Congressmen had coerced the move with some not too subtle hints about Organized Baseball's desire to maintain its antitrust exemption. In the course of pretrial discovery, counsel for the City of San Diego examined a number of very interesting documents. Among them was a copy of a press release issued by Speaker of the House Carl Albert in November, 1971 which stated,

> "I have discussed with Representative B. F. Sisk his forthcoming trip to the Baseball Owners' Winter Meeting in company with Members of Congress and civic leaders of the District of Columbia and have assured him that I strongly support the objectives of his group.
>
> "There is such great concern regarding the failure of organized baseball to maintain a franchise in Washington that I have requested Congressman Sisk to convey to the baseball owners the views of Members of the

[19] Memorandum dated 12/15/71, at page 6, attached as Exhibit D to Affidavit of Robert J. Logan [Deputy City Attorney] in support of motion for preliminary injunction, San Diego v. National League of Professional Baseball Clubs, et al., U.S.D.C., S.D.Cal., No. 73-529-T.

House of Representatives, as well as my personal view, in this regard. I have also asked Congressman Sisk to report to me and the House of Representatives upon his return and I am very hopeful he will bring back some indication of a willingness on the part of the owners to restore a franchise to the Capital City.

"Many Members of the House have come to me urging an investigation of organized baseball and urging quick action on the proposals to remove the anti-trust exemption for organized sports. I feel the owners should know first-hand the attitude of the House and, therefore, have asked Mr. Sisk to undertake this mission." [20]

Following the 1971 baseball Winter Meeting, Congressman Sisk sent Commissioner Kuhn a letter which read,

"Dear Bowie:

"I just wanted to send a note to let you know how much I sincerely appreciate the cooperation shown by you, the two major league presidents, the baseball owners and your staff as a result of the Washington delegation's request to meet with you at your recent meetings in Phoenix.

"I want to again stress that not only am I interested in returning major league baseball to the Nation's Capital but I am also interested in being of assistance to major league baseball with its overall problems. Hopefully the Congressional group that we have established can be a further vehicle in establishing the necessary communication between major league baseball and the Congress. As a long time fan I would hope

---

[20] Exhibit B-1 to Logan affidavit, *supra* note 19.

that our upcoming meetings will provide a solution to both our problems.

"With kindest personal regards.

Sincerely,

/s/ Bernie
B. F. Sisk
Member of Congress" [21]

Inasmuch as baseball had long been held to be exempt from the antitrust laws,[22] and had never been seriously threatened with legislation depriving it of that exemption,[23] it does not appear that baseball was ever in need of "a further vehicle" for communication with Congress. Nor is it apparent what "problems" baseball may have had which Congressman Sisk hoped that "upcoming meetings" would "provide a solution to"—unless those problems were ones that arose from the urgings of Congressmen with respect to the removal of its antitrust exemption.

Indeed, after the National League owners had voted to approve the sale of the Padres to Danzansky, Padres President Buzzie Bavasi told reporters that Commissioner Kuhn had strongly influenced the vote. "He stressed that baseball would need the goodwill of Congress in holding off antitrust legislation and in dealing with the energy crisis," Bavasi said.[24] Bavasi also reported that he had accused Commissioner Kuhn of wanting to use the Padres "to bribe the government." [25] According to the Padres'

---

[21] Exhibit C to Logan affidavit, *supra* note 19.

[22] See § 1.1, *supra.*

[23] See § 1.2(c), *supra.*

[24] L.A. Times, Dec. 14, 1973, Part III.

[25] *Id.*

President, Commissioner Kuhn replied with a laugh, "You might say that." [26]

When informed of the League's decision to transfer the team to Washington, the Mayor of San Diego, Pete Wilson, issued a colorful and impassioned statement. "The U.S. Congress, as watchdog of the public purse, has decided that subsidizing the piracy of the San Diego Padres is an urgent national priority, warranting the expenditure of federal taxpayers' dollars," he said. "It's a modern version of the public be damned. The city will wage war against the league on both legal and political fronts to keep the team in San Diego." [27]

On the legal front, San Diego's first step was to file a federal antitrust action on December 12, 1973, naming as defendants the National League, all of its teams, all of their presidents, Commissioner Bowie Kuhn, National League President Charles "Chub" Feeney, American League President Joseph Cronin, C. Arnholt Smith, Joseph Danzansky and his partners, and Congressmen B. F. Sisk, Joel Broyhill, Frank Horton, and Melvin Price. Named as unsued co-conspirators were Gerald Ford, Speaker of the House Carl Albert, Congressman Emanuel Celler, Congressman Peter Rodino, Senator Thomas Eagleton, and District of Columbia Mayor Walter Washington.[28] The complaint alleged that the defendants had conspired to restrain and monopolize major league baseball and the business of operating sports arenas. It asserted that the defendants had agreed with one another to use their monopoly power to move the Padres franchise from San Diego to Washington without regard to the existing legal

[26] *Id.*

[27] L.A. Times, Dec. 7, 1973, Part III.

[28] San Diego v. National League, *supra* note 19.

commitments of the team to remain in San Diego. With respect to those defendants who were Congressmen, the complaint charged that they had "improperly and illegally used their congressional positions to support, condone and continue the monopoly position of major league baseball," and that Congressman B. F. Sisk "in particular" had conspired with the other defendants "to delay, postpone and in fact prevent any legislation from being passed which would adversely affect baseball's antitrust exemption." This agreement to delay, postpone and prevent legislation, the complaint alleged, was the "consideration for moving the baseball franchise to Washington, D.C." [29]

As expected, Organized Baseball immediately filed a motion to dismiss, citing *Flood* v. *Kuhn*[30] and its predecessors.[31] Oral argument on the motion, and on a motion by San Diego for a preliminary injunction, was scheduled for January 30, 1974. But before that date arrived, the entire problem was resolved, and the case eventually dismissed.

The ultimate solution came after a quick series of developments, the first of which took place on December 21, 1973. That was the date by which Danzansky was to have arranged for indemnification of the National League and its teams, owners and executives, so as to protect them from any liability to San Diego that might be assessed in the pending lawsuits. When Danzansky had not arranged for the indemnity by then, the franchise was "shifted" back to San Diego by the National League owners who "met" that very day by conference telephone call. National League President Charles Feeney issued a statement in

[29] Complaint ¶ 38c and ¶ 39f, San Diego v. National League, *supra* note 19.

[30] 407 U.S. 258 (1972), discussed in § 1.3(b), *supra.*

[31] See §§ 1.1(a) and 1.1(d), *supra.*

which he said that the League was considering "all aspects" of the situation, including the possibility that the League might operate the Padres itself during 1974.[32]

A week later, on December 29, 1973, Padres owner C. Arnholt Smith announced that he had sold the team—without League consent—to a group headed by Mrs. Marjorie Everett. Of course, League rules provide that such sales must be approved by nine of the twelve clubs; and thus, as a spokesman for Commissioner Kuhn said following Smith's announcement, "nothing is official" until the League voted.[33] It voted on January 9, 1974, in a special meeting called for that purpose in Chicago. The vote, however, was against approving the sale; no reason was given to the public, nor was the exact vote disclosed. Immediately however, newspapers began to report the interest of other parties. The Houston Chronicle, for example, said that Texas financier Reuben Askanase was heading a group that would seek to buy the Padres.[34]

The vote against Everett left the franchise in Smith's beleaguered hands, with $71,000 in bonus payments to ten players about to become due on January 15, 1974. Smith was reportedly unable to make the payments. If the bonuses were not paid on time, the ten players would become free agents, legally entitled to negotiate with all of the other teams in baseball for future employment. One of the ten was rookie outfielder Dave Winfield, a highly thought of player. His loss, and the loss of the other players, would have made the Padres less attractive to potential buyers, San Diego Mayor Pete Wilson thought. And so, in a move reported to be without precedent in the

[32] L.A. Times, Dec. 22, 1973, Part III.
[33] L.A. Times, Dec. 29, 1973, Part III.
[34] Reported by the L.A. Times, Jan. 11, 1974, Part III.

history of baseball, the San Diego City Council voted to advance the Padres the money necessary for the player bonuses.[35]

The $71,000 advance was a portion of a $300,000 per year subsidy San Diego had contracted to pay the team for the first seven years of its lease. The agreement provided that in the event the Padres had attendance in excess of 800,000 per season during the last 13 years of the lease, the money would be repaid. Naturally, when San Diego learned that the team was to be moved to Washington, it stopped making the subsidy payments. Thus, the $71,000 advance was money that would have been paid had there been no talk of movement, and San Diego gave it to the Padres hoping the team would stay. Had the team gone to Washington anyway, the $71,000 simply would have been added to the $12 million San Diego was already claiming in damages.

The first hint of the ultimate solution came on January 22, 1974, when it was reported that McDonald Corp.'s board chairman Ray Kroc was inspecting the Padres' books with the assistance of two lawyers.[36] On January 23rd, Kroc announced that his negotiations to buy the team were "98% complete"[37] and two days later they were. At a joint news conference with San Diego Mayor Pete Wilson, Kroc announced that he would keep the Padres in San Diego at least until 1980 and said that he would personally pay any indemnity if the Padres were moved thereafter. The approval of the National League was voted on January 31st, and months of controversy should then have been at an end.

[35] L.A. Times, Jan. 16, 1974, Part III.
[36] L.A. Times, Jan. 22, 1974, Part III.
[37] L.A. Times, Jan. 24, 1974, Part III.

A complication arose, however, which threatened to create a new round of problems. The Internal Revenue Service was considering attaching Kroc's check, because of some $22.8 million in back taxes it allegedly claimed Smith owed. Kroc reported that he had been told by Smith's attorney that if the IRS were going to attach the check, Smith would not want to sell the team after all. Kroc, however, said that his agreement to buy the Padres made no mention of any of Smith's personal tax problems. "There were only two conditions," he told reporters. "I had to gain approval from the league, and I had to negotiate a lease with the city. I've met both conditions. The deal has gone through. Mr. Smith's problems are his problems." [38]

Eventually the matter of the IRS tax lien against Smith was settled, and the sale was concluded. San Diego's lawsuits were dismissed in February of 1974—their interesting issues left unresolved.

§8.4 The economics of team moves

The conclusion of the trial judge in the *Milwaukee Braves* case,[1] that the team was being supported by the city quite well, probably came as something of an affront to the Braves' management. The Braves' management, it can be assumed, undoubtedly felt that it knew as well as anyone how their own business was doing.

Interestingly, the Braves' conclusion that they could do better in Atlanta was not the only conclusion of a similar nature to be questioned by outside observers. In 1973,

---

[38] L.A. Times, Feb. 1, 1974, Part III.

[1] Wisconsin v. Milwaukee Braves, Inc., 1966 CCH Trade Cases ¶ 71,738 (Wisc. Cir. Ct. 1966), *reversed,* 144 N.W.2d 1 (Wisc. S.Ct. 1966), discussed in § 8.3(a), *supra.*

James Quirk, a Professor of Economics at the California Institute of Technology, conducted a detailed study of the ten baseball franchise shifts that took place between the Braves' move from Boston to Milwaukee in 1953 and the Senators' move from Washington to Texas in 1972. The results of his study were quite surprising. Professor Quirk found, for example, that the traditional justification offered for most moves—"lack of fan support"—was of "dubious validity" and not borne out by the figures.[2] In five of the ten cases, the teams were doing so poorly on the field that they "would have had difficulty drawing wherever they were located."[3] In three instances, including that of the Milwaukee Braves, "Lack of fan support also rings a little hollow [because the teams were in fact drawing substantial crowds] . . . unless two or three years attendance is projected into the indefinite future. . ."[4]

In addition, the reasonable expectations of the moving teams were also questionable. It is generally assumed that all other things being equal, the greater the population of a team's home town, the greater the possibility of its financial success. (This assumption seems to have been substantiated by major league baseball's attendance data for the 1962 through 1971 seasons which show for example, that although Kansas City's *per capita* home attendance was two to three times as great as the *per capita* home attendance of the New York Yankees, the New York team had more than a million customers every one of those ten seasons while Kansas City did not draw more than a

[2] Quirk, An Economic Analysis of Team Movements in Professional Sports, 38 Law and Contemporary Problems, 42, 52, 60 (1973).

[3] *Id.* at 52.

[4] *Id.* at 52-53.

million even once.[5]) Nevertheless, in seven of the ten moves studied, the teams' new home towns were smaller than the cities they had left. Furthermore, in eight of the ten cases, the cities to which the teams moved were smaller than the League average.

Finally, when Professor Quirk studied the actual success of the moves, he found that they "have not been particularly successful in terms of long-run viability at the new locations." [6] Home attendance of approximately one million is usually considered necessary for a baseball team to break even financially.[7] Thus, using that figure as a "crude yardstick," [8] it can be said that five of the ten moves were successful. Interestingly, however, four of the five "successful" moves were accompanied by above-average playing records on the field. However, two of the other teams which also enjoyed above-average playing records were unable to parlay those records into attendance "success." One of the moves classified as "successful"—that of the Braves from Boston to Milwaukee—resulted of course in a second move, to Atlanta. And while the move to Atlanta also qualified as a success—using one million in home attendance as the measure—it did so only by realizing *per capita* attendance which was a full fifteen percentage points higher than its nearest competitor—a standard of *per capita* attendance that is "highly unlikely to continue over time," [9] in Professor Quirk's judgment.

[5] *Id.* at 61.
[6] *Id.* at 60.
[7] *Id.* at 59.
[8] *Id.*
[9] *Id.* at 63.

Chapter 9

PROFESSIONAL SPORTS AND THE TAX LAWS: TAX ASPECTS OF TEAM AND LEAGUE OPERATIONS

§9.1 Professional sports teams as tax shelters

For years, certain kinds of investments have been thought of as "tax shelters," because they enable those who invest in them to avoid, at least temporarily, some of the taxes they would otherwise have to pay. Real estate investments are probably the most common tax shelters, for even the ownership of a single-family home provides income tax savings that are not available to apartment dwellers. However, more exotic forms of shelter are also well known. Oil and gas drilling ventures, cattle ranching, fruit farming, and motion picture production are some of the forms of investment that have long been considered traditional tax shelters. In recent years, ownership of a professional sports team has also been thought of as a tax shelter, although the extent to which tax benefits are available to team owners generally may have been overestimated.[1]

Most "tax shelters" are investments which permit deductions to be taken earlier than their investors are required to expend cash. Because the deductions are taken before the investor spends his or her cash, a portion of the investor's income goes untaxed—and hence is "sheltered"—at least until some later time. With respect to some tax shelters, deductible expenses are paid with bor-

[1] An article explaining these benefits, using the ABA's Utah Stars as an example, was published only a few months before the Stars went out of business, for financial reasons, in December of 1975. See, Comment, Professional Sports Teams as a Tax Shelter—A Case Study: The Utah Stars, 1974 Utah L.Rev. 556 (1974).

rowed money, rather than with the investor's money, but the deductions are taken by the investor nevertheless.

Other kinds of tax shelters are structured so that money actually spent by their investors is tax deductible, even though similar expenditures by non-investors are not. For example, apartment rent paid by tenants is not deductible, while real property taxes and mortgage interest paid by home owners are. Another example is that money invested in depreciable or amortizable property is deductible, while money invested in non-depreciable and non-amortizable property is not. It is these concepts, depreciation and amortization, that are at the heart of the income tax aspects of professional sports team and league operations.

§9.2 Depreciation and amortization

§9.2(a) The general principle

Federal income tax, in general, is payable upon *net* income. That is, ordinary and necessary expenses incurred in order to produce income may be deducted from the income in fact produced in calculating the amount of income upon which federal tax must be paid.[1] In order for a business to earn income, it is usually necessary for it to use assets, such as machinery and other equipment, which wear out even under ordinary use. The cost of replacing such worn out assets would therefore be an ordinary and necessary expense. However, where the process of wear and tear is gradual, the law requires the deduction to be taken gradually rather than all at once. Thus, the Internal Revenue Code provides that a reasonable allowance for "exhaustion, wear and tear" of property used to produce income may be deducted each year.[2]

[1] I.R.C. §§ 161 *et seq.*

[2] I.R.C § 167(a).

Generally, such deductions are usually spread over the estimated useful life of the asset in question. Thus, if a particular piece of machinery wears out over ten years, a portion of its cost is deductible each year for the entire period. In such cases, ten percent per year will frequently be the amount deducted; although the law does permit greater amounts to be deducted in earlier years and lesser amounts in later years, under certain circumstances.[3]

Where the asset in question is *tangible,* such as a building or a machine, the deductions permitted by law are referred to as "depreciation." When the assets involved are *intangible,* such as patents and copyrights, the deductions are commonly referred to as "amortization." Intangible assets must be amortized uniformly each year of their useful lives;[4] but so long as they do in fact have useful lives, deductions are permitted just as with tangible objects.

Of course, in order for deductions for depreciation or amortization to be taken, the assets in question must truly have "useful lives" that will come to an end. Thus, buildings may be depreciated because buildings wear out. Unimproved land, on the other hand, does not wear out, and therefore cannot be depreciated.

§9.2(b) Depreciation and amortization in professional sports

The assets of a professional sports team are of three types: a franchise from a league; athletic and office equipment; and contracts employing players (and other team personnel such as coaches).[1] Under the tax law, each of

[3] I.R.C. § 167(b).

[4] I.R.C. § 167(c).

[1] Klinger, Tax Aspects of Buying, Selling and Owning Professional Sports Teams, 48 Los Angeles Bar Bulletin 162, 164 (1973), reprinted in The Journal of Taxation, Nov. 1973 at 276 *et seq.*

these three types of assets is considered differently from the others.

§9.2(b)(1) League franchise

A league franchise is an intangible contract right. Once issued, it never expires; and, because it never expires, the cost of acquiring it cannot be deducted as amortization.[1]

§9.2(b)(2) Athletic and office equipment

Athletic and office equipment are personal property which wear out over a definite period which can be estimated with a great deal of accuracy. Thus, such equipment is a classic example of property which may be depreciated for income tax purposes.[1]

§9.2(b)(3) Player contracts

The contracts used to employ professional athletes give teams intangible rights which have a definite and limited useful life. This is so not only because all contracts contain a specific term—anywhere from two to five years or more, including the option year—but also because players themselves are only able to compete professionally for a definite number of years. An actual statistical study conducted by the Internal Revenue Service showed that the average remaining playing life of players on the 1961 rosters of National Football League teams was 4.7 years.[1] Therefore, the cost of acquiring player contracts may be

[1] Rev. Rul. 66-140, 1966-1 C.B. 45; Dunn v. United States, 400 F.2d 679, 681 (10th Cir. 1968); Toledo TV Cable Co., 55 T.C. 1107 (1971); Victor E. Stromsted, 53 T.C. 330, 343-44 (1969).

[1] Klinger, Tax Aspects of Buying, Selling and Owning Professional Sports Teams, 48 Los Angeles Bar Bulletin 162, 164 (1973).

[1] Internal Revenue Service, Audit Coordination Digest No. 65 (Jan. 2, 1973).

deducted as amortization over the useful estimated life of the player or players involved.

The amortizable cost of acquiring a player contract should not be confused with the salary payable to the athlete under his contract. Salaries paid to athletes are fully deductible by the team for the year in which they were paid.[2] Amortizable costs of *acquiring* player contracts are of two varieties: bonuses paid to athletes at the time of signing, and amounts paid to other teams to purchase player contracts.

Back in the 1930's, major league baseball teams deducted the full costs of acquiring player contracts in the year such costs were incurred. Although the Internal Revenue Service objected even then to teams deducting these costs in full in one year, the teams were successful in persuading the courts that it was proper.[3] The basis for the teams' judicial victories was that player contracts had a useful life of one year only, despite the reserve clause, because there was no certainty that the team would be able to utilize its renewal rights.

Ultimately, the Internal Revenue Service formally agreed with the old cases that the cost of acquiring a single player contract could be deducted currently in full.[4] (However, the Internal Revenue Service went on to take the position that when several player contracts were acquired together, they constituted an indivisible asset the cost of which could

---

[2] I.R.C. § 162(a).

[3] Commissioner v. Pittsburgh Athletic Co., 72 F.2d 883 (3d Cir. 1934); Commissioner v. Chicago National League Ball Club, 74 F.2d 1010 (7th Cir. 1935); Helvering v. Kansas City American Assn. Baseball Co., 75 F.2d 600 (8th Cir. 1935).

[4] Rev. Rul. 54-441, 1954-2 C.B. 101.

not be deducted currently, but had to be amortized over the average useful life of the baseball players involved.)

In 1967, the Internal Revenue Service reasserted its opposition to the practice of deducting player contract acquisition costs on a current basis. The I.R.S. stated that it had reconsidered the court decisions dealing with player contracts and had come to the conclusion that,

> "The uniform player contract currently in use in the baseball industry contains a 'reserve' clause giving the baseball club the right to renew the contract upon expiration of the one-year term at a salary negotiated by the player and the club. . . . By virtue of the renewal or reserve clause, which confers the exclusive right to the player's services during his baseball career, the purchaser of a player contract obtains an asset which has a useful life extending substantially beyond the taxable year in which the contract is acquired." [5]

As a result, the Internal Revenue Service ruled that the cost incurred by a major league baseball team in acquiring a player contract had to be amortized over the estimated useful life of the player involved.[6]

In 1971, the Internal Revenue Service issued a virtually identical ruling requiring the amortization of the costs of acquiring professional football player contracts.[7] Amortization, rather than current deductions, were said to be necessary in football as well, even though the National Football League's option clause was ostensibly less binding than Organized Baseball's reserve clause.[8] The Internal Revenue

[5] Rev. Rul. 67-379, 1967-2 C.B. 127, 128-129.
[6] *Id.* at 129.
[7] Rev. Rul. 71-137, 1971-1 C.B. 104.
[8] See §§ 2.2(a) and 2.2(c)(1), *supra.*

Service found that, "In many cases . . . notwithstanding the fact that the team only has a one year option, the player remains with the team with which he originally contracted for the duration of his playing career." [9]

Generally speaking, taxpayers prefer to deduct expenses currently, as they are incurred, rather than to capitalize the asset acquired and depreciate or amortize its cost over its useful life. Therefore, by its rulings, the Internal Revenue Service intended to increase the amount of income tax it could expect to receive from professional sports teams. And, for the most part, it probably did.

Interestingly, however, it has been pointed out that the amortization of bonuses paid to players upon signing may provide "tax shelter" under certain circumstances.[10] For example, an especially large signing bonus might be paid over a period of years by agreement between the athlete and his team. The athlete would benefit by avoiding the higher income taxes he would have to pay if the entire bonus was received in one year; and the team would benefit by the reduced burden on its cash flow that payment of the bonus in one year would necessarily impose. If the estimated playing career of the athlete involved was four years, one-fourth of the agreed-upon bonus could be deducted by the team each year, even if the bonus itself was to be paid over five or more years. Thus, in such a case, deductions could be taken more quickly than expenses actually paid—one of the classic "tax shelters."

The extent to which this classic tax sheltering opportunity has in fact been taken advantage of is another

---

[9] Rev. Rul. 71-137, *supra* note 7.

[10] Klinger, Tax Aspects of Buying, Selling and Owning Professional Sports Teams, 48 Los Angeles Bar Bulletin 162, 162-163 fn. 2, 165 (1973). But see, H. Rep. 94-658, 94th Cong., 1st Sess. 80 (1975).

question. "Cash bonuses are usually very small." [11] It has been reported that only ten of the fourteen top rookies signed by American Basketball Association teams in 1971 received bonuses, and those bonuses ranged from $7,500 to $55,000 and averaged about $31,000.[12] Moreover, the extent to which teams are even complying with the amortization requirement is also an open question. The Baltimore Orioles' "Report to Stockholders" for 1970 accurately noted that the cost of acquiring player contracts and the payment of signing bonuses are required to be amortized, but went on to state, "The Company, however, has always charged these type expenditures to operations as they were incurred and is continuing to do so." [13] Also, one team official has stated that his practice is to deduct bonuses of $20,000 or less currently and to amortize only those over $20,000.[14]

In any event, the amortization requirement does not make its most significant impact in connection with the payment of bonuses upon signing or the occasional acquisition of a player from another team. According to Benjamin Okner of The Brookings Institution,

> "If a team does expense bonus payments [i.e., deduct them for the year in which they are paid], its net income and tax liability for the year will not normally be appreciably affected. . . . Since the average bonus amount is quite small and would be written off over a short period, whether it is expensed or capitalized has little effect on annual expenses as long as the team's

[11] Okner, Taxation and Sports Enterprises, in Government and the Sports Business (Washington, D.C.: The Brookings Institution, 1974), at Pg. 170.

[12] *Id.* at 170 fn. 23

[13] Quoted in Okner, *supra* note 11, at 171.

[14] *Id.* at 171 fn. 26.

experience in writing and renewing new contracts does not vary much over a period of years." [15]

The most significant impact the amortization requirement has had is in connection with the sales of entire teams to new owners and in connection with league expansions. When an existing team is sold to a new owner, the buyer receives the team's league franchise, its athletic and office equipment, and its player contracts. A portion of the purchase price paid may therefore be considered to be in consideration for each one of these distinct elements. Furthermore, the purchase price paid may be, and always is, allocated between these elements for the purpose of computing income tax liability. This is done because the buyer is permitted to take amortization deductions with respect to that portion of the purchase price allocated to player contracts and is permitted to take depreciation deductions with respect to that portion allocated to athletic and office equipment. However, the buyer is not permitted to take amortization deductions with respect to that portion of the purchase price allocated to the league franchise.[16]

The seller of a team also has an interest in the allocation that is made. The portion of the purchase price which the seller receives in consideration for the league franchise is taxed at favorable capital gains rates. While the amounts received in consideration for athletic and office equipment and player contracts may also be taxed at favorable capital gains rates, those amounts will be taxed at the higher ordinary income rates to the extent that the seller previously took depreciation and amortization deductions.[17]

---

[15] *Id.* at 171.

[16] Klinger, *supra* note 10, at 179-180.

[17] I.R.C. § 1245.

Thus, for example, if the assets sold included athletic and office equipment which originally cost $50,000, and if the seller had taken $10,000 in depreciation deductions, and if the portion of the purchase price allocated to athletic and office equipment was $75,000, then the seller would realize $10,000 in gains taxed at ordinary income rates and $25,000 in capital gains taxed at lower capital gains rates. This is referred to as the "recapture" of depreciation, because, to the extent that depreciation has been taken, it must be "recaptured" in the form of ordinary income before the taxpayer is entitled to receive more favorable capital gains treatment.

The theory behind the "recapture" requirement is that depreciation deductions reduce income which would have been taxed at ordinary rates. Thus, those tax savings should be "repaid" by the taxpayer, in full, before the taxpayer takes advantage of the lower capital gains rates.

The recapture rules applicable to the sale of athletic and office equipment also apply to the sale of player contracts.[18] Thus, for example, if the sale of a team includes the sale of player contracts which cost the seller $50,000 (either because the players were paid signing bonuses, or because their contracts were purchased from another team), and if the seller took $10,000 in amortization deductions, and if the portion of the purchase price allocated to those contracts is $75,000, then the seller will realize $10,000 in gain taxed at ordinary rates and $25,000 in gains taxed at lower capital gains rates.

Because of this "recapture" requirement, if the seller has in fact taken any depreciation or amortization deductions, the seller will wish to allocate enough of the purchase price

[18] Rev. Rul. 67-380, 1967-2 C.B. 291; Rev. Rul. 71-137, *supra* note 7, at 105.

to the league franchise so that no gain whatsoever is realized on the sale of athletic and office equipment and player contracts. Obviously, if no gain is realized on the sale of equipment and contracts, there is nothing to be "recaptured." On the other hand, the buyer will wish to allocate as much of the purchase price as possible to equipment and player contracts, and as little as possible to the league franchise, because the buyer will be able to depreciate and amortize equipment and contracts, but will not be able to amortize the league franchise.[19]

Current law does not require the parties to specify in their agreement the allocation they have made. Buyers and sellers may simply make the allocation on their income tax returns in the manner most favorable to each. However, conflicting allocations would signal the Internal Revenue Service that audits could profitably be made of both returns; and therefore, if the allocation is significant to one party or the other, it should be bargained for and incorporated into the written agreement of purchase and sale. Moreover, the proposed Tax Reform Bill of 1974 contained a provision requiring both the seller and the buyer to agree on the amount allocated by them to player contracts.[20]

The extent to which the allocation may be significant depends upon several factors, including the total purchase price, the tax bracket of the buyer, and the number of years over which depreciation and amortization are to be taken. The potential significance may be seen by considering one example. If a buyer in the fifty percent tax bracket were to purchase a team for $10,000,000, the buyer's ability to

---

[19] On strategy generally, see, Klinger, *supra* note 10, at 167 *et seq.*

[20] Jones, Amortization and Nonamortization of Intangibles in the Sports World, 53 Taxes 777, 786 (1975); see also, § 9.6, *infra*.

allocate $5,000,000 to player contracts to be amortized over five years would result in approximately $2,000,000 in tax savings. If the buyer was in the seventy percent bracket, his tax savings would be approximately $2¾ million.[21]

Similar principles are involved in the tax aspects of league expansions, for expansions are conceptually quite similar to the sale of an existing team. An expansion team purchases a newly-issued franchise rather than an old one, and purchases two or three players from every team in the league (pursuant to an expansion draft) rather than an entire roster of contracts from one team. The amount paid by the expansion team for player contracts acquired in the expansion draft is amortizable, while the amount the expansion team pays for its newly-issued franchise is not. The amount received by the league and by existing teams in exchange for the newly issued franchise is taxed at capital gains rates,[22] and the amount received by existing teams in exchange for the players given up in the expansion draft is taxed at ordinary rates to the extent of recaptured amortization and thereafter at capital gains rates.[23]

(It is interesting to note that the Tax Reform Act of 1969 added a section to the Internal Revenue Code which has the effect of taxing gains realized on the sale of franchises at ordinary income rates, rather than at lower capital gains rates, if the seller retains any significant power, right, or continuing interest in or to the franchise.[24] Professional sports leagues certainly do retain significant powers, rights, and continuing interests in franchises issued by them. However, the provision added by the Tax

---

[21] See, *id.* at 778 for a table facilitating the calculation of such savings.

[22] Rev. Rul. 71-123, 1971-1 C.B. 227.

[23] *Id.*

[24] I.R.C. § 1253.

Reform Act of 1969 contained a subsection indicating that it did not apply to franchises to engage in professional football, basketball, baseball or other professional sports.[25])

§9.3 Player contract amortization and the potential for tax shelter

During the Congressional hearings concerning the proposed basketball merger bill,[1] it was learned that The Brookings Institution was conducting an independent study of professional sports as part of its series of Studies in the Regulation of Economic Activity. The Senate Subcommittee on Antitrust and Monopoly invited Roger G. Noll and Benjamin A. Okner, the two Brookings senior fellows who were in charge of the study, to testify; and it was their testimony which first resulted in the widespread knowledge that ownership of a professional sports team could provide certain tax shelter benefits.

The written statement submitted to the Subcommittee by Noll and Okner included several statistical tables, one of which (Table 8) compared the before-tax and after-tax status of a hypothetical basketball team owner with that of a hypothetical non-owner. The table showed that if the team had a \$200,000 book loss, its owner would be \$240,000 better off after taxes than the non-owner. It further showed that even if the team had an \$800,000 book loss, its owner would still be \$60,000 better off after taxes than the non-owner.[2] Clearly this was heady stuff, suggesting that to

---

[25] I.R.C. § 1253(e).

[1] See § 6.2(d), *supra.*

[2] Hearings on S.2373 before the Subcomm. on Antitrust and Monopoly of the Senate Comm. on the Judiciary, 92d Cong., 1st and 2d Sess. 412 (1971-72), published also in Okner, Taxation and Sports Enterprises, in Government and the Sports Business (Washington, D.C.: The Brookings Institution, 1974) at 168.

own a professional sports team was to truly have a Midas touch.

The table was assembled in the following fashion. It was assumed that the team owner was in the 70% bracket; that he had purchased the team for $2,000,000; that he had allocated 75% of the purchase price to player contracts; and that the contracts were being amortized over a five year period. It was also assumed that both the owner and the non-owner had taxable income from sources other than the team of $1,000,000 per year.

A non-owner in the 70% bracket with taxable income of $1,000,000 in a year would pay approximately $671,000 in income tax, leaving the non-owner with $329,000 in after-tax income.

Assuming, as the illustration did, that 75% of the $2,000,000 purchase price had been allocated to player contracts, $1.5 million was thus deductible at the rate of $300,000 per year for the assumed five-year period. If the team's book loss (taking into account $300,000 for amortization) were to be $200,000, then the team showed a $100,000 cash flow profit. The team owner would be able to deduct his team's $200,000 book loss from his $1,000,000 in income from other sources, leaving taxable income of $800,000. Taxes on $800,000 would be approximately $531,000, leaving the team owner with $569,000 in after-tax income ($1,000,000 from other sources, plus $100,000 cash flow income from the team, minus $531,000 in taxes). Thus, the team owner with $569,000 in after-tax income is $240,000 better off than the non-owner with $329,000 in after-tax income.

Similarly, if the owner's team had an actual cash flow loss of $500,000 plus $300,000 in amortization, the total book loss would be $800,000. An owner with $1,000,000 in income from other sources would have taxable income of $200,000 after accounting for this $800,000 book loss. The income tax payable on $200,000 is $111,000, leaving the owner with $389,000 in after-tax income ($1,000,000 from other sources minus $500,000 actual cash flow loss minus $111,000 in income taxes). Thus, the owner of a team with an $800,000 book loss and $389,000 in after-tax income is $60,000 better off than the non-owner with $329,000 in after-tax income.

Although the table was based upon an accurate application of federal tax law, the significance of its conclusions was immediately disputed by Robert R. Nathan, the consulting economist who had been retained by the National and American Basketball Associations. He told the Congressional subcommittee,

> "I cannot recall a discussion of taxation which comes nearer to characterizing a 'get-rich-quick-through-losses scheme' than the figures and illustrations in the Noll-Okner testimony, especially table 8. One can only conclude from these figures and observations that the best way in the world to make a lot of money is to invest in a losing sports team. The more you lose the more you make—up to some astronomical levels of losses—according to Dr. Noll and Dr. Okner." [3]

Nathan then went on to explain why, in his judgment, the table was "about as remote from reality and sound economic principles" [4] as any he had encountered in a long time.

> "In their examples, Dr. Noll and Dr. Okner take no account of the fact that the investors who buy basketball teams lay out cash or obligate themselves to finance

[3] *Id.* at 632.

[4] *Id.* at 608.

> their investment. When one buys a venture, whether it is a factory, a department store, an apartment house, or a basketball team, the money used to buy the venture is an investment . . . . In their table 8, Dr. Noll and Dr. Okner completely ignore the fact that the investors have put up money to buy a basketball team, and they therefore draw wrong conclusions.
>
> "Dr. Noll and Dr. Okner have failed to take into consideration the fact that individuals do much better to invest their money in profitable ventures than in losing ventures, even with all the tax gimmicks in the world. It would have been proper and useful to have added a column to table 8 to show the financial status of an individual who invested his money in some venture other than basketball, a venture that would have been a profit-maker rather than a loser." [5]

Nathan did outline for the subcommittee the financial status of a hypothetical individual who had invested $2,000,000, not in basketball, but in some other venture which produced $400,000 in book profit, after accounting for $300,000 in depreciation. Assuming the investor had $1,000,000 in income from other sources, his total taxable income would be $1,400,000, upon which he would be required to pay taxes of approximately $950,000. Since his total income would be $1,700,000 ($1,000,000 from other sources plus $700,000 in cash before deducting $300,000 for depreciation), he would have an income, after taxes, of $750,000—a much greater income, in other words, than Dr. Noll and Dr. Okner's hypothetical basektball team owner.

While Nathan's testimony demonstrated that actual losses are not necessary to achieve tax shelter, he did not neces-

[5] *Id.* at 633.

sarily disprove the validity of the point made by Noll and Okner. Noll and Okner used hypothetical money-losing teams as illustrations, because they wanted to indicate that merger of the National and American Basketball Associations should not be legislatively approved simply because basketball teams were losing money. Their point was that because of the amortization deductions team owners may take under certain circumstances, those owners may not have been in dire financial straits *themselves,* even if their teams were losing money.

Nathan's response demonstrated that given the ability to take the same amortization deductions, investors would be better off with profits than with losses. It should be noted, however, that even Nathan's hypothetical example was based upon the assumption that the alternate, non-basketball investment was one which would permit amortization deductions to be taken. If, for example, the $2,000,000 had been invested in a venture which did not give rise to depreciation or amortization deductions—such as corporate bonds or preferred stock—then, although the team non-owner would have been better off than Noll and Okner indicated in their table, that non-owner would not necessarily have been better off than the owner whose team suffered book losses. In particular, in order for an alternate $2,000,000 investment which does not give rise to amortization deductions to be as valuable as Noll and Okner's hypothetical $200,000 book loss basketball team, the alternate investment would have to yield 12% per year *after taxes.* A $2,000,000 investment yielding 12% after taxes would be an excellent investment, indeed.

Of course, the extent to which any real basketball team owner had in fact been able to realize the benefits illustrated by Noll and Okner's hypothetical example was another question. One hundred percent of the losses sustained by their hypothetical $200,000 book loss team were attributable to player contract amortization. Similarly, 37½% of the losses sustained by the $800,000 book loss team were attributable to player contract amortization. However, Nathan testified that amortization of player contracts accounted for only 7% of the total losses sustained to that time by members of the American Basketball Association,[6] and in no year did player contract amortization amount to as much as 20% of book losses.[7]

On the other hand, National Basketball Association teams, in the aggregate, seem to have come closer to Noll and Okner's hypothetical example, for in his testimony, Nathan acknowledged that the total amount of player contract amortization taken by NBA teams (since the ABA was formed) exceeded the aggregate total of the book losses sustained by NBA teams to the extent that they averaged $130,000 per team per year in cash flow profits.[8]

After their initial testimony, Noll and Okner were retained by the Senate Subcommittee in order to assist it in digesting and analyzing a large amount of financial information requested of the individual NBA and ABA teams. Following their compilation and analysis of the data submitted, Noll and Okner testified a second time concerning their findings and conclusions. They found, for example, that although zero percent of the cost of acquiring teams was allocated to player contracts in some five instances, one NBA team had allocated fully 100% of the cost to player contracts. In the American Basketball Association, the average allocation to player contracts was

[6] *Id.* at 640.
[7] *Id.* at 1133.
[8] *Id.*

69.4%; and in the National Basketball Association, the average allocation to player contracts was 85.4%.[9] They also found that one National Basketball Association expansion team submitted actual figures illustrating "the reality of using our 'theory' to make money by 'losing' it."[10] This particular team, which was not identified by name, had a $1.6 million book loss for its first year of operations. More than $1.5 million of that loss was attributable to player contract amortization, however, so that if the owner of the team were in the 50% tax bracket, he would have been almost $1,000,000 better off, after taxes, than had he not owned the team at all.

Noll and Okner did acknowledge that this one unidentified NBA team was most unusual in that it took in one year 10% of all of the amortization taken by professional basketball teams during the preceding 5 years.[11] They further acknowledged that to the extent teams have large book losses attributable to player contract amortization, it "most probably" signified "that the club's books have not yet been examined by the Internal Revenue Service!"[12]

§9.4 I.R.S. technical study concerning purchase price allocation

The basketball team financial information for 1967 through 1971 which Dr. Noll and Dr. Okner studied while acting as special counsel to the Senate Subcommittee on Antitrust and Monopoly[1] revealed only one Internal Revenue Service audit, even though the period consisted of a

---

[9] *Id.* at 1034.
[10] *Id.* at 1036.
[11] *Id.* at 1037.
[12] *Id.* at 1035.
[1] See § 9.3, *supra.*

total of 97 team-years.[2] The I.R.S.' apparent disinterest in professional sports was soon to give way to very serious interest, however.

In 1972, the Internal Revenue Service conducted a technical study of the allocation of purchase prices of professional sports teams, and published the results in its Audit Coordination Digest.[3] The Digest is a publication distributed to I.R.S. examiners for their official use in connection with auditing income tax returns, but it does not have the force of law and examiners do not use it as authority for making adjustments. Rather, the Digest is similar to a law review, except that it is published by the government for government-employed readers.

The study began by noting that when an established or expansion team in any of the major professional sports is acquired, it is common for the purchaser to allocate a nominal amount to the non-depreciable franchise or league membership and to allocate the balance to depreciable player contracts. This practice, the study said, ". . . is clearly in error and runs counter to the requirements of section 1.167(a)-5 of the Income Tax Regulations."[4]

Section 1.167(a)-5 provides that when a combination of depreciable and non-depreciable property is acquired for a lump sum, the portion of the purchase price allocated to the depreciable property may not exceed the depreciable property's proportion of the total value of the assets acquired. Thus, for example, if land worth $25,000 and a

[2] Okner, Taxation and Sports Enterprises, in Government and the Sports Business (Washington, D.C.: The Brookings Institution, 1974) at 166.

[3] Internal Revenue Service, Audit Coordination Digest No. 65 (Jan. 2, 1973).

[4] *Id.* at 1.

building on it worth $75,000 were purchased for a total of only $80,000, the purchaser could not allocate $75,000 of the purchase price to the building and only $5,000 to the land. Rather, Regulation §1.167(a)-5 requires that no more than 75% of the purchase price—here $60,000—be allocated to the building and at least 25%—here $20,000—be allocated to the land.

The I.R.S. study reported that owners sometimes attempt to demonstrate, either by means of an actual purchase offer or by the opinion of knowledgable sports figures, that the value of a particular superstar is several hundred thousand dollars. The values of other players on the team are then established relative to the superstar. Using this method, the total value of the players involved is then said to be in excess of the total price paid for the team; and that is claimed to be the justification for attributing little or no value to the league franchise itself.

The Internal Revenue Service was not convinced that franchises have little or no value, however. It said:

> "It would be difficult to argue that the value of a major professional sports franchise is not substantial. Some of the items that contribute to franchise value are as follows:
>
> Territorial rights
> Specified location
> Share of TV income
> Radio income
> Gate receipts
> Concessions
> Advertising
> Parking fees
> Pay TV

Films
Player slots to be continuously filled
League membership
(a) Participation in draft
(b) Future expansion
(c) Personnel to officiate
Going concern
(a) Scouting system
(b) Operating business management structure
(c) Affiliation agreements
(d) Lease arrangements" [5]

In order to make a proper allocation between the value of player contracts and the value of the franchise itself, the study recommended the use of what it called the "Prudent Investor Approach." This approach is based upon the theory that a prudent investor expects a certain rate of return, and therefore the amount such an investor is willing to pay depends upon that rate and the amount of income expected from the investment. In order to calculate how much money such a prudent investor would be willing to pay for player contracts, the following formula was suggested: [6]

"S=RP"

In words, this formula means that the amount attributable to player contracts ("S") equals the annual cash flow profit (without regard to depreciation or amortization) ("R") times the present value of a one dollar annuity ("P"). The amount of annual cash flow profits would be determined by looking at the books and records of the team involved (or, presumably, the hoped for profits of a

[5] *Id.*
[6] *Id.* at 3.

new expansion team). The present value of a one dollar annuity depends upon the expected rate of return and the number of years over which the player contracts are to be amortized. The I.R.S. study included a table setting forth such present values at various rates of return for periods from one through twenty years. The table showed, for example, that the present value of a one dollar annuity at 6% is approximately $4.21 for 5 years, and approximately $2.67 for 3 years. Similarly, the value of a one dollar annuity at 10% is approximately $3.79 for 5 years and $2.49 for 3 years.[7]

At the time the I.R.S. study was prepared, the 1961 rosters of several NFL teams were chosen on a random basis, and each player was checked to see how many more years he actually played professional football. In addition, the expansion rosters of the 1960 Dallas Cowboys, the 1961 Minnesota Vikings, the 1966 Atlanta Falcons, and the 1967 New Orleans Saints were similarly checked. In this fashion, the I.R.S. determined that the average remaining playing life of a player on an established team was 4.7 years, and the average remaining playing life of a player selected in an expansion draft was 2.5 years. The I.R.S. also found that the average annual cash flow profit (without regard to depreciation or amortization) of the teams studied was approximately $1.2 million.[8]

Assuming that a prudent investor would expect a 6% rate of return on money invested in player contracts, and assuming that all of the cash flow profits realized by a team were attributable to player contracts until those contracts had been fully amortized, the I.R.S. formula indicates that

[7] *Id.* at 4.
[8] *Id.* at 3.

the amount that may be allocated to player contracts to be amortized over 5 years is approximately $5,052,000. The balance of any purchase price paid for a team would have to be allocated to the non-amortizable league franchise (and other assets, if any). (The present value of a one dollar annuity at 6% for 5 years is approximately $4.21. $1,200,000 ("R") x 4.21 ("P") = $5,052,000 ("S").)

According to the I.R.S. formula, the amount that may be allocated to player contracts decreases as the number of years over which those contracts are to be amortized decreases. Likewise, the amount that may be allocated to player contracts decreases as the expected rate of return increases (because the present value of a one dollar annuity decreases as the expected rate of return increases).

§9.5 The Atlanta Falcons case

§9.5(a) Facts and contentions

In 1966, the National Football League issued an expansion franchise to a Georgia corporation known as The Five Smiths, Inc., permitting it to own and operate the Atlanta Falcons. The total price paid by The Five Smiths, Inc., was $8.5 million, of which $50,000 was the cost of the NFL franchise itself, and $8,450,000 (including interest on deferred payments) was the cost of 42 veteran player contracts acquired in an expansion draft.

The Five Smiths, Inc., estimated the useful playing lives of the players acquired to be 5.25 years, and therefore took amortization deductions of almost $1.5 million per year for 1967 and 1968. Although the Falcons had cash flow profits in each of those years, the amortization taken resulted in losses, for tax purposes, of more than a half million dollars both years.

The Five Smiths, Inc., was a "Subchapter S Corporation," and as a result its losses were passed through to its shareholders[1] each of whom reported his proportionate share on his respective personal income tax return. Thereafter, the Internal Revenue Service audited The Five Smiths, Inc., for 1967 and 1968, and determined that only $1,050,000 should have been allocated to player contracts rather than the much larger sum that had been. As a result, annual amortization was reduced from almost $1.5 million to only $200,000 ($1,050,000 divided by 5.25 years). With only $200,000 in annual amortization, the Falcons showed not only a cash flow profit, but substantial taxable income as well. A proportionate share of its taxable income was added to the income of each shareholder in The Five Smiths, Inc., and additional taxes were assessed against them accordingly. One shareholder, E. Cody Laird, Jr., paid the additional tax and then, along with his wife Joanne, filed an action for its refund in the United States District Court in Atlanta.[2]

The manner in which the Internal Revenue Service determined that only $1,050,000 should have been allocated to player contracts has not been publicly explained. It is interesting to note that in making this determination, the I.R.S. apparently failed to follow even its own Audit Coordination Digest Technical Study.[3] According to the formula set forth in that study, approximately $4.4 million properly could have been allocated to player contracts. (The actual cash flow profit of the Falcons for 1967 and 1968 was approximately $1 million each year. The present value of a one dollar annuity at 6% is approximately $4.40.

[1] I.R.C. §§ 1371-1379.

[2] Laird v. United States, 391 F.Supp. 656 (N.D. Ga. 1975).

[3] See § 9.4, *supra*.

$1 million x 4.4 = $4.4 million.) In order to arrive at the Internal Revenue Service's $1,050,000 allocation, using the formula set forth in the I.R.S. Audit Coordination Guide, given approximately $1 million in cash flow profits, one would have to assume, for example, an expected rate of return of 25% and an estimated useful playing life of less than 1½ years, or other assumptions equally removed from any expectations reasonably attributable to the shareholders of The Five Smiths, Inc.

Furthermore, other determinations made by the Internal Revenue Service in similar matters offer no insight into the drastic reduction made by it with respect to the Atlanta Falcons. When the Atlanta Braves baseball team moved to Atlanta from Milwaukee,[4] the purchasers allocated approximately $5.5 million—99% of the price—to player contracts. Following an I.R.S. audit, an additional $450,000 was allocated to the franchise, in effect reducing the portion allocated to contracts from 99% to approximately 90%.[5]

The only audit that seems to have been made of a basketball team for the years 1967 through 1971 reportedly resulted in a reduction of the proportion allocated to player contracts from 90% to 50%.[6] Subsequent basketball team audits have upheld an allocation of 75% to player contracts and have been compromised by agreement on 60% allocations to contracts. Never, prior to the Atlanta Falcon's audit, does it appear that the I.R.S. had ever sought an allocation as small as the 12⅓% allocation to contracts sought there.

---

[4] See §8.3(a), *supra.*

[5] Okner, Taxation and Sports Enterprises, in Government and the Sports Business (Washington, D.C.: The Brookings Institution, 1974) at 166.

[6] *Id.*

In court, the Lairds introduced four kinds of evidence to prove that the amount that had been allocated to player contracts was proper for tax purposes. First, evidence was introduced showing the arm's length nature of the negotiations that had preceded agreement on the price. This included an exhibit (apparently a letter or memorandum) indicating that some team owners had investigated the tax consequences of the prices negotiated and had realized that their own tax position would be more favorable if those prices were renegotiated so that a higher value was assigned to the league franchise. When this was suggested, however, the proposed renegotiation was promptly and conclusively rebuffed, according to the testimony offered during trial.

Evidence was also introduced showing the costs that had been incurred in acquiring players in comparable transactions during 1965 and 1966. It was shown that the first 53 players selected in the college draft in December of 1965 were paid almost $10,000,000 in bonuses and no-cut salaries. Per player, this was almost as much as The Five Smiths, Inc., paid for the 42 veterans they acquired in the expansion draft. Yet, the testimony indicated that the veteran players obtained by The Five Smiths, Inc., were more valuable than the first 53 rookies drafted, because of the veteran's experience, proven ability and generally lower salaries.

In addition, it was shown that in 1965, the owners of the then new Miami Dolphins paid $7.7 million for the right to select only 32 veteran players from existing American Football League teams. In 1967, the owners of the then new Cincinnati AFL franchise paid $7.65 million for the right to select 32 veterans. And in 1967, the owners of the then new New Orleans franchise paid $7.7 million for the right to select 42 veterans in that year's NFL expansion draft. Given this evidence, the Lairds vigorously contended that The Five Smiths, Inc., did no more than pay what was then the "going price" for football players.

Evidence was also introduced to establish that the cost that would have been incurred in developing players comparable in experience and ability to those selected in the expansion draft would have been quite comparable to the amount that had been allocated to player contracts. Tex Schramm, General Manager of the Dallas Cowboys, testified that by the time a college rookie had earned a place on the Cowboys' active roster, Dallas had spent an average of $150,000 to scout, draft and sign the player to a contract, to put the player through training camp, to analyze his skills and potential, to determine his ability relative to others trying out for his position, and to train and equip him for the regular season. Thereafter, further costs had to be incurred in order to bring the player to the level of experience of the 42 veterans selected by the Atlanta Falcons in the expansion draft. Computed in this fashion, the cost of developing players comparable in experience and ability to those selected in the veteran draft would have been far greater than the sum actually allocated by The Five Smiths, Inc., to player contracts.

Finally, Tex Schramm and Jim Finks, both General Managers of NFL teams and, therefore, very experienced in negotiating with football players, offered testimony as experts that they would have paid the amount allocated to player contracts in order to acquire the veteran player selection rights set forth in the expansion agreement. Furthermore, both of them supported this general testimony with valuations of each player actually selected by the Falcons in the expansion draft. The total of the individual prices that Schramm would have paid for the players actually selected was $7.3 million, and the total that Finks would have paid was $6.8 million. Although both figures were somewhat less than the sum actually allocated to player contracts, the figures were close and were said to attest to the economic reality of the amount allocated to player contracts by The Five Smiths, Inc.

In addition to this evidence concerning the substantial value of the players acquired by the Falcons in the expansion draft, evidence was also introduced designed to establish that the franchise issued to The Five Smiths, Inc., had little value, in and of itself, in excess of the $50,000 that had been allocated to it. This was said to be so because of the "war" that existed between the NFL and AFL at the time the Atlanta Falcons were added to the NFL.[7] And, this was said to be the case because the League franchise imposed burdens on The Five Smiths, Inc., as well as benefits. That is, it was argued that the true purchase price of the franchise itself was not simply the $50,000 in cash The Five Smiths paid, but also the assumption of all of the obligations that are imposed by the NFL Constitution and By-Laws on all NFL members.

Alternatively, the Lairds argued that if the amount allocated to player contracts was excessive, then The Five Smiths, Inc., should be permitted to allocate a portion of the purchase price to the value of a CBS television contract, and they further argued that the amount allocated to the television contract is itself amortizable. The contract in question was for the years 1966 through 1969, and as a result of it, the Atlanta Falcons received almost $5,000,000 over those four years. Since the contract would

---

[7] See § 6.1(a), *supra*.

expire by its own terms after those four years, the Lairds argued that one-fourth of the contract's value should be deductible each year.

In court, the government abandoned the position that had been taken at first by the Internal Revenue Service (which allocated $1,050,000 to player contracts), and instead took the position that what The Five Smiths, Inc., actually purchased from the NFL was a bundle of indivisible assets having no determinable useful life. It was therefore the government's contention at trial that none of the purchase price was amortizable. These assets were said to consist of a number of rights, all of which had perpetual life: the exclusive right to provide professional football in Atlanta, Georgia, the right to share revenues from network television contracts; the right to receive additional income from such sources as radio broadcasts, gate receipts, NFL merchandise and films, and program advertising and sales; the right to participate in college drafts, to trade players with other teams, and to obtain players cut from other teams; and the right to the administrative services provided all teams by the NFL office.

There were two items of evidence which the government contended supported its position. First, in 1966, the National and American Football Leagues agreed to merge with one another.[8] One element of that agreement required the AFL to pay NFL teams $22,500,000 over a period of years. Within the NFL, it was agreed that the New York Giants would receive $10,000,000 and the San Francisco 49ers would receive $8,000,000, while the $4,500,000 balance would be divided equally among the other teams (except for the Atlanta Falcons and the New Orleans Saints, which

[8] *Id.*

were brand new teams at the time).[9] The merger of the two leagues did not involve the sale of any veteran players to AFL teams, and thus the amount paid was strictly in consideration for NFL franchise rights. The New York Giants and San Francisco 49ers received far more than any other NFL team, because AFL teams—the New York Jets, and the Oakland Raiders—were located within what would have otherwise been the Giants' and 49ers' exclusive territories under the NFL Constitution and By-Laws.

The Internal Revenue Service ruled that the amounts received by the Giants and 49ers were to be taxed at favorable capital gain rates, because exclusive territorial rights were held to be capital assets.[10] In the Atlanta Falcons' case, the government argued that the amounts previously received by the Giants and the 49ers solely in exchange for relinquishing a portion of their exclusive territorial rights proved the great value such rights have.

The second item of evidence was a letter written by an attorney for the NFL to the judge in an unrelated antitrust action[11] which said,

> "The 'valuation' of player contracts by the three expansion franchises [Atlanta, New Orleans and Cincinnati] was done solely for tax purposes and is subject to change by a ruling of the I.R.S., supported by the appropriate court.
>
> . . .
>
> "The irrelevance of the expansion club tax information is also demonstrated when it is realized that there are a number of factors which determine the price of

[9] Weill, Depreciation of Player Contracts—The Government Is Ahead at the Half, 53 Taxes 581, 584 (1975).

[10] Rev. Rul. 71-583, 1971-2 C.B. 312.

[11] Smith v. Pro-Football, Inc., (D.C.D.C. Civ. No. 1643-70).

an expansion franchise. These include, among others, the intensity of the desire of the purchaser to become a part of professional football; the fact that he is acquiring the exclusive rights to play professional football in the NFL within a specified territory; the fact that he is acquiring valuable television and radio rights; the size and nature of the city in which the franchise is to be located; the right to select 'experienced' players from the other clubs; and, as indicated, tax depreciation privileges." [12]

§9.5(b) District Court opinion

District Judge Frank Hooper awarded neither the Lairds nor the government a complete victory.[1] On the one hand, Judge Hooper agreed with the Lairds that some portion of the purchase price properly could be allocated to player contracts. On the other hand, he did not agree that the full amount allocated by The Five Smiths, Inc., to player contracts represented their true value. Instead, Judge Hooper found that the actual value of the player contracts acquired by the Falcons in the expansion draft was $3,035,000.[2] This finding was based upon the testimony of the Falcons' first coach, Norb Hecker, which had been intended to prove the minimum value of the players actually acquired by the Falcons.

Judge Hooper also agreed with the Lairds that a portion of the purchase price could be allocated to the value of the CBS television contract, but held that the amount so allocated was not amortizable. It was not, he said, because he found that the Falcons were entitled to share in tele-

[12] Laird v. United States, Post-Trial Brief for the Defendant 51, 72; Weill, *supra* note 9, at 589-590.

[1] Laird v. United States, 391 F.Supp. 656 (N.D. Ga. 1975).

[2] *Id.* at 666.

vision revenue for so long as they were a member of the NFL and "Since it was impossible to determine how long Atlanta would continue as a member of the league, it was impossible to determine the useful life of Five Smiths' rights to share in the league television pool." [3] Apparently, Judge Hooper assumed that the League itself would always enjoy television income and that, therefore, it was irrelevant that the particular contract in existence at the time the Falcons joined the League had only a four year term.

After subtracting the amounts thus allocated to the amortizable player contracts and to the non-amortizable television contract, just over $410,000 remained; and that sum Judge Hooper allocated to the non-amortizable League franchise.[4] Both sides thereafter appealed. The government appealed on the grounds that player contracts are not capable of valuation separate from the rest of the franchise assets, and on the grounds that there was no evidence in the record to support the $3,035,000 valuation given to them. The Lairds appealed Judge Hooper's conclusion that the amount allocated to the CBS television contract was not amortizable.[5]

The impact the Atlanta Falcons case is likely to have on professional sports is difficult to assess at this time, because a number of factors remain unsettled. If the Court of Appeals agrees with the government that no portion of the purchase price of a professional sports team may be allocated to player contracts, it is quite likely that the value of professional teams will decrease. In economic theory, a

[3] *Id.* at 665.
[4] *Id.* at 671.
[5] Jones, Amortization and Nonamortization of Intangibles in the Sports World, 53 Taxes 777, 785 (1975).

purchaser willing to pay $5,750,000 for a team if 90% of the price may be allocated to player contracts should be willing to pay only $3,000,000 for it if none of the purchase price may be so allocated.[6]

If, on the other hand, the Court of Appeals agrees with the Lairds that the amount allocated to the CBS television contract is amortizable, then there should be little impact on the value of NFL teams because the value of television rights in the NFL is substantial. However, such a ruling may not be of as much help to the value of teams in other leagues, because other leagues have relatively less income from television. For example, the National Hockey League no longer has a network television contract, though it once did—thus suggesting that Judge Hooper's apparent assumption that the NFL would always have television income is not as certainly accurate as it seems at the present moment.

In addition, the Falcons case may well have a greater impact on allocations made in connection with the purchase of expansion franchises than on allocations made in connection with the purchase of existing established teams. This is so because the valuation arguments made by The Five Smiths, Inc. were based on the effects of the then-existing AFL-NFL "war." Since that "war" was settled by the merger of the two leagues, the cost of developing players from rookies, for example, has been said to be substantially less. Evidence admitted during the Falcons trial showed that the Falcons paid rookies $828,454 in bonuses in 1966, the last year before the AFL-NFL merger, and only $164,150 in 1967, the year after the merger.[7] Since the

---

[6] Weill, Depreciation of Player Contracts—The Government Is Ahead at the Half, 53 Taxes 581, 589 (1975).

[7] *Id.* at 583.

very best players in a league are not usually available to be selected in an expansion draft, it would be difficult for any new expansion team to argue that any of the particular players acquired by it had exceptional value.

On the other hand, when an established existing team is sold, its roster may contain some superstars for which a large portion of the purchase price might reasonably be allocated. It has been found, for example, that the loss of Rick Barry cost the San Francisco Warriors of the NBA $404,000 in gate receipts in a single season.[8] Thus, assuming a five year playing life—something Rick Barry in particular has already far exceeded—Barry alone would be worth more than $2,000,000.

Another factor which leaves the impact of the Atlanta Falcons case in doubt is Congressional activity in the area of sports team taxation which could entirely supersede the ultimate outcome of the case.

§9.6 Proposed tax legislation concerning professional sports

Since the testimony of Dr. Roger Noll and Dr. Benjamin Okner before the Senate Subcommittee on Antitrust and Monopoly,[1] Congress has shown serious interest in the question of sports team taxation. In both 1974 and 1975, the House Ways and Means Committee approved legislation intended to eliminate at least some of the tax shelter benefits available from team ownership.[2] Had the 1975 bill been enacted, Committee Staff members estimated that it

---

[8] Lemat Corp. v. Barry, 80 Cal.Rptr. 240, 243 (1969), discussed in § 2.3(b)(1), *supra.*

[1] See § 9.3, *supra.*

[2] Jones, Amortization and Nonamortization of Intangibles in the Sports World, 53 Taxes 777, 786-788 (1975).

would have cost team owners $150 million or more over the next six years.[3]

The 1975 bill would have accomplished this result by providing that no more than 50% of the purchase price of a professional sports team could be allocated to player contracts, unless the buyer could establish, under the facts and circumstances of the case, that the player contracts involved had a greater value. In no event, however, could the amount allocated to player contracts by a purchaser exceed the amount allocated to player contracts by the seller.[4]

In addition, the House Ways and Means Committee also considered applying the "limitation on artificial losses" provisions of the Tax Reform Bill to the amortization of player contracts, and it considered treating any gain realized on the sale of player contracts as ordinary income rather than as capital gain. However, the Committee deferred making any decision in these areas until a later time.[5]

It is interesting to note that although the legislation which has been proposed is intended to diminish the tax benefits of team ownership, if enacted, it could restore benefits that may be abolished by the forthcoming decision of the Court of Appeals in the Atlanta Falcons case.[6] This is so because the government has asked the Court of Appeals to rule that no portion of the purchase price of a professional team may be allocated to player contracts, on the

---

[3] L.A. Times, Sept. 18, 1975, Part III.

[4] Release No. 5, Comm. on Ways and Means, Tax Reform Legislation Tentative Decisions, Sept. 17, 1975; see also, Jones, *supra* note 2, at 786-788.

[5] *Id.*

[6] See § 9.5, *supra.*

theory that a team consists of a single indivisible asset under current tax law. If the current Internal Revenue Code is amended to provide that no more than 50% of the purchase price of a team may be allocated to player contracts, except under special circumstances, the amendment would clearly create authority for the proposition that some portion may be so allocated. Thus, depending upon the decision of the Court of Appeals in the Falcons case, the proposed legislation may be adverse to the interests of professional sports team owners, or it may, in fact, preserve a great deal of the value teams have at the present time.

Chapter 10
PROFESSIONAL SPORTS BROADCASTING

§10.1 Significance of television to sports

On May 17, 1939, Columbia and Princeton Universities played a baseball game which, it is apparent in retrospect, was one of the greatest moments in sports. For although the game was to decide nothing more significant than fourth place in the Ivy League, it was nevertheless the first athletic event ever to be shown on television. Only 5,000 people saw that historic broadcast, according to one estimate,[1] but it ushered in an entirely new era.

Three decades later, some 70,000,000 people would watch the Super Bowl on television, and by then it would be said that the "impact of television . . . has produced more revolutionary—and irrevocable—change in sports than any other force since men began playing organized games."[2] Some of these changes have been the way games themselves are played. For example, most commercials televised during football games are broadcast during natural breaks in play when the game clock is stopped by football's own rules. But a couple of times during each game, the referees themselves call time outs for no other purpose than to permit the networks to show commercials.[3] During the 1967 Super Bowl game, there were actually two kickoffs to start the second half of play, because the net-

---

[1] W. Johnson, Super Spectator and the Electric Lilliputians (Boston: Little, Brown and Co., 1971), at 38.

[2] *Id.* at 26.

[3] Why Pro Football Insists on TV Blackouts—Interview with Commissioner Pete Rozelle, U.S. News & World Report, Sept. 10, 1973, at Pg. 62.

work was in the middle of a commercial when the first kick-off was inadvertently permitted.[4]

The principal reason for these changes is the money television has meant to athletics. As Vince Lombardi once said, "We can't be penny-wise and pound-foolish. Given today's budgets, there wouldn't be a single franchise left in the National Football League without television." [5] NFL Commissioner Pete Rozelle concurred.

> "There are twenty-six pro football franchises active now. Without television, half of them would not exist at all. The rest would be struggling to survive. From a practical standpoint, I doubt that the American Football League would be in business at all without television. There would be no Super Bowl without television." [6]

The accuracy of these assessments can be seen in the dollar figures themselves. In 1933, major league baseball teams each received, on the average, only $1,000 per year for radio rights. In 1950, when television was in its infancy, each team received an average of $210,000 per year. And by 1971, teams were receiving some $1,335,000 each.[7] Similarly, National Football League teams each received only $70,000 per year in broadcast revenue in 1952; but by 1971, that figure had increased to approximately $1,755,000.[8]

Television is considered to be a mixed blessing by sports executives, however. While it offers significant income, it

---

[4] W. Johnson, *supra* note 1, at 59.

[5] *Id.* at 27.

[6] *Id.* at 57.

[7] Horowitz, Sports Broadcasting, in Government and the Sports Business (Washington, D.C.: The Brookings Institution, 1974) at Pg. 287.

[8] *Id.* at 288.

also enables fans to see games without buying admission tickets. Television's potential threat to game attendance was perceived immediately, and rules were adopted as long ago as the late 1940's in efforts to minimize that feared impact.

§ 10.2 The blackout controversy

§ 10.2(a) Early blackout practices

§ 10.2(a)(1) Organized Baseball

Organized Baseball's first Commissioner, Kenesaw Mountain Landis, perceived a need to protect minor league teams even from radio broadcasts of major league games, and therefore he issued an order in the 1930's prohibiting major league teams from permitting their games to be broadcast in minor league cities and towns where the local clubs objected. In December of 1946, the major leagues formalized and expanded this order by adopting Major League Rule 1(d) which prohibited major league teams from authorizing radio or television broadcasts of their games from stations located outside of their own home territories and within the home territory of any other major or minor league team, without the other team's consent.[1]

In October of 1948, after the rule had been in effect for almost two years, Baseball Commissioner Albert "Happy" Chandler was asked to submit information to the Department of Justice concerning Organized Baseball's broadcasting practices. During the course of the following year, a number of conferences were held between Justice Department and baseball representatives which resulted in an amendment to Major League Rule 1(d) adopted in October of 1949. Under the amended rule, the prohibition against a

[1] S.Rep. 387, 83d Cong., 1st Sess. 4 (1953).

team's authorizing a broadcast of its games within the home territory of another team, without its consent, was limited to the time the other team was actually playing a home game or was telecasting one of its away games back to its home territory.[2]

In May of 1951, the Department of Justice reopened its investigation of Organized Baseball's broadcasting practices. During conferences between Department of Justice and baseball representatives held between May and September of 1951, the Department of Justice asked Organized Baseball to consent to a decree which would, in effect, restrain the major leagues from exercising any control over the use and sale of radio and television rights to major league games. From Organized Baseball's point of view, the timing of that request could not have been worse. During April, May, June and July of 1951, six antitrust lawsuits had been filed against it seeking treble damages, five of which attacked the legality of the reserve clause[3] and one of which attacked baseball's broadcasting rule. Faced with that great burden of private litigation, and threatened with an antitrust prosecution by the Department of Justice, Organized Baseball repealed Major League Rule 1(d) on October 8, 1951, despite its consistently held belief that the rule was both reasonable and lawful.[4]

Organized Baseball then turned to Congress for relief, seeking passage of a bill specifically authorizing reinstatement of Rule 1(d). Though such a bill was recommended to the full House of Representatives by the Committee on Interstate and Foreign Commerce,[5] it was never enacted.

---

[2] *Id.*

[3] See § 1.1(d), *supra.*

[4] S.Rep. 387, *supra* note 1, at 5.

[5] *Id.*

§10.2(a)(2) National Football League

Like Organized Baseball, the National Football League also adopted a broadcasting rule early in the life of television. Article X of the NFL Constitution and By-Laws, as it read in those years, provided that no team could permit any radio or television station located within 75 miles of another "League City" to broadcast its games when the other city's team was playing at home or broadcasting one of its away games back to its own territory, without permission. The Department of Justice contended that this rule was a contract among NFL members in restraint of trade and commerce among the several states, and thus illegal as a violation of Section 1 of the Sherman Act. Like Organized Baseball, the National Football League disagreed with the Department of Justice and believed its rule to be both reasonable and legal. Unlike Organized Baseball, the National Football League did not repeal its rule in the face of the Justice Department's threatened antitrust prosecution. Instead, the NFL chose to litigate.

United States District Judge Allan K. Grim agreed with the Department of Justice. He held,

> "There can be little doubt that this provision constitutes a contract in restraint of trade. The market for the public exhibition of football no longer is limited to the spectators who attend the games. Since the advent of television and radio, the visual and aural projections of football games can be marketed anywhere in the world where there are television or radio facilities to transmit and receive them. When a football team agrees to restrict the projection of its games in the home areas of other teams it thereby cuts itself off from this part of its potential market. Since the clubs

> of the National Football League have agreed at certain times not to project their games into the home territories of other clubs they have given that part of their market at those certain times exclusively to other teams. In return, each of them has been given the right to market its own games without competition in its own home area under the same circumstances. The purpose and effect of this is to restrict outside competition on the part of other teams in the home area of each club. This, therefore, is a clear case of allocating marketing territories among competitors, which is a practice generally held illegal under the antitrust laws." [1]

Judge Grim went on to state, however, that though the allocation of marketing territories was generally illegal, the "rule of reason" should be applied.[2] (Interestingly, two years before, the United States Supreme Court had held that the allocation of marketing territories between competitors is a practice which is not only "generally" illegal, but is in fact illegal *per se*.[3] When Judge Grim ruled that the "rule of reason" should be used in the case then before him, he cited as authority and quoted from the *dissenting* opinion of Justice Frankfurter in that Supreme Court case!) He therefore analyzed separately the reasons for and effects of Article X as it applied to (1) a television blackout of all other games when a team was playing at home, (2) a television blackout of all other games when a team was playing away, but televising its own game in its home territory, and (3) radio blackouts.

---

[1] United States v. National Football League, 116 F.Supp. 319, 322 (E.D. Pa. 1953).

[2] See § 2.4(b)(3)(A), *supra*.

[3] Timken Roller Bearing Co. v. United States, 341 U.S. 593 (1951).

Not at issue in that case were the sorts of blackouts which have been the subject of contention in recent years: the home territory blackout of games being played at home, and local blackouts of championship games.

Judge Grim did hold illegal and did enjoin all radio blackouts and television blackouts of other games in the home territory of a team simply because the home team was itself televising its own game in its territory. However, Judge Grim agreed with the National Football League that it was legal for teams to agree that when one is playing at home none of the others would permit the televising of their games by a station in the home team's territory. In so holding, Judge Grim found, as a matter of fact, that attendance at home games would decrease if other games were available on television. However, in the more than twenty years that have passed since Judge Grim's decision on this issue, conditions in professional football have changed to such an extent that even the "rule of reason" might bring a different result today.[4] Indeed, in 1966 the National Football League voluntarily ceased blacking out other games in cities where the home team was playing at home. Nevertheless, as of 1953, home territory television blackouts on days when teams were playing at home were held to be legal.

§10.2(a)(3) Organized Baseball revisits the Justice Department

After the repeal of Major League Rule 1(d) in October of 1951,[1] every major league team had the unlimited right to broadcast its games into the territories of all minor and

[4] Comment, Professional Football Telecasts and the Blackout Privilege, 57 Cornell L.Rev. 297 (1972).

[1] See § 10.2(a)(1), *supra*.

major league teams, and many did so. The CBS and NBC television networks carried selected major league games nationwide, causing attendance at minor league games to drop drastically. In 1949, almost 42,000,000 people attended minor league games, but by 1957 attendance was only 15½ million. When CBS announced its intention to broadcast a Sunday game-of-the-week during the 1958 season, Paul Porter, Organized Baseball's attorney, wrote a letter to Assistant Attorney General Victor Hansen, seeking authorization for a new rule prohibiting teams from televising their games in the territory of another club "during the day that such other club is scheduled to play a home game." [2] According to Porter, the proposed rule followed the one approved by Judge Grim in *United States* v. *National Football League*.[3] "All that is asked," Porter wrote, "is that baseball be given the same authority as was granted to football by this decision." [4] The rule was necessary, Porter argued, because during the period from 1949 through 1956, diminished attendance had caused the number of minor leagues in existence to drop from 59 to 26 and the number of minor league clubs from 448 to 205. In the opinion of baseball's Commissioner, Porter reported, the number of minor league teams then in existence was "at or below the minimum needed for the successful development of major league talent." [5]

Hansen, however, refused to give Porter assurance that the proposed rule would not subject Organized Baseball

---

[2] Correspondence published in Hearings on H.R. 10378 and S.4070 before the Subcomm. on Antitrust and Monopoly of the Senate Comm. on the Judiciary, 85th Cong., 2d Sess. 686 (1958).

[3] 116 F.Supp. 319 (E.D. Pa. 1953), discussed in § 10.2(a)(2), *supra*.

[4] Hearings, *supra* note 2, at 687.

[5] *Id.* at 688.

to an antitrust suit. In Hansen's view, *United States* v. *National Football League* upheld broadcasting restrictions agreed to by members of only one league, because they were thought by the court to be necessary to keep that league in fairly even balance. Organized Baseball's proposed new rule, on the other hand, was primarily aimed at preserving the minor leagues by restricting the operations of the major leagues. Further, the proposed new rule would prohibit, for example, a night broadcast into a territory where the home team had already played that afternoon. Finally, by virtue of the number and geographic location of minor league teams, the rule "might well preclude the American public from all chance to view on television the bulk of professional baseball games," Hansen said.[6]

Although Organized Baseball's exemption from the antitrust laws had been reaffirmed by the Supreme Court only five years before, nevertheless, it again acquiesced.[7]

§10.2(a)(4) National Football League revisits court

Prior to 1961, each team in the National Football League entered into individual contracts for the televising of its own games. Typically, these contracts granted individual stations the right to televise a team's away games back to that team's home territory (though during the 1950 season, the Los Angeles Rams granted a local station the right to televise Rams home games as well, seriously diminishing, it has been said, the attendance at Rams home games that year).

In 1961, the National Football League realized what the motion picture industry and even other sports leagues had

[6] *Id.* at 689.

[7] See §§ 1.1(d) and 1.4, *supra*.

discovered long before: that total revenue could be increased by tying the sale of less desirable products to the sale of more desirable ones. In professional sports, this meant the sale of television rights to a package of games; and, in order to create such a package, each NFL team ceased selling its games separately and authorized the Commissioner to sell the rights to all NFL games together. The American Football League had sold the television rights to its games in a package to a network for the 1960 and 1961 seasons, and the National Basketball Association and the National Hockey League had previously entered into such package contracts as well.[1]

In the motion picture industry, this practice is known as "block-booking" and was held illegal by the United States Supreme Court in 1948.[2] There does not seem to be any reason why block-booking of football, basketball or hockey games would have fared any better under the antitrust laws, but the issue was apparently never raised against the American Football League, National Basketball Association, or National Hockey League; nor was it ever reached when a court reviewed the National Football League's proposed package contract for the 1961 season.

Fearing that its package agreement with the CBS television network might violate Judge Grim's 1953 decree, whether or not it violated statutory law, the National Football League petitioned Judge Grim for a construction of his decision. Without reaching the question of whether the agreement was legal under statutory law, Judge Grim ruled that his earlier order prohibited the package deal the NFL had negotiated with CBS, because under the contract CBS would have the right to determine which games would be

---

[1] H.Rep. 1178, 87th Cong., 1st Sess. 2 (1961).

[2] United States v. Paramount Pictures, 334 U.S. 131 (1948).

televised where.[3] As a result, the contract restricted individual teams from determining the areas within which telecasts of their games could be made, and this was precisely the restriction Judge Grim had ruled illegal and prohibited in his 1953 order.

§ 10.2(b) Legislative relief for the NFL

§ 10.2(b)(1) Package contract authorization

As soon as Judge Grim handed down his 1961 ruling,[1] the National Football League immediately turned to Congress for relief and, in the incredibly short period of 72 days, obtained it in the form of an amendment to Title 15 of the United States Code. Section 1291 was added. It provides:

> "The antitrust laws . . . shall not apply to any joint agreement by or among persons engaging in or conducting the organized professional team sports of football, baseball, basketball, or hockey, by which any league of clubs participating in professional football, baseball, basketball or hockey contests sells or otherwise transfers all or any part of the rights of such league's member clubs in the sponsored telecasting of the games of football, baseball, basketball, or hockey, as the case may be, engaged in or conducted by such clubs."

In other words, package contracts were made legal, and Judge Grim's 1961 order was overruled legislatively.

---

[3] United States v. National Football League, 196 F.Supp. 445 (E.D. Pa. 1961).

[1] United States v. National Football League, 196 F.Supp. 445 (E.D. Pa. 1961), discussed in § 10.2(a)(4), *supra.*

§ 10.2(b)(2) Codification of anti-blackout rule

The bill that was submitted to Congress immediately following Judge Grim's 1961 ruling would have added §1291 only, and left the matter at that. Its proponents maintained that the bill's only purpose was to authorize and legitimize the National Football League-CBS package contract, and that no other aspect of Judge Grim's 1953 ruling was intended to be affected by it. Nevertheless, certain members of Congress and the Department of Justice were very much concerned that the bill's sweeping language might overrule Judge Grim's anti-blackout decree as well.

Since Congress was concerned about preserving the anti-blackout portion of the ruling, and since the National Football League expressly disclaimed any intention of doing away with it,[1] it was agreed that the pending bill could and would be amended to codify that portion of it.[2] Section 1292 of Title 15 was the result, and it provides:

> "Section 1291 of this Title shall not apply to any joint agreement described in such section which prohibits any person to whom such rights are sold or transferred from televising any games within any area, except within the home territory of a member club of the league on a day when such club is playing a game at home."

In other words, package contracts are permissible, so long as they do not require any kind of a blackout other than a home territory blackout on a day when a team is

[1] See, Hearings on H.R. 8757 before the Antitrust Subcomm. of the House Comm. on the Judiciary, 87th Cong., 1st Sess. 30-32 (1961).

[2] H.Rep. 1178, 87th Cong., 1st Sess. 5 (1961).

playing at home, in which case the antitrust exemption does not apply, and the package contract once again violates Judge Grim's rulings and, possibly, statutory prohibitions against block-booking as well.

§10.2(b)(3) Mandatory blackouts for college protection

Although Congress was careful to preserve the anti-blackout provisions of Judge Grim's 1953 decree, it did not act with total consistency on the blackout question. On the one hand, it codified the prohibition against all kinds of blackouts except home territory blackouts on days when home teams were playing at home. But on the other hand, it also acted to *require* blackouts in certain areas of the country during one season of the year.

The provision requiring certain blackouts was added to the bill at the request of the National Collegiate Athletic Association. Just as minor league baseball teams had felt the effects of major league telecasts, so had NCAA schools felt some effects from broadcasts of National Football League games. Generally speaking, most NFL games are played on Sundays, while most college football games are played on Saturdays and Friday evenings. However, occasionally NFL games are also played on Friday evenings and Saturdays, particularly at the beginning of the season when professional baseball games are still being played and result in scheduling conflicts.

NCAA representatives told Congress that its members spend more than $81 million every year in order to provide intercollegiate, intramural and recreational activities for more than one million students. They also told Congress that a principal source of financial support for these programs was gate receipts from intercollegiate athletic events, especially football. They said that uncontrolled televising of professional football games "can be ruinous of 'in person' attendance at college games," "that reasonable devices to protect the colleges' sources of income and their athletic programs are in the public interest," and that therefore "professional football should not be granted exemption from the antitrust laws for package television contracts at the possible expense of intercollegiate football games." [1]

Although Congress had not seen fit in 1953 to protect minor league baseball from the same sort of competition,[2] it was receptive to the urgings of the National Collegiate Athletic Association. Section 1293 was added to Title 15 of the United States Code. As originally enacted, it provided that the antitrust exemption for package contracts would not apply to any package contract which permitted the telecasting of professional football games on Friday evenings or Saturdays, between mid-September and mid-December, within 75 miles of an intercollegiate football game scheduled to be played on the same date. In 1966, when the merger of the American and National Football Leagues was authorized,[3] §1293 was amended to provide the same protection for high school football games as well.

Because of the enormous number of locations where high school and college football games are played on Friday nights and Saturdays, the effect of §1293 is to require the blacking out of virtually every professional football game played on Friday nights and Saturdays from mid-September to mid-December.

---

[1] H.Rep. 1178, 87th Cong., 1st Sess. 4 (1961).

[2] See § 10.2(a)(1), *supra.*

[3] See § 6.1, *supra.*

The NCAA vigorously guards the protection conferred by §1293. In the summer of 1972, for example, it was announced that the Hughes Sports Network intended to broadcast on Friday nights for 16 weeks beginning September 15, 1972, a half hour program entitled "NFL Game of the Week" consisting of some 25 minutes of film of an NFL game played the preceding weekend. In correspondence with the Department of Justice, the NCAA took the position that this program violated §1293, and it asked that the Department intervene and take action to prevent the violation.[4] The NCAA argued that §1293 prohibits "the telecasting of all or a *substantial part* of any professional football game" on Friday nights and Saturdays, and that the legislative history of the section specifically provided that the "term 'telecasting' as used in this section covers both live and delayed telecasts of professional football games." [5] According to the NCAA, a study done by its Football Rules Committee indicated that during the course of an entire game, the ball is actually in play for only 12 minutes. Therefore, the NCAA argued, "a telecast of twenty-five minutes of film provides twice as much time as would be needed to show at normal speed every play in a professional football game." [6]

The NCAA's legal position with respect to the "NFL Game of the Week" appears to be correct. The wisdom of a law allowing it to take such a position is of course another question altogether. But the existence of such a law does indicate the inconsistency of Congress' attitude towards blackouts. Examples of live games that actually

---

[4] Correspondence published in Hearings on H.R. 1206 et al., before Antitrust Subcomm. of the House Comm. on the Judiciary, 92d Cong., 2d Sess. 293-296 (1972).

[5] H.Rep. 1178, *supra* note 1, at 5.

[6] Hearings on H.R. 1206, *supra* note 4, at 296.

had to be blacked out illustrate the point in dramatic fashion. On Saturday, September 9, 1972, the Kansas City Chiefs played the Green Bay Packers in Milwaukee. The game would have been broadcast in both Kansas City and Green Bay, but was not in either city, because Washington State played the University of Kansas in Lawrence, Kansas, and Stout State played St. Norbert College in West DePere, Wisconsin. On the same day, the Chicago Bears played the St. Louis Cardinals in St. Louis in a game that could not be televised live in Chicago because Illinois was playing Benedictine in Lisle, Illinois, and Illinois State was playing Northern Illinois in DeKalb, Illinois. Finally, the New York Jets played the San Diego Chargers in San Diego in a game that began at 11:00 P.M., New York time, which could not be broadcast in New York, because earlier that day Hofstra played Lehigh in Bethlehem, Pennsylvania.[7]

§10.2(c) NFL championship game cases

While §1292 of Title 15 of the United States Code prohibits most blackouts, it does expressly authorize the practice of blacking out the home territory on days when the home team is playing there.[1] Since other games may be blacked out (even though they no longer are) in the home territory of a team when it is playing there, it certainly followed that prior to the enactment of the anti-blackout act in 1973[2] the home game itself could be blacked out in the home territory. The question arose some time ago, however, whether championship games were not another matter.

[7] *Id.* at 293-294.

[1] See § 10.2(b)(2), *supra.*

[2] See § 10.2(d), *infra.*

The first reported challenge to a championship game blackout was in the pre-Super Bowl year of 1962. In *Blaich v. National Football League,*[3] three New York Giants fans sought to enjoin the blackout of that year's NFL Championship Game which was being played in New York. Since the Giants were playing in their home territory, §1292 appeared to legitimize the blackout. However, the fans argued that championship games were not covered by §1292, because Judge Grim's 1961 ruling concerned only regular season games, and the legislative history of the section states that it was designed to meet the problems created by that ruling. The court responded by saying that §1292 uses the "all-embracing term 'game' " and that to exclude championship games from its sweep would amount to a judicial amendment to it. The court therefore refused to ban that blackout.

The court's response overlooked two facts, however—perhaps because the lawsuit was filed the Friday before the Sunday of the game. The first is that the *judgment* entered by Judge Grim in 1953 specifically stated that "the term 'games' means regular season and exhibition professional football games between member clubs of the defendant National Football League; it does not include conference playoff games or the 'World Professional Championship Game' between the first place clubs in the two conferences of the National Football League." [4]

Thus, since §1292 was enacted for the specific purpose of preserving the anti-blackout portion of Judge Grim's 1953 decision, and since Judge Grim himself defined "games" so as not to include championship games, a read-

[3] 212 F.Supp. 319 (S.D.N.Y. 1962).

[4] Hearings on H.R. 8757 before the Antitrust Subcomm. of the House Comm. on the Judiciary, 87th Cong., 1st Sess. 24 (1961).

ing of §1292 which excluded championship games would not be a judicial amendment of the section. Rather, it would simply be judicial recognition of a legislative adoption of a judicial ruling in which the word "games" was assigned a particular meaning. Unfortunately, only the decision and not the judgment was published. Thus, it is probable that the judge who decided *Blaich* was unaware of Judge Grim's definition. However, Congress presumably was, for the judgment was published in the transcript of the hearings before the House Antitrust Subcommittee that considered the bill that became §1292.

The decision in *Blaich* v. *National Football League* not only overlooked Judge Grim's own definition of "games," it also overlooked the fact that only a few years before, the United States Supreme Court specifically ruled that championship sporting events may constitute an entirely different market from ordinary events, even within the same sport. In *International Boxing Club of New York* v. *United States,*[5] the Government charged the defendants with monopolization of world championship boxing contests. The defendants argued that it was improper to consider the relevant market to be championship boxing contests rather than all professional boxing events; but the Supreme Court did not agree and held that non-championship fights were not "reasonably interchangeable for the same purpose" with championship fights. Championship boxing was characterized as the "cream" of the professional boxing business; and though the decision did not turn upon whether a particular word in a statute covered both championship and non-championship events alike, it does suggest that a statute designed to deal with one type event ought not be applied to the other without some justification.

---

[5] 348 U.S. 236 (1955) and 358 U.S. 242 (1959), discussed in § 1.2(a), *supra.*

Without the protective exemption of §1292, championship game blackouts would seem to have violated antitrust laws on two grounds. First, if the television rights to such games were sold as part of a package, the package agreement itself may have violated Judge Grim's 1953 decree and possibly statutory law prohibiting block-booking as well. Second, though the blackout of a championship game is not a *horizontal* allocation of territories, as was the sort of blackout held illegal by Judge Grim in 1953, it would seem to be an illegal *vertical* allocation of territories.

This is so because the "manufacturer" of the championship football game, the National Football League, sells its "product," the game, to an independent "distributor," the television network, reserving for itself the exclusive right to sell that "product" within a 75-mile radius of the game site by prohibiting the "distributor" from selling there by requiring that area to be blacked out. The "manufacturer" in effect agrees to give its "distributor" the exclusive right to the rest of the country, because the distances involved make it unlikely that any resident of the territory outside the 75-mile radius would buy from the "manufacturer" by attending in person.

In *United States* v. *Arnold, Schwinn & Co.,*[6] a case not unlike a blackout case except that a different product was involved, the United States Supreme Court held that it is a *per se* antitrust violation for a manufacturer to sell its products to a distributor subject to territorial restrictions on resale. Even when goods are distributed by consignment (where the manufacturer retains title, dominion and risk of loss, as distinguished from sales to distributors, where the manufacturer retains none of those things), territorial restraints are not necessarily legal. They are

[6] 388 U.S. 350 (1967).

simply subject to the "rule of reason," rather than being *per se* illegal.

The National Football League's sale of television rights to its games certainly appears to be a "sale" within the meaning of the *Arnold, Schwinn* case. The NFL has neither dominion nor control over the broadcast itself, and the risk of an electronic malfunction that might destroy the broadcast is undoubtedly borne by the network. If so, a championship game blackout would be a *per se* violation of the antitrust laws.

Moreover, even if the sale of television rights did not constitute a sale within the meaning of the *Arnold, Schwinn* case, the blackout would still have to satisfy the rule of reason which, according to the standards enunciated by the Supreme Court in that case, it might not. The Court held that Arnold, Schwinn's territorial restrictions on resale by consignees were not unreasonable restraints of trade because (1) other bicycles were available to distributors and retailers, (2) Schwinn distributors handled other brands as well, (3) there was no evidence of price fixing, and (4) competition made the program necessary and justified its extent, and the program actually preserved competition in the bicycle market. Insofar as championship professional football games are concerned, (1) there are none other than those produced by the NFL, (2) television networks handle no kind of professional football other than NFL football, (3) the higher price of championship game tickets in years past may have been due in part to blackouts, and (4) the reasons given for blacking out championship games have been deemed to be unpersuasive by many of those who have studied the question.[7]

---

[7] See, for example, S.Rep. 92-1151, 92d Cong., 2d Sess. 6-7 (1972); and Comment, Professional Football Telecasts and the Blackout Privilege, 57 Cornell L.Rev. 297, 301-303, 308-312 (1972).

Since at least 1967, when the first Super Bowl game was played, the question of whether §1292 applies to championship games being played in the home territory of one of the participating teams has been largely academic. Super Bowl games are played in pre-selected warm-weather cities, not necessarily the home city of either participant. When neither participant is "at home" for the Super Bowl, its blackout is not authorized by §1292.

Between 1966 and 1973, when the anti-blackout statute was enacted, at least five lawsuits were filed in attempts to enjoin Super Bowl blackouts. Despite the seeming illegality of Super Bowl blackouts, the National Football League won all five cases. Only one of the five resulted in a published opinion, the 1972 game in New Orleans, Super Bowl VI.[8] In that case it was held that the plaintiff did not have standing to assert that the blackout violated the antitrust laws, because he was not within an area of the economy that could be endangered by a breakdown of competitive conditions in the industry and, therefore, could not be directly or proximately injured by the lessening of competition in that industry.[9] Lack of standing was also the basis for the NFL's victory in federal cases filed in Los Angeles in 1966 involving the very first Super Bowl,[10] and in Miami in 1971 involving Super Bowl V.[11]

On the merits, it has been reported that a judge in a Florida state court ruled that the blackout of Super Bowl V was a clear violation of the Sherman Act, but he also

---

[8] Campo v. National Football League, 334 F.Supp. 1181 (E.D. La. 1971).

[9] On standing generally, see § 8.2(b), *supra.*

[10] Minter v. National Football League, No. 66-2072-WPG, U.S. Dist.Ct. (C.D. Cal. 1967).

[11] Rubin v. Reese, No. 70-1489-Civ-TC, U.S. Dist.Ct. (S.D. Fla. 1970).

said that he did not have jurisdiction to enjoin it on that ground.[12] In the 1966 case in Los Angeles, the court specifically held "that the conduct of defendants herein does not constitute a violation of any of the antitrust laws of the United States," [13] though no reasons for that conclusion were stated. The court's failure to articulate any reasons for its conclusions may well have been why the decision was never published, despite the obvious novelty and significance of the issue involved. Nevertheless, in 1972, a California Superior Court judge in Los Angeles also stated, in the course of his ruling denying plaintiffs a preliminary injunction and granting defendants' motion for summary judgment, that the planned blackout of Super Bowl VII did not violate the antitrust laws.[14]

§ 10.2(d) The anti-blackout statute

§ 10.2(d)(1) Congressional action

Despite the National Football League's courtroom victory in the case designed to enjoin the blackout of Super Bowl VII,[1] the game was televised live in Los Angeles—the first Super Bowl to be televised locally in the history of that event. NFL Commissioner Pete Rozelle announced in October of 1972 that the customary blackout would be lifted, as an experiment, in the event the game was sold out at least ten days in advance. It was. In agreeing to abandon the local blackout, Rozelle was not responding so much to the lawsuit, or even to the possibility of future lawsuits, as he was to pending activity in the Congress. For by the time the 92nd Congress had convened in 1971,

---

[12] Comment, *supra* note 7, at fn. 23.

[13] Minter v. National Football League, *supra* note 10.

[14] Schneider v. Rozelle, LASC No. C32005 (1972).

[1] See § 10.2(c), *supra*.

the popularity of professional football had become so great that pressure to eliminate blackouts, particularly of sold-out games, had resulted in the introduction of several bills intended to do just that.[2] Indeed, the speculation which followed Rozelle's announcement was that the experiment was designed to head-off enactment of those bills.

If the speculation was correct, the tactic was successful—all of the bills died with the close of the 92nd Congress—but only temporarily so. Following the announcement that the Super Bowl blackout would be lifted if the game was sold out ten days in advance, pressure immediately built for a lifting of the blackouts of the play-off games as well. Spearheading that pressure was President Nixon himself, but the National Football League nevertheless resisted. Thus, Attorney General Richard Kleindienst was prompted to issue the following statement on December 20, 1972:

> "Following a recent discussion with the President, and at his direction, I have had a series of conversations with Commissioner Rozelle of the National Football League to request that arrangements be made so that all remaining play-off games would be televised locally in cases where they are sold out forty-eight hours in advance of the kick-off.
>
> "Commissioner Rozelle advised me this morning that it would not be possible for the NFL to comply with the President's request.
>
> "I advised Mr. Rozelle that, as a result of the League's decision, the Nixon Administration would strongly urge the new Congress to re-examine the

---

[2] See, Hochberg, Second and Goal To Go: The Legislative Attack in the 92d Congress on Sports Broadcasting Practices, 18 New York Law Forum 841 (1973), 26 Federal Communications Bar Journal 118 (1973).

entire antitrust exemption statute and seek legislation that is more in keeping with the public interest."[3]

When the 93rd Congress convened shortly thereafter, several new bills were introduced dealing with the blackout question.[4] In the Senate, Senator John O. Pastore introduced a measure which would have prevented television stations from performing any contract which prohibited it from broadcasting any home football, basketball, baseball or hockey game for which tickets were no longer available for purchase forty-eight hours in advance.[5] No hearings were immediately scheduled on the bill, and as matters developed, none was ever held. On July 1, 1973, CBS's Baltimore affiliate announced that it had been prohibited from broadcasting any of the Washington Redskins' home games that coming season even though in previous years it had shown as many as five. At first, it was not clear whether this decision had been made by CBS, the National Football League, or the Redskins. Within days, however, the National Football League accepted responsibility, "eagerly" according to one observer.[6] In an interview published in the *Washington Post,* Robert Cochran, the NFL's Broadcast Coordinator, said:

> "We are well within our rights to order the blackout . . . nor are we going to listen to fan mail saying 'I want this' and 'I want that!' . . . In this society, people are

---

[3] C.C.H. Trade Regulation Reports, No. 52 at 5 (Dec. 26, 1972).

[4] See, Hochberg, Congress Kicks A Field Goal: The Legislative Attack in the 93d Congress on Sports Broadcasting Practices, 27 Federal Communications Bar Journal 27 (1974).

[5] S.1841, 93d Cong., 1st Sess. (1973), discussed in Hochberg, *supra* note 4, at 40-45, and in Shooshan, Confrontation with Congress: Professional Sports and the Television Antiblackout Law, 25 Syracuse Law Rev. 713, 722-724 (1974).

[6] Shooshan, *supra* note 5, at 723.

always wanting to get something they shouldn't necessarily have to get . . . they're so spoiled." [7]

According to Congressman Torbert Macdonald's Administrative Assistant, Harry Shooshan, "Cochran's intemperate outburst destroyed what little remained of a willingness to compromise on the part of Congress." [8] Senator Pastore's bill was reported out of committee without any hearings whatsoever and was passed by a vote of 76 to 6 on September 6, 1973.

In the House of Representatives, several bills were introduced in July of 1973, including one by Congressman Macdonald, Chairman of the House Subcommittee on Communications and Power. This bill provided that any football, baseball, basketball or hockey game broadcast pursuant to a package television contract must be made available for television broadcasting in the local area if admission tickets to the game were no longer available for purchase forty-eight hours or more in advance.[9]

Although Senator Pastore's and Congressman Macdonald's bills appeared similar to one another, there was in fact a significant distinction between them. Congressman Macdonald's bill prohibited the blacking out of sold-out games only if the game was being broadcast pursuant to a league package contract. Senator Pastore's bill, on the other hand, would have prohibited the blacking out of sold-out games even if they were being broadcast pursuant to a television contract individually negotiated between a single team and a single television station. As a result, Senator Pastore's bill would have had far greater impact

[7] *Id.* at 723-724.

[8] *Id.* at 724.

[9] H.R. 9553, 93d Cong., 1st Sess. (1973), discussed in Hochberg, *supra* note 4, at 63-75, and Shooshan, *supra* note 5, at 725-744.

on professional sports broadcasting. This is so because although the National Football League sells all of its regular season and post-season games to television pursuant to a package contract, baseball, basketball and hockey teams sell relatively few games to television pursuant to a network contract. In fact, most baseball, basketball and hockey games shown on television are broadcast pursuant to contracts negotiated by individual teams, usually with their local stations. For the most part, the only baseball, basketball and hockey games shown on television pursuant to a league package contract are the "Games of the Week" and post-season play-off and championship games. According to FCC Chairman Dean Burch, baseball, basketball and hockey games broadcast pursuant to league package contracts amount to only two or three percent of the total number of games played.[10]

For this reason, it was thought that these three sports might support Congressman Macdonald's bill during the hearings conducted by his Subcommittee in July, August and September of 1973. In fact, that support never developed. Although Don Ruck, Vice President of the National Hockey League, did testify that Congressman Macdonald's bill "is the most reasonable approach," he stated that his League was actually opposed to any legislation.[11]

Baseball Commissioner Bowie Kuhn took an even more aggressive stand. "First off," he said, "we would oppose any bill which would compel any team sports, whether it is baseball, football, or basketball, or hockey, to make games

---

[10] Hearings on S.4007 et al. before the Subcomm. on Communications of the Senate Comm. on Commerce, 92d Cong., 2d Sess. 130 (1972).

[11] Hearings on H.R. 9536 et al. before the Subcomm. on Communications and Power of the House Interstate and Foreign Commerce Comm., 93d Cong., 1st Sess. 26-27 (1973).

available for television under certain circumstances." But, he added, "if the Congress should feel that a bill is necessary, notwithstanding, then in my judgment the bill should have no application to professional baseball."[12] Thus, rather than support Congressman Macdonald's bill which would have had little or no impact on baseball, over Senator Pastore's bill which might have had some impact on it, Kuhn sought an exemption for baseball from the proposed statute. While Congress had treated Organized Baseball with kindness in earlier years, by 1973 it was no longer inclined to give it special treatment.

National Basketball Association Commissioner Walter Kennedy also attacked all of the bills with equal vigor. He stated,

> "As a general matter, the NBA and its member teams oppose all of the proposed legislation, which we believe will have a serious financial impact on our member teams. . . . It is a well-established principle of fairness and equity that no business should be forced to give away its product. No other form of entertainment is deprived of the right to make the decision as to whether to sell—professional sports should not be deprived of this right either. We find it particularly disturbing that a basis for support of this legislation is the allegation that it would cost the teams no money, since the blackout is not prohibited until the game has been sold out. But the question of whether it will cost money must basically be one of business judgment. The supporters of the legislation should not assume that they know better what is good for the professional sports business than do the owners whose investment is at stake. It should be assumed instead that the

---

[12] *Id.* at 158.

> owners know their own business and have made the decision to blackout because the decision is a necessary one."[13]

Congressman Macdonald, for one, was apparently not prepared to assume that the NBA owners know their own business. "I am rather surprised at your testimony," he told Kennedy. "As a matter of fact," he added,

> "I won't say just rather surprised, I am very surprised. . . . You start off rather unharmoniously telling us that we assume that we know better what is good for the professional sports business than do the owners whose investments are at stake. Now, that is not the case. Nobody here thinks that they know more about professional sports than the people involved in it. However, I would point out that if I were looking at any professional sport that is not noted for its astuteness, I think I would pick the NBA."[14]

By the time NFL Commissioner Rozelle testified on September 6, 1973, a Report had been issued by the House Special Subcommittee on Investigations which concluded that "the NFL clubs no longer need the degree of protection presently provided by the antitrust exemptions granted by Congress in 1961." This conclusion was "based on the fact that the original justification for permitting blackouts, i.e., to assist the clubs in obtaining financial stability, is no longer necessary."[15]

---

[13] *Id.* at 119.

[14] *Id.* at 122.

[15] Evaluation of the Necessity for Television Blackouts of Professional Sporting Events, Report by the Special Subcomm. on Investigations of the House Comm. on Interstate and Foreign Commerce, 93d Cong., 1st Sess. (1973).

As a result, Rozelle felt, even before he testified, that Congress was likely to enact anti-blackout legislation, and he told a reporter that if it did, the National Football League would "just have to accept it." [16] Rozelle's statement to Congressman Macdonald's Subcommittee was viewed as being "generally hostile," [17] and it concluded with his observation that he believed "that any realist making an objective review of this situation will conclude that the proposed legislation is unfair and unjustified." [18]

While the Subcommittee members had not been persuaded to abandon the proposed legislation, Congressman Macdonald, for one, did not wish to impose the heavier burdens the Pastore bill would have required. Thus, his Subcommittee reported out Congressman Macdonald's own bill (with some modifications[19]), rather than the House counterpart to the Pastore bill; and on September 11, 1973, the full Commerce Committee reported the measure to the House itself, concluding as follows:

> "Your Committee believes that professional sports clubs have benefited substantially from legislation previously enacted by the Congress, exempting certain of their activities from the operation of the Federal antitrust laws. The legislation herein reported exacts for these previously conferred benefits the requirement that sold-out games of such clubs which are televised pursuant to a league television contract must be made available for live television showing in the area in which the game is being played. While the legislation may result in some additional 'no shows'

[16] Shooshan, *supra* note 5, at 734.

[17] *Id.*

[18] Hearings on H.R. 9536, *supra* note 11, at 198.

[19] See Shooshan, *supra* note 5, at 737-739.

> at sold-out games which are televised under its provisions, with some consequential diminution of revenues from such sources as parking fees and concessions, the benefits that flow from its enactment far outweigh these shortcomings. Your Committee is convinced that this legislation serves the public interest and urges its speedy enactment." [20]

With the National Football League season scheduled to begin on September 16th, speedy enactment was precisely what Congress wished to accomplish. Yet, because of the significant differences that existed between the Pastore bill that had been passed by the Senate and the Macdonald bill that had been reported to the House, it appeared that a Conference Committee meeting would be necessary unless some compromise could be worked out in advance. One was. As noted above, the Pastore bill would have affected all sports broadcasts, even those that were not part of a league-wide, package contract. However, the Pastore bill would have remained in effect by its own terms, for only one year. The Macdonald bill would affect only those broadcasts made pursuant to a league package contract, but it was permanent legislation. The compromise worked out between Senator Pastore and Congressman Macdonald was this: Senator Pastore agreed to the substantive provisions of Congressman Macdonald's bill; and Congressman Macdonald agreed to limit the term of his bill to three full football seasons.[21]

Thus, when the Macdonald bill was brought up on the floor of the House of Representatives, an amendment was added pursuant to which the legislation would expire by

[20] H.Rep. 93-483, 93d Cong., 1st Sess. (1973).

[21] Shooshan, *supra* note 5, at 743.

its own terms on December 31, 1975. Although some Congressmen spoke in opposition to the bill, the measure passed on September 13, 1973 by a vote of 336 to 37. It was then returned to the Senate which passed it by a voice vote. And on Friday, September 14, 1973, it was signed by President Nixon and became law.

Thereafter, any professional football, baseball, basketball or hockey game broadcast pursuant to a league package television contract had to be shown in the area where the game was being played if all of the admission tickets which were available for purchase five days before the game were sold 72 hours or more before it began[22] (unless the broadcast would conflict with the playing of a college or high-school football game in the same area and would therefore be prohibited by §1293 of Title 15 of the United States Code[23]).

From the point of view of those who opposed blackouts, the legislation actually passed during the 93rd Congress was superior to the bills that had been considered but not enacted during the 92nd Congress. This is so because the legislation actually enacted amended the Communications Act of 1934,[24] while the measures that had been considered during the 92nd Congress would have amended §1292 of Title 15 by eliminating its antitrust exemption if sold out games were nevertheless blacked out. The deficiency with such an amendment, is that eliminating the antitrust exemption for home territory blackouts would not necessarily have made those blackouts illegal. It would simply have made illegal the package contracts by which the league sold television rights to the networks. But the legality of

[22] 47 U.S.C. § 331.

[23] See § 10.2(b)(3), *supra.*

[24] 47 U.S.C. §§ 301 *et seq.*

the blackouts would still have had to have been litigated, and the National Football League had won on that issue before.[25] Furthermore, if §1292 had been amended, fans would not have had standing to object, even if the leagues blatantly violated the law.[26]

Although it has been said that the bills introduced in the 93rd Congress were designed to amend the Communications Act of 1934 so as to enable Senator Pastore and Congressman Macdonald to acquire jurisdiction over them in their own subcommittees[27] (jurisdiction over amendments to Title 15 would have been in the Judiciary Committees of the Senate and House), this change also permitted Congress to resolve the "standing" problem. As enacted, the law contained a simple subsection providing,

> "If any person violates . . . this section, any *interested person* may commence a civil action for injunctive relief restraining such violation in any United States District Court for a district in which the defendant resides, or has an agent. In any such action, the court may award the cost of the suit including reasonable attorneys' fees." [28]

While such a subsection conceivably could have been included in an amendment to §1292 of Title 15 as well, it would have been a very significant departure from the usual rules concerning "standing" in antitrust cases.[29]

---

[25] See § 10.2(c), *supra.*

[26] Campo v. National Football League, 334 F.Supp. 1181 (E.D. La. 1971), discussed in § 10.2(c), *supra.*

[27] Hochberg, *supra* note 4, at 41; and Shooshan, *supra* note 5, at 723.

[28] 47 U.S.C. § 331(b).

[29] See § 8.2(b), *supra.*

§10.2(d)(2) The law's effects

The anti-blackout statute requires the Federal Communications Commission to conduct a continuing study of the effect of the law and to submit an annual report to the Senate and House.[1] The first such report was submitted on April 15, 1974, after the law had been in effect one full football season, and for most of a basketball and hockey season as well. As expected, the law had no significant effect on basketball or hockey leagues. At the time of the FCC report, the National Basketball Association expected that only 39 of its 757 games that season would be broadcast pursuant to a league television contract. Of those 39, the NBA thought that 24 would be legally blacked out and only 15 televised locally as a result of the law. Of those 15, it was expected that 8 or 9 would be play-off games;[2] and, therefore, it was the FCC's conclusion that "the effect of the legislation on season and individual ticket sales, and on overall team and concession revenues would appear minimal."[3]

In the American Basketball Association, only 6 of its 499 games that season were to be broadcast pursuant to a league television package contract, and none of those were sold out 72 hours in advance and, therefore, none had to be broadcast locally. The ABA also reported that none of the 9 games that had been broadcast pursuant to a package contract the previous season were sold out 72 hours in advance, and therefore none would have had to have been broadcast locally, even if the law had been in effect the previous season.[4]

---

[1] 47 U.S.C. § 331(d).

[2] The Sports Anti Black-out Issue—A Federal Communications Report 38-39 (1974).

[3] *Id.* at 40.

[4] *Id.* at 40-41.

The World Hockey Association did not have a league package contract during the 1973-1974 season, and therefore the anti-blackout law had no effect on it whatsoever.[5] During the preceding season, 5 of its games were shown on the CBS Network, but none of those was sold out and therefore none would have been affected, had the law been in effect at that time.[6]

The law's effect on the National Hockey League appears to be equally minimal. Only 15 of its 624 regular-season games were broadcast pursuant to a league package contract in both the 1972-1973 and 1973-1974 seasons. Moreover, none of those broadcast during the 1972-1973 season were blacked out, even though the law was not then in effect. Nor were any blacked out during the 1973-1974 season, although it is not clear whether the National Hockey League voluntarily showed those games locally or was required to do so by the law. Of the 38 post-season games played during the 1972-1973 season, only 6 were broadcast pursuant to a league package contract, and of those 6, only 3 were blacked out, again even though the law was not then in effect.[7]

Although the 1973 baseball season was almost over when the law was enacted, and although the 1974 season had not yet begun when the FCC submitted its report, the FCC was nevertheless able to reach some conclusions concerning the law's expected impact on that sport. The only league package television contract which Organized Baseball had was one with NBC, pursuant to which the World Series, the National and American League Championship Series, the All-Star Game, the Saturday Afternoon "Games of the Week," and 15 mid-season Monday night games were

---

[5] ***Id.* at 43.**

[6] ***Id.* at Appendix XIII.**

[7] ***Id.* at 42.**

nationally telecast. The contract itself affirmatively required NBC to telecast the World Series and All-Star Game nationally without any blackouts whatsoever. In addition, during the 1972 and 1973 seasons, the World Series and the National and American League Championship Series were not blacked out in any area of the country. Because none of these games had been blacked out, the FCC concluded that the law would not have any effect on baseball with respect to them. "Games of the Week" are blacked out in the home territories of both teams playing. However, had the law been in effect during the 1972 and 1973 baseball seasons, it would not have required any "Games of the Week" to be televised locally because none was sold out at least 72 hours in advance.[8]

The law did have a significant effect on the broadcasting of National Football League games. Of the 182 regular-season NFL games, 109 were televised locally during the 1973 season. By comparison, none of the NFL's regular-season games had been televised locally the season before.[9]

According to the National Football League, the immediate and most important result of the televising of these 109 sold-out games was a dramatic increase in the number of no shows (i.e., people who purchased admission tickets but did not attend the game). There was 1,017,337 no-shows during the regular season in 1973 as compared to only 624,686 during the regular season in 1972. This would have represented a 64% increase in no-shows. However, the FCC detected that the Dallas Cowboys and the San Diego Chargers had not provided the National Football League with statistics concerning their no-shows during the 1972 season, and as a result there were really more no-shows in

[8] *Id.* at 36-37.

[9] *Id.* at 5.

1972 than the NFL reported. When the FCC excluded the Dallas and San Diego no-shows for 1973, the total for that season dropped to 967,362—a 54.6% increase over 1972.[10]

Clearly a 54.6% increase in the number of no-shows would have been very significant had the increase been due to the anti-blackout law. However, the FCC concluded that this increase in the number of no-shows was not due mainly to the anti-blackout law, but was probably due to other factors such as weather, league standings, and the unimportance of particular games. The FCC concluded that this was so because of other relevant comparisons it made. For example, 9 teams televised all of their home games locally in 1973, and the average number of no-shows at those games was 5,665. Five teams were able to blackout all of their home games, because none was sold out in advance, and the average number of no-shows at those games was 5,218—only about 8% fewer than at the televised games.[11] Moreover, the percentage of no-shows at all of the games televised locally during the 1973 season was 9.8%, while the percentage of no-shows at all of the games blacked out locally that season was 9.1%.[12] In other words, the difference was slight.

With respect to post-season games, the statistics were similarly inconclusive. The FCC reported that the largest number of no-shows, 4,277, was tallied at a game that was blacked out locally. There were 18,489 no-shows for the Pro Bowl, and that game, too, was blacked out locally.[13]

As a result, the FCC concluded that, "At least in the first season, there is little evidence to support the NFL claim that the antiblackout law will result in football be-

[10] *Id.* at 6.
[11] *Id.* at 8.
[12] *Id.*
[13] *Id.* at 9.

coming a television, or studio, sport as a result of increasing no-shows."[14]

The FCC's 1975 report again concluded that the fear that professional football would be turned into a "studio sport" by the anti-blackout law was unfounded.[15] Although the number of no-shows increased somewhat over 1973, they increased at blacked out and televised games alike. In fact, the percentage difference between the average number of no-shows at televised games (6,413) and at blacked out games (5,965) was only about 7½%, slightly less than the difference the year before.[16] According to FCC calculations, 46% of the increase in the number of no-shows could be explained by rain or snow, while only 2.2% of the increase was the result of the lifting of blackouts.[17]

The number of season tickets sold did decline slightly—by 6%—from the year before, but the FCC explained that ". . . these sales could have been affected by, among other things, the players' strike, the weakening of the economy, and the competitive threat of the World Football League."[18]

§10.3 Cable television and sports

§10.3(a) Nature of television rights

In the early minutes of every NFL television broadcast, the following announcement is made by one of the game commentators:

---

[14] *Id.*

[15] Maher, FCC Denies "Studio Sport" Danger, L.A. Times, May 2, 1975, Part III.

[16] *Id.*

[17] *Id.*

[18] *Id.*

> "This telecast is presented by authority of the National Football League. It is intended for the private use of our audience, and any rebroadcast or other use of this telecast without the express written consent of the National Football League is prohibited."

This announcement is virtually identical to one that Organized Baseball began making in connection with radio broadcasts even before television was in widespread use.[1] For unauthorized sports broadcasts are a problem that has plagued team owners since at least the mid-1930's. As long ago as 1936, the Federal Communications Commission considered whether it should refuse to renew the license of a radio station in Jamestown, New York, because it had rebroadcast the 1934 World Series in violation of the Communications Act. The station's announcer had listened to the authorized radio broadcast of the game and, using the information he heard, he gave a running account of the game to his own listeners. The FCC ultimately decided to renew the license, because the unauthorized recreation had occurred only once.[2] But, in the course of its opinion, the FCC noted,

> "However, it is not inappropriate to observe that the production of programs by a radio station calls for the exercise of creative faculties and the outlay of funds for the employment of talent—the preparation and planning of the broadcast and the employment of persons trained and qualified for their particular duties. When, therefore, a station engages in the practice here involved, its conduct is inconsistent with fair dealing, is dishonest in nature, and amounts to an unfair utilization of the results of another's labor.

[1] S.Rep. 387, 83d Cong., 1st Sess. 10 (1953).

[2] Matter of Newton, 2 F.C.C. 281 (1936).

> Moreover, the practice is deceptive to the public upon the whole, and contrary to the interest thereof." [3]

A similar case was filed in federal court two years later by the Pittsburgh Pirates against radio station KQV to prevent it from broadcasting play-by-play descriptions of the Pirates' games. There, KQV did not obtain its information from another radio broadcast. Rather, KQV stationed observers at vantage points outside of the Pirates' Forbes Field who were able to see over the fences and observe the plays as they were made. The Pirates had sold the exclusive right to broadcast play-by-play descriptions of their games to General Mills which in turn had entered into an agreement with NBC for the broadcast of the games over two of its radio stations.

The court granted a preliminary injunction restraining KQV from broadcasting Pirates' games, holding that the right to broadcast these games was a property right with which KQV had interfered.[4] It explained,

> "The Athletic Company [the Pirates] has, at great expense, acquired and maintains a baseball park, pays the players who participate in the games, and have, as we view it, a legitimate right to capitalize on the news value of their games by selling exclusive broadcasting rights to companies which value them as advertising mediums for their merchandise. This right the defendant interferes with when it uses its broadcasting facilities for giving out the identical news obtained by its paid observers stationed at points outside Forbes Field for the purpose of securing in-

---

[3] *Id.* at 284.

[4] Pittsburgh Athletic Co. v. KQV Broadcasting Co., 24 F.Supp. 490 (W.D. Pa. 1938).

> formation which it cannot otherwise acquire. This, in our judgment, amounts to unfair competition, and is a violation of the property rights of the plaintiffs. For it is our opinion that the Pittsburgh Athletic Company, by reason of its creation of the game, its control of the park, and its restriction of the dissemination of news therefrom, has a property right in such news, and the right to control the use thereof for a reasonable time following the games." [5]

Probably because of this case, a committee of Congress once reported that sports teams are entitled to protection against the misappropriation of the radio and television broadcasting rights to their games, and that the "committee understands that these property rights are supported by well-established principles of law, including principles of common law copyright and the principles of equitable protection against unfair competition." [6] The same opinion has been expressed more recently by at least one communications law commentator.[7]

When cable television systems began picking up sports broadcasts and carrying them to other cities, despite the objections of team owners, "unfair competition" theories may have given team owners a basis for preventing the practice. Apparently, however, no such lawsuit has ever been filed. Instead, team owners sought a remedy in Congress and from the Federal Communications Commission.

---

[5] *Id.* at 492; but see National Exhibition Co. v. Teleflash, 24 F.Supp. 488 (S.D.N.Y. 1936), refusing to enjoin play-by-play descriptions over telephone wires under similar circumstances.

[6] S.Rep. 387, *supra* note 1, at 11.

[7] Hochberg, Second and Goal To Go: The Legislative Attack in the 92d Congress on Sports Broadcasting Practices, 18 New York Law Forum 841 (1973), 26 Federal Communications Bar Journal 118 (1973), at fn. 99 and accompanying text.

They were not successful in Congress,[8] but were, at least partially so, with the FCC.[9]

It is interesting to consider whether an unfair competition lawsuit by team owners against cable television systems would have succeeded or might now succeed. On the one hand, it has been held by the United States Supreme Court that cable television systems do not infringe the copyrights to copyrighted television programming they pick up and carry to their subscribers.[10] Live sporting events are not copyrighted. Thus, it could be argued that if cable television systems may legally carry copyrighted programming, they certainly may carry uncopyrighted programming as well.

On the other hand, the owners of copyrighted television programming apparently have never asserted an unfair competition cause of action against cable television systems, probably because of 1964 Supreme Court decisions which strongly suggested that the Copyright Act had preempted unfair competition claims, at least with respect to the kinds of programming that qualified for copyright protection in the first place.[11] However, in 1973, the Supreme Court ruled that the Copyright Act does not pre-empt the entire field of law concerning the protection of literary, musical and artistic property.[12] Moreover, it has been sug-

[8] See Hochberg, *supra* note 7, at text accompanying footnotes 95 through 103; and Hochberg, Congress Kicks A Field Goal: The Legislative Attack in the 93d Congress on Sports Broadcasting Practices, 27 Federal Communications Bar Journal 27, 33-40 (1974).

[9] See § 10.3(c), *infra*.

[10] Teleprompter Corp. v. Columbia Broadcasting System, Inc., 415 U.S. 394 (1974).

[11] Sears, Roebuck & Co. v. Stiffel Co., 376 U.S. 225 (1964); Compco Corp. v. Day-Brite Lighting, Inc., 376 U.S. 234 (1964).

[12] Goldstein v. California, 412 U.S. 546 (1973).

gested, accurately it seems, that even if the Copyright Act does pre-empt certain areas of the law, it would not pre-empt an unfair competition theory for the protection of the broadcast of sporting events, because live sporting events are not "writings" and therefore are not eligible for copyright protection.[13] Team owners may have weakened their position in this regard by seeking copyright protection for their broadcasts, however.[14] In any event, team owners decided to seek a remedy from the Federal Communications Commission.

§10.3(b) The cable-sports dispute

In their early years, cable television systems enabled subscribers who lived in areas where television reception was poor, because of nearby mountains or tall buildings for example, to enjoy clear television pictures broadcast by local stations. As cable systems matured and developed, however, they also began to pick up television signals in cities quite distant from the places their subscribers lived. As a result, it became possible, for example, for Philadelphia residents who were cable subscribers to watch television programs broadcast by New York City stations. When cable systems began to carry sporting events broadcast in one city to subscribers located in another city, team owners quickly began to object.

There were essentially two reasons for the team owners' dispute with cable television systems. First, except when games are broadcast nationwide pursuant to a league package contract, teams generally permit their games to be broadcast in and around their own home territory only.

---

[13] Hochberg, *supra* note 7, at fn. 99.

[14] In S.644, 92d Cong., 1st Sess. (1971), and in S.1361, 93d Cong., 1st Sess. (1973), discussed in Hochberg, *supra* note 8. See also, Copyright Protection for Sports Broadcasts and the Public's Right of Access, 15 Idea 385 (1971).

In particular, one team would never sell broadcasting rights to its games to a television station located in the home territory of another team in the same league. Thus, a game being played or televised in a team's home territory does not usually compete with televised games between other teams in the league. The absence of such competition maximizes the value of each team's television rights, and, according to team owners, protects live attendance at home games. Cable television has the ability to, and has in fact, destroyed this exclusive territory concept. For example, the broadcasts of New York City television stations are carried to Philadelphia by a cable television system operating in Philadelphia. Thus, when the game of any New York team is being shown on television in New York, Philadelphia cable subscribers may choose to watch the New York game rather than to watch or attend the Philadelphia game, thereby making the two games competitive.

Second, it often happened that the competing game being imported from a distant city by a cable television system was in fact a game being played and blacked out in the city where the cable system operated. Thus, the away games of the New York Mets have been broadcast in New York City and carried by a cable television system to its subscribers in Philadelphia. When the New York Mets played the Philadelphia Phillies in a blacked out game in Philadelphia, and permitted the game to be broadcast in New York City, Philadelphia cable subscribers have been able to view the game, even though it has been blacked out there. In other words, cable television systems can and have frustrated blackouts which were perfectly legal under §1292 of Title 15 of the United States Code.[1]

---

[1] See § 10.2(b)(2), *infra*.

In an effort to head off what they characterized as this growing threat from cable television systems, team owners appealed to both Congress and the Federal Communications Commission for restrictions on the ability of cable television systems to carry sporting events. While testifying before the Senate Communications Subcommittee in June of 1971, the Chairman of the Federal Communications Commission promised to provide the Subcommittee with a written summary of the FCC's proposals for the then "near-term" regulation of cable television. On August 5, 1971, he did so in a letter which stated, "Sports events stand on a separate footing from other programming presented on commercial television." [2] Noting that Congress had enacted a law which permitted blackouts of home games in the home territory of the team concerned, the letter continued, "Certainly, cable systems should not be permitted to circumvent the purpose of the law by importing the signal of a station carrying the home game of a professional team if that team has elected to blackout the game in its home territory." [3] The letter stated that the FCC intended "to issue very shortly a notice of proposed rule making directed to this specific area," and it stated that the FCC would "give this proceeding expedited treatment. . . ." [4]

A notice of proposed rule making was in fact issued in February of 1972, soliciting comments on a proposed rule governing the carriage of sports programs by cable television systems.[5] The notice advised interested parties

[2] In re Commission Proposals for Regulation of Cable Television, 31 F.C.C. 2d 115, 124 (1971).

[3] *Id.*

[4] *Id.*

[5] Notice of Proposed Rule Making in Docket 19417. 36 F.C.C. 2d 641 (1972).

that the FCC intended to complete the proceeding expeditiously and that requests for extensions of time to file comments would have to be accompanied by a very strong showing of unusual circumstances. The proceeding, however, was not completed by September of 1973, when Congress enacted the anti-blackout law.[6] Nor was it completed by 1974 when Congress considered, but rejected, an amendment to the Copyright Act which would have afforded copyright protection to televised sporting events.[7] Because of this Congressional activity, the FCC issued a Further Notice of Proposed Rule Making in December of 1974, requesting comment on what impact, if any, Congress' actions might have on the pending proceeding.[8]

Over one hundred comments and replies were filed with the Federal Communications Commission in response to the two notices. The cable television interests argued that in enacting §1291 through §1293 of Title 15, Congress merely wanted to place the National Football League on an equal footing with the American Football League, by allowing the NFL to sell its television rights in a package as was already being done by the AFL, and to make clear that television blackouts were not to be extended further than what Judge Grim had considered to be reasonable in his 1953 decision. Congress had not intended, the cable television interests argued, to assure television blackouts, and therefore it did not intend to protect professional sports from the impact of cable television operations.[9]

---

[6] See § 10.2(d), *supra.*

[7] See § 10.3(a), *supra.*

[8] Further Notice of Proposed Rule Making in Docket 19417, 50 F.C.C.2d 48 (1974).

[9] Report and Order in Docket 19417, 54 F.C.C.2d 265 (1975), 40 Fed.Reg. 30641, 30644 (1975).

Team owners, on the other hand, argued that §1291-§1293 of Title 15 indicated a Congressional policy that went far beyond the desire to place the NFL on an equal footing with the AFL. They argued that the purpose of these sections was to permit teams to re-establish control over their own patterns of telecasts and could be regarded as a Congressional mandate to afford protection not only to the gate receipts of professional sports teams, but also to the value of their television packages.[10]

Similarly, cable television interests argued that the anti-blackout law indicated a Congressional intent to reduce the favored position previously given professional sports and represented a clear expression of policy to reduce the control sports leagues had over their telecasts and to expand the number of events offered to television viewers. Therefore, cable television interests contended that because cable television offers additional viewing choices, any FCC rule which would reduce the cable television carriage of sports events would be contrary to the policy of the anti-blackout law. This view is supported, they argued, by the refusal of the Senate to afford sports teams copyright protection in the Copyright Act which it passed (but which was not passed by the House).[11]

On the other hand, team owners and conventional broadcasters asserted that the anti-blackout law evidenced Congressional intent to give professional sports teams and leagues absolute control over their telecasts, except for the one limited situation when games are sold out seventy-two hours in advance. They argued that the fact that the anti-blackout law was narrowly applied only to games telecast by virtue of a package contract, indicated Congress' con-

---

[10] ***Id.***
[11] ***Id.***

cern was one limited to the public's criticism of football blackouts and was not meant to reverse the policy established when home territory blackouts had been sanctioned by §1292 of Title 15.[12]

Organized Baseball and the National Hockey League urged the Federal Communications Commission to adopt a rule which would have prevented cable television systems from importing *any* game of *any* sport from a distant city to a team's home territory, when it was playing at home or was broadcasting one of its games at home.[13]

The National Collegiate Athletic Association proposed that a rule be adopted which would parallel §1293 of Title 15, that is, prohibit a cable television system located within seventy-five miles of the site of a college or high school football game to be played on Friday evening or Saturday from carrying a professional football game on the same date.[14] The NCAA also proposed that the rule prohibit cable television systems from carrying NCAA events which are not available on local television broadcast stations.[15]

The cable television interests naturally opposed rules which would prohibit the importation of all sporting events. They denied that the importation of distant sporting events affected gate receipts or eroded advertiser support for conventional television broadcasts. They contended that restrictions on their ability to carry sporting events would have a substantial impact on the cable television industry. The National Cable Television Association asserted that a rule which merely prohibited cable television systems from importing a game of the *same sport* (unless

---

[12] *Id.*

[13] *Id.* at 40 Fed.Reg. 30645.

[14] See § 10.2(b) (3), *supra*.

[15] Report and Order, *supra* note 9, at 40 Fed.Reg. 30645.

the game was available on conventional television) on a day when a professional baseball, basketball, football or hockey team was playing at home would result in the blacking out of a substantial number of sports events in more than three million American homes and would have a drastic impact on the future development of cable television in the country's major television markets.[16]

§10.3(c) FCC regulations

The Federal Communications Commission concluded that when Congress passed §§1291-1293 of Title 15 of 1961, it believed that professional football, baseball, basketball and hockey needed financial protection in order to survive. Television blackouts in home territories were believed to be necessary in order to protect gate receipts, it explained. But, it added, the circumstances of professional sports in 1975 were vastly different from what they were in 1961. Revenues from both gate receipts and the sale of broadcast rights were running into the tens of millions of dollars. Nevertheless, the FCC said, the Congressional policy established in §1292 is still valid in many respects and indicates a need for some, although a quite limited, restriction on the importation of sporting events by cable television. Therefore, the FCC believed that a rule restricting the importation of sports by cable television in a manner consistent with Judge Grim's 1953 opinion and §1292 "would be in the public interest and would reflect Congressional policy as applied to today's sports practices."[1]

The FCC went on to explain that Judge Grim and Congress concluded that sports leagues should have the right

[16] *Id.*

[1] Report and Order in Docket 19417, 54 F.C.C.2d 265 (1975), 40 Fed.Reg. 30641, 30647 (1975).

to restrict the telecasting of *other* league games in the home territory of member teams when they were playing at home. But, the FCC pointed out, this right has not always been exercised, and many teams now play at home on the same day that other league games are televised in their home territories. This practice led the FCC to believe that prohibiting the importation of *other* games by cable television into the home territory of teams playing at home is not necessary to protect the home team's gate receipts. Therefore, it decided to adopt a rule prohibiting cable systems from importing only the *same* game which is being played locally. "This rule is consistent with the policy established by Congress and helps to assure the continued availability of sport telecasts to the public," the FCC explained.[2]

The rule which the FCC adopted on July 9, 1975, provides that no cable television system located within thirty-five miles of a community in which a sports event is taking place shall carry the live television broadcast of that event, if the event is not available live on a conventional television station in that community.[3]

Although §1292 of Title 15 and the anti-blackout law deal with the professional team sports of football, basketball, baseball and hockey only, the FCC felt that the need to maximize live audiences is shared by all spectator sports, college and high school, as well as professional, individual as well as team sports. Therefore, its rule was made to apply to all sports telecasts where the event is not exhibited on local conventional television.[4]

[2] *Id.*

[3] 47 C.F.R. § 76.67. Petitions for reconsideration were denied, except as to certain specific suggested alterations, 40 Fed.Reg. 53027 (1975).

[4] Report and Order, *supra* note 1, at 40 Fed.Reg. 30648.

In conclusion, the FCC stated that the rule which it had adopted would have only minimal impact on present and future cable television viewers. Where events are made available for local telecasts, it explained, either voluntarily or by virtue of the anti-blackout law, both cable and non-cable viewers will be able to watch home game telecasts. Only when a game is not televised locally, but is broadcast by a distant television station carried by a local cable system, will the rule affect cable subscribers. Finally, the FCC noted,

> "We emphasize that our interest is not to assure the profitability of organized sports. Our concern is with the availability of television broadcast programming to the general public, which is of vital importance to the larger and more effective use of the airwaves." [5]

§10.4 Pay television and sports

Pay television, which is sometimes referred to as subscription television, dates back to at least 1950, when a New York City television station conducted an early pay television test. As its name implies, subscription television viewers are required to pay for the programs they watch, and today this is accomplished in one of two ways. Some systems charge their subscribers a flat monthly fee for which they may watch as much or as little programming as they like. Others charge their viewers on a per-program basis.[1]

Physically, pay television signals are delivered to subscribers' homes in one of two ways. The most common method is over cable. That is, virtually all pay television

---

[5] *Id.*

[1] First Report and Order in Dockets 19554 and 18893, 52 F.C.C. 2d 1, 2 (1975).

stations in operation at this time are simply a channel on existing cable television systems. Obviously, the growth of pay television in this form has depended upon the prior installation of cable television systems. As a result, pay television is sometimes available to some of the residents of a city, but not to others even in the same city. For example, Los Angeles' pay television station, which is known as "Z Channel," is available only in those areas of the city that have been wired for cable television, and that is by no means most of the city. Cable subscribers pay a monthly fee for the basic cable service, and they pay an additional fee in order to be able to receive the pay television channel. As of 1974, approximately 100,000 subscribers in the United States were receiving pay television service by cable.[2]

Pay television signals have also been broadcast over the air in the same fashion as conventional television signals. As a matter of fact, one of the earliest pay television systems in regular operation was an over-the-air station located in Hartford, Connecticut. As of 1974, there were no over-the-air pay stations in operation, but the Federal Communications Commission had granted applications by then for over-the-air pay stations to be located in Newark, Milwaukee, and Boston, and applications to operate such stations in a number of other cities were then pending as well.

Over-the-air pay television stations broadcast a scrambled signal. A decoder is necessary to unscramble the signal, and payment is collected from those who have the decoders, either on a monthly or per-program basis.

From its earliest days, pay television has been explosively controversial. Conventional broadcasters, whose

---

[2] *Id.*

revenue is derived from advertising, have feared that they will be out-bid for programming material by pay television operators; and conventional broadcasters have long argued that as a result television viewers will someday be required to pay for the same programs they now view for free. Therefore, conventional broadcasters (supported by motion picture theater owners who also fear the development of pay television) sought to block the development of pay stations.

In 1968 the Federal Communications Commission concluded that pay television operations could add significantly to the quality and diversity of television programming available to the public, and it therefore adopted rules both authorizing and regulating over-the-air pay television operations.[3] These rules became known as the "anti-siphoning rules," because they provided that sports events regularly broadcast by conventional television in the pay television station's community during the preceding two years could not be shown by the pay station; that feature films more than two years old could not be shown (except for twelve films per year that were more than ten years old); that no series type of program could be shown; that commercial advertising announcements could not be shown; and that no more than 90% of total pay programming could consist of feature films and sporting events combined.

In 1970, virtually identical anti-siphoning rules were adopted governing pay cable television operations (that is, cable operations for which an additional per-program or per-channel fee was charged).[4]

---

[3] Fourth Report and Order in Docket 11279, 15 F.C.C.2d 466 (1968).

[4] Memorandum Opinion and Order in Docket 18397, 23 F.C.C.2d 825 (1970).

While these rules made it substantially less likely that popular sporting events would ever be shown on pay television, rather than on conventional television, many members of Congress expressed doubts that the two-year period was sufficient. They believed that team owners might be willing to withhold sporting events from conventional television long enough to make them eligible for pay television under the then existing anti-siphoning rules. And in 1970, the House Committee on Interstate and Foreign Commerce favorably reported a bill which would have lengthened the period from two to five years.[5] That is, the bill proposed to amend the Communications Act to provide that sports events could not be broadcast over pay television, if they had been televised on a regular basis in the community by conventional television during any period in the five years preceding their proposed pay television broadcast.

Although the 91st Congress adjourned without enacting the measure into law, the Federal Communications Commission nevertheless took note of the information furnished during the hearings on the bill, and in 1972 it amended its regulations to provide, in essence, that over-the-air pay television stations could not broadcast live sporting events which have been shown on conventional television during any one of the preceding five years.[6]

Finally, in 1975, the FCC completely revised its pay television rules, including those applicable to sporting events, and issued regulations which generally treat pay cable and over-the-air pay stations alike. The portion of those rules which deal with sports are as complex as federal tax law and incorporate by reference several paragraphs

[5] H.R. 91-1110, 91st Cong., 2d Sess. (1970).

[6] Report and Order in Docket 18893, 34 F.C.C.2d 271 (1972).

of the FCC Report and Order by which they were adopted, something no other FCC regulation has done.[7] Given the volatile nature of the issue, however, simpler regulations were probably impossible to develop; and, as a matter of fact, the regulations actually adopted were a good deal more direct than some that had been recommended by team owners, leagues and conventional broadcasters.[8]

Current anti-siphoning rules classify sporting events as "specific events" or "non-specific events."[9] Specific events are those such as the World Series, the Sugar Bowl, the NBA Championship Game, the Rose Bowl and other college bowl games, the Kentucky Derby and the Olympic Games.[10] A specific event may not be shown on pay television unless it has *not* been broadcast live on conventional television in the pay station's market during any of the five preceding seasons. But if a regularly recurring event takes place less frequently than annually, such as the Olympic Games which take place every four years, it may not be shown on pay television unless it has *not* been broadcast on conventional television during any of the preceding ten years. Furthermore, if a new specific sports event is created as a result of the restructuring of an existing sport, that event may not be shown on pay television during its first five seasons; thereafter, the general rules concerning existing specific events apply.

---

[7] Prepared Remarks of Philip R. Hochberg, Esq., for American Law Institute/American Bar Association Seminar on Cable and Pay Television, Chicago, Illinois, April 20, 1974, at Pg. 3.

[8] See, for example, First Report and Order, *supra* note 1 at 31-35; and Further Report and Order in Dockets 19554 and 18893, 40 Fed.Reg. 34341, 34344-34346 (1975).

[9] Pay Over-the-Air, 47 C.F.R. § 73.643; Pay Cable, 47 C.F.R. § 76.225.

[10] First Report and Order, *supra* note 1, at 59, and Fourth Report and Order, *supra* note 3, at paragraphs 293-297.

Some examples of the effects of these rules are these. Because the Super Bowl has been broadcast on conventional television during the preceding five years, it cannot be shown on pay television unless the National Football League should decide to withhold the Super Bowl from conventional television for the next five seasons; and then it could only be shown on pay television beginning with the sixth season thereafter. Similarly, because the Olympics have been broadcast on conventional television within the last ten years, the Olympics may not be shown on pay television, unless they should be withheld from conventional television for the next ten years.

If a basketball super-event were to result from the merger of the National and American Basketball Associations, or if a hockey super-event were to result from the merger of the National Hockey League and the World Hockey Association, such events could not be shown on pay television during their first five seasons. Thereafter, whether or not such an event could be shown on pay television would depend upon whether or not it had been broadcast on conventional television during its first five seasons. If it had been broadcast on conventional television during its first five seasons, then it could not be shown on pay television immediately thereafter; but if it had been withheld from conventional television throughout its first five seasons, then it could be shown on pay television beginning with its sixth season.

Non-specific events are games or other contests which are part of a regular series, such as football or baseball games played during a regular season, and pre-season practice games.[11] Non-specific events are divided into four

[11] *Id.*

"categories": pre-season home games; pre-season away games; regular season home games; and regular season away games.[12] If fewer than 25% of the events in a category were broadcast on conventional television in the pay television station's market during each one of the preceding five seasons, then it is permissible to show some events in that category on pay television.

The maximum number that may be shown is the number of "remainder games" that existed during the "highwater mark" season. Remainder games are those that are not shown on conventional television; and the highwater mark season is that season during which the greatest number of games is shown on conventional television.

If 25% or more of the events in a category were broadcast on conventional television during any one of the preceding five seasons, it is still permissible to show some games on pay television. But, the maximum number that may be shown in that case is only 50% of the number of remainder games there were during the highwater mark season. (However, if the number of games broadcast on conventional television is reduced from the number shown during the highwater mark season, then the number that may be shown on pay television is proportionately reduced as well.)

The application of these rules concerning non-specific events may be illustrated with the following examples. There are approximately 40 home games in a National Hockey League season. Twenty-five percent of the events in that home game category is ten games. Thus, if 9 or fewer home games of a National Hockey League team have been broadcast on conventional television in that team's home territory during each of the preceding five seasons,

[12] First Report and Order, *supra* note 1, at 61.

the number of games that could be shown on pay television in that territory would be 31 (or more). If 9 games were the most that had been broadcast on conventional television during the preceding five seasons, then 9 would be the "highwater mark season" and 31 would be the number of "remainder games." If, for example, 5 games were the most that had been broadcast on conventional television during the preceding five seasons, then 5 would be the highwater mark season and 35 would be the number of remainder games and the number that could be shown on pay television.

If, however, 10 or more home games had been broadcast on conventional television during any one of the preceding five seasons, then only 50% of the number of remainder games that existed during the highwater mark season could be shown. For example, if during the preceding five seasons, a National Hockey League team had permitted 8, 9, 10, 11 and 12 games to be broadcast on conventional television each season, then the following season only 14 games could be shown on pay television (50% of: 40 minus 12).

In order to minimize the possibility that team owners might gradually reduce the number of games broadcast on conventional television so as to get below the 25% mark, the number of games that may be shown on pay television in any season is reduced in proportion to the extent to which the number of games broadcast on conventional television that season is fewer than the number that was broadcast on conventional television during the highwater mark season. For example, if 20 out of 40 home games were broadcast on conventional television during the highwater mark season of the preceding five, the number of remainder games is 20 of which 50%, or 10, may be shown on pay television. But if the number of games to be broadcast on conventional television this season is fewer than 20, then the number that may be shown on pay television is fewer than 10. Thus, if the number of games to be broadcast on conventional television this season is 18, a 10% reduction from the 20 that were shown during the highwater mark season, then the number of games that may be shown on pay television this season is only 9, also a 10% reduction.

As complex as these rules are, they do not in and of themselves fairly deal with all possible circumstances. It was pointed out, for example, that a team might arrange to have only 23% of its home games broadcast on conventional television, thereby reserving the right to show all of its remainder games in that category on pay television. However, it might develop that by virtue of a league package contract, over which a team has no control, an additional 2% of its home games might be broadcast on a network. If so, a total of 25% of its home games would have been broadcast by conventional television, and then the team would only be permitted to show 50% of its remainder games on pay television. When asked whether this should happen, the Federal Communications Commission answered, "Possibly not."[13] Therefore, if the FCC were presented with such a situation, it would consider granting a waiver of the rule, so as to permit more games to be shown on pay television than strict application of the rule would otherwise allow.

Another difficulty exists with respect to events that consist of more than one game or match, such as the World Series or a golf tournament, or which take several hours to complete, such as a twenty-four hour auto race. All of

[13] *Id.* at 64.

the games of the World Series are broadcast on conventional television, and therefore that event clearly is shown on conventional television. However, it is common for only selected games or matches, or only portions of an event, to be broadcast on conventional television; and then it is not as clear that the event has been shown on conventional television. The FCC's response to this problem was that if a substantial number of games or matches, or portions thereof, were broadcast on conventional television, it would consider the event to have been broadcast on conventional television within the meaning of the rule.[14] Similarly, if a golf tournament ran for three days, for example, and a conventional television station broadcast one to two hours per day for two or three days, it would consider the event to have been covered by conventional television, even though only portions of play would have in fact been broadcast. Also, a twenty-four hour auto race would be considered to have been broadcast by conventional television, even if the entire twenty-four hours were not shown. Naturally, the distinction between a "substantial" portion of an event and an insubstantial portion is a matter of judgment, about which reasonable people may differ (especially, it seems, if the people are not fans of the event to the same degree).

One of the most interesting questions that exists with respect to these anti-siphoning rules is whether they are triggered by conventional broadcasts which are required by the anti-blackout law.[15] For example, prior to the enactment of the anti-blackout law, no National Football League home games were ever broadcast in the home territory. Thus, prior to the enactment of the anti-blackout

---

[14] Fourth Report and Order, *supra* note 3, at paragraph 295.
[15] See § 10.2(d), *supra*.

law, NFL teams would have been permitted to sell the television rights to all of their home games to pay television stations located in their home territories. Since the enactment of the anti-blackout law, however, all of the home games of several NFL teams have been shown in their home territories. As a result, strict application of the FCC's anti-siphoning rules would prohibit these teams from selling any of their home games to pay television.

One commentator construed statements made by Congressman Macdonald during the hearings on his bill as indicating that he did not intend the anti-blackout statute to have that result.[16] But Congressman Macdonald's statements are not altogether clear on that point. And there is nothing whatsoever in either the anti-blackout law or the anti-siphoning rules to indicate that games broadcast on conventional television because of the anti-blackout law will not be barred from pay television because of the anti-siphoning rules.

Indeed, it seems that the vigor with which team owners and leagues opposed the anti-blackout law was due far more to the impact that law has on their ability to sell games to pay television than to the effect the anti-blackout law may have on in-person attendance at their games.

---

[16] Hochberg, Congress Kicks A Field Goal: The Legislative Attack in the 93d Congress on Sports Broadcasting Practices, 27 Federal Communications Bar Journal 27, 67-69 (1974).

APPENDIX A

SHERMAN ANTITRUST ACT

Sections 1 and 2

(Title 15 United States Code §§ 1, 2)

Section 1. Every contract, combination in the form of trust or otherwise, or conspiracy, in restraint of trade or commerce among the several States, or with foreign nations, is hereby declared to be illegal. . . . Every person who shall make any such contract or engage in any such combination or conspiracy shall be deemed guilty of a misdemeanor, and, on conviction thereof, shall be punished by fine not exceeding fifty thousand dollars, or by imprisonment not exceeding one year, or by both said punishments, in the discretion of the court.

Section 2. Every person who shall monopolize, or attempt to monopolize, or combine or conspire with any other person or persons, to monopolize any part of the trade or commerce among the several States, or with foreign nations, shall be deemed guilty of a misdemeanor, and, on conviction thereof, shall be punished by fine not exceeding fifty thousand dollars, or by imprisonment not exceeding one year, or by both said punishments, in the discretion of the court.

APPENDIX B

CLAYTON ACT

Sections 6 and 20

(Title 15 United States Code § 17;
Title 29 United States Code § 52)

Section 6. "The labor of a human being is not a commodity or article of commerce. Nothing contained in the antitrust laws shall be construed to forbid the existence and operation of labor, agricultural, or horticultural organizations, instituted for the purposes of mutual help, and not having capital stock or conducted for profit, or to forbid or restrain individual members of such organizations from lawfully carrying out the legitimate objects thereof; nor shall such organizations, or the members thereof, be held or construed to be illegal combinations or conspiracies in restraint of trade, under the antitrust laws."

Section 20. "No restraining order or injunction shall be granted by any court of the United States, or a judge or the judges thereof, in any case between an employer and employees, or between employers and employees, or between employees, or between persons employed and persons seeking employment, involving, or growing out of, a dispute concerning terms or conditions of employment, unless necessary to prevent irreparable injury to property, or to a property right, of the party making the application, for which injury there is no adequate remedy at law, and such property or property right must be described with particularity in the application, which must be in writing and sworn to by the applicant or by his agent or attorney.

"And no such restraining order or injunction shall prohibit any person or persons, whether singly or in concert, from terminating any relation of employment, or from ceasing to perform any work or labor, or from recommending, advising, or persuading others by peaceful means so to do; or from attending at any place where any such person or persons may lawfully be, for the purpose of peacefully obtaining or communicating information, or from peacefully persuading any person to work or to abstain from working; or from ceasing to patronize or to employ any party to such dispute, or from recommending, advising, or persuading others by peaceful and lawful means so to do; or from paying or giving to, or withholding from, any person engaged in such dispute, any strike benefits or other moneys or things of value; or from peaceably assembling in a lawful manner, and for lawful purposes; or from doing any act or thing which might lawfully be done in the absence of such dispute by any party thereto; nor shall any of the acts specified in this paragraph be considered or held to be violations of any laws of the United States."

APPENDIX C

NATIONAL LABOR RELATIONS ACT

Sections 2, 7, 8, 9, 10, and 14

(Title 29 United States Code §§ 152, 157, 158, 159, 160, 164)

Definitions

Section 2. When used in this Act—

(5) The term "labor organization" means any organization of any kind, or any agency or employee representation committee or plan, in which employees participate and which exists for the purpose, in whole or in part, of dealing with employers concerning grievances, labor disputes, wages, rates of pay, hours of employment, or conditions of work.

(6) The term "commerce" means trade, traffic, commerce, transportation, or communication among the several States, or between the District of Columbia or any Territory of the United States and any State or other Territory, or between any foreign country and any State, Territory, or the District of Columbia, or within the District of Columbia or any Territory, or between points in the same State but through any other State or any Territory or the District of Columbia or any foreign country.

Rights of Employees

Section 7. Employees shall have the right to self-organization, to form, join, or assist labor organizations, to bargain collectively through representatives of their own choosing, and to engage in other concerted activities for the purpose of collective bargaining or other mutual aid or protection, and shall also have the right to refrain from any or all of such activities except to the extent that such right may be affected by an agreement requiring membership in a labor organization as a condition of employment as authorized in section 8(a)(3).

Unfair Labor Practices

Section 8. (a) It shall be an unfair labor practice for an employer—

(1) to interfere with, restrain, or coerce employees in the exercise of the rights guaranteed in section 7;

(2) to dominate or interfere with the formation or administration of any labor organization or contribute financial or other support to it: *Provided,* That subject to rules and regulations made and published by the Board pursuant to section 6, an employer shall not be prohibited from permitting employees to confer with him during working hours without loss of time or pay;

(3) by discrimination in regard to hire or tenure of employment or any term or condition of employment to encourage or discourage membership in any labor organization: . . .

(5) to refuse to bargain collectively with the representatives of his employees, subject to the provisions of section 9(a).

(d) For the purposes of this section, to bargain collectively is the performance of the mutual obligation of the employer and the representative of the employees to meet at reasonable times and confer in good faith with respect to wages, hours, and other terms and conditions of employment, or the negotiation of an agreement, or any question arising thereunder, and the execution of a written contract incorporating any agreement reached if requested by either party, but such obligation does not compel either party to agree to a proposal or require the making of a concession: . . .

Exclusive Representatives

Section 9. (a) Representatives designated or selected for the purposes of collective bargaining by the majority of the employees in a unit appropriate for such purposes, shall be the exclusive representatives of all the employees in such unit for the purposes of collective bargaining in respect to rates of pay, wages, hours of employment, or other conditions of employment: . . .

(c)(1) Whenever a petition shall have been filed, in accordance with such regulations as may be prescribed by the Board—

(A) by an employee or group of employees or any individual or labor organization acting in their behalf alleging that a substantial number of employees (i) wish to be represented for collective bargaining and that their employer declines to recognize their representative as the representative defined in section 9(a), or (ii) assert that the individual or labor organization, which has been certified or is being currently recognized by their employer as the bargaining representaive, is no longer a representative as defined in section 9(a); or

(B) by an employer, alleging that one or more individuals or labor organizations have presented to him a claim to be recognized as the representative defined in section 9(a);

the Board shall investigate such petition and if it has reasonable cause to believe that a question of representation affecting commerce exists shall provide for an appropriate hearing upon due notice. Such hearing may be conducted by an officer or employee of the regional office, who shall not make any recommendations with respect thereto. If the Board finds upon the record of such hearing that such a question of representation exists, it shall direct an election by secret ballot and shall certify the results thereof.

Prevention of Unfair Labor Practices

Section 10. (a) The Board is empowered, as hereinafter provided, to prevent any person from engaging in any unfair labor practice (listed in section 8) affecting commerce. . . .

(b) Whenever it is charged that any person has engaged in or is engaging in any such unfair labor practice, the Board, or any agent or agency designated by the Board for such purposes, shall have power to issue and cause to be served upon such person a complaint stating the charges in that respect, and containing a notice of hearing before the Board or a member thereof, or before a designated agent or agency, at a place therein fixed, not less than five days after the serving of said complaint: *Provided*, That no complaint shall issue based upon any unfair labor practice occurring more than six months prior to the filing of the charge with the Board and the service of a copy thereof upon the person against whom such charge is made, unless the person aggrieved thereby was prevented from filing such charge by reason of service in the armed forces, in which event the six-month period shall be computed from the day of his discharge. Any such complaint may be amended by the member, agent, or agency conducting the hearing or the Board in its discretion at any time prior to the issuance of an order based thereon. The person so complained of shall have the right to file an answer to the original or amended complaint and to appear in person or otherwise and give testimony at the place and time fixed in the complaint. In the discretion of the member, agent, or agency conducting the hearing or the Board, any other person may be allowed to intervene in the said proceeding and to present testimony. Any such proceeding shall, so far as practicable, be conducted in accordance with the rules of evidence applicable in the district courts of the United States under the rules of civil procedure for the district courts of the United States, adopted by the Supreme Court of the United States pursuant to section 2072 of Title 28.

(c) The testimony taken by such member, agent, or agency or the Board shall be reduced to writing and filed with the Board. Thereafter, in its discretion, the Board upon notice may take further testimony or hear argument. If upon the preponderance of the testimony taken the Board shall be of the opinion that any person named in the complaint has engaged in or is engaging in any such unfair labor practice, then the Board shall state its findings of fact and shall issue and cause to be served on such person an order requiring such person to cease and desist from such unfair labor practice, and to take such affirmative action, including reinstatement of employees with or without back pay, as will effectuate the policies of this Act: . . . If upon the preponderance of the testimony taken the Board shall not be of the opinion that the person named in the complaint has engaged in or is engaging in any such unfair labor practice, then the Board shall state its findings of fact and shall issue an order dismissing the said complaint.

(e) The Board shall have power to petition any court of appeals of the United States, or if all the courts of appeals to which application may be made are in vacation, any district court of the United States, within any circuit or district, respectively, wherein the unfair labor practice in question occurred or wherein such person resides or transacts business, for the enforcement of such order and for appropriate temporary relief or restraining order, and shall file in the court the record in the proceedings, as provided in section 2112 of Title 28. Upon the filing of such petition, the court shall cause notice thereof to be served upon such person, and thereupon shall have jurisdiction of the proceeding and of the question determined therein, and shall have power to grant such temporary relief or restraining order as it deems just and proper, and to make and enter a decree enforcing, modifying, and enforcing as so modified, or setting aside in whole or in part the order of the Board. . . .

(f) Any person aggrieved by a final order of the Board granting or denying in whole or in part the relief sought may obtain a review of such order in any United States court of appeals in the circuit wherein the unfair labor practice in question was alleged to have been engaged in or wherein such person resides or transacts business, or in the United States Court of Appeals for the District of Columbia, by filing in such court a written petition praying that the order of the Board be modified or set aside. . . .

Limitations

Section 14. * * *

(c)(1) The Board, in its discretion, may, by rule or decision or by published rules adopted pursuant to the Administrative Procedure Act, decline to assert jurisdiction over any labor dispute involving any class or category of employers, where, in the opinion of the Board, the effect of such labor dispute on commerce is not sufficiently substantial to warrant the exercise of its jurisdiction: Provided, That the Board shall not decline to assert jurisdiction over any labor dispute over which it would assert jurisdiction under the standards prevailing upon August 1, 1959.

APPENDIX D

TELECASTING OF PROFESSIONAL SPORTS CONTESTS

Title 15 United States Code Sections 1291-1295

Section 1291. *Exemption from antitrust laws of agreements covering the telecasting of sports contests and the combining of professional football leagues.*

The antitrust laws, as defined in section 12 of this title or in the Federal Trade Commission Act, as amended shall not apply to any joint agreement by or among persons engaging in or conducting the organized professional team sports of football, baseball, basketball, or hockey, by which any league of clubs participating in professional football, baseball, basketball, or hockey contests sells or otherwise transfers all or any part of the rights of such league's member clubs in the sponsored telecasting of the games of football, baseball, basketball, or hockey, as the case may be, engaged in or conducted by such clubs. In addition, such laws shall not apply to a joint agreement by which the member clubs of two or more professional football leagues, which are exempt from income tax under section 501(c)(6) of Title 26, combine their operations in expanded single league so exempt from income tax, if such agreement increases rather than decreases the number of professional football clubs so operating, and the provisions of which are directly relevant thereto. (Pub. L. 87-331, § 1, Sept. 30, 1961, 75 Stat. 732; Pub. L. 89-800, § 6(b)(1), Nov. 8, 1966, 80 Stat. 1515.)

Section 1292. *Area telecasting restriction limitation.*

Section 1291 of this title shall not apply to any joint agreement described in the first sentence in such section which prohibits any person to whom such rights are sold or transferred from televising any games within any area, except within the home territory of a member club of the league on a day when such club is playing a game at home. (Pub. L. 87-331, § 2, Sept. 30, 1961, 75 Stat. 732; Pub. L. 89-800, § 6(b)(2), Nov. 8, 1966, 80 Stat. 1515.)

Section 1293. *Intercollegiate and interscholastic football contest limitations.*

The first sentence of section 1291 of this title shall not apply to any joint agreement described in such section which permits the telecasting of all or a substantial part of any professional football game on any Friday after six o'clock postmeridian or on any Saturday during the period beginning on the second Friday in September and ending on the second Saturday in December in any year from any telecasting station located within seventy-five miles of the game site of any intercollegiate or interscholastic football contest scheduled to be played on such a date if—

(1) such intercollegiate football contest is between institutions of higher learning both of which confer degrees upon students following completion of sufficient credit hours to equal a four-year course, or

(2) in the case of an interscholastic football contest, such contest is between secondary schools, both of which are accredited or certified under the laws of the State or States in which they are situated and offer courses continuing through the twelfth grade of the standard school curriculum, or the equivalent, and

(3) such intercollegiate or interscholastic football contest and such game site were announced through publication in a newspaper of general circulation prior

to August 1 of such year as being regularly scheduled for such day and place.

(Pub. L. 87-331, § 3, Sept. 30, 1961, 75 Stat. 732; Pub. L. 89-800, § 6(b)(3), Nov. 8, 1966, 80 Stat. 1515.)

Section 1294. *Antitrust laws unaffected as regards to other activities of professional sports contests.*

Nothing contained in this chapter shall be deemed to change, determine, or otherwise affect the applicability or nonapplicability of the antitrust laws to any act, contract, agreement, rule, course of conduct, or other activity by, between, or among persons engaging in, conducting, or participating in the organized professional team sports of football, baseball, basketball, or hockey, except the agreements to which section 1291 of this title shall apply. (Pub. L. 87-331, § 4, Sept. 30, 1961, 75 Stat. 732.)

Section 1295. *"Persons" defined.*

As used in this chapter, "persons" means any individual, partnership, corporation, or unincorporated association or any combination or association thereof. (Pub. L. 87-331, § 5, Sept. 30, 1961, 75 Stat. 732.)

APPENDIX E

BROADCAST OF GAMES OF PROFESSIONAL SPORTS CLUBS

Title 47 United States Code Section 331

Section 331. (a) If any game of a professional sports club is to be broadcast by means of television pursuant to a league television contract and all tickets of admission for seats at such game which were available for purchase by the general public one hundred and twenty hours or more before the scheduled beginning time of such game have been purchased seventy-two hours or more before such time, no agreement which would prevent the broadcasting by means of television of such game at the same time and in the area in which such game is being played shall be valid or have any force or effect. The right to broadcast such game by means of television at such time and in such area shall be made available, by the person or persons having such right, to a television broadcast licensee on reasonable terms and conditions unless the broadcasting by means of television of such game at such time and in such area would be a telecasting which section 3 of Public Law 87-331, as amended (15 U.S.C. 1293), is intended to prevent.

(b) If any person violates subsection (a) of this section, any interested person may commence a civil action for injunctive relief restraining such violation in any United States district court for a district in which the defendant resides or has an agent. In any such action, the court may award the cost of the suit including reasonable attorneys' fees.

(c) For the purposes of this section:

(1) The term 'professional sports club' includes any professional football, baseball, basketball, or hockey club.

(2) The term 'league television contract' means any joint agreement by or among professional sports clubs by which any league of such clubs sells or otherwise transfers all or any part of the rights of such league's member clubs in the sponsored telecasting of the games engaged in or conducted by such clubs.

(3) The term 'agreement' includes any contract, arrangement, or other understanding.

(4) The term 'available for purchase by the general public', when used with respect to tickets of admission for seats at a game or games to be played by a professional sports club, means only those tickets on sale at the stadium where such game or games are to be played, or, if such tickets are not sold at such stadium, only those tickets on sale at the box office closest to such stadium.

(d) The Commission shall conduct a continuing study of the effect of this section and shall, not later than April 15 of each year, submit a report to the Committee on Commerce of the Senate and the Committee on Interstate and Foreign Commerce of the House of Representatives with respect thereto. Such report shall include pertinent statistics and data and any recommendations for legislation relating to the broadcasting of professional football, baseball, basketball, and hockey games which the Commission determines would serve the public interest.

APPENDIX F

CABLE TELEVISION PROGRAM RULES

Title 47 Code of Federal Regulations Section 76.67

Section 76.67. *Sports Broadcasts.*

(a) No cable television system located in whole or in part within the specified zone of a television broadcast station licensed to a community in which a sports event is taking place, shall, on request of the holder of the broadcast rights to that event, or its agent, carry the live television broadcast of that event if the event is not available live on a television broadcast signal carried by the system pursuant to the mandatory signal carriage rules of this Part. For the purposes of this Section, if there is no television station licensed to the community in which the sports event is taking place, the applicable specified zone shall be that of the television station licensed to the community with which the sports event or local team is identified, or, if the event or local team as not identified with any particular community, the nearest community to which a television station is licensed.

(b) Notification of the programming to be deleted pursuant to this section shall include the following information:

(1) As to programming to be deleted from television broadcast signals regularly carried by the cable system:

(i) The name and address of the party requesting the program deletion;

(ii) The date, time and expected duration of the sports event the television broadcast of which is to be deleted;

(iii) The call letters of the television broadcast station(s) from which the deletion is to be made.

(2) As to programming to be deleted from television broadcast signals not regularly carried by the cable system:

(i) The name and address of the party requesting the program deletion;

(ii) The date, time and expected duration of the sports event the television broadcast of which is to be deleted.

(c) Notifications given pursuant to this section must be received, as to regularly scheduled events, no later than the Monday preceding the calendar week (Sunday-Saturday) during which the program deletion is to be made. Notifications as to events not regularly scheduled and revisions of notices previously submitted, must be received within twenty-four (24) hours after the time of the telecast to be deleted is known, but in any event no later than twenty-four (24) hours from the time the subject telecast is to take place.

(d) Whenever, pursuant to this section, a cable television system is required to delete a television program on a signal regularly carried by the system, such system may, consistent with the rules contained in Subpart F of this part, substitute a program from any other television broadcast station. A program substituted may be carried to its completion, and the cable system need not return to its regularly carried signal until it can do so without interrupting a program already in progress.

(e) The provisions of this section shall not be deemed to require the deletion of any portion of a television signal which a cable television system was lawfully carrying prior to March 31, 1972.

APPENDIX G

SUBSCRIPTION TV PROGRAM RULES

Title 47 Code of Federal Regulations Sections 73.643 and 76.225

Section 73.643 *General Operating Requirements.* [Applicable to over-the-air broadcasting]

Subscription television broadcast programming shall comply with the following requirements:

(b) Sports events shall not be broadcast live except as provided in this paragraph.

(1) A specific event may be broadcast if the event has not been broadcast live over conventional television in the market of the subscription television broadcast station during any one of the five (5) seasons preceding the proposed subscription broadcast. If a regularly recurring event takes place at intervals of more than one year (*e.g.,* summer Olympic games), the event shall not be broadcast on a subscription basis if it has been broadcast live over conventional television in the market of the subscription television broadcast station during any one of the ten (10) years preceding the proposed subscription broadcast.

(2) New specific sports events that result from the restructuring of existing sports shall not be broadcast on a subscription basis until five (5) seasons after their first occurrence. Thereafter, subscription broadcasts shall be governed by subparagraph (b)(1).

(3) The number of non-specific events which may be broadcast on a subscription basis in any given season shall be determined as follows:

(i) If less than twenty-five (25) percent of the events in a category of non-specific events were broadcast live over conventional television in the market of the subscription television broadcast station during each of the five (5) seasons preceding the proposed subscription broadcast, the number of events in the category broadcast on a subscription basis shall not exceed the number of events in the category not conventionally broadcast in that season among the preceding five (5) seasons when the largest number of events in the category were broadcast over conventional television.

(ii) If twenty-five (25) percent or more of the events in a category of non-specific events were broadcast live over conventional television in the market of the subscription television broadcast station during any one of the five (5) seasons preceding the proposed subscription broadcast, the number of events in the category broadcast on a subscription basis shall not exceed fifty (50) percent of the number of events in the category not broadcast in that season among the preceding five (5) seasons when the largest number of events in the category were broadcast over conventional television. However, if the number of events in the category to be broadcast over conventional television in the current season is a reduction from the number of events broadcast in that season among the preceding five (5) seasons when the largest number of events in the category were broadcast, the number of events in the category which may be broadcast on a subscription basis pursuant to this subparagraph shall be reduced in proportion to the reduction in events broadcast over conventional television.

NOTE.—The manner in which this paragraph will be administered and in which "sports events," "new sports events," "specific events," "non-specific events," "live telecast" and "category" will be construed is explained in paragraphs 186-208 of the *First Report and Order in Docket 19554,* FCC 75-369, 40 Fed. Reg. ——.

(d) No commercial advertising announcements shall be carried during subscription television operations except for promotion of subscription television broadcast programs before and after such programs.

(e) Not more than 90 percent of the total subscription programming hours shall consist of feature films and sports events combined. The percentage calculations may be made on a yearly basis, but, absent a showing of good cause, the percentage of such programming hours may not exceed 95 percent of the total subscription programming hours in any calendar month.

(g) Except as they may be otherwise waived by the Commission in authorizations issued hereunder, the rules and policies applicable to regular television broadcast stations are applicable to subscription television operations.

NOTE.—As referred to in this section "the market" of a subscription broadcast station includes all commercial broadcast stations which place a Grade A contour over the entire community to which the subscription station is licensed.

Section 76.225 *Subscription Cablecasting.*

Cable television system operators or channel lessees engaging in origination or access cablecasting operations for which a per-program or per-channel charge is made shall comply with the following requirements:

(b) Sports events shall not be cablecast live by a cable television system subject to the mandatory signal carriage requirements of Subpart D of Part 76, except as provided in this paragraph.

(1) A specific event may be cablecast if the event has not been broadcast live over conventional television in the market of the cable television system during any one of the five (5) seasons preceding the proposed cablecast. If a regularly recurring event takes place at intervals of more than one year (*e.g.*, summer Olympic games), the event shall not be cablecast if it has been broadcast live over conventional television in the market during any one of the ten (10) years preceding the proposed cablecast.

(2) New specific sports events that result from the restructuring of existing sports shall not be cablecast until five (5) seasons after their first occurrence. Thereafter, subscription cablecasts shall be governed by subparagraph (b)(1).

(3) The number of non-specific events which may be cablecast in any given season shall be determined as follows:

(i) If less than twenty-five (25) percent of the events in a category of non-specific events were broadcast live over conventional television in the market of the cable television system during each of the five (5) seasons preceding the proposed cablecast, the number of events in the category cablecast shall not exceed the number of events in the category not broadcast in that season among the preceding five (5) seasons when the largest number of events in the category were broadcast.

(ii) If twenty-five (25) percent or more of the events in a category of non-specific events were broadcast live over conventional television in the market of the cable television system during any one of the five (5) seasons preceding the proposed cablecast, the number of events in the category cablecast shall not exceed fifty (50) percent of the number of events in the category not broadcast in that season among the preceding five (5) seasons when the largest number of events in the category were broadcast. However, if the number of events in the category to be broadcast in the current season is a reduction from the number of events broadcast in that season among the preceding five (5) seasons when the largest number of events in the category were broadcast, the number of events in the category which may be cablecast pursuant to this subparagraph shall be reduced in proportion to the reduction in events broadcast.

Note.—The manner in which this paragraph will be administered and in which "sports events," "new sports events," "specific events," "non-specific events", "live telecast," and "category" will be construed is explained in paragraphs 186-208 of the *First Report and Order in Docket 19554,* FCC 75-369, 40 Fed. Reg. ——.

(d) Not more than ninety (90) percent of the total cablecast programming hours shall consist of feature films and sports events combined. The percentage calculations may be made on a yearly basis, but absent a showing of good cause, the percentage of such programming hours may not exceed ninety-five (95) percent of the total cablecast programming hours in any calendar month.

(e) No commercial advertising announcements shall be carried on subscription channels during such operations except before and after such programs for promotion of other programs for which a per-program or per-channel charge is made.

NOTE.—As referred to in this section, "the market" of a cable television system includes all commercial broadcast stations which must be carried by the cable television system upon request pursuant to Subpart D of Part 76.

APPENDIX H

FORM 1

Uniform Player's Contract

THE NATIONAL LEAGUE
OF PROFESSIONAL BASEBALL CLUBS

Parties

Between .... herein called the Club,

and ....

of ...., herein called the Player.

Recital

The Club is a member of The National League of Professional Baseball Clubs, a voluntary association of twelve member Clubs which has subscribed to the Major League Rules with The American League of Professional Baseball Clubs and its constituent Clubs and to The Professional Baseball Rules with that League and the National Association of Baseball Leagues.

Agreement

In consideration of the facts above recited and of the promises of each to the other, the parties agree as follows:

Employment

1. The Club hereby employs the Player to render, and the Player agrees to render, skilled services as a baseball player during the year .... 197 .... including the Club's training season, the Club's exhibition games, the Club's playing season, the League Champion-

ship Series and the World Series (or any other official series in which the Club may participate and in any receipts of which the Player may be entitled to share).

Payment

2. For performance of the Player's services and promises hereunder the Club will pay the Player the sum of

$...

....

....,

in semi-monthly installments after the commencement of the playing season covered by this contract except as the schedule of payments may be modified by a special covenant. Payment shall be made on the day the amount becomes due, regardless of whether the Club is "home" or "abroad". If a monthly rate of payment is stipulated above, it shall begin with the commencement of the Club's playing season (or such subsequent date as the Player's services may commence) and end with the termination of the Club's scheduled playing season and shall be payable in semi-monthly installments as above provided.

Nothing herein shall interfere with the right of the Club and the Player by special covenant herein to mutually agree upon a method of payment whereby part of the Player's salary for the above year can be deferred to subsequent years.

If the Player is in the service of the Club for part of the playing season only, he shall receive such proportion of the sum above mentioned, as the number of days of his actual employment in the Club's playing season bears to the number of days in said season.

Notwithstanding the rate of payment stipulated above, the minimum rate of payment to the Player for each day of service on a Major League Club shall be at the rate of $15,000 per year for the 1973 and 1974 playing seasons and $16,000 per year for the 1975 playing season.

Payment to the Player at the rate stipulated above shall be continued throughout any period in which a Player is required to attend a regularly scheduled military encampment of the Reserve of the Armed Forces or of the National Guard during the Club's playing season.

Loyalty

3.(a) The Player agrees to perform his services hereunder diligently and faithfully, to keep himself in first-class physical condition and to obey the Club's training rules, and pledges himself to the American public and to the Club to conform to high standards of personal conduct, fair play and good sportsmanship.

Baseball Promotion

3.(b) In addition to his services in connection with the actual playing of baseball, the Player agrees to cooperate with the Club and participate in any and all reasonable promotional activities of the Club and its League, which, in the opinion of the Club, will promote the welfare of the Club or professional baseball, and to observe and comply with all reasonable requirements of the Club respecting conduct and service of its team and its players, at all times whether on or off the field.

Pictures and Public Appearances

3.(c) The Player agrees that his picture may be taken for still photographs, motion pictures or television at such times as the Club may designate and agrees that all rights in such pictures shall belong to the Club and may be used by the Club for publicity purposes in any manner it desires. The Player further agrees that during the playing season he will not make public appearances, participate in radio or television programs or permit his picture to be taken or write or sponsor newspaper or magazine articles or sponsor commercial products without the written consent of the Club, which shall not be withheld except in the reasonable interests of the Club or professional baseball.

Player Representations

Ability

4.(a) The Player represents and agrees that he has exceptional and unique skill and ability as a baseball player; that his services to be rendered hereunder are of a special, unusual and extraordinary character which gives them peculiar value which cannot be reasonably or adequately compensated for in damages at law, and that the Player's breach of this contract will cause the Club great and irreparable injury and damage. The Player agrees that, in addition to other remedies, the Club shall be entitled to injunctive and other equitable relief to prevent a breach of this contract by the Player, including, among others, the right to enjoin the Player from playing baseball for any other person or organization during the term of his contract.

Condition

4.(b) The Player represents that he has no physical or mental defects known to him and unknown to the appropriate representative of the Club which would prevent or impair performance of his services.

Interest in Club

4.(c) The Player represents that he does not, directly or indirectly, own stock or have any financial interest in the ownership or earnings of any Major League Club, except as hereinafter expressly set forth, and covenants that he will not hereafter, while connected with any Major League Club, acquire or hold any such stock or interest except in accordance with Major League Rule 20(e).

Service

5.(a) The Player agrees that, while under contract, and prior to expiration of the Club's right to renew this contract, he will not play baseball otherwise than for the Club, except that the Player may participate in post-season games under the conditions prescribed in the Major League Rules. Major League Rule 18 (b) is set forth herein.

Other Sports

5.(b) The Player and the Club recognize and agree that the Player's participation in certain other sports may impair or destroy his ability and skill as a baseball player. Accordingly, the Player agrees that he will not engage in professional boxing or wrestling; and that, except with the written consent of the Club, he will not engage in skiing, auto racing, motorcycle racing, sky diving, or in any game or exhibition of football, soccer, professional league basketball, ice hockey or other sport involving a substantial risk of personal injury.

Assignment

6.(a) The Player agrees that this contract may be assigned by the Club (and reassigned by any assignee Club) to any other Club in accordance with the Major League Rules and the Professional Baseball Rules.

No Salary Reduction

6.(b) The amount stated in paragraph 2 and in special covenants hereof which is payable to the Player for the period stated in paragraph 1 hereof shall not be diminished by any such assignment, except for failure to report as provided in the next subparagraph (c).

Reporting

6.(c) The Player shall report to the assignee Club promptly (as provided in the Regulations) upon receipt of written notice from the Club of the assignment of this contract. If the Player fails so to report, he shall not be entitled to any payment for the period from the date he receives written notice of assignment until he reports to the assignee Club.

Obligations of Assignor and Assignee Clubs

6.(d) Upon and after such assignment, all rights and obligations of the assignor Club hereunder shall become the rights and obligations of the assignee Club; provided, however, that

(1) The assignee Club shall be liable to the Player for payments accruing only from the date of assignment and shall not be liable (but the assignor Club shall remain liable) for payments accrued prior to that date.

(2) If at any time the assignee is a Major League Club, it shall be liable to pay the Player at the full rate stipulated in paragraph 2 hereof for the remainder of the period stated in paragraph 1 hereof

and all prior assignors and assignees shall be relieved of liability for any payment for such period.

(3) Unless the assignor and assignee Clubs agree otherwise, if the assignee Club is a National Association Club, the assignee Club shall be liable only to pay the Player at the rate usually paid by said assignee Club to other Players of similar skill and ability in its classification and the assignor Club shall be liable to pay the difference for the remainder of the period stated in paragraph 1 hereof between an amount computed at the rate stipulated in paragraph 2 hereof and the amount so payable by the assignee Club.

Moving Allowances

6.(e) The Player shall be entitled to moving allowances under the circumstances and in the amounts set forth in Article VII of the Basic Agreement between the Major League Clubs and the Major League Baseball Players Association, effective January 1, 1973.

"Club"

6.(f) All references in other paragraphs of this contract to "the Club" shall be deemed to mean and include any assignee of this contract.

Termination

By Player

7.(a) The Player may terminate this contract, upon written notice to the Club, if the Club shall default in the payments to the Player provided for in paragraph 2 hereof or shall fail to perform any other obligation agreed to be performed by the Club hereunder and if the Club shall fail to remedy such default within ten (10) days after the receipt by the Club of written notice of such default. The Player may also terminate this contract as provided in subparagraph (g) (4) of this paragraph 7.

By Club

7.(b) The Club may terminate this contract upon written notice to the Player (but only after requesting and obtaining waivers of this contract from all other Major League Clubs) if the Player shall at any time:

(1) fail, refuse or neglect to conform his personal conduct to the standards of good citizenship and good sportsmanship or to keep himself in first-class physical condition or to obey the Club's training rules; or

(2) fail, in the opinion of the Club's management, to exhibit sufficient skill or competitive ability to qualify or continue as a member of the Club's team; or

(3) fail, refuse or neglect to render his services hereunder or in any other manner materially breach this contract.

7.(c) If this contract is terminated by the Club by reason of the Player's failure to render his services hereunder due to disability resulting directly from injury sustained in the course and within the scope of his employment hereunder and notice of such injury is received by the Club as provided in the Regulations set forth herein, the Player shall be entitled to receive his full salary for the season in which the injury was sustained, less all workmen's compensation payments received by the Player as compensation for loss of income for the specific period for which the Club is compensating him in full.

7.(d) If this contract is terminated by the Club during the training season, then, except in the case provided for in subparagraph (c) of this paragraph 7, the Player shall be entitled to receive as full payment hereunder the Player's board, lodging and/or expense allowances during the training season to the date of termination, the reasonable traveling expenses of the Player, including first-class jet air fare and meals en route to his home city, and the expert training and coaching provided by the Club to the Player during the training season, provided, however, that if this contract is terminated under subparagraph (b) (2) of this paragraph 7 for failure to exhibit sufficient skill or competitive ability, the Player shall be entitled to an additional amount (termination pay) equal to thirty (30) days payment at the rate stipulated in paragraph 2 hereof.

7.(e) If this contract is terminated by the Club during the playing season, then, except in the case provided for in subparagraph (c) of this paragraph 7, the Player shall be entitled to receive as full payment hereunder such portion of the amount stipulated in paragraph 2 hereof as the number of days of his actual employment in the Club's playing season bears to the total number of days in said season, provided, however, that if this contract is terminated under subparagraph (b) (2) of this paragraph 7 for failure to exhibit sufficient skill or competitive ability, the Player shall be entitled to an additional amount (termination pay) equal to sixty (60) days payment at the rate stipulated in paragraph 2 hereof and the reasonable traveling expenses of the Player, including first-class jet fare and meals en route to his home city, provided further, however, that if this contract is terminated under said subparagraph (b) (2) for failure to exhibit sufficient skill or competitive ability, on or after May 15, the additional amount (termination pay) which the Player shall be entitled to receive shall be the unpaid balance of the full salary stipulated in paragraph 2 for that season.

7.(f) Subparagraphs (c), (d) and (e) of this paragraph 7 shall be applied regardless of the number of times the Player may be released during a year, subject to the following limitations:

(1) The maximum amount of termination pay which the Player shall be entitled to receive for any year shall not exceed the amount by which (a) the salary stipulated in the Player's original contract for such year exceeds (b) the aggregate amount which the Player earns during that year from any Club or Clubs, including amounts deferred to later years, if any, and bonuses.

(2) In the event a released Player refuses to accept a reasonable Major League contract offered by a Club other than the Club which released him, such Player shall forfeit that portion of the termination pay which would not have been payable if such contract had been accepted.

Procedure

7.(g) If the Club proposes to terminate this contract in accordance with subparagraph (b) of this paragraph 7, the procedure shall be as follows:

(1) The Club shall request waivers from all other Major League Clubs. Such waivers shall be good for six (6) days only. Such waiver request must state that it is for the purpose of terminating this contract and it may not be withdrawn.

(2) Upon receipt of the waiver request, any other Major League Club may claim assignment of this con-

tract at a waiver price of $1.00, the priority of claims to be determined in accordance with the Major League Rules.

(3) If this contract is so claimed, the Club shall, promptly and before any assignment, notify the Player that it had requested waivers for the purpose of terminating this contract and that the contract had been claimed.

(4) Within 5 days after receipt of notice of such claim, the Player shall be entitled, by written notice to the Club, to terminate this contract on the date of his notice of termination. If the Player fails so to notify the Club, this contract shall be assigned to the claiming Club.

(5) If the contract is not claimed, the Club shall promptly deliver written notice of termination to the Player at the expiration of the waiver period.

7.(h) Upon any termination of this contract by the Player, all obligations of both Parties hereunder shall cease on the date of termination, except the obligation of the Club to pay the Player's compensation to said date.

Regulations

8. The Player accepts as part of this contract the Regulations set forth herein.

Rules

9.(a) The Club and the Player agree to accept, abide by and comply with all provisions of the Major League Agreement, the Major League Rules, the Rules or Regulations of the League of which the Club is a member, and the Professional Baseball Rules, in effect on the date of this Uniform Player's Contract, which are not inconsistent with the provisions of this contract or the provisions of any agreement between the Major League Clubs and the Major League Baseball Players Association, provided that the Club, together with the other Clubs of the American and National Leagues and the National Association, reserves the right to modify, supplement or repeal any provision of said Agreement, Rules and/or Regulations in a manner not inconsistent with this contract or the provisions of any then existing agreement between the Major League Clubs and the Major League Baseball Players Association.

Disputes

9.(b) All disputes between the Player and the Club which are covered by the Grievance Procedure as set forth in the Basic Agreement, effective January 1, 1973, shall be resolved in accordance with such Grievance Procedure.

Publication

9.(c) The Club, the League President and the Commissioner, or any of them, may make public the findings, decision and record of any inquiry, investigation or hearing held or conducted, including in such record all evidence or information, given, received, or obtained in connection therewith.

Renewal

10.(a) On or before December 20 (or if a Sunday, then the next preceding business day) in the year of the last playing season covered by this contract, the Club may tender to the Player a contract for the term of that year by mailing the same to the Player at his address following his signature hereto, or if none be given, then at his last address of record with the Club. If prior to the March 1 next succeeding said December 20, the Player and the Club have not agreed upon the terms of such contract, then on or before 10 days after said March 1, the Club shall have the right by written notice to the Player at said address to renew this contract for the period of one year on the same terms, except that the amount payable to the Player shall be such as the Club shall fix in said notice; provided, however, that said amount, if fixed by a Major League Club, shall be an amount payable at a rate not less than 80% of the rate stipulated for the next preceding year and at a rate not less than 70% of the rate stipulated for the year immediately prior to the next preceding year.

10.(b) The Club's right to renew this contract, as provided in subparagraph (a) of this paragraph 10, and the promise of the Player not to play otherwise than with the Club have been taken into consideration in determining the amount payable under paragraph 2 hereof.

Governmental Regulation — National Emergency

11. This contract is subject to federal or state legislation, regulations, executive or other official orders or other governmental action, now or hereafter in effect respecting military, naval, air or other governmental service, which may directly or indirectly affect the Player, Club or the League and subject also to the right of the Commissioner to suspend the operation of this contract during any national emergency during which Major League Baseball is not played.

Commissioner

12. The term "Commissioner" wherever used in this contract shall be deemed to mean the Commissioner desig-

nated under the Major League Agreement, or in the case of a vacancy in the office of Commissioner, the Executive Council or such other body or person or persons as shall be designated in the Major League Agreement to exercise the powers and duties of the Commissioner during such vacancy.

Supplemental Agreements

The Club and the Player Covenant that this contract, the Basic Agreement effective January 1, 1973 and the Agreement Re Major League Baseball Players Benefit Plan effective April 1, 1973 fully set forth all understandings and agreements between them, and agree that no other understandings or agreements, whether heretofore or hereafter made, shall be valid, recognizable, or of any effect whatsoever, unless expressly set forth in a new or supplemental contract executed by the Player and the Club (acting by its President or such other officer as shall have been thereunto duly authorized by the President or Board of Directors as evidenced by a certificate filed of record with the League President and Commissioner) and complying with the Major League Rules and the Professional Baseball Rules.

Special Covenants

Approval

This contract or any supplement hereto shall not be valid or effective unless and until approved by the League President.

Signed in duplicate this .... day of ...., A.D. 197.... .

.... (Player)	.... (Club)
.... (Home address of Player)	By .... (Authorized Signature)
.... (City and State)	

Social Security No. ....

Approved ...., 197....

....

President The National League of Professional Baseball Clubs

Regulations

1. The Club's playing season for each year covered by this contract and all renewals hereof shall be as fixed by The National League of Professional Baseball Clubs, or if this contract shall be assigned to a Club in another League, then by the League of which such assignee is a member.

2. The Player, when requested by the Club, must submit to a complete physical examination at the expense of the

Club, and if necessary to treatment by a regular physician or dentist in good standing. Upon refusal of the Player to submit to a complete medical or dental examination the Club may consider such refusal a violation of this regulation and may take such action as it deems advisable under Regulation 5 of this contract. Disability directly resulting from injury sustained in the course and within the scope of his employment under this contract shall not impair the right of the Player to receive his full salary for the period of such disability or for the season in which the injury was sustained (whichever period is shorter), together with the reasonable medical and hospital expenses incurred by reason of the injury and during the term of this contract; but only upon the express prerequisite conditions that (a) written notice of such injury, including the time, place, cause and nature of the injury, is served upon and received by the Club within twenty days of the sustaining of said injury and (b) the Club shall have the right to designate the doctors and hospitals furnishing such medical and hospital services. Failure to give such notice shall not impair the rights of the Player, as herein set forth, if the Club has actual knowledge of such injury. All workmen's compensation payments received by the Player as compensation for loss of income for a specific period during which the Club is paying him in full, shall be paid over by the Player to the Club. Any other disability may be ground for suspending or terminating this contract at the discretion of the Club.

3. The Club will furnish the Player with two complete uniforms, exclusive of shoes, unless the Club requires the Player to wear non-standard shoes in which case the Club will furnish the shoes. The uniforms will be surrendered by the Player to the Club at the end of the season or upon termination of this contract.

4. The Player shall be entitled to expense allowances under the circumstances and in the amounts set forth in Article VI of the Basic Agreement between the Major League Clubs and the Major League Baseball Players Association effective January 1, 1973.

5. For violation by the Player of any regulation or other provision of this contract, the Club may impose a reasonable fine and deduct the amount thereof from the Player's salary or may suspend the Player without salary for a period not exceeding thirty days or both. Written notice of the fine or suspension or both and the reason therefor shall in every case be given to the Player.

6. In order to enable the Player to fit himself for his duties under this contract, the Club may require the Player to report for practice at such places as the Club may designate and to participate in such exhibition contests as may be arranged by the Club, without any other compensation than that herein elsewhere provided, for a period beginning not earlier than March 1 or ten days prior to the second Saturday in March, whichever is earlier, provided, however, that the Club may invite pitchers and catchers to report at an earlier date on a voluntary basis. The Club will pay the necessary traveling expenses, including the first-class jet air fare and meals en route of the Player from his home city to the training place of the Club, whether he be ordered to go there directly or by way of the home city of the Club. In the event of the failure of the Player to report for practice or to participate in the exhibition games, as required and provided for, he shall be required to get into playing condition to the satisfaction of the Club's team manager, and at the Player's own expense, before his salary shall commence.

7. In case of assignment of this contract the Player shall report promptly to the asignee Club within 72 hours from the date he receives written notice from the Club of such assignment, if the Player is then not more than 1600 miles by most direct available railroad route from the assignee Club, plus an additional 24 hours for each additional 800 miles.

Post-Season Exhibition Games. Major League Rule 18 (b) provides:

(b) EXHIBITION GAMES. No player shall participate in any exhibition game during the period between the close of the Major League championship season and the following training season, except that, with the consent of his club and permission of the Commissioner, a player may participate in exhibition games for a period of not less than thirty (30) days, such period to be designated annually by the Commissioner. Players who participate in barnstorming during this period cannot engage in any Winter League activities. Player conduct, on and off the field, in connection with such post-season exhibition games shall be subject to the discipline of the Commissioner. The Commissioner shall not approve of more than three (3) players of any one club on the same team. The Commissioner shall not approve of more than (3) players from the joint membership of the World Series participants playing in the same game. No player shall participate in any exhibition game with or against any team which, during the current season or within one year, has had any ineligible player or which is or has been during the current season or within one (1) year, managed and controlled by an ineligible player or by any person who has listed an ineligible player under an assumed name or who otherwise has violated, or attempted to violate, any exhibition game contract; or with or against any team which, during said season or within one (1) year, has played against teams containing such ineligible players, or so managed or controlled. Any player violating this Rule shall be fined not less than Fifty Dollars ($50.00) nor more than Five Hundred Dollars ($500.00), except that in no event shall such fine be less than the consideration received by such player for participating in such game.

FORM 2

Uniform Player's Contract

THE AMERICAN LEAGUE OF PROFESSIONAL BASEBALL CLUBS

Parties

Between .... herein called the Club,

and ....

of ...., herein called the Player.

Recital

The Club is a member of The American League of Professional Baseball Clubs, a voluntary association of twelve member Clubs which has subscribed to the Major League Rules with The National League of Professional Baseball Clubs and its constituent Clubs and to The Professional Baseball Rules with that League and the American Association of Baseball Leagues.

Agreement

In consideration of the facts above recited and of the promises of each to the other, the parties agree as follows:

Employment

1. The Club hereby employs the Player to render, and the Player agrees to render, skilled services as a baseball player during the year .... 197 .... including the Club's training season, the Club's exhibition games, the Club's playing season, the League Championship Series and the World Series (or any other official

series in which the Club may participate and in any receipts of which the Player may be entitled to share).

Payment

2. For performance of the Player's services and promises hereunder the Club will pay the Player the sum of

$..

....

....,

in semi-monthly installments after the commencement of the playing season covered by this contract except as the schedule of payments may be modified by a special covenant. Payment shall be made on the day the amount becomes due, regardless of whether the Club is "home" or "abroad". If a monthly rate of payment is stipulated above, it shall begin with the commencement of the Club's playing season (or such subsequent date as the Player's services may commence) and end with the termination of the Club's scheduled playing season and shall be payable in semi-monthly installments as above provided.

Nothing herein shall interfere with the right of the Club and the Player by special covenant herein to mutually agree upon a method of payment whereby part of the Player's salary for the above year can be deferred to subsequent years.

If the Player is in the service of the Club for part of the playing season only, he shall receive such proportion of the sum above mentioned, as the number of days of his actual employment in the Club's playing season bears to the number of days in said season.

Notwithstanding the rate of payment stipulated above, the minimum rate of payment to the Player for each day of service on a Major League Club shall be at the rate of $15,000 per year for the 1973 and 1974 playing seasons and $16,000 per year for the 1975 playing season.

Payment to the Player at the rate stipulated above shall be continued throughout any period in which a Player is required to attend a regularly scheduled military encampment of the Reserve of the Armed Forces or of the National Guard during the Club's playing season.

Loyalty

3.(a) The Player agrees to perform his services hereunder diligently and faithfully, to keep himself in first-class physical condition and to obey the Club's training rules, and pledges himself to the American public and to the Club to conform to high standards of personal conduct, fair play and good sportsmanship.

Baseball Promotion

3.(b) In addition to his services in connection with the actual playing of baseball, the Player agrees to cooperate with the Club and participate in any and all reasonable promotional activities of the Club and its League, which, in the opinion of the Club, will promote the welfare of the Club or professional baseball, and to observe and comply with all reasonable requirements of the Club respecting conduct and service of its team and its players, at all times whether on or off the field.

Pictures and Public Appearances

3.(c) The Player agrees that his picture may be taken for still photographs, motion pictures or television at such times as the Club may designate and agrees that all rights in such pictures shall belong to the Club and may be used by the Club for publicity purposes in any manner it desires. The Player further agrees that during the playing season he will not make public appearances, participate in radio or television programs or permit his picture to be taken or write or sponsor newspaper or magazine articles or sponsor commercial products without the written consent of the Club, which shall not be withheld except in the reasonable interests of the Club or professional baseball.

Player Representations

Ability

4.(a) The Player represents and agrees that he has exceptional and unique skill and ability as a baseball player; that his services to be rendered hereunder are of a special, unusual and extraordinary character which gives them peculiar value which cannot be reasonably or adequately compensated for in damages at law, and that the Player's breach of this contract will cause the Club great and irreparable injury and damage. The Player agrees that, in addition to other remedies, the Club shall be entitled to injunctive and other equitable relief to prevent a breach of this contract by the Player, including, among others, the right to enjoin the Player from playing baseball for any other person or organization during the term of his contract.

Condition

4.(b) The Player represents that he has no physical or mental defects known to him and unknown to the appropriate representative of the Club which would prevent or impair performance of his services.

Interest in Club

4.(c) The Player represents that he does not, directly or indirectly, own stock or have any financial interest in the ownership or earnings of any Major League Club, except as hereinafter expressly set forth, and covenants that he will not hereafter, while connected with any Major League Club, acquire or hold any such stock or interest except in accordance with Major League Rule 20(e).

Service

5.(a) The Player agrees that, while under contract, and prior to expiration of the Club's right to renew this contract, he will not play baseball otherwise than for the Club, except that the Player may participate in post-season games under the conditions prescribed in the Major League Rules. Major League Rule 18 (b) is set forth herein.

Other Sports

5.(b) The Player and the Club recognize and agree that the Player's participation in certain other sports may impair or destroy his ability and skill as a baseball player. Accordingly, the Player agrees that he will not engage in professional boxing or wrestling; and that, except with the written consent of the Club, he will not engage in skiing, auto racing, motorcycle racing, sky diving, or in any game or exhibition of football, soccer, professional league basketball, ice hockey or other sport involving a substantial risk of personal injury.

Assignment

6.(a) The Player agrees that this contract may be assigned by the Club (and reassigned by any assignee Club) to any other Club in accordance with the Major League Rules and the Professional Baseball Rules.

No Salary Reduction

6.(b) The amount stated in paragraph 2 and in special covenants hereof which is payable to the Player for the period stated in paragraph 1 hereof shall not be diminished by any such assignment, except for failure to report as provided in the next subparagraph (c).

Reporting

6.(c) The Player shall report to the assignee Club promptly (as provided in the Regulations) upon receipt of written notice from the Club of the assignment of this contract. If the Player fails so to report, he shall not be entitled to any payment for the period from the date he receives written notice of assignment until he reports to the assignee Club.

Obligations of Assignor and Assignee Clubs

6.(d) Upon and after such assignment, all rights and obligations of the assignor Club hereunder shall become the rights and obligations of the assignee Club; provided, however, that

(1) The assignee Club shall be liable to the Player for payments accruing only from the date of assignment and shall not be liable (but the assignor Club shall remain liable) for payments accrued prior to that date.

(2) If at any time the assignee is a Major League Club, it shall be liable to pay the Player at the full rate stipulated in paragraph 2 hereof for the remainder of the period stated in paragraph 1 hereof

and all prior assignors and assignees shall be relieved of liability for any payment for such period.

(3) Unless the assignor and assignee Clubs agree otherwise, if the assignee Club is a National Association Club, the assignee Club shall be liable only to pay the Player at the rate usually paid by said assignee Club to other Players of similar skill and ability in its classification and the assignor Club shall be liable to pay the difference for the remainder of the period stated in paragraph 1 hereof between an amount computed at the rate stipulated in paragraph 2 hereof and the amount so payable by the assignee Club.

Moving Allowances

6.(e) The Player shall be entitled to moving allowances under the circumstances and in the amounts set forth in Article VII of the Basic Agreement between the Major League Clubs and the Major League Baseball Players Association, effective January 1, 1973.

"Club"

6.(f) All references in other paragraphs of this contract to "the Club" shall be deemed to mean and include any assignee of this contract.

Termination

By Player

7.(a) The Player may terminate this contract, upon written notice to the Club, if the Club shall default in the payments to the Player provided for in paragraph 2 hereof or shall fail to perform any other obligation agreed to be performed by the Club hereunder and if the Club shall fail to remedy such default within ten (10) days after the receipt by the Club of written notice of such default. The Player may also terminate this contract as provided in subparagraph (g) (4) of this paragraph 7.

By Club

7.(b) The Club may terminate this contract upon written notice to the Player (but only after requesting and obtaining waivers of this contract from all other Major League Clubs) if the Player shall at any time:

(1) fail, refuse or neglect to conform his personal conduct to the standards of good citizenship and good sportsmanship or to keep himself in first-class physical condition or to obey the Club's training rules; or

(2) fail, in the opinion of the Club's management, to exhibit sufficient skill or competitive ability to qualify or continue as a member of the Club's team; or

(3) fail, refuse or neglect to render his services hereunder or in any other manner materially breach this contract.

7.(c) If this contract is terminated by the Club by reason of the Player's failure to render his services hereunder due to disability resulting directly from injury sustained in the course and within the scope of his employment hereunder and notice of such injury is received by the Club as provided in the Regulations set forth herein, the Player shall be entitled to receive his full salary for the season in which the injury was sustained, less all workmen's compensation payments received by the Player as compensation for loss of income for the specific period for which the Club is compensating him in full.

7.(d) If this contract is terminated by the Club during the training season, then, except in the case provided for in subparagraph (c) of this paragraph 7, the Player shall be entitled to receive as full payment hereunder the Player's board, lodging and/or expense allowances during the training season to the date of termination, the reasonable traveling expenses of the Player, including first-class jet air fare and meals en route to his home city, and the expert training and coaching provided by the Club to the Player during the training season, provided, however, that if this contract is terminated under subparagraph (b) (2) of this paragraph 7 for failure to exhibit sufficient skill or competitive ability, the Player shall be entitled to an additional amount (termination pay) equal to thirty (30) days payment at the rate stipulated in paragraph 2 hereof.

7.(e) If this contract is terminated by the Club during the playing season, then, except in the case provided for in subparagraph (c) of this paragraph 7, the Player shall be entitled to receive as full payment hereunder such portion of the amount stipulated in paragraph 2 hereof as the number of days of his actual employment in the Club's playing season bears to the total number of days in said season, provided, however, that if this contract is terminated under subparagraph (b) (2) of this paragraph 7 for failure to exhibit sufficient skill or competitive ability, the Player shall be entitled to an additional amount (termination pay) equal to sixty (60) days payment at the rate stipulated in paragraph 2 hereof and the reasonable traveling expenses of the Player, including first-class jet air fare and meals en route to his home city, provided further, however, that if this contract is terminated under said subparagraph (b) (2) for failure to exhibit sufficient skill or competitive ability, on or after May 15, the additional amount (termination pay) which the Player shall be entitled to receive shall be the unpaid balance of the full salary stipulated in paragraph 2 for that season.

7.(f) Subparagraphs (c), (d) and (e) of this paragraph 7 shall be applied regardless of the number of times the Player may be released during a year, subject to the following limitations:

(1) The maximum amount of termination pay which the Player shall be entitled to receive for any year shall not exceed the amount by which (a) the salary stipulated in the Player's original contract for such year exceeds (b) the aggregate amount which the Player earns during that year from any Club or Clubs, including amounts deferred to later years, if any, and bonuses.

(2) In the event a released Player refuses to accept a reasonable Major League contract offered by a Club other than the Club which released him, such Player shall forfeit that portion of the termination pay which would not have been payable if such contract had been accepted.

Procedure

7.(g) If the Club proposes to terminate this contract in accordance with subparagraph (b) of this paragraph 7, the procedure shall be as follows:

(1) The Club shall request waivers from all other Major League Clubs. Such waivers shall be good for six (6) days only. Such waiver request must state that it is for the purpose of terminating this contract and it may not be withdrawn.

(2) Upon receipt of the waiver request, any other Major League Club may claim assignment of this con-

tract at a waiver price of $1.00, the priority of claims to be determined in accordance with the Major League Rules.

(3) If this contract is so claimed, the Club shall, promptly and before any assignment, notify the Player that it had requested waivers for the purpose of terminating this contract and that the contract had been claimed.

(4) Within 5 days after receipt of notice of such claim, the Player shall be entitled, by written notice to the Club, to terminate this contract on the date of his notice of termination. If the Player fails so to notify the Club, this contract shall be assigned to the claiming Club.

(5) If the contract is not claimed, the Club shall promptly deliver written notice of termination to the Player at the expiration of the waiver period.

7.(h) Upon any termination of this contract by the Player, all obligations of both Parties hereunder shall cease on the date of termination, except the obligation of the Club to pay the Player's compensation to said date.

Regulations

8. The Player accepts as part of this contract the Regulations set forth herein.

Rules

9.(a) The Club and the Player agree to accept, abide by and comply with all provisions of the Major League Agreement, the Major League Rules, the Rules or Regulations of the League of which the Club is a member, and the Professional Baseball Rules, in effect on the date of this Uniform Player's Contract, which are not inconsistent with the provisions of this contract or the provisions of any agreement between the Major League Clubs and the Major League Baseball Players Association, provided that the Club, together with the other Clubs of the American and National Leagues and the National Association, reserves the right to modify, supplement or repeal any provision of said Agreement, Rules and/or Regulations in a manner not inconsistent with this contract or the provisions of any then existing agreement between the Major League Clubs and the Major League Baseball Players Association.

Disputes

9.(b) All disputes between the Player and the Club which are covered by the Grievance Procedure as set forth in the Basic Agreement, effective January 1, 1973, shall be resolved in accordance with such Grievance Procedure.

Publication

9.(c) The Club, the League President and the Commissioner, or any of them, may make public the findings, decision and record of any inquiry, investigation or hearing held or conducted, including in such record all evidence or information, given, received, or obtained in connection therewith.

Renewal

10.(a) On or before December 20 (or if a Sunday, then the next preceding business day) in the year of the last playing season covered by this contract, the Club may tender to the Player a contract for the term of that year by mailing the same to the Player at his address following his signature hereto, or if none be given, then at his last address of record with the Club. If prior to the March 1 next succeeding said December 20, the Player and the Club have not agreed upon the terms of such contract, then on or before 10 days after said March 1, the Club shall have the right by written notice to the Player at said address to renew this contract for the period of one year on the same terms, except that the amount payable to the Player shall be such as the Club shall fix in said notice; provided, however, that said amount, if fixed by a Major League Club, shall be an amount payable at a rate not less than 80% of the rate stipulated for the next preceding year and at a rate not less than 70% of the rate stipulated for the year immediately prior to the next preceding year.

10.(b) The Club's right to renew this contract, as provided in subparagraph (a) of this paragraph 10, and the promise of the Player not to play otherwise than with the Club have been taken into consideration in determining the amount payable under paragraph 2 hereof.

Governmental Regulation — National Emergency

11. This contract is subject to federal or state legislation, regulations, executive or other official orders or other governmental action, now or hereafter in effect respecting military, naval, air or other governmental service, which may directly or indirectly affect the Player, Club or the League and subject also to the right of the Commissioner to suspend the operation of this contract during any national emergency during which Major League Baseball is not played.

Commissioner

12. The term "Commissioner" wherever used in this contract shall be deemed to mean the Commissioner designated under the Major League Agreement, or in the case of a vacancy in the office of Commissioner, the Executive Council or such other body or person or persons as shall be designated in the Major League Agreement to exercise the powers and duties of the Commissioner during such vacancy.

Supplemental Agreements

The Club and the Player Covenant that this contract, the Basic Agreement effective January 1, 1973 and the Agreement Re Major League Baseball Players Benefit Plan effective April 1, 1973 fully set forth all understandings and agreements between them, and agree that no other understandings or agreements, whether heretofore or hereafter made, shall be valid, recognizable, or of any effect whatsoever, unless expressly set forth in a new or supplemental contract executed by the Player and the Club (acting by its President or such other officer as shall have been thereunto duly authorized by the President or Board of Directors as evidenced by a certificate filed of record with the League President and Commissioner) and complying with the Major League Rules and the Professional Baseball Rules.

Special Covenants

Approval

This contract or any supplement hereto shall not be valid or effective unless and until approved by the League President.

Signed in duplicate this .... day of ...., A.D. 197.... .

....

(Player) (Club)

.... By ....

(Home address of Player) (Authorized Signature)

....

(City and State)

Social Security No. ....

Approved ...., 197....

....

President, The American League of Professional Baseball Clubs

Regulations

1. The Club's playing season for each year covered by this contract and all renewals hereof shall be as fixed by The American League of Professional Baseball Clubs, or if this contract shall be assigned to a Club in another League, then by the League of which such assignee is a member.

2. The Player, when requested by the Club, must submit to a complete physical examination at the expense of the

Club, and if necessary to treatment by a regular physician or dentist in good standing. Upon refusal of the Player to submit to a complete medical or dental examination the Club may consider such refusal a violation of this regulation and may take such action as it deems advisable under Regulation 5 of this contract. Disability directly resulting from injury sustained in the course and within the scope of his employment under this contract shall not impair the right of the Player to receive his full salary for the period of such disability or for the reason in which the injury was sustained (whichever period is shorter), together with the reasonable medical and hospital expenses incurred by reason of the injury and during the term of this contract; but only upon the express prerequisite conditions that (a) written notice of such injury, including the time, place, cause and nature of the injury, is served upon and received by the Club within twenty days of the sustaining of said injury and (b) the Club shall have the right to designate the doctors and hospitals furnishing such medical and hospital services. Failure to give such notice shall not impair the rights of the Player, as herein set forth, if the Club has actual knowledge of such injury. All workmen's compensation payments received by the Player as compensation for loss of income for a specific period during which the Club is paying him in full, shall be paid over by the Player to the Club. Any other disability may be ground for suspending or terminating this contract at the discretion of the Club.

3. The Club will furnish the Player with two complete uniforms, exclusive of shoes, unless the Club requires the Player to wear non-standard shoes in which case the Club will furnish the shoes. The uniforms will be surrendered by the Player to the Club at the end of the season or upon termination of this contract.

4. The Player shall be entitled to expense allowances under the circumstances and in the amounts set forth in Article VI of the Basic Agreement between the Major League Clubs and the Major League Baseball Players Association effective January 1, 1973.

5. For violation by the Player of any regulation or other provision of this contract, the Club may impose a reasonable fine and deduct the amount thereof from the Player's salary or may suspend the Player without salary for a period not exceeding thirty days or both. Written notice of the fine or suspension or both and the reason therefor shall in every case be given to the Player.

6. In order to enable the Player to fit himself for his duties under this contract, the Club may require the Player to report for practice at such places as the Club may designate and to participate in such exhibition contests as may be arranged by the Club, without any other compensation than that herein elsewhere provided, for a period beginning not earlier than March 1 or ten days prior to the second Saturday in March, whichever is earlier, provided, however, that the Club may invite pitchers and catchers to report at an earlier date on a voluntary basis. The Club will pay the necessary traveling expenses, including the first-class jet air fare and meals en route of the Player from his home city to the training place of the Club, whether he be ordered to go there directly or by way of the home city of the Club. In the event of the failure of the Player to report for practice or to participate in the exhibition games, as required and provided for, he shall be required to get into playing condition to the satisfaction of the Club's team manager, and at the Player's own expense, before his salary shall commence.

7. In case of assignment of this contract the Player shall report promptly to the asignee Club within 72 hours from the date he receives written notice from the Club of such assignment, if the Player is then not more than 1600 miles by most direct available railroad route from the assignee Club, plus an additional 24 hours for each additional 800 miles.

Post-Season Exhibition Games. Major League Rule 18 (b) provides:

(b) Exhibition Games. No player shall participate in any exhibition game during the period between the close of the Major League championship season and the following training season, except that, with the consent of his club and permission of the Commissioner, a player may participate in exhibition games for a period of not less than thirty (30) days, such period to be designated annually by the Commissioner. Players who participate in barnstorming during this period cannot engage in any Winter League activities. Player conduct, on and off the field, in connection with such post-season exhibition games shall be subject to the discipline of the Commissioner. The Commissioner shall not approve of more than three (3) players of any one club on the same team. The Commissioner shall not approve of more than (3) players from the joint membership of the World Series participants playing in the same game. No player shall participate in any exhibition game with or against any team which, during the current season or within one year, has had any ineligible player or which is or has been during the current season or within one (1) year, managed and controlled by an ineligible player or by any person who has listed an ineligible player under an assumed name or who otherwise has violated, or attempted to violate, any exhibition game contract; or with or against any team which, during said season or within one (1) year, has played against teams containing such ineligible players, or so managed or controlled. Any player violating this Rule shall be fined not less than Fifty Dollars ($50.00) nor more than Five Hundred Dollars ($500.00), except that in no event shall such fine be less than the consideration received by such player for participating in such game.

FORM 3

STANDARD PLAYER CONTRACT

FOR

THE NATIONAL FOOTBALL LEAGUE

BETWEEN

....

a .... Corporation, (a limited Partnership), hereinafter called "Club," which Club operates under the name and style of .... and which Club is presently a member of the National Football League, hereinafter called "League" and ...., hereinafter called "Player."

In consideration of the respective promises herein the parties agree as follows:

1. The term of this contract shall be from the date of execution hereof until the first day of May following the close of the football season commencing in the calendar year 19 ......, subject, however, to termination, extension or renewal as specified herein.

2. The Player agrees that during the term of this contract he will play football and engage in activities related to football only for the Club and as directed by the Club according to: this contract; the Constitution and By-Laws, Rules and Regulations of the League and of the Club; and the Club, subject to the provisions hereof, agrees during such term to employ the Player as a skilled football player. The Player agrees during the term of this contract to report promptly for the Club's training sessions and, at

the Club's direction, to render his full time services during such training sessions and to participate in all practice sessions and in all League and other football games scheduled for or by the Club.

Professional Sports and the Law

3. For: the Player's services as a skilled football player during the term of this contract: his agreement not to play football or engage in activities related to football for any other person, firm, corporation or institution during the term of this contract; the option hereinafter set forth giving the Club the right to renew this contract; and all other undertakings of the Player herein; the Club promises, subject to Paragraph 7 hereof, to pay the Player each football season during the term of this contract, unless the compensation is changed under Paragraph 10 hereof, the amount of $................ to be payable as follows:

> ....% of "said amount in equal semi-monthly installments commencing with the first regularly scheduled League game played by the Club during each season and continuing each semi-monthly period thereafter; the balance of ....% of said amount shall be paid on the date of the last regularly scheduled League game.

In addition, the Club agrees to pay: the reasonable board and lodging expenses of the Player incurred in pre-season training and/or while playing pre-season and/or regularly scheduled League games for the Club in other than the Club's home city; and all proper and necessary traveling expenses of the Player en route to and from said games in other than the Club's home city. Any advances made to the Player shall be repaid promptly to the Club by means of deduction from payments coming due to the Player hereunder, the amounts of such deductions to be determined by the Club unless otherwise agreed by the parties.

The Player hereby authorizes the Club to make such deductions.

If, either this agreement is executed, or the Player reports for play and thereafter is placed on the Active List of the Club after the Club has played one or more regularly scheduled games in the applicable season, the obligation of the Club to pay Player the salary prescribed in Paragraph 3 hereof shall be reduced in the proportion that the number of said games already played by the Club bears to the total number of regularly scheduled games to be played by the Club in the applicable season.

4. The Player agrees at all times to comply with and be bound by: the Constitution and By-Laws, Rules and Regulations of the League, of the Club, and the decisions of the Commissioner of the League (hereinafter called "Commissioner"), which shall be final, conclusive and unappealable. The enumerated Constitution, By-Laws, Rules and Regulations are intended to include the present Constitution, By-Laws, Rules and Regulations as well as all amendments thereto, all of which are by reference incorporated herein. If the Player fails to comply with said Constitution, By-Laws, Rules and Regulations, the Club shall have the right to terminate this contract as provided in Paragraph 6 hereof or to take such other action as may be specified in said Constitution, By-Laws, Rules and Regulations, or as may be directed by the Commissioner. The Player agrees to submit himself to the discipline of the League and of the Club, for any violation of said Constitution, By-Laws, Rules and Regulations, subject, however, to the right to a hearing by the Commissioner. All matters in dispute between the Player and the Club shall be referred to the Commissioner and his decision shall be accepted as final, conclusive, binding and unappealable,

by the Player and by the Club. The Player, if involved or affected in any manner whatsoever by a decision of the Commissioner, whether the decision results from a dispute between the Player and the Club or otherwise, hereby releases and discharges the Commissioner, the League, each Club in the League, each Director, Officer, Stockholder, Owner or Partner of any Club in the League, each employee, agent, official or representative of the League or of any Club in the League, jointly and severally, individually and in their official capacities, of and from any and all claims, demands, damages, suits, actions and causes of action whatsoever, in law or in equity, arising out of or in connection with any decision of the Commissioner, except to the extent of awards made by the Commissioner to the Player. The Player hereby acknowledges that he has read the present said Constitution, By-Laws, Rules and Regulations, and that he understands their meaning.

5. The Player promises and agrees that during the term of this contract he will not play football or engage in activities related to football for any other person, firm, corporation or institution, or on his own behalf, except with the prior written consent of the Club and the Commissioner, and, that he will not, during the term of this contract, without the prior consent of the Club, engage in any other sport. The knowledge of the Club or the Commissioner of any of the foregoing activities by the Player shall not be deemed to be a consent thereto. Such activities if engaged in by the Player shall be at his own risk and any injury suffered therein shall not be deemed to be in the performance of his services under this contract. The Player likewise promises and agrees that, during the term of this contract, when, as and if he shall receive an invitation to participate in any All-Star football

game which is sponsored by the League, he will play in said game in accordance with all of the terms and conditions relating thereto, including the player compensation therein set forth, as are agreed to between the League and the Sponsor of such game. The Player likewise promises and agrees that during the term of this contract, he will not participate in any other outside football game not sponsored by the League unless such game is first approved by the League; despite such approval by the League, the Player shall not be obligated to participate therein.

6. The Player represents and warrants that he is and will continue to be sufficiently skilled in all types of football team play, to play professional football of the caliber required by the League and by the Club, and that he is and will continue to be in excellent physical condition, and agrees to perform his services hereunder to the complete satisfaction of the Club and its Head Coach. Player shall undergo a complete physical examination by the Club physician at the start of each training session during the term hereof. If Player fails to establish his excellent physical condition to the satisfaction of the Club physician by the physical examination, or (after having so established his excellent physical condition) if, in the opinion of the Head Coach, Player does not maintain himself in such excellent physical condition or fails at any time during the football seasons included in the terms of this contract to demonstrate sufficient skill and capacity to play professional football of the caliber required by the League, or by the Club, or if in the opinion of the Head Coach the Player's work or conduct in the performance of this contract is unsatisfactory as compared with the work and conduct of other members of the Club's squad of players, the Club shall have the right to terminate this contract.

7. Upon termination of this contract the Club shall pay the Player only the balance, if any, remaining due him for traveling, board and lodging expenses and for football seasons completed prior to termination, and if termination takes place during a football season, the balance, if any, remaining due him on that portion of his total compensation for that season as provided in ¶3 or ¶10 hereof, whichever is applicable, which the number of regularly scheduled League games already played by the Club during that season bears to the total number of League games scheduled for the Club for that season.

8. The Player hereby represents that he has special, exceptional and unique knowledge, skill and ability as a football player, the loss of which cannot be estimated with any certainty and cannot be fairly or adequately compensated by damages and therefore agrees that the Club shall have the right, in addition to any other rights which the Club may possess, to enjoin him by appropriate injunction proceedings against playing football or any other professional sport, without the consent of the Club, or engaging in activities related to football for any person, firm, corporation, institution, or on his own behalf, and against any other breach of this contract.

9. It is mutually agreed that the Club shall have the right to sell, exchange, assign or transfer this contract and the Player's services hereunder to any other Club in the League. Player agrees to accept such assignment and to report promptly to the assignee Club and faithfully to perform and carry out this contract with the assignee Club as if it had been entered into by the Player with the assignee Club instead of with this Club.

10. The Club may, by sending notice in writing to the Player, on or before the first day of May following the

football season referred to in ¶1 hereof, renew this contract for a further term of one (1) year on the same terms as are provided by this contract, except that (1) the Club may fix the rate of compensation to be paid by the Club to the Player during said further term, which rate of compensation shall not be less than ninety percent (90%) of the sum set forth in ¶3 hereof and shall be payable in installments during the football season in such further term as provided in ¶3; and (2) after such renewal this contract shall not include a further option to the Club to renew the contract. The phrase "rate of compensation" as above used shall not include bonus payments or payments of any nature whatsoever and shall be limited to the precise sum set forth in ¶3 hereof.

11. Player acknowledges the right and power of the Commissioner (a) to fine and suspend, (b) to fine and suspend for life or indefinitely, and/or (c) to cancel the contract of, any player who accepts a bribe or who agrees to throw or fix a game or who, having knowledge of the same, fails to report an offered bribe or an attempt to throw or fix a game, or who bets on a game, or who is guilty of any conduct detrimental to the welfare of the League or of professional football. The Player, if involved or affected in any manner whatsoever by a decision of the Commissioner in any of the aforesaid cases, hereby releases and discharges the Commissioner, the League, each Club in the League, each Director, Officer, Stockholder, Owner, Partner, employee, agent, official or representative of any Club in the League, jointly and severally, individually and in their official capacities, of and from any and all claims, demands, damages, suits, actions, and causes of action whatsoever, in law or in equity, arising out of or in connection with any such decision of the Commissioner.

12. Any payments made hereunder to the Player, for a period during which he is entitled to workmen's compensation benefits by reason of temporary total, permanent total, temporary partial, or permanent partial disability shall be deemed an advance payment of workmen's compensation benefits due the Player, and the Club shall be entitled to be reimbursed the amounts thereof out of any award of compensation.

13. Should Player become a member of the Armed Forces of the United States or any other country; or fail or refuse to perform his services as provided in this contract; or retire from professional football as a player prior to the expiration of this contract or any option renewal term hereof, and subsequently be released from the Armed Forces or return to professional football as a player, then, and in either event, the time elapsed between Player's induction into the Armed Forces and his discharge therefrom, or between the date of his failure or refusal to perform his services as provided in this contract, or between the date of his retirement from professional football as a player, and his return thereto, shall be tolled, and the term of this contract shall be for a period beginning with Player's failure or refusal to perform his services hereunder, release from the Armed Forces, or his return to professional football as a player, as the case may be, and ending after a period of time equal to the portion of the term of this contract which was unexpired at the time Player entered the Armed Forces, failed or refused to perform his services hereunder, or retired from professional football as a player. The renewal option contained herein shall be continuously in effect from the date of this contract until the end of such extended term. During the period of such services in the Armed Forces or such retirement, or while failing or refusing to perform his services hereunder,

the Player shall not be entitled to any compensation, expenses or other payments under this contract.

14. In the event that Player is injured in the performance of his services under this contract, and if Player gives written notice to the Club Physician of such injury within thirty-six (36) hours of its occurrence, the Club will: (1) provide, during the term of this contract, such medical or hospital care as, in the opinion of the Club Physician, may be necessary; and (2) continue, during the term of this contract, to pay Player his salary as provided in ¶3 or ¶10 hereof, whichever is applicable if and so long as it is the opinion of the Club Physician that Player, because of such injury, is unable to perform the services required of him by this contract. Player, may, within seventy-two (72) hours after his examination by the Club Physician submit at his own expense to an examination by a physician of his choice. If the opinion of such physician with respect to Player's physical ability to render the services required of him by this contract is contrary to that of the Club Physician, the dispute shall be submitted to a disinterested physician to be selected by the Club Physician and Player's physician or, if they are unable to agree, by the Commissioner, and the opinion of such disinterested physician shall be conclusive and binding upon the Player and the Club. Except as provided in this paragraph, Player's failure for any reason whatsoever to perform this contract or the services required of him by this contract, or his failure to comply with: the Constitution and By-Laws, Rules and Regulations of the League, or of the Club, shall entitle the club, at its option, to terminate such contract, such termination to be effective when the Club sends to the Player written notice of such termination, or shall entitle the Club at its option to terminate Player's salary under this contract. The Player's death shall auto-

matically terminate this contract. The rights of termination set forth in this paragraph shall be in addition to the rights of termination set forth in ¶6 hereof, and any other rights of termination allowed by law.

If Player is injured in the performance of his services under this contract, this contract shall remain in full force and effect despite the fact that Player, following injury, is either carried by the Club on its Reserve List or is waived out as an injured player while injured; when such Player is, in the opinion of the Club physician, again physically able to perform his services under this contract, the Club shall have the right to activate such Player, and Player shall be obligated to perform his services hereunder in accordance with the terms hereof.

15. Any notice, request, demand, approval or consent required or permitted under this contract to be given by one party to the other shall be deemed sufficiently given if delivered in person or mailed (registered or first-class) to such other party at his or its address set forth in this contract or to such other address as such other party may previously have furnished to the sender in writing.

16. This contract sets forth the entire agreement between the parties. The signing of this agreement by the parties constitutes their mutual recognition that no other contract or agreements, oral or written, except as attached hereto or specifically incorporated herein, exists between them, that, if any such oral or written contracts or agreements exist, such are hereby cancelled; each party hereby represents to the other that it will not rely upon any agreement or understanding not reduced to writing and incorporated in this agreement prior to the execution hereof.

17. This contract shall be valid and binding upon the parties hereto immediately upon its execution. A copy of such contract shall be filed by the Club with the Commissioner within ten (10) days after execution. The Commissioner shall have the right to terminate this contract by his disapproval thereof within ten (10) days after the filing thereof in his office; such action by the Commissioner shall be exercised in accordance with and pursuant to the power vested in the Commissioner by the Constitution and By-Laws of the League; in such event, the Commissioner shall give both parties written notice of such termination, and thereupon, both parties shall be relieved of their respective rights and liabilities hereunder.

18. This agreement has been made under and shall be governed by the laws of the State of ....

In Witness Whereof the Player has hereunto set his hand and seal and the Club has caused this contract to be executed by its duly authorized officer on the date set opposite their respective names.

....
Name of Club

By ....
Date

....
Player Date

....
Player's Address

Telephone No. ....

League Office Copy

CLUB RULES AND REGULATIONS

1. All players must be on time for all meetings, practice sessions, meals, and all types of transportation. The curfew must be observed. Players must keep all publicity appointments and be on time.

2. Drinking of intoxicants is forbidden.

3. Players must not frequent gambling resorts nor associate with gamblers or other notorious characters.

4. Players must report all injuries to a coach and the club physician or trainer immediately, and be prompt in keeping appointments.

5. Players must wear coats and neckties in hotel lobbies, public eating places, and on all public conveyances.

6. Players must familiarize themselves with their contract, especially paragraph 11 thereof.

7. Players shall not write or sponsor magazine or newspaper articles, or endorse any product or service or appear on or participate in any radio or television program without the consent of the club.

FORM 4

WORLD FOOTBALL LEAGUE*

PLAYER'S CONTRACT

1. PARTIES AND CONSIDERATION.

This Contract is between .... (Club), a Member of the World Football League playing football as the ".."; and .... (Player). The consideration for this Contract includes the mutual promises, and performance rendered and to be rendered in accordance with those promises, as set forth below.

2. DEFINITIONS.

2.1. *League.*

The World Football League (WFL, or, the League) is a California nonprofit Corporation of which the Club is a member.

2.2. *Club.*

The Club is the WFL Franchise holder which operates a WFL football Club in a designated territory.

2.3. *Player.*

A Player is a football player, who represents that he is capable of playing Major League football and who, by executing this Contract, agrees to play football exclusively with Club.

---

* The World Football League is now defunct, but the form has been included as useful for reference and comparison purposes.—Ed.

2.4. *League By-Laws, Playing and Operating Rules.*

The League by-laws, playing rules and operating rules are those adopted, and from time to time amended, by the League.

2.5. *Club Rules.*

Club rules are those adopted, and as from time to time amended, by each individual WFL Club.

2.6. *Contract.*

The Contract referred to is this Contract, of which there are four copies: The League's copy, Club's copy, Player's copy and Player's temporary copy (held by the Player until the Player's copy is executed by the League President and returned to Player). If there is any discrepancy between or among the copies, the copy on file in the League Office shall control.

2.7. *Contract Year.*

Contract Year is the twelve consecutive month period from February 1 to January 31 each year during the term of this Contract.

2.8. *Season.*

Season is that period of time in the Contract Year, not to exceed eight months, during which WFL Clubs practice and play regular season, playoff, championship and all-star games.

2.9. *Effective Date.*

This Contract shall be effective on the date which it is signed by Club and Player as set out in the signatory paragraph on the last page. In order to preserve the integrity of the League by-laws, operating rules, playing rules and Presidential authority, the President shall have the right to approve or disapprove this Contract within 10 days after its filing in his office. In the absence of a written notice of disapproval to both Club and Player, the Contract remains in effect. On disapproval, neither Club nor Player shall be further obligated under this Contract.

3. COMPENSATION.

3.1. Except as modified by any other paragraph of this Contract, Club will pay to Player, for the performance described hereunder the following salary:

3.2. Club will provide Player with reasonable lodging and meals for preseason training, and while Club is on the road for games in other than Club's home territory. Club will also provide necessary transportation en route to and from away games.

3.3. Payments under pargaraphs 3.1 and 3.2 above shall be in accordance with Club's normal payroll practices.

3.4. After the Effective Date, if Club defaults in any salary payment admittedly due to Player, and fails to make such payment within forty-eight (48) hours after written demand to Club, with a copy to League Office, then, payment of the amount in default will be mailed by certified or registered mail to Player by the League within seventy-two (72) hours after receipt by the League of written notice that Club has failed to respond to Player's demand.

3.5. If the League is required to and does make any payment to Player hereunder, this Contract may, at the

League's option, be assigned to and become the property of the League.

4. Employment and Services.

Club employs Player as a Major League football player, and Player accepts such employment and agrees to perform to the best of his ability and provide, by way of illustration and not limitation, the following services:

4.1. To report to Club in good physical condition and training at the time and place fixed by Club at the beginning of each Season.

4.2. To play and participate in, to the best of his ability, all practice sessions, scrimmages, League and other games scheduled by or for Club.

4.3. To comply with and be bound by League by-laws, operating rules, playing rules, Club rules and decisions of the League President, and to submit to discipline of the League and Club for any violation thereof.

4.4. To stay in the best physical condition possible during the Season.

4.5. To give his loyalty to the League and Club and to participate in their promotions and publicity and to cooperate with their football and business activities.

4.6. If invited, and if physically able, to play and participate in, to the best of his ability, any all-star games sponsored by the League, in accordance with the terms and player compensation established for such game.

4.7. When requested by the League or Club, to submit himself, at a mutually convenient time and place, for medical examination to be conducted by a physician selected by the League or Club. The League or Club will pay all expenses connected with such examination.

5. Publicity.

5.1. Player grants and assigns to Club the non-exclusive right to take his picture, alone or with others, to use his name, initials, likeness, signature facsimile and biographical sketch in connection with any matter associated with Club's or League's business on publicity. These items granted and assigned shall hereafter be called "intangible property." This intangible property shall not include radio or television commercials involving Player.

5.2. Speaking engagements, newspaper, radio and television interviews are hereby excluded from the definition of intangible property, and money paid to Player for such services, which services shall not conflict with any obligation hereunder, shall belong to Player.

6. Exclusivity.

6.1. Player will not play football, nor engage in activities related to football, for any entity other than Club, without Club's prior written consent, and will not, without prior written consent of the Club, engage in any other sport. Neither the Club's nor the President's knowledge of of a violation of this clause shall be deemed consent thereto. Player will not participate in any football game other than with Club or one sponsored by the League, unless such game is first approved by the League.

6.2. Player has represented to Club, and agrees that he has unique skill, experience, knowledge, and ability, all of which contribute to his being an exceptional Major League football player. Player acknowledges that the services he will perform under this Contract cannot be replaced or duplicated by the services of any other player. In addition, he acknowledges that should Club lose his services by any breach or threatened breach of this Contract, or any other agreement with the Player, Club cannot properly or adequately be compensated for his loss by the mere payment of money. Player agrees, therefore, that in the event of a breach or threatened breach of this Contract by Player, Club or its assignees, in addition to any other remedies that may be available to them judicially or by way of arbitration, shall have the right to obtain from any competent court or arbitrator a decree enjoining any further breach of this Contract, and enjoining the Player from playing football for any other entity during the term of this Contract or any extension or renewal hereof.

7. Physical Condition; Injury; Death.

7.1. If Player, in the sole judgment of Club's physician, is not in appropriate physical condition at the commencement of the Season, or if, during the Season, Player fails to remain in appropriate physical condition, unless such condition results directly from performance under this Contract, so as to render Player in the sole judgment of Club's physician, unfit to play football, Club shall have the right to suspend Player until such time as, in the sole judgment of Club's physician, Player is in condition to play skilled football. On any such suspension, the salary payable to Player shall be proportionately reduced as the length of the period of disability during which, in the sole judgment of the Club's physician, the Player is not fit to play bears to the WFL Season. If Player believes the decision of Club's physician is unreasonable, Player has the right to be examined by an independent medical specialist mutually selected by the Club physician and Player's physician, or, if they are unable to agree, by the League President. The opinion of the independent medical specialist so selected shall be binding on Club and Player.

7.2. If Player is injured as a direct result of participating in any practice or game played for Club, Club will pay Player's hospitalization until Player is discharged from the hospital, as well as related medical expenses and doctor's bills, provided the hospital and doctor are selected or approved by Club.

7.3. If Player suffers any injury in any practice or game for Club, and this injury renders Player, in the sole judgment of Club's physician, unfit to play for the balance of the season or any part thereof, then during such time Player is so unfit, but in no event beyond the end of the season in question, Club shall pay Player the compensation herein provided, less any workmen's compensation benefits or insurance proceeds provided through Club, whether paid or payable to Player, and Player releases Club from any and every additional obligation, liability, claim or demand, except as set out in paragraph 7.2 above.

7.4. If Player is declared by Club's physician to be physically able to play, and refuses to do so, Player agrees to submit for examination by an independent medical specialist, mutually acceptable to both parties (or if the parties cannot agree, one selected by the President), operating in the field commonly known as specializing in the treatment of the injury of which Player complains. If, in the opinion of this independent medical specialist, Player is again declared physically able to play and refuses to do so, Player shall be liable to immediate suspension without pay, or termination of this Contract, at Club's option.

7.5. If Player is injured in any practice or game played by Club, this Contract shall remain in full force and effect despite the fact that Player, following the injury, is either carried by Club on its reserve list or injured list. When such Player is, in the opinion of the Club physician, again physically able to perform his services under this Contract, Club shall have the right to activate Player, and Player shall be obligated to perform the services promised hereunder.

7.6. Player's death shall automatically terminate this Contract.

8. Gambling.

If the League President shall, in his sole judgment, find that Player has bet, or has offered or attempted to bet, money or anything of value on the outcome of any game participated in by any Club which is a member of the League, the President shall have the power, in his sole discretion, to suspend without pay and/or fine the Player, and the President's finding and decision shall be binding and conclusive. Player hereby releases the President and waives every claim he may have against the President and/or the League, and against every Club in the League, and against every director, officer or stockholder of every Club in the League, for damages and for all claims and demands arising out of or in connection with the decision of a gambling matter by the President. If Player feels the President's decision in this regard is unreasonable, Player has the right to have the decision reviewed by an independent arbitrator mutually acceptable to both Player and the President. The decision of this arbitrator shall be binding on both Player and the League. The arbitrator shall also determine who shall pay the costs of this arbitration procedure.

9. Drugs.

Player warrants that at no time during the term of this Contract will he use any drugs unless prescribed for him by a licensed physician. Player agrees that the League President shall have the sole power and discretion to suspend, terminate, and/or fine Player for violation of this Paragraph, and the President's finding and decision shall be binding and conclusive on all parties. Player hereby releases the President and waives every claim he may have against the President and/or the League and against Club and every director, officer, or stockholder of a Club, for damages and for all claims and demands arising out of, or in connection with, the decision of this matter by the President.

10. Confidential Agreement.

Player agrees with Club that no information regarding the existence or the terms and conditions of this Contract shall be released to any third party without the mutual consent of both.

11. Deductions.

Player hereby authorizes Club to deduct from payments due him hereunder amounts required for Player's income tax, and other lawfully required withholdings. Player agrees to promptly pay any Club or League fine levied against him, either in cash or by deduction from any payment due him hereunder.

12. Standards of Performance.

Player understands that he is competing with other players for positions on Club's roster and that the number of players on the roster is limited by League rules and practical necessity. If, at any time during the term of this Contract, in the sole opinion of Club, Player's skill, performance, or conduct is not sufficient to enable him to stay on Club's active roster, or within some other League authorized numerical limit, Club shall have the right to terminate this Contract. Upon any such termination Club shall be liable to Player only for accrued expenses due him and that part of the compensation due him hereunder which the number of League games already played by Club during the Season of the termination bears to the total number of League games for that Season scheduled for Club.

13. Waiver.

Player understands that he, Club, or this Contract might be affected by a decision of the League President or Board of Governors. Player hereby releases and discharges the President, League, each Club in the League, each officer, director, shareholder, owner or partner of any Club and each employee or representative of the League or of any Club, jointly and severally, individually and in their official capacities, from and of any and all claims, demands, damages, causes of action, or suits, arising out of or in connection with any decision of the President or of the Board on any matter within their jurisdiction.

14. Arbitration.

14.1. Any dispute or controversy arising under, out of or in connection with this Contract shall be submitted to arbitration under the provisions of this Paragraph. The arbitration shall be held within Club's territory before an arbitrator acceptable to both parties. If Club and Player are unable to agree on an arbitrator within 10 days after either party requests arbitration, the American Arbitration Association shall be requested by either party to submit a list of arbitrators from which the arbitrator shall be selected by agreement between Club and Player. If the parties still fail to agree on an arbitrator, they shall each strike off the names of potential arbitrators who are unacceptable and shall indicate the order of preference of those remaining. They will then request the American Arbitration Association to appoint an arbitrator from the names remaining on the list, after considering preference, qualifications and availability.

14.2. The arbitrator shall determine by whom and in what proportion the cost of arbitration shall be paid. Player and Club hereby grant such arbitrator full power to determine their dispute in such manner as he shall direct, and under such rules of procedure as he shall in his sole discretion adopt, and his award shall be final, binding and conclusive and may be enforced in any court having competent jurisdiction.

14.3. Demand for arbitration hereunder shall be forever barred unless made within one (1) year from the date when the alleged dispute arose, and shall be made by notice in writing given to the other party. Notwithstanding the foregoing, Club shall have the right in its sole discretion to waive arbitration and to institute judicial proceedings for the purpose of obtaining an injunction or other equitable relief.

15. Term, Termination and Extension.

15.1. The Term of the Contract shall be for .... Contract Years. The initial Contract Year shall commence on the effective date hereof and shall conclude on January 31, 1975.

15.2. Club may terminate this Contract at any time that Player fails to perform the services or comply with the agreements he has made under paragraphs 4 and 12 above, or any other paragraph of this Contract and, on such termination, Player's sole remedy shall be payment of his salary and expenses accrued to the date of such termination.

15.3. Club and Player shall each have the option to extend the term of this Contract, beyond that set out in paragraph 15.1 above, for an additional one year period, on the following conditions:

15.3.1. The option may be exercised, at any time prior to December 31 of the final Contract Year by giving written notice to the other party of intent to exercise the option. Giving such notice shall automatically bind the other party, under the terms of this paragraph 15.3, and the term of this Contract shall automatically be extended for one (1) additional Contract Year.

15.3.2. All terms and conditions of this Contract except for salary and termination, shall remain in effect for the option year.

15.3.3. This shall be a single option, for one year only. If Player and Club do not enter into a new contract before the termination of this Contract and its one year option, neither Player nor Club shall have any further right or obligation to further extend the term hereof.

15.3.4. After the termination of this Contract (whether or not the one year option has been exercised by either party) Club shall have no right to compensation, arising from this Contract, from any other Club which subsequently employs Player.

15.3.5. Player's compensation during the option year shall be determined in accordance with this subparagraph 15.3.5: On exercise of this option Player and Club agree to make a good faith effort to agree on Player's compensation for the option year in the event the option is exercised. If, however, they are unable to agree by May 1 of the option year, the following procedure shall automatically control:

15.3.5.1. On or before May 10 of the option year, Player and Club shall each submit to the League Office one compensation figure, together with any reasons each might have on the fairness of the proposed compensation.

15.3.5.2. The League President shall submit each party's offer, together with supporting data, to an arbitrator selected in accordance with paragraph 14.1 above. The arbitrator so selected must choose either the compensation figure submitted by Player, or the compensation figure submitted by Club. The decision shall be made on the basis of the material submitted to him or he may, in his sole discretion, hold a hearing. The arbitrator's decision regarding compensation shall be final, binding and conclusive and may be enforced in any court having competent jurisdiction. Each party shall bear his own costs and expenses in this arbitration.

15.4. If Player becomes a member of the armed forces of any country, or retires or withdraws from playing professional football prior to the termination of this Contract, and subsequently returns to professional football as a player, then the time elapsed between such retirement or withdrawal and such return shall be considered as tolled, and the term of this contract shall be considered as extended for a period of time beginning with such return and ending after a period of time equal to the portion of the term of this Contract which was unexpired at the time of such retirement or withdrawal. In addition, the renewal option of paragraph 15.3 above contained herein shall be considered as continuously in effect from the date of this Contract until the end of such extended term. During the period of such retirement or withdrawal, Player shall not be entitled to any compensation, expenses or other payments under this Contract.

16. Transferability of Contract.

16.1. Club shall have the right to sell, assign, trade and transfer this Contract to another Club in the League, and Player agrees to accept and be bound by such sale, exchange, assignment or transfer and to report promptly to his new Club, and to faithfully perform and carry out his obligations under this Contract as if it had been entered into between Player and the new Club. If Player is transferred, Player's reasonable moving expenses shall be paid by the acquiring Club.

16.2. If this Contract is assigned, Club shall immediately send notice to Player of the name and address of the Club to which he has been assigned, and specify the time and place of reporting to such Club. If Player fails to report to such other Club, he may be suspended by such other Club and no salary shall be payable to Player during the period of such suspension.

17. MISCELLANEOUS AND PROCEDURAL.

17.1. Any notice required or permitted to be given under this Contract shall be sufficient if in writing, sent by certified mail, return receipt requested, to Player's residence or any other address he notices to Club, or to Club's office.

17.2. This Contract contains the entire understanding between the parties and it cannot be terminated or changed orally.

17.3. This Contract shall be governed and construed according to the laws of ....

17.4. If any part, paragraph or provision of this agreement should be held or become invalid, then all remaining parts, paragraphs and provisions shall continue to be fully effective.

17.5. Waiver by Club or the League of any breach by Player of this Contract shall not be construed as a waiver of any other breach.

17.6. Player represents to Club that he is not under contract or option to play football for any professional football organization for any period of time which conflicts with this Contract, and that he is not a party to any contract which prevents him from signing or performing under this Contract.

17.7. Immediately upon execution of this Contract by Club and Player, it is Club's responsibility to file a copy with the League President for his review and approval or disapproval.

CLUB AND PLAYER ACKNOWLEDGE THAT THEY EACH HAVE READ THIS CONTRACT, AND THAT, BY SIGNING BELOW, DESIRE

TO MAKE IT EFFECTIVE THIS .... DAY OF ...., 197..........

CLUB	PLAYER
....	....
(Club)	(Player)

By:

....	....
	(Player's address)

By:

....

CERTIFICATION OF PRESIDENT

I have examined and hereby approve this Contract, effective ...., 197.....

....
GARY L. DAVIDSON, President
World Football League

FORM 5

NATIONAL BASKETBALL ASSOCIATION

Uniform Player Contract

This Agreement made this .... day of ...., 19....... by and between ....
....
(hereinafter called the "Club"), a member of the National Basketball Association (hereinafter called the "Association") and ....
....
whose address is shown below (hereinafter called the "Player").

Witnesseth:

In consideration of the mutual promises hereinafter contained, the parties hereto promise and agree as follows:

1. The Club hereby employs the Player as a skilled basketball player for the term of one year from the 1st day of October, 19........ The Player's employment shall include attendance at training camp, playing the games scheduled for the Club's team during the schedule season of the Association, playing all exhibition games scheduled by the Club during and prior to the schedule season, and playing the playoff games subsequent to the schedule season. Players other than rookies will not be required to attend training camp earlier than four weeks prior to the first game of the Club's schedule season. Rookies may be required to attend training camp at an earlier date. Exhibition games shall not be played on the three days prior to the opening of a team's regular season schedule, nor on the day prior to a regularly scheduled game, nor on the

day prior to and the day following the All Star Game. Exhibition games prior to the schedule season shall not exceed twelve (including intra-squad games for which admission is charged) and exhibition games during the regularly scheduled season shall not exceed three.

2. The Club agrees to pay the Player for rendering services described herein the sum of $
(less all amounts required to be withheld from salary by Federal, State and local authorities and exclusive of any amount which the Player shall be entitled to receive from the Player Playoff Pool) in twelve equal semi-monthly payments beginning with the first of said payments on November 1st of the season above described and continuing with such payments on the first and fifteenth of each month until said sum is paid in full; provided however, if the Club does not qualify for the playoffs, the payments due subsequent to the conclusion of the schedule season shall become due and payable immediately after the conclusion of the schedule season.

3. The Club agrees to pay all proper and necessary expenses of the Player, including the reasonable board and lodging expenses of the Player while playing for the Club "on the road" and during training camp if the Player is not then living at home. The Player, while "on the road" (and at training camp only if the Club does not pay for meals directly) shall be paid $19.00 per day as meal expense allowance. In addition, the Club agrees to pay $50.00 per week to the Player for the four weeks prior to the first game of the Club's schedule season that the Player is either in attendance at training camp or engaged in playing the exhibition schedule.

4. The Player agrees to observe and comply with all requirements of the Club respecting conduct of its team

and its players, at all times whether on or off the playing floor. The Club may, from time to time during the continuance of this contract, establish reasonable rules for the government of its players "at home" and "on the road", and such rules shall be part of this contract as fully as if herein written and shall be binding upon the Player; for any violation of such rules or for any conduct impairing the faithful and thorough discharge of the duties incumbent upon the Player, the Club may impose reasonable fines upon the Player and deduct the amount thereof from any money due or to become due to the Player. The Club may also suspend the Player for violation of any rules so established, and during such suspension the Player shall not be entitled to any compensation under this contract. When the Player is fined or suspended, he shall be given notice in writing, stating the amount of the fine or the duration of the suspension and the reason therefor. Disputes under this paragraph shall be resolved in the manner provided for in paragraph 21 hereof.

5. The Player agrees (a) to report at the time and place fixed by the Club in good physical condition; (b) to keep himself throughout the entire season in good physical condition; (c) to give his best services, as well as his loyalty to the Club, and to play basketball only for the Club and its assignees; (d) to be neatly and fully attired in public and always to conduct himself on and off the court according to the highest standards of honesty, morality, fair play and sportsmanship; and (e) not to do anything which is detrimental to the best interests of the Club or of the Association or of professional sports.

6. If the Player, in the sole judgment of the physician designated for that purpose by the Club, is not in good physical condition at the date of his first scheduled game for the Club, or if, during the season, he fails to remain

in good physical condition, unless such condition results directly from playing basketball for the Club, so as to render him, in the sole judgment of the Club's physician, unfit to play skilled basketball, the Club shall have the right to suspend such Player until such time as, in the sole judgment of the Club's physician, the Player is in sufficiently good physical condition to play skilled basketball, and in the event of such suspension, the annual sum payable to the Player shall be reduced in the same proportion as the length of the period of disability during which, in the sole judgment of the Club's physician, the Player is unfit to play skilled basketball, bears to the length of the season. If the Player is injured as a direct result of participating in any basketball practice or game played for the Club, the Club will pay the Player's reasonable hospitalization until he is discharged from the hospital and his reasonable medical expenses and doctor's bills, provided the hospital and the doctor are selected by the Club, and provided further, that the Club's obligation to pay said medical expenses and said doctor's bills shall terminate at a period not exceeding eight (8) weeks after the injury. If, in the sole judgment of the physician designated for that purpose by the Club, the Player's injuries resulted directly from playing for the Club and render him unfit to play skilled basketball, then, so long as such unfitness continues, but in no event beyond the term of one year referred to in paragraph 1 of this agreement, the Club shall pay to the Player the compensation prescribed in paragraph 2 of this agreement. The Club's obligations hereunder shall be reduced by any workmen's compensation benefits and any insurance provided for by the Club whether paid or payable to the Player, and the Player hereby releases the Club from any and every other obligation or liability arising out of any such injuries.

7. The Player agrees to give to the Club's coach, or to the Club's physician, immediate notice of any injury suffered by him, followed by written notice thereof within 48 hours after such injury occurs, each such written notice to state the time, place, cause and nature of such injury.

8. Should the Player become disabled as provided in the preceding section, he will submit himself to a medical examination and treatment by a physician designated by the Club. Such examination when made at the request of the Club shall be at its expense, unless made necessary by some act or conduct of the Player contrary to the terms of this contract.

9. The Player represents and agrees that he has extraordinary and unique skill and ability as a basketball player, that the services to be rendered by him hereunder cannot be replaced or the loss thereof adequately compensated for in money damages, and that any breach by the Player of this contract will cause irreparable injury to the Club and to its assignees. Therefore, the Player agrees that in the event of a breach of this contract by the Player, the Club and its assignees (in addition to any other remedies that may be available to them judicially or by way of arbitration) shall have the right to obtain from any court or arbitrator having jurisdiction, such equitable relief as may be appropriate, including a decree enjoining any further breach of this contract, and enjoining the Player from playing basketball for any other person, firm, corporation or organization during the term of this contract. In any suit, action or arbitration proceeding brought to obtain such relief, the Player does hereby waive his right, if any, to trial by jury, and does hereby waive his right, if any, to interpose any counterclaim or set-off for any cause whatever.

10. The Club shall have the right to sell, exchange, assign or transfer this contract to any other professional basketball club and the Player agrees to accept such sale, exchange, assignment or transfer and to faithfully perform and carry out this contract with the same force and effect as if it had been entered into by the Player with the assignee club instead of with this Club.

11. In the event that the Player's contract is sold, exchanged, assigned or transferred to any other professional basketball club, all reasonable expenses incurred by the Player in moving himself and his family from the home city of the Club to the home city of the club to which such sale, exchange, assignment or transfer is made, as a result thereof, shall be paid by the assignee club. Such assignee club hereby agrees that its acceptance of the assignment of this contract constitutes agreement on its part to make such payment.

12. In the event that the Player's contract is assigned to another club the Player shall forthwith be notified orally or by a notice in writing, delivered to the Player personally or delivered or mailed to his last known address, and the Player shall report to the assignee club within forty-eight hours after said notice has been received or within such longer time for reporting as may be specified in said notice. If the Player does not report to the club to which his contract has been assigned within the aforesaid time, the Player may be suspended by such club and he shall lose the sums which would otherwise be payable to him as long as the suspension lasts.

13. The Club will not pay and the Player will not accept any bonus or anything of value for winning any particular Association game or series of games or for attaining a certain position by the Club's team in the standing of the

league operated by the Association as of a certain date, other than the final standing of the team.

14. This contract shall be valid and binding upon the Club and the Player immediately upon its execution. The Club agrees to file a copy of this contract with the Commissioner of the Association prior to the first game of the schedule season or within forty-eight (48) hours of its execution, whichever is later; provided, however, the Club agrees that if the contract is executed prior to the start of the schedule season and if the Player so requests, it will file a copy of this contract with the Commissioner of the Association within thirty (30) days of its execution, but not later than the date hereinabove specified. If pursuant to the Constitution and By-Laws the Commissioner disapproves this contract within ten (10) days after the filing thereof in his office, this contract shall thereupon terminate and be of no further force or effect and the Club and the Player shall thereupon be relieved of their respective rights and liabilities thereunder.

15. The Player and the Club acknowledge that they have read and are familiar with Section 35 of the Constitution of the Association, a copy of which, as in effect on the date of this Agreement, is attached hereto. Such section provides that the Commissioner and the Board of Governors of the Association are empowered to impose fines upon the player and/or upon the Club for causes and in the manner provided in such section. The Player and the Club, each for himself and itself, promises promptly to pay to the said Association each and every fine imposed upon him or it in accordance with the provisions of said section and not permit any such fine to be paid on his or its behalf by anyone other than the person or club fined. The Player further authorizes the Club to deduct from

his salary payments any fines imposed on or assessed against him.

16. Notwithstanding any provisions of the Constitution or of the By-Laws of the Association, it is agreed that if the Commissioner of the Association shall, in his sole judgment, find that the Player has bet, or has offered or attempted to bet, money or anything of value on the outcome of any game participated in by any club which is a member of the Association, the Commissioner shall have the power in his sole discretion to suspend the Player indefinitely or to expel him as a player for any member of the Association and the Commissioner's finding and decision shall be final, binding, conclusive and unappealable. The Player hereby releases the Commissioner and waives every claim he may have against the Commissioner and/or the Association, and against every member of the Association, and against every director, officer, stockholder, trustee and partner of every member of the Association, for damages and for all claims and demands whatsoever arising out of or in connection with the decision of the Commissioner.

17. The Player and the Club acknowledge and agree that the Player's participation in other sports may impair or destroy his ability and skill as a basketball player. The Player and the Club recognize and agree that the Player's participation in basketball out of season may result in injury to him. Accordingly, the Player agrees that he will not engage in professional boxing or wrestling; and that, except with the written consent of the Club, he will not engage in any game or exhibition of basketball, football, baseball, hockey, lacrosse, or other athletic sport, under penalty of such fine and suspension as may be imposed by the Club and/or the Commissioner of the Association. Nothing contained herein shall be intended to require the Player to obtain the written consent of the Club in order

to enable the Player to participate in, as an amateur, the sport of golf, tennis, handball, swimming, hiking, softball or volleyball.

18. The Player agrees to allow the Club or the Association to take pictures of the Player, alone or together with others, for still photographs, motion pictures or television, at such times as the Club or the Association may designate, and no matter by whom taken may be used in any manner desired by either of them for publicity or promotional purposes. The rights in any such pictures taken by the Club or by the Association shall belong to the Club or to the Association, as their interests may appear. The Player agrees that, during the playing season, he will not make public appearances, participate in radio or television programs or permit his picture to be taken or write or sponsor newspaper or magazine articles or sponsor commercial products without the written consent of the Club, which shall not be withheld except in the reasonable interests of the Club or professional basketball. In addition to the foregoing, the Player agrees to participate, upon request, in all other reasonable promotional activities of the Club and the Association.

19. The Player agrees that he will not, during the term of this contract, directly or indirectly entice, induce, persuade or attempt to entice, induce or persuade any player or coach who is under contract to any member of the Association to enter into negotiations for or relating to his services as a basketball player or coach, nor shall he negotiate for or contract for such services, except with the prior written consent of such member of the Association. Breach of this paragraph, in addition to the remedies available to the Club, shall be punishable by fine to be imposed by the Commissioner of the Association and to be payable to the Association out of any compensation due or to become due

to the Player hereunder or out of any other moneys payable to him as a basketball player. The Player agrees that the amount of such fine may be withheld by the Club and paid over to the Association.

20. (a) If the Club shall default in the payments to the Player provided for in paragraph 2 hereof or shall fail to perform any other material obligation agreed to be performed by the Club hereunder, the Player shall notify both the Club and the Association in writing of the facts constituting such default or failure. If neither the Club nor the Association shall cause such default or failure to be remedied within ten (10) days after receipt of such written notice, the Player shall have the right, by a further written notice to the Club and Association, to terminate this contract.

(b) The Club may terminate this contract upon written notice to the Player (but only after complying with the waiver procedure provided for in subparagraph (f) of this paragraph 20) if the Player shall do any of the following:

(1) at any time, fail, refuse or neglect to conform his personal conduct to standards of good citizenship, good moral character and good sportmanship, to keep himself in first class physical condition or to obey the Club's training rules; or

(2) at any time during the year, except during the period from February 2 through April 30 of any year, fail, in the sole opinion of the Club's management, to exhibit sufficient skill or competitive ability to qualify to continue as a member of the Club's team; or

(3) at any time, fail, refuse or neglect to render his services hereunder or in any other manner materially breach this contract.

(c) If this contract is terminated by the Club by reason of the Player's failure to render his services hereunder due to disability resulting directly from injury sustained in the course and within the scope of his employment hereunder and written notice of such injury is given by the Player as provided herein, the Player shall be entitled to receive his full salary for the season in which the injury was sustained, less all workmen's compensation benefits and any insurance provided for by the Club paid or payable to the Player by reason of said injury.

(d) If this contract is terminated by the Club during the period designated by the Club for attendance at training camp, payment by the Club of the Player's board, lodging and expense allowance during such period to the date of termination and of the reasonable travelling expenses of the Player to his home city and the expert training and coaching provided by the Club to the Player during the training season shall be full payment to the Player.

(e) If this contract is terminated by the Club during the playing season, except in the case provided for in subparagraph (c) of this paragraph 20, the Player shall be entitled to receive as full payment hereunder a sum of money which, when added to the salary which he has already received during the season, will represent the same proportionate amount of the total sum set forth in paragraph 2 hereof as the number of days of the season then past bear to the total number of days of the schedule season, plus the reasonable travelling expenses of the Player to his home.

(f) If the Club proposes to terminate this contract in accordance with paragraph (b) of this paragraph 20, the applicable waiver procedure shall be as follows:

(1) The Club shall request the Association Commissioner to request waivers from all other clubs. Such

waiver request must state that it is for the purpose of terminating this contract and it may not be withdrawn.

(2) Upon receipt of the waiver request, any other club may claim assignment of this contract at such waiver price as may be fixed by the Association, the priority of claims to be determined in accordance with the Association's Constitution or By-Laws.

(3) If this contract is so claimed, the Club agrees that it shall, upon the assignment of this contract to the claiming club, notify the player of such assignment as provided in paragraph 12 hereof, and the Player agrees he shall report to the assignee club as provided in said paragraph 12.

(4) If the contract is not claimed, the Club shall promptly deliver written notice of termination to the Player at the expiration of the waiver period.

(5) To the extent not inconsistent with the foregoing provisions of this subparagraph (f) the waiver procedures set forth in the Constitution and By-Laws of the Association shall govern.

(g) Upon any termination of this contract by the Player, all obligations of the Club to pay compensation shall cease on the date of termination, except the obligation of the Club to pay the Player's compensation to said date.

21. In the event of any dispute arising between the Player and the Club relating to any matter arising under this contract, or concerning the performance or interpretation thereof (except for a dispute arising under paragraph 9 hereof), such dispute shall (by notice in writing given to the other party and to the Commissioner of the Association) first be submitted to the Commissioner or a person

designated by the Commissioner in writing for such purpose, acting as a mediator. No other action shall be taken with respect to such dispute for a period of 30 days following the date of such submission for mediation. If mediation is unsuccessful, the parties shall have a period of 15 days to agree on a method of arbitration. In the absence of such agreement, either party shall have the right to bring an action with respect to such dispute in a State or Federal court of competent jurisdiction of the county or district whose territorial jurisdiction includes the home city in which the Club is located. Such action shall be forever barred unless brought within one year from the date when the alleged dispute arose. Each of the parties does hereby waive his and its right to trial by jury in any such action. Each party shall have the right to designate a representative to appear before the Commissioner on its behalf.

22. On or before September 1 next following the last playing season covered by this contract and renewals and extensions thereof, the Club may tender to the Player a contract for the next succeeding season by mailing the same to the Player at his address shown below, or if none is shown, then at his address last known to the Club. If the Player fails, neglects or omits to sign and return such contract to the Club so that the Club receives it on or before October 1st next succeeding, then this contract shall be deemed renewed and extended for the period of one year, upon the same terms and conditions in all respects as are provided herein, except that the compensation payable to the Player shall be the sum provided in the contract tendered to the Player pursuant to the provisions hereof, which compensation shall in no event be less than 75% of the compensation payable to the Player for the last playing season covered by this contract and renewals and extensions thereof.

The Club's right to renew this contract, as herein provided, and the promise of the Player not to play otherwise than for the Club and its assignees, have been taken into consideration in determining the amount of compensation payable under paragraph 2 hereof.

23. Nothing contained in this agreement or in any provision of the Constitution or By-Laws of the Association shall be construed to constitute the Player a member of the Association or to confer upon him any of the rights or privileges of a member thereof.

24. This agreement contains the entire agreement between the parties and there are no oral or written inducements, promises or agreements except as contained herein.

EXAMINE THIS CONTRACT CAREFULLY BEFORE SIGNING IT.

In Witness Whereof the Player has hereunto signed his name and the Club has caused this contract to be executed by its duly authorized officer.

Witnesses:

....

....

By ....

Title:

....

....

Player

Player's Address ....

EXCERPT FROM CONSTITUTION OF THE ASSOCIATION

MISCONDUCT OF OFFICIALS AND OTHERS

35. (a) The provisions of this Section shall govern all members, and officers, managers, coaches, players and other employees of a member, and all officials and other employees of the Association, all hereinafter referred to as "persons." Each member shall provide and require in every contract with any of its officers, managers, coaches, players or other employees that they shall be bound and governed by the provisions of this Section. Each member, at the direction of the Board of Governers or the Commissioner, as the case may be, shall take such action as the Board or the Commissioner may direct in order to effectuate the purposes of this Section.

(b) The Commissioner shall direct the dismissal and perpetual disqualification from any further association with the Association or any of its members, of any person found by the Commissioner after a hearing to have been guilty of offering, agreeing, conspiring, aiding or attempting to cause any game of basketball to result otherwise than on its merits.

(c) Any person who gives, makes, issues, authorizes or endorses any statement having, or designed to have, an effect prejudicial or detrimental to the best interests of basketball or of the Association or of a member or its team, shall be liable to a fine not exceeding $1,000, to be imposed by the Board of Governors. The member whose officer, manager, coach, player or other employee has been so fined shall pay the amount of the fine should such person fail to do so within ten (10) days of its imposition.

(d) If in the opinion of the Commissioner any other act or conduct of a person at or during a pre-season, championship, playoff or exhibition game has been prejudicial to or against the best interests of the Association or the game of basketball, the Commissioner shall impose upon such person a fine not exceeding $1,000 in the case of a member, officer, manager or coach of a member, or $500 in the case of a player or other employee, or may order for a time the suspension of any such person from any connection or duties with pre-season, championship, playoff or exhibition games, or he may order both such fine and suspension.

(e) The Commissioner shall have the power to suspend for a definite or indefinite period, or to impose a fine not exceeding $1,000, or inflict both such suspension and fine upon any person who, in his opinion, shall have been guilty of conduct prejudicial or detrimental to the Association.

(f) The Commissioner shall have the power to levy a fine of $1,000 upon any Governor or Alternate Governor who, in the opinion of the Commissioner, has been guilty of making statements to the press damaging to the Association.

(g) Any person who, directly or indirectly, entices, induces, persuades or attempts to entice, induce, or persuade any player, coach, trainer, general manager or any other person who is under contract to any other member of the Association to enter into negotiations for or relating to his services or negotiates or contracts for such services shall, on being charged with such tampering, be given an opportunity to answer such charges after due notice and the Commissioner shall have the power to decide whether or not the charges have been sustained; in the event his decision is that the charges have been sustained, then the Commissioner shall have the power to suspend such person for a definite or indefinite period, or to impose a fine not exceeding $5,000, or inflict both such suspension and fine upon any such person.

(h) Any person who, directly or indirectly, wagers money or anything of value on the outcome of any game played by a team in the league operated by the Association shall, on being charged with such wagering, be given an opportunity to answer such charges after due notice, and the decision of the Commissioner shall be final, binding and conclusive and unappealable. The penalty for such offense shall be within the absolute and sole discretion of the Commissioner and may include a fine, suspension, expulsion and/or perpetual disqualification from further association with the Association or any of its members.

(i) Except for a penalty imposed under subparagraph (h) of this paragraph 35, the decisions and acts of the Commissioner pursuant to paragraph 35 shall be appealable to the Board of Governors who shall determine such appeals in accordance with such rules and regulations as may be adopted by the Board in its absolute and sole discretion.

FORM 6

AMERICAN BASKETBALL ASSOCIATION UNIFORM PLAYER CONTRACT

AGREEMENT made this .... day of ...., 19...., between ...., (hereinafter called the "CLUB"), a member of the AMERICAN BASKETBALL ASSOCIATION, (hereinafter sometimes called the "ASSOCIATION"), and .... of the City of ...., (hereinafter called the "PLAYER").

IT IS AGREED AS FOLLOWS:

1. Employment and Term Thereof. The CLUB hereby employs the PLAYER as a skilled Basketball Player for the term of .... years from the first (1st) day of October, 19........, subject, however, to termination, extension or renewal as specified herein. The PLAYER's employment shall include attendance at training camp, playing the games scheduled for the team during the schedule season of the American Basketball Association, playing all exhibition games scheduled by the team during and prior to the schedule season, and playing the playoff games for which the player is to receive such additional compensation as is provided by the ASSOCIATION. Additionally, if selected, the Player will play in the All-Star games without additional compensation. Regular players will not be required to attend training camp earlier than four (4) weeks prior to the season starting date of the team of which the player is a member. "Rookies" may be required to attend training camp at an earlier date. Exhibition games shall not be played on the three (3) days prior to the opening of a team's regular season schedule nor on a day prior to a regularly scheduled game. The All-Star game shall for

the purpose of this paragraph not be considered an exhibition game. Exhibition games during the regularly scheduled season shall not exceed three (3).

2. Compensation.

a. Salary. For the PLAYER's rendering services described herein, and for his agreement not to play basketball or engage in activities related to basketball for any other person, firm, corporation or institution during the term of this contract, and for the option hereinafter set forth giving the right to renew this contract, and for the other undertakings of the PLAYER herein, the CLUB agrees to pay the PLAYER each year during the term of this contract the sum of $.. in twelve (12) equal semi-monthly payments beginning with the first of said payments on November 1st of the season above described and continuing with such payments on the first and fifteenth of each month until said sum is paid in full. Provided, however, if the CLUB does not qualify for the playoffs, the payments due subsequent to the conclusion of the schedule season shall become due and payable immediately after the conclusion of the schedule season.

b. Expenses. The CLUB promises and agrees to pay the reasonable board and lodging expenses of the PLAYER while playing for the CLUB in other than the CLUB's home city and will pay all proper and necessary expenses of the PLAYER and his meals enroute.

3. PLAYER's Duties and Obligations:

a. Duties. The PLAYER agrees:

(1) To report at the time and place fixed by the CLUB in good physical condition; and

(2) To keep himself throughout the entire season in good physical condition; and

(3) To give his full time and best services, as well as his loyalty, to the CLUB, and to play basketball only for the CLUB unless he is released or his contract is sold, exchanged or assigned by the CLUB; and

(4) To be neatly and fully attired in public and always to conduct himself on and off the court according to the highest standards of honesty, morality, fair play and sportsmanship; and

(5) Not to do anything which is detrimental to the best interests of the CLUB or of the American Basketball Association or of professional sports.

b. Compliance With CLUB. The CLUB may from time to time during the continuance of this contract establish reasonable rules for the government of its players "at home" and "away from home," and such rules shall be a part of this contract as fully as if herein written and shall be binding upon the player; and for violation of such rules or for any conduct impairing the faithful and thorough discharge of the duties incumbent upon the player, the CLUB may impose reasonable fines upon the player and deduct the amount thereof from any money due or to become due to the player. The CLUB may also suspend the player for violation of any rules so established, and during such suspension the player shall not be entitled to any compensation under this contract. All of the foregoing shall be in addition to any other rights and remedies the Club may have at law, equity or otherwise. When the player is fined or suspended, he shall be given notice in writing, stating the amount of the fine or the duration of the suspension and the reason therefor.

c. Participation in Other Sports. The PLAYER and the CLUB recognize and agree that the PLAYER's participation in other sports may impair or destroy his ability and skill as a basketball player and his participation in basketball out of season may result in injury to him. Accordingly, the PLAYER agrees that he will not engage in professional boxing or wrestling; and that, except with the written consent of the CLUB, he will not engage in any game or exhibition of basketball, football, baseball, hockey, lacrosse, or other athletic sport, under penalty of such fine and suspension as may be imposed by the CLUB and/or the Commissioner of the ASSOCIATION.

4. Physical Condition and Injuries.

a. Physical Condition. If the PLAYER, in the judgment of the CLUB's physician, is not in good physical condition at the date of his first scheduled game of the regular playing season scheduled by the ASSOCIATION for the CLUB, or if, during such regular playing season, he fails to remain in good physical condition, unless such condition is a direct result of participating in any basketball practice or game for the CLUB, it is mutually agreed that the CLUB shall have the right to suspend such PLAYER until such time as, in the judgment of the CLUB's physician, the PLAYER is in sufficiently good physical condition to play skilled basketball. In the event of such suspension:

(1) The annual sum payable to the PLAYER shall be proportionately reduced as the length of the period the PLAYER is unfit to play skilled basketball bears to the season; and

(2) The CLUB shall not become obligated to pay hospital and medical expenses, and salary continuation, as provided in paragraph 4.b hereof.

b. Injuries.

(1) Salary Continuation. If the PLAYER is injured after the start of the regular playing season scheduled by the ASSOCIATION and the injury was a direct result of participating in any basketball practice or game for the CLUB and written notice of such injury is given by the PLAYER as provided below, and the PLAYER's injury renders him unfit to play skilled basketball, then, so long as such unfitness continues, but in no event beyond the playing season during which such injury occurred, the CLUB shall pay to the PLAYER the compensation prescribed in paragraph 2 of this agreement, less any workmen's compensation benefits and any insurance provided for by the CLUB whether paid or payable to the PLAYER.

(2) Notice of Injury. The PLAYER agrees to give to the CLUB's coach, or to the CLUB's physician, immediate notice of any injury suffered by him, followed by written notice thereof within forty-eight (48) hours after such injury occurs; each such written notice to state the time, place, cause and nature of such injury.

(3) Medical Examination. Should the PLAYER become injured, as provided in this section, he will upon request by the CLUB, submit himself to a medical examination and treatment by a regular physician, in good standing, to be selected by the CLUB. Such examination when made at the request of the CLUB shall be at its expense, unless made necessary

by some act or conduct of the PLAYER contrary to the terms of this agreement or rules and regulations made under it.

e. Appeal. In the event the PLAYER does not agree with any decision and opinion of the CLUB physician as to his fitness to play skilled basketball, then the PLAYER may petition the Commissioner of the ASSOCIATION to appoint a disinterested physician to examine said PLAYER and render an opinion to the Commissioner. The decision of the Commissioner after such opinion by such disinterested physician shall be final, binding and conclusive on all the parties.

5. Injunctive Relief. The PLAYER hereby represents that he has special, exceptional and unique knowledge, skill and ability as a basketball player, the loss of which cannot be estimated with any certainty and cannot be fairly or adequately compensated by damages and therefore agrees that the CLUB shall have the right, in addition to any other rights that the CLUB may possess, to enjoin him by appropriate injunction proceedings against playing basketball, or engaging in activities related to basketball for any person, firm, corporation or institution, or injunction against any other breach of this contract.

6. Assignment.

a. Right to Assign. The CLUB shall have the right to sell, exchange, assign and transfer this contract to any other American Basketball Association club only and the PLAYER agrees to accept such assignment and to faithfully perform and carry out this contract with the same force and effect as if it had been entered into by the PLAYER with the assignee Club instead of with this CLUB.

b. Moving Expenses. In the event that the PLAYER's contract is sold, exchanged, assigned or transferred to any other American Basketball Association club only during the schedule season of the American Basketball Association, all reasonable expenses incurred by the PLAYER in moving himself and his family from the home city of the CLUB to the home city of the Club to which such sale, exchange, assignment or transfer is made, as a result thereof, shall be paid by the assignee Club. Such assignee Club hereby agrees that its acceptance of the assignment of this contract constitutes agreement on its part to make such payment.

c. Notice to PLAYER. In the event that the PLAYER's contract is assigned to another Club, the PLAYER shall be forthwith notified, by a notice in writing, delivered to the PLAYER personally or delivered or mailed to his last known address and the PLAYER shall report to the assignee CLUB within forty-eight (48) hours after said written notice has been personally delivered or received at his last known address or within such longer time for reporting as may be specified in said written notice. If PLAYER does not report to the CLUB to which his contract has been assigned within the aforesaid time, PLAYER may be suspended by either Club and he shall lose the sums which would otherwise be payable to him as long as the suspension lasts. The foregoing shall be in addition to all other remedies of the Club by reason of Players failure to so report.

7. ASSOCIATION Fines. The PLAYER and the CLUB expressly acknowledges that the Commissioner and/or the Board of Trustees of the ASSOCIATION are and may be empowered by present and future provisions of the Certificate of Incorporation and Bylaws and action of said

Association to impose fines upon the Player and/or upon the Club for causes and in the manner provided in such Certificate of Incorporation and Bylaws and such action. The Player and the Club, each for himself and itself, promises promptly to pay to the said Association each and every fine imposed upon him or it in accordance with the said provisions of said Certificate of Incorporation and Bylaws and said action and not to permit any such fine to be paid on his or its behalf by anyone other than the person or Club fined. The Player further authorizes the Club to deduct any fines imposed on or assessed against him from his salary payments.

8. Bonus, Bets, Bribes.

a. Bonus. It is mutually agreed that the Club will not pay and the Player will not accept any bonus or anything of value for winning any particular Association game.

b. Bets. Notwithstanding any provision of the Certificate of Incorporation or of the Bylaws of the American Basketball Association, it is agreed that if the Commissioner of the Association shall in his sole judgment find that the Player has bet, or has offered or attempted to bet, money or anything of value on the outcome of any game participated in by any club which is a member of the Association or has accepted a bribe or has agreed to "throw" or "fix" a game or, having knowledge of the same, fails to report an offered bribe or an attempt to "throw" or "fix" a game, the Commissioner shall have the power in his sole discretion to suspend the Player indefinitely or to expel him as a player for any member of the Association, and the Commissioner's finding and decision shall be final, binding, conclusive and unappealable.

9. Association Approval of Contract. This contract, if not inconsistent with the Certificate of Incorporation and Bylaws of the Association, shall be valid and binding upon the Club and the Player immediately upon its execution. The Club agrees to file a copy of this contract with the Commissioner of said Association within ten (10) days of the signing of said contract by the Player. If pursuant to said Certificate of Incorporation and Bylaws, the Commissioner disapproves this contract within ten (10) days after the filing thereof in his office, this contract shall thereupon terminate and be of no further force or effect and the Club and the Player shall thereupon be relieved of their respective rights and liabilities thereunder.

10. Pictures of Player. Pictures of the Player alone or together with others may be taken for still photographs, motion pictures, television, or otherwise, at such times as the Club or the Association may designate, and no matter by whom taken, may be used by the Club or the Association in any manner desired by either of them. All rights in such pictures shall belong to the Club or the Association, as their interests may appear. The Player further agrees that during the playing season he will not make public appearances, participate in radio or television programs or permit his picture to be taken or write or sponsor newspaper or magazine articles or sponsor commercial products without the written consent of the Club, which shall not be withheld except in the reasonable interests of the Club. In addition, the Player agrees to participate, upon request of the Club, in all other promotional activities of the Club and the Association.

11. Inducing Breach of Contract. The Player agrees that he will not, during the term of his contract, directly or indirectly entice, induce, persuade or attempt to entice,

induce or persuade any player or coach who is under contract to any member of the ASSOCIATION to enter into negotiations for or relating to his services as a basketball player or coach; nor shall the PLAYER negotiate for or contract for such services, except with the written consent of such member of the ASSOCIATION. Breach of this paragraph, in addition to the remedies available to the CLUB, shall be punishable by fine to be imposed by the Commissioner of such ASSOCIATION and to be payable to the ASSOCIATION out of any compensation due or to become due to the PLAYER hereunder or out of any other moneys payable to him as a basketball player. The PLAYER agrees that the amount of such fine may be withheld by the CLUB and paid over to such ASSOCIATION.

12. Default, Termination.

a. If the CLUB shall default in the payments to the PLAYER provided for in paragraph 2 hereof or shall fail to perform any other material obligation agreed to be performed by the CLUB hereunder, the PLAYER shall notify both the CLUB and the American Basketball Association in writing of the facts constituting such default or failure. If neither the CLUB nor the ASSOCIATION shall cause such default or failure to be remedied within ten (10) days after receipt of such written notice, the PLAYER shall have the right, by a further written notice to the CLUB and ASSOCIATION, to terminate this Contract.

b. Upon any termination of this contract by the PLAYER, all obligations of both parties hereunder shall cease on the date of termination, except the obligation of the CLUB to pay the PLAYER's compensation to said date.

c. The CLUB may terminate this contract upon written notice to the PLAYER if the PLAYER shall at any time:

(1) fail, refuse or neglect to keep himself in first class physical condition; or

(2) fail, in the opinion of the CLUB's management, to exhibit sufficient skill or competitive ability to qualify to continue as a member of the CLUB's team; or

(3) fail, refuse or neglect to render his services hereunder or in any other manner materially breach this contract.

d. If this contract is terminated by the CLUB during the training season for any reason other than as stated in c. (3) above, payment by the CLUB of the PLAYER's board, lodging and expense allowance during the training season to the date of termination and of the reasonable traveling expenses of the PLAYER to his home city and the expert training and coaching provided by the CLUB to the PLAYER during the training season shall be full payment to the PLAYER.

e. If this contract is terminated by the CLUB during the playing season, except for the reasons provided in c. (3) above and in subparagraph f. of this paragraph 12, the PLAYER shall be entitled to receive as full payment hereunder a sum of money which, when added to the salary which he has already received during the season, will represent the same proportionate amount of the total sum set forth in paragraph 2 hereof as the number of days of the season then past bear the total number of days of the playing season, plus the reasonable traveling expense of the PLAYER to his home.

f. If this contract is terminated by the CLUB by reason of the PLAYER's failure to render his services hereunder due to disability resulting directly from participating in any basketball practice or game for the CLUB after the start of the regular playing season scheduled by the ASSOCIATION for the CLUB and written notice of such injury is given by the PLAYER as provided herein, the PLAYER shall be entitled to receive his full salary for the season in which the injury was sustained, less all workmen's compensation payments paid or payable by reason of said injury.

g. If the CLUB proposes to terminate this contract in accordance with subparagraph c. of this paragraph 12 the procedure shall be as set forth in the regulations promulgated therefore by the Commissioner.

(1) If, however, this contract is claimed by any other club pursuant to waiver, the CLUB agrees that it shall, upon the assignment of this contract to the claiming club, notify the PLAYER in writing of such assignment as provided for in paragraph 6 hereof and the PLAYER agrees he shall report to the assignee club as provided in said paragraph 6.

(2) If the contract is not claimed, the CLUB shall promptly deliver written notice of termination to the PLAYER at the expiration of the waiver period.

13. Arbitration. In the event of any dispute arising between the PLAYER and the CLUB relating to any matter or thing whatever, whether or not arising under this Contract, or concerning the performance or interpretation thereof, such dispute shall be determined by arbitration before the Commissioner of the American Basketball Association, or a person designated by such Commissioner in writing for

such purpose, acting as Arbitrator. The Arbitrator shall determine by whom and in what proportion the cost of arbitration shall be paid. The PLAYER and the CLUB hereby grant such Arbitrator full power to determine such dispute in such manner as he shall direct, and under such rules of procedure as he shall in his sole discretion adopt, and his decision shall be final, binding and conclusive and may be enforced in any court, state or Federal, having competent jurisdiction. Demand for arbitration hereunder shall be made by notice in writing given to the other party and to the Commissioner of the ASSOCIATION. Notwithstanding the foregoing, the CLUB shall have the right in its sole discretion to institute judicial proceedings for the purpose of obtaining an injunction or other equitable relief pursuant to paragraph 5 hereof.

14. ASSOCIATION Certificate of Incorporation and Bylaws Binding. The CLUB and the PLAYER agree to be bound by the Certificate of Incorporation and Bylaws of the American Basketball Association and by all the terms and provisions thereof, copies of which are and shall remain open and available for inspection by the CLUB, its directors, officers and stockholders and by the PLAYER at the main office of the ASSOCIATION and at the main office of the CLUB.

15. Option to Renew. On or before the date of the expiration of this contract, the CLUB may, upon notice in writing to the PLAYER, renew this contract for the further term of one (1) year following said expiration date on the same terms as are provided by this contract, except that:

a. The CLUB may fix the rate of compensation to be paid by the CLUB to the PLAYER during said period of renewal, which compensation shall not be less than ninety per cent (90%) of the amount paid by the CLUB to the PLAYER during the preceding season, and

b. After such renewal, this contract shall not include any further option to the CLUB to renew the contract. The compensation in subsection a. herein shall mean only the salary prescribed in paragraph 2 above.

16. Retirement. If by reason of his becoming a member of the Armed Forces of the United States or any other country, or if for any other reason whatsoever (including, without limitation, illness or injury not incurred in the performance of services under this contract), the PLAYER shall retire or withdraw from professional basketball as a player prior to the expiration of the term of this contract, and subsequently shall return to professional basketball as a player, then the time lapsed between such retirement or withdrawal and such return shall be considered as tolled, and the term of this contract shall be considered as extended for a period of time beginning with such return and ending after a period of time equal to the portion of the term of this contract which was unexpired at the time of such retirement or withdrawal; and the option to renew hereof contained in paragraph 15 shall be considered as continuously in effect from the date of this contract until the end of such extended term. During the period of such retirement or withdrawal the PLAYER shall not be entitled to any compensation, expenses or other payments under this contract.

17. Waiver of Claims. The parties to the contract, if involved or affected in any manner whatsoever by a decision of the Commissioner and/or the Board of Trustees and/or the Member Clubs, as provided in the Bylaws and Rules and Regulations of the Association, agree to release the Commissioner individually and in his official capacity and to waive every claim he or they may have against the Commissioner and the ASSOCIATION, and every Member

Club and its directors, officers, stockholders or partners, for damages and for all claims and demands arising out of said decision.

18. Whole Agreement. This agreement contains the entire agreement between the parties and there are no oral or written inducements, promises or agreements except as contained herein. No change, termination or attempted waiver of any of the provisions of this contract shall be binding unless in writing and signed by the party against whom the same is sought to be enforced and approved by the ASSOCIATION as provided in paragraph 9.

19. Governing Law. This contract shall be governed by the laws of the State of ....

EXAMINE THIS CONTRACT CAREFULLY BEFORE SIGNING IT.

IN WITNESS WHEREOF the PLAYER has hereunto set his hand and the CLUB has caused this contract to be executed by its duly authorized officer.

WITNESSES: ....

CLUB

By..

....

....

Player

....

Player's Address..

FORM 7

IMPORTANT NOTICE TO PLAYER

Before signing this contract you should carefully examine it to be sure that all terms and conditions agreed upon have been incorporated herein, and if any has been omitted, you should insist upon having it inserted in the contract before you sign.

NATIONAL HOCKEY LEAGUE

STANDARD PLAYER'S CONTRACT

(1974 FORM)

THIS AGREEMENT

BETWEEN:

....

hereinafter called the "Club", a member of the National Hockey League, hereinafter called the "League"

—AND—

....

hereinafter called the "Player"

of .... in (Province, State) of ....

WITNESSETH:

That in consideration of the respective obligations herein and hereby assumed, the parties to this contract severally agree as follows:—

1. The Club hereby employs the Player as a skilled Hockey Player for the term of .... year(s) commencing

October 1st, 19........ and agrees, subject to the terms and conditions hereof, to pay the Player a salary of

.... Dollars ($...................)

Payment of such salary shall be in consecutive semi-monthly instalments following the commencement of the regular League Championship Schedule of games or following the date of reporting, whichever is later; provided, however, that if the Player is not in the employ of the Club for the whole period of the Club's games in the National Hockey League Championship Schedule, then he shall receive only part of the salary in the ratio of the number of days of actual employment to the number of days of the League Championship Schedule of games.

And it is further mutually agreed that if the Contract and rights to the services of the Player are assigned, exchanged, loaned or otherwise transferred to a Club in another League, the Player shall only be paid at the rate of

.... Dollars in the .... League.

or .... Dollars in the .... League.

or .... Dollars in the .... League.

2. The Player agrees to give his services and to play hockey in all League Championship, Exhibition, Play-Off and Stanley Cup games to the best of his ability under the direction and control of the Club for the said season in accordance with the provisions hereof.

The Player further agrees,

(a) to report to the Club training camp at the time and place fixed by the Club, in good physical condition,

(b) to keep himself in good physical condition at all times during the season,

(c) to give his best services and loyalty to the Club and to play hockey only for the Club unless his contract is released, assigned, exchanged or loaned by the Club,

(d) to co-operate with the Club and participate in any and all promotional activities of the Club and the League which will in the opinion of the Club promote the welfare of the Club or professional hockey generally.

(e) to conduct himself on and off the rink according to the highest standards of honesty, morality, fair play and sportsmanship, and to refrain from conduct detrimental to the best interests of the Club, the League or professional hockey generally.

The Club agrees that in exhibition games played after the start of the regular schedule (except where the proceeds are to go to charity, or where the player has agreed otherwise) the player shall receive his pro rata share of the gate receipts after deduction of legitimate expenses of such game. This provision re exhibition games is applicable in the National Hockey League only.

3. In order that the Player shall be fit in proper condition for the performance of his duties as required by this contract the Player agrees to report for practice at such time and place as the Club may designate and participate

in such exhibition games as may be arranged by the Club within thirty days prior to the first scheduled Championship game. The Club shall pay the travelling expenses and meals en route from the Player's home to the Club's training camp. In the event of failure of the player to so report and participate in exhibition games a fine not exceeding Five Hundred Dollars may be imposed by the Club and be deducted from the compensation stipulated herein. At the conclusion of the season the Club shall provide transportation direct to the Player's home.

4. The Club may from time to time during the continuance of this contract establish rules governing the conduct and conditioning of the Player, and such rules shall form part of this contract as fully as if herein written. For violation of any such rules or for any conduct impairing the thorough and faithful discharge of the duties incumbent upon the Player, the Club may impose a reasonable fine upon the Player and deduct the amount thereof from any money due or to become due to the Player. The Club may also suspend the Player for violation of any such rules. When the Player is fined or suspended he shall be given notice in writing stating the amount of the fine and/or the duration of the suspension and the reason therefor.

5. Should the Player be disabled or unable to perform his duties under this contract he shall submit himself for medical examination and treatment by a physician selected by the Club, and such examination and treatment, when made at the request of the Club, shall be at its expense unless made necessary by some act or conduct of the Player contrary to the terms and provisions of this contract or the rules established under Section 4.

If the Player, in the sole judgment of the Club's physician, is disabled or is not in good physical condition at the commencement of the season or at any subsequent time during the season (unless such condition is the direct result of playing hockey for the Club) so as to render him unfit to play skilled hockey, then it is mutually agreed that the Club shall have the right to suspend the Player for such period of disability or unfitness, and no compensation shall be payable for that period under this contract.

If the Player is injured as the result of playing hockey for the Club, the Club will pay the Player's reasonable hospitalization until discharged from the hospital, and his medical expenses and doctor's bills, provided that the hospital and doctor are selected by the Club and provided further that the Club's obligation to pay such expenses shall terminate at a period not more than six months after the injury.

It is also agreed that if the Player's injuries resulting directly from playing for the Club render him, in the sole judgment of the Club's physician, unfit to play skilled hockey for the balance of the season or any part thereof, then during such time the Player is so unfit, but in no event beyond the end of the current season, the Club shall pay the Player the compensation herein provided for and the Player releases the Club from any and every additional obligation, liability, claim or demand whatsoever. However if upon joint consultation between the Player, the Club's physician and the Club General Manager, they are unable to agree as to the physical fitness of the Player to return to play, the Player agrees to submit himself for examination by an independent medical specialist and the Parties hereto agree to be bound by his decision. If the Player is declared to be unfit for play he shall continue to receive the full benefits of this Agreement. If the Player is declared to be physically able to play and refuses to do so he shall be liable to immediate suspension without pay.

If upon joint consultation between the Player, the Club's Physician and the Club General Manager, they are unable to agree upon the physical fitness to return to play following an injury not resulting directly from playing for the Club, the Player agrees to submit himself for examination by an independent medical specialist and the Parties hereto agree to be bound by his decision. If the Player is declared to be fit for play, he shall be entitled to receive the full benefits of this agreement. If he is declared to be not physically able to play, he shall not be entitled to the benefits of this agreement until he has been declared to be physically fit to play by the independent medical specialist.

6. The Player represents and agrees that he has exceptional and unique knowledge, skill and ability as a hockey player, the loss of which cannot be estimated with certainty and cannot be fairly or adequately compensated by damages. The Player therefore agrees that the Club shall have the right, in addition to any other rights which the Club may possess, to enjoin him by appropriate injunction proceedings from playing hockey for any other team and/or for any breach of any of the other provisions of this contract.

7. The Player and the Club recognize and agree that the Player's participation in other sports may impair or destroy his ability and skill as a hockey player. Accordingly the Player agrees that he will not during the period of this Contract and during any period when he is obligated under this contract to enter into a further contract with the Club engage or participate in football, baseball, softball, hockey, lacrosse, boxing, wrestling or other athletic sport without the written consent of the Club.

8. (a) The Player hereby irrevocably grants to the Club during the period of this Contract and during any period

when he is obligated under this contract to enter into a further contract with the Club the exclusive right to permit or authorize any person, firm or corporation to take and make use of any still photograph, motion pictures or television of himself, and agrees that all rights in such pictures and television shall belong to the Club exclusively and may be used, reproduced, distributed or otherwise disseminated by the Club directly or indirectly in any manner it desires.

(b) The Player further agrees that during the period of this Contract and during any period when he is obligated under this contract to enter into a further contract with the Club he will not make public appearances, participate in radio or television programs, or permit his picture to be taken, or write or sponsor newspaper or magazine articles, or sponsor commercial products without the written consent of the Club which consent shall not be withheld unreasonably. Where the Club grants its written consent to any of the activities recited in this sub-section the Player shall receive his proper share of the proceeds of such activities.

9. It is mutually agreed that the Club will not pay, and the Player will not accept from any person, any bonus or anything of value for winning any particular game or series of games except as authorized by the League By-Laws.

10. The Player agrees that during the period of this contract and during any period when he is obligated under this contract to enter into a further contract with the Club he will not tamper with or enter into negotiations with any player under contract or reservation to any Club of the League for or regarding such player's current or future

services, without the written consent of the Club with which such player is connected under penalty of a fine to be imposed by the President of the League.

11. It is mutually agreed that the Club shall have the right to sell, assign, exchange and transfer this contract, and to loan the Player's services to any other professional hockey club, and the Player agrees to accept and be bound by such sale, exchange, assignment, transfer or loan, and will faithfully perform and carry out this contract with the same purpose and effect as if it had been entered into by the Player and such other Club.

It is further mutually agreed that in the event that this contract is assigned, or the Player's services are loaned, to another Club, the Club shall, by notice in writing delivered personally to the Player or by mail to the address set out below his signature hereto advise the Player of the name and address of the Club to which he has been assigned or loaned, and specifying the time and place of reporting to such club. If the Player fails to report to such other Club he may be suspended by such other Club and no salary shall be payable to him during the period of such suspension.

The Club shall pay the actual moving expenses incurred by a player during the playing season when such move is directed by the Club and is not part of disciplinary action.

12. If the Club shall default in the payments to the Player provided for in Section 1 hereof or shall fail to perform any other obligation agreed to be performed by the Club hereunder, the Player may, by notice in writing to the Club, specify the nature of the default, and if the Club shall fail to remedy the default within fifteen (15) days from receipt of such notice, this contract shall be

terminated, and upon the date of such termination all obligations of both parties shall cease, except the obligation of the Club to pay the Player's compensation to that date.

13. The Club may terminate this contract upon written notice to the Player (but only after obtaining waivers from all other League clubs) if the player shall at any time:

(a) fail, refuse or neglect to obey the Club's rules governing training and conduct of players,

(b) fail, refuse or neglect to render his services hereunder or in any other manner materially breach this contract.

In the event of termination under sub-section (a) or (b) the Player shall only be entitled to compensation due to him to the date such notice is delivered to him or the date of the mailing of such notice to his address as set out below his signature hereto.

In the event that this contract is terminated by the Club while the Player is "away" with the Club for the purpose of playing games the instalment then falling due shall be paid on the first week-day after the return "home" of the Club.

14. The Player further agrees that the Club may carry out and put into effect any order or ruling of the League or its President for his suspension or expulsion and that in the event of suspension his salary shall cease for the duration thereof and that in the event of expulsion this contract, at the option of the Club, shall terminate forthwith.

15. The Player further agrees that in the event of his suspension pursuant to any of the provisions of this con-

tract, there shall be deducted from the salary stipulated in Section 1 hereof an amount equal to the exact proportion of such salary as the number of days' suspension bears to the total number of days of the League Championship Schedule of games.

16. If because of any condition arising from a state of war or other cause beyond the control of the League or of the Club, it shall be deemed advisable by the League or the Club to suspend or cease or reduce operations, then:

(a) in the event of suspension of operations, the Player shall be entitled only to the proportion of salary due at the date of suspension,

(b) in the event of cessation of operations, the salary stipulated in Section 1 hereof shall be automatically cancelled on the date of cessation, and

(c) in the event of reduction of operations, the salary stipulated in Section 1 hereof shall be replaced by that mutually agreed upon between the Club and the Player.

17. (a) The Club may no later than August 10th of the final year of this contract, tender the Player a Player's Termination Contract and notify him that he has the choice of executing said Player's Termination Contract and delivering it to the Club on or before September 10th of that year or automatically being unconditionally released from any further obligation to provide services under this contract as of midnight, September 10th of that year. The Player's Termination Contract shall be on the same terms and conditions as this contract except that it shall be for only one additional season at the Player's previous year's salary and shall provide for the Player's unconditional

release from any further obligation to provide services under said Player's Termination Contract effective the following June 1st.

(b) If the Club does not take the action permitted under subsection (a), it shall no later than September 1st of the final year of this contract (August 10th if the Player is a "protected" player or played at least fifty NHL games in the preceding season), tender the Player a new Standard Player's Contract upon the same terms and conditions (including this Section 17) as this Standard Player's Contract except that salary and the number of years of its fixed term may be different.

(c) Without regard to any action taken by the Club under subsections (a) or (b), the Player may notify the Club no later than September 10th of the final year of this contract that he wishes to sign a Player's Option Contract. If the Player gives such notice, the Club shall no later than September 25th of that year tender the Player's Option Contract, and the Player shall forthwith enter into said contract. The Player's Option Contract shall be on the same terms and conditions as this contract except that it shall be for only one additional season at the Player's previous year's salary and shall provide that effective the following June 1st the Player will be a free agent, without any further obligation to provide services under said Player's Option Contract, and as such will have the right, as provided by Section 9A of the League By-Laws, the text of which Section is printed on the reverse side hereof, to negotiate and contract with any club in the League, or with any other club.

(d) If the Club does not take the action permitted under subsection (a) and the Player does not give notice to the

Club in accordance with subsection (c), then the parties shall enter into a new Standard Player's Contract by mutual agreement or, failing such agreement, the parties shall enter into a new one-year Standard Player's Contract for the succeeding season upon the same terms and conditions (including this Section 17) as this Standard Player's Contract, except as to salary, which shall be determined by neutral arbitration under the applicable collective bargaining agreement providing a mechanism for such arbitration, provided, however, that if no such collective bargaining agreement is then in effect, the Player's salary shall be the same as his salary for the previous year.

(e) As used in this Section 17, the phrase "final year of this contract" means the final year of the term specified in Section 1 of this contract, unless there is attached to this contract a special option provision agreed to by the parties, in which case the phrase "final year of this contract" means the last year which any exercised special option adds to the fixed term specified in Section 1.

(f) The Club's notice and tender obligations under this Section 17 shall be deemed fulfilled if the Club delivers the required written notification and/or the proposed contract to the Player in person on or before the applicable deadline date or mails same by registered mail postmarked no later than said deadline date to the Player at the address set forth below his signature hereto. The Player's notice and delivery obligations under this Section 17 shall be deemed fulfilled if the Player hand delivers the required written notification or the executed contract on or before the applicable deadline date or mails it by registered mail postmarked no later than said deadline date to the Club at its address set forth below.

18. The Club and the Player severally and mutually promise and agree to be legally bound by the Constitution and By-Laws of the League and by all the terms and provisions thereof, a copy of which shall be open and available for inspection by Club, its directors and officers, and the Player, at the main office of the League and at the main office of the Club.

The Club and the Player further agree that in case of dispute between them, except as to the compensation to be paid to the Player on a new contract, the dispute shall be referred within one year from the date it arose to the President of the League as an arbitrator and his decision shall be accepted as final by both parties.

The Club and the Player further agree that all fines imposed upon the Player under the Playing Rules, or under the provision of the League By-Laws, shall be deducted from the salary of the Player and be remitted by the Club to the N.H.L. Players' Emergency Fund.

19. The parties agree that the rights provided in Section 17 and in any Addendum hereto and the promise of the Player to play hockey only with the Club, or such other club as provided in Section 2 and Section 11, and the Club's right to take pictures of and to televise the Player as provided in section 8 have all been taken into consideration in determining the salary payable to the Player under Section 1 hereof.

20. It is severally and mutually agreed that the only contracts recognized by the President of the League are the Standard Player's Contracts, Player's Termination Contracts, and Player's Option Contracts which have been duly executed and filed in the League's office and approved by him, and that this Agreement contains the entire agree-

ment between the Parties and there are no oral or written inducements, promises or agreements except as provided herein.

IN WITNESS WHEREOF, the parties have signed this .... day of ....

A.D. 19......

WITNESSES:

....
Club

....
Address of Club

.... By ....
President

....
Player

....
Home Address of Player

I hereby certify that I have, at this date, received, examined and noted of record the within Contract, and that it is in regular form.

Dated .... 19......

....
President NATIONAL HOCKEY LEAGUE

NATIONAL HOCKEY LEAGUE

By-Law Section 9A

FREE AGENTS AND EQUALIZATION

(Adopted November 27, 1973)

Free Agents

9A. 1. A player who becomes a "free agent" pursuant to subsections 2 or 3 of this By-Law shall have the right to negotiate and contract with any Member Club or with any club in any other league.

9A. 2. A player who enters into a 1974 Form Standard Player's contract shall have the right to become a free agent in accordance with the terms of Section 17 of said contract and in accordance with the Player's Option contract to which said Section 17 refers.

9A. 3. Any other player under contract to any Member Club on the date this By-Law is adopted, the final year of whose contract ends on or after September 30, 1974, shall become a free agent on June 1 of the final year of that contract, except that any such player whose contract is a 1972 Form Standard Player's contract whose final year ends on September 30, 1974, shall become a free agent on June 1, 1975. For purposes of this subsection 3, the "final year" of a contract shall be the last year of its fixed term specified in Section 1 of said contract, including, however, any period added to that term by any addendum or exercised special option contracted for by the Member Club and player.

9A. 4. The foregoing subsection 3 shall not be construed to derogate in any way from the rights of any player under any contract but constitutes instead a waiver of any and all rights by each Member Club under the contracts to which said subsection is applicable to require the services of players for periods beyond those set out in said subsection.

Free Agent List

9A. 5. On or before May 15 in each year each Member Club shall deliver to the President a report in writing, by TWX, telegram or by mail (which report shall remain confidential until the issuance of the Free Agent List described below), setting forth the name of each player under contract to it who, unless signed to a new contract with said Club prior to June 1 of that year, will become a free agent as of that date. Each Member Club shall also furnish to the President after May 15 of each year, by immediate TWX or telegram, information as to any change of status of any such player. The President shall, on June 1 of such year, issue to all Member Clubs a Free Agent List setting forth the names of all players he finds to be free agents as of such date, together with the name of the Member Club with which each such player was last under contract, and shall thereafter promptly issue such bulletins correcting, amending, or updating such list as may be necessary to ensure its accuracy and currency. Except during a period that a player's name remains on the Free Agent List, no Member Club other than the Club with which he was last under contract may sign a contract or negotiate with such player, directly or indirectly, without the prior written consent of the Member Club with which he was last under contract, or otherwise take any action which would violate Section 15 of these By-Laws.

Obligation to make equalization payment

9A. 6. Each time that a player becomes a free agent and the right to his services is subsequently acquired by any

Member Club other than the club with which he was last under contract or by any club owned or controlled by any such Member Club, the Member Club first acquiring the right to his services, or owning or controlling the club first acquiring that right, shall make an equalization payment to the Member Club with which such player was previously under contract, as prescribed by subsection 8 of this By-Law. Each Member Club may acquire the right to the services of as many free agents as it wishes, subject to the provisions of subsection 9 of this By-Law.

Determination of Equalization Payment
Purpose

9A. 7. The purpose of the equalization payment shall be to compensate a player's previous Member Club fairly for loss of the right to his services when that player becomes a free agent and the right to his services is acquired by another Member Club or a club owned or controlled by another Member Club.

Procedure

9A. 8. (a) The Member Club acquiring the services of a free agent, or owning or controlling the club acquiring such services, shall immediately notify the player's previous Member Club and the President of that fact by TWX or telegram. The equalization payment shall be determined, if possible, by mutual agreement of the two Member Clubs involved. If no such agreement is reached within three business days after the date on which the player's services are acquired, each of the Member Clubs involved shall within two additional business days submit by TWX or telegram its proposal for an equalization payment to a neutral arbitrator selected from time to time by majority vote of the Board of Governors of the League.

9A. 8. (b) Within two business days after the deadline for receipt of the Clubs' proposals, the arbitrator shall, unless notified by both Clubs in writing, by TWX or by telegram that they have reached agreement on the equalization payment, select without change one of the proposals submitted to him, and his determination shall be final and not subject to review.

9A. 8. (c) The Clubs' proposals and the arbitrator's determination of equalization must be limited to:—

(i) the assignment of a contract or contracts for the services of a player or players binding upon such player or players for at least the next season; and/or

(ii) choices in any intra-league, inter-league and/or amateur drafts to be held at any time subsequent to such proposal and/or unsigned draft choices or negotiation nominees; and/or

(iii) cash.

In making his selection the arbitrator shall be governed by the policy that cash shall be used for equalization purpose only as a last resort.

9A. 8. (d) The contracts of all players under contract to the acquiring Club at the time a free agent is acquired shall be available for equalization purposes.

9A. 8. (e) The cost of the arbitrator shall be borne by the League.

9A. 8. (f) To facilitate a good faith effort to reach agreement on the equalization payment, the acquiring Club shall furnish to the Club entitled to that payment such information as may reasonably be required with respect to any player the assignment of whose contract is proposed by either party as an equalization payment, in whole or in part, including, but not limited to, the salary, bonus, and other compensation of such player, a copy of the player's contract, and any adverse information with respect to the physical, mental, or emotional condition of such player.

9A. 8. (g) The details of the procedure to be followed in the event arbitration is required shall be set forth in the agreement entered into by the League and the arbitrator.

Satisfaction of Equalization Obligation

9A. 9. No Member Club, or any club owned or controlled by such Member Club, shall be entitled to sign or acquire the right to the services of any free agent until it has satisfied in full its equalization obligation under these By-Laws as to each other free agent, the right to whose services it has acquired, by assigning the player contracts and/or draft rights and otherwise consummating the equalization payment required by mutual agreement or by arbitration. It shall be the responsibility of the acquiring Club to notify the President that it has satisfied its equalization obligation.

9A. 10. The President shall disallow the right of any acquiring Member Club to use the services of any signed free agent if he has not received the notice specified in subsection 9 or otherwise finds that the equalization payment for that player or for any other free agent previously signed has not been fully satisfied by said Member Club in accordance with this By-Law.

FORM 8

WORLD HOCKEY ASSOCIATION

Player's Contract

By this contract,

....

(hereafter "Club") employs

....

(hereafter "Player"), to perform in or on behalf of the Club's participation in the World Hockey Association (hereafter the "League").

This Contract is based on the following facts:

1. The Club is a member and holds a franchise in the League and will participate in exhibitions, regularly scheduled and championship games sponsored by the League.

2. Player has the skill, or potential skill, and training to enable him to compete with other players in the League.

Agreement

1. Compensation.

1.1. The Club agrees to pay the Player for rendering the services described herein the following salary:

1.2. If the Player is not on the Club's roster for the whole period of the Club's WHA League games, then he shall receive only part of the salary in the ratio of the number of games during which he is on the Club roster, to the number of games in the League schedule. If the Player is assigned, exchanged or otherwise transferred to a club in a lower classification league, the Player shall only be paid at the rate of $.......................... for that period in which he is on the roster of the lower classification league. However, if the Player is on the roster of the Club for at least twenty-five (25) regular WHA League and/or play-off games, he shall receive his full WHA salary as provided in Paragraph 1.1.

1.3. If the League is required to and does make any payment due the Player hereunder, this contract, and all its rights and obligations, is immediately and automatically assigned to and becomes the property of the League, subject to the Player's rights set out hereunder.

2. Employment and Duties.

During the term of this agreement, the Club employs Player as a skilled hockey player, subject to all the provisions of this contract. Player's duties under this contract shall include, but not be limited to:

2.1. The participation in and playing of practice sessions, exhibition, league and play-off games, to the best of his ability, under the direction and control of the Club during the term of this contract.

2.2. To report, in good physical condition and training at the time and place fixed by the Club, and to render full time services required of a skilled hockey player.

2.3. To keep himself in appropriate physical condition at all times during the training, exhibition, league and play-off season in which the Club participates.

2.4. At the request of the Club or League to participate in promotional activities and cooperate in general with Club and League activities.

2.5. To give his best services, best performance and loyalty to the Club and League both in and out of season, and to play hockey only for the Club, unless he is released or his contract is sold or exchanged by the Club, or unless he is assigned by the Club to another team or affiliate of the Club.

2.6. To keep and abide by such rules of gentlemanly conduct, dress and deportment in public as either the Club or the WHA may impose.

3. Travel Expenses, Per Diem.

3.1. The Club shall pay traveling expenses and meals reasonably incurred by the Player in his travel from his home to the Club's training camp. At the conclusion of the season, the Club shall provide transportation direct to the Player's home.

3.2. Each Player while "on the road" shall be paid a minimum of $18.00 per day as per diem.

3.3. The Club shall pay reasonable lodging expenses of the Player while playing for the Club in other than the Club's home city.

4. Club Rules; Fines.

The Club may from time to time during the continuance of this contract establish reasonable rules which shall be uniformly applied to all Players for the government of its Players "at home" and "on the road," and such rules shall be a part of this contract as fully as if herein written and shall be binding upon the Player; and for violation of such rules or for any conduct impairing the faithful and thorough discharge of the duties incumbent upon the Player, the Club may impose reasonable fines upon the Player and deduct the amount thereof from any money due or to become due to the Player. The Club may also suspend the Player for violation of any rules so established, and during such suspension the Player shall not be entitled to any compensation under this contract. When the Player is fined or suspended, he shall be given notice in writing, stating the amount of the fine or the duration of the suspension and the reason therefor. In the event the Player believes the fine or suspension to be unreasonable, he may, within forty-eight (48) hours of notice of the fine or suspension, request the League President to rule on its reasonableness, and the President's decision shall be binding on Player and Club.

5. Physical Condition, Injury.

5.1. If the Player, in the sole judgment of the Club's physician, is not in good physical condition at the date of his first scheduled game for the Club, or if, during the season, he fails to remain in good physical condition, unless such condition results directly from playing hockey for the Club, so as to render him, in the sole judgment of the Club's physician, unfit to play skilled hockey, it is mutually agreed that the Club shall have the right to suspend such Player until such time as, in the sole judgment of the Club's physician, the Player is in sufficiently good physical condition to play skilled hockey. In the event of such suspension, the annual salary payable to the Player shall be proportionately reduced as the length of the period of disability, during which, in the sole judgment of the Club's physician, the Player is not fit to play skilled hockey, bears to the season. In the event the Player believes the decision of the Club's physician is unreasonable, he has the right to be examined by an independent medical specialist operating in the field commonly known as specializing in the treatment of the alleged injury to the Player. If this independent medical specialist determines that, in his opinion, the Player is in sufficiently good physical condition to play skilled hockey, the Player's suspension shall be terminated.

5.2. If the Player is injured as a direct result of participating in any hockey practice or game played for the Club, the Club will pay the Player's hospitalization until he is discharged from the hospital and his medical expenses and doctor's bills, provided the hospital and the doctor are selected or approved by the Club.

5.3. If the Player suffers any injury in any practice or game played for the Club, and this injury renders him, in the sole judgment of the Club's physician, unfit to play skilled hockey for the balance of the season or any part thereof, then during such time the Player is so unfit, but in no event beyond the end of the current season, the Club shall pay the Player the compensation herein provided, less any workmen's compensation benefits and insurance proceeds provided by the Club, whether paid or payable to the Player, and the Player releases the Club from any and every additional obligation, liability, claim or demand.

5.4. If a Player is declared, by the Club's physician, to be physically able to play, and refuses to do so, he agrees to submit himself for examination to an independent medical specialist operating in the field commonly known as specializing in the treatment of the injury of which the Player complains. If, in the opinion of this independent medical specialist, Player is again declared physically able to play and refuses to do so, he shall be liable to immediate suspension without pay.

6. Exceptional Skill, No Competition.

Player has represented to the Club, and agrees that he has unique skill, experience, knowledge, and ability, all of which contribute to his being an exceptional hockey player. Player acknowledges that the services he will perform under this contract cannot be replaced or duplicated by the services of any other Player. In addition, he acknowledges that should the Club lose his services, by any breach or threatened breach of this agreement, or any other agreement with the Player, the Club cannot properly or adequately be compensated for this loss by the mere payment of money. Player agrees, therefore, that in the event of a breach of this contract by the Player, the Club and its assignees, in addition to any other remedies that may be available to them judicially or by way of arbitration, shall have the right to obtain from any court or arbitrator having jurisdiction, such equitable relief as may be appropriate, including a decree enjoining any further breach of this contract, and enjoining the Player from playing hockey for any other person, firm, corporation or organization during the term of this contract. In any suit, action or arbitration proceeding brought to obtain such relief, the Player hereby waives his right, if any, to trial by jury or to interpose any counterclaim or set-off.

7. Other Sports.

The Player and the Club recognize and agree that the Player's participation in other sports may impair or destroy his ability and skill as a hockey player. Accordingly the Player agrees that he will not during the period of this contract, or its renewal, engage or participate in soccer, basketball, football, baseball, softball, lacrosse, boxing, wrestling or other sport without the written consent of the Club.

8. PUBLICITY.

8.1. Player acknowledges that his picture, alone or with others, may be taken for motion pictures, television, still photographs or other display, at such times as the Club or the League may designate. No matter by whom taken, these pictures belong to and may be used by the Club or the League in any manner desired by either of them.

8.2. The Player further agrees that during the playing season he will not make public appearances, participate in radio or television programs or permit his picture to be taken, write or sponsor newspaper or magazine articles, or sponsor commercial products without the written consent of the Club, which shall not be withheld except in the reasonable interests of the Club or professional hockey. If such consent is given, all compensation for such appearances shall belong to the Player. If the Player feels the Club has unreasonably withheld its consent, he may request the League President to rule on the reasonableness of the Club's decision. The President must make such a decision within ten (10) days of receiving notice of the Player's request.

9. TRANSFERABILITY OF CONTRACT.

9.1. It is mutually agreed that the Club shall have the right to sell, assign, exchange and transfer this contract, and thereby transfer the Player's services to any other professional hockey club, and the Player agrees to accept and be bound by such sale, exchange, assignment, transfer or loan, and to faithfully perform and carry out his obligation under this contract as if it had been entered into by the Player and such other club.

9.2. If this contract is assigned the Club shall notice to the Player, the name and address of the club to which he has been assigned, and specify the time and place of reporting to such club. If the Player fails to report to such other club, he may be suspended by such other club and no salary shall be payable to him during the period of such suspension.

9.3. The Club shall pay the actual moving expenses incurred by a Player during the playing season when such move is directed by the Club.

10. Term and Termination.

10.1. The term for this contract shall be for .... years, commencing October 1, 19......, and expiring September 30, 19.......

10.2. The Club may terminate this contract upon written notice to the Player (but only after obtaining waivers from all other League clubs) if the Player shall at any time:

10.2.1. fail, refuse or neglect to obey the Club's rules governing training and conduct of Player;

10.2.2. fail, refuse or neglect to render his services hereunder or in any other manner materially breach this contract;

10.3. If this contract is terminated under Subparagraphs 10.2.1 and 10.2.2 above, the Player's sole remedy shall be to receive the compensation due him to the date of notice of termination, and the Club agrees to pay such compensation.

10.4. If the Club proposes to terminate this contract in accordance with Subparagraph 10.2 above, Player agrees to abide by such waiver and other procedures as are part of the League's by-laws or other governing documents.

11. League Rules.

The Club and the Player agree to abide and be bound by the Certificate of Incorporation and by-laws of the League. The Club agrees that copies thereof shall be open and available for inspection at the League office or the main office of the Club.

12. Disputes—Arbitration.

In the event of any dispute arising between the Player and the Club relating to any matter arising under this contract, or concerning the performance under or interpretation hereof, such dispute shall be determined by arbitration before the League President, or a person designated by the President in writing for such purpose, acting as arbitrator. The arbitrator shall determine by whom and in what proportion the cost of arbitration shall be paid. The Player and the Club hereby grant such arbitrator full power to determine such dispute in such manner as he shall direct, and under such rules of procedure as he shall in his sole discretion adopt, and his award shall be final, binding and conclusive and may be enforced in any court having competent jurisdiction. Demand for arbitration hereunder shall be forever barred unless made within one (1) year from the date when the alleged dispute arose, and shall be made by notice in writing given to the other party and to the President of the League. Notwithstanding the foregoing, the Club shall have the right in its sole discretion to waive arbitration and to institute judicial proceedings for the purpose of obtaining an injunction or other equitable relief pursuant to Paragraph 6 hereof. If arbitration of any dispute which is arbitrable under this Paragraph 12 is waived by the parties hereto, or, for any reason, any such dispute is not submitted to arbitration, as provided herein, and judicial proceedings are instituted by the Club or its assignees against the Player or by the Player against the Club or its assignees, the Player does hereby waive his right to trial by jury, if any.

13. GAMBLING.

Notwithstanding any provision of the League Certificate of Incorporation or by-laws, it is agreed that if the League President shall in his sole judgment find that the Player has bet, or has offered or attempted to bet, money or anything of value on the outcome of any game participated in by any club which is a member of the League, the President shall have the power in his sole discretion to suspend the Player, and the President's finding and decision shall be binding and conclusive. The Player hereby releases the President and waives every claim he may have against the President and/or the League, and against every club in the League, and against every director, officer or stockholder of every club in the League, for damages and for all claims and demands arising out of or in connection with the decision on this matter by the League President. If the Player feels the President's decision in this regard is unreasonable, he has the right to have the decision reviewed by an independent arbitrator mutually acceptable to both the Player and the League President. The decision of this arbitrator shall be binding on both the Player and the League. The arbitrator shall also determine who shall pay the costs of this arbitration procedure.

14. ACT OF GOD.

If, because of any condition arising from a state of war or other similar cause beyond the control of the League or of the Club, it shall be deemed advisable by the League or the Club to suspend or cease or reduce operations, then:

14.1. in the event of reduction of operations, the Player's salary shall be renegotiated;

14.2. in the event of suspension of operations, the Player shall be entitled only to the proportion of salary due at the date of suspension;

14.3. in the event of cessation of operations the Player's salary shall be automatically cancelled on the date of cessation.

15. Approval by League President.

This contract, if not inconsistent with the League's Certificate of Incorporation and by-laws shall be valid and binding upon the Club and the Player immediately upon its execution. The Club agrees to file this contract with the League President within ten (10) days after its execution.

If pursuant to the Certificate of Incorporation or by-laws, the President disapproves this contract within ten (10) days after its filing in his office, this contract shall thereupon terminate and be of no further force or effect and the Club and the Player shall thereupon be relieved of their respective rights and liabilities hereunder.

16. Player Negotiations.

16.1. If the Player and the Club fail to sign a new contract for the season following the termination of this contract before June 1, the mediation procedure outlined in this Paragraph 16 shall automatically go into effect.

16.2. *Mediation Procedure.*

16.2.1. On or before July 4 following the last playing season of this contract, in the event the Player and the Club fail to enter into a new contract, the Player and the Club shall each appoint one person to hear and determine the dispute preventing the signing of such new contract. If these persons are able to reach agreement on or before July 15 of the year of the dispute, no further proceedings are necessary. If they are unable to reach agreement on or before that date, then they shall immediately select a third impartial mediator whose decision shall be reached on or before July 31 of the year of the dispute.

16.2.2. Player and Club agree to mediate in good faith.

16.2.3. If the Player and Club agree that the decision of the impartial mediator is fair, a new contract will be executed embodying the terms of his decision.

16.2.4. If either the Player or the Club disagree with the decision of the impartial mediator, they may refuse to enter into a contract and the Player automatically enters into a special "secondary draft" pool on August 1 of the year of the dispute.

16.3. *Secondary Draft.*

16.3.1. Once a Player enters the secondary draft pool, he may not sign a contract with any other club until he is drafted.

16.3.2. The League will hold, in accordance with its normal draft procedure, a "secondary draft" on or about August 15 of each year. Teams will draft in the same order as in the normal yearly draft.

16.3.3. The Club with which the Player was under contract immediately prior to the secondary draft may not draft the Player in this manner.

16.4. *Subsequent Secondary Drafts.*

In the event the Player and the club that drafted him in the secondary draft are unable to reach an agreement by September 1, the Player will enter a pool for a new secondary draft, the date of which will be determined by the League President.

16.5. *Costs of Mediation.*

The costs of the mediation, including costs expended by the President and his staff if his services are required, will be borne equally by the Club and the Player, and the Player hereby authorizes his employing club to deduct his share of the expenses from the first payment due the Player under the next contract he signs.

17. MISCELLANEOUS AND PROCEDURAL PROVISIONS.

17.1. Any notice required or permitted to be given under this agreement shall be sufficient if in writing, sent by certified mail, return receipt requested, to the Player's residence or to the Club's office.

17.2. This agreement contains the entire understanding between the parties and it cannot be terminated or changed orally.

17.3. This agreement shall be governed and construed according to the laws of the State of ....
(Province of ....).

17.4. If any part, paragraph or provision of this agreement should be held or become invalid, then all remaining parts, paragraphs and provisions shall continue to be fully effective.

THE PARTIES ACKNOWLEDGE THAT THEY HAVE EACH READ THIS AGREEMENT AND THAT, BY ADDING THEIR SIGNATURES BELOW, DESIRE TO MAKE IT EFFECTIVE THIS .... DAY OF ...., 19......

....
(CLUB)

By: ....

....
Witness to Signature

By: ....

....
Witness to Signature

....
(PLAYER)

....
Witness to Signature

....
(PLAYER'S ADDRESS)

FORM 9

WORLD TEAM TENNIS, INC.

STANDARD PLAYER'S CONTRACT

By This Contract,

....

("Club") employs

....

("Player")

to perform in or on behalf of the Club's participation in WORLD TEAM TENNIS, INC. ("WTT" or "League").

This contract is based on the following facts:

1. The Club is a member and holds a franchise in the League and will participate in exhibitions, regularly scheduled and championship matches sponsored by the League.

2. Player has the skill, or potential skill, and training to enable Player to compete in the League.

AGREEMENT

1. *Compensation.*

1.1. The Club agrees to pay Player for rendering the services described herein, the following salary:

1.2. If the League is required to and does make any payment to player hereunder, this contract and all its rights and obligations, may, at the League's option, be assigned to and become the property of the League, subject to the Player's rights set out hereunder.

2. *Employment and Duties.*

During the periods covered by this contract, Club employs Player as a skilled tennis player, subject to all the provisions of this contract. Player's duties under this contract shall include, but not be limited to:

2.1. The participation in and playing of practice sessions, exhibitions, league and play-off matches, under the direction and control of the Club during the periods covered by this contract.

2.2. To report, in good physical condition and training at the time and place fixed by the Club, and to render services required of a skilled tennis player.

2.3. To keep in appropriate physical condition at all times during the training, exhibition, league and play-off season in which the Club participates.

2.4. At the request of the Club or League, to participate in promotional activities and cooperate in general with Club and League activities.

2.5. To give best services, best performances and loyalty to the Club both in and out of season and to play team tennis only for the Club during the WTT season, unless released or unless Player's contract is sold or exchanged by the Club.

3. *Travel Expenses, Per Diem.*

3.1. Each Player while "on the road" for the Club shall be paid a minimum of Eighteen Dollars ($18.00) per day for expenses.

3.2. The Club shall pay reasonable lodging expenses of the Player while playing for the Club in other than the Club's home city.

4. *Physical Condition, Injury.*

4.1. If Player, in the sole judgment of the Club's physician, is not in appropriate physical condition at the date of Player's first scheduled match for the Club, or if, during the season, Player fails to remain in appropriate physical condition, unless such condition results directly from performance under this contract, so as to render Player, in the sole judgment of the Club's physician, unfit to play skilled tennis, it is mutually agreed that the Club shall have the right to suspend such Player until such time as, in the sole judgment of the Club's physician, the Player is in sufficiently good physical condition to play skilled tennis. In the event of such suspension, the salary payable to Player shall be proportionately reduced as the length of the period of disability, during which, in the sole judgment of the Club's physician, the Player is not fit to play skilled tennis, bears to the WTT season. In the event the Player believes the decision of the Club's physician is unreasonable, Player has the right to be examined by an independent medical specialist, mutually acceptable to both parties, operating in the field commonly known as specializing in the treatment of the alleged injury to the Player. If this independent medical specialist determines that, in his opinion, the Player is in sufficiently good physical condition to play skilled tennis, the Player's suspension shall be terminated.

4.2. If the Player is injured as a direct result of participating in any tennis practice or match played for the Club, the Club will pay the Player's hospitalization until Player is discharged from the hospital and Player's medical expenses and doctor's bills, provided the hospital and doctor are selected or approved by the Club.

4.3. If Player suffers any injury in any practice or match played by the Club, and this injury renders Player, in the sole judgment of the Club's physician, unfit to play skilled tennis for the balance of the season or any part thereof, then during such time the Player is so unfit, but in no event beyond the end of the current season, the Club shall pay the Player the compensation herein provided, less any workmen's compensation benefits and insurance proceeds provided by the Club, whether paid or payable to the Player, and the Player releases the Club from any and every additional obligation, liability, claim or demand.

4.4. If Player is declared, by the Club's physician, to be physically able to play, and refuses to do so, Player agrees to submit for examination by an independent medical specialist, mutually acceptable to both parties, operating in the field commonly known as specializing in the treatment of the injury of which the Player complains. If, in the opinion of this independent medical specialist, Player is again declared physically able to play and refuses to do so, Player shall be liable to immediate suspension without pay, or termination of this contract, at Club's option.

5. *Publicity and Promotion.*

Player acknowledges that his or her picture, alone or with others, may be taken for motion pictures, television, still photographs or other display, at such times as the Club or the League may designate. No matter by whom taken, these pictures belong to and may be used by the Club or League solely for promoting the Club or the League. In addition, Player acknowledges that his or her name, likeness, facsimile and biographical sketch may be used by the Club or League to promote the Club or League. In no event shall any of these uses by Club or League be for individual endorsement purposes, except as set forth above, without Player's written consent.

6. *Transferability of Contract.*

6.1. It is mutually agreed that the Club shall have the right to sell, assign, trade and transfer this contract to another Club in the League, and the Player agrees to accept and be bound by such sale, exchange, assignment or transfer and to faithfully perform and carry out his or her obligations under this contract as if it had been entered into by the Player and such other Club. In the event Player is transferred, the Player's reasonable moving expenses shall be paid by Club.

6.2. If this contract is assigned, the Club shall immediately send notice to the Player of the name and address of the Club to which he or she has been assigned, and specify the time and place of reporting to such club. If the Player fails to report to such other club, he or she may be suspended by such other club and no salary shall be payable to Player during the period of such suspension.

7. *Term and Termination.*

7.1. This contract shall bind Player for .... consecutive WTT playing seasons to be composed of thirteen (13) playing weeks, plus playoff. The initial playing season covered by this contract shall be the 197.... season.

7.2. Club shall have an option to renew this contract on the same terms and conditions as were in effect under this contract during the WTT playing season immediately preceding the termination date of this contract, except for this paragraph, for an additional one (1) year period. If Club chooses to exercise this option, it must give player notice of such no later than three (3) months prior to the

Club's first scheduled WTT match for the year in question. Should Club exercise this option, it shall have no further option to Player's services under the terms and conditions of this contract.

7.3. The Club may terminate this contract upon written notice to the Player if the Player shall at any time:

7.3.1. fail, refuse or neglect to obey the Club's rules governing training and conduct of Players;

7.3.2. fail, refuse or neglect to render his services hereunder or in any other manner materially breach this contract;

7.3.3. fail, in the opinion of the Club's management, to exhibit sufficient skill or competitive ability to warrant further employment as a member of the Club's team.

8. *League Rules.*

The Club and the Player agree to abide by the WTT Articles of Incorporation, By-Laws and League rules. The Club agrees that copies thereof shall be open and available for inspection at the League office or the main office of the Club.

9. *League Wide Benefits to Player.*

Club acknowledges that Player shall be entitled to all Player benefits offered by the Club and League, including but not necessarily limited to, pension plans, life insurance and hospitalization plans, and bonuses for team league finish and play-off positions.

10. *Disputes—Arbitration.*

In the event of any dispute arising between the Player and the Club relating to any matter arising under this contract, or concerning the performance under or interpretation hereof, such dispute shall be determined by arbitration before an arbitrator mutually acceptable to both parties. In the event the parties cannot agree on an arbitrator, both agree to the use of an independent arbitrator chosen by the American Arbitration Association. The arbitrator shall determine by whom and in what proportion the cost of arbitration shall be paid. The Player and the Club hereby grant such arbitrator full power to determine such dispute in such manner as he shall direct, and under such rules of procedure as he shall in his sole discretion adopt, and his award shall be final, binding and conclusive and may be enforced in any court having competent jurisdiction. Demand for arbitration hereunder shall be forever barred unless made within one (1) year from the date when the alleged dispute arose, and shall be made by notice in writing given to the other party. Notwithstanding the foregoing, the Club shall have the right in its sole discretion to waive arbitration and to institute judicial proceedings for the purpose of obtaining an injunction or other equitable relief.

11. *Nondisclosure of Information.*

Player and WTT agree that no information regarding the existence for the terms and conditions of this contract shall be released to any third party without the mutual consent of both WTT and Player.

12. *Gambling.*

Notwithstanding any provision of the League Articles of Incorporation or By-laws, it is agreed that if the League Commissioner shall in his sole judgment find that the Player has bet, or has offered or attempted to bet, money or anything of value on the outcome of any match participated in by any Club which is a member of the League, the Commissioner shall have the power in his sole discretion to suspend without pay and/or fine the Player, and the Commissioner's finding and decision shall be binding and conclusive. The Player hereby releases the Commissioner and waives every claim he may have against the Commissioner and/or the League, and against every Club in the League, and against every director, officer or stockholder of every club in the League, for damages and for all claims and demands arising out of or in connection with the decision of this matter by the League Commissioner. If the Player feels the Commissioner's decision in this regard is unreasonable, Player has the right to have the decision reviewed by an independent arbitrator mutually acceptable to both the Player and the League Commissioner. The decision of this arbitrator shall be binding on both the Player and the League. The arbitrator shall also determine who shall pay the costs of this arbitration procedure.

13. *Act of God.*

If, because of any condition arising from a state of war or other similar cause beyond the control of the League or of the Club, it shall be deemed advisable by the League or the Club to suspend or cease or reduce operations, then:

13.1. In the event of reduction of operations, the Player's salary shall be renegotiated;

13.2. In the event of suspension of operations, the Player shall be entitled only to the portion of salary due at the date of suspension;

13.3. In the event of cessation of operations, the Player's salary shall be automatically cancelled on the date of cessation.

14. *Approval by League Commissioner.*

This contract, if not inconsistent with the League's Articles of Incorporation and By-Laws shall be valid and binding upon the Club and the Player immediately upon its execution. The Club agrees to file this contract with the League Office within ten (10) days after its execution.

If pursuant to the Articles of Incorporation or By-Laws, the Commissioner disapproves this contract within ten (10) days after its filing in his office, this contract shall thereupon terminate and be of no further force or effect and the Club and the Player shall thereupon be relieved of their respective rights and liabilities hereunder.

15. *Miscellaneous and Procedural Provisions.*

15.1. Any notice required or permitted to be given under this agreement shall be sufficient if in writing, sent by certified mail, return receipt requested, to the Player's residence or to the Club's office.

15.2. This agreement contains the entire understanding between the parties and it cannot be terminated or changed orally.

15.3. This agreement shall be governed and construed according to the laws of the State of ....

15.4. If any part, paragraph or provision of this agreement should be held or become invalid, then all remaining parts, paragraphs and provisions shall continue to be fully effective.

IMPORTANT NOTICE TO PLAYER

Before signing this agreement, you should carefully examine it to be sure all terms and conditions agreed upon have been incorporated herein, and if any has been omitted, you should insist upon having it inserted in the contract before you sign. "WTT" DOES NOT GUARANTEE PAYMENT OF ANY SUMS DUE UNDER THIS CONTRACT.

THE PARTIES ACKNOWLEDGE THAT THEY HAVE EACH READ THIS AGREEMENT AND THAT, BY ADDING THEIR SIGNATURES BELOW, DESIRE TO MAKE IT EFFECTIVE THIS .... DAY OF ...., 197.......

CLUB	PLAYER
....	....
(Club)	(Player)
BY:	
....	....
	(Player's Address)
BY:	
....	....

BIBLIOGRAPHY

Books

Barry, Rick, with Bill Libby. *Confessions of a Basketball Gypsy: The Rick Barry Story* (Englewood Cliffs: Prentice-Hall, 1972).

Blackman, Martin E., Editor. *Counselling Professional Athletes—Course Handbooks* (New York: Practising Law Institute).

Davidson, Gary, with Bill Libby. *Breaking The Game Wide Open* (New York: Atheneum, 1974).

Durso, Joseph. *The All-American Dollar: The Big Business of Sports* (Boston: Houghton Mifflin, 1971).

Flood, Curt, with Richard Carter. *The Way It Is* (New York: Trident Press, 1971).

Gallner, Sheldon M. *Pro Sports: The Contract Game* (New York: Charles Scribner's Sons, 1974).

Johnson, William R., Jr. *Super Spectator and the Electric Lilliputians* (Boston: Little, Brown & Company, 1971).

Libby, Bill, and Spencer Haywood. *Stand Up For Something: The Spencer Haywood Story* (New York: Grosset & Dunlap, 1972).

Noll, Roger G., Editor. *Government and the Sports Business* (Washington: The Brookings Institution, 1974).

Parrish, Bernie. *They Call It A Game* (New York: The Dial Press, 1971).

Paul, William Henry. *The Gray-Flannel Pigskin: Movers and Shakers of Pro Football* (Phliadelphia: J. B. Lippincott Company, 1974).

Rentzel, Lance. *When All The Laughter Died In Sorrow* (New York: Saturday Review Press, 1972).

Rothenberg, Alan I., Editor. *Representing Professional Sports Teams—Course Handbook* (New York: Practising Law Institute, 1974).

Wolf, David. *Foul! The Connie Hawkins Story* (New York: Holt, Rinehart and Winston, 1972).

Congressional Hearings and Reports

Study of Monopoly Power—Organized Baseball. Hearings before the Subcommittee on the Study of Monopoly Power, House Committee on the Judiciary, 82nd Congress, 1st Session, Ser. 1, Pt. 6 (1951).

Organized Baseball. House Report No. 2002, 82nd Congress, 2nd Session (1952).

Broadcasting and Televising Baseball Games. Hearings before a Subcommittee of the Committee on Interstate and Foreign Commerce, U.S. Senate, 83rd Congress, 1st Session, on S.1396 (1953).

Broadcasting and Telecasting Baseball Games. Senate Report 387, 83rd Congress, 1st Session (1953).

Organized Professional Team Sports. Hearings on H.R. 5307, et al., before the Antitrust Subcommittee of the House Committee on the Judiciary, 85th Congress, 1st Session (1957).

Applicability of Antitrust Laws to Organized Professional Team Sports. House Report 1720, 85th Congress, 2nd Session (1958).

Organized Profesional Team Sports. Hearings on H.R. 10378 and S.4070 before the Subcommittee on Antitrust and Monopoly of the Senate Committee on the Judiciary, 85th Congress, 2nd Session (1958).

Organized Professional Team Sports. Hearings on S.616 and S.886 before the Subcommittee on Antitrust and Monopoly of the Senate Committee on the Judiciary, 86th Congress, 1st Session (1959).

Organized Professional Team Sports—1960. Hearings on S.3483 before the Subcommittee on Antitrust and Monopoly of the Senate Committee on the Judiciary, 86th Congress, 2nd Session (1960).

Professional Sports Act of 1960. Senate Report 1620, 86th Congress, 2nd Session (1960).

Telecasting of Professional Sports Contests. Hearings on H.R.8757 before the Antitrust Subcommittee of the House Committee on the Judiciary, 87th Congress, 1st Session (1961).

Telecasting of Professional Sports Contests. House Report 1178, 87th Congress, 1st Session (1961).

Telecasting of Professional Sports Contests. Senate Report 1087, 87th Congress, 1st Session (1961).

Professional Sports Antitrust Bill—1964. Hearings on S. 2391 before a Subcommittee on Antitrust and Monopoly of the Senate Judiciary Committee, 88th Congress, 2nd Session (1964).

Applicability of the Antitrust Laws to Certain Aspects of Designated Organized Professional Team Sports. Senate Report 1303, 88th Congress, 2nd Session (1964).

Professional Sports Antitrust Bill of 1965. Hearings on S.950 before Subcommittee on Antitrust and Monopoly of the Senate Judiciary Committee, 89th Congress, 1st Session (1965).

Professional Sports Act of 1965. Senate Report 462, 89th Congress, 1st Session (1965).

Football Merger Bill. Hearings on S.3817 before the Antitrust Subcommittee of the House Committee on Judiciary, 89th Congress, 2nd Session (1966).

Report on Football Merger Bill. Senate Report 1654, 89th Congress, 2nd Session (1966), 1966 U.S. Code and Administrative News 4378.

Professional Basketball. Hearing on S.2373 before the Subcommittee on Antitrust and Monopoly of the Senate Judiciary Committee, 92nd Congress, 1st and 2nd Sessions (1971 and 1972).

Authorizing the Merger of Two or More Professional Basketball Leagues and For Other Purposes. Senate Report 92-1151, 92nd Congress, 2nd Session (1972).

Federal Sports Act of 1972. Hearings on S.3445 before the Senate Committee on Commerce, 92nd Congress, 2nd Session (1972).

The Antitrust Laws and Organized Professional Team Sports Including Consideration of the Proposed Merger of the American and National Basketball Associations. Hearings on H.R. 1206, et al., before the Antitrust Subcommittee of the House Committee on the Judiciary, 92nd Congress, 2nd Session (1972).

Labor Relations in Professional Sports. Hearings before the Special Subcommittee on Labor of the House Committee on Education and Labor, 92nd Congress, 2nd Session (1972).

Blackout of Sporting Events on TV. Hearings on S.4007 and S.4010 before the Subcommittee on Communications of the Committee on Commerce of the U.S. Senate, 92nd Congress, 2nd Session (1972).

TV Blackout—Professional Sports. Senate Report 93-347, 93rd Congress, 1st Session (1973).

Evaluation of the Necessity for Television Blackouts of Professional Sporting Events. Report of the Special Subcommittee on Investigations of the Committee on Interstate and Foreign Commerce, House of Representatives, 93rd Congress, 1st Session (1973).

Professional Sports Blackouts. Hearings on H.R. 9536, et al., before the Subcommittee on Communications and Power of the House Committee on Interstate and Foreign Commerce, 93d Congress, 1st Session (1973).

Television—Professional Sports. House Report 93-483, 93d Congress, 1st Session (1973).

Law Review Articles

After the Fall, by A. M. Rosenblatt. 5 Trial 44 (1969).

Amortization and Nonamortization of Intangibles in the Sports World, by Jones. 53 Taxes 777 (1975).

Antitrust and Professional Sport: Does Anyone Play By the Rules of the Game? 22 Catholic University Law Review 403 (1973).

Antitrust Law—Baseball Reserve System . . . 48 Notre Dame Law Review 460 (1972).

Antitrust Law: Procedural Safeguard Requirements in Concerted Refusals To Deal: An Application to Professional Sports. 10 San Diego Law Review 413 (1973).

Antitrust Law—Professional Football Immune From Sherman Act As Team Sport Not Constituting Interstate Commerce. 105 University of Pennsylvania Law Review 110 (1956).

Antitrust Law—Sherman Antitrust Act—Exemption of Professional Football, 2 Villanova Law Review 120 (1956).

Antitrust Laws—The Applicability of Federal and State Antitrust Laws to the Sport of Baseball, 1971 University of Toledo Law Review 594 (1971).

Antitrust Laws—Interstate Commerce—Professional Football. 11 Southwestern Law Journal 516 (1957).

Antitrust Laws and Professional Baseball, 19 NYU Intra. Law Review 235 (1964).

Antitrust Laws—Sherman Antitrust Act—Professional Sports. 36 North Carolina Law Review 315 (1958).

Antitrust Principles and Collective Bargaining by Athletes: of Superstars in Peonage, by M. S. Jacobs and R. K. Winter, Jr. 81 Yale Law Journal 1 (1971).

Antitrust Threat to Professional Team Sports, by Keating. 1959 Antitrust Law Symposium 23 (1959).

Applicability of the Antitrust Laws to Baseball. 2 Memphis State University Law Review 299 (1972).

Athletics Symposium Forward, by John C. Weistart. 38 Law and Contemporary Problems 1 (1973).

Balance of Power in Professional Sports. 22 Maine Law Review 459 (1970).

Ball, Bat and Bar, by Seymour. 6 Cleveland-Marshall Law Review 534 (1957).

Baseball—An Exception to the Antitrust Laws. 18 University of Pittsburgh Law Review 131 (1956).

Baseball and the Antitrust Laws, by Neville. 16 Fordham Law Review 208 (1947).

Baseball and the Antitrust Laws, by Gromley. 34 Nebraska Law Review 597 (1955).

Baseball and the Law. 19 Case and Comment 151 (1912).

Baseball and the Law, by Johnson. 73 United States Law Review 252 (1939).

Baseball and the Law—Yesterday and Today. 32 Virginia Law Review 1164 (1946).

Baseball and the Reserve Clause. 1 NYLS Student Law Review 159 (1952).

Baseball As Interstate Commerce Within the Meaning of Antitrust Laws. 5 NYU Intra. Law Review 206 (1950).

Baseball Jurisprudence, by Stratton. 44 American Law Review 374 (1910).

Baseball Law. 17 Law Notes 207 (1914).

Baseball Not A "Game" But A National Recreation. 68 Century Law Journal 341 (1909), 54 Ohio Law Bulletin 255 (1909).

Baseball Players and the Antitrust Laws. 53 Columbia Law Review 242 (1953).

Baseball, Professional Sports and the Antitrust Acts, by Johnson. 2 Antitrust Bulletin 678 (1957).

Baseball—Sport or Commerce? 17 University of Chicago Law Review 56 (1949).

Baseball's Antitrust Exemption and the Reserve System: Reappraisal of an Anachronism. 12 William and Mary Law Review 859 (1971).

Baseball's Antitrust Exemption—How Many Times Will the Supreme Court Throw the Federal Baseball Past

Unwary Players? 2 Ohio Northern University Intra. Law Review 16 (1972).

Baseball's Antitrust Exemption: The Limits of Stare Decisis. 12 B.C. Industrial and Commercial Law Review 737 (1971).

The Business of Pro Sports: A Reexamination in Progress, by Carlson. 18 New York Law Forum 915 (1973).

Case Note on Eastham v. Newcastle United Football Club, Ltd., 27 Modern Law Review 210 (1964).

Case Note on Flood v. Kuhn. 43 Mississippi Law Journal 718 (1972).

Case Note on Wisconsin v. Milwaukee Braves. 35 Fordham Law Review 350 (1966).

Case Note on Wisconsin v. Milwalkee Braves. 8 B.C. Industrial and Commercial Law Review 341 (1967).

Collective Bargaining in Professional Athletics—The NFL Money Bowl, by D. S. Shulman and B. M. Baum. 50 Cincinnati Bar Record 173 (1969).

Collective Bargaining and the Professional Team Sports Industry, by Cym H. Lowell. 38 Law and Contemporary Problems 3 (1973).

Common Law Origins of the Infield Fly Rule. 123 University of Pennsylvania Law Review 1474 (1975).

Confrontation With Congress: Professional Sports and the Television Antiblackout Law, by H. M. Shooshan, III. 25 Syracuse Law Review 713 (1974).

Congress Kicks A Field Goal: The Legislative Attack in the 93d Congress on Sports Broadcasting Practices, by Philip R. Hochberg. 27 Federal Communications Bar Journal 27 (1974).

Constitutional Law—Baseball and the Antitrust Laws—A Game Or A Conspiracy. 27 Notre Dame Law Review 372 (1949).

Constitutional Law — Preemption — Baseball's Immunity From State Antitrust Law. 13 Wayne Law Review 417 (1967).

Contractual Rights and Duties of the Professional Athlete —Playing the Game in a Bidding War. 77 Dickinson Law Review 352 (1973).

Copyright Protection for Sports Broadcasts and the Public's Right of Access. 15 Idea 385 (1971).

Curt Flood At Bat Against Baseball's "Reserve Clause." 8 San Diego Law Review 92 (1971).

Depreciation of Player Contracts—The Government is Ahead at the Half, by J. R. Weil. 53 Taxes 581 (1975).

Developments in the Application of Antitrust Laws to Professional Team Sports, by Keith. 10 Hastings Law Journal 119 (1968).

Discipline in Professional Sports: The Need for Player Protection. 60 Georgetown Law Journal 771 (1972).

An Economic Analysis of Team Movements in Professional Sports, by James Quirk. 38 Law and Contemporary Problems 42 (1973).

Economic Discrimination in Professional Sports, by Gerald Scully. 38 Law and Contemporary Problems 67 (1973).

Enforcement Problems of Personal Service Contracts in Professional Athletics. 6 Tulsa Law Journal 40 (1969).

Extra-Contractual Aspects of Canadian Professional Football. 16 Fac. Law Review 38 (1958).

Federal Antitrust Laws—Monopolies—Professional Football. 62 Dickinson Law Review 96 (1957).

Federal Control of Baseball. 28 Law Notes 202 (1925).

The First Great Leap: Some Reflections on the Spencer Haywood Case, by Richard K. Simon. 48 Los Angeles Bar Bulletin 149 (1973).

Flood in the Land of Antitrust: Another Look at Pro Athletics, The Antitrust Laws and the Labor Exemption. 7 Indiana Law Review 541 (1974).

Footnotes to Baseball Salary Arbitration, by Peter Seitz. 29 Arbitration Journal 98 (1974).

In the Grand Stand. 24 Law Note 5 (1920).

In the Wake of the Flood, by John P. Morris. 38 Law and Contemporary Problems 85 (1973).

Injunction Against Professional Athletes Breaching Their Contracts, by J. T. Brennan. 34 Brooklyn Law Review 61 (1967).

Injunctions in Professional Athletes Contracts—An Overused Remedy. 43 Connecticut Bar Journal 538 (1969).

Is the NLRB Going to Play the Ball Game?, by R. B. Hoffman. 20 Labor Law Journal 239 (1969).

Judicial Criticism of Baseball Playing. 47 Chicago Legal Notes 277 (1915).

Labor Controversy in Professional Baseball: The Flood Case, by P. L. Martin. 23 Labor Law Journal 567 (1972).

The Law of Baseball. 113 New York Law Journal 1832, 1848, 1864, 1880 (1945).

Law of Sports: The Unique Performer's Contract and the Antitrust Laws, by Johnson. 2 Antitrust Bulletin 251 (1957).

The Landis Case. 7 American Bar Association Journal 87 (1921).

Legal Aspects of Sports. 24 Record 306 (1969).

Legalization of Gambling on Sports Events, by Samuels. 18 New York Law Forum 897 (1973).

Medical Practices in Sports, by Allan J. Ryan. 38 Law and Contemporary Problems 99 (1973).

Modern Trend in Antitrust and Professional Sports. 22 Albany Law Review 272 (1958).

Monopoly in Professional Sports, by Topkis. 58 Yale Law Journal 691 (1949).

Monopoly in Manpower: Organized Baseball Meets the Antitrust Laws. 62 Yale Law Journal 576 (1953).

More Baseball Law. 18 Law Notes 22 (1914).

Municipal Promotion of Play. 19 Case and Comment 184 (1912).

NBA's Four Year Rule: A Technical Foul? 1972 Law and Social Order 489 (1972).

National Football League Restrictions on Competitive Bidding for Players' Services. 24 Buffalo Law Review 613 (1975).

The Nature and Effect of Major Sports Restrictions on Radio and TV Broadcasting Rights Under the Sherman Act. 21 George Washington Law Review 466 (1953).

Negative Covenant in Baseball Contracts. 18 Law Notes 83 (1914).

Note on Brooklyn National League v. Pasquel. 22 Notre Dame Law Review 226 (1947).

Note on Denver Rockets v. All-Pro Management. 10 San Diego Law Review 413 (1973).

Notes on Gardella v. Chandler. 37 Georgetown Law Journal 618 (1949), 62 Harvard Law Review 1240 (1949), 44 Illinois Law Review 493 (1949), 47 Michigan Law Review 1214 (1949), 28 Nebraska Law Review 616 (1949), 20 Tennessee Law Review 770 (1949), 18 University of Cincinnati Law Review 203 (1949).

Note on Toolson v. Yankees. 29 New York University Law Review 213 (1954).

Note on Unreported American Baseball v. Harper. 1902 Century Law Journal 449.

Organized Baseball and the Law. 46 Yale Law Journal 1386 (1937).

Organized Baseball and the Law, by Halligan. 19 Notre Dame Law Review 262 (1944).

Organized Professional Team Sports and the Antitrust Laws, by Pierce. 43 Cornell Law Quarterly 566 (1958).

Player Control Mechanisms in Professional Team Sports. 34 University of Pittsburgh Law Review 645.

Positively Mr. Kipling? Absolutely, Mr. Kuhn!, by Keeffe. 58 American Bar Association Journal 651 (1972).

Professional Athlete: Liberty or Peonage?, by D. I. Shapiro. 13 Alberta Law Review 212 (1975).

Professional Athletic Contracts and the Injunctive Dilemma. 8 John Marshall Law Journal 437 (1975).

Professional Football Held Within Purview of Sherman Act. 57 Columbia Law Review 725 (1957).

Professional Football Telecasts and the Blackout Privilege. 57 Cornell Law Review 297 (1972).

Professional Sport: Involuntary Servitude and the Popular Will, by M. Schneiderman. 7 Gonzaga Law Review 63 (1971).

Professional Sports, by J. P. Eppel. 33 ABA Antitrust Law Journal 69 (1967).

Professional Sports and the Antitrust Laws: Status of the Reserve System, by J. R. Allison. 25 Baylor Law Review 1 (1973).

Professional Sports and the Antitrust Laws, by O'Dea. 9 Hastings Law Journal 18 (1957).

Professional Sports Contracts and the Players' Association, by K. Alyluia. 5 Man. Law Journal 359 (1973).

Professional Sports Franchising and the IRS. 14 Washburn Law Journal 321 (1975).

Professional Sports Team As a Tax Shelter—A Case Study: The Utah Stars. 1974 Utah Law Review 556 (1974).

Pros Offside? The Antitrust Laws and Professional Sports, by Ducker. 76 Case and Comment 32 (1971).

Pugilist and the Law. 20 Law Notes 182 (1917).

Release Clause in Baseball Contracts. 18 Law Notes 82 (1914).

Reserve Clauses in Athletic Contracts. 2 Rutgers Camden Law Journal 302 (1970).

Sale of Minor League Baseball Players During Liquidation—The Application of Corn Products to Depreciable Property. 45 Temple Law Quarterly 291 (1972).

Second and Goal to Go: The Legislative Attack in the Ninety-Second Congress on Sports Broadcasting Practices, by Philip R. Hochberg. 18 New York Law Forum 841 (1973), 26 Federal Communications Bar Journal 118 (1973).

Sherman Act: Football's Player Controls—Are They Reasonable? 6 California Western Law Review 133 (1969).

Sherman Act and Professional Sports Association's Use of Eligibility Rules, by M. F. Anderson. 47 Nebraska Law Review 82 (1968).

Some Modest Proposals for Collective Bargaining in Professional Sports, by David G. Miller. 48 Los Angeles Bar Bulletin 155 (1973).

Sport: A Philosophical Perspective, by Howard Slusher. 38 Law and Contemporary Problems 129 (1973).

Sporting Suit. 53 American Bar Association Journal 58 (1967).

Sports and the Law: An Overview, by Koppett. 18 New York Law Forum 815 (1973).

Sunday Baseball. 11 Law Notes 69 (1907).

Super Bowl and the Sherman Act: Professional Team Sports and the Antitrust Laws. 81 Harvard Law Review 418 (1967).

Supreme Court of Baseball. 23 Case and Comment 665 (1917).

Take Me Out To The Ball Game. 25 Fordham Law Review 793 (1956).

Tax Aspects of Buying, Selling and Owning Professional Sports Teams, by Leslie S. Klinger. 48 Los Angeles Bar Bulletin 162 (1973), 39 Journal of Taxation 276 (1973).

Television Sports Blackouts: Private Rights vs. Public Policy, by Lionel S. Sobel. 48 Los Angeles Bar Bulletin 169 (1973).

Trade Regulation and Professional Sports, by J. F. Leavell and H. L. Millard. 26 Mercer Law Review 603 (1975).

Trade Regulation—Antitrust Acts—Unlawful Conspiracy —Non-coverage of Professional Football. 25 University of Cincinnati Law Review 519 (1956).

Trade Regulation—Sherman Act—Amenability of Organized Baseball. 34 Iowa Law Review 545 (1949), 33 Minnesota Law Review 428 (1949).

Tying Arrangements in the Sale of Season Tickets. 47 Temple Law Quarterly 761 (1974).

Unionization and Professional Sports, by Krasnow and Levy. 51 Georgetown Law Journal 749 (1963).

Violence in Professional Sports. 1975 Wisconsin Law Review 771 (1975).

What Constitutes Interstate Commerce. 34 Harvard Law Review 559 (1921).

Who's on First?, by Neville. 36 Michigan State Bar Journal 13 (1957).

TABLE OF CASES

(References are to page numbers in text which contain official citations of cases noted)

SUBJECT INDEX

(References are to page numbers)

ABOUT THE AUTHOR

Lionel S. Sobel received a Bachelor of Arts Degree in Economics from the University of California, Berkeley, in 1966, and graduated from the U.C.L.A. School of Law in 1969. He teaches Professional Sports Law at the University of Southern California Law School, and has lectured on that subject for the Practising Law Institute. He also testified before the House of Representatives Select Committee on Professional Sports and consulted with U.S. Senator Gart Hart on proposed antitrust legislation concerning professional athletes. Mr. Sobel practices law in Beverly Hills, California, where he is counsel for college athletic conferences and athletic directors as well as for those involved in professional sports.